To Karen Silva! –
Happy Secretary's Day!
Pastor Paul Davis

The Encyclopedia for Today's Christian Woman

The Encyclopedia for Today's Christian Woman

Fleming H. Revell Company
Old Tappan, New Jersey

Scripture quotations identified RSV are from the Revised Standard Version of the Bible, copyrighted 1946, 1952, © 1971 and 1973.

Acknowledgments for the use of copyrighted material continued on page 11.

Library of Congress Cataloging in Publication Data
Main entry under title:
The Encyclopedia for Today's Christian Woman.
    Includes bibliographies and index.
    1. Women—Life skills guides—Dictionaries. 2. Women—
Religious life—Dictionaries. 3. Women's encyclopedias.
I. Fleming H. Revell Company.
HQ1115.E49   1984   305.4'03'21   83-21305
ISBN 0-8007-1393-1

CONTENTS

5

Introduction

Who is today's Christian woman? She's a homemaker or a business executive, a wife and mother or a single, an adventurer or an introvert. It's as impossible to paint a single portrait of her as it is to define all snowflakes in terms of one's design. For each Christian woman has been created by God as a unique person—a very special testimony to His handiwork and limitless imagination.

Today each of us has more freedom to express our God-given talents than at any other time in history. It's difficult to think in terms of "traditional" roles because times have changed so dramatically that traditions are constantly being redefined. Becoming a homemaker and raising children—once the most common path taken by Christian women—has now become a life choice of the minority. Working outside the home is an economic necessity or a conscious choice of the majority of Christian women today.

As a result of all these wonderful options, Christian women are now faced with a whole new set of problems and difficult decisions. Every day seems to bring a dizzying array of choices.

At one time or another all of us pause to ask the same question: How can I best serve God by using my talents and by exercising my options as a Christian woman today?

This book is written to help answer that question. It is a compilation of some of the very best wisdom any Christian woman would hope to draw upon. It is meant to be a valuable resource in advice ranging from marriage to menus. And it can provide the very practical ideas necessary to help every Christian woman deal with such diverse problems as a dependent friend or meddling in-law.

In its pages you will find the words of men and women who care about resolving the dilemmas today's Christian woman faces. You will discover that they have collectively offered an invaluable resource for solving today's problems and answering tomorrow's questions. And best of all, they offer their thoughts from a Christian perspective.

Not only will you find advice by today's foremost Christian writers—Joyce Landorf, James Dobson, Elisabeth Elliot, Edith Schaeffer—but you will also find words by "ordinary" women. These women, like you and me, are struggling with everyday problems. Here they share some of their thoughts and advice for practically resolving those problems.

The practical nature of this volume is probably its greatest asset. It is simply filled with tips, checklists, and guidelines for putting ideas into action. And at the end of each section a valuable resource list points the reader to additional sources of information.

This is more than a book; it is truly an encyclopedia that every Christian woman will refer to again and again. We hope it will help you today and for many years to come as you grow into the woman God wants you to be.

DALE HANSON BOURKE
Editor
Today's Christian Woman

Acknowledgments

Material in this volume was compiled by Cecil and Shirley Murphey. Cecil Murphey is minister of the Riverdale (Georgia) Presbyterian Church. He holds master's degrees in divinity and education and is the author of over twenty books and hundreds of articles. His most recent books include *Getting There From Here*, *Press On*, and *Seven Daily Sins*. He is the compiler of *The Encyclopedia of Christian Marriage*. Shirley Murphey holds bachelor's degrees in religious education and journalism and is an editor for *These Days* and *Older Youth/Young Adult Bible Studies*. She is the contributor of articles to *These Days* and to church-school publications.

Acknowledgment is made to the following for permission to reprint copyrighted material:

ABINGDON: Excerpts from WOMEN IN CHURCH AND SOCIETY by Georgia Harkness. Copyright © 1972 by Abingdon Press. Used by permission. Excerpts from GIFTS OF THE SPIRIT by Kenneth Kinghorn. Copyright © 1976 by Abingdon Press. Used by permission. Excerpts from LETTERS TO KAREN by Charlie W. Shedd. Copyright © 1965 by Abingdon Press. Used by permission. Excerpts from TELL ME AGAIN, I'M LISTENING by Richard B. Wilke. Copyright © 1973 by Abingdon Press. Used by permission.

ACROPOLIS BOOKS LTD.: Excerpts reprinted with permission from COLOR ME BEAUTIFUL by Carole Jackson, copyright © 1980 by Acropolis Books Ltd.

CAROL AMEN: For "How to Keep a Journal," copyright © 1980 by Lutheran Church Women, Lutheran Church in America.

AMERICAN CANCER SOCIETY: For "Cancer-Related Checkup Guidelines."

AMERICAN HEALTH FOUNDATION: Excerpts from THE BOOK OF HEALTH, Ernest L. Wynder, M.D., editor-in-chief, published by Franklin Watts, Inc. 1981.

SARAH FRANCES ANDERS: For "Others, Caring for Shut-in Adults."

BAKER BOOK HOUSE: Excerpts from MONEY IN THE COOKIE JAR by Edith Flowers Kilgo. Copyright © 1980 by Edith Flowers Kilgo and used by permission of Baker Book House. Excerpts from MONEY MANAGEMENT. Copyright © 1980 by Edith Flowers Kilgo and used by permission of Baker Book House.

BEACON PRESS: Excerpts from SUICIDE: PREVENTION, INTERVENTION, POSTVENTION by Earl A. Grollman. Copyright © 1971 by Earl A. Grollman. Reprinted by permission of Beacon Press.

VERNE BECKER: For "Gossip: One of the Lesser Sins?" and "The Big Put-Off Game."

BETHANY HOUSE PUBLISHERS: Excerpts reprinted by permission from FREE TO BE THIN by Marie Chapian, published and copyright 1979, Bethany House Publishers, Minneapolis, Minnesota 55438. Excerpts reprinted by permission from YOU WILL NEVER BE THE SAME by Basilea Schlink, published and copyright 1972, Bethany House Publishers, Minneapolis, Minnesota 55438.

HUGH BURNS, TH.M.: For "Don't Make Your Child Your Confidant," "Burnout Housewife," "Jealousy Jeopardizes," "Cancer and Resentment," and "Hooked on a Person."

GARY R. COLLINS: For "Color Me Shy" and "Is Competition Killing Your Family?"

CONCORDIA PUBLISHING HOUSE: Excerpts from THE POSSIBLE YEARS by Donald L. Deffner, copyright © 1973 Concordia Publishing House. Used by permission.

JIM AND SALLY CONWAY: For "The Mystery and Meaning of Mid-Life."

DOUBLEDAY & COMPANY, INC.; Excerpts from WHAT'S SPECIAL ABOUT OUR STEPFA-MILY? by Mala Schuster Burt and Roger B. Burt, Ph.D. Copyright © 1983 by Mala Schuster Burt and Rogert B. Burt. Reprinted by permission of Doubleday & Co., Inc. Excerpts from THE TRAVELING WOMAN by Dena Kaye. Copyright © 1979 by Dena Kaye. Reprinted by permission of Doubleday & Co., Inc. Excerpts from TALK TO ME by Charlie W. Shedd. Copyright © 1975 by Charlie W. Shedd and the Abundance Foundation. Reprinted by permission of Doubleday & Co., Inc. Excerpts from THE PARENTING ADVISOR, by Frank Caplan, copyright © 1977 by the Princeton Center for In-fancy. Reprinted by permission of Doubleday & Company, Inc. Excerpts from THE COMPLETE WOMAN by Patricia Gundry. Copyright © 1981 by Patricia Gundry. Reprinted by permission of Doubleday & Co., Inc. Excerpts from MODERN WOMAN'S MEDICAL ENCYCLOPEDIA by Anna M. Fishbein. Copyright © 1966 by Doubleday & Co., Inc.

JUDY DOWNS DOUGLASS: For "Now We Are Three."

DAVID AND VIRGINIA EDENS: Excerpts from MAKING THE MOST OF FAMILY WORSHIP by David and Virginia Edens, Broadman Press, 1968.

ANTHONY FLORIO, Ph.D.: Excerpts from TWO TO GET READY by Anthony Florio, copyright © 1974 by Anthony Florio.

DALE E. GALLOWAY: Excerpts from WE'RE MAKING OUR HOME A HAPPY PLACE by Dale E. Galloway.

DOROTHY GISH: For "Single, Sane and Satisfied."

GREEN LEAF PRESS: Excerpts from CREATIVE HOSPITALITY by Bruce A. Rowlison.

GUIDEPOSTS ASSOCIATES, INC.: For "The Good Habit of Breaking Bad Habits" by Norman Vincent Peale. Reprinted with permission from Guideposts Magazine. Copyright © 1983 by Guide-posts Associates, Inc., Carmel, New York 10512.

CHARLOTTE HALE: Excerpts from FULL-TIME LIVING by Charlotte Hale Allen, copyright © 1978 by Charlotte Hale Allen.

GEORGE AND MARGARET HARDISTY: Excerpts from HOW TO PLAN YOUR ESTATE by George and Margaret Hardisty.

HARPER & ROW, PUBLISHERS, INC.: Excerpts from BECOMING WOMAN: THE QUEST FOR WHOLENESS IN FEMALE EXPERIENCE by Penelope Washbourn. Copyright © 1977 by Pene-lope Washbourn. Reprinted by permission of Harper & Row, Publishers, Inc. Excerpts from NATU-RAL CHILDBIRTH AND THE FAMILY, Revised Edition, by Helen Wessel. Copyright © 1963, 1973 by Helen S. Wessel. Reprinted by permission of Harper & Row, Publishers, Inc.

HERALD PRESS: Excerpts from CHERISHABLE: LOVE AND MARRIAGE by David W. Augs-burger, Herald Press, 1971.

HODDER AND STOUGHTON LIMITED: Excerpts from THE SEX THING by Branse Burbridge; copyright © 1972 by Branse Burbridge. Published by Hodder and Stoughton, Ltd., London. Reprinted by permission of Hodder and Stoughton Limited.

HOLT, RINEHART AND WINSTON, CBS COLLEGE PUBLISHING: Excerpts from WOMEN: AN ANTHROPOLOGICAL VIEW by Evelyn S. Kessler. Copyright © 1976 by Holt, Rinehart and Winston. Reprinted by permission of Holt, Rinehart and Winston, CBS College Publishing. Excerpts from LOVE AND SEXUALITY by Mary Perkins Ryan and John Julian Ryan. Copyright © 1967 by Mary Perkins Ryan and John Julian Ryan. Reprinted by permission of Holt, Rinehart and Winston, Publishers.

ELIZABETH HORMANN: For "Single Parents" and "Open Adoption."

INTERVARSITY PRESS: Excerpts taken from PARENTS IN PAIN by John White. © 1979 by Inter-Varsity Christian Fellowship of the USA and used by permission of InterVarsity Press, Downers Grove, IL 60515.

JOAN JACOBS: Excerpts from FEELINGS by Joan Jacobs.

BRUCE JOFFE: For "Soap Operas."

GRAHAM KERR: Excerpts from THE LOVE FEAST by Graham Kerr copyright © 1978 by Graham Kerr.

SHARREL KEYES: For "Start a Home Bible Study."

EDITH FLOWERS KILGO: For "What Every Woman Should Know About Obtaining a College Degree at Home," "What Every Woman Should Know About Home Mortgages," and "Five Things You Need to Know About Banks." Excerpts from HANDBOOK FOR CHRISTIAN HOMEMAKERS, copyright © 1982 by Edith Flowers Kilgo, published by Baker Book House.

ALFRED A. KNOPF, INC.: Excerpts from THE SEASONS OF A MAN'S LIFE by Daniel J. Levinson, et al. Copyright © 1978 by Daniel J. Levinson. Reprinted by permission of Alfred A. Knopf, Inc.

JOHN KNOX PRESS: Excerpts from CASEBOOK FOR CHRISTIAN LIVING by Robert A. and Alice F. Evans and Louis and Carolyn Weeks, John Knox Press, 1977. Excerpts from WHEN IN DOUBT, HUG 'EM by Cecil B. Murphey, John Knox Press, 1978.

MARLENE LEFEVER: For "Breaking into a New Neighborhood."

METROPOLITAN LIFE INSURANCE COMPANY: Excerpts from *Four Steps to Weight Control,* © 1969, and *Exercise,* © 1979.

MILADY PUBLISHING CORPORATION: Excerpts from A WOMANS GUIDE TO BUSINESS AND SOCIAL SUCCESS.

EVELYN MINSHULL: For "When Ministering Turns to Meddling."

WILLIAM MORROW & COMPANY, INC.: Excerpts from THE WOMAN DOCTOR'S MEDICAL GUIDE FOR WOMEN by Barbara Edelstein, M.D. Copyright © 1982 by Barbara Edelstein, M.D., P.C. Used by permission of William Morrow & Company.

THE NATIONAL COUNCIL ON THE AGING, INC.: Excerpts from FACTS AND MYTHS ABOUT AGING, 1981, published by The National Council on the Aging, Inc.

THOMAS NELSON PUBLISHERS: Excerpts reprinted by permission of Thomas Nelson Publishers from the book I LOVE BEING MARRIED TO A GRANDMA by Ken Berven. Copyright © 1978 by Thomas Nelson, Inc., Publishers.

PRENTICE-HALL, INC.: Excerpts from COPING by Martha Yates. Copyright © 1976 by Prentice-Hall, Inc. Published by Prentice-Hall, Inc., Englewood Cliffs, NJ 07632. Excerpts from THE MANAGEMENT OF TIME by James T. McCay. Copyright © 1959 by Prentice-Hall, Inc., Englewood Cliffs, NJ 07632. Excerpts from THE WOMAN DOCTOR'S DIET FOR WOMEN by Barbara Edelstein, M.D. Copyright © 1977 by Barbara Edelstein, M.D. Published by Prentice-Hall, Inc., Englewood Cliffs, NJ 07632.

RAWSON ASSOCIATES: Excerpts from PARENTS AFTER THIRTY by Murray M. Kappelman and Paul R. Ackerman are reprinted with the permission of Rawson, Wade Publishers, Inc. Copyright © 1980 by Murray M. Kappelman, M.D., and Paul R. Ackerman, Ph.D.

READER'S DIGEST: Excerpts from FAMILY HEALTH GUIDE AND MEDICAL ENCYCLOPEDIA, prepared in association with Benjamin F. Miller, M.D., 1970.

REGAL BOOKS: Excerpts from CARING ENOUGH TO CONFRONT by David Augsburger. Copyright © 1981, Regal Books, Ventura, CA 93006. Used by permission. Excerpts from EMOTIONS, CAN YOU TRUST THEM? by Dr. James Dobson. Copyright © 1980, Regal Books, Ventura, CA 93006. Used by permission. Excerpts from THE MEASURE OF A WOMAN by Gene Getz. Copyright © 1977, Regal Books, Ventura, CA 93006. Used by permission. Excerpts from SEX BEGINS IN THE KITCHEN by Dr. Kevin Leman. Copyright © 1981, Regal Books, Ventura, CA 93006. Used by permission. Excerpts from COMMUNICATION: KEY TO YOUR MARRIAGE by H. Norman Wright. Copyright © 1974, Regal Books, Ventura, CA 93006.

FLEMING H. REVELL COMPANY: Excerpts from THE SECRET OF ABUNDANT LIVING by Charles L. Allen, copyright © 1980 by Charles L. Allen: Excerpts from DEVOTIONS FOR INSOMNIACS by Phillip Barnhart, copyright © 1982 by Fleming H. Revell Company. Excerpts from EMOTIONALLY FREE by Rita Bennett, copyright © 1982 by Rita Bennett. Excerpts from YOU ARE VERY SPECIAL by Verna Birkey, copyright © 1977 by Verna Birkey. Excerpts from FOR SUCH A TIME AS THIS by Vonette Zachary Bright, copyright © 1976 by Fleming H. Revell Company. Excerpts from FINDING GOD'S WILL by Dwight L. Carlson, copyright © 1976 by Fleming H. Revell Company. Excerpts from HOW TO WIN OVER FATIGUE by Dwight L. Carlson, copyright © 1974 by Fleming H. Revell Company. Excerpts from LOVE AND BE LOVED by Marie Chapian, copyright © 1983 by Marie Chapian. Excerpts from FUN TO BE FIT by Marie Chapian, copyright © 1983 by Marie Chapian. Excerpts from BETWEEN MOTHER AND DAUGHTER by Sheila Schuller

Coleman, copyright © 1982 by Sheila Schuller Coleman. Excerpts from WOMEN WHO WIN by Mary C. Crowley, copyright © 1979 by Mary C. Crowley. Excerpts from DISCIPLINE: THE GLAD SURRENDER by Elisabeth Elliot, copyright © 1982 by Elisabeth Elliot Gren. Excerpts from YOU CAN BE FINANCIALLY FREE by George Fooshee, Jr., copyright © 1976 by George Fooshee, Jr. Excerpts from YOU CAN BEAT THE MONEY SQUEEZE by George and Marjean Fooshee, copyright © 1980 by George and Marjean Fooshee.

Excerpts from THE SUPER YEARS by Charlotte Hale, copyright © 1984 by Charlotte Hale. Excerpts from THE FOREVER PRINCIPLE by Maxine Hancock, copyright © 1980 by Maxine Hancock. Excerpts from PEOPLE IN PROCESS by Maxine Hancock, copyright © 1978 by Maxine Hancock. Excerpts from FEELING FREE by Archibald D. Hart, copyright © 1979 by Archibald D. Hart. Excerpts from SHAPE UP by O. Quentin Hyder, M.D., copyright © 1979 by O. Quentin Hyder, M.D. Excerpts from HOW TO TEACH YOUR CHILD ABOUT SEX by Grace H. Ketterman, M.D., copyright © 1981 by Grace H. Ketterman, M.D. Excerpts from THE COMPLETE BOOK OF BABY AND CHILD CARE FOR CHRISTIAN PARENTS by Grace H. Ketterman, M.D., and Herbert L. Ketterman, M.D., copyright © 1982 by Grace H. Ketterman, M.D., and Herbert L. Ketterman, M.D. Excerpts from FLAB: THE ANSWER BOOK, by Jim Krafft, M.D., copyright © 1983 by Fleming H. Revell Company. Excerpts from CHANGEPOINTS by Joyce Landorf copyright © 1981 by Joyce Landorf. Excerpts from FAMILY DEVOTIONS WITH SCHOOL-AGE CHILDREN by Lois E. LeBar, copyright © 1973 by Fleming H. Revell Company. Excerpts from RUBY MACDONALD'S FORTY PLUS AND FEELING FABULOUS BOOK, copyright © 1982 by Ruby MacDonald. Excerpts from THE PEACEMAKERS by Ella May Miller, copyright © 1977 by Ella May Miller. Excerpts from HEADACHES: THE ANSWER BOOK by Joan Miller, Ph.D., copyright © 1983 by Joan Miller, Ph.D. Excerpts from DEVOTIONS FOR GRANDPARENTS by Cecil B. Murphey, copyright © 1983 by Fleming H. Revell Company. Excerpts from DEVOTIONS FOR TRAVELERS by Cecil B. Murphey, © 1982 by Fleming H. Revell Company. Excerpts from DEVOTIONS FOR WORRIERS by Cecil B. Murphey, copyright © 1982 by Fleming H. Revell Company.

Excerpts from THE POWER OF A WOMAN'S LOVE by Barbara Rice, copyright © 1983 by Barbara Rice. Excerpts from WOMAN by Dale Evans Rogers, copyright © 1980 by Dale Evans Rogers. Excerpts from HAVE YOU HUGGED YOUR TEENAGER TODAY by Patricia H. Rushford, copyright © 1983 by Patricia H. Rushford. Excerpts from FROM MONEY MESS TO MONEY MANAGEMENT by Patricia H. Rushford, copyright © 1984 by Patricia H. Rushford. Excerpts from A WAY OF SEEING by Edith Schaeffer, copyright © 1977 by Edith Schaeffer. Excerpts from SELF TALK by David Stoop, Ph.D., copyright © 1982 by David Stoop, Ph.D. Excerpts from FED UP WITH FAT by Jim Tear and Jan Houghton Lindsey, copyright © 1978 by Jim Tear and Jan Houghton Lindsey. Excerpts from DRESS WITH STYLE by Joanne Wallace, copyright © 1983 by Joanne Wallace. Excerpts from THE IMAGE OF LOVELINESS by Joanne Wallace, copyright © 1978 by Joanne Wallace. Excerpts from INTENDED FOR PLEASURE, Revised Edition, by Ed Wheat, M.D., and Gaye Wheat, copyright © 1977, 1981 by Ed Wheat and Gaye Wheat. Excerpts from MARIJUANA by Don Wilkerson, copyright © 1980, 1983 by Don Wilkerson. Excerpts from THE CHRISTIAN USE OF EMOTIONAL POWER by H. Norman Wright, copyright © 1974 by Fleming H. Revell Company. Excerpts from THE ENCYCLOPEDIA OF CHRISTIAN MARRIAGE copyright © 1984 by Fleming H. Revell Company.

RODALE PRESS: Excerpts reprinted from THE WOMAN'S ENCYCLOPEDIA OF HEALTH AND NATURAL HEALING © 1981 by Rodale Press, Inc. Permission granted by Rodale Press, Inc., Emmaus, PA 18049.

ROBERTA ROESCH: For "Ten Steps to Take You Back to Work."

LINDA SCHWITZ: For "A Resume for Success."

MARILU SECKINGER: For "But What Will I Wear?"

SERVANT BOOKS: Excerpts from THE ANGRY CHRISTIAN by Bert Ghezzi, Servant Books, 1980. Excerpts from GETTING FREE by Bert Ghezzi, Servant Books, 1982. Excerpts from TAMING THE TV HABIT, © 1982 by Kevin Perrotta. Published by Servant Publications, Box 8617, Ann Arbor, Michigan 48107. Used with permission.

HAROLD SHAW PUBLISHERS: Excerpts reprinted from SO YOU'RE SINGLE by Margaret Clarkson by permission of Harold Shaw Publishers. Copyright © 1978 by Harold Shaw Publishers.

SIMON & SCHUSTER, INC.: Excerpts from OUR BODIES, OURSELVES by The Boston Women's Health Book Collective. Copyright © 1971, 1973, 1976 by The Boston Women's Health Collective, Inc. Reprinted by permission of Simon & Schuster, a division of Gulf & Western Corporation. Excerpts from WOMAN'S BODY by The Diagram Group. Revision copyright © 1981 by Simon & Schuster, Inc. Reprinted by permission of Wallaby Books, a Simon & Schuster division of Gulf & Western Corporation. Excerpts from MAN'S BODY by The Diagram Group. Revision copyright © 1981 by Simon & Schuster, Inc. Reprinted by permission of Wallaby Books, a Simon & Schuster division of Gulf & Western Corporation. Excerpts from THE NEW YOU by Wilhelmina. Copyright © 1978 by Wilhelmina Cooper. Reprinted by permission of Simon & Schuster, a division of Gulf & Western Corporation.

THE SUNDAY SCHOOL BOARD OF THE SOUTHERN BAPTIST CONVENTION: "How to Meet Men" by Dan Runyon from *Christian Single*, February 1983. © Copyright 1982 The Sunday School Board of the Southern Baptist Convention. All rights reserved. Used by permission. "God Don't Make No Junk" by Cecil Murphey from *Christian Single*, February 1983. © Copyright 1982 The Sunday School Board of the Southern Baptist Convention. All rights reserved. Used by permission. "Others, Caring for Shut-ins" by Sarah Anders from *Christian Single*, February 1983 copyright © 1982 The Sunday School Board of the Southern Baptist Convention. All rights reserved. Used by permission. Excerpts from TEN GOOD THINGS I KNOW ABOUT RETIREMENT by J. Winston Pearce (Nashville: Broadman Press 1982) pp. 38–42. All rights reserved. Used by permission.

TODAY'S CHRISTIAN WOMAN: "Start a Hospitality Notebook," Fall 1982, and "How to Talk to Your Mother," Winter 1980, by Dale Hanson Bourke; "Budget: Where Has All the Money Gone," Summer 1980. How to Help a Dependent Friend," Fall 1982, and "What Every Woman Should Know About Car Repairs," Spring 1981, by Kelsey Menehan; "Let Yourself Be Loved," Summer 1982, by Ron Wilson.

KRISTINE MILLER TOMASIK: "Divorced But Not Defeated" reprinted by permission of the author.

TYNDALE HOUSE PUBLISHERS: Excerpts from YOUR MONEY: FRUSTRATION OR FREEDOM? by Howard L. Dayton, Jr. Published by Tyndale House Publishers, Inc., © 1971 by Howard L. Dayton, Jr. Used by permission. Excerpts from WHAT WIVES WISH THEIR HUSBANDS KNEW ABOUT WOMEN by Dr. James Dobson. Published by Tyndale House Publishers, Inc., © 1975. Used by permission. Excerpts from A PIECE OF ME IS MISSING by Marilyn Cram Donahue. Published by Tyndale House Publishers, Inc., © 1978 by Marilyn Cram Donahue. Used by permission. Excerpts from LET ME BE A WOMAN by Elisabeth Elliot. Published by Tyndale House Publishers, Inc., © 1976. Used by permission. HOW TO HANDLE PRESSURE by Clyde and Ruth Narramore. Published by Tyndale House Publishers, Inc., © 1975. Used by permission. FOR FAMILES ONLY by J. Allan Petersen. Published by Tyndale House Publishers, Inc., © 1977. Used by permission.

THE UNITED PRESBYTERIAN CHURCH OF THE USA: "Myths and Facts About Rape and Battering," by the Council on Women and the Church.

UNITED STATES COMMISSION ON CIVIL RIGHTS: Excerpts from "Child Care and Equal Opportunity for Women."

VICTOR BOOKS: Excerpts from WHAT HUSBANDS WISH THEIR WIVES KNEW ABOUT MONEY by Larry Burkett, Victor Books, 1977. Excerpts from HOW TO REALLY LOVE YOUR CHILD by Dr. Ross Campbell, Victor Books, 1977. Excerpts from YOU CAN BE THE WIFE OF A HAPPY HUSBAND by Darien B. Cooper, Victor Books, 1974. Excerpts from 19 GIFTS OF THE SPIRIT by Leslie B. Flynn, Victor Books, 1974. Excerpts from CURE YOUR DEVOTIONAL BLAHS by Harland A. Hill, Victor Books, 1974. Excerpts from THE FRAGRANCE OF BEAUTY by Joyce Landorf, Victor Books, 1973. Excerpts from OVERCOMING STRESS by Jan Markell, Victor Books, 1982. Excerpts from DISCOVER YOUR WORTH by Mariam Neff, Victor Books, 1979. Excerpts from LONELINESS: LIVING BETWEEN THE TIMES by Nancy Potts, Victor Books, 1978.

VOLCANO PRESS, INC.: Excerpts from BATTERED WIVES, Revised, Updated, by Del Martin, © Del Martin, 1976, 1981; Volcano Press, Inc., San Francisco, CA.

FRANKLIN WATTS, INC.: Excerpts from THE BOOK OF HEALTH, Ernest L. Wynder, M.D., editor-in-chief. Published by Franklin Watts, Inc., 1981.

WESTMINSTER PRESS: Excerpts from AFTER SUICIDE by John H. Hewett. Copyright © 1980 The Westminster Press. Reprinted and used by permission. Excerpts from MARRIAGE AND THE MEMO METHOD by Paul A. Hauck and Edmund S. Kean. Copyright © 1975 The Westminster Press. Reprinted and used by permission.

ROBERT L. WISE: Excerpts from YOUR CHURNING PLACE by Robert L. Wise.

NYLA JANE WITMORE: Excerpts from I WAS AN OVER COMMITTED CHRISTIAN by Nyla Jane Witmore. .

WORD BOOKS, PUBLISHER: Excerpts from RADICAL RECOVERY by Janie Clausen, copyright © 1982, pp. 141–45; used by permission of Word Books, Publisher, Waco, Texas 76796. Excerpts from Billy Graham, TILL ARMAGEDDON, copyright © 1981 by Billy Graham, pp. 198–206; used by permission of Word Books, Publisher, Waco, Texas 76796. Excerpts from GETTING THERE FROM HERE by Cecil M. Murphey, copyright ©1981, pp. 11–15; 19–21; used by permission of Word Books, Publisher, Waco, Texas 76796. Excerpts from THE GIFT OF SEX by Clifford and Joyce Penner, copyright © 1981, pp. 195–200; 227–230; used by permission of Word Books, Publisher, Waco, Texas 76796.

THE ZONDERVAN CORPORATION: Excerpts taken from HOW TO WIN IN A CRISIS by Creath Davis. Copyright © 1976 by Creath Davis. Used by permission of the Zondervan Publishing House. Excerpts taken from THE ACT OF MARRIAGE by Tim and Beverly LaHaye. Copyright © 1976 by the Zondervan Corporation. Excerpts taken from DARE TO LIVE NOW! by Bruce Larson. Copyright © 1965 by Zondervan Publishing House. Excerpts taken from A WOMAN'S WORLD by Clyde M. Narramore. Copyright © 1963 by Zondervan Publishing House. Used by permission. Excerpts taken from THE ART OF LEARNING TO LOVE YOURSELF by Cecil Osborne. Copyright © 1976 by the Zondervan Corporation. Used by permission. Excerpts taken from THE ART OF UNDERSTANDING YOURSELF by Cecil Osborne. Copyright © 1967 by Zondervan Publishing House. Used by permission. Excerpts taken from A WOMAN'S CHOICE: Living Through Your Problems by Eugenia Price. Copyright © 1962 by Zondervan Publishing House. Used by permission. Excerpts taken from WOMAN TO WOMAN by Eugenia Price. Copyright © 1959 by Zondervan Publishing House. Used by permission. Excerpts taken from CHRISTIAN WOMEN AT WORK by Patricia Ward and Martha Stout. Copyright © 1981 by the Zondervan Corporation. Used by permission.

The
Encyclopedia
for Today's
Christian Woman

A

ABILITIES

WHAT GIFTS will you develop during your Super Years? What special powers do you possess? What is there about yourself that you can begin to foster, nurture, and enjoy?

Perhaps in the past you considered your own giftedness too slight to bother about. Or perhaps you *know* you hide your light (your talents for art, organization, public speaking, compassionate outreach, your gift for anything at all) under a bushel. Whatever the case, you can use the *3-D* approach.

Define your gifts. Begin with the simple recognition that you probably take for granted most of your giftedness and much about yourself that's unique. It's not easy to take an objective look at one's attributes, but do it anyhow. Remember, the outcome of this exercise should excite and even *ennoble* you, as you discover old and new personal treasures with which to bless others.

How, exactly, can you define your gifts? How to recognize your own latent talents? There are several ways to begin that personal search, but the best place to start might be with *desire. Which of my deep personal desires tie in directly with my special giftedness?*

There's an easy and graphic way you can answer such questions (not an answer, actually, but a thought process that could begin today and continue forever). Divide a large sheet of paper into three columns. Write:

1. I Want to *Be* . . .
2. I Want to *Do* . . .
3. I Want to *Own* . . .

Jot your thoughts beneath the appropriate headings as rapidly as they come to mind. Don't stop to think, just write. You'll be surprised at what emerges.

Then take another large sheet. At the top, write "My Gifts." List your accomplishments, beginning with walking, talking, singing, and other such fundamental functions. These are *gifts?* you ask. Of course! Try getting along without speech, sight, or a sense of smell.

As you write, begin to appreciate exactly how talented and well trained you've become. Driving a car: *Millions of people in this world could envy you that skill.* Reading: *Any illiterate man or woman would love to have such abilities!* Cooking: *Not only can you recognize dozens of foodstuffs, herbs, and condiments, you know how to use them. American supermarkets and food know-how would bewilder residents of this world's other six continents. Never take such skills for granted.*

You get the picture. Leave your lists where you can add to them regularly. You'll soon feel elated and amazed at what you see. You are gifted, talented, and superbly trained: it's all there in black and white! Obviously you're ready to give yourself away.

At that point, it's important to realize that *you begin exactly where you are.* Even without exceptional training, expensive tuition, or ponderous exercise, life by now has showered you with gifts beyond measure. You can relate to a widow who emerged on the American art scene a generation ago—a spare, simple housewife, who eventually astounded millions with her acute powers of observation.

Anna Mary Robertson Moses was past sixty when she picked up a brush and began to paint her memories of idyllic times and places in our national scene. Untrained, she never pretended to education she didn't possess. Throughout her sixties, seventies, eighties, nineties, and into her centennial year, Grandma Moses enchanted and enriched art critics and ordinary folk alike.

Special gifts? You can argue that Grandma Moses had them, or you can insist that she did not. That's really not the question. The point is, her decision to give herself away has enlarged us all.

Even had Grandma Moses never painted a lick, however, she possessed a God-given ability to see and share the sort of things that stir and touch us.

Develop your gifts. "Taste and quality can be self-taught," declared Stanley Marcus, former chairman of Neiman-Marcus. Beyond that teaching, though, lies a vitally important schooling common to every genius you've ever admired: persistency. *You can teach yourself to persist.* Through simply becoming persistent, you can develop your gifts. Indeed, there's no other way to do so!

Take a look at your own impressive list of personal gifts. Which do you consider your best strengths? How much did you *persist* in order to ski, play the piano, or use hand tools? Which lesser gifts on your list could you maximize through a simple decision to persist?

George Washington Carver, towering scientist, educator, and humanitarian, was born during America's Civil War into a world that could offer virtually no encouragement toward fostering his considerable talents. Lawrence Elliott's book, *George Washington Carver: The Man Who Overcame,* records the incredible exploits Carver derived from sheer persistence. Born black, choosing to cast his lot with other blacks in the rural South; struggling to educate himself and others during the bleak and hungry years of postwar reconstruction; it's incredible to

imagine Carver gaining even a toehold on life, despite his genius.

George Washington Carver, by dint of assiduous self-directed work and study, became a giant in American science even as he helped develop a struggling black college in rural, backwoods Alabama. At Tuskegee Institute, the rustic school which would become world-famous through his influence, Carver studied the lowly peanut. Before he died, the homely "goober pea" had more than three hundred industrial uses!

Yes, develop your gifts. Like Dr. Carver, you can learn to continue feeding and exercising your talents. You do not require genius to learn persistency. However, every genius has learned to persist.

Decide to become a giver. In *Priceless Gifts: How to Give the Best to Those You Love,* author and clinical psychologist Dr. Daniel A. Sugarman says our capacity for happiness is only as great as our ability to give and express love. . . . What's more, you'll never become too old to give, or too feeble, or too poor.

Lydia Niebuhr, mother of the noted theologian Reinhold Niebuhr, personified the giver of truly precious gifts, the gifts of self. "Even in her mid-eighties, she was a Pied Piper to the children on the McCormick Seminary campus who visited her several times a week to paint and carve, to sew and make designs out of stained glass, to cook and eat," Niebuhr's biographer recounted. *Lydia Niebuhr knew how to give herself away.*

Define your gifts. Develop your gifts. Decide to give. That's the 3-D approach to life beyond your wildest dreams!

—From Charlotte Hale, *The Super Years.* Old Tappan, N.J.: Revell, 1984.

Possess and Use Your Talents

You cannot impress God with your human abilities. He knows all about what you can and can't do in your own strength. If you want to make a real imprint on this world, do something great in life, count yourself as worthwhile, use your Talent.

Put aside those aspirations that vaunt your own natural abilities over the power of God in your life (including in your ministry). Almost everyone has some sort of natural talent. God wants *you.*

The reward for the two servants who used their talents is what every person on earth wants: joy, delight, blessedness. ". . . Enter into and share the joy—the delight, the blessedness—which your master [enjoys]" (Matthew 25:23 AMPLIFIED).

The investment of the Holy Spirit in a human life has incomparable rewards. The master told the servants who invested wisely, "Well done, good and faithful servant; you have shown you can be faithful in small things, I will trust you with greater. . . ."

How do you apply the truths in this parable to your life? Let me give you a progression to bring you to the point where you will unquestionably "enter into the joy of the Lord."

How to possess and use your talent:

1. Receive the Talent, which is the Holy Spirit within you.
2. Exercise the Talent so He will multiply within you. This is done by believing in Him and who He is through faithful meditating (walking and talking) the Word of God.
3. Give yourself as a gift to God. You're a Spirit-filled, Spirit-multiplied person and you belong to Him. He promises to enter you into His joy.
4. Receive your interests, skills, fruitful endeavors, labors, and works. (Here's where you can develop your dream of skydiving for Jesus or heavenly hairdressing or writing, singing, cooking, mule packing—whatever!) Because He has found you faithful in a little, He can give you much.
5. Now because your main Talent and lifeline is the power of the Holy Spirit, all that you do you do with the joy of the Lord as your strength. Though things get rough and you find yourself in difficult straits, you have entered into the Master's joy and you don't quit or despair.

6. You continue to multiply and multiply. "For to everyone who has will be given more, and he will have more than enough."
7. He gives unto you good measure, running over for the purpose of your giving to others. You're now able to obey the Holy Spirit as He moves you into the realm of the Lord's New Commandment. "Then shall the righteous shine forth as the sun in the kingdom of their Father . . ." (Matthew 13:43).

You're shining with a dazzling light of power and love, multiplying the power of the Holy Spirit within you and through you.

Now you're *really* Talented.

—From Marie Chapian, *Love and Be Loved.* Old Tappan, N.J.: Revell, 1983.

ABORTION

THE DICTIONARY defines the word *abortion:* "Expulsion of a fetus from the womb before it is sufficiently developed to survive." *Fetus* is defined as "the offspring in the womb from the end of the third month of pregnancy until birth."

When we look at the use of words in the English language, we discover they can be used to change the meaning of an act. Dr. C. Everett Koop, chief surgeon of Children's Hospital in Philadelphia, said, "I am convinced that we are using certain words to depersonalize the unborn baby. It doesn't pose such a problem when you decide to kill it. It's easier to kill a fetus than an unborn baby" (*Christianity Today,* December 15, 1978).

If we substituted, "unborn child" every time we saw the word *fetus,* we might get a different perspective on the subject of abortion.

Woman is designed to bear children. When a woman becomes pregnant, everything in her starts to prepare for nurturing and carrying a child to term in pregnancy. From a purely biological standpoint, I believe abortion is destructive to the woman, because it halts a very fast development within her. It is contrary to nature.

It's significant that some cancer specialists believe women who nurse their babies are less apt to develop breast cancer than those who take pills to dry up. Perhaps this is a poor parallel, but in my honest opinion there are unpleasant effects, physical, mental, and spiritual to abortion.

First of all, there is the guilt trauma. Somehow a woman feels she has foiled and failed her womanhood in aborting her child. Years ago, when abortion was illegal, many women died from infection. Today there is less danger, physically, since abortion is legal in many areas. A Christian doctor said, "Just because it's legal doesn't make it right."

However, there is no real way of telling what long-term damage abortion does to a woman physically, particularly when she has more than one. Today, where it is legal, some women have come to depend upon abortion as a form of birth control, and see it as something no worse than taking the "pill."

Freewheeling sex outside of wedlock most certainly is not helping to curb abortion. I have known women who have had abortions and then found it next to impossible to conceive or carry a child when they wanted a family.

ARE THERE EXCEPTIONS?

There are pros and cons about the issue, and no one case is exactly the same as another. However, the Bible says, "Thou shalt not kill," and there is penalty somewhere, sometime for killing.

God is not mocked, and we shouldn't kid ourselves about this. He sees all and knows all. This is not to say He will not forgive, if one is truly repentant. This is what the Cross is all about.

I cannot understand anyone aborting after the end of three months, legal or not, unless something happens in the pregnancy where the mother's life is in jeopardy.

In the case of rape or incest, I believe the woman should be taken care of immediately, for if a pregnancy should develop, that little unborn child, having been conceived by violence in rape, or by deception of the incestuous parent, faces a pretty dim future. Many criminals have this kind of background. Such a child as this has been conceived in conditions contrary to the loving creativity of God.

Many times when a woman has aborted a child because she didn't want it, or the man didn't, she later begins to wonder what she gave up. Was it a boy or girl? If he or she had lived, who would the child resemble? I meet many women who have opened their hearts to me, knowing that I will not divulge their secret guilt feelings. I know that abortion is not the will of God, and that there is penalty somewhere along the line.

IS THERE AN ALTERNATIVE?

Abortion is sad, for so many reasons. In my book, it should only be considered in the most dire, bizarre, and impossible situations.

There are many childless couples who desire to adopt, love, and raise a baby. If at all possible, a woman who is unwed, or unable to raise a child alone, should carry the child and place it for adoption.

Here is where Christians can be of great help. If we understand the grace of God, we should extend our help and love to those girls who have the courage to have their babies, even in the face of the worldly trend toward destructive abortion.

Adoption is God's way. He invented the idea and we are all adopted. The Bible says, ". . . we should behave like God's very own children, adopted into the bosom of his family. . ." (Romans 8:15 TLB).

Where do you stand on this subject? Are you firm enough in your convictions about the worth of a human life? This is one of the biggest issues facing women today. It could affect generations to come.

—From Dale Evans Rogers, *Woman*. Old Tappan, N.J.: Revell, 1980.

FOR FURTHER READING:

Koop, C. Everett. *The Right to Live; The Right to Die.* Wheaton, Ill.: Tyndale, 1976.

LaHaye, Beverly. *I Am a Woman By God's Design.* Old Tappan, N.J.: Revell, 1980.

Martin, Walter. *Abortion: Is It Always Murder?* Ventura, Calif.: Vision House, 1977.

Schaeffer, Francis A., and C. Everett Koop, M.D. *Whatever Happened to the Human Race?* Old Tappan, N.J.: Revell, 1979.

ACCEPTANCE

Of Husband

God has a plan through which you can learn to accept your husband. It is clearly outlined in Philippians 4:4, 6–8 (BECK): "Be happy in the Lord always! . . . Don't worry about anything, but in everything go to God, and pray to let Him know what you want, and give thanks. Then God's peace, better than our thinking, will guard your hearts and minds in Christ Jesus. . . . Keep your minds on all that is true or noble, right or pure, lovely or appealing, on anything that is excellent or that deserves praise."

The first step in God's plan is to commit all of your problems to Him. Regardless of what has worried, upset, or irritated you, Christ says you should tell Him about it. Then let Him work it out. Resist the impulse to return to the problem because you've "thought of something else that might work." Trust Him for the solution. If you don't, you're saying in effect, "God, You are not able to handle my problem."

Don't be like the man who was walking along the road with a heavy load on his back. A farmer stopped to give him a ride. The man climbed onto the farmer's truck but left the load on his back. "Why don't you put your load down on the truck?" the farmer called out to him.

"It was so kind of you to give me a ride," the man answered, "I don't want to ask you to carry my load too."

How foolish! But that is what you do when you do not let Jesus Christ carry all of your burdens. He died for you and paid for your sins. He offers you victory over each problem and is pleased when you claim it (see 1 Corinthians 10:13).

How do you commit your burdens or problems to God? By talking to Him about them. That's prayer—simply opening up to God, knowing He understands perfectly. God will not force His solutions on you even though He is God of the universe. Instead, He waits for you to come to Him and share with Him and ask for His help.

Since He sees things from a different viewpoint and knows what's best for you, don't limit Him by telling Him when and how to answer your prayers. Let Him work out your problems according to His timing and plan. Then thank Him for answering, trusting Him to do what is best.

After giving your problems to God and thanking Him for taking care of them, fix your mind on whatever pure, honorable, and praiseworthy qualities your husband has (if your problem involves him). Does he get up each morning, regardless of how he feels, and go to work? Thank God. Is he kind and gentle to the children? Thank the Lord. Is he a sociable guy? Be grateful.

If you have a hard time thinking of some positive traits, think back to the qualities that drew you to him before marriage. Those traits are still in him but may have been buried during the years of your marriage. Concentrate on his positive traits and his weaknesses will diminish. This idea is different from a "self-improvement" plan because you're trusting God to improve you and your husband as you follow His formula.

It might be comforting to realize that negative traits are distorted positive traits. If negative traits can be modified or channeled in the right direction, they can become strengths. Stubbornness can become perseverance. Cowardice can be turned to gentleness. Tactlessness can be turned to frankness. If you trust Jesus Christ to take care of your husband's problems, and fix your mind on his assets, you can help him turn bad traits into good ones.

The results you can expect are described in Philippians 4:8. You will experience God's peace which is more wonderful than the human mind can understand. It is a deep, inner quietness that depends not on circumstances, but on your relationship with Jesus Christ.

The formula can be stated in this way: Problems transferred to Christ, plus focusing on the positive, equals peace.

APPLICATION

Now that you know you should accept your husband as he is, try to apply the principle in your own marriage relationship. Look for opportunities to tell your husband that you are glad he is the kind of man he is. Tell him you know you have made many mistakes and are willing to correct them. Explain that you realize you have not been the loving, understanding, submissive wife you should have been.

Do not confess past immorality. You may relieve your own guilt but hurt your husband. If you have made such mistakes, simply confess them to Jesus Christ and accept His forgiveness. He forgives and forgets and so should you. Show your husband through your actions as well as your words that you accept him as he is. Both of you will begin to experience the sheer joy and freedom that comes from following God's principles.

—From Darien B. Cooper, *You Can Be the Wife of a Happy Husband.* Wheaton, Ill.: Victor Books, 1974.

Of Others

We must make allowances for the faults or mistakes of others. Love requires this as a part of our behavior.

Some years ago, I wrote my personal paraphrase of 1 Corinthians 13:4–7. "I am very patient and kind, never jealous or envious, never boastful or proud, never haughty or selfish or rude. I do not demand my own way. I am not irritable or touchy. I do not hold grudges and will hardly even notice when my husband does me wrong. I am never glad about injustice, and rejoice whenever truth wins out. Because I love my husband (or child or friend) I will be loyal to him no matter what the cost. I will always stand my ground in defending him."

When we live these characteristics on a daily basis, we do not nitpick. Minor personal habits do not become a source of arguments. We give each other room to have different habits from our own. When the other fails, I see him through sympathetic eyes of love rather than an "I told you so" attitude. If he has a certain weakness, I protect him from criticism rather than expose his inability.

Many people think it is funny to cut down their mate or children. If you have a little humor, it's good for lots of laughs. But it isn't good for your relationships. Cutting down another person isn't "making room."

Have you developed the habit of being down on people, seeing weaknesses rather than strengths? Do you dwell on failures rather than another's abilities and potential? Read 1 Corinthians 13—the personalized version—every morning for a month or so. Memorize it. You will develop the ability to make room for your child, for your mate, for your friend.

—From Mariam Neff, *Discover Your Worth.* Wheaton, Ill.: Victor Books, 1979.

FOR FURTHER READING:

Osborne, Cecil G. *The Art of Learning to Love Yourself.* Grand Rapids: Zondervan, 1976.

Powell, John S. *Why Am I Afraid to Tell You Who I Am?* Allen, Tex.: Argus, 1970.

Powell, John S. *Unconditional Love.* Allen, Tex.: Argus, 1978.

Wallace, Joanne. *The Image of Loveliness.* Old Tappan, N.J.: Revell, 1978.

Wilke, Richard B. *Tell Me Again, I'm Listening.* Nashville: Abingdon, 1973.

24

ADOPTION

PERHAPS YOU and your husband are unable to, or have, for reasons of your own, chosen not to have children. Prayerfully you have decided that with all the homeless babies in the world, adoption *is* a part of God's plan for you.

To you I say, "Bravo!" I really do hope and pray you take up the option of adoption. I can think of no people in the world better suited to adopt children than a man and woman who love God and each other.

Only eternity will tell the full story of what *might* have happened to that baby had he *not* been adopted by Christian parents. Parents who gave him God's unconditional love, nurtured him physically, mentally, and spiritually, and then released him as an adult to serve the Lord.

In my Bible study and in seminars, I have asked women who have adopted a child this question: "What did people say when they found out you were adopting?" Generally, the answers have been frustratingly familiar. They went something like this: "It's nice you adopted a baby (or child), but you can never know how a real mother feels until you've actually given birth."

Hog wash! Three times I discovered I was pregnant. And two out of the three times I reacted by throwing up my hands (and my dinner) and hollering, "Oh, no!" Fortunately, by the end of the sixth month I changed my mind, but not so with a woman who wants to adopt. She takes a flying leap at loving that child *long, long* before she's even sure she's going to get him. Her head start on motherhood eclipses mine in an instant. Also, according to friends of ours who have one natural child and one adopted— *there is no difference in their parental love for each child.*

Besides the tactless, unfounded response about a mother of an adopted child never really being able to know how a "real" mother feels, here are some of the other typical questions frequently asked of a couple who is considering adoption:

"Are you really sure you want to get involved with someone else's child?"

"If the baby turns out to be sickly or retarded, can you give it back?"

"How much did this adoption cost you?"

All of these questions are positively humiliating to the couple who has prayed and waited out the long procedures involved in adopting. All this couple needs to hear from us as they are "expecting their child" is, "Praise the Lord! Children are a gift from God, and we'll be praying that you become very special parents to this very special child!"

I just love it during a baby dedication at church when the pastor turns from the couple and their child, faces the audience and asks, "Do you pledge, before God, to prayerfully uphold this couple as they train and nurture this child? Do you promise to be supportive to this child in case this marriage is dissolved by death or divorce? And finally, do you see how very much this young couple needs the loving approval of this congregation—especially in times like these?"

When the audience's answer to these questions is a resounding yes—heaven records the ringing joy! And then the who's, what's and how's of this couple's adoption should be put to rest.

Not too long ago, I heard a young man talk about his parents. He had been adopted by them as a baby, and when asked if he would be interested in someday meeting his biological mother, he answered kindly, "Yes, I'd be interested in meeting her. She gave birth to me, and saw that I was placed in a good home; but those things in themselves did not make her my mother. While I'm grateful to her—still, it was my adoptive parents who sat up nights with me when I was little and sick; worried with me when things weren't going well in school; fed me—both physically and spiritually; laughed and cried with me; and shared my heartaches, disappointments, joys, and triumphs. They are my *real* parents."

Nobody, absolutely nobody, is better equipped, darling Christian woman, to be a mother to an adopted child than you! Even if you are on the foster-care mother program, and have babies and children for only a short time—you still have a portion of the mind of Christ, and that alone sets you miles ahead in the wisdom department. And who knows— since all children are only *loaned* to us— maybe this brief time with you will be the one and only time when this child touches base with the loving Lord.

Go to it, in all joy!

—From Joyce Landorf, *Changepoints.* Old Tappan, N.J.: Revell, 1981.

Special Children

The availability of children for adoption has decreased dramatically in the past decade. Due to freely available contraceptives and the legalization of abortions, but mainly due to the removal of social stigma against unwed parenthood, there are few babies to be found for adoption. To be sure, there are some and, tragically, "black-marketing" (selling babies) has become all too common. But the average waiting time in this country for adopting an infant is about three and a half years.

OLDER CHILDREN

More easily found, however, are older children. Many of these were children of unwed mothers who desperately tried to care for them and couldn't. They had to give them up. Some of these babies, due to the immense stress and inexperience of their young mothers, received a less-than-ideal start in life, and thus present special needs and handicaps. Many times these can be overcome. But the first eighteen months are crucial ones in a child's habit patterning and development. We may wish that a toddler were just as easy to accept, love, and raise as an infant, but that simply is not so, especially when he has been neglected or abused. We may empathize and care about the heroic

young mothers, too, but that doesn't change the facts, either. In many large cities, one out of every five births is to a teenage mother (often unmarried). Rarely have they gained the maturity and experience it takes to successfully parent a child. Every community needs to take action about such a deplorable situation.

HANDICAPPED CHILDREN

But that is not the purpose of this book. There are many adoptable children of two or three years. There are also a number who have various physical or emotional handicaps who may be adopted. Many of these require costly medical attention and certainly need parents who can manage to honestly accept and love them as they are. They demand a fine balance in empathy and concern, but firmness and consistency in expecting them to help overcome the handicap as fully as possible.

CHILDREN FROM OVERSEAS

There also are children from other countries who need parents. After the Korean War, there were many Korean children, fathered by American servicemen, who were brought to America for adoption. This has continued with full-blooded Koreans, half-American Vietnamese, as well as children from various other countries. The death rates in some impoverished countries leave a disproportionate number of orphans, and there are several adoption agencies which can help you find such children. There is, unfortunately, a great length of red tape to untangle in bringing such a child to this country.

CHILDREN OF OTHER RACES

In many communities, there is still some racial prejudice. This is tragic but true. So

26

before you decide on adopting a child of another race, be careful that you are doing him a favor. Sound out your friends, neighbors, schools, and church. See if they will accept, love, and help you raise this special child with sincerity. If not, you may even move to a community that is more democratic. A child may be better off in poverty in his own country than to live in prosperity yet suffer the rejection of prejudice.

Considerations in Adoption

Telling the Child He's Adopted

If you decide to adopt a child, there are several ideas you must consider. First, how and when should you tell him he is adopted? If he is older or of another nationality, he may well know from the start that he is adopted. If not, you will want to tell him before he hears from someone else. For some reason, it is shocking to a child to learn that his parents did not give birth to him.

In a well-meant effort to save children from such a shock, adoptive parents many years ago tried very hard to keep children from finding out that they had been adopted. Fortunately, that practice gave way to a better one (in our opinion). Adoptive parents started, when the child was one year of age, to have a biological birthday celebration and an adoptive anniversary party. They would explain to this small child about their search for him and how very much they loved and wanted him. This helped the child to view his adoption as a happy event. It is likely that some parents overplayed this, and perhaps a more ideal plan is to simply begin to explain as soon as the parents wish.

Have Information About Biological Parents

Adoptive parents need to understand their feelings about not having a child of their own. They must get over any sense of failure,

inferiority, or guilt if they are to be free to be really confident parents. In the case of adoption, *it is also urgent that adoptive parents know something and feel comfortable about the child's biological parents.* Sooner or later, many adoptive children become curious about their background. They will want to know how their mothers or fathers looked, what they did for a living, what their interests were, and rarely spoken, but extremely important: *Why did they give me away?*

—From Grace H. Ketterman, M.D., and Herbert L. Ketterman, M.D., *The Complete Book of Baby and Child Care for Christian Parents.* Old Tappan, N.J.: Revell, 1982.

Open Adoption

Open adoptions range from the sharing of identifying information without a face-to-face meeting, to arrangements in which there is ongoing contact between the two families. The variations are designed to meet the needs of all members of the adoption triangle.

The move away from secrecy and "sealed records" grows out of the changing nature of adoption itself. It has been assumed that older children who are adopted have developed ties to their biological family that should be maintained. "Sunday's Child," a weekly profile of adoptable children that runs in the *Boston Globe* newspaper, frequently notes that a particular child or sibling group will need to have a continuing relationship with siblings, with members of their extended family, or with their foster parents. The best interest of the child, not standard practice or custom, dictates the amount of openness appropriate for each adoption.

Activist groups such as Orphan Voyage (a support group for adoptees) and Concerned United Birthparents (CUB) have raised the public consciousness that adoptees do have roots. And birthparents do *not* just go home and forget they have ever had a child. The need for the two to know about each other goes beyond mere curiosity.

Recognizing these needs, some agencies have begun to experiment with open adoption. As early as 1976, a report on successful placements of this sort appeared in the professional press ("Open Adoption," *Social Work*, Vol. 21, No. 2, March 1976). Catholic Charities in Green Bay, Wisconsin, has been quietly and effectively arranging open adoptions for some time.

Adoptive parents sometimes express fear that in an open adoption they will risk losing their children or will feel "demoted" to babysitting for the "real" parents. Orphan Voyage, CUB, and the agencies involved in open adoptions stress that adoption is a permanent and legally-binding relationship between adoptive parents and their children. But they point to a growing number of open adoptions that demonstrate that these fears, for the most part, are unfounded.

Last winter, a coalition of adoptees, birthparents, adoptive parents, and agency representatives met in Cambridge, Massachusetts, to draft a statement on placement philosophy. That statement, when it is completed, may form the basis for more widespread experimentation with the new modes of adoption.

For more information about open adoption, write:

Concerned United Birthparents, Inc.
P.O. Box 396
Cambridge, MA 02138

Orphan Voyage
c/o Jean Paton
Cedaredge, CO 81413

—ELIZABETH HORMANN, books editor for *Single Parent*, single parent of five, an adoptive parent, and social worker.

FOR FURTHER READING:

Dennis, Muriel, ed. *Chosen Children*. Westchester, Ill.: Good News Publisher, 1978.
Small, Dwight Hervey. *Design for Christian Marriage*. Old Tappan, N.J.: Revell, 1959.

Strauss, Richard L. *Confident Children and How They Grow*. Wheaton, Ill.: Tyndale, 1975.

ADULTERY

Can a Person Truly Be Forgiven of Adultery?

The sins of adultery, homosexuality, and murder were held as capital crimes in the Bible, as evidenced by the death penalty (Leviticus 20:10). Clearly, human life is of prime importance in the Word of God, and these sins affect the perpetuity of life. In spite of that, Jesus Christ's sacrifice on the cross is sufficient to cleanse these or any other sins (1 John 1:7, 9). Further evidence of God's pardon of this sin appears in Jesus' forgiveness of the woman taken in adultery (John 8:1–11) and the woman with five husbands who was living with still another (John 4:1–12).

—From Tim and Beverly La Haye, *The Act of Marriage*. Grand Rapids: Zondervan, 1976.

FOR FURTHER READING:

LaHaye, Tim and Bev. *Spirit-Controlled Family Living*. Old Tappan, N.J.: Revell, 1978.
Murphey, Cecil B., compiler. *Encyclopedia of Christian Marriage*. Old Tappan, N.J.: Revell, 1983.
Penner, Clifford and Joyce. *The Gift of Sex*. Waco, Tex.: Word Books, 1981.
Small, Dwight Hervey. *Your Marriage Is God's Affair*. Old Tappan, N.J.: Revell, 1979.
White, Mel. *Lust: The Other Side of Love*. Old Tappan, N.J.: Revell, 1980.

AGING

Facts and Myths

One out of every 7 Americans is over 60. In this century (thanks to a baby boom between 1900 and 1910, and declining mortality rates thereafter), the number of older

Americans has increased two-and-a-half times as fast as the overall population.

If you're 35 years old, and a man, the chances are 8 in 10 you'll live to be 60—9 in 10 if you're a woman. And when you reach your sixties and seventies, you don't automatically arrive at death's door. At 65, the average life expectancy is 16 more years; at 75, another 10.

The percentage and number of people who live to be 80 and beyond is growing. Not only are old people *not* alike—they are growing more diverse every day. Their lifestyles are becoming more varied. The old have more time than ever for leisure.

But less opportunity for work.

Because of stereotypes about old age, older Americans are kept from participating actively—as wage earners, as volunteer workers, as neighbors, as sources of wisdom—in the mainstream of American life.

In 1900, 2 out of 3 men past 65 worked for a living. Today, only 1 in 5 does.

Mandatory retirement (along with a decline in self-employment) has helped separate many older Americans from the workplace. And many, many older Americans are far from happy with the situation.

This problem doesn't affect just people over 65. According to the U.S. Department of Labor, you're an older worker if you're 45-plus. (You even have your own "week"— "Hire the Older Worker Week.")

Some people, of course, do look forward to retirement. But many others do not. And more and more people who *want* to work are being deprived of the *option* to work.

If so many people want to work past 60 or 65, what's the problem?

The problem is that many employers have accepted the stereotype of older workers as being less capable than younger workers.

As studies have shown, the opposite is the case.

Older workers have *less* absenteeism than younger workers. They have *fewer* on-the-job accidents. They are *more* satisfied with their jobs and no less efficient.

Younger workers report *more* stress than

older workers, show *higher* rates of admission to psychiatric facilities and use psychotropic drugs more often.

Contrary to myth, older workers are no more subject to depression than younger workers.

Mandatory retirement may actually force people out of work at the height of their careers or even *before* they've reached their full productive powers.

Some employers (Bankers Life & Casualty of Chicago, for example) have recognized that optional or conditional retirement works and works well.

Unfortunately, the drift over the last 75 years has been toward earlier, forced retirement.

One of the arguments offered in defense of early retirement is that older people can get by on less than younger people.

Many older people *do* get by on less. They have to—they have less money. But financial needs don't suddenly taper off at 65. As a result, many older people have financial problems.

This does *not* mean, however, that older people as a whole are a negligible market. *One in 9 Americans is over 65; yet, older Americans account for 1 of every 5 dollars spent for food consumed at home. In addition, they spend about 20 percent of all dollars spent for nonprescription drugs.*

Yes, old people have more chronic ailments than young people. But in most cases, these ailments aren't terribly limiting.

Only 10 percent of people over 65 are confined in any serious way. An even smaller proportion requires unusual attention. Only 1 over-65 person in 20 lives in an institution.

For most older people, there's no reason to regard the years past 60 as a time for rest and curtailed activity. Indeed, there is every reason *not* to. For the old as well as the young, exercise is basic to health and well-being.

So is sex—for the old no less than the young. Some older people, conditioned to associate sexuality with youth, are embarrassed by their sexual desires and try to deny them. Others equate "old" with "unattractive" and retire from the field. In most cases, there is no physiological basis for this loss of interest.

Of the many myths about old age, the image of all older people as sick, fragile, disabled and sexless is the most inaccurate of stereotypes.

Like most minorities, old people are victims of language. The word *senile*, for example, has a long history of medical abuse.

What doctors now call schizophrenia used to be known as *dementia praecox* or "premature madness"—as opposed to *senile dementia* or the "madness of old age."

In other words:

"Sure he's crazy. He's old."

There *are* degenerative diseases of the brain which afflict old people. But senility is not, by any means, an inevitable consequence of growing old. And not every mental disorder in old people is the result of brain damage.

Often doctors as well as laymen fail to grasp this point. What is diagnosed as "senility" may actually be the by-product of anemia, malnutrition or infection. Such conditions may be fully reversible. There may be no organic disease whatsoever, in which case psychotherapy may help. More often than not, old people do respond to psychotherapy—contrary to popular belief.

Learning ability does not decline significantly with age. Vocabulary and conceptual skills often grow after 60. In the absence of brain disease, old people are not notably more forgetful than young people. Depression is an unfortunate fact of American life, not a peculiarity of the aged. Old neurotics are no more "infantile" than young neurotics. The majority of older people are *not* "set in their ways." On the contrary, they can be remarkably adaptable. They've had to be. They've lived through more technological and social change than any other group in history—from the horse and buggy to the supersonic transport.

In short, the stereotype of dotty old age is just that—a stereotype. The sooner we all learn to do without it, the better, because it can obscure the real medical and social causes of distress affecting millions of older people.

—From *Facts and Myths About Aging*, 1981, published by The National Council on the Aging, Inc.

Qualities of the Aging

Let's take a look at these six special qualities of older people.

TEMPERATE

We should be temperate and cool under pressure. We older ones are to set the pace in being self-controlled and moderate in our actions. Often we have seen two young men engage in verbal or outright physical conflict, and someone will call for the "older heads to prevail." People really do expect something better from us. The temperate, moderate, self-controlled older person is the way he is because this quality of life in the Spirit is gained only through years of experience. Grandparent, be a model of temperate living for others.

DIGNIFIED

In redeeming us from our subhuman state and restoring us to full humanity, God gives back our dignity and intrinsic worth as persons. Because we are valuable to God, an older person is to be one marked by dignity, a stately person with an elevated character. An older person should not be proud and pretentious, but one who has a place of honor among others. Our "hoary heads" speak of an honor of age that God has placed upon us. While not thinking of yourself more highly than you ought, thank the Lord for the dignity which accompanies your length of years.

SENSIBLE

"Be sensible!" How many times I heard that in my youth when I came up with what

I thought was a great idea. But the sensibleness of older men around me kept me from getting into the errors they had previously made. Their experience gave them a ready discernment that often prevented me from doing "that which was right in my own eyes." There were times when I would be jealous of their years and would strive to be as sensible as they were. But you have to pay your dues and let good sense come with experience. Job was absolutely right when he stated, "Wisdom is with aged men, With long life is understanding" (Job 12:12).

SOUND IN FAITH

The stalwarts of the faith are recorded in Hebrews 11. This Hall of Fame of Faith contains the names of men and women who believed God, and it was counted unto them as righteousness. People like Noah and Abraham were examples of how walking with God for many years was rewarded. They were sound in faith, having been tested and tried in the most difficult circumstances.

In my experience I can think of many older Christians whom I followed—I've ridden on the coattails of their faith. These men and women seemed to have been through it all in their walk with God; and I knew that if *they* could trust God in a tough situation, *I* could too.

SOUND IN LOVE

Being sound in love also comes from a maturing and lasting walk with God. There is an unusual emotion that comes to you when you are loved by an older person. The older the person, the more significant the love. You see, the older person can best spot a phony, and you can be sure that if he loves you, it will be sound!

SOUND IN PERSEVERANCE

Webster says perseverance is "a continuance in a state of grace until it is succeeded

by a state of glory." This definition properly describes the quality of life I have found in older Christian brothers. These men are counting on God to bring them to a state of glory as they now are persevering in a state of grace. How often we have been encouraged by those who are looking for the blessed hope. These older saints of God, persisting in spite of the counter influences of the enemy, exhibit a quiet confidence that they will be taken by the Lord when He comes.

—From Ken Berven, *I Love Being Married to a Grandma.* Nashville: Nelson, 1978.

AGING PARENTS

NO ONE HAS absolute statistics on the number of singles or formerly marrieds who have major care for declining and/or disabled parents. Estimates are that 70 percent of senior adults live in their own homes; 20 percent live in hotels, rooming houses, or with relatives; and 5 percent need some kind of institutional care. But how many of the 23 million senior adults will need some direct or indirect attention and assistance from a daughter or son? It could be 5 or 6 million, but probably the number is higher. Numbers are of no concern here; rather, concern focuses on *who* and *what* is involved in caring for shut-in parents. . . .

A part of this initial and continuing appraisal is determining the level of dependency of a parent. This is not simply nor entirely a medical diagnosis. Mother Nature often brings us full circle from total dependency to almost full independency to eventual dependency again. Seldom does any change come drastically or immediately. How does a parent-child relationship gracefully switch roles? Parents are always parents; children remain offspring forever. That simple fact can make it difficult to be objective about the proper time for discreet checks on parents from some distance to protect their self-assurance, the time for intermediate care or change of residence, even finally to the time for nursing care in your home or a health facility. . . .

No short article could offer you solutions to all of the unique decisions and situations you may face with your shut-in adult. As one who has "walked in a similar pair of shoes," may I condense some of what I learned (sometimes the hard way!) into the "Ten Commandments for Caretakers for Shut-Ins":

1. *Don't expect to be superhuman!* None of us can be all things to all people—not even ourselves. If you trust your help, *let go* of their tasks. Recognize your priorities, make a semi-flexible time schedule, and don't feel guilty when you fail or fall short occasionally—as you surely must.

2. *Expect stress.* Every normal, thinking, alive person lives with some stress. With a shut-in, you will have more. Oftentimes, physical activities will help relieve mental anxieties, as well as the reverse. Frustration may come out in your tone of voice as anger. It is important to explain to an elder parent that the resentment, anger, or frustration is not personally directed toward the parent. Reassure the parent that he or she did not necessarily contribute to your frustration. But it is important to your mental health to ventilate a general sense of stress occasionally.

3. *Combine tasks with communication.* I often explained to my shut-in, friends, and visitors that the tasks I could do manually while I talked with them were made easier. I often moved my blind mother or sat in her den to chat while I mended or sorted clothing, prepared something for a meal, or did my nails.

4. *Plan an outside activity for yourself at least once a week.* Vary the event as well as your companions. You will discover that you will bring a fresh perspective and new topics of conversation to your homebound loved one.

5. *Talk openly and frequently to a confidante,* but seldom should you dwell on the negatives of your situation. A true friend or counselor will understand your joys and resentments without passing judgment on you.

6. *Provide multigenerational contacts for your shut-in.* As precious as her age-mates were to my shut-in, she delighted in the preschoolers who came by with their parents. Some of her favorite night-sitters were responsible high-school seniors who came when I had night meetings. They loved her anecdotes, learned to manipulate the potty-chair, and played the guitar for her.

7. *Prepare for your visits with the doctor.* Make a list of questions and jot down carefully all instructions about medication and care. Your doctor can be on par with the pastoral friend.

8. *Vary the kind of help you use.* We had two different practical nurses (retired) in the daytime and two college girls to sleep in on alternate nights, plus a list of teenagers and singles who asked to come now and then. It was a bit more difficult at payroll time—but what an interesting array of people from the outside world!

9. *Use your church ministries.* Almost every church program—Sunday School, WMU, social ministries committees, family ministry—sincerely wants to help. Let them have the thrill of knowing your shut-in and helping you.

10. *Keep your own spiritual resources vital.* For one year I took a leave of absence from teaching my Bible class, returning once monthly to teach the entire department. One neighbor relieved me each Sunday night so I could attend worship services. I gave and I took spiritually. You should, too. Your spiritual health will be a

reservoir and preparation for the adjustment when your shut-in is released.

—SARAH FRANCES ANDERS, PH.D., "Others, Caring for Shut-in Adults," *Christian Single,* February 1983.

FOR FURTHER READING:

Berven, Ken. *I Love Being Married to a Grandma.* Nashville: Nelson, 1978.

Hyder, O. Quentin. *The People You Live With.* Old Tappan: N.J.: Revell, 1975.

Ortlund, Ray and Anne. *The Best Half of Life.* Waco, Tex.: Word Books, 1976.

Tournier, Paul. *Learn to Grow Old.* New York: Harper & Row, 1972.

AGORAPHOBIA

PANIC. TERROR. Fear. Fortunately, for most people, these feelings only rarely get a grip—and when they do, it's often in response to some voluntary confrontation like one of Hitchcock's greatest hits. But for a growing number of people—of which as many as 80 percent are women—a disabling panic attack complete with pounding heart, rapid pulse and cold sweat can strike anytime, anywhere. And, usually, it is in response to nothing at all—just a fleeting concern gone absolutely haywire.

It's called agoraphobia, which, literally translated, means fear of places of assembly but which actually encompasses a fear of many things. Fear of being hemmed in by crowds. Fear of disease and death. Eventually, even fear of leaving the house lest an attack should strike in unfamiliar surroundings. . . .

What brings on this curious array of symptoms is not entirely understood. But it appears to be triggered by stress. For example, a major operation, especially a gynecological one in which hormone balance is suddenly disturbed. An accident. A drastic life change—such as the birth of a child or the death of a loved one. Or even the more gradual stress of an upsetting life situation such as an unhappy marriage, or stressful work condition. Much hinges, of course, on how sensitive the person is and how well she can cope with stress.

"Your Emotional System Bulges at the Seams"

A person with an excitable personality and very strong feelings soon learns that our world doesn't tolerate intensity or people who dramatize, explains Arthur Hardy, M.D., director of the Territorial Apprehension Program, Inc. (TERRAP), a desensitization program for agoraphobics. "When you keep your feelings in, your body keeps score. Eventually your emotional system begins to bulge at the seams. When suppressed feelings finally come out in the open, they lead to a severe anxiety attack or panic."

Dr. Hardy says agoraphobia is a growing problem—1 out of every 100 persons may be affected to some degree. "We move faster. The world is more complicated. We have to know more people and go to school to know more things. Life requires a lot more coping skills than it used to."

Despite the increase in the number of cases, doctors often don't even know that any kind of treatment is available for this disorder. "It's like a secret disease," says Dr. Hardy. "Agoraphobia affects a lot more people than muscular dystrophy. It cripples more people than arthritis, and devastates more lives than other diseases, but it is not researched. You'd think an enlightened society like ours would know more about it, wouldn't you?"

With all of the mystery surrounding agoraphobia, some facts are known. Only a small percentage of agoraphobics become totally housebound, for instance. "A lot of agoraphobics get around and do things but at a great expense," says Dr. Hardy. "They feel nervous, upset, tense and tightened up all the while they're doing things."

A woman also is more likely to become an agoraphobic than a man. "About 76 percent of the patients we see are women," says Dr. Hardy. He has several theories on why it strikes females so often. Among them, he suggests that our culture requires more perfection from women. "They are taught to be ladylike and told not to swear or do naughty things," he says. There may be other cultural reasons or it may stem from biological differences between the sexes, he adds.

Although some people associate the condition with older women, agoraphobia actually begins at an average of 23.9 years. The problem is that young people may ignore early warning signs thinking they will outgrow them. Shyness or an extreme sensitivity to ordinary things in the world, like noise, may foreshadow problems that could get worse, says Dr. Hardy. Yet people can have agoraphobia for years before they finally get help.

The interesting thing about all this is that agoraphobia with its easily misunderstood symptoms and difficulty in diagnosis is primarily a problem that affects women. And, at least according to one survey conducted by Dr. Sheehan, 98 percent of the agoraphobia victims are being treated with minor tranquilizers—most commonly Valium, the one prescribed more than twice as frequently for women as for men.

Do Tranquilizers Really Help?

Now you might say tranquilizers are intended to ease anxiety and there's probably no one filled with more anxiety than an agoraphobia victim. But the truth of the matter is, that Valium isn't the answer. According to Dr. Sheehan's article, the hoopla over minor tranquilizers like Valium for the treatment of agoraphobia is greatly exaggerated. In his study, 57 patients together had consumed a total of nearly two-thirds of a million minor tranquilizer tablets and still continued to be stricken by the panic attacks. What's more, he adds, "No reliable evidence supports the use of antipsychotic drugs (so-called *major* tranquilizers), although they are prescribed for nearly half of all persons afflicted with agoraphobia."

What, then, does provide effective treatment?

Dr. Hardy, working with TERRAP for the past 18 years, has provided desensitization techniques for agoraphobics with notable success.

"We educate people about their agoraphobia and assure them that there is nothing wrong with their mind or their body," says Dr. Hardy. Patients are taught some basic psychology and relaxation techniques. Slowly their inhibited feelings come to the surface.

"They must be able to recognize and identify their feelings and to learn how to express them in socially acceptable ways to avoid criticism," says Dr. Hardy. "We tell them if they can openly express themselves and speak up for themselves, they will have no problems. If they begin to inhibit themselves again, they'll revert back to their old habits."

It takes a lot for some agoraphobics to go through a desensitization program. "It can be frightening to even attempt it," a recovered agoraphobic working at TERRAP told us. She had suffered from agoraphobia for nine years, spending the last year housebound. "It took me a long time to be able to walk into a TERRAP meeting," she recalls. "I stood outside the door and listened for two months. I didn't want to walk into a room with so many people in it. It was too frightening for me." Now she travels, skis and throws parties without any difficulty.

"We have a success rate of 80 to 85 percent," says Dr. Hardy. People with agoraphobia don't go crazy, and panic attacks do not injure their bodies or minds in any way. Agoraphobia also is not fatal, he adds. He attributes his success rate to using psychological techniques to treat a "personality disorder." But what about the other 15 to 20 percent? Is it possible that some of those agoraphobics might respond favorably to a nutritional approach?

Laraine Abbey, R.N., a nurse practitioner who specializes in orthomolecular nutrition and clinical ecology in East Windsor, New Jersey, thinks so.

Nutritional Deficiencies and Fear

"I think all agoraphobics probably have nutritional deficiencies of one kind or another," Laraine Abbey told us. "I previously had worked with a number of people who had fears and anxieties and found they invariably cleared up on a nutritional program."

—From Emrika Padus, *The Woman's Encyclopedia of Health and Natural Healing.* Emmaus, Pa.: Rodale, 1981.

FOR FURTHER READING:

Marks, Isaac M., M.D. *Living With Fear.* New York: McGraw-Hill, 1978.

Weekes, Claire. *Simple Effective Treatment of Agoraphobia.* New York: Hawthorn.

ALCOHOL

ALMOST 10 MILLION Americans are either outright alcoholics or "problem drinkers" whose consumption is enough to cause serious problems both to themselves and others. This still leaves 70 to 80 million men and women in this country, many of them Christians, who drink in moderation, and are rather proud of the fact that they never get drunk. Whereas I do not share the view that if someone partakes of alcohol, he cannot be a Christian, I nevertheless am committed to the belief that temperance is a personal quality to be aimed at by all who profess Christ as Lord in their lives.

Although Christians differ in their opinions as to whether or not drinking alcohol is a sin, most would agree that the Christian virtue of self-control is required of all of us. Although total abstention is the perfect standard, Christians who do drink are obligated to be strict with their own self-discipline. We are in danger of losing the protective and guiding influence of the Holy Spirit when alcohol, in clouding intellectual functioning and loosening emotional restraint, usurps the control the Spirit should have

over us, thereby forming a barrier between us and God.

There is no guaranteed "safe" level of drinking because individuals differ widely in their vulnerability. Alcohol, being extremely water soluble, is rapidly absorbed through the stomach, enters the bloodstream in seconds, and immediately is carried to the brain, a few heartbeats later. There it interferes with the release of oxygen to the brain cells, many of which die as a result. Alcohol, even in very small doses, causes blood cells to clump together, or sludge, and these can block minute capillaries, depriving local areas of the brain of vital nutrients. For reasons not yet clearly understood, some people are apparently much more sensitive than others to this highly destructive mechanism.

Alcohol is broken down in the liver to sugars which are then stored as fat, leading to undesirable weight gain, unless adequate exercise prompts further breakdown to waste products. Taken daily, even in small doses, it eventually begins to damage the liver, especially if taken on an empty stomach. Fortunately, unlike the brain, liver cells can regenerate, but only during periods of abstinence, when they are not being overwhelmed with yet more alcohol. These periods of relief are essential to recovery. It is less harmful to the liver to have a binge on a Saturday night and then abstain totally for the rest of the week, than to inflict it daily with no letup. This doesn't mean that the binge is okay. It still kills brain cells, but daily, small amounts of alcohol can cause the liver to become fatty, and, after about fifteen years of continuous abuse, it may become the victim of cirrhosis, an irreversible and potentially fatal degenerative condition.

How can you tell if a family member or friend is in danger of progressing from a social drinker to a problem drinker? When should such a one either quit completely or at the least seek professional help? Here's what to look for:

1. He/she makes stronger drinks for himself than for his guests.
2. He seems to be able to enjoy drinking

alone, as much or more than if in the company of family or friends.

3. He craves his first drink of the day, and may even have it before noon. Morning drinking is an especially sinister symptom.

4. He tends to be evasive about his habit and usually divides his admitted number of drinks by two or three when stating his consumption.

5. He may slip alcohol into his orange juice or coffee or otherwise try to disguise his intake.

6. He may have had an alcohol-related traffic violation.

7. He may be unable to sleep without a stiff drink.

Two or more of these signs are strong indications that something firm must be done at once to halt an otherwise irreversible downward spiral.

Whereas I am personally convinced that alcohol is harmful, I recognize that some Christians are less concerned. I have, therefore, a few words of caution for Christians who do not feel convinced that they ought or need to be total abstainers. By these comments I am in no way condoning the use of alcohol in any form, but rather advising of some vital principles to be remembered by those Christians who do choose to drink.

Morris Chafetz, M.D., former director of the National Institute on Alcohol Abuse and Alcoholism, has stated that one and a half ounces of pure alcohol per twenty-four hours must be regarded as the upper limit of "safe" drinking. (This is, of course, only a statistical average. For thousands of alcoholics now in Alcoholics Anonymous, and many other people, even one drop is too much.) This one and a half ounces is contained in three one-ounce shots of 100-proof liquor (which is 50% alcohol), or in twelve ounces of wine, or in thirty-two ounces of any light beer. More than this consumption will increase the concentration of alcohol in the blood to above 0.05%, at which point many brain functions begin to be adversely affected. It would take the liver at least two hours to fully metabolize the one and a half ounces, if taken all at once.

—From O. Quentin Hyder, M.D., *Shape Up.* Old Tappan, N.J.: Revell, 1979.

Alcoholism

Are You an Alcoholic?

To answer this question, ask yourself the following questions and answer them as honestly as you can.

1. Do you lose time from work due to drinking?

2. Is drinking making your home life unhappy?

3. Do you drink because you are shy with other people?

4. Is drinking affecting your reputation?

5. Have you ever felt remorse after drinking?

6. Have you gotten into financial difficulties as a result of drinking?

7. Do you turn to lower companions and an inferior environment when drinking?

8. Does your drinking make you careless of your family's welfare?

9. Has your ambition decreased since drinking?

10. Do you crave a drink at a definite time daily?

11. Do you want a drink the next morning?

12. Does drinking cause you to have difficulty sleeping?

13. Has your efficiency decreased since drinking?

14. Is drinking jeopardizing your job or business?

15. Do you drink to escape from worries or troubles?

16. Do you drink alone?

17. Have you ever had a complete loss of memory as a result of drinking?

18. Has your physician ever treated you for drinking?

19. Do you drink to build up your self-confidence?

20. Have you ever been to a hospital or institution on account of drinking?

—From Donald L. Deffner, *The Possible Years.*
St. Louis: Concordia, 1973.

FOR FURTHER READING:

Davis, Creath. *How to Win in a Crisis.* Grand
Rapids, Mich.: Zondervan, 1976.

Padus, Emrika. *The Woman's Encyclopedia of
Health and Natural Healing.* Emmaus, Pa.: Rodale, 1981.

Wilkerson, Don. *Fast Track to Nowhere.* Old
Tappan, N.J.: Revell, 1979.

ALONENESS

ACCEPTING ONE'S particular individuality as
unique involves trusting our *aloneness,* the
essential separateness of ourselves from one
another. Each of us has a particular destiny.
We come into the world alone, and we die
alone. Realizing our uniqueness involves a
recognition that we cannot finally be dependent on any other person for our being.
Emerging from a crisis we often see loneliness as the only promise. There is a distinction though between aloneness and loneliness, and we need to trust that through the
negative experience of loneliness will
emerge the positive experience of being
alone. Being alone is a positive state, an understanding that we are unique, creative
centers of life, essentially separate persons.
Ultimately we cannot submerge our identity
into others. Being alone is not loneliness; it is
tragic in some respects, but it is also our opportunity for life and for expressing ourselves. The grace that we discover as we
grow into this new sense of aloneness is that
we are indeed related to others.

—From Penelope Washbourn, *Becoming
Woman.* New York: Harper & Row, 1977.

FOR FURTHER READING:

Clarkson, Margaret. *So You're Single.* Wheaton, Ill.: Shaw Pubs., 1978.

Fix, Janet, with Zola Levitt. *For Singles Only.*
Old Tappan, N.J.: Revell, 1978.

Hulme, William E. *Creative Loneliness.* Minneapolis: Augsburg, 1977.

Hunter, Brenda. *Beyond Divorce.* Old Tappan, N.J.: Revell, 1978.

Smoke, Jim. *Suddenly Single.* Old Tappan,
N.J.: Revell, 1982.

Stewart, Suzanna. *Parent Alone.* Waco, Tex.:
Word Books, 1978.

ANGER

ANGER IS a part of our lives which can be
controlled and directed. Consider these
principles for dealing with anger.

1. *Be aware of your emotional reactions.* Recognize the emotion and
   admit to yourself that you are feeling irritated or angry. Do not repress or deny
   the feeling. Admitting it does not mean
   that you have to act on it.

2. *Try to understand why you are
   angry.* What brought it about? Can
   you isolate the cause or reason? Is it one
   that occurs often?

3. Can you *create other situations in which
   anger won't occur?* What were you
   doing that might have contributed to
   this problem or difficulty? Did you do
   anything to cause the other person to
   react in such a way that you became
   angry?

4. *Ask yourself, "Is anger the best response?"* You can be rational at this
   point and discuss this question with
   yourself. What are the consequences of
   becoming angry and letting it out?
   Write down your answer. Can you think
   of a better response? Write that down.
   What would be accomplished by kindness, sympathy, and understanding toward the other person? Can you confess
   your feelings to him?

5. *Is your anger the kind that rises too soon?* If so, when you start to get angry take some deep breaths or count to ten. Concentrate on the strengths and positive qualities of the other person instead of his defects. Remember that it is possible to control your thoughts. (*See* Ephesians 4:23; 1 Peter 1:13.)

6. *Do you find yourself being critical of others?* What does this do for you? Be less suspicious of the other person. *Listen* to what he says and feels. Evaluate his comments instead of condemning him. Does your faultfinding or anger come from a desire to make yourself feel better? Are your opinions always accurate or could they be improved? The other person may have something to offer you. Slow down in your speech and reactions toward others. Watch your gestures and expressions which may convey rejection and criticism of the other person. Can you express appreciation and praise in place of criticism?

7. *You may have a time when your anger or criticism is legitimate.* Plan ahead how you will express it and do it in such a way that the other person can accept what you say. Use timing, tact, and have a desire to help the other person instead of tearing him down.

8. *Find a friend with whom you can talk over your feelings and gain some insight from his suggestions.* Admit how you feel and ask for his guidance.

9. *Spend time praying for the difficulty that you have with your feelings.* Openly admit your situation to God. Ask for His help. Understand and memorize the Scriptures that speak of anger and those that speak of how we should behave toward others. Put them into practice.

—From H. Norman Wright, *The Christian Use of Emotional Power.* Old Tappan, N.J.: Revell, 1974.

Anger Generates More Anger

Expressing anger indiscriminately fails to resolve it. A person does not need to be promiscuous to make the commonsense observation that ordinary sexual experience tends to stimulate sexual desire. And anger, like sexual desire, increases rather than decreases when indulged without discipline.

Even when expressed under control, anger may generate more of its kind. I observed a person, quite rightly I think, angrily reprove a newspaper columnist who had slandered him. The individual explained to me later that he did not feel very angry at the moment, but expressed himself hotly to convince the journalist of her wrongdoing. He left the meeting, and as he climbed into his car, which momentarily blocked traffic, a taxi driver announced his impatience by leaning on his horn. The man, overcome with anger, growled, "I'd like to go back and punch his lights out." His controlled expression of anger had induced an inappropriate and intemperate reaction.

How much more anger results from promiscuously letting it all hang out by punching pillows and shrieking obscenities? The follow-your-feelings people admit in print that their approach inclines to excess. One of the frankest, Jane Howard has written: "Most of the angry gestures amounted to ritual murders. Many people had to be reminded: 'Remember, it's only a pillow!' "

Admissions such as this indicate that even if it worked to let anger out, Christians would have to be extremely wary of the method. Uncontrolled expression of anger contradicts the spiritual teaching on anger: "Be angry, but do not sin . . . give no opportunity to the devil" (Ephesians 4:26). Following your feeling of anger—letting it out of control or putting it in control—leads to grave emotional and spiritual problems. Among these are rage, resentment, hostility, broken relationships and domination by evil spirits.

There is hardly anyone who does not have a friend or relative who has bought into the follow-your-feelings approach. Dignified and reserved people who have patiently struggled with personal problems have been persuaded that their panacea lies in venting their anger. The cure is often worse than the disease. Expressing anger indiscriminately may result in name-calling, name-calling can lead to quarrels, quarrels can degenerate into fights, fights can cause enmity, and enmity can culminate in murder. Better to end up in heaven with some unresolved emotional problems, than to end up in hell because we followed our feelings there.

—From Bert Ghezzi, *The Angry Christian.* Ann Arbor: Servant, 1980.

FOR FURTHER READING:

Augsburger, David. *Caring Enough to Confront.* Ventura, Calif.: Regal, 1981.

Hauck, Paul A., Ph.D., and Edmund S. Kean, M.D. *Marriage and the Memo Method.* Philadelphia: Westminster, 1975.

LaHaye, Tim. *Anger Is a Choice.* Grand Rapids: Zondervan, 1982.

Rubin, Theodore Isaac, M.D. *The Angry Book.* New York: Collier, 1969.

ANOREXIA NERVOSA

THERE ARE some women who can't quit dieting. They become obsessed with weight loss and reduce themselves to an empty encasement of skin and bones. Some eventually starve themselves to death.

The problem was named "anorexia nervosa," meaning loss of appetite due to anxiety, back at a time when the condition was misunderstood. In true anorexia nervosa there is no loss of appetite, only a deliberate avoidance of food—a sort of self-induced hunger strike. The object is to become thin at all costs. And the results pitifully demonstrate the severity of the problem. A fifteen-year-old girl weighing sixty-five pounds refuses more than three tablespoons of cottage cheese a day. A thirteen-year-old is threatened into eating a meal, only to slip away afterwards and stick her finger down her throat until she vomits every last trace of food.

Like alcoholism, anorexia nervosa is a disease. It primarily strikes attractive, perfection-oriented females aged eleven to twenty-four from upper- or upper-middle-class backgrounds. An off-the-cuff estimate is that one in 300 adolescent girls is affected. And thousands of young women may be afflicted with a sister syndrome, bulimarexia, a term coined by two Cornell University psychologists to describe a seesaw form of anorexia. "Women suffering from bulimarexia alternately gorge themselves with food and then empty themselves, whether by fasting, vomiting, or through self-induced diarrhea," says Marlene Boskind-Lodahl, Ph.D. "In most cases it leaves its victims little time or energy for any sort of life beyond its own binges and purges" (*Psychology Today,* March, 1977).

Understandably, both diseases were considered rarities fifty years ago—before Twiggy ushered in the era of the envied toothpick physique. It's also easy to understand why 98 percent of their victims are women (especially impressionable adolescent girls), since they are the primary targets of Madison Avenue advertising ploys.

But how do otherwise sensible young women become bent on self-destruction? "When they begin to diet, they seem to be doing nothing different from what thousands of other women are doing," says Hilde Bruch, M.D., professor of psychiatry at Baylor College of Medicine in Texas and author of numerous articles and books on this topic. "Not one of the patients I have known had intended to pursue the frightening road of life-threatening emaciation—and to sacrifice the years of youth to this bizarre goal. They had expected that being slimmer would improve not only their appearance but their way of living." Isn't that how we all feel?

Strange Self-Perception

Yes, but there are recognizable peculiarities in their logic. For one thing, only about two percent of these young women are over-weight to begin with. Most are slender, at-tractive girls. But for some unknown reason, they perceive themselves as "too fat"—even after severe starvation has reduced them to a faded image of what they once were. "I have stood in front of a mirror with an anorexic girl who at sixty-five pounds was so thin you could pick her up by her pelvic bones," Steven Levenkron, M.S., a New York City psy-chotherapist and author of *The Best Little Girl in the World* (Contemporary, 1978), a book on anorexia nervosa, told us. "No mat-ter how I'd try to point out that it isn't pretty to have protruding ribs or a concave abdomen, she'd insist that she looked just fine. It was as if we were seeing two dis-tinctly different images in the mirror."

Also, according to Dr. Bruch, the *way* the girls experience hunger will determine whether dieting remains what it was in-tended to be—a means of losing a few extra pounds—or whether it becomes a compul-sive force that dominates their whole life. "The fact that they are able to tolerate the sensation of hunger (and thus achieve the miracle of losing weight rapidly) seems to induce these girls to go on and on," says Dr. Bruch.

Truth is, however, that all that worry over dieting and losing weight, the obsession with thinness, and the twisted perspective of self-image are not causes of anorexia nervosa. They are symptoms—early warning signs of the drastic weight loss that will follow. The actual cause is much more deeply rooted.

"The real illness has to do with the way you feel about yourself," Dr. Bruch explains to a young patient. "There is a peculiar con-tradiction—everybody thinks you're doing so well and everybody thinks you're great, but your real problem is that you think you're not good enough. . . . This peculiar dieting begins with such anxiety. You want to prove that you have control, that you can do it. The peculiar part of it is that it makes you feel 'I can do something nobody else can do.' There is only one problem with this feeling of superiority. It doesn't solve your problem because what you really want is to feel good about yourself while feeling happy and healthy. The paradox is that you have started to feel good for being unhealthy."

The Symptoms . . . and Real Danger

Along with the weight loss comes a whole host of unhealthful and not-so-pretty symp-toms. Menstrual periods stop. Hair falls out. The skin becomes very dry. Constipation be-comes a problem. Heartbeat drops to 50 to 55 (72 is average for normal women) and blood pressure to 80/50 (120/70 is normal for a young woman). The sensation of cold is always present.

But the real danger is the upset of water balance in the body caused by bouts of vo-miting combined with the repeated inges-tion of laxatives and diuretics. It is often this and not the weight loss per se that causes death.

Until recently, standard treatment wasn't too successful. Drugs administered to im-prove appetite or tranquilize the senses have been outright failures. Psychoanalysis proved to be a meaningless and time-consuming ex-ercise. And behavior modification tech-niques—in which an anorexic is put in a sparsely furnished hospital room without TV, books or visitors and forced to earn priv-ileges by gaining weight—have successfully fattened up the patient, but not for long. Soon after release from the hospital, most girls get on with their dietary regimen all over again. Some are even worse off for the experience, feeling bitter about being coerced and attempting suicide afterward.

Anorexia nervosa is a psychological as well as a nutritional problem. Both are equally important in treatment. And both demand professional assistance.

Current trends in psychological counsel-ing for anorexia nervosa involve the whole family. "In every anorexic's family, there is always somebody else who is the problem," says Steven Levenkron. Usually it's another child, perhaps a slow learner or a hyperac-tive child who demands and gets all the par-ents' attention. The anorexic child, on the other hand, is usually the model child—a docile girl, straight-A student, active in sports, and fairly sociable. She doesn't appear to need any special attention. As a result, she is all but ignored by her parents. "This is a mistake," the psychotherapist explains. "To avoid anorexia nervosa, parents should make sure their well-behaved children get as much attention as the poorly behaved ones. The family must move closer. And there must be trust."

—From Emrika Padus, *The Woman's Encyclopedia of Health and Natural Healing.* Emmaus, Pa.: Rodale, 1981.

FOR FURTHER READING:

Edelstein, Barbara. *The Woman Doctor's Medical Guide for Women.* New York: Morrow, 1982.

The Diagram Group. *Woman's Body.* New York: Simon & Schuster, 1981.

17 Women Doctors, with D. S. Thompson, M.D., as consulting editor. *Everywoman's Health.* Garden City, N.Y.: Doubleday, 1980.

ANXIETY

ANXIETY IS THE RESULT of internal confusion. When we are uncertain or confused we feel anxious. Often this emotional turmoil is a secondary result that comes as a spin-off of another emotion. The original feeling gets displaced, and we lose touch with our principle apprehension. We're not sure exactly what's wrong, but we feel upset. Anger and fear are particularly devastating when we fail to face them honestly.

Anger can be a powerful undercurrent that stirs up anxiety. If I vent my anger I may do some very harmful things to those around me. But I can't *deny* that I'm angry without turning the anger inward on myself. And anger turned inward becomes the substance of depression. I can't escape the fire in my stomach; to let it smolder is to burn myself and to become victimized by an unnecessary anxiety born of my own hostility.

So what do I do about this? I keep from putting labels on my emotions until after I have fully faced them! Good or bad doesn't count until I can honestly be in touch with what's happening inside my churning place. I must recognize what I am feeling whenever it hits and I must face it fully. I can't bring the power of Christ to bear on my life until I open myself to the real place it must work. Then both my anger and the anxiety it causes can be attacked by God's power.

Fear has the same potential for creating chaos, yet it has an important place in my life. Fear is a very valid emotion, for it is a barometer that warns me of danger. Fright causes me to think about things in my life which may require adjustment. I must sort through and find appropriate responses to those things that could be destructive.

But what if we lose perspective on our fears? Then anxiety is born! When we fail to look our fears in the eye, we are captured by their consequences.

Look at the relationship between fear and anxiety. Fear always has an object; you know where there is something of which you are afraid; you can pinpoint a valid reason for your concern. Anxiety, on the other hand, is nameless. There is no object for its apprehension; all perspective has been lost.

Anxiety is like a strange animal inside us that moves in all directions but has no center. This devourer roams aimlessly across our every concern, contaminating all he touches. His journey seems to have no purpose but to make us miserable. In the end we are completely defeated because of his nameless, directionless churning.

Look anxiety in the eye! Face the facts! Before you decide on the good or the bad, get the basics of your concern in sight. When you hide the truth from yourself, you will find it impossible to defeat anxiety. But when you confront your fears you allow the Holy Spirit to deal with the real issues of your life, and this is where anxiety is starved to death!

—From Robert L. Wise, *Your Churning Place.* Ventura, Calif.: Regal, 1977.

How to Deal With Worry and Anxiety

1. Be sure you have had a complete physical by your physician. Have him check glands, vitamin deficiencies, allergies, exercise schedule and fatigue.
2. Be aware of all of your emotions. Face your worries. Don't run from them for they will return to haunt you. Admit that you do worry or have anxiety (but only if you really do). Do not worry about worrying. That just reinforces and perpetuates the problem.
3. Write down the worries and anxieties that you have on a piece of paper. Be very specific and complete as you describe them.
4. Write down the reason or cause for your worry. Investigate the source. *Is there any possibility that you can eliminate the source or cause for your worry? Have you tried? What have you tried specifically?*
5. Write down how much time you spend each day worrying.
6. What has your worry accomplished in your life? Describe in detail. Describe the benefits of worrying.
7. Make a list of the following:
   (a.) How many times has my worrying prevented a situation from occurring?
   (b.) In what way did my worry increase the problem?
8. If you are nervous or jumpy try to eliminate any sources of irritation. Stay away from situations that increase this until you learn how to react differently. Try to remove the source of irritation. For example, if the troubled world situation gets to you why listen to so many newscasts! What do you do to try to relax? Can you read, work in the garden, ride a bike for several miles? Avoid rushing yourself. If you worry about being late plan to arrive at a destination early. Give yourself more time.
9. Avoid any type of fatigue—physical, emotional, or intellectual. When a person is fatigued difficulties can loom out of proportion.
10. When you do get involved in worry is it over something that really pertains to you and your life *or* does it properly belong to someone else? Remember that often our fears or worries may be disguised forms of the fear of what *others* think of us!
11. When a problem arises, face it and make a decision as to what you can do about it. Make a list of all of the possible solutions and decide which you think is the best one. If these are minor decisions, make your decision fairly quickly, taking more time for major ones. A person who is a worrier usually says, "I can't decide. I go over and over these problems and cannot decide which is best." Look at the facts and then decide, but do not continue to worry about it. After you have looked at the facts and made your decision, do not question your choice. Otherwise the worrying pattern erupts all over again. Do not begin to debate your own decision. Practice this new pattern of making decisions. If you do fail in the beginning do not give up. Your old pattern has been locked in because of long use and you need to practice the new pattern of thinking for a while before it begins to work successfully. As soon as possible act upon your decision and get rid of the problem.

If it is a major problem it may be a difficult decision. As questions arise you may have to seek advice. Make a plan for obtaining this advice. It may take a day or a week, but when you have made the plans, dismiss the problem from your mind until that time, until you obtain the information you need. What good will it do to keep running over and over the problem until the time you gain this new information? With any kind of problem including those where the matter is out of your hands (such as the illness of a family member) you can leave the problem with the Lord. Do not carry the weight around on your own shoulders.

THE PRINCIPLES OF SCRIPTURE

Matthew 6:25–34: *Learn how to live a day at a time.* Deal with your problems a step at a time. Do not allow worry to creep in. Focus upon Christ and not the problem. Write out a description of how you will put this into daily practice in your own life.

1 Peter 5:7: *Unload your worry on God and you will be strengthened* because of His love and care for you. Write down the specific cares and worries that you have at this time and then spend time in prayer giving these to the Lord.

Isaiah 26:3: *Direct your thoughts toward God and His teachings.* Describe how you will put this principle into practice in your life and how you will remember to do this each day.

Psalms 37: *Replace fretting with trust, delight, commitment and resting in the Lord.* Describe what each of these words means to you and how each one will help you release your worries and anxieties to God so you will be free of them.

Philippians 4:6, 7: *Stop worrying, give everything to God in prayer and supplication and peace will be yours.* Describe how you need to pray for this to happen. Discuss the specific steps you will take to stop yourself from worrying.

—From H. Norman Wright, *The Christian Use of Emotional Power.* Old Tappan, N.J.: Revell, 1974.

FOR FURTHER READING:

Collins, Gary. *Overcoming Anxiety.* Ventura, Calif.: Vision House, 1975.

Murphey, Cecil B. *Devotions for Worriers.* Old Tappan, N.J.: Revell, 1982.

Osborne, Cecil G. *The Art of Understanding Yourself.* Grand Rapids: Zondervan, 1967.

ASSERTIVENESS

ASSERTIVENESS IS . . . neither passive nor aggressive. It is neither motivated by fear nor by anger. True assertive behavior is motivated by the emotion of love. You care enough about yourself and about others that you will speak up for your rights and be careful not to violate anyone else's rights at the same time. In my work with Dr. Frank Freed, we describe this handling of emotions as *confession.* We do not repress, suppress, or express our emotions. We confess them.

In the Greek, the meaning of the word *confess* is "to agree with." When you confess your feelings and emotions, you are verbally agreeing with what you are feeling inside. When you confess these emotions and feelings, you are describing to another person what is going on inside of you.

One of the mistakes often encountered in attitudes regarding assertiveness is that it is a way to get what you want. You cannot do that with assertiveness! Perhaps by being aggressive that goal could be accomplished. But with assertiveness, the major reason for acting assertively is that you regain that sense of self-control. You are not pushing someone else around at his expense, and you are not being pushed around—both ways of reacting to life. You are now experiencing self-control, and are able to *act* the way you choose, not *react!* This eventually leads you to greater feelings of self-confidence and self-control, which reduces your need to be either passive or aggressive with other people. And since assertiveness is motivated by the emotion of love, your goal in acting assertively is to maximize the possibility that all parties in a situation are able to partially achieve their goals. And this leads to a closer, more satisfying type of relationship with others.

Once again, the battle for assertive behavior begins in your mind—in your Self-Talk. Nonassertive people are dominated in their Self-Talk by "SHOULDs" and these "shoulds" lead to the feelings of "I CAN'T!"

Whenever you nonassertively say or think, "I SHOULD," you set in motion the following:

I - Immobilization

S - Saying—not doing
H - Hung up on guilt
O - Overly anxious
U - Underlying anger
L - Lowered self-esteem
D - Depression

That's not a very satisfying pattern. Non-assertive behavior patterns feed right into feelings of guilt, anger, worry, anxiety, and depression. The result is always a lowering of self-esteem, and a feeling of being paralyzed, or immobilized. You sit and *talk* about what you should have done. Or you sit and *brood* about what you shouldn't have done. And nothing happens to change you or the situation—you're paralyzed.

The "I SHOULDs" always lead to the "I CAN'Ts." The "I CAN'Ts" create the following pattern:

I - Inadequate feelings about myself

C - Controlled instead of being in control
A - Apathetic
N - Negative results
T - Total despair

No wonder you say "I CAN'T!" You're inadequate, out of control, and tired of negative results to what you do attempt, which leads you to become even more apathetic, until you give up in total despair.

Four D's of Assertive Living

So what can you do? Let me describe for you the four *D*'s of assertive living. This is a way to monitor your Self-Talk, turning it into a force for change.

DESCRIBE - First, sit down and describe the kinds of situations in which you react nonassertively. Take the time to write out the description of the conflict.

DEFINE - Second, define what is happening to you. What are you saying, doing, and thinking? What is your Self-Talk? What are your expectations in this situation? Define as clearly as possible your feelings, fears, hostilities, and behavior.

DISCERN - Third, try to discern what the other person, or persons, may be thinking. What might be their motives? What might they be feeling? What is going on inside the others involved in this situation?

DECIDE - Fourth, make a decision about what you *can* do about this situation. What new assertive strategy can you use to break out of the trap you feel caught in? What one thing can you begin doing differently in love, which would create the possibility of change?

Try it right now. Don't listen to those old patterns of Self-Talk that say it *can't* be done. Become a believer in "I CAN!" The "I CAN" pattern looks like this:

I - Initiate change by acting not reacting

C - Confess my feelings
A - Ask for what I want and need
N - Negotiate for positive results

—From David Stoop, Ph.D., *Self-Talk*. Old Tappan, N.J.: Revell, 1982.

FOR FURTHER READING:

Crowley, Mary C. *Women Who Win*. Old Tappan, N.J.: Revell, 1979.
Dobson, Dr. James. *Hide or Seek*. Old Tappan, N.J.: Revell, 1974.
Ruby MacDonald's Forty Plus and Feeling Fabulous Book. Old Tappan, N.J.: Revell, 1982.
Schuller, Robert H. *Self Esteem*. Waco, Tex.: Word Books, 1982.

B

BATTERED WIVES

Facts and Myths

Battering is the "use of forceful and repetitive behavior in order to coerce a person into doing what the batterer wants without regard to the person's rights (or body or health)." Battering may be both psychological and physical.

MYTHS:

Women are basically masochistic and enjoy being battered; that's why they stay in battering situations.

No human being enjoys being beaten or harassed. Women generally stay in battering relationships because they are economically dependent on the batterer and because they are emotionally ambivalent about the relationship. Community, family and sometimes the church encourage her to stay.

Battering is a lower class problem.

Battering is a serious social problem among all classes, races, professions and religious groups.

Battering is directly related to alcoholism; only drunk men batter.

One-third of batterers don't drink at all. One-third have an alcohol problem, but batter whether drunk or sober. One-third batter only when drunk.

The woman provokes the beatings.

Some batterers report what they see as "provocative" behavior on the part of the woman. Many also report that she did nothing to provoke them.

Men who batter are out of control.

Most men are in control of their actions: when someone enters the room, they stop: they focus on very specific parts of the victim's body. They choose to direct their violence at their "partner," even though the source of their hostility may be elsewhere. **"Uppity" assertive women are beaten more often than submissive women.**

Some men report beating their partners because they were too assertive; other men report beating because their partners were too passive and agreeable. There seems to be a high incidence of battering in relationships in which sex roles are narrowly defined and the man insists upon being completely in charge of the household.

Men are battered as much as women. What about husband beating?

Men are sometimes battered by their partners: we have no conclusive data as to how much because men tend not to report it. However, the seriousness of the abuse seems to be much greater when directed toward women. Serious physical injury is more likely to occur. Also women generally have far fewer options to leave an abusive relationship.

FACTS:

• One incident of "wife-beating" is reported every minute in the U.S. (3 times higher than rape.) This rate represents less than 10 percent of actual incidents.

• One out of every two women will experience some form of violence in relationships with other adults (spouse/lover) at some point in their lives.

• 60 percent of couples will experience some degree of physical violence at some point in their relationship.

—From Council on Women and the Church, United Presbyterian Church, U.S.A., *Myths and Facts About Rape and Battering.*

Who Is the Batterer?

What kind of man beats up his wife? What are the underlying psychological and social causes of wife-beating, and what triggers this behavior? Are men naturally violent creatures? Or is aggressive behavior learned? These are key questions, but we can only really speculate as to the answers. Few wife-beaters admit to their own cruel and violent behavior, let alone discuss the reasoning behind it. They rarely see the problem *as* a problem and seek help for it. Therefore, few people outside the immediate family know when a man is a wife-beater. The police may know, but to them he is just a DD—a statistic and a nuisance. To unsuspecting friends he is probably a nice guy. But to his wife he is a dangerous, explosive man who can fly into a rage without warning.

Much of what is known about wife-batterers has been learned from their victims. A random sample of descriptions from battered women shows that the wife-beater can come from any walk of life. . . .

Battering husbands are described by their wives as angry, resentful, suspicious, moody, and tense. Though they may be terrifying, they often have about them an aura of helplessness, fear, inadequacy, and insecurity. The battering husband is likely to be a "loser" in some basic way. He is probably angry with himself and frustrated by his life. He may put up a good front in public, but in the privacy and intimacy of his home he may not be able to hide, either from himself or his wife, his feelings of inadequacy and low self-esteem. The man who is losing his grip on his job or his prospects may feel compelled to prove that he is at least the master of his home. Beating his wife is one way for him to appear a winner.

These general impressions have been gleaned from conversations with battered women. In the professional social-science literature, little concrete data on the batterer is to be found. Case histories exist on the wife/victims, but not on the husbands. Only when wife-beaters are charged with assault and battery and actually prosecuted in court—and this happens very rarely . . . do batterers come under any sort of official scrutiny. Even then we learn little about these men except that they do indeed perform violent acts.

During the years 1957 through 1962, thirty-seven men charged by their wives with assault and battery were referred by the court and the police to the Framingham Court Clinic in Massachusetts for psychiatric evaluation and possible treatment. Three doctors at the clinic—John E. Snell, Richard J. Rosenwald, and Ames Robey—routinely interviewed these men and their wives. The men, they soon learned, resisted the interviews and tended to deny that any problems warranting outside help existed in their marriages. The women, on the other hand, were much more willing to talk about their marriages and to seek counseling. The three doctors decided to take the easy way out. Though they had been charged with the responsibility of finding out more about wife-batterers, they ended up writing a paper on "The Wifebeater's Wife," which was published in the *Archives of General Psychiatry*. Needless to say, this paper did not contribute substantially to our understanding of wife-beaters.

What Triggers the Batterer?

In my own conversations with battered women, I have discovered that however a batterer may rationalize his actions to himself, those actions never seem warranted by the actual triggering event. For example, one woman told me she was beaten unmercifully for breaking the egg yolk while cooking her husband's breakfast. Another said her husband blew up because at their child's birthday party she instructed the youngster to give the first piece of cake to a guest, not to him. Another wife was battered because her *husband's* driver's license was suspended. Other women reported these reasons: she prepared a casserole instead of fresh meat for dinner; she wore her hair in a pony tail; she mentioned that she didn't like the pattern on the wallpaper. These incidents seem trivial in the extreme; in no way do they warrant a violent response. To my way of thinking, these are irrational attacks, even if they can be attributed, as Richard Gelles argues, to the husband's stress and frustration.

Some women report that they just don't know what triggers their husbands' violent outbursts. Husbands have been known to come home and just start flailing away. Several women told me that their husbands started beating them as they lay asleep in bed. Ray Fowler, executive director of the American Association of Marriage and Family Counselors, describes the wife-abuser as "generally an obsessional person who has learned how to trigger himself emotionally." A man may interpret a reasonable comment by his wife as a nagging remark or a whining complaint. "Why is she treating me like this?" he might say to himself. "I deserve better than this." The man might allow this sort of inner conversation to escalate until it triggers his hostility. At the same time the interior monologue provides him with a justification for his violent acts.

Battered wives report that when the husband erupts in a volcanic rage he generally uses his fists, not his open hand. And the practiced batterer knows how to aim his blows at the places that don't show, the women say. He goes for the breasts, the stomach (even during pregnancy), the base of the spine, and parts of the head where bumps and bruises will be covered by hair. Gelles says that slapping, scratching, or grabbing are most common when both parties actively participate in a fight, but that husbands predominate when it comes to pushing (downstairs, for instance), choking, shoving, punching, kicking—even throwing things.

Threats of violence can be as frightening as an actual physical attack. Many husbands punch holes in the wall, break down doors, and fire guns to demonstrate their potential destructiveness. Gelles noted that "violent threats are typically used by the husband to intimidate or coerce deference from the wife," but he found no instances of a wife threatening a husband with violence. But both Gelles and M. Komarovsky, another investigator, found that wives threatened their husbands with other possibilities: that they would withhold sexual favors, call the police, or leave and take the children.

Wife-Abuse: The Skeleton in the Closet

Common sense tells us that statistics relating to domestic violence reflect, to some extent, the incidence of wife-beating. "Wife-beating has been so prevalent that all of us must have been aware of its existence—if not in our own lives, at least in the lives of others, or when a wife-beating case that resulted in death was reported in the press," states Betsy Warrior. But, although governmental agencies and social scientists have begun to concentrate on social violence in recent years, wife-battering has merited no special attention in those quarters. Nor has it aroused the shocked indignation it should have from the women's movement until very recently. The fact is, the issue has been buried so deeply that no real data exist on the incidence of wife-beating.

The news media have often treated wife-abuse as a bizarre and relatively rare phenomenon—as occasional fodder for sensationalistic reporting, but rarely as a social issue worthy of thorough investigation....

From one point of view, the battered wife in her secrecy conspires with the media, the police, the social scientists, the social reformers, and the social workers to keep the issue hushed up. We can picture a very thick door locked shut. On the inside is a woman trying hard not to cry out for help. On the other side are those who could and should be helping, but instead are going about their business as if she weren't there.

—From Del Martin, *Battered Wives* (revised and updated). San Francisco: Volcano Press, © 1976, 1981.

FOR FURTHER READING:

17 Women Doctors, with D. S. Thompson, M.D., as consulting editor. *Everywoman's Health.* Garden City, N.Y.: Doubleday, 1980.

BEAUTY

A FULL CUP OF BEAUTY

⅔ cup loving personality

¼ cup proper posture and positive body language

1½ tablespoons of good grooming and pleasing appearance

Mix well, and you will have plenty of beauty—enough to serve almost everyone.

Watching thousands of just-average women bloom into beautiful ladies in my classes by following that recipe, I am convinced that it works. Glow, charm, your interest in others—these are all invisible, but they represent fully two-thirds of the qualities that are essential for making others see you as beautiful. Some women naturally have a loving personality. Most of us don't. We have to work at it. Almost anyone, through self-study and a right relationship with God, can acquire one.

In my opinion, posture and positive body language represent about 25 percent of the ingredients of beauty. But I am talking about more than just the basics of sitting gracefully and standing straight. You need a way of walking that tells everyone, "I like myself." You should be able to touch a friend's shoulder in such a gentle way that you deliver the message, "I like you," without spoken words.

In fact, communications experts now believe that 60 to 80 percent of all messages are relayed nonverbally. If you make a conscious effort to send messages of love to another by leaning toward him or maintaining eye contact while he is talking, you are telling that person, "Both you and I are beautiful people."

I believe that only 10 percent of your beauty quotient depends on your grooming—your makeup, hairstyle and wardrobe selection. And if this is so, you may be wondering why so many books have been written about makeup and why American women

spend millions for beauty aids. The reason is that, while a pleasing appearance may be a relatively insignificant part of beauty, *it is important.* Without it, we are like a cracker minus those few but tasty grains of salt—or the drooping houseplant that misses its tiny dollop of fertilizer.

We go by visual impressions. When a woman enters a room, we instantly form an impression. We don't wait until she utters a brilliant thought—we humans don't work that way.

If you owned a famous masterpiece, you would be sure to choose the best possible frame for it. Of course you would enjoy the painting itself (the inner part) most of all. But you would spoil the whole effect if you surrounded it with a frame that clashed in color, or looked drab, faded or peeling.

I hope you will try the suggestions that are made here, so that you may frame your inner beauty in the most attractive way. I'm excited about your prospects!

WHO, ME?

You may have an endless list of excuses for why the Full Cup of Beauty formula won't work for you, but let's look at some of the more common problems and determine their validity.

Reason Number One. "How can I be beautiful when I've got this *problem?*" you say, bemoaning bow legs, a big nose, an unfortunate ability to gain weight on mere sips of water. Maybe you have thin hair, or too much hair; a bad complexion, or crooked teeth.

Sometimes we magnify our problems until they are mountains big enough to hide behind, when we could be minimizing them into molehills so tiny no one would notice. Why? It's hard work to learn to be beautiful. It is easier to give up, than to try.

Reason Number Two. "My husband wouldn't like me to change." I have found that such husbands are a rarity. The usual male reaction is one of delight.

One of my students had not warned her husband that she was going to try wearing false eyelashes. Usually when he came home for supper, he found her grubbing in the garden or cleaning up the clutter left by their three youngsters. This particular evening, when he walked in the door, he saw that she was setting the table for supper. He spotted her long, luxurious eyelashes immediately. "I like it! I like it!" he exclaimed, running toward her across the room.

Perhaps your husband may say, "You don't need a self-improvement course," or "You don't need to read a book on beauty." These words could be a compliment, but they could also mean that he cannot take the risk of seeing you become beautiful, because he has a low image of himself. He may be afraid you will become so attractive that he will lose you. (We are planning a self-improvement course for men, because so many have admitted that they, too, feel unattractive and uncertain about themselves.)

If your husband discourages you, tell him you want to learn to be beautiful inside as well as out. Explain that when this happens, you will know how to love him in a new and better way.

Reason Number Three. "Beauty is a sexist idea. If God put hair on my legs, why should I bother to remove it?" In my classes I have seen a lot of women who started out with this idea. Often they wore tailored, masculine clothes. Their expressions, hair and skin held no softness. They usually wore no makeup. In fact, they were nothing but plain!

"How I wish your classes had been available to me twenty-five years ago. Perhaps a traumatic divorce could have been avoided," said one middle-aged woman who discovered the value of femininity only after she lost her husband.

Another one of my students wrote to me, "I know there are a lot of us 'out here' who need these classes to give us a little boost in

confidence and courage to accept our right and step out into a new freedom. Perhaps this is really what 'women libbers' are reaching for, without having fully defined their needs."

Reason Number Four. "I haven't the time." True, we must spend minutes, even hours, each week manicuring nails, following a skin-care program and keeping our clothes in good order if we would be beautiful. But you can learn organization that will magically stretch the hours.

Reason Number Five. "I'm not the type. Maybe others can wear paint and polish, but I'm a tomboy. Glamour is not for me." Watch it! Are these the same old negative thoughts—the inability to love and believe in yourself—putting these words in your mouth? Haven't you always secretly envied the Snow Whites in your class and the Sleeping Beauties in your neighborhood, who captured the prince just because they were lucky enough to have perfect teeth, shining hair and sparkling eyes? It is not as impossible for you to look like them as you think.

Maybe you have other reasons, ones you feel that are legitimate barriers to improving yourself. I am writing for you, to help you, because as a woman—God's lovely creation—it is possible for you to be beautiful in the eyes of many beholders. I have gone through all the same struggles that you are going through. And if I can improve, there is hope for anyone!

—From Joanne Wallace, *The Image of Loveliness.* Old Tappan, N.J: Revell, 1978.

FOR FURTHER READING:

Jones, Candy. *Finishing Touches.* New York: Harper & Brothers, 1961.

Landorf, Joyce. *The Fragrance of Beauty.* Wheaton, Ill.: Victor Books, 1973.

Pierre, Clara. *Looking Good.* New York: Reader's Digest Press, 1976.

Wallace, Joanne. *Dress With Style.* Old Tappan, N.J.: Revell, 1983.

BIBLE

Reading

Christianity is a living relationship with the Person Jesus Christ. However, as in any relationship which has meaning, it must be worked at. As we are available to talk to, listen to, and do things for those we love, so must we spend time in the same manner getting to know Jesus Christ.

The most important source of information about Christ is the Bible. Consequently, it is necessary to study Scripture to know what it has to say. When we experience spiritual birth, it is extremely important that we have spiritual nourishment, just as in the first few hours after a baby is born he's fed with sugar and water. Then he moves on to a formula, and later, orange juice is added to his diet and then pablum.

So should it be with us as spiritual babies. After we first become Christians, we should begin to study His Word and act upon what we know. Just as babies are not concerned with what they can't eat but concentrate on what they can, so should new Christians concentrate on what they understand in the Word of God.

Tragically, there are many people who remain spiritual babies though they have been Christians long enough to be quite mature in their spiritual walk. A person who does not spend time alone with the Lord or time with other believers limits himself. He cannot know the rewards of a spiritually productive or abundant life as the person who spends more time with the Lord can.

I have known individuals who received Christ and began their spiritual walk on the same day. They got into the Word of God and began to apply spiritual truth to their lives and really "took off" as Christians. Others were slow, for they gave Bible study a low priority in their lives and consequently did not learn how to apply spiritual truths.

Scripture is relevant to every phase of our lives. I believe that one of the great needs of this hour is for us to know what the Bible has to say. Today, when no authority seems to rule our conduct, we need to get back to God's textbook for man.

God's Word speaks explicitly about topics ranging from our personal relationships to decisions in court. For instance, a friend of mine who operated her own business was taken to court and sued. Her lawyer assured her that the individual who was suing didn't have a case, but my friend lost. After the trial, one of the jurors came up to her to say she was sorry the decision had to be made against my friend. The juror said, "We knew you weren't guilty, but we also knew that you could afford to pay this penalty. Since there was financial need on the part of the other person, we decided in his favor." In executing justice, an understanding of the Word of God would have led the jurors to render a different decision.

In Exodus 23:3 we have clear instruction: "Nor shall you be partial to a poor man in his dispute." This would, of course, apply to the rich man as well.

A schoolteacher tells of a problem she faced in her classroom. A little boy had lost twenty-five cents and was quite distressed over his loss. Trying to comfort him, she instructed the class to look for the quarter. After the children had been looking for a while, she thought, *Surely someone should have found it by now.* When she inquired, one little boy spoke up and said he had found the quarter. The teacher suggested he return it, but the little boy said, "I will not. He lost it and I found it. So the quarter is mine." She then found she could not exert any real pressure to cause the young man to give it back to the boy who had lost it.

The teacher left the classroom bewildered about what to do. Obviously, according to the value system of the class, the response aptly expressed was, "Tough luck for the guy who loses it."

In the Bible we see a different set of values. We are told that that which is lost is to be returned to the owner, even if the owner is your enemy. (*See* Exodus 23:4.)

Only as we know God's Word can we apply it to our lives, and learning takes time and attention. Hebrews 4:12 tells us, "The word of God is living and active and sharper than any two-edged sword, piercing as far as the division of soul and spirit, of both joints and marrow, and able to judge the thoughts and intentions of the heart." God's Word is strengthening. It brings peace to our hearts and gives direction to our lives. Decisions which are made in the light of God's Word are stable and show wisdom.

In 2 Chronicles 34, the story of Josiah and the impact the Word of God had on him and on the nation of Israel is recorded. After Josiah became king, he sought to know about Jehovah, the God his grandfather David worshiped. After learning about Him, Josiah embraced the God of Israel as his God and began to tear down all the pagan temples and rebuild the Temple of the Lord. In the Temple's reconstruction, the original scroll of Moses was discovered and taken to Josiah. As Josiah read the Scriptures, he began to understand that God's judgment would be upon the people of Israel because they had disobeyed and dishonored Him by worshiping idols and forsaking Him.

Josiah took the Scripture to Huldah, the prophetess, and she told him if he humbled himself before the Lord, interceding for his people, God would hear. Josiah called the people of Judah and the inhabitants of Jerusalem together and read them the Word of God. He then publicly declared that he would follow Jehovah and asked the others in the nation to do so, too. Because of their actions, God spared Israel during Josiah's lifetime.

Just as Josiah realized the importance of knowing what the Word of God had to say and then following it, so we must realize there are ramifications for us even today if we do not know and obey Him.

As we read the Bible, we find explicit direction in many matters which concern us. For instance, we learn what kind of husband a man is to be, the kind of wife a woman is to be, how to discipline and rear children, how to handle our relationships with other people. If we neglect the Bible, we cannot expect to benefit from the wisdom and direction which results from learning what God has to say.

Any time my husband and I have an important decision to make and the direction is not clear, we always seek the answer from Scripture. There was a time when we desired to have a third child. We had voiced this to some friends, and one day when Bill was away, I received a telephone call that someone wished to place a baby girl in our home for adoption. Already having two boys, I thought this was an absolute answer to prayer.

Bill was enroute home from a trip and I could hardly wait to tell him. I was certain that he would be excited because we had talked about having a little girl, but when I did get to tell him he completely surprised me by not immediately saying yes.

For hours we discussed the pros and cons of taking a new baby into our home. After consideration it seemed wisest not to take her, but I was emotionally involved and wanted to have a little girl. As we went to bed that night, I prayed that if God wanted us to adopt her, He would confirm it in my heart. But if we were not to have her, I asked to know from His Word that this was definitely His plan for us.

Within a few days, a staff member came to visit. Our guest had just purchased an Amplified Old Testament and enthusiastically read Proverbs 31 to me. As I listened, one verse (v. 16) caught my attention: "She considers a new field before she buys or accepts it—expanding prudently [and not courting neglect of her present duties by assuming others]. With her savings [of time and strength] she plants fruitful vines in her vineyard."

Suddenly I realized that I had all I could handle with the family God had given me and the increasing responsibilities of an expanding ministry. This verse confirmed to me the decision we should make, and as soon as God confirmed that fact, it took all my intense emotion of wanting a daughter away.

If you find that studying the Bible is uninteresting and that it is difficult to arrange time to do it, I understand. As a new Christian, I had to concentrate on finding time to read my Bible, and then discipline myself to do it. But today, reading the Scripture is an absolute necessity to me, and I can't function well without prolonged times of Bible study and Bible reading. When my children were small, reading even a verse or two would sustain me through times of weariness. But today, with the special pressures of decisions and administrative responsibilities, that time in God's Word is vital in sensing His direction and guidance.

Because the reading of the Bible can be an overwhelming experience for many, with its histories, lineages, and strange names, let me give you some suggestions to begin. The Gospel of John is a good place to start your reading. I have found it helpful to underline all the verses that admonish us to believe and emphasize what we are to believe.

After studying the Book of John, you may wish to study the Books of Acts and Romans. Acts is a particularly important book because it tells of the early church, its leaders, and God's miracles. The Book of Romans explains what man is like without God, his need for a Savior, why it was necessary that Jesus Christ come, and the difference between a life governed by self and a life governed by the Holy Spirit.

When you've finished, read the New Testament through as quickly as possible. It can be read in about twenty-five hours. Read it two or three times before you go on to the Old Testament, and then read the Old Testament as quickly as possible.

To learn more about the Bible, you may want to consider purchasing a study book. You can work on your own or attend a Bible-study group. However, nothing can take the place of your personal reading and study. You need time alone to communicate with God. Try to spend time daily with the Lord, even if it's just five to fifteen minutes. As you mature in your walk, you will want to spend an hour or more reading and studying God's Word.

—From Vonette Zachary Bright, *For Such a Time as This.* Old Tappan, N.J.: Revell, 1976.

Home Bible Study

Joyce was a part of a home Bible study group for six years and had taken her turn at leading the studies and hosting the group at her home. Then her husband was transferred halfway across the country. Once they were settled in their new community, Joyce began looking for some sort of neighborhood group to join. She called churches and asked new Christian friends she had met, but no one knew of such a group. "Help!" she wrote to her friends in the community she had left. "What am I going to do without a Bible study group?"

Perhaps you're in Joyce's position—you've had a good experience with a Bible study-discussion in the past, and are now in a place where there aren't any. Or perhaps you have friends who've given you glowing reports about the fellowship and deepening understanding that have come through group study, and you'd like to share in that excitement. What can you do? Just what Joyce ended up doing—start your own group!

Did you just say, "But I could never do that"? Of course you can. Armed with some of the helps you'll find at your local Christian bookstore, you can prepare a study, invite others, and before you know it, you'll have a thriving group. And then you'll wonder why you waited so long.

Your first step is to find another person to share your goal with. The two of you (or perhaps two or three more who are interested) will want to talk about the purposes of your study, the kind of study you'd like to have, who you'd like to invite, and what materials you might use. And you'll want to pray for guidance. Those prayers may be pretty general when you first start meeting, but before long, you'll be asking for specific insight about study guides, babysitters, and who the Lord is preparing to accept your invitation.

WHAT'S YOUR PURPOSE?

Groups calling themselves "home Bible studies" can vary greatly in their purposes, their material, and their method; there's not just one model to follow. For example, you may want to gain more *knowledge* about a particular book of the Bible. Or you may have a deep desire to share Jesus' love with some women who do not yet know Him— an evangelistic study-discussion. Perhaps your goal is *personal growth;* or you want to see a loving, caring support group develop—*fellowship.* You may have questions, either doctrinal or those dealing with emotions or relationships, for which you'd like to find answers.

For each one of these purposes, there are a number of good study guides available. (See pp. 55–56 for a partial list of publishers with a particularly good selection. Your Christian bookstore is also a valuable resource.)

Of course, in most cases, we join a Bible study for more than one reason: we want to learn something, we hope to make new friends or deepen already existing relationships, we want to grow emotionally and spiritually, and we would like to share the good news with others. But which one of these, right now, is the priority for you and the one or two others with whom you are praying? Which of these areas touches a need or deep desire in you? Your own commitment to the study will be stronger if you have a personal, vested interest. And remember, when you complete one guide or discussion series, you can always reevaluate and choose another area for emphasis next time.

Who Will Come?

Besides thinking about your own needs and interests, you'll want to consider who'll be coming to the study. Women in your neighborhood who may not have heard the Gospel might be ready to see what the Bible has to say about being fully alive in God's world. Their eyes might be opened by a short study on the life of Jesus. Women at various places in their relationships to God, but sharing the same frustrations of young motherhood or some rocky places in a marriage or the stresses of a career could well be

ready for a topical study dealing with one of these issues. Experienced Christians might be challenged to rediscover the God of Abraham, Isaac, and Jacob with a study in Genesis or to worship the Christ revealed in Hebrews or Revelation.

By now, you and your friend(s) have voiced your own interests, and thought about who you could invite to join you. You have some idea what you'd like to study. You may be tempted at this point to start calling people: "We're going to start a Bible study. Can you come?" That enthusiasm is great, but hold on for a few more paragraphs. Some of your hardest work is yet to come.

What Next?

Most experienced leaders would agree that it works best, at least at first, to iron out all the details before you get your group together. Group decision-making can take a lot of time and leave some people feeling frustrated (Someone put it: God so loved the world that he didn't send a committee). If you have a clear idea of the material you're going to use, when you're going to meet, and why you're inviting people to join you, you're likely to get more positive responses. Someone not familiar with Bible study groups would feel more secure if you could say, "A group of us in the neighborhood is going to meet for coffee (juice, cocoa) and see what some of the Psalms have to say about our emotional ups and downs. We'll be meeting at my house on Mondays from nine to eleven for the next eight weeks. Would you like to come along and share your ideas? We have a babysitter lined up and we don't assume we'll all come believing the same thing." That's a lot less threatening because it's more specific than, "Would you like to come to my Bible study?"

Preparing to Lead

You're probably familiar with some of the different formats groups use. They range

53

from a teacher-instructed class to a free-flowing sharing group that emphasizes the relational approach. While these two ends of the spectrum have their place, what I'd like to steer you toward is a *discussion Bible study.* There are many Christian books on the market, many of them with study guides for individual or group use. A lot of them are just great and many of the following guidelines can apply to these sorts of books. But there are books, and then there's *THE* Book. I don't know anyone who thinks she spends enough time in Scripture study, so I encourage groups to study the Bible firsthand.

The other half of that phrase was *discussion.* Not a series of lectures by a Bible teacher, nor a series of questions asked by the leader with one definite answer in mind, but a real discussion, where several people have the opportunity to contribute ideas. As group members look at Scripture together, think about what they read, and then ask each other questions to try to determine the meaning of the passage and its application to their lives, everybody grows. Educators tell us that we remember about ten percent of what we are told, but about ninety percent of what we say ourselves.

Worried that somebody will come up with a way-out interpretation? You have at least a couple of safeguards. First, since you're studying a Scripture passage, you can always refer back to the text and ask, "What in these verses leads you to that conclusion?" or "Does the context support that interpretation?" Second, the discussion format will allow the group to be self-correcting and balancing. If another view is not offered, you can ask, "Mary, do you agree with what Joan just said?" or, "Who else can suggest a possible meaning?" While not putting anybody's answer down, the discussion leader can draw out responses based on the passage. Sometimes, you'll need to ask, "Is that what the text says, or is that what you *wished* it said?" (If we're honest, we're not always comfortable with what God says in the Bible.)

Many study guides use a basic question-discussion format, with extra helps for the leader. Browse through several to find one that fits your purpose and the kind of group you hope to have. Probably two or three of you will want to share the responsibility of being the discussion leader. You could rotate weekly, each taking a couple of turns, and at the same time looking for others within the group who would be willing to be a leader or co-leader. Remember, as a leader your job is to keep the discussion going, on track, and involving as many in the group as are ready to share. In many ways, your function is like that of an officer directing traffic—not a lawyer arguing a case or a judge pronouncing sentence.

After you have used discussion guides a few times, you may be interested in creating your own questions—after all, somebody made up the ones in the books. If you feel adventurous, study the format of two or three guides that have worked well in your group. You'll find that the questions are neither too large nor too small, too general nor too specific. (There's no sense in asking the name of the man Jesus was talking to. That's too easy. But something as undefined as "What sort of things did Jesus talk about?" won't help your discussion move toward its goal.)

A good set of questions will help the group *observe* the specific details of the passage, *understand* the author's main point, and *apply* the main point to their own lives in a personal, practical way. With a little practice, you can work out your own set of questions on a book or a topic that can follow that format.

DETAILS THAT MAKE A DIFFERENCE

Working out a few administrative details in advance will make everything go more smoothly. Probably tops on the list is being sure you have a babysitter lined up and a good place to keep the children. Frequently, you can find an older woman from your church who, for the extra income, would be glad to love your children for one morning a week. It's an extra plus if she can share a simple Bible story or activity with the boys and girls while the mothers are studying together.

Many groups have found that a local church will make one of its Sunday school rooms available for such a purpose, and that seems to be an ideal place. Groups are unanimous in agreeing that the children should *not* be kept in the same home in which the study group meets. There's too much chance for distraction and interruption. Lining up a reliable sitter, and perhaps one as a reserve, coordinating her ride to and from the centrally located sitting spot, and arranging for juice and crackers for the children covers the major areas of this detail.

Because having a babysitter is a service to the whole group, it seems fair to pass the hat (or a jar for donations) around to everyone, rather than putting the whole burden of paying the sitter on the young mothers.

You may say, "But we don't plan on inviting any mothers with pre-school children." Perhaps not, but sooner or later, someone will invite a friend who does, and if the group has already made plans for a sitter, she is more likely to feel welcome and be willing to come.

Ideally, your group will meet every week. This gives a feeling of continuity. The relaxed atmosphere of a home is recommended, but don't stick one member with hostessing all the time. A good rule of thumb is to change homes each month (any more frequently makes it hard to remember where you're supposed to go each week). It's important, too, to keep the format simple. This is not the time to try to outdo each other in coffee cake baking. A pot of coffee and a pitcher of juice on a serve-yourself basis helps break the ice without putting anyone to undue trouble.

One of the most important pieces of advice from old-timers is to decide on a time to start and a time to end and stick to your commitment. A good rule of thumb is ten minutes of initial sharing and settling down, an hour for the study itself, ten minutes for sharing anything that hasn't come out in the study that really needs to be said, and ten to fifteen minutes for praying together. It's the leader's responsibility to guard the time for prayer (it's so easy to keep on talking and never get around to praying) as well as keep the study-discussion itself moving along so the group can get to the application section. If you get sloppy about keeping to your time schedule, you will start losing people; they'll drift in and out, early and late, and then not at all.

ARE YOU READY?

You've found one or two others who share your desire for a home Bible study. You've prayed together, talked about your purpose and who you'll invite, and you've chosen your materials. You know when and where you're meeting, one of you has volunteered to coordinate the babysitting service, and the ones who are leading the discussion for the first two or three weeks have already started studying the material. (You might see if your local bookstore will let you take out a number of the study guides on consignment to sell at your first meeting. That's a good way to be sure everybody has one.)

What's left to do? Call the people you've been praying about. A good group can work with as little as four; when it gets to be more than ten or twelve, you are ready to have two groups. Thank the Lord for the ones who are ready to give it a try. And don't pay too much attention to those butterflies in your stomach; remember it's God's group and you're just a part of it. He's able to handle even the things you haven't thought of!

—SHARREL KEYES

MATERIALS TO GET YOU STARTED

Publishers of discussion-format Bible studies include:

InterVarsity Press
Harold Shaw Press (Fisherman Bible Study Guides)
NavPress (Design for Discipleship)

Tyndale House (Neighborhood Bible Studies; New Life Bible Studies)

Zondervan Publishing Company (Woman's Workshop Series)

Books on how to start and lead studies:

Winnie Christianson: *Caught With My Mouth Open* (Harold Shaw)

Gladys Hunt: *How-to Handbook* (Harold Shaw)

James Nyquist: *Leading Bible Discussions* (Inter-Varsity Press)

Kunz and Schell: *How to Start a Neighborhood Bible Study* (Tyndale)

Lead Out—A Guide for Leading Bible Discussion Groups (NavPress)

FOR FURTHER READING:

Edens, David and Virginia. *Making the Most of Family Worship.* Anderson, Ind.: Warner Press, 1968.

LeBar, Lois E. *Family Devotions With School-Age Children.* Old Tappan, N.J.: Revell, 1973.

Murphey, Cecil B. *Press On!* Ann Arbor: Servant, 1983.

Scanlan, Betsey, ed. *The Family Bible Study Book.* Old Tappan, N.J.: Revell, 1975.

————. *The Family Bible Study Book* #2. Old Tappan, N.J.: Revell, 1977.

BIOLOGY OF WOMEN

X and Y Chromosomes

Every human being possesses twenty-three chromosomes in one's sex cells. Only one is a sex chromosome, which determines the sex of the child to be born. Females produce eggs containing sex chromosomes of only one kind—the X chromosome. Males produce sperm of two kinds, some containing the X chromosome, others containing the Y chromosome. Thus, in the act of reproduction, the embryo necessarily receives an X chromosome from the ovum of the mother, but may receive either an X or a Y chromosome from the sperm of the father. A female is determined by the combination XX; a male by the combination XY.

The X chromosome is a relatively large one and bears genes that influence the development of many traits. The Y chromosome, on the other hand, is very small, and we do not know at this time precisely what genes it carries. We do know, however, that the Y chromosome does not carry the same genes as the X chromosome, because certain diseases, such as hemophilia, appear only in the male, but are passed on by the female. Evidently the gene for hemophilia appears only on the X chromosome and is a recessive trait. This explains why a female who has a gene for hemophilia on one X chromosome and a gene for normal blood clotting on the other X chromosome does not develop the disease herself, but a son that she bears who receives the X chromosome carrying the defect will show the disease, since there is no alternative gene on the Y chromosome. Work is proceeding to determine which genes are carried on the Y chromosome. It has been suggested that males who, through defective cell division, carry several Y chromosomes tend to be more aggressive than other males; however, this theory needs much further testing.

Since the Y chromosome is very small and light as compared with the X chromosome, its light weight makes the sperm carrying it more mobile than the sperm carrying X chromosomes. As a result, the actual number of male fertilizations which occur is higher than female fertilizations.

Differential Viability of Males Versus Females in the United States

Ashley Montagu (1974) estimates the number of male embryos as 120 to 150 compared to 100 female embryos at fertilization. However, during the embryological process, these embryos show less viability. During gestation, many die so that at birth the number of males born is 106 to 100 females. This suggests that there may be a disadvantage to the embryo possessing the Y chromosome. Such a disadvantage may be of the type known for hemophilia, an inability to counter recessive deleterious genes on the X chromosome. Or the disadvantage may lie in some as yet unknown quality. Whatever that disability is, it continues throughout the population curve, in that more males than females die in every age grouping, until, in old age, the predominant number of survivors are females. Montagu states that in the first year of life, three male infants die for every female; by the age of 21 the ratio is down to two to one. At 35, 1,400 males die for every 1,000 females; at 55 the ratio is up to 1,800 to 1,000. After that the ratio declines; however, the life expectancy of the female is always greater than that of the male.

For the Western world, Montagu lists 63 diseases which appear in males more frequently than in females, whereas there are only 31 diseases which afflict women more frequently than men. The diseases to which males are subject are diseases of stress.

Coronary insufficiency occurs 30 times more frequently in men than in women. Coronary sclerosis affects men 25 times as often as it does women. Ulcers are six times more prevalent among men than women. Angina pectoris affects men five times more frequently than women. Women appear to be slightly more subject to carcinomas of the gall bladder and genitalia.

Hormones

It has been shown that the possession of the Y chromosome alone is not sufficient to create maleness. The differentiation of the sexes is a process which occurs *in utero*, during fetal development. In the embryological process, various biological systems develop at various times. Apparently, early in pregnancy the reproductive tissue of the embryo is undifferentiated. During the course of development, anatomical sexual differentiation of the male occurs in response to androgens secreted by the fetal testis. Hamburg and Lunde (1972) state: "The recent but already classic experiments of Jost have shown that there is a critical period during which the development of internal reproductive structures takes place. The testis must secrete a

masculinizing hormone (androgen) during this period if differentiation is to take a male course."

Both sexes are exposed to female hormones secreted *in utero* by the mother. It has been noted that in cases where pregnant women have been treated with a synthetic form of testosterone (the male hormone) in order to prevent miscarriage, there have been reports of masculinization of the fetus. This has been shown by Wilkins *et al.* (1958) in 18 out of 21 cases of female pseudohermaphrodism (the enlargement of the clitoris and partial fusion of the labial folds) which causes the female sexual organs to resemble male sexual organs. Wilkins (1965) has shown that in cases where the embryo starts out as a genetic male, and the masculinization continues so that the internal genitalia are differentiated, a failure of androgen secretion by the fetal testes causes the external genitalia to develop in feminine fashion.

It may be that the role played by androgens during pregnancy contributes to the discrepancy between the number of males conceived and those born. A male may fail to develop normally due to lack of androgens. With the exception of the artificial introduction of testosterone during the pregnancy, the course of sexual differentiation for the female is less hazardous than that for the male.

At birth there are notable differences between male and females. Male neonates raise their heads higher than females. Females are more sensitive to the removal of covering, showing a higher degree of skin sensitivity.

The role of sex hormones in patterning the behavior of males and females is less clearly understood. Since there is a feedback mechanism in operation between the glands which secrete hormones and the hypothalamus, which is part of the brain, it is not clear what role in human behavior is played by hormones alone. Thus Money (1961) reports that sex hormones have little or no influence in patterning human behavior, but that such behavior is culturally defined and taught. Hamburg and Lunde (1966) are less certain of this and do seem to see some basic hormonal patterning, although they state that the "complexity of the inter-reactions between genetic, endocrinological, and environmental variables" needs further study.

Throughout childhood there is a minimal secretion of gonadotrophins, regulators of sex hormones. Research (Donovan 1963) tends to show that certain cells in the hypothalamus portion of the brain lose their sensitivity to gonadotrophins gradually throughout childhood, and eventually allow the presence of sufficient amounts of these regulators to stimulate puberty; environmental factors may be involved in the timing of this event. It has been noted that the onset of puberty has decreased from the ages of 16 to 17 one hundred years ago to 12 to 13 years at present. The reasons for this are unknown at present, although better nutrition has been suggested. In any event, the onset of puberty is marked in both sexes by the development of secondary sexual characteristics. These include the growth of body hair characteristic of each sex, lowered pitch of the voice in boys, and the development of the breasts in girls. This is also accompanied by a spurt in growth which usually occurs a year or two earlier in girls than in boys. According to chemical assays (Hamburg and Lunde 1972), both boys and girls secrete estrogens, the female hormone, and testosterone, the male hormone. The difference between the sexes is marked by the proportion of each. Moreover, estrogens become cyclic for the female, with the onset of the menstrual cycle, but not for the male.

The female menstrual cycle is marked by a buildup of the estrogen levels, followed by a cessation of estrogen production and the onset of progesterone secretion. During pregnancy, progesterone levels remain high. It is possible that the minor fluctuations in behavior, which mark both the menstrual cycle and the birth cycle for some women, might have their origin in the sudden cessation of progesterone production with the onset of the menses or immediately postpartum.

Experimentation on monkeys has shown that monkeys maintained on a high level of testosterone tend to be more aggressive than untreated monkeys. They have a higher level of threat behavior; they initiate more play, and their play tends to be rougher. Since human behavior is always mediated by culture, it cannot be stated that the presence of testosterone alone will suffice to make the human male more aggressive. As to the effects of estrogen-progesterone cycles on females, much less is known. Aside from the occasional swings in mood and minor discomforts which accompany the alternations of the cycle, little in female behavior can be directly attributed to hormonal activity. Progesterone has been found to raise the pain threshold in the brain, a most adaptive feature for childbirth. Sex motivation in the female seems to be influenced by androgens, a secretion of the adrenal glands, rather than either estrogen or progesterone. Maccoby (1972) and others have measured intellectual activity, intelligence, creativity, and areas of intellectual interest among males and females for evidence to support a claim that what differences exist are either consistent or biological in nature. The fact that some boys may excel in science while some girls excel in literature or art is a result of the cultural norms of male-female behavior established in our society rather than of hormonal influence.

Puberty

There are, however, certain differences which are intrinsically biological, and upon which culture has elaborated. Primary among these is the fact that the female reproductive period is marked by the visible symptoms of menarche and menopause. The male reproductive period is not. This has had an effect upon the means used by various cultures to establish adult status in its members. Many societies have found it necessary to create elaborate puberty rituals to mark the passage from boyhood to manhood. Since the time used is culturally rather than biologically determined, the age varies from culture to culture.

Birth and Lactation

Birth and lactation are also biological attributes of women, and here too, the ritual involved is manifold. . . . Despite the fact that childbirth in itself is a natural process, most societies recognize that it is fraught with danger for both mother and child under primitive conditions. Pregnant women are often permitted special foods, and denied others in order to ease childbirth. There are few societies which do not have a ritual specialist, either a man or, more frequently, a woman, whose task it is to see a woman through a difficult childbirth. In some societies, men are strictly barred from the house in which a woman is giving birth. In others, as in Mexico, the husband is often asked to hold the wife, to support her through the final stage of parturition. There are various rituals connected with the disposal of the afterbirth, as well. In many societies, it is buried either in the floor of the house or close by.

Finally, there are restrictions on intercourse between husband and wife during pregnancy and lactation. These range from the extreme of complete abstinence during the entire period, which may last as long as six years, to the milder injunctions against intercourse during the final months of pregnancy and almost always during lactation.

Biologically, then, the differences between males and females are real and of significant order. Cultural elaborations have served to widen the gap. In one instance, however, there is evidence of decreasing differentiation between men and women. This brings us to the question of sexual dimorphism.

Sexual Dimorphism

In most species, it is possible to distinguish the male from the female visually. Almost always, particularly in mammals, the male is significantly larger. He is often endowed with certain physical traits which differ from the female, such as the mane of the lion or the larger canine teeth of baboons. Most of these traits, including greater physical strength, are correlated with the function of the male as protector of the females and young. Although sexual dimorphism is less obvious among humans than among other species, men usually have heavier bones and muscles than women. They also have a higher rate of heart efficiency. Such differences are not highly significant in the light of modern complex technology. However, they must have been much more significant for early humans, and thus men were endowed with the responsibility of acting as protectors of women and children. Some anthropologists have argued that *Australopithecus robustus* may be the male of the same species of which the smaller, more gracile *Australopithecus africanus* is the female. This theory has not been generally accepted by anthropologists. Certainly, by the time we deal with *Homo erectus*, the differences between males and females are more difficult to discern, except, of course, in the pelvic structure. This implies that, for man, culture replaced physical weapons for defense. A woman armed with a heavy stick could do as much damage to an intruder as a man. With the development of cultural means of defense and offense, the differences in physical stature between men and women became relatively less important. In discussing athletic training programs for women, De Vries (1966) notes that those sports which depend upon power more than skill have fewer women as star performers. However, he also notes that women athletes respond to a conditioning program in much the same way as men. Barron, Heeschen and Widman (1968) state that men have heavier muscles and bones than women, that they tend to be five to six inches taller than women, and that they have less subcutaneous fat. Women have more rapid pulse rates. In a measure of heart efficiency, known as the oxygen pulse, men and women show the same efficiency until the age of about 15. At that time, the male efficiency triples, while that of the female remains the same: this factor may have been very significant to early man. De Vries,

(1966), however, points out that women have greater manual dexterity than men:

> A review of the literature in this area (physical training) seems to indicate that there are probably no real sex differences in regard either to motor learning rate or capacity, unless strength is a factor.

In contemporary life, strength plays a smaller role than it did in the past. Few modern industries depend upon brute strength, and dexterity is probably at least as important.

Today, there are women who are taller than men, and men who are lighter in weight than women. Some women show greater athletic ability than some men. Both men and women of one society may be taller than both men and women of other societies. The question of greater physical strength is also debatable. In many societies, the women do the heavy work, carry the heavy loads, and walk while men ride. Therefore, sexual dimorphism in humans is less significant now than in the earlier times. This can be regarded as the result of the development of cultural strategies for survival.

The Relation Between Culture and Biology

. . . The human species, although certainly a biological entity, has, through the use of culture, divorced itself from biological imperatives to a greater extent than any other species. Humans are preeminently creatures of learning and culture, which modifies even the most demanding needs of biology. We fulfill our need for nourishment according to the dictates of our society as to appropriate food and proper time to eat. Our sexual desire similarly follows culture's guidelines, which attempt to restrict it to a lasting emotional attachment that has adaptive value for the culture. Even the ultimate biological fact of death has for many people been culturally translated into a transferral to a new and better life. The important factor in this cultural involvement with biology is that the culture sets up a feedback system between the biological fact and the societal values.

If we use the simple factor of the biological attainment of puberty, we can readily see how culture constrains the biological effects. Weatherley (1964) reports that boys who show signs of an early puberty readily become leaders among their peers in middle-class Western society. Group acceptance is easily granted to the taller, stronger, more masculine boy. Late maturing boys are less dominant and more in need of reassurance. Precocious boys are sure of themselves; they are sure of society's approval, they become confident, secure men. Precocious girls, on the other hand, often feel the weight of their society's approbation. They are often frightened and embarrassed by the early onset of menstruation and tend to be timid and withdrawn; however, girls who matured late showed anxiety. This proves the point that a thoroughly encultured member of a society incorporates the values of that society. Women themselves have been taught by tradition that being a woman is not desirable, despite the biological facts which tend to disprove this.

Summary

There are very real biological differences between men and women. Although men are usually larger and stronger, evidence shows that in our society women tend to live longer and be less subject to diseases of stress. This condition may change as more women enter the stressful public sphere.

The factor of maleness is due not only to the presence of a Y chromosome, which must be inherited from the father, but also to the production of androgens by the fetal reproductive system.

Boys attain manhood through a culturally defined ritual or form of recognition; girls reach womanhood through menarche. Many societies regard menstrual blood as dangerous, and therefore women are considered potential defilers during menstruation.

Concern with childbirth and lactation is evident in most societies. Specialists exist to aid the mother, and most cultures observe specific customs during this period. Central to the differentiation of men and women is woman's function as a childbearer. Many of the attitudes and behavior patterns of the sexes are structured around this core.

—From Evelyn S. Kessler, *Women: An Anthropological View.* New York: Holt, Rinehart & Winston, 1976.

FOR FURTHER READING:

Edelstein, Barbara, M.D. *The Woman Doctor's Diet for Women.* Englewood Cliffs, N.J.: Prentice-Hall, 1977.

Fishbein, Anna Mantel, ed. *Modern Women's Medical Encyclopedia.* New York: Doubleday, 1966.

The Diagram Group. *Woman's Body.* New York: Simon & Schuster, 1981.

BIRTH CONTROL

Common Methods of Birth Control

The first type of birth control we will consider is called the "rhythm method." You will remember that ovulation takes place about midway between a woman's menstrual periods and it is possible to become pregnant only within a very few days after ovulation. To abstain from sexual intercourse, then, would prevent pregnancy. The problem with this method is the erratic nature of ovulation. Sometimes it occurs earlier and sometimes later. There is now the possibility of taking one's temperature every morning before rising. This is called the "basal temperature" and it is one degree higher at the time of ovulation. This knowledge helps the user of this method to be more accurate in timing. It is also known that during ovulation, the degree of acidity and alkalinity of the vaginal area changes. There are simple ways by which a woman may test this, and again, the chance of preventing pregnancy is increased. The rhythm method at best, however, is not a sure one.

THE DIAPHRAGM

Another method of birth control is the use of a mechanical barrier over the cervix or the penis. In common use today is the diaphragm, a cuplike structure made of soft rubber and held in shape by a firm rim. It is inserted into the vagina before each sexual contact and left in place for six to eight hours after intercourse. It covers the cervix and prevents the entry of sperm into the womb. It is used with a gelatinous preparation that tends to destroy sperm as well. The diaphragm, to be effective, must be precisely fitted by a physician. This is 96 percent effective in preventing conception.

PROPHYLACTICS

Condoms or rubbers have been used by men for many decades. These are also made of soft rubber and are slipped over the penis just before sexual intercourse is completed. Not only do they prevent pregnancy but they also protect men from most venereal diseases. Condoms are about 99 percent effective as a birth-control measure but they are inconvenient and spoil the spontaneity of lovemaking.

NONPRESCRIPTION PREPARATIONS

Various foams, gels, and vaginal suppositories as well as douches have been widely used as a form of birth control. They generally work by killing the sperm cells, washing them out, or preventing them from entering the womb. These preparations can be purchased without a doctor's prescription, are usually harmless, but are not very effective in preventing pregnancy. Often young people experiment with them, falsely thinking that they are safe from a pregnancy.

THE PILL

For about three decades, birth control has been possible through hormonal intervention in the form of a pill. By understanding accurately the complex hormone cycle that begins menstruation at puberty, doctors have discovered how to safely prevent the process of ovulation. The ovaries are simply put at rest, until a couple is ready for a child. By stopping "the Pill," as it is commonly called, in a few weeks or months, the woman has reestablished her normal cycle and may become pregnant. This is almost 100 percent effective, is relatively safe, and only requires that a woman never forget her pill. According to her normal cycle, she will take a pill every day for twenty-one days. Upon stopping them, she will have a menstrual period and will again take the pill for twenty-one days. She needs to have regular medical examinations to be sure that she is not having any negative reactions.

The few side effects of the Pill need to be understood. Some women suffer mild nausea and tend to eat more to get rid of that uncomfortable sensation, causing weight gain. Most women gain a few pounds of fluid in their tissues, similar to that just before their menstrual period, and on lower doses, about midway through the month's supply of pills, they may have a little vaginal bleeding, called "breakthrough" bleeding. This means that the doctor needs to adjust the dosage. All of these problems may be solved by medical advice. The much-publicized possibility of blood clots being caused by the Pill is less than the risks of a normal pregnancy. Pills that may stop the manufacture of sperm by men are under study, but are not yet perfected or available.

It is also probable that in the next few months or years, a tiny pellet of the chemical contained in the Pill may be inserted through a tiny incision in the skin, and will slowly release the substance without a person's even having to take a pill!

There is a hormone, commonly called the "morning-after pill," that can destroy the fertilized ovum as long as three days after intercourse. It is especially useful in cases of rape or incest. This pill does not prevent conception and therefore is less desirable than the methods previously mentioned. It also causes such severe nausea and discomfort that it could not be used on a regular basis.

THE IUD

The most common method for preventing the implantation of the ovum is the IUD, or intrauterine device. It is a coil of fine plastic that is inserted into the womb. Without injuring the tissues, it moves about just enough to prevent the egg from settling into that soft lining, establishing its nurturing system of blood vessels, and instead it causes the egg to be discharged from the womb. Recently, there has been concern among some medical authorities about the safety of the IUD. Women who use or are considering the use of this method should consult their doctors for more information.

Medical science has studied and perfected safe methods of birth control. By the use of these proven methods, the sexual enjoyment of a husband and wife may be greatly enhanced. The ability of today's couple to plan the size of their family may enrich the quality of life for everyone.

—From Grace H. Ketterman, M.D., *How to Teach Your Child About Sex.* Old Tappan, N.J.: Revell, 1981.

THE DOUCHE

The word *douche* comes from a French word meaning to gush or pour. It is a mistake to douche after intercourse in the hope of washing out sperm that have already been deposited—even if only minutes earlier. Sperm are deposited at ejaculation in a forceful spray that lands at or slightly into the opening of the uterus. An average sperm travels an inch in eight minutes. Therefore, some sperm will probably have penetrated beyond the reach of the douche fluid. Furthermore, the pressure of the douche water may push some droplets of semen farther into the cervix without harming the sperm.

It is not really necessary to douche at any time. The vagina is well supplied with glands and a surface which produces its own fluids that are sufficient to cleanse the vagina, much as tears are designed to cleanse the eye.

Almost all odor from the female genital area comes from fluids which have dried on the outside of the vagina. So, thorough washing with soap and water is all that is needed to remove almost any odor. Additional cleansing can be done simply by cupping your hands and splashing clean water up into the vaginal opening several times.

The morning after intercourse some women find the vaginal drainage of their own secretions mixed with their husband's semen to be uncomfortable. If this is a bother, they may sometimes want to use a cleansing douche.

Here is the proper procedure for douching. You may use any one of several solutions: two tablespoons white vinegar to two quarts of water; or two teaspoons of salt to two quarts of water; just plain water; or one of the commercial preparations, following label directions.

The two main types of douching equipment are the bag (or fountain) and the bulb syringe. The bag type can be hung from a wall hook, so that it is about two feet above hip level. Never hold the lips of the vulva together so that you put water into the vagina under pressure. Water can be forced up through the cervical opening and possibly out the fallopian tubes, causing an inflammatory reaction, which could become a severe pelvic infection.

The douche liquid should be at a comfortable temperature and should be allowed to flow in gently, until the vagina feels slightly distended. Then, allow the fluid to gush out. Repeat this procedure, until you use all of the two quarts of solution.

After each use, your douche equipment should be washed thoroughly with soap and water, rinsed, and dried. Do not allow it to touch a wall as it hangs to dry. Some vaginal infections come from candida (monilia) growing on damp bathroom walls. Your

douche equipment should never be used by anyone else, and, of course, it should never be used for enemas.

The decision to douche is a personal preference, but you should understand that it has little value as a form of birth control.

COITUS INTERRUPTUS (WITHDRAWAL METHOD)

Coitus interruptus means the withdrawal of the penis from the vagina just prior to ejaculation. This method attempts to prevent pregnancy by depositing the semen outside the genital tract.

The withdrawal method is discussed in chapter 38 of Genesis—the only direct reference to birth control in the Bible. Verses 8 through 10 read: "And Judah said unto Onan, Go in unto thy brother's wife and marry her, and raise up seed to thy brother. And Onan knew that the seed should not be his; and it came to pass, when he went in unto his brother's wife, that he spilled it on the ground, lest that he should give seed to his brother. And the thing which he did displeased the Lord; wherefore he slew him also."

We know that the Hebrew custom of that day dictated that if Onan fathered a child by Tamar, his dead brother's wife, the child would not legally have been his, but would have been considered the child of his brother. Even though Onan complied with the command to marry his brother's wife, he perverted the purpose of the marriage, which was to produce a child; he deliberately disobeyed this order given by his father, Judah; therefore, he did not fulfill his spiritual and moral responsibility to his dead brother. It was not just the physical act, but the spiritual disobedience that displeased the Lord. This disobedience demanded the most severe discipline God could give.

Requiring Onan to marry his brother's wife apparently was done for two reasons. One, to provide an offspring for the deceased brother and preserve his name and his memory; and to provide an heir for his property.

The second reason was to serve the interest of the wife; otherwise, she would be destitute. I think we can be safe in assuming that some of the most interested people involved would be the brothers of the fellow considering marriage in that day. He could probably expect much help in choosing a wife!

Today *coitus interruptus* is frequently used by those who have convictions against using artificial contraceptives. Unfortunately, it is one of the most ineffective of all methods. This is because some sperm are usually present in the slight lubricating fluid secreted from the penis during sexual excitement before ejaculation. Only one sperm is actually needed to fertilize the ovum, and that one may be well on its way before ejaculation occurs. To attempt to use this method the man must withdraw completely from any contact with the woman's genitalia before he actually ejaculates.

Coitus interruptus is not only ineffective, but it is undesirable, because it imposes great restrictions on both partners at the very time each should feel the most free in the sex act.

NATURAL FAMILY PLANNING
(RHYTHM AND SYMPTO-THERMAL METHODS)

Three commonly known biological facts provide the scientific basis for natural family planning, in which pregnancy is spaced or controlled without using any of the artificial contraceptives.

1. A woman normally produces only one ovum during each menstrual cycle.

2. The ovum has an active life of only about twenty-four hours, and it is only during this twenty-four hours that it can be fertilized by the male sperm.

3. The male sperm is capable of living for only about forty-eight hours after it is released into the vagina. It is only during this two-day interval that it can fertilize the female ovum.

The conclusion from these three facts is that there are really only three days each month when intercourse can lead to pregnancy—the two days before the ovum is released and the full day afterward. If a woman could avoid having intercourse during this time, then, *theoretically*, she would be in no danger of becoming pregnant.

The idea behind all natural family planning is that a woman must simply refrain from having intercourse on the days when she can become pregnant. What makes this simple idea so difficult to put into practice, however, and what limits the effectiveness of this method, is that no fail-safe way has yet been found to determine just which days are safe for intercourse. The old **rhythm method** simply assumed that most women would be safe one week before their period, during their period, and for about five days after their period. However, the method-failure rate for the rhythm system was quite high.

Today, more and more couples are learning to use what has been called the **sympto-thermal method,** because it is far more precise in predicting the fertile period each month. Understanding and carefully charting your own monthly cycle is the key to using this method successfully. This method is equally helpful when you want to conceive a child, and even as an aid in selecting the sex of your baby through careful planning and accurate timing.

The sympto-thermal method is based on the fact that during a woman's periodic monthly cycle, certain bodily signs occur just before, during, and after the fertile phase of her cycle. The couple using this method learn to observe and interpret the signs to avoid sexual intercourse during the fertile time.

This method includes calendar calculations, daily temperature taking, cervical mucus observations, and observation of other signs that indicate the time when the woman is ovulating (releasing the ovum).

Calendar watching with daily record keeping is important, because ovulation usually takes place between twelve and sixteen days before the beginning of a woman's next menstrual flow. The problem lies in knowing for sure when the next menstrual period will begin. The number of days between periods may vary from one cycle to another, and may vary at different times of a woman's life. Irregularity in the menstrual cycle is common among very young women, and also in the years prior to menopause. Menstrual irregularities may occur when a woman experiences physical or emotional stress—or at any time.

A woman must learn just how much variation there is in the length of her own menstrual cycles. Over a period of months a pattern does emerge. With this detailed record, one can begin to predict the first day of the next menstrual bleeding, called Day 1 of the menstrual cycle. When such a record is available, she can subtract fourteen days from the next predicted date of onset of menstruation to find the day of ovulation. Then she should avoid the four days just before ovulation and the three days after it. [For details about this method, see your physician.]

TUBAL LIGATION

A tubal ligation is a surgical operation performed by a doctor to prevent a woman from being able to become pregnant. This is done by cutting and tying off each of the two tubes that carry an ovum from the ovary to the uterus. If the ovum cannot get to the uterus and sperm cannot reach the ovum, then there is no chance for the woman to conceive.

A tubal ligation must be performed in a hospital under anesthesia. There are three ways your doctor can perform a tubal ligation:

1. He can make an incision in the abdominal wall.

2. He can make an incision through the back of the vagina.

3. He can use a special instrument called the Laparoscope.

Many tubal ligations are now being done using the first method, because the operation is performed within twenty-four hours after the birth of a baby. The uterus is enlarged during pregnancy; therefore, the tubes are raised high in the abdomen, making it easier to reach the tubes within the first day after delivery. When a woman has a tubal ligation performed shortly after she has given birth to a baby, it is relatively easy for her and rarely prolongs her hospital stay more than a day or two. If the birth is by caesarean section, a tubal ligation takes only a few minutes more at the time of the caesarean section, and does not prolong the hospital stay at all.

The tubal ligation has no physical effect, other than to prevent pregnancy. There is no change in the woman's menstrual cycle, and personality and sexual responsiveness will be generally unchanged. However, some women, relieved of their fear of pregnancy, become more responsive sexually.

Because of its simplicity and lower cost, vasectomy is usually chosen by most couples who desire a permanent form of birth control. However, personal preferences sometimes favor the tubal ligation, especially when it is to be done following the birth of a baby, and particularly when the woman's health seems to indicate an avoidance of pregnancy in the future.

Again, I must stress that husband and wife should consider this surgical procedure as *permanent* and *irreversible*, and such a decision should be very carefully weighed.

Advantages of Tubal Ligation

1. There is no need to interrupt lovemaking with use of contraceptives.

2. The sterilization procedure is permanent.

Disadvantages of Tubal Ligation

1. Tubal ligation is considered a major operation and carries some operative risk, as well as considerable expense.

65

2. There is always the initial risk of problems with bleeding, infection, or poor healing.

3. There will be pelvic discomfort for a few days.

4. Only under rare circumstances can a woman get pregnant again, if she later decides she wants to have another child.

VASECTOMY

The vasectomy involves removing a section of the tube called the vas deferens, which ordinarily carries the sperm to be stored in the seminal vesicles to await ejaculation. This prevents the sperm from leaving the scrotum, thus producing sterility. The operation is usually performed in a doctor's office, and requires only a small injection of local anesthetic to deaden a small area on the front and side of the scrotum. If a man has a desk job, he can usually return to work the next day; men whose work requires more physical exertion may need to take two or three days off. Thus, this operation is simpler, safer, and less expensive than the tubal ligation.

To prepare for the operation a man should shave the hair from the skin of the scrotum and bathe before going to the doctor's office. This advance preparation helps decrease the chance for infection.

The vas deferens proceeds from the testicle upward to the seminal vesicles above and behind the prostate gland. This little tube, about the size of the lead in a pencil, can be felt by grasping the loose skin of the scrotum in the area between the testicle and the body, and rolling the tube between thumb and fingers.

The doctor begins by grasping this cord-like tube between his fingers, and then catching a loop of the tube with a sharp grasping instrument. A small incision, about one-half inch, is made in the skin of the scrotum, and a loop of the tube (the vas) is brought to the outside. This skin incision is sometimes so small that it does not even require suturing after the operation.

A section of the tube is then removed, varying from one-half inch up to two inches in length. An older man, who is absolutely certain he will never want to try to reverse the operation, may ask his doctor to take out an extra-long section of vas. The length of the section of the vas which is removed determines more than any other single factor the success rate of the operation, for the longer the section removed, the less chance there is of a new channel developing. Even the best-performed operation can fail, when a new channel develops through the scar tissue between the two cut ends. The failure rate for all vasectomies is about two per one thousand men. Therefore, you may wish to have a semen specimen checked every one or two years, if your wife desires this for her peace of mind.

The most urgent question is: *How soon after vasectomy is the risk of pregnancy no longer a problem?* This will be when there are no sperm in the fluid you ejaculate. Time is not the main factor, but the number of ejaculations is. Sterility occurs after ten or twelve ejaculations. If any sperm are then left, reexamine after five more ejaculations. It is possible to be sterile within one week, but it may take six to eight weeks, or even longer, for this to occur. Never depend on your vasectomy for conception control, until you have had at least one sperm-free specimen examined.

There is a form of microsurgery, which can possibly rejoin the cut ends of the vas, but this operation is expensive, tedious, and often fails to produce the desired results.

Probably the greatest misunderstanding about vasectomy is fear that it will adversely affect a man's sex drive. While all the possible psychological factors cannot be predicted, the vasectomy does *not* have any physical influence upon a man's sex drive or his ability to perform. The tubes which have been cut have no other fuction than to transport the microscopically small sperm cells from the testicles. The fluid material that is ejaculated comes from the seminal vesicles and prostate gland, so that the amount of ejaculation fluid released after the vasectomy is not visibly decreased. The physical sensations and enjoyment during orgasm will remain the same.

There is some data now to suggest that vasectomy may be a risk factor for arthritis and for atherosclerosis, commonly called "hardening of the arteries." We really are not sure of the long-term health effects of a vasectomy, but the question is being studied.

Advantages of Vasectomy

1. It is the simplest means of permanent sterilization for couples who definitely want no more children.

2. A couple are no longer bothered with using other methods of contraception.

3. It is relatively painless and takes only a short time to perform.

Disadvantages of Vasectomy

1. The operation required to reverse the surgery is expensive, difficult, and often unsuccessful. Permanent sterility must be expected.

2. Possibility of some adverse long-term effects to the man's health.

ABSTINENCE

The one method of birth control which the Bible forbids is continuing abstinence in a marriage. As 1 Corinthians 7:3-5 tells us, "Let the husband render unto the wife her due; and likewise also, the wife unto the husband. The wife hath not power of her own body, but the husband; and likewise also the husband hath not power of his own body, but the wife. Defraud ye not one the other, except it be with consent for a time, that ye may give yourselves to fasting and prayer; and come together again, that Satan tempt you not for your incontinency."

Couples should strive to be sensitive and considerate of each other's sexual needs and desires, and to satisfy them regularly and lovingly.

—From Ed Wheat, M.D., and Gaye Wheat, *Intended for Pleasure*, Rev. ed. Old Tappan, N.J.: Revell, 1981.

FOR FURTHER READING:

LaHaye, Tim and Beverly. *The Act of Marriage.* Grand Rapids: Zondervan, 1976.

Penner, Clifford and Joyce. *The Gift of Sex.* Waco, Tex.: Word Books, 1981.

Roetzer, Josef, M.D. *Family Planning the Natural Way.* Old Tappan, N.J.: Revell, 1981.

Ryan, Mary Perkins, and John Julian Ryan. *Love and Sexuality: A Christian Approach.* New York: Holt, Rinehart & Winston, 1967.

BLAME

WHAT REALLY causes more marital unhappiness than anything else is blame. By this we mean making judgments about your mate on the basis of what he or she has done. Suppose your wife has failed to live up to her domestic obligations and this has disappointed you greatly. You would then be correct in assuming that she is a poor housekeeper, and if you stopped your criticisms at that point, you would be a healthy person. You would not be angry, and your wife might learn something from your rebuke. However, what most people do is to go one step farther. They conclude that not cleaning the house is a bad thing, and therefore the *mate is bad.* This interpretation confuses the person with the person's behavior. Whenever you attack what a person has done *and* the person himself, that is what we refer to as blame. So far as we can see, no good comes from this kind of attack. Most people simply do not improve when they are repeatedly told they are worthless. No matter what the issue might be, separate the behavior of the person from the person himself.

You might now ask, How is it possible to separate a person's fresh talk or impolite conduct from the person himself? After all, you will insist that what a person does *is* that person. We insist that this is not so. Your behavior is not you. Your mate's behavior is not your mate. They are two distinctly separate entities.

Examine for a moment whether or not it is

impossible to dislike something about you without also disliking yourself as a person. Can you, for example, dislike your shoes without hating yourself? And if that is possible, it is just as easy to dislike the shape of your ear without damning yourself as a human being. If these two acts are possible, then why can't we also include our behavior? In other words, if you do not like the way you dance, can't you disapprove of your dancing without hating yourself as a human being? The answer is, Of course you can! If you can do this for yourself, can't you also do this for others? In fact, we do this frequently where children or handicapped persons are concerned. Children frequently behave badly, making messes, breaking things, embarrassing us, and we all feel quite irritated at what they do. However, that hardly means that they are worthless or bad. If you do not accept this view, you will wind up being uncontrollably angry with your children and perhaps even beating them. Most beatings are done out of resentment and bitterness in an attempt to get a supposedly bad child to behave well. But the child is not bad, his actions are bad. Why must he and his actions be the same?

There are excellent reasons why we can be most forgiving even though we do not like what happened. Three basic reasons for behavior that we usually regard as bad are: (1) lack of ability to do what is expected, (2) lack of skill and training, (3) emotional disturbance.

1. Let us take as an example a woman who is married to a businessman who is slowly but surely getting up in the world. She comes from a humble, rural background and has never been fully introduced to the sort of life their more affluent friends have adopted. They all play tennis, and tennis, in particular, is something she cannot master. She is grossly uncoordinated and will probably never be able to improve her game because she is so awkward. She loses games and is sometimes laughed at by their friends, although not nearly as much as her husband imagines. He blames her for this deficiency,

when in reality there is nothing she can do about it.

In counseling, this woman was told not to allow his accusations to bother her. He was entirely wrong to insist that she was a bad person simply because she was not able to improve her game in order to please him. By the same logic her husband, who is very poor at languages, would have to conclude that he is a worthless person simply because he cannot learn a foreign tongue. This is something that *he* is innately incapable of grasping. No amount of schooling is going to make him a good linguist. Once the woman saw the absurdity of such a position she was better able to accept herself as a decent person even though she remained a poor tennis player. Most of all, she was able to reject her husband's judgment of her even though he still held to it quite firmly. She recognized that this was his problem, not hers.

2. Let us now consider a woman who appears to have good physical coordination but who has never been exposed to intensive tennis and therefore plays badly. What she obviously needs is more practice, many more lessons. In this way she will be able in time to improve her game. Her impatient husband, however, may scold her and blame her for being a poor tennis player. He fails to realize that she has never had the opportunity to practice tennis and therefore has not mastered the game. Again it could be pointed out to the husband that he too is a failure because he does not know how to speak Russian. Yet he obviously cannot be blamed for not speaking Russian if he was never taught the language nor had the opportunity to practice it.

3. Emotional disturbance is the third reason why people will frequently behave badly and for which they should not be blamed. In this case, a woman might have great tennis skills. She has taken lessons for years and has achieved a high degree of perfection in the game. But she sometimes plays badly because she is so intent upon winning that she makes herself nervous. She is not a bad person because she makes herself ner-

vous, she is simply neurotic. Isn't that also an excellent reason to play tennis poorly? How can she possibly play well when she is a bundle of nerves? If she could get hold of herself and learn how to control her anxiety, she would calm down, use her fine experience and training, and play a decent game of tennis. Until she knows how to get hold of herself, she is bound to play badly simply because she is a disturbed human being, not an evil human being. Therefore, if her husband condemns her *and* her playing, he is nothing less than a fool. It would be no different if the husband were to forget his speech before a business group because of nervousness. He would not be a bad person because he forgot what he wanted to say. He would simply be a disturbed person—that and nothing more. To hate someone for being disturbed is positively absurd and makes no sense whatsoever.

For these reasons blame is never rational. Persons will behave badly some of the time during their lives. We do this simply because we are either unskilled, uneducated, or disturbed. Next time your mate frustrates you in some way that you feel deserves blame, we suggest that you immediately ask yourself why your spouse did this unreasonable thing. He or she must have been incapable, ignorant, or disturbed. These are the reasons why this act was committed, not because your mate is bad. Therefore he or she does not deserve to be hounded, put down, punished, or screamed at. The behavior is *not* the person, and therefore we do not need to damn the entire human being for a few flaws.

—From Paul A. Hauck, Ph.D., and Edmund S. Kean, M.D., *Marriage and the Memo Method.* Philadelphia: Westminster, 1975.

FOR FURTHER READING:

Augsburger, David. *Caring Enough to Confront.* Ventura, Calif.: Regal, 1981.

Hart, Archibald D. *Feeling Free.* Old Tappan, N.J.: Revell, 1979.

Wilke, Richard B. *Tell Me Again, I'm Listening.* Nashville: Abingdon, 1973.

BLENDED FAMILIES

MAKING A MARRIAGE is like weaving a richly textured fabric. The memories and experiences of the couple, and the family after children arrive, create a constantly changing pattern of care and conflict that lengthens daily. When one of the spouses dies or a divorce occurs, the fabric is torn. Especially when a divorce occurs, there are often so many bad feelings that people forget, in their eagerness to end the old relationship, that there are some ties that are better left unbroken. Children need to know that there were loving feelings between their parents and that they themselves were a part of that affection. If a parent denies any good in a previous marriage, the child of that union is likely to make negative assumptions about himself or herself.

There are experiences in previous marriages that should not be denied. My stepchildren love to hear the story of their arrivals into this world; of how their father watched as they slipped into his life. This is important to them, and it is a part of Roger's life with his first wife that should not be forgotten. It is very difficult for people who are divorcing to consider that there may still remain ties to a previous mate—as long as there are children, some ties remain. A new marriage partner needs to be understanding of the children's need for this continuity.

This is part of the emotional baggage we carry, lightly or with effort. All members of stepfamilies come with this luggage; some bring more than others, and some of the things we bring to a new marriage are harder to deal with than others.

The Stepfamily Means Many Simultaneous Adjustments

The new stepfamily is a family of people, all of whom are in a crisis of adjustment to some degree. The children may be adjusting to having a new parenting figure in their lives, they may have to get used to a new house, a new neighborhood, stepsiblings.

They may have to share their parent, not only with the new spouse, but perhaps with stepsiblings who either live in or visit.

The remarriage is a signal to the child that his fantasy of a parental reunion is just that—a fantasy. Children may react explosively. Often couples who lived together before remarriage in peace and harmony are surprised and overwhelmed at the strength of feelings that emerge from their children when the remarriage takes place. The negative reaction will subside when the child recognizes that this is how it will be. He can begin to adjust.

Another common occurrence in stepfamilies is that the anger of the child toward his own biological parents is displaced onto the stepparent. The child is angry at major changes in which he feels he has had no choice. The anger needs to be directed somewhere, and it feels emotionally safer for a child to be angry at his stepparent than at his biological parent. Unfortunately, this can make life fairly miserable for the stepparent—and for the child who may not understand why he is acting the way he is. For children who are old enough, this reaction can be discussed. . . . Remember, the child's negative reaction will not last forever. Guard against your own feelings that your life will always be this complicated.

During all the changes in the child's life there is a need for continuity and security. Do not add more changes than necessary. This would not be the best time to send a child to overnight camp or even day camp, for the first time. Your child may need to be close to you for a while to feel safe; let your child's reactions guide you. If you have no choice about day care or nursery school, for example, explain to the person who will be caring for your child what the situation is. Discuss the arrangements with your child and let him participate in the planning. What can he take with him that will make him feel more secure?

Another adjustment for children involves differences in living styles. Suddenly there is another person who is making decisions in the house. For some kids this can be a culture shock. And children can experience the same discontinuity when they go from custodial home to the home of the noncustodial parent. They have to get used to two sets of rules and two different ways of doing things. It takes time.

They may be confused about which household is "right." What is the right way to eat soup? At one house you have to use your spoon a certain way, and at another house you drink soup out of mugs. This question of which house is right brings out the loyalty dilemma that crops up so frequently for stepchildren. You can help by letting them know that people do things in many different ways, and different doesn't mean wrong—it means different.

—From Mala Schuster Burt and Roger B. Burt, Ph.D. *What's Special About Our Stepfamily?* Garden City, N.Y.: Doubleday, 1983.

BODY

A Temple of God

I wish that the clergy, who have equal if not greater influence than physicians on people's minds, would preach sermons more often exhorting the spiritually faithful to be also physically fit to the glory of God. Though preaching much about sin, they rarely give any practical, workable definition of it. Sin for me is to do, or not do, anything which could harm my body, my self-esteem, or any relationships with God or others. To be perfectly blunt, I consider that to malnourish my body with excess food or allow it to deteriorate through lack of exercise are very serious sins. Preachers should have the guts to tell their Christian listeners when they see that they are sinning in these areas. Physical fitness and true spirituality are interrelated and inseparable.

A famous high school in England, dating back to the thirteenth century, has as its motto the Latin statement, *Mens Sana in*

Corpore Sano. "A healthy mind in a healthy body."

Quoting the ancient Greeks, then-President-elect John F. Kennedy in the December 26, 1960, issue of *Sports Illustrated* wrote, "Physical fitness is not only one of the most important keys to a healthy body, it is the basis of dynamic and creative intellectual activity. Intelligence and skill can only function at the peak of their capacity when the body is healthy and strong; hardy spirits and tough minds usually inhabit sound bodies."

It has been said that the advent of the automobile in America has killed more people by inactivity than by accidents. We are so often in such a hurry to get to the corner drugstore and back that our impatience leads us to jump into the car instead of enjoying and benefiting from a few minutes exercise by walking. An average of fifty thousand people die each year in highway accidents, whereas almost a million die annually of heart attacks. Many of these are either preventable altogether or at least postponable in individuals whose hearts are maintained in good shape through regular exercise.

The medical signs and symptoms of inactivity are scary. A body that isn't used, quickly deteriorates. Astronauts have to do vigorous exercises out in space to compensate for the ease of living in a weightless environment. If the extent of your exercise consists of walking from your car to the television set, you will eventually literally fall apart: Your lungs will become less effective in the task of oxygen and carbon-dioxide exchange; your heart will grow less efficient; you will lose muscle tone; your bones will become more brittle due to loss of calcium; your blood vessels will become less pliable, and your body will become weaker, especially in the matter of the blood's ability to resist infection. You will then become much more vulnerable to colds and other upper-respiratory infections. If you suffer any injury to bone or muscle, you will take longer to heal. Worst of all, your mind will become affected, as evidenced by yawning and a drowsy feeling all day, slowed thought processes, a frequent sense of being "too tired" to do even minor tasks, and eventually by failing memory and declining ability to think logically and rationally.

. . . .

A healthy body is fun to have, but to be unhealthy is miserable. A healthy body is delightful, comfortable, and pleasant to look at; while an unhealthy or fat body is ugly, or even grotesque. God often permits some suffering in the Christian experience for the purpose of restoring a rebellious, or more often, a lazy or neglectful follower back into a more intimate fellowship with Himself. Some pain and discomfort, therefore, either in physical or emotional form, can happen to anyone; but much that we suffer is *not* God's will. We have brought it upon ourselves by our own neglect. Whereas God sometimes uses sickness as a loving means of bringing back a lost sheep, He is not to be held responsible for all the results of our own stupidity in not living within the limits of natural laws.

If we don't exercise sufficiently and regularly, we are highly vulnerable to a sudden, fatal heart attack. If we persist in smoking over a pack of cigarettes a day, natural law decrees that our lungs will suffer. If we drink alcohol at a higher rate than our livers can metabolize it, we know that they will eventually develop cirrhosis. If we continue to eat sugar-filled junk food in calorific excess of our energy expenditure, we cannot blame God if we gain weight. And let's not blame Him either if we have a tough time giving up all these self-destructive habits. We know the rules. We know the penalties for breaking them. "Cause and effect" is one of the inexorable principles of natural law in any form. Cause and effect is the first fundamental of the scientific method, and the overruling essence of general revelation in all of space and time. We ignore it at our peril.

One of the slogans of the American Health Foundation is, "Nobody takes better care of you than you." It stresses that, since many of the diseases of man as yet unconquered are in fact man-made, it follows that they are therefore preventable. But let us not think of it as being the responsibility of organized medicine or government departments of health to deliver to us the well-being we desire. True, some progress has been made in prevention, especially in the area of infectious diseases, with immunization programs. But remember that throughout history no illness or disease has ever been eliminated by curing it. Curing merely restores the individual to health. The disease survives to afflict others, until preventive methods eventually conquer it, and even then only for as long as our guards remain up.

We need, therefore, as individuals, to take upon ourselves the responsibility of practicing our own preventive medicine. The attitude of "it can't happen to me" is unrealistic, foolish, and dangerous. Yes it *can* happen to me, to you, to any one of us who ignorantly or willfully defies natural law. We live within the confines of nature as God made it, and He does not make exceptions. ". . . for he . . . sendeth rain on the just and on the unjust" (Matthew 5:45).

—From O. Quentin Hyder, M.D., *Shape Up*. Old Tappan, N.J.: Revell, 1979.

Recommended Annual Physical Examinations

In addition to the basic stethoscope-on-the-chest clinical evaluation, people over thirty-five should have several special tests done annually. An electrocardiogram (EKG), for example, done lying down is only useful for revealing a heart that is already damaged. Many a middle-aged man has had an EKG lying down and, after receiving reassurance of no abnormality, has dropped dead of a heart attack on leaving his doctor's office. A "stress" EKG, done while exercising, on the other hand, can much more readily reveal potential damage before it actually happens. Leads are attached to the chest of the patient while he is walking on a treadmill with a progressively increasing incline or pace; the heartbeats are displayed on an oscilloscope which is scrutinized by a doctor. An imminent coronary-artery block and

most other cardiac abnormalities can be immediately visualized. If any such abnormality occurs, the treadmill is promptly stopped, a fatal heart stoppage is averted, and the patient is initiated into a treatment program to strengthen his heart and restore it to full health.

A useful blood test which can alert one to the danger of a heart attack is the measurement of high-density lipoproteins (HDLs). A strong inverse relationship exists between high-density lipoproteins and coronary heart disease (CHD), which means that decreased concentrations of HDL in plasma lead to an increased risk of CHD, whereas raised concentrations exert a protective effect.

A proctosigmoidoscopy (rectal examination with instrument) is also an annual must, especially for men over thirty-five. Thousands of very early cancers of the bowel or prostate have thereby been detected, long before the patient would have become aware of any symptoms, and swift surgery has averted death at far too early an age. The hemoccult slide test detects minute presence of blood in feces and represents a double check against intestinal cancer.

Other annual cancer detection tests for men should include chest X ray, GI series (X rays of esophagus, stomach, and upper intestine) and examination of urine for occult (unseen) blood.

For women over thirty-five an annual Papanicolaou (Pap test) for cervical cancer (of the uterus) and a thyroid-function test are essential for good preventive care. Women should examine their own breasts regularly and bring any lump or firm area to the attention of their doctors immediately. Breast cancer can occur rarely in men also. Although there are some reservations about the effect of X rays on the breast, a mammography should be done if any tumor is suspected, because the risk of failing to detect a cancer there then becomes greater than any possible damage that could be done by the radiation. All these tests can be lifesaving when pathology is discovered before symptoms are experienced, thereby giving early treatment a chance to prevent serious illness, or even death.

Special blood tests essential annually to all over thirty-five should include evaluations of cholesterol, triglycerides, and lipoprotein levels. These determine the status of fat metabolism with any consequent potential threat of arteriosclerosis, or narrowing of the blood vessels by fat-related deposits along their inner walls. Liver-function tests (transaminase, alkaline phosphatase, and bilirubin levels) are important year by year for all "social" drinkers to monitor and expose any unrecognized (or unconfessed!) increase in alcohol intake. Other blood chemistries should include measurements of sugar, urea nitrogen (kidney function), uric acid (gout, arthritis, and so forth), and several others such as lactic dehydrogenase (LDH), albumin-globulin ratio, total protein, and concentrations of calcium, creatinine, and inorganic phosphates. A blood-serology test warns of any venereal disease.

A pulmonary (lung) function analysis is important for all smokers or people exposed to occupational or environmental breathing hazards. Again, early detection leading to change of habits or avoidance of further exposure can prevent serious problems later. Have your eyes and ears checked regularly too. Both vision and hearing can often decline imperceptibly and can many times be treated. Finally, don't forget your teeth. See your dentist regularly, every six months at least, for evaluation, treatment, and preventive care.

—From O. Quentin Hyder, M.D., *Shape Up.* Old Tappan, N.J.: Revell, 1979.

FOR FURTHER READING:

Chapian, Marie. *Fun to Be Fit.* Old Tappan, N.J.: Revell, 1982.

Morehouse, Laurence E., and Leonard Gross. *Total Fitness in 30 Minutes a Week.* New York: Simon & Schuster, 1975.

Murphey, Cecil B. *Fitness: The Answer Book.* Old Tappan, N.J.: Revell, 1983.

Murphey, Cecil B. *Devotions for Joggers.* Old Tappan, N.J.: Revell, 1982.

BODY LANGUAGE

Face

A minister looked out at his congregation on Sunday morning and said, "I know there are lots of happy, joyous people here this morning." He paused a minute and then went on. "I just wish they'd notify their faces." Whoops! The congregation's body language was showing. The pastor, without seeing any smiles, could not feel his flock's happiness.

Others can be drawn to us through our body language—which includes walking, sitting and standing properly. We can also lose one to two inches in the waist and hips, if need be, simply by practicing correct posture. Our clothes will look better, too.

Let's look at how body language can affect your appearance. Almost everyone I know is concerned to some degree with looking interesting and attractive to others. Yet many are labeled "expendable" even before they open their mouths. How can this happen?

Let's say a new member of your club is introduced to you. She slouches on one leg, letting her shoulders slump dejectedly. While being presented to you, she takes a step backward, without even smiling. Her eyes focus *not on you*, but on a spot on the wall over your left shoulder.

"What an aloof person!" you are thinking. "She's trying to freeze me out—probably thinks she's better than I am." But you are wrong. Like Mrs. Lowly, this woman wants your friendship more than anything but doesn't know how to receive it.

Our body language also includes the movement of our eyes and our hands, the glow or dullness in our faces. It is a universal language that says everything about our acceptance or rejection of ourselves and others. To a certain extent, we all can understand it, but sometimes we send out garbled messages.

When counselors and psychologists tell us that 60 to 80 percent of all communication is nonverbal, they mean that we are often say-

73

ing more with our bodies than with our tongues. Nothing is wrong with that, if we like ourselves, for our bodies will faithfully report that fact. But if we don't accept ourselves, if we feel anxious or worthless, our bodies automatically deliver that message, too.

If you have days when you feel like a Mrs. Lowly, don't despair. Just as you can learn to speak French by studying it from a book and then practicing, you can also become fluent in the kind of body language that says, "I like myself, and I also like you." As you act out this self-confident behavior, you will almost miraculously come to like yourself better. I wish I could see the wonderful changes that are going to be made in you!

Posture

Facial expressions are important in delivering the message that you love others. But the rest of your body also speaks loudly and clearly.

If you are speaking body language with the same kind of misleading accent, don't despair. As you learn to improve your outer appearance with the right makeup and hairstyle, you will also gain a better feeling about yourself. As you practice listening attentively or leaning toward someone, rather than away from him, your body language will improve.

How many times have you heard that you should stand tall, with your tummy tucked in, shoulders straight and head level? "Oh, you mean posture? I heard all about that in junior high." Probably you did. But what I see so often is that few actually practice what's been preached so often. You can look so much lovelier if you practice good posture each day.

Here's an easy way to see if your body lines up properly when you stand. Tape a six-foot long string to a full-length mirror and weight it with a heavy object that will keep it taut. Then line your body up with the string.

If it is hard for you to see if your body is really lined up, ask someone else to check

you. Start with your head. Pull it up tall and stretch it. Then check the rest of your body, to see if it is in line with the string.

Once you have your body lined up in a tall, poised stance, you are ready to learn to walk gracefully. It helps to have someone check out your walk, because many people have developed bad walking habits, of which they are not even aware. Your walk may demonstrate self-consciousness, shyness, fear, carelessness or a manner of being too forward. Instead, you want your walk to speak of grace and ease.

There is a lovely way to sit, too, though it is not done often enough. Many times an attractive girl spoils the whole effect of her beauty by sitting with her lower limbs wrapped around the chair legs, or twisted into awkward pretzel shapes under the chair. Or there are those who don't keep their skirts down.

The best position is to sit with your ankles crossed. Bring them over to the side of the leg which is in front. Hold your knees tightly together and point your feet to the side.

If you must cross your legs, cross them at the knees, then pull both legs to the side. Keep your ankles closely together and point your toes down. Tuck your skirt closely to your knees. Warning: Crossing your legs at the knees *incorrectly* can cause varicose veins and cut off the circulation in your legs. It also destroys poise.

Practice standing and sitting correctly until these ways become natural to you. Practice much at home, to look relaxed and at ease in public.

—From Joanne Wallace, *The Image of Loveliness*. Old Tappan, N.J.: Revell, 1978.

BOREDOM

BOREDOM isn't static. It feeds upon itself, growing larger and fatter until it earns enough names to look impressive. How about depression, hypertension, chronic fatigue, hypochondria? Do those sound interesting? How about the everyday ones like overweight, chewed fingernails, vague fears, vertigo, and irritability?

Now wait a minute. We all have those days when we get up in the morning with a vague feeling of wishing we could spend the day in a hammock with a good book. That's not the kind of boredom I'm talking about. That's a healthy rest stop.

But if your life is dull a little too often, if you get tired too soon, if the things you do are uninteresting, if you find yourself annoyed, even with those you love, and especially if you catch yourself sighing a lot (don't laugh . . . I don't know why women sigh when they're bored, but they do) you'd better read on.

A piece of you is definitely missing. An important piece, because you have an emptiness deep inside. Like Old Mother Hubbard, your cupboard is bare. Worse than that, it's a vacuum.

Unfortunately, you're not alone. In days when smallpox is all but wiped out, and people get excited over a case of measles, we have a new epidemic. But you can't slap a bandage on boredom. It's more than a break in the skin. There's no vaccination. There's no pat answer.

But I do have some clues. Call them guidelines, if you want, and give them a try. Remember . . . there is not one single thing about the world we live in that is boring. Only your attitude toward it makes it unexciting. So take the month of September to rid yourself of rust. Get your creative gears oiled, and let your enthusiasm roll. Here's how to break the boredom habit:

1. *This First Step Is an Important One.* It's an emergency measure. It gets you pointed immediately in the right direction. The very next time you feel bored, stop whatever it is that you've been doing, and do something else.

Come on now! You can leave almost any job for a few minutes. Unless you're performing surgery (in which case you wouldn't be bored), break away, and try something new. Anything. Go outside and walk around the house. Play the piano. Clean the medi-

cine cabinet. Bake a cake and give it to a neighbor. Call a friend. Go somewhere on the spur of the moment.

Now you have a head start on anti-boredom, but don't stop. Busy-ness is not the whole answer. It's only the beginning. Getting out of bed in the morning is just the starting line for the race. It's necessary, of course, and you'll feel better as soon as you do it, but it's not enough. So move right on to the second step . . .

2. *Come Out of Exile.* Don't be like the squirrel who got his seasons mixed up and hid in the tree trunk all summer long. "Why do you stay cooped up in there?" asked the woodchuck. "It's so exciting out here in the world!"

The squirrel poked his nose out and looked around carefully. "But it's so safe in here," he whispered. And it was . . . until his food ran out!

It must have been boring, spending the whole glorious summer in a tree trunk. But don't feel too sorry for that squirrel. Boredom is a cop-out, an excuse for living. When you turn your back on life, you always get backed into a corner.

Safety, you see, can't be your primary concern. Neither should a security blanket be your prized possession. We were made, like ships, to sail, not to sit at anchor in some snug harbor, or worse, in dry dock, with rusted hinges and chipped paint.

Don't you agree? Perhaps you're thinking of the person who said that we have to get rid of all our fears *before* we can begin to live. Well, that's not entirely true. Sometimes we get rid of our fears by *beginning* to live. The thing is, all of us have fears of one kind or another. We don't want them. We try to get rid of them. But the little devils seem to keep popping up. I'm not telling you to learn to live with them. They ought to be cleaned out as quickly as you can find the dustpan. But if you wait around for a completely clean house, you're going to spend a lot of time sweeping. My point is this: you have to get out there and live in *spite* of whatever it is you're afraid of.

Come out of your tree trunk, and splash right on in, just like the small boy who went to the beach. He didn't know the water was going to be so cold. But the chill didn't last. After a while, it even felt pretty good. Most important, cold water didn't keep him from splashing in again and again.

3. *Have a Survival Kit.* I can remember one Sunday, some years ago, when I was sitting next to our youngest son in church. No matter how quietly he tried to move, he crackled. It wasn't until later that I discovered his pants pockets were stuffed with edibles and his coat was lined with comic books. "At least," my husband said, "he came prepared."

Your survival kit doesn't have to be that drastic. I think a list will be enough. Write down all the things you really want to do, but have never had the time (or courage) to try. I have a friend named Elizabeth who started a list like that years ago. She keeps it in a drawer as a reminder that there's plenty left out there in the world for her to explore. This year she summoned up her courage and took a glider ride as a birthday gift from her family. What will she do when all the items are checked off? She's not worried about that. Her "survival kit" list is better than a wish book, because it doesn't have a last page. With enthusiasm like hers, the list will grow and grow. And you can bet that looking forward to each new experience goes a long way toward burying boredom.

If you want something more concrete than a list, be ready with a large box. Fill it as you go along with things you want to do: that special book you've been wanting to read; a piece of material you can make into a long-awaited evening skirt; a stack of pretty cards to write on and send to friends; a pillow cover to embroider, a package of seeds to plant. There is only one restriction on your survival kit. These must be things you really *want* to do. You should feel that you can hardly wait. If you're still bored when you're busy, you're not busy at the right kind of

things. You made the choices; you have no one to blame but yourself.

4. *Carry a Mental Compass.* Know your directions: enthusiasm is up; depression is down.

We used to think, thanks to Newton and his falling apple, that the law of gravity was infallible. What goes up, must come down. Isn't that what we were taught? Too bad Newton couldn't have lived long enough to see the age of space travel, when what goes up sometimes stays up forever.

That's the way your attitude about life should be. As high as the sky, with no need for falling. Remember the story of Chicken Little, who went around announcing that the sky was falling? What a gloom machine he must have been. Children love the story, because it is so ridiculous. In their innate wisdom, they wonder who in the world would spend his days waiting for the sky to fall in. Some of us adults do.

How wise to see things like the little boy who gazed up at the altar and asked, "What's that big plus sign doing up there?" He recognized the cross as a positive symbol. His mental compass was right on target.

Where's *your* mental compass? Make your choice. Don't be like the crooked man who built a crooked house. Once he got started, everything he did was crooked. He didn't have any sense of direction at all.

5. *Get in There and Hustle!* If you don't, you're liable to become a dull person. That's what happened to Ann Murphy. I watched her as she sat one morning in her kitchen, her elbows on the sill, while she stared out the window.

"I never should have poured the coffee," she complained. "I should have left it in the pot until it had oily film on top. I should have gone to Siberia on a fast plane. It's been that kind of morning."

"What on earth happened?" I asked. From her tone, I expected the worst.

"Nothing!" she muttered. "Nothing ever happens. That's the trouble. I got up and poured the coffee, and everybody else got up and grumbled around the way they always do." She looked at me with tear-filled eyes. "Is this it? Is this all I can expect from life?"

My answer could only be, "Yes. That's all there is . . . if you stop right there and go back to bed, that's all you can expect out of life."

Ann was a gray person. The only way to break out of her nest of boredom was to get out and hustle. I told her so. At first she looked insulted.

"How?" she demanded.

I couldn't help laughing. "A good place to start is by getting out of your chair," I said. Ann didn't know that life wasn't passing out favors. She didn't realize that if you want hot tamales, you have to add some chili to the sauce!

About one hundred years ago, a man named Josiah Gilbert Holland had a few choice words to say on the matter of getting out and hustling.

God gives every bird his food,
but He does not throw it into the nest.

By the way, did you ever see a bored bird? I did, only once. For some reason he took a liking to our bedroom window. He came every day that spring, arriving about 4:30 A.M. to peck at the glass. He kept it up until mid-afternoon, when he began collecting bits of straw and leaves, which he tried to apply to the window's surface. Of course, everything dropped to the ground. He never accomplished a thing. And . . . listen to this . . . he never tried a new tactic. Toward the end of the season, he was beginning to lose his feathers, his eyes looked glazed, his head drooped. Like Ann Murphy, he probably wondered if this was it! All the equipment was available. He just couldn't seem to put things together.

You can't just sit through life and expect everything to come up roses. Ecclesiastes puts it this way: "Whatever your hand finds to do, do it with your might" (9:10). This doesn't include moping at the kitchen win-

dow or dropping loose straw on the ground.

It does include having a workable goal. Only when you have a definite aim in sight, so that you can place your feet firmly on the stepping stones of productivity, is your busyness going to keep you vitalized. It's no good being as busy as a bee unless you produce a little honey. It's no good collecting straw unless you eventually come up with a nest.

6. *Be a People Watcher.* It's a wonderful way to jerk yourself up by the bootstraps. Just look at the faces around you. How many look preoccupied, disinterested . . . bored? How many look vital and alive, their faces animated, their eyes sparkling? Watch them all. Try to imagine what makes people look the way they do. Discover the infinite variety of the human countenance. Then ask yourself what *you* look like. Is your mouth turned up in a smile? Or sagging at the corners? Are you staring blankly . . . or are you looking at what you see? If you can decide which way you *want* to look, it's five spare minutes well spent.

7. *Don't Be a Bore.* I wish I could have met the man who said, "The man who rows the boat generally doesn't have time to rock it." Show me a troublemaker, and I'll show you a bored person. The sad fact is that most bored people soon become bores. You never catch one picking up an oar. They're too busy thinking about themselves. Watch for these warning signals in *your*self:

A bore talks when he should listen.
A bore nags.
A bore is selfish.
A bore turns his back on life, but is interested
*   in your business.*

Watch for the red light. Don't let yourself fall into the boredom trap. Be a rower, not a rocker.

8. *Stop Looking Out at the World Through Dirty Windows.* Here's a little exercise to help you. Pick an object, any object.

Anything from a bowl of sugar to a picket fence. Stare at it. Let its edges grow hazy. Let your eyes go out of focus. Exciting? Not very. Can you imagine how you look? That's not very exciting either. Now, pull yourself back into focus and have a good look at that bowl of sugar or picket fence. Concentrate on its fine points. Keep your vision edges sharp. Can you *feel* the difference? Notice how your eyes are actually moving, even darting, as they take in the smallest details. If you could see yourself now, you'd *notice* a difference.

Remember this experiment the next time you're bored. You alone can wipe your dirty windows clean. Don't stare blankly; it fogs your windows. Try looking at things around you with interest and enthusiasm, and wipe the glass clean.

9. *Be Good for Something.* "But I try to be a good person," I can hear you saying. "Isn't that enough? I make a real effort to do all the right things. I don't rob, lie, cheat, or steal!"

So why do you get bored? Henry David Thoreau tells it the way it is: "Be not simply good . . . be good for something." Doesn't that imply more than good behavior? Of course it does! It implies action. It implies purpose.

The key word is *change.* I'm reminded of the woodcarver I once watched for a long period of time. The artist was so talented that, as the shape of the figure emerged, I could have sworn that it had been there all along, and all the artisan had to do was strip away the extra covering. It looked so easy, the change he created. But it wasn't a hit-and-miss affair. It involved, he told me, visualizing the total result before beginning. It also involved his total commitment. In other words, he didn't just hack away at the life of his wood. He had a plan, and he was part of it.

You can be a moving force, an impetus. You can change things. If you can't think of anything else for starters, why not move the furniture and put a fresh bouquet on the cof-

fee table. That's change, and it involves you—because you're a little different each time you act. How ambitious are you? Write a letter to the editor. Join the church choir. Run for office. Wherever you go, make your presence felt.

Hans Christian Andersen had a wonderful philosophy. "To be of use in this world," he believed, "is the only way to be happy." Take a tip from him and make yourself useful. Don't turn your back on life. Stand right up and be counted. You'll never be the same again.

10. *Use It or Lose It.* I'm talking about life. Approach it with enthusiasm. It's the only way anything good gets done. Never crawl into a tree trunk to hide. Instead, "Let your light so shine before men, that they may see your good works and give glory to your Father who is in heaven" (Matthew 5:16).

Life's a little like love. The more you spend, the more there is. And it's a little like a kiss. It's more fun when you share it. So take your pent-up energy and spend it on the month of September. Put on your thinking cap and let imagination flow. Fight boredom with action, and it won't have a chance to thrive. Know that every hour *is* a miracle. How can you be bored with that?

—From Marilyn Cram Donahue, *A Piece of Me Is Missing.* Wheaton, Ill.: Tyndale, 1978.

FOR FURTHER READING:

Allen, Charlotte Hale. *Full-Time Living.* Old Tappan, N.J.: Revell, 1978.

Fried, Barbara. *The Middle-Age Crisis.* New York: Harper & Row, 1976.

BREAST

Cancer Prevention

Current statistics are that fourteen out of every fifteen women will never get breast cancer. However, every woman needs to guard against the disease with regular physical examinations and a monthly breast self-examination. When breast cancer is found early, before it has spread, the chances of cure are very high. ALL CHANGES—lumps, nipple discharge, unusual sensation or other breast change—should always receive prompt, expert medical examination.

Bathing or showering is your moment to take care of yourself, to take time for a breast self-examination. As you wash, while your skin is slippery, it's a simple thing to do. Keep your fingers flat and touch every part of each breast. Feel gently for a lump or thickening. Why? Because it could save your life. After your shower, take a moment for a more thorough check.

Monthly self-examination helps a woman know the normal consistency of her breasts, enabling her to identify any change.

Ninety-five percent of all breast cancers are discovered by women themselves.

Despite the fact that a high percentage of breast lumps will prove to be harmless, it is important to see your physician as soon as possible if you discover a lump or thickening.

Breast cancer is highly curable. The odds are in your favor and they'll improve, if you act on what you know right now.

The above information has been taken from a small pamphlet put out by the American Cancer Society.

The February 15, 1976, issue of *Modern People* carried a number of interesting findings on the relation of cancer and stress. There exists the possibility that cancer may in some few cases be psychosomatic. Cancer researchers working at Johns Hopkins University are finding increasing indications that cancer is mental, or that cancer can be triggered by mental or emotional causes.

V. R. Riley of the Northwest Research Foundation in Seattle, Washington, found that the crucial factor in the development of cancers was stress. He completed some astounding laboratory experiments in that regard on mice.

Many researchers have observed the same thing where people are concerned. Naturally, some of us are able to handle stress and don't develop cancers. But many people cannot.

The connection between emotions and cancer has been talked about for over a generation now. In his book *No Miracles Among Friends*, written in the 50s, a British surgeon, Sir Heneg Ogilvie, said: "The happy man never gets cancer." Of course, what makes one person happy, might make another unhappy. But his point was this: It now seems almost certain that if something in your life changes to make you much less happy or permanently unhappy, you are a prime candidate for cancer. And, if you can keep in your life that which makes you basically happy, you are going a long way toward protecting yourself against cancer.

One thing seems sure—mental state is crucial in dealing with cancer.

The same issue of *Modern People* mentioned above also stated that the National Institute of Cancer in Milan, Italy, is working on a report called "Toward an Understanding of Cancer as a Psychosomatic Phenomenon." The main author of the study, Dr. Filippo Beringheli, was said to be a prime candidate for the Nobel Prize.

Greece is working on a similar study. At the University of Athens, Dr. N. C. Rassidakis has shown cancer, diabetes, and schizophrenia all to be linked by a strong mental factor. One of the proofs for this is "the frequent appearance of these diseases when there is the greatest mental turmoil" together with "the disappearance of anxiety once the disease is established."

—From Janie Clausen, *Radical Recovery*, copyright © 1982, pp. 141–43; used by permission of Word Books, Publisher, Waco, Texas 76796.

Self-Examination

The possibility that you may have or will get breast cancer is very real. There is rarely pain in the early stages, so it is important that you examine your breasts regularly. Ignorance is *not* bliss if a lump in your breast goes unheeded, whereas attention to the lump in its early stages can usually mean successful treatment of cancer.

The first principle of self-examination is *regularity*. Once a month, at the same time of the month, is sufficient: more often can become an obsession, and breasts tend to change during the month, causing undue alarm to the examiner. A few days after menstruation is a good time because the breasts will then be at their smallest and anything unusual can be detected easily. If you have passed menopause, pick a time of the month when your breasts are the least full and tender. You still have a monthly cycle even though menses have ceased.

Visual Exam

First stand in front of a mirror with your hands at your sides; then raise your hands above your head; place palms against each other and lower them to chin level, pressing them against each other. Look for differences in shape (not size); look for unusual bulges or puckering of the skin; gently squeeze each nipple and watch for a discharge (if you are breastfeeding, omit this step); look for a scaly crust on the nipple or a reddening of the skin immediately surrounding the nipple. Of course, a sore on the nipple should be examined by a doctor as soon as possible.

Manual Exam

Lie on a bed and raise one arm above your head, placing your hand under your head. Feel your breast with the flat of the fingers of the opposite hand, moving them in small circles and covering the entire breast, including the joining of breast and armpit. Then change hands and examine the other breast. Anything that is abnormal compared to previous examinations should be reported to your doctor. Pain, a thickening in one area of the breast, or a hard lump should be checked by your doctor. All lumps are not

cancerous, and the doctor may be able to draw fluid out of a cyst with a special needle. If the lump is not a cyst, the doctor will want to arrange for its removal for tests. This will require surgery, but should not throw you into a panic, because the majority of lumps will be found to be nonmalignant.

—Shirley Murphey

FOR FURTHER READING:

Clausen, Janie. *Radical Recovery*. Waco, Tex.: Word Books, 1982.

The Diagram Group. *Woman's Body*. New York: Simon & Schuster, 1981.

BUDGET

Where Has All the Money Gone?

The money squeeze is putting a pinch on young and old, singles and marrieds, in all income brackets. Howard L. Dayton in his book *Your Money: Frustration or Freedom* says, "Invariably, whether a family earns $8,000 or $80,000 a year, it probably will have too much month at the end of the money unless there is a carefully planned and disciplined approach to spending."

George and Marjean Fooshee have counselled many people in their home, and while conducting financial seminars across the country. They often encounter people who have consistently and unknowingly overspent their income. George's position as president of a credit adjustment company in Wichita, Kansas, brings him in direct contact with dozens of families whose financial difficulties have pushed them to the edge of despair.

Is there hope? The Fooshees say yes. But getting "unsqueezed" for these people requires brutal honesty, planning, and discipline. Yet it can be done, and it begins with a budget.

"Not one person who has come to us with financial difficulties has had a budget," George said. "A budget is simply 'planned spending,' or my favorite definition, 'telling your money where to go instead of wondering where it went.' " Without a budget, it is relatively easy, George says, for a family to overspend by $50 or more a month. But with a plan, it's easier to say no to spending. A budget is not a "straight-jacket that restricts your life and makes a miserable miser of you," George Ford says in his book *All the Money You Need.* "A budget properly used . . . will set you free."

A budget also motivates family members to work and pray together about their spending. "A successful budget," Dayton says, "should be a 'team effort.' Budgeting can help each member of the family participate in deciding what should be purchased and what the goals of the family should be. It is a good tool for the husband and wife to use for communicating together."

In the following steps taken from their book, *You Can Beat the Money Squeeze* (Fleming H. Revell, 1980), the Fooshees describe how to set up a budget and make it work for you.

GET THE FACTS

"Getting the facts is the hardest thing we have to do," George said. When George and Marjean counsel people, first they have them fill out a financial summary. Often seeing the facts in black and white is shocking. But, according to George, getting the facts is an oft-repeated Biblical principle.

"When Jesus was about to feed the 5,000 he first asked his disciples 'What do we have?' When they responded, 'Five loaves and two fishes,' Jesus then used them to feed the people." (Mark 6:38).

The Proverbs repeat this admonition to get the facts. See Proverbs 1:29, 31; 14:8,15; 18:13; 19:2; 23:23; and 27:23,24.

SET GOALS

After getting the facts, set financial goals. Determine what you will spend in the following categories:

1. **Tithes and offerings**—all charitable giving: church, United Way, etc.
2. **Federal Income Tax**—all amounts withheld, plus estimates paid, plus any amounts due with tax return.
3. **State Income Tax**—all amounts withheld, plus estimates paid, plus any amounts due with tax return.
4. **Social Security Tax 1983 Figures**—6.7% of your first $35,700 earned.
5. **Other Taxes**—taxes on your wages such as city income taxes.
6. **Shelter**
   a. If renting—include rent, heat, lights, telephone, household supplies, appliance repairs, magazine and newspaper subscriptions, other home related expenses.
   b. If buying—include house payments, interest, insurance, real estate taxes, repairs and maintenance, other items listed under renting.
7. **Food**—grocery store items, paper goods, cleaning supplies, pet foods. Include all eating out and carry-out items and school lunches. May also include entertainment.
8. **Clothing**—purchases, cleaning, repairs. May be divided with separate budget for each family member.
9. **Health**—health insurance premiums, medical, dental, hospital expenses, drug items, medicines, cosmetics.
10. **Education**—school supplies, books, lessons, college expenses, uniforms, equipment.
11. **Life insurance**—all premiums whether paid monthly, annually, or quarterly.
12. **Gifts**—birthdays, anniversaries, special occasions, Christmas, weddings, funerals, office collections, dues for organizations.
13. **Transportation**—gas, oil, repairs, licenses, personal property tax, insurance, car payments or an amount set aside to purchase your next car.
14. **Personal Allowances**—for each family member to spend personally. Hair care, recreation, baby sitting, hobbies, and children's allowances.

15. **Vacations**—trips, camps, weekend outings. Trips for weddings, funerals, family visits.
16. **Savings**—amounts set aside now for future needs.
17. **Household purchases**—for major appliances, furniture, carpeting, and major home maintenance such as roofing and painting.
18. **Debt Reduction**—all payments on debt not included in other categories such as school loans, amounts due relatives, banks or others.
19. **Special Categories**—anything tailored to your own needs or desires. May include a boat, cabin, airplane, or hobby.

If you have a monthly estimate, multiply it by twelve for the annual figure. If you have an annual figure, divide it by twelve for the monthly figure. You may need to refer to your checkbook to obtain previous expenditures to make accurate estimates for future amounts.

BALANCE THE BUDGET

If you're like most people, what you planned to spend will be more than your income. Many people overspend like this without realizing it—until they're severely in debt. For your budget to be effective, you must either increase your income, decrease your expenses, or both. No category should be above scrutiny in cutting expenses, according to the Fooshees.

For example, the Fooshees have found they can cut driving expenses by setting up a mileage budget. "We have car-less days," Marjean explained. "On those days we walk to the grocery store or the shopping center or ride our bikes." From May to October, George rides his bike to work. It not only helps relieve tension from job pressures, but saves $800 a year in gas and car maintenance.

"I asked the businessmen at a civic club once how many had bicycles at home," George recalled. "Fifty percent raised their hands, but not one rode his bike to work."

Marjean stays within a car allowance by planning her week. She does all her shopping and errands in one trip. If she and George are going out in the evening, she catches a bus to his office, so they will be able to take just one car to their destination.

These are just some of the ways the Fooshees have found to cut the seemingly uncuttable expenditures.

KEEP RECORDS

Purchase a budget book and enter the amount you have allotted yourself for each category. When you buy something, deduct the expense from that category. According to George, it's like setting up a checking account for each category, except it's all in one book. You can always see how well you are doing against your plan.

Are you in debt? Budget in your debt payments just like other expenses.

SET LIFETIME GOALS

If you are not yet in debt, determine that your lifetime goal will be to live debt-free. If you begin with this goal you need not ever go through the prolonged agony of working your way back to financial freedom.

Twenty-five years ago, when George and Marjean got married they set a life-time goal of remaining out of debt. In twenty-five years, they have never borrowed for anything except for the two houses they bought. Early in their marriage, sticking to this lifetime commitment meant that several rooms in their house didn't have a stick of furniture. But they were content because they were spending only what they had.

LEARN TO BE CONTENT

Advertisements, friends, and even your family members will try to convince you that you can't possibly be happy with what you have. Why wait if you can have it now?

George Fooshee urges people to fill out this financial summary before tackling a budget. Try it . . . you might be surprised at how much you're really worth (and how much you owe)!

WHERE WE ARE NOW   DATE _____

A. What we own
   1. Money in the bank   _____
   2. Cash value of life insurance (call agent on each policy)   _____
   3. Savings (savings & loan, credit union, etc.)   _____
   4. Stocks and Bonds (present market value)   _____
   5. Real estate
      a. Home (price home would readily sell for on today's market)   _____
      b. Other real estate   _____
   6. Other investments   _____
   7. Personal possessions (for each room you have that is nicely furnished multiply by $500.00)   _____
   8. Automobiles (call car dealer and ask for average retail price of your car/cars)   _____
   9. Other property (boats, trailers, cabins, etc.)   _____
  10. Special property (cameras, guns, hobbies, motorcycles, silver, camping equipment, stereo equipment)   _____
  11. Interest in retirement or pension plan   _____

        What We Own Totals   (1-4)   Cash & Other Savings
                              (5)   Real Estate
                              (6-11)   Other Property

GRAND TOTAL OF WHAT WE OWN   _____

B. What we owe	Amount Due	Monthly Payment	
1. To the mortgager of our home	_____	_____	_____
2. To others			
a. Bank	_____	_____	_____
b. Loan company	_____	_____	_____
c. Credit union	_____	_____	_____
d. Insurance companies	_____	_____	_____
3. Credit card companies	_____	_____	_____
4. Other businesses	_____	_____	_____
5. Other—family loans, etc.	_____	_____	_____
6. Medical, dental, hospital	_____	_____	_____

GRAND TOTAL OF WHAT WE OWE   _____

A. What We **Own** Grand Total   _____
B. Less What We **Owe** Grand Total   _____
C. What We Have Accumulated (Net Worth)   _____
D. Number of Years of Accumulation   _____
E. Average Annual Accumulation of Resources (C divided by D)   _____

But God instructs us to be "anxious for nothing" and let our requests be known to God. Marjean has discovered that she can remain much more content if she doesn't spend too much time shopping. "Many times a woman gets down—I do—and then feels that she owes it to herself to buy something. But then later she feels guilty for spending thoughtlessly and she gets down all the more."

When you feel depressed, Marjean suggests you do something for somebody. Or listen to a tape about God's character or just praise Him. It's a much less expensive way to get out of the dumps.

Dayton contrasts two philosophies: "Society says, 'You will find happiness and peace as you accumulate enough wealth to support your desired standard of living.' Scripture says, 'As you learn and follow the scriptural principles of how to handle your money and possessions, you can be content in every circumstance.'"

There is a special joy that comes from following God's principles in money management. "God wants us to be free," George says, "free of guilt and free of debt. It reduces all sorts of tensions in marriages. If you have no debts, you have no worries."

The Bible offers hope for our lives, including our finances. If we follow the principles found there, we won't have to ask, "Where has our money gone?" We'll know. "For everything that was written in the past was written to teach us, so that through endurance and encouragement of the Scriptures we might have hope" (Romans 15:4 NIV).

—By Kelsey Menehan, *Today's Christian Woman*, Summer 1980, including material from George and Marjean Fooshee. *You Can Beat the Money Squeeze*, Old Tappan, N.J.: Revell, 1980.

The Management of Necessary Expense

There is not a great deal you can do about the bills to which you have already committed yourself. The car payment, the mortgage, and your health insurance are fairly fixed expenses. These things are the unavoidable bites out of your income. Other equally unavoidable expenditures are such things as utility bills, medical expenses, and school lunch money. These things can be manipulated to a certain extent, but even if they are trimmed they still exist. Eradicate the installment payments you are making as soon as you can. No stable financial base can be built on the misuse of credit.

Having the obvious expenses out of the way, you are left with such things as grocery money, gasoline money, school money, and money for the paper boy, the barber, and the Avon lady. Typically, when all these things are subtracted from the remaining funds not much remains for savings, entertainment, gift giving, unexpected repair bills, eating out occasionally, annual payments of car insurance, license plates, and taxes. How can we possibly budget in so many directions?

The answer lies in setting more priorities. The temptation is to put every available cent into paying the current bills in an effort to rid ourselves of them. In order to spread the money in all the directions it must go, bill paying day may leave the checking account with no money left for other vital expenses. As a consequence it becomes necessary to skimp on the groceries and maybe even resort to charging the gasoline necessary for the days left before the next paycheck comes in. While it is commendable to apply as much cash as possible to the paying off of troublesome installment payments, it is not commendable to do so at the expense of having to resort to making even more charges.

Most women who are having troubles with the finances take the obvious step to juggling the grocery money. Of all the items to be paid this is the one most women think of as being the most flexible. But is it really?

Few Americans have had the experience of going without food entirely, but in many homes the food on the table is of poor quality and variety. Since energy and good health are two of the most valuable assets anyone can possess, does it really save money to stint on the grocery allowance?

Certainly it is possible to eat well on a small food budget, but too many people don't know enough about nutrition to make this happen. Their money is spent, not for low cost protein food such as beans, cheese, or eggs, but for an increase in starches and carbohydrates. Inevitably, the price of ignoring the body's demands for proper fuel will have to be met. It is senseless to save money on groceries if the only way one knows how to do so is by creating less than nutritious meals, which, in the long run, will only cause expenditures for medical and dental treatments.

The first step then in bringing the grocery expenses into line is to learn everything you can about nutrition in order to save money. Anyone can serve a balanced meal when she has the funds for an ample roast, fresh vegetables, specialty breads, and out of season fresh fruit. The challenge comes when she doesn't have the funds for that kind of fare, yet must still meet her family's nutritional needs.

Since the family health is such a vital issue, the grocery allowance should receive primary attention. After tithes have been paid and the mortgage and utility bills taken out, the grocery money should come next. This is not to suggest that an outrageous amount be spent on groceries, but rather that you set aside a reasonable amount of grocery money and then use it for that purpose even if doing so means paying only a minimum amount on some installment loan bill.

Two other expenditures should also be taken care of before applying money to other expenses—gasoline money and your "running" money. (My husband calls this the "running" money because he says it is what we use to run our family on from one payday until the next.) You know gasoline expenses will have to come out of each paycheck, but, unless you set aside a specific amount for this purpose immediately, it may be spent in other ways and you will be left with no alternative other than resorting to the use of credit cards. And you can't get yourself out of debt by creating new charges while you are struggling to pay off old ones.

"Running" money is another essential which can only result in problems if you don't set aside a specific amount before all your available funds are used elsewhere. Nobody can get by without a certain amount of small expenses which nibble away at the budget. You will be able to curtail considerably in this area, but don't make the mistake of assuming you can get by without any "running" money at all. If you try this, you will wind up having to borrow necessary funds from another allotment, which in turn will make it necessary to readjust still another budget category. Once this chain starts your entire budget will be in ruins. Rather than face this, start off by allotting yourself a realistic amount of money to cover the small expenses which inevitably crop up. No two families will have quite the same circumstances in this area so you will have to judge for yourself how much you will need after taking into consideration such things as buying newspapers, getting a haircut, putting a dollar into the Salvation Army kettle at Christmas, buying your mother a birthday card, giving your children their allowances and lunch money, paying your club dues, chipping in on a friend's going away present, or paying parking fees. Certainly the category of "running" money presents a real opportunity for trimming the budget because many of the things we spend money on in this way may be unnecessary. Only you can decide which things are to be eliminated.

Another priority, if at all possible, is personal spending money. If you are up against a wall financially, you will want to exercise moderation here, but, if possible, allot yourself something that you can spend without having to account for it to anyone. The amount you set aside here can be whatever you can reasonably afford, but don't get carried away. The purpose of this spending money is to make you feel good about having some "free" money and the amount is not important.

—From Edith Flowers Kilgo, *Money Management.* Grand Rapids: Baker Book, 1980.

FOR FURTHER READING:

Burkett, Larry. *What Husbands Wish Their Wives Knew About Money.* Wheaton, Ill.: Victor Books, 1977.

Dayton, Howard L. Jr. *Your Money: Frustration or Freedom?* Wheaton, Ill.: Tyndale, 1979.

Fooshee, George, Jr. *You Can Be Financially Free.* Old Tappan, N.J.: Revell, 1976.

Fooshee, George and Marjean. *You Can Beat the Money Squeeze.* Old Tappan, N.J.: Revell, 1980.

BURNOUT

THEY CALL IT the "burnout syndrome." It refers to extreme reactions to occupational stress on the job, but it can happen at home too.

It comes on gradually. It develops from excessive demands on our time and energy.

Someone has even suggested that there is a "Sunday night stress." It has symptoms such as headaches, stomach knots, restlessness, and insomnia. What causes it? You guessed it: having to go back to work on Monday!

Some persons burn out quicker than others. The overachiever and the perfectionist go the quickest. And some occupations are more prone to it: nursing, social work, and teaching.

And it's good that attention is being paid to this stress on the job. Good things can come of it.

But how about *stress at home?* How about the burnout housewife? Who's studying her? Who's recommending ways to help her on her "job"?

Do you know her? She's the *ideal* wife and mother. She has a spotless house. She goes more than eight hours per day. She is the one who can't say no. She's everyone's leaning post. Everyone cries on her shoulder. She's busy, busy, busy. Most certainly a perfectionist. Has to do everything right. Feels guilty if she relaxes. Never spends money on herself. Never goes anywhere without the kids. Super mom. Super responsible. Super woman.

Until, she burns out and becomes physically ill. Diagnosis: worn out. Or, hopefully, she suddenly asks herself: "What am I doing all this for?" before the body and mind give way.

Best approach: prevention. Here are some questions which warn that it's close.

1. Do you tire easily?
2. Do people tell you, "You don't look so good lately"?
3. Are you working harder and accomplishing less?
4. Are you increasingly cynical and disenchanted?
5. Are you often invaded by sadness you can't explain?
6. Are you increasingly irritable? Short-tempered? Disappointed in the people around you?
7. Are you suffering from aches, pains, headaches, a lingering cold?
8. Does sex seem to be more trouble than it's worth?
9. Do you have very little to say?

Some ways to help yourself:

1. Make a list of all you *have* to do; then cut it in half; keep one half and throw the other half away!
2. Give equal time to yourself, as to the kids and husband.
3. Make up a catchy saying to humor your slave driver, such as "What difference will it make fifty years from now if I don't. . . ."
4. Make a motto and put on the refrigerator: "Work less, enjoy more!"
5. Find a fun part-time job, and spend the money on yourself.
6. Join an exercise class, but don't *work* at it.
7. Take a college class that interests you.
8. Lie around.
9. Spend some time with friends, without the kids.
10. Be kinder to yourself.
11. Plan, schedule, and guard some personal time for yourself.

12. Listen to your kind of music.
13. Begin doing some of those "If I only had time for . . ." things.
14. Laugh at least three times a day.

—HUGH BURNS, Th.M., psychotherapist, Clayton Professional Building, Riverdale, GA 30274.

FOR FURTHER READING:

Freudenberger, Herbert J., Ph.D. *Burn Out.* Garden City, N.Y.: Doubleday, 1980.
Markell, Jan. *Overcoming Stress.* Wheaton, Ill.: Victor Books, 1982.
Narramore, Clyde and Ruth. *How to Handle Pressure.* Wheaton, Ill.: Tyndale, 1975.

BUSYNESS

MOST PEOPLE are just too busy. This is a point for quick agreement, but the subtle danger involved in our *busyness* is that most of us never stop to realize that in most cases we can do something about it!

. . . We tend to look wildly and unrealistically in every other direction for the cause of our trouble. Most of us feel like helpless victims where our work and activity schedules are concerned. For five or six years, this was entirely true of me.

Then one day, when I had actually fallen asleep on someone's sofa in the middle of a conversation, I began to take stock.

What was actually important? How much of this activity was God actually instigating? How much of it was the consequence of my own bad judgment, and how much was simply to keep people liking me? How much of it was guided by the Holy Spirit within me? What was really gained that evening I fell asleep during what to me was no longer "sweet fellowship"?

. . . . .

Learning to be an orderly person is a slow process for most of us. And unless for some reason, you have no control over your life at all, you should begin to organize by *eliminating* everything possible to eliminate.

If your friends and fellow church members don't understand, it won't be the first time. But how do you know you couldn't start something valuable in your group by admitting to them that you feel guilty about your over-busyness? Nine times out of ten, they do, too. Ask their understanding and cooperation with you as you sincerely attempt to rescue your life from its present whirl. If you are criticized after honesty of this kind, skip it. Don't fall into the trap of false guilt.

I am convinced that most women are disorganized simply because they are trying to pack more into one 24-hour period than is possible. We never get through when we tackle too much to begin with. Then we feel guilty, and it is, if we are facing facts—false guilt.

It is almost impossible for an alcoholic to say "no." This is due mainly because he or she feels basically guilty at all times for being an alcoholic. When an alcoholic is sober, he or she is the easiest person to impose upon! I know a man who, before his conversion to Christ, was a real alcoholic. He is a fairly balanced Christian now—except for the fact that he still cannot say "no." The pattern of *doing* to try to make up for not *being* has been with him for so long, he is still trapped in it most of the time. He is no longer drinking, but he is mistreating his body and his mind and neglecting his family because he *never stops working!*

If we are honest, much of what we do, we do so that people will like us.

"We just don't think we'll ever forgive you if you refuse the presidency of the Missionary Guild again!"

Oh, yes they will. If God has convinced you by the very circumstances of your life and the jumpy state of your nerves, that someone else should take the load this year, you can trust the ladies to Him! If they don't forgive you, the guilt they are attempting to heap on you is *falsely* based, so forget it.

A woman's *ego* often pushes her into a whirlwind life of busyness, too. If you are capable, and if the ladies adore you and heap

87

compliments on your pretty head every time you teach the class or preside at the circle meeting, just be wary. It is easy to mistake the voice of flattery for the voice of God. Especially if you've been busy for so long, there hasn't been a really quiet time to hear God speak.

It could be that you're not too busy. Some women aren't busy enough. Either excess can cause multiple troubles. One thing sure, no woman is her balanced best, no woman can think clearly and make wise decisions when she's physically and nervously exhausted. And still woman after woman chastises herself, pleads with God in prayer, and wonders why her temper doesn't vanish like an April snowflake, when she only needs to slow down! Woman after woman blames her husband or her children when their communication breaks down, and all the time, she is perhaps just too exhausted to communicate.

Excessive *busyness* affects single women as well as housewives. The whole atmosphere of a small business office changed when the Christian woman, who was office manager, finally tallied up her score before God. This took some doing. She had fired three new typists and a file clerk the month before God got at her with the reminder that she could not expect to have patience and show love and understanding toward those who worked under her as long as she was running every night to either a library board meeting, a church function or a fellowship meeting! She legislated quiet nights at home for herself. Among them were reading nights, music nights, or just nights to relax and watch T.V. She began to go to sleep before midnight, and she got up half an hour earlier so there was time to enjoy the sun in her small apartment during breakfast. Soon a "new" woman was arriving at the office, and with her, a new atmosphere.

I now keep my "reading nights" as definitely as I keep speaking engagements. This is not unspontaneous, it is creative. I now feel somewhat true to myself. My relationship with God is much more meaningful than when I was exhausting myself in "full time service." When I "give" now, I have something to *give*.

True, most Christians are over-busy with church activities. I realize this presents a real problem for both minister and flock. However, recently I have spoken with several pastors who share my concern over the fact that Christians are just too busy to take advantage of the *rest* Jesus promised to His people. These men, in some instances, are planning and setting aside "family nights." *Not* family nights at the church—but family nights at home! One man urges his people every Sunday to keep one night free that week for rediscovering each other within the family circle.

These are wise, wise men. Their people are receiving wise counsel. The voice of God is always speaking to us, always trying to get our attention. But His voice *is* a "still, small voice," and we must at least slow down in order to listen.

—From Eugenia Price. *A Woman's Choice.* Grand Rapids: Zondervan, 1962.

FOR FURTHER READING:

Jacobsen, Marion Leach. *How to Keep Your Family Together and Still Have Fun.* Grand Rapids: Zondervan, 1972.

Renich, Fred. *The Christian Husband.* Wheaton, Ill.: Tyndale, 1976.

Tchividjian, Gigi. *A Woman's Quest for Serenity.* Old Tappan, N.J.: Revell, 1981.

C

CANCER

What Is Cancer?

Cancer is one of several disorders which can result when the process of cell division in a person's body gets out of control. Such disorders produce tissue growths called "tumors." A cancer is a certain kind of tumor.

Cancer attacks one in every five people.

NORMAL CELL DIVISION

The body is constantly producing new cells for the purposes of growth and repair—about 500,000 million daily. It does this by cell division: one parent cell divides to form two new cells. When this process is going correctly, the new cells show the same characteristics as the tissue in which they originate. They are capable of carrying out the functions that the body requires that tissue to perform. They do not migrate to parts of the body where they do not belong; and if they were placed in such a part artificially they might not survive.

TUMORS

In a tumor, the process of cell division has gone wrong. Cells multiply in an uncoordinated way, independent of the normal control mechanisms. They produce a new growth in the body, that does not fulfill a useful function. This is a tumor, or "neoplasm." A tumor is often felt as a hard lump, because its cells are more closely packed than normal.

Tumors may be "benign" or "malignant." A cancer is a malignant tumor. That is, it may go on growing until it threatens the continued existence of the body.

Benign Tumors. In a benign tumor, the cells reproduce in a way that is still fairly orderly; they are only slightly different from the cells of the surrounding tissue. Their growth is slow and may stop spontaneously; the tumor is surrounded by a capsule of fibrous tissue; and does not invade the normal tissue; and its cells do not spread through the body.

A wart is a benign tumor. Benign tumors are not fatal unless the space they take up exerts pressure on nearby organs which proves fatal. This usually only happens with some benign tumors in the skull.

Malignant Tumors. In a malignant tumor, the cells reproduce in a completely disorderly fashion. The cells differ considerably from those of the surrounding tissue. (Generally, they show less specialization.) The tumor's growth is rapid, compared with the surrounding tissue.

The tumor has no surrounding capsule, and can therefore invade and destroy adjacent tissue. The original tumor is able to spread to other parts of the body by metastasis, and produce secondary growths there. A malignant tumor is usually fatal if untreated, because of its destructive action on normal tissue.

BIOPSY

A biopsy is the most certain way of distinguishing between benign and malignant tumors. A piece of the tumor is surgically removed, and then studied under a microcope.

Causes of Cancer

CHROMOSOME DAMAGE

In cancerous cells, the characteristics of malignant growth are passed on from one generation to another. This means that the genetic code must have been damaged. This, in fact, is seen, if the chromosomes of cancerous cells are examined. Normal cells have 46 chromosomes arranged in 23 pairs. Almost all cancer cells are abnormal in the number and/or structure of these chromosomes.

NORMAL DEVIANCY

Cells with genetic defects appear in the body every day; so many millions of cells are being made, that some mistakes are inevitable. But most die almost immediately, because they are too faulty to survive, or because they are recognized as abnormal and eaten by white blood corpuscles. Others are only slightly defective, and not malignant. Only very rarely do malignant cells survive and reproduce successfully.

Appearance of cancer in a person may simply be due to this unlucky chance. Alternatively, it may be that the body has "immunity" to such malignant cells, and that this sometimes breaks down. This would explain why cancer can sometimes remain "dormant" in a person for many years.

SPECIAL FACTORS

A few factors have been recognized that make genetic damage in cells more likely. But they only explain a tiny proportion of cancers.

a) Certain chemicals can cause cancer to form, if they are repeatedly in contact with the body over a period of time. Such chemicals are called carcinogens; but apart from

tobacco smoke, they usually only affect workers whose job brings them into regular contact with them. (However, atmosphere pollution may also be slightly carcinogenic.)

b) Certain viruses can pass malignant tumors from one animal to another, and the same may occur in humans. But so far only one very rare form of cancer is thought to be caused this way. Apart from this, human cancer seems not to be virus induced—and therefore not infectious.

c) Ionizing radiation. Without correct protection, X rays can cause skin cancer, and radiation can cause leukemia. Also ultraviolet rays (as in sunlight) may cause skin cancer in some circumstances.

d) Continued physical irritation. There is disagreement over this, but some experts believe that continued physical disturbance of the skin or mucous membrane can cause cancer (not just accelerate it).

CORRELATIVE FACTORS

Some individuals are more likely to develop cancer than others.

a) Heredity. Actual cancerous growths are not inherited. But a predisposition for cancer can be passed on. It may be that some inherited characteristics make a person's cells more likely to become malignant.

b) Age. Most cancers occur in the 50 to 60 age group. However, children and adolescents are susceptible to leukemia, brain tumors, and sarcomas of the bone.

c) Sex. In almost all countries, cancer occurs more frequently in men than in women.

d) Geographical location. For example, for some unknown reason, gastric cancer is most frequent in coastal countries with cold climates.

e) Cultural habits. For example, cancer of the penis is much less common in societies where circumcision is usual.

Cancer-Related Checkup Guidelines

Guidelines for the early detection of cancer in people without symptoms follow.

Speak with your doctor about how these guidelines relate to you.

Age 20–40:
Cancer-Related Checkup Every 3 Years
Should include the procedures listed below plus health counseling (such as tips on quitting cigarettes) and examinations for cancers of the thyroid, testes, prostate, mouth, ovaries, skin and lymph nodes. Some people are at higher risk for certain cancers and may need to have tests more frequently.

Breast
- Exam by doctor every 3 years
- Self-exam every month
- One baseline breast X-ray between ages 35–40.

(Higher Risk for Breast Cancer: Personal or family history of breast cancer, never had children, first child after 30)

Uterus
- Pelvic exam every 3 years
- Cervix: Pap test—after 2 initial negative tests 1 year apart—at least every 3 years, includes women under 20 if sexually active.

(Higher Risk for Cervical Cancer: Early age at first intercourse, multiple sex partners)

Age 40 and Over:
Cancer-Related Checkup Every Year
Should include the procedures listed below plus health counseling (such as tips on quitting cigarettes) and examinations for cancers of the thyroid, testes, prostate, mouth, ovaries, skin and lymph nodes. Some people are at higher risk for certain cancers and may need to have tests more frequently.

Breast
- Exam by doctor every year
- Self-exam every month
- Breast X-ray every year after 50 (between ages 40–50, ask your doctor)

(Higher Risk for Breast Cancer: Personal or family history of breast cancer, never had children, first child after 30)

Uterus
- Pelvic exam every year
- Cervix: Pap test—after 2 initial negative tests 1 year apart—at least every 3 years (Higher Risk for Cervical Cancer: Early age at first intercourse, multiple sex partners)
- Endometrium: Endometrial tissue sample at menopause if at risk.

(Higher Risk for Endometrial Cancer: Infertility, obesity, failure of ovulation, abnormal uterine bleeding, estrogen therapy)

Colon and Rectum
- Digital rectal exam every year
- Guaiac slide test every year after 50
- Procto exam—after 2 initial negative tests 1 year apart—every 3 to 5 years after 50.

(Higher Risk for Colorectal Cancer: Personal or family history of polyps in the colon or rectum, ulcerative colitis)

—Checkup Guidelines reprinted with permission of the American Cancer Society.

Symptoms

a) Any unusual bleeding or discharge from mouth, genitals, or anus (including, in women, bleeding from the breast and menstrual bleeding between periods).

b) Any lump or thickening or swelling on the body surface, or any swelling of one limb.

c) Any increase in size or change in color or appearance in a mole or wart.

d) A sore that will not heal normally.

e) Persistent constipation, diarrhea, or indigestion that is unusual for the person.

f) Hoarseness or dry cough that lasts more than three weeks.

g) Difficulty in swallowing or urinating.

h) Sudden unexplained loss in weight.

If you develop any of these symptoms, you should visit your doctor. Nearly always, the cause will be something else, not cancer. But do not delay. If it is cancer, quick diagnosis is essential.

Treatment

Treatments for cancer have a good chance of success only if the tumor is still localized.

Early diagnosis is vital. Once a tumor has metastasized, successful treatment is almost impossible.

Surgery. Surgical removal of localized malignant tumors at an early stage is the only completely successful form of treatment known at present. In later stages, surgery may be attempted in conjunction with other techniques.

Radiotherapy. Cancer cells are killed by radiation more easily than normal cells. Radiotherapy seeks to destroy cancerous tissue by focusing a stream of radiation on it. This can be done only if the cancer is still localized, and can be destroyed without causing radiation damage to the rest of the body.

The rays used are either X rays or those of radioactive materials such as radium or cobalt.

Chemotherapy. This is treatment by the administration of chemicals. Again, the major difficulty is finding drugs that will destroy cancer cells without harming normal cells. Three main types of chemical are used: those that interfere with the cancer cells' reproductive processes; those that interfere with the cells' metabolic processes; those that increase the natural resistance of the body to the tumor cells.

These chemicals can affect the whole of the body, specific regions, or the tumors themselves, depending on how they are applied.

Hormone Therapy is used mainly for tumors of the endocrine glands and related organs. It is also useful in the treatment of metastases originating from these areas (for example in women, against disseminated breast cancer). Success depends on whether the cancerous cells still have the specialized relationship with the hormone that the original tissue had. In women hormone therapy may include removal of the ovaries.

—From The Diagram Group, *Woman's Body.* New York: Simon & Schuster, 1981.

Resentment

Cancer frightens us all. It's like a mysterious evil force that constantly threatens us. It comes in many disguises: dyes, cigarettes, food additives; and it seems each day a new something is added to the list.

That's not all. You can start another list. A different kind of list, one that deals with the world inside us. The world within—of attitudes, emotions, and feelings.

At the top of this new list write in big letters the word *stress*—a word much used these days, and now applied to cancer.

Stress is very significant in some persons who develop cancer. These persons are unable to handle a cluster of stressful situations. They become overwhelmed, feel helpless, give up, and the immune system of the body is suppressed. They become victims of cancer.

And underneath their helplessness and hopelessness festers resentment: a strong negative mood, the infectious remains of aborted anger never expressed but swallowed time and again until it poisons the spring of hope and life.

According to Dr. Carl Simonton, resentments re-create, relive, and replay the painful memories of stressful situations, causing again a restressing of the body and its protective systems. And this restressing diminishes the ability of the immune system to function. Cancerous cells are ignored and are allowed to reproduce.

In his book *Getting Well Again,* Dr. Simonton says that resentful persons can and need to forgive old hurts and make peace with the past. Not easy to do, to give up old grudges, but it can be done, and here's how Dr. Simonton says to do it. Sit in a quiet place, relax, picture in your mind the person or persons you are resentful of, then picture good things happening to that person or persons. Then think about your own part in the stressful situations, and how it looked from the other person's point of view.

This little exercise can take only five minutes to do. It can be done as often as resentment comes into your mind. It's worth doing whether or not you fear cancer!

—HUGH BURNS, Th.M., psychotherapist, Clayton Professional Building, Riverdale, Ga. 30274.

FOR FURTHER READING:

Derbyshire, Caroline. *The New Woman's Guide to Health and Medicine.* New York: Appleton-Century-Crofts, 1980.

Fishbein, Anna Mantel, ed. *Modern Woman's Medical Encyclopedia.* New York: Doubleday, 1966.

Padus, Emrika. *The Woman's Encyclopedia of Health and Natural Healing.* Emmaus, Pa.: Rodale, 1981.

CARS

THE AUTOMOBILE is one item that keeps many families in a financial pinch. How easy it is to become discontented with your present car and succumb to the fever to trade for a newer model. New-car fever can't be cured with an aspirin, but it may be cooled by looking at some cold, hard facts about car costs.

Automobiles are seldom worn out when they are traded for later models. The proof of this is the fact that someone will buy your trade-in (probably for several hundred dollars more than you received for it), expecting to drive it many thousands of miles. Consider the reasons usually given for trading in a car: age, mileage, and needed repairs.

Age is no reason to trade in a car. My mother's car is now over thirteen years old, but it still has less than 40,000 miles on it. Having spent most all of its nondriving time in a garage, the condition of its body is better than that of most cars half its age. While some cars are old after one year a car can be relatively new after several years if it has had excellent care.

A recent experience dramatically illustrated that the age of a car is no reason for trading it. I serve communion monthly to a couple who are eighty-five and eighty-six years old. When I arrived one Sunday the woman was out in the garage. There I saw the car that they had bought in 1940—a 1940 Master Deluxe Chevrolet. It has been driven a total of 57,000 miles, and the engine has never had any major repairs. The car is still providing useful transportation for these folks.

That the car is still powerful was proven when the lady went to back the car out of the garage. Unintentionally she left the car in low gear instead of reverse. After the car was started, she released the clutch, and the car shot straight forward, removing the back of the garage in one big piece. Not one dent or scratch was on the front of the car, even though the entire back of the garage had been moved about ten feet forward into the backyard.

When the couple drives the car, they find people oohing and aahing over it. They have even had people follow them home and ask about buying the car. Would you advise these folks to trade for a newer model just because the car is thirty-six years old?

Age is not necessarily a reason to trade a car.

Mileage is usually not sufficient justification to trade in cars. The chairman of our deacons is a mechanic. He tells me that with proper maintenance and repairs most cars can be expected to perform satisfactorily up to 150,000 miles or more. A survey that I made at one automobile dealership revealed that, during a recent three-month period, the average number of miles on the cars that were traded in was 60,285 miles. Of a substantial number of cars only four had mileage in excess of 100,000; the highest mileage on any trade-in was 112,112 miles. That's hardly driving your car to a successful conclusion. These facts support the proposition that most people trade in when their cars still have over half of their useful life remaining.

Repairs. Buying a new car because your present car needs repairs seems almost as absurd as committing suicide because you need surgery.

A youth director was sent to me by her father for counsel about her car. Her present vehicle had under 100,000 miles on it, was less than ten years old, but was suddenly in need of about $200 worth of repairs. Her father thought she should not waste any more money repairing the old clunker but should buy a new one. As we studied the facts of the two alternatives, we clearly saw that the economics favored fixing up the car she had.

You can seldom justify on a financial basis the purchase of a new car to replace one that needs repairs.... Check with your car dealer, bank or credit union, and insurance agent to assemble your facts. The facts usually prove that in almost every case it costs more to own and operate a newer car than an older one.

The principle in Scripture is that of gathering facts before making major purchases. God calls fact-finders *wise men:* "The wise man looks ahead. The fool attempts to fool himself and won't face facts" (Proverbs 14:8).

Facing facts is one very effective way to purge the urge to splurge. A little splurge here and there is most often the disaster that keeps you from making ends meet in your finances.

—From George Fooshee, Jr., *You Can Be Financially Free.* Old Tappan, N.J.: Revell, 1976.

Automobile Loans

Most families borrow to buy a car, the second largest purchase they will make (a house is the largest). Car purchases, however, will usually consume more family dollars than a house. An average of ten to twelve cars per family will be bought and then sold at a loss, while only two or three homes will be traded, usually at increased worth.

In general, auto loans have a unique feature. Interest is calculated on the entire amount of money borrowed for the entire period of the loan. Also, for the first third of the loan period, most of the payment goes to

interest. If, after one year of a three-year loan, the buyer wishes to trade the car or pay off the loan, he or she would quickly discover that almost nothing but interest had been paid.

—From Larry Burkett, *What Husbands Wish Their Wives Knew About Money.* Wheaton, Ill.: Victor Books, 1977.

Car Repairs

A young man, with a penchant for practical joking, was talking to a woman friend after church about the problems she was having with her car. As they parted, he said, "Next time you're at a gas station, have them check the water in the radiator."

Trusting his advice instinctively, the woman drove into a service station and asked the attendant to make the check. He looked at her incredulously, then at her aging Volkswagen and back again. "Lady," he said with disdain, "you don't have no radiator."

For many women, like this one, the area under the hood of the car has been a mysterious, metallic, greasy jungle, best left to the exploration of the male of the species. But as traditional male/female roles shift, women are discovering for the first time just what makes their cars run—and stop running. Being alert to the symptoms of common automobile malfunctions can help you keep your car on the road and out of the repair shop.

The working parts of most cars are outlined below, plus the more common signals that a car needs service. For more exact information, consult your owner's manual.

CARBURETOR

The carburetor, which delivers a mixture of fuel and air to the engine cylinders, requires periodic checking. Generally the idle speed and automatic choke are checked and adjusted, if necessary, at each tune-up. This is particularly important in the spring and fall because of seasonal changes in gasoline formulas. *Service signals:* Hard starting, hesitation when you press the accelerator, stalling at stop lights, idling too fast or too slow, a sluggish feel at road speeds, a tendency to "run on" after you turn off the ignition, or poor gasoline mileage.

CARBURETOR AIR CLEANER

If your carburetor has a dry air cleaner, the filter element should be replaced periodically. Between replacements, check occasionally to see that the filter has no holes and tap it gently to dislodge dirt. Never wash it or try to clean it with air under pressure.

If the carburetor has a wet (oil bath) filter, it should be cleaned and the oil changed as the automobile manufacturer recommends. *Service signals:* Hard starting, poor mileage, or loss of power.

ENGINE VALVES

The intake valves admit the fuel/air mixture from the carburetor into the engine cylinders. The exhaust valves permit the escape of waste gases after the gasoline burns. Mechanical lifters to open and close the valves should be adjusted at every tune-up or as the manufacturer recommends. Hydraulic valve lifters do not normally require adjustment. *Service signals:* Loss of power, a ragged or uneven feel to engine performance, a light clattering noise, or hard starting—especially when the engine is cold.

ELECTRICAL CHARGING SYSTEM

When you start your car, the source of electric current is the battery. After the car is running, the source is the alternator or generator, and a voltage regulator protects the battery from overcharge. Check the battery water level often and add water, preferably distilled, as needed. Battery cable connections should be kept clean and tight. *Service signals:* Sluggish starting, dim lights when the engine isn't running, or the battery frequently needs water.

IGNITION SYSTEM

Electricity from the battery, alternator, or generator flows on to the coil where it is stepped up to higher voltage. From the coil, the current travels to the distributor, which channels it to the spark plugs in the engine cylinders. At each plug, the current ignites the fuel/air mixture. Periodically, the ignition system should be checked and the spark plugs and distributor points changed as needed. *Service signals:* Hard starting, uneven acceleration, loss of power at high speed, rough idle, or a partial or complete "miss" in one or more cylinders causing rough performance and a severe loss of power.

TIMING SYSTEM

For efficient engine operation, the spark plug must fire in each cylinder at precisely the right moment. This firing is regulated by the distributor, which can be adjusted to advance or retard the timing of the spark. *Service signals:* Hard starting, "pinging," or a rough feel during driving if the timing is too "fast"; hard starting, sluggish performance, excessive gasoline consumption, or overheating if the timing is too "slow."

GASOLINE

Gasoline with too low an octane rating for your engine will burn unevenly, or explode, inside the cylinders, instead of smoothly producing power. The usual symptom is a light clattering or pinging during acceleration or when the engine is pulling hard. Continued use of the wrong gasoline could result in serious damage.

Gasoline with an unnecessarily high rating, however, costs you extra money and wastes energy. If your car accelerates without ping on the gas you use now, try a tankful of the next lower octane. After the car has warmed up, accelerate hard from a full stop. If the engine pings, go back to the higher octane. If it doesn't, repeat the test with gas with a still lower rating.

ENGINE OIL, OIL FILTER, AND LUBRICATION

Have the oil level checked at least every other time you fill up with gasoline. If the level is at or below the "add" mark on the dipstick, put in oil of the type specified for your particular model of car. Do not use additives unless they are called for by the automobile manufacturer. Have the oil changed at recommended intervals.

Generally, the filter is changed every other time the oil is changed; but if you live in a dusty climate or do a lot of stop-and-start driving, your mechanic may suggest a filter change with every oil change.

For lubrication, follow the manufacturer's recommendations. *Service signals:* If the oil warning light shows red while the engine is running at or above idle speed, turn the engine off immediately. Oil is not reaching all the engine parts, and continued operation will result in major engine damage.

TRANSMISSION FLUID

Check the fluid level at intervals in either a manual or an automatic transmission, and replace the fluid at recommended mileages with the type specified for your car model. Learn the correct checking procedures. For example, if you have an automatic transmission, the engine must be running and, usually, the shift should be in the "park" position. *Service signals:* Whine during driving, uneven growling noises, or jerky acceleration.

CLUTCH

In a car with a manual transmission, depressing the pedal disengages the clutch,

slows the transmission gear rotation, and permits you to shift gears. Clutch linkage should be checked and adjusted at regular intervals. *Service signals:* A tendency for the gears to clash when you shift, clutch slippage under startup or hard acceleration, or clutch "chatter" at startup.

BRAKES

All late-model, U.S.-built automobiles using conventional drum and shoe brakes have assemblies that adjust automatically for wear unless mechanical troubles develop. Disc brakes, also, need no adjustment. All brakes, however, should be inspected as recommended by the manufacturer, and the brake linings or disc pads should be replaced as needed. Occasionally, brake fluid must be replenished. *Service signals:* A spongy feel when you press the brake pedal, longer pedal movement, scraping noises, or the car pulls to one side when slowing or stopping. Uneven or grabby brakes are especially dangerous on slippery surfaces.

TIRE PRESSURE

Correct tire pressure is necessary for safe driving, good tire mileage, and responsive steering. Check at least monthly that your tires (and the spare) are at the recommended pressure. Buy a good tire gauge and learn to use it; air towers at service stations are frequently incorrect. Occasionally inspect the tire treads. Wear on the edges indicates too little pressure; too much causes excessive wear in the center. When the car is on a lift for an oil change, have the tires inspected for cuts, bruises, or tread separations. The precaution could prevent a blowout. *Service signals:* Pulling to right or left, uneven braking, or excessive squealing on corners.

TIRE BALANCE

Tires should be kept in balance for comfortable and safe driving and for long tread life. For the best results, have the tires spin balanced on the car whenever vibration becomes objectionable. Follow the recommended tire rotation for your automobile make and model and the type of tire. *Service signals:* Vibration, usually felt through the steering wheel for the front tires or through the seat for the rear tires.

FRONT SUSPENSION

Front wheel suspensions should be properly aligned at all times for safe handling and economical tire wear, but pot holes and other rough road conditions may gradually throw wheels out of alignment. *Service signals:* Abnormal or uneven tire wear, or the car pulls hard to the right or left during driving even when tire pressure and balance are correct.

LIGHTS

Headlamps must be set to provide maximum road illumination and minimum glare for oncoming motorists. Check periodically to be sure all lights are in working order.

AIR ENGINE-COOLING SYSTEM

Air-cooled cars have a powerful fan, driven by a belt from the engine, that forces a large volume of air over the hot engine. The fan belt should be regularly checked for correct tension and freedom from wear. If the fan belt should break while you are driving, *stop the engine immediately or it will overheat.*

AIR CONDITIONER

Just before the operating season, have the drive belt checked for correct tension and examine the liquid in the sight glass for bubbles that could mean the system needs more refrigerant. During the winter, most condi-

tioners will benefit from a five minute workout every two or three weeks as long as the temperature is above forty degrees Fahrenheit. Check with your mechanic to see if this is good advice for your particular car. *Service signals:* A drop in cooling power, unusual noises from the fan, or rapid cycling of the compressor. You can hear the compressor click off and on or detect the added load on the engine.

LIQUID ENGINE-COOLING SYSTEM

All the car engines presently manufactured in the United States are cooled by a liquid-circulating system assisted by a fan. The system includes a liquid coolant (water plus antifreeze), hoses, a water pump, a thermostat, and a radiator.

Ask the service attendant to check the coolant level in the system every other time you fill up with gasoline. Whenever you have the car in for routine maintenance, have the mechanic check the hoses for soundness and the belt that drives the fan for correct tension. Have the belt replaced if it is frayed. Each spring and fall have the concentration of the antifreeze-water mixture tested; if too little of the antifreeze is present, you are inviting either a freezeup or a boilover. *Service signals:* The temperature gauge often reads high, or you must frequently add liquid to the system.

HOW TO GET THE BEST SERVICE

When your car is in the shop, you want an honest judgment of the service needed plus skilled, careful workmanship. This combination can extend the life of your car, save you money and time, and enable you to drive safely and confidently. The following tips should help you obtain such services:

Observe the Warranty. During the warranty period, have the car serviced exactly as recommended. Routine maintenance may be performed at an independent garage or service station without violating the warranty agreement; but be sure to keep a receipt showing the mileage reading, the date, and the nature of the service.

For repairs under warranty, you must take the car to an authorized dealer.

Use Business Safeguards. When repair or service is necessary after the warranty period, be sure to take the following steps:

Inquire if the shop offers a warranty on service and replacement parts and how long it is effective.

Tell the service manager, the service advisor, or the mechanic all the car's symptoms and problems, and be sure he understands what you are saying. Master mechanics complain that they often have to "read the customer's mind."

Then, find out exactly what work is to be done and, if possible, obtain a written estimate. At least write out a list for yourself and keep it. *Insist that the shop obtain your approval before doing any additional work.*

If you suspect the shop's estimate includes unnecessary repairs, either obtain another estimate from a different shop or take the car to a diagnostic center—one that charges a fee for diagnosis but does no repairs.

When you pick up the car after repairs, check each item on the list or estimate. Do not accept the car unless everything is complete and satisfactory.

Road test the car before you drive home, and return it to the garage immediately if it is not performing well.

Cultivate Car Friends. Try to use the same mechanic every time you have your car serviced. This may not be possible if you deal with a large garage; but you can establish a relationship with the service manager or one particular service advisor so that he remembers your car and its special needs.

When work is good, stop by and tell the dealer or the service manager, and ask him to pass on your compliment to the mechanic. It will be time well invested.

If you would prefer an independent ga-

rage or service center, you can write to the Automatic Service Councils, Inc., 4001 Warren Boulevard, Hillside, Ill. 60162, for information on their National Warranty Program. Participating shops give a customer a written guarantee covering labor and parts. A faulty repair may be corrected at any other participating shop if the customer is not able to return to the original one.

Or you can purchase a copy of *Where to Find a Certified Mechanic,* a nationwide list of shops whose employees have passed special tests on automotive repairs. Write to Employers Director, National Institute for Automotive Service Excellence, Suite 515, 1825 K Street, N.W., Washington, D.C. 20006.

Know How to Complain. At a dealership, talk to the owner about poor service or inadequate repairs. If he refuses to give you satisfaction, consult your owner's manual or the warranty for the address of the nearest district office of the company, and write or telephone the customer service representative. The next step, if you must take it, is to talk with or write to the vice president for sales at the company headquarters. Keep copies of all repair orders, receipts, and correspondence.

If these steps fail, you may wish to contact one of the pilot project AUTOCAP's—or Automotive Consumer Action Panels—in which local or state automotive trade associations and consumer representatives seek to resolve customer difficulties. To learn if an AUTOCAP has been established in your locality and if it can handle your particular problem, write to the National Automobile Dealers Association, 1640 Westpark Drive, McLean, VA 22101. AUTOCAP's were initiated at the request of the U.S. Office of Consumer Affairs.

At a private garage or service center, also talk with the owner about a complaint. If the problem is not resolved, check to see if a municipal, county, or state consumer agency can help you. You can also appeal to the local office of the Better Business Bureau or write to the U.S. Office of Consumer Affairs, Washington, D.C. 20201.

As a last resort, pay the bill and then see a lawyer.

—From "What Every Woman Should Know About Car Repairs," *Today's Christian Woman*, Spring, 1981 (including information from *Car Care and Service*, U.S. General Services Administration).

FOR FURTHER READING:

Dayton, Howard L., Jr. *Your Money: Frustration or Freedom?* Wheaton, Ill.: Tyndale, 1979.

Fooshee, George and Marjean. *You Can Beat the Money Squeeze.* Old Tappan, N.J.: Revell, 1980.

CHILDBIRTH

1. *The First Stage of Labor.* Civilization has imposed one handicap upon us that primitive women did not have to contend with. Women have to puzzle over whether labor has or has not begun, in order to know whether to go or not to go to the hospital. In the majority of women the beginning of true labor is signaled by contractions that occur at regular intervals. But for some this is not an infallible sign of true labor. Contractions are occurring every three and a half minutes. She is told to report to the hospital. She packs her bag and goes. Several hours later she is dismissed, the regular contractions having ceased. She is told that she was in "false" labor.

Then again, a woman thinks she is in labor. She calls the doctor. "Are the contractions regular?" he asks, and she replies that they are not. She is told to call again as soon as they become regular. An hour later the parents and doctor rush to the hospital, and the baby appears shortly. Her contractions never did become regular.

For those who have this difficulty, how is it possible to know whether labor is "true" or "false"? A safer criterion is especially necessary for the mother who has learned to relax, as some contractions may pass unnoticed, and she will not think they are "regular."

Because this may be a problem, certain sensations that are true indications of labor should be recognized. The surest way to tell if the contractions are real or "practice" ones, is by noticing whether or not there is this mild feeling of tightening *down in the area of the pubic bone and lower spine*. This is a sign that the uterine muscles are pushing *down*. A false contraction will often be much larger, expanding the abdomen up and out, rather than giving this sensation of tightening *low* in the abdomen. This sensation disappears when one relaxes, so *do not go to bed* to relax if you think that you are really in labor. Wait to relax completely until you are in the hospital.

Once in the hospital, consciously allowing all muscles of the abdomen and pelvic area to be limply relaxed, many contractions may pass unnoticed.

.   .   .   .   .

When in the hospital in labor, one must rest quietly, ignoring the contractions during the first stage of labor. If they begin to cause discomfort, it helps to change to the left lateral position, with a pillow under one's upper knee. It is *most* important for the right knee and thigh to be supported, so that the abdomen sags loosely toward the bed, while the upper leg and knee support one's weight. Sometimes a mild sedative is given if one has difficulty in relaxing.

.   .   .   .   .

It is impossible to remain in one position for long periods of time. For those who seem unable to get comfortable in the lateral position and prefer to lie in the reclining-chair position, their back and knees must be elevated and supported to prevent tension on the abdominal muscles. Sometimes the labor-room bed is too narrow for lying in the lateral position. In this case, a mother can lie on her side with a large pillow between her knees. This will hold them apart, keep the weight of the upper leg from resting on the lower one, and help her keep the pelvic floor relaxed.

As transition approaches, it may become necessary to concentrate on controlled breathing to stay relaxed. It is most important, however, for attendants to remember that the woman before them is an individual.

. . . . .

2. *The Transition Period.* There are certain emotional signs of the progress of labor that a woman shows. These make it possible for attendants to tell how her labor is advancing without frequent rectal examinations, which always interfere with relaxation. By observing these phenomena, both mother and attendants can tell when the transition period is near.

. . . . .

These emotional guideposts have been outlined as follows: The mother appears mildly euphoric and frequently likes to carry on conversation between contractions until the cervix is dilated to about four centimeters; at three to four centimeters she becomes more serious about her labor; as transition approaches, the mother may find difficulty in relaxing, experience some backache, and she may also feel chilled to the point where her legs will tremble. When this happens, the attendants will probably wrap her warmly in blankets and give her a hot water bottle and have her change to the reclining-chair position on the bed.

Transition contractions usually last a full minute or more, and they may come so close together that they seem almost continuous. This is the point in labor when an uninstructed woman may go all to pieces emotionally and remain out of control for the rest of the time. *No woman should ever be left alone after labor has begun.*

During transition (eight to ten centimeters until complete dilation) there is often a feeling of confusion between the need to *relax,* as for first-stage contractions, and the need to *push,* as for second-stage contractions. The mother should be reminded not to bear down until the doctor gives his permission, since pushing too soon can damage the cervix. It helps to be raised to a sitting position during transition, with the knees raised and supported by pillows or the stirrups, so the legs can remain limp.

The strength of transition contractions may alarm a woman having her first baby. If she has had a relaxed, comfortable first stage, the sensation of the strong contractions will be similar to that of tensing her biceps firmly in the upper arm. She should be reminded that transition is very short and that she will soon be more comfortable.

As the transition stage ends, the bearing-down reflex begins. This reflex may not begin immediately after the cervix is completely dilated; the uterine muscles need time to shorten, since the baby is now farther down. If pushing causes any discomfort, the mother should be told to wait and not push until it does not hurt. If her body is ready, bearing down will feel good.

3. *The Birth of the Baby.* The second stage of labor is the really exciting period. At last one can *do* something to help bring this baby into the world!

. . . . .

Frequently a young mother needs to be reminded not to "squeeze up" the muscles of her pelvic floor as she feels the baby's head coming down, but to keep them slack. Often she will hesitate to relax this birth outlet and bear down properly because of shyness and embarrassment over this part of her body. Turning her attention to her baby as soon as possible helps to relieve her selfconsciousness and relax the outlet by taking her mind off herself. If the muscles of the outlet remain tense, she will have pain.

A common mistake that is made is instructing the woman to bear down "as if moving the bowels." This increases her embarrassment and is confusing. This advice causes the woman to tighten the vagina in order to open the anus. This hinders, rather than helps, her efforts.

As the baby's head descends and the initial stretching of the vulva begins, the mother may appear alarmed. Although this "pins and needles" sensation is only mildly uncomfortable, it brings all the negative influences of our culture to mind. The common belief that the approaching moment of birth *will* be painful causes the mother to hesitate with doubt at this crucial point.

It is a wise attendant who can reassure her with confidence that the birth outlet will be insensitive in a moment, and that she will feel only the bulging of the baby's head. She will be grateful to him after the birth is over, if he does not rob her of the wonderful orgasm of birth by administering an anesthetic, or pudendal block, or hypnotic analgesia, against her wishes.

One cannot feel either the incision for an episiotomy, or minor laceration during the birth, once the baby's head has cut off circulation of the blood to the perineum. What one *does* feel is the thrilling expansion of the vagina to its maximum capacity.

—From Helen Wessel, *Natural Childbirth and the Family,* Rev. Ed. New York: Harper & Row, 1963, 1973.

FOR FURTHER READING:

Ketterman, Grace H., M.D., and Herbert L. Ketterman, M.D. *The Complete Book of Baby and Child Care for Christian Parents.* Old Tappan, N.J.: Revell, 1982.

The Diagram Group, *Woman's Body,* N.Y.: Simon & Schuster, 1981.

Todd, Linda. *Labor and Birth.* Minneapolis: International Childbirth Education Association, 1981.

Washbourn, Penelope. *Becoming Woman.* New York: Harper & Row, 1977.

CHILDREN—YES OR NO?

My husband, Steve, and I were in our mid-thirties, and had been married four years when we sensed it was time to decide—will we seek to have children or not?

We realized the high value Scripture placed on children. We knew it was a fairly normal biblical and social practice to have children. Yet we also believed the answer would be individual, based on God's plan for us, and not on whether it was convenient for us or allowed me to do all that I might in developing my career. Our first step was to list the following pros and cons in seeking God's wisdom:

Pros

1. We have a small but growing desire.
2. Many people are praying that we will have children.
3. What an opportunity to raise disciples!
4. Children present a creative challenge.
5. It would please our parents.
6. It would provide loved ones for us in our old age.
7. Children are a source of joy.
8. It will give us experiences that enable us to empathize in speaking, writing, and ministering to others.
9. Children provide a source of meaningful illustrations.
10. It is God's normal plan.
11. It would demonstrate that we believe that God could bring revival to this country.

Cons

1. Children would cut back on time to help reach others for Christ, particularly for Judy.
2. Considering the urgency of the hour and the need to reach the world for Christ, it could be a bad example to others.
3. It would limit the continuation of Judy's career.
4. Judy's health has not been excellent.
5. Children are a constant distraction.
6. Children are a source of sorrow.
7. Children would create more housework for Judy, which she doesn't like.

Though we had listed more pros than cons, the weight of the cons was heavy in our eyes. Therefore we evaluated each one. Here's what we decided:

1. Some ministry opportunities would continue, and children would provide chances for new contacts.
2. It's an act of faith to bring a child into this world, but we believed God would be sufficient to meet that child's needs.
3. My skills in writing and editing could continue to be used in an informal capacity.
4. My doctor assured me that my health was adequate both to bear and to raise children.
5. We could live with Steve working some evenings at the office rather than at home.
6. Yes, children are a source of sorrow just as they are a source of joy. But God is sufficient to sustain us and use both to draw us closer to him.
7. Though the idea of more housework did not appeal to me, I was willing to trust God to give me grace in that area.

With these thoughts in mind, we decided we could live with each of the cons. And the pros seemed of significant value that we believed God wanted us to have children.

We did apply a final test, though. We waited three months, during which we asked God to answer according to Colossians 3:15, "And let the peace of Christ rule in your hearts. . . ." During those three months each of us had a growing peace that this was definitely God's plan for us.

Today I have no regrets. I love and enjoy Debbie. I am in awe as I watch this little human being develop. I am learning so much about myself and about God and about people. I am still editing. I am writing. I am doing some speaking. But Debbie is my priority, and I'm stimulated and excited to be working in cooperation with God to mold a human life.

—JUDY DOWNS DOUGLASS, a former editor of *Worldwide Challenge.*

FOR FURTHER READING:

Ketterman, Grace H., M.D., and Herbert L. Ketterman, M.D. *The Complete Book of Baby and Child Care for Christian Parents.* Old Tappan, N.J.: Revell, 1982.

LaHaye, Beverly. *I Am a Woman by God's Design.* Old Tappan, N.J.: Revell, 1980.

Landorf, Joyce. *Changepoints.* Old Tappan, N.J.: Revell, 1981.

CHURCH

IN THE "hang loose" mood of our day, the importance of firm commitment to a local church is often overlooked. The result is that Christian commitment becomes highly individualized, and thus impoverished. Commitment to *the* Church is best affirmed in commitment to *a* church. Many young believers find themselves frustrated with the church as they find it, and rather than attempting to make a contribution within the structure as it exists, they opt out of the church family. The church, of course, may take one of many forms: the house group, the assembly, the huge congregation. But commitment must be made to fellowship regularly with other believers, if a person is to truly disciple himself to Jesus Christ. The writer of the book of Hebrews advises sternly that we are not to be ". . . forsaking the assembling of ourselves together, as the manner of some is . . ." (Hebrews 10:25).

There are, of course, no perfect churches. There is no one fellowship that has a corner on the only New Testament model. Indeed, it seems as though perhaps the best understanding of denominational choices was voiced by a friend who said, "You choose a church according to your spiritual temperature. Some people like to run hot, some like to run cool." Accepting this diversity within the Body is a mark of maturity. But simply drifting from one fellowship to another, in search of perfection or a fresh charge for spiritual batteries, can never create the experience of "Body life" that is meant to be a very vital part of the Christian experience.

Commitment to the Church carries with it many of the benefits of commitment to family. In the larger family of the Church, in friendships and caring that cross generational, racial, spatial, and even time boundaries, a sense of the continuity of life is gained. The little particle of life of each individual becomes a part of a great whole: not lost, but given a setting, a meaning, and an extension. Within the Church, ". . . ye are all the children of God by faith in Christ Jesus. . . . There is neither Jew nor Greek, there is neither bond nor free, there is neither male nor female: for ye are all one in Christ Jesus" (Galatians 3:26, 28).

It is by the *communication* of the Gospel—the good news that ". . . God so loved the world, that he gave his only begotten Son . . ." (John 3:16)—that we are invited into *communion*. It is no accident that the table of the Lord, by whatever name and through whatever form of service it is approached, is central to the worship of believers. Paul, in reviewing the Lord's Supper for the Corinthian believers, reminds, "For as often as ye eat this bread, and drink this cup, ye do shew the Lord's death till he come" (1 Corinthians 11:26). In the communion fellowship, we look back to Christ's death with gratitude and forward to His coming with anticipation, and we are strengthened to go on sharing with our brothers and sisters in the task of bearing witness "till He come." Whether as Eucharist at an ornate altar, or as the loaf broken at a simple table, this remembrance meal binds all who have named the name of Jesus Christ into one vast fellowship. It is a fellowship that stretches around the world. It stretches back through all the ages of Church history, to that moment in the Upper Room, when our Lord Himself broke bread and offered the cup "in remembrance of Me." It stretches out ahead of us, until the consummation of the age in the coming of Jesus Christ as King of kings and Lord of lords. And it wonderfully presages yet another supper, at which our Lord will preside; a supper at which all Christians of all centuries, all the great "Company of the Committed" will celebrate their unity with one another and be finally fully united with their Lord (*see* Revelation 19:7–9).

If the human family lends meaning and continuity to life, how much more so "the whole family in heaven and earth" (*see* Ephesians 3:15). In the Church Universal, one finds oneself as part of Christ's continuing presence here on this earth. In the local fellowship, one has opportunity to interpret this in practical relationships of caring and sharing.

Not only should the Church contribute to continuity and extension of the individual life; it also should help to provide purpose and meaning. For the Church does not exist just for the comfort of Christians. It is through the Church and by the Church that God continues to reveal His truth from generation to generation. And every member of the Church, every committed Christian, is part of that vital transmission of truth. We have a job to do, and we find it expressed within the context of the Church. The Church fellowship should be concerned about identifying and giving opportunity for the use of the gifts of the Holy Spirit among its members. And here again, a sense of personal mission, fused with the great, overall mandate of the Church to "Go . . . teach . . . baptize . . . preach . . ." (*see* Matthew 28:19 and Mark 16:15), lends meaning and order to life.

Commitment to the community of believers that is the Church is not a way of ducking out of commitment to the "global village" of mankind. It is a way of finding and harnessing my abilities and gifts to God's redemptive purposes for His fallen creation. It is a way of finding out what I can do to witness for Jesus Christ, as part of a whole fellowship similarly committed. It is a way of being strengthened to serve God by serving mankind.

It is through a deep and enduring commitment to a fellowship of believers—a community of the faithful—that we learn how to feel our kinship to others, and ultimately to all humans. Peter Jenkins, who

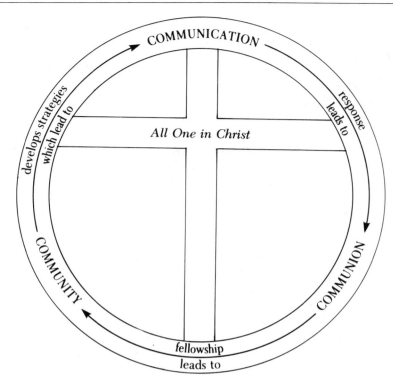

*The Unity of the Witness, Worship & Work of
the Church*

found a personal relationship with Jesus Christ during his walk across America, had expected that those who would try to help him along the way would be "young, hip, long-haired, college-type people." But this was not the case. "You know, I'm kind of thick headed. But it began to get to me that every person that reached out to me was a Christian. . . . The young, hip, intellectual college generation of our time . . . were very rarely the ones who tried to reach out and help me."

Through the caring of committed Christians, Jenkins found himself surrounded by the love and care of God and made part of the very community he had attempted to reject.

Learning through the Sunday-by-Sunday worship and week-by-week sharing of life with other believers, we finally come to an understanding of what it means to be "members one of another." And in awareness of both our unique personal identities and our corporate identification with all believers, we are enabled to become serving, caring people in our communities.

—From Maxine Hancock, *The Forever Principle.* Old Tappan, N.J.: Revell, 1980.

FOR FURTHER READING:

LaHaye, Tim and Bev. *Spirit-Controlled Family Living.* Old Tappan, N.J.: Revell, 1978.

CLOTHES

Basic Wardrobe

Here are the essentials for a coordinated wardrobe (with all colors and fabrics working together):

1 three-piece basic solid-color suit (jacket, pants, skirt) in a quality fabric

1   light-colored pants to coordinate
1   light-colored skirt to coordinate
3   colored (plain, floral, or stripe) blouses
2   sweaters (up-to-date cardigan and pullover)
1   basic (solid color) coat
1   shirtwaist basic dress (long or short) in quality, year-round fabric
1   long hostess skirt
1   vest
2   pairs of basic shoes with style and versatility
Lots of scarves
A few pieces of good jewelry

Discipline may have to be learned in buying clothes. Once you see how wonderful you can look, you may really catch the buying fever! But be careful not to overspend.

One day while reading, I noticed that one of the best stores in town was having a tremendous fur sale. Now, it has always been a dream of mine to have a real fur coat. I just *had* to attend that sale, so I asked Jim to come along "just in case" we found a fantastic bargain.

Trying on all those fantastic furs made me feel like the richest lady in town! Every one of them *was* a fantastic bargain, but the price tags were still terribly steep. Yet each touch of those furs was like a caress. I was feeling awfully covetous, so I bowed my head and said. "Lord, should I? You know how much I've loved things like red fingernail polish and furs all my life!"

Getting no real answer, I looked at Jim, who was waiting patiently and not saying a word about expenses and budgets. Typically kind and loving, Jim just said, "It's up to you." That wasn't fair! Wasn't God supposed to work through my husband? And then I almost laughed out loud as the truth hit me. The big stack of dollar bills that would have to be paid for a fur coat could really be used to better advantage for a lot of other things.

Hadn't I been trying to learn discipline and self-control? The fact that Jim granted permission to buy a fur coat gave me an excellent opportunity to learn self-control. Some day the Lord may provide a fur coat.

But for now, He has other things to accomplish in my life. Leaving that store without the coat gave me a new peace and a feeling that I was still the richest lady in town! No amount of money can buy that kind of satisfaction.

There is nothing wrong with buying pretty things, but you can have lots of pretty clothes that will make you look pleasingly attractive—while sticking to the budget. I trust that you will learn to spend time on yourself. Study your wardrobe coordination, then go shopping for pretty clothes, wear them and carry the fragrance of our Lord wherever you go.

Accessories

There are some general accessory rules which I try to follow. These may be somewhat different from those dictated by fashion magazines, but I feel they are especially suitable for the tasteful Christian woman.

Shoes—should be the same color as the hem of the garment, or darker. With a casual dress or sportswear, you may wear brighter, but not lighter-colored shoes. (You want the entire look to *blend*.) Only wear white shoes with an outfit that is predominantly white. If you wear winter white, you must select a shoe that is suitable for the winter months. You should not wear your white summer sandals in cold months. Actually a leg-colored shoe is more attractive and versatile with summer pastel clothing. Since fashion varies in different areas of the nation, check your local practices for the times when summer white may be used.

Nylon stockings—If you wear dark colors, your stockings should be the same color tone as the shoes or blend with them. Dark stockings are usually worn only in the fall and winter months with dark clothing. Avoid wearing navy or black hose with red shoes. It is always safe to wear leg colors—but *do* be fashionable.

Gloves—used to be on the necessities list, but now are off. For most women, a pair of leather gloves and a pair of warm wool gloves are enough, with perhaps the addition of a long glove for formal evening functions. Avoid pastel and bright colors. Use neutral and deep shades.

Handbags—do not have to match your shoes as long as they blend with your outfit. Invest in a good handbag. If need be, you can dress stylishly with only two good leather bags a year. One might be in tan or deep beige, the other black, navy or brown. Cloth bags are usually worn with sportswear. Straw and linen are generally reserved for spring and summer.

Jewelry—should be button or loop-type earrings in medium sizes for round-the-clock wear. Save anything dangly or sparkly for evening. Earrings and bracelets can effectively add a fresh look to a garment.

Hats—as a whole, are being worn less and less, with the exception of rain hats, beach and straw hats. But, if you love hats, wear them! Choose one according to your proportions. Suede, leather, feathers, fur and velvet are for September through March (in clothing selections as well). Felt may be worn all year round.

Boots—should follow fashion trends. Watch carefully!

Skirt length—should move with fashion. You do not have to go to the extremes shown in fashion magazines, at least until such lengths have become accepted in your area. The goal is to wear a length in which you won't appear to be out of step. And remember, if a longer or shorter length puts your legs at a disadvantage, you don't have to follow the crowd. Wear what is best for you, without going to extremes.

Pants length—should never be high enough to reveal the ankle unless you are wearing a strappy sandal that you *want* to show. Short pants and/or cuffs make your legs look choppy. The best length is to have the hem down on the heel of the shoe, but not dragging on the floor.

—From Joanne Wallace, *The Image of Loveliness.* Old Tappan, N.J.: Revell, 1978.

Working Woman's Wardrobe

So you're going back to work? Great. You'll need a working woman's wardrobe, one that tells people you know who you are and where you are going, one that projects the self-confidence of someone on her way up.

Look through your closet. Not so great?

After years of working at home, raising babies, driving kids to and from soccer practice and ballet lessons, you may have very little to wear to work in an office, let alone to project a career image.

Now, before you call your new employer to say you've changed your mind, let me help you begin to put together a working woman's wardrobe that projects the right image for you. The image you present is as important as a good resume was when you were looking for a job. Just as your resume told the prospective employer who you were, the image you project through your clothes will tell your boss and your co-workers who you want to be, even before you prove yourself to be the sharpest, most dedicated member of the staff.

THE WRONG IMAGE

To determine what is the right image for a working woman let's consider what it is *not:*

—*Young and "cutesy."* You don't want to look inexperienced.
—*Frumpy.* Frumpiness indicates a lack of dynamism and self-assurance.
—*Sexy.* Seductiveness at the office has always been in poor taste and is even more so today.
—*Masculine.* You are not and will never be a man. Nor would you want to be.

THE RIGHT IMAGE

The image you want to project, then, is one of a self-assured, efficient professional who happens to be a woman. An image that is right for your particular job and ultimately right for you. A balance of femininity and no-nonsense efficiency not easily attained, but one achieved successfully by hundreds of working women today. So why not you?

Developing your own image should be the first challenge of your new career. Let's analyze your particular situation and then determine your wardrobe needs.

First, consider your working environment. In what type of office will you be working? An established law firm downtown? A sales-oriented company in a suburban area? A high-powered public relations firm with lots of media contact? An up-and-coming group of young graphic artists? The type of office will determine the kind of wardrobe you need: Clothes in established law firms tend to be formal and conservative, while a sales-oriented job requires a more updated appearance. A stylish look is appropriate for a job with media exposure, while the atmosphere of an artistic firm allows for more casual attire.

Second, consider your position in the office. Are you part of the support staff? Or are you starting at a managerial or professional level? If you are a professional or supervisor, your wardrobe should be more businesslike than if you are a secretary. Furthermore, if you are starting in a supporting position but plan to rise to a managerial or professional job, the way you dress should say just that.

Third, consider your own looks and personality. What kind of figure do you have? What colors look best on you? What kind of fabrics or styles make you feel comfortable?

Each of these considerations plays an important part in determining what kind of working wardrobe you need. Being able to choose the appropriate attire for a particular set of circumstances is another way of showing good judgment.

GETTING YOUR WORKING WARDROBE

The next step is deciding how to attain the look you have chosen.

First, go to your closet again and take a slower inventory of what you actually own. Carefully examine each article of clothing. Is it in good condition? Does it fit well? Can it be made to fit your working image? You will be surprised to see how many pieces you will be able to use in your new career—if you shorten a hemline, get a new belt, buy a new sweater. If, after considering all the possibilities, an item can't be made to work—or if you have to spend too much money to make it work—discard it. Better to have fewer good pieces than a closet full of mediocre ones. This will not only assure that you always look good, but it will save you time in the morning rush.

After you have separated the salvageable items, make a list of what you need to complete your wardrobe.

Your basic working fall wardrobe—the minimum to get you started—is made up of the following pieces:

2   skirts
1   pair of trousers
3   tops
2   jackets
1   dress
2   pairs of shoes
1   handbag/attache case
1   raincoat
1   coat
Accessories: belts, scarves, jewelry, stockings

These items, to work well for you, should be coordinated to make the greatest possible number of outfits. You might like to select most of your wardrobe from one designer's collection or from one label so that the separates work well together. Or, you might like to seek the help of a fashion consultant who can coordinate a wardrobe that will give you a polished look.

BOTTOMS

Start with skirts since they are harder to fit and more expensive than tops. Shape is very important because it determines the silhouette of your outfit. Regardless of what is in fashion, a working skirt should be *slim*—not necessarily straight, but close to the body.

The trouser skirt with fly front and kick-pleat looks good with any top. For most versatility it should be made of lightweight wool or gabardine in a solid, neutral color such as taupe.

Your other skirt should be pleated or narrow dirndle. It could be a small plaid or subtle tweed or another solid color. Avoid large plaids—which may make you look fat and unprofessional.

If pants are acceptable in your office and your figure can handle them, a pair of good trousers should be your next choice. They could be pleated in front and should have straight legs. They should *never* be tight. The most versatile pair of pants is of black wool crepe or gabardine, since you can make them very businesslike for the day and very chic for the evening by using different tops and accessories. A dark shade of taupe or charcoal gray is also appropriate. Narrow herringbone tweeds will be smart but not as versatile. Definitely no plaids or other patterns, which are too suburban for the office.

TOPS

You should own at least one light-colored blouse in a soft fabric, preferably silk or at least tissue faille polyester. Its lines should be classic so that it can be worn with anything.

You should have another blouse in a second color or in a pattern. Again, the pattern should be subtle, preferably a small print.

Your third top should be a crew neck sweater in a rich color which could be worn by itself or with a blouse underneath. A narrow belt worn over the sweater will pull together this look for the office.

JACKETS

You need at least two because you should wear one every day, especially if you are a supervisor or professional (or want to be one).

One of your jackets should be a classic blazer. It should coordinate with all of your bottoms—ideally of the same fabric of one of the skirts so you can have a "suit."

Your other jacket can be less versatile—perhaps one of the sweater-jackets. These are soft and youthful and often can be made to look quite chic.

DRESS

No working wardrobe is complete without a basic dress. A silk or wool challis shirtwaist in a solid shade or little print will be perfect. One of the jackets should coordinate with the dress for a day-into-evening look.

SHOES

You need at least two pairs of shoes for comfort. They should be of the best possible quality. The colors should compliment your wardrobe, and the style should be simple with a comfortable heel height.

Protect your shoes with a pair of weather boots. Unless you are in a very informal, "artsy" environment, boots should not be worn at the office.

RAINCOAT

Buy a good classic one, and you won't have to buy another for several years. A trench coat in any shade of tan or taupe is always stylish and youthful. *Never* buy a black raincoat.

COAT

As with the raincoat, this should be an investment to last several years. A dark wool is the best choice since it can be dressed up or down with wool or silk scarves.

ACCESSORIES

Buy the scarves, belts, and jewelry which will finish your look at the same time and pull together your wardrobe. *A pulled together outfit is always accessorized.* Few accessories are needed, since they should compliment rather than match your clothes. The same scarf or belt can be used with several outfits.

Think of stockings as accessories because they too give you a finished look. Buy them to coordinate with your skirts and shoes. Unless you are very sure of your taste, avoid colored stockings.

HANDBAG/ATTACHE CASE

You should look for an attache case that will hold your wallet and cosmetic bag, since it is awkward to carry both a case and a handbag. Many are made specifically for this purpose. As with the raincoat and coat, you should buy a good attache case so you won't have to buy another for a long time.

After you've made a list of what you need to put together your working wardrobe, go on a shopping spree. If possible buy all at once, early in the season. Buy only what you need, but buy the best possible quality. Keep in mind what your objective is: to look self-assured at all times.

—MARILU SECKINGER, Washington, D.C., fashion consultant.

Communication Through Clothes

Some people are so *nice* I'm not comfortable around them. I can't believe they are really that nice all the time, and I'm waiting for the big blowup. Or else I figure if they really are that nice, they won't bother with me for long because I know I'm not that nice. I dread the letdown when they discover it. There is also a type of person who *looks* too nice to be real. Sometimes they are both the same person. I keep wondering why they need to try so hard. Do they want attention? Or what?

I knew a lady, a pastor's wife, who was the picture of perfect fashion every time I ever saw her. She was eye-catching in a crowd, the only peacock in a flock of doves. She had the monochromatic color scheme down to perfection in several different colors. Her pink straw hat (usually in a congregation of hatless women) matched her pink purse and shoes, the pink gloves were just a shade lighter. And the outfit always had the requisite color emphasis of some item in a brighter shade. It was always that way. I had the distinct impression that she wasn't real, that somewhere under all that clothing was a plastic woman. That's what's really wrong with ostentation or out-of-place overdressing, it draws attention to the clothing. It makes the wearer seem only an accessory worn by the clothes.

But the woman who dresses so drably that she draws attention to herself is as far off the track as the peacock. Good dressing has something in common with driving with the traffic. If you go thirty miles an hour when everyone else is going fifty you are as likely to get a ticket as if you are going seventy. Maybe more likely, because you are a rarer bird, and so unexpected.

In some circles it is thought to be a mark of spiritual substance to look drab and be at least ten years out of style. I know that sounds catty, and I don't mean it to be. It is just an honest assessment of the reality of living as though women are to look old-fashioned, that somehow it is holy to do so. I went to a college where there were several representatives of this school of thought. I don't put them down for it. Someone taught them this, they didn't think it up themselves. But it doesn't work. If you look so out of step as all that, you draw as much attention to yourself as the woman with the wild-and-crazy outfit or the scanty one.

If you go to excess in either direction you are saying by your dress, "Look at me, I'm different." And you may also be saying, "Look at me, I'm a little weird." If you don't want to look weird, then don't do it, even if someone who looks and sounds important says you should. You should be deciding clothing for yourself.

WHO AND HOW ARE YOU?

Who do your clothes say you are? What do they say to *you?* Do they say that you are the martyr of the family, that your needs come last? Do they say you are afraid to look as good as you can, because you don't know how to handle friendship and closeness? Are clothes a barrier between you and others? Do you want your clothes to say what they do? Or would you rather change the message?

How about dressing to say both to yourself and to the world, "I'm okay, I'm neither so drab that I want everyone to feel sorry for me or not see me at all, nor do I want to say by my gaudy clothing, 'Hey look at me, I want lots of attention, I'm insecure.' "

Can you dress so that your clothes say, "I'm me, I'm happy about it. I wear what I feel good and happy in and comfortable in and about. I am free to be a whole person in this area, too"?

If you can't say that now, you can work toward it. How can you make one small or medium-sized change that will be more like the real you and the message you want to send to you and to others? Can you do it soon? Today?

—From Patricia Gundry, *The Complete Woman.* Garden City, N.Y.: Doubleday, 1981.

How to Shop for Clothing

Throughout the years I have learned a few workable shortcuts that help make clothes shopping easier for me. I'll pass them on for you to try:

1. *Know what you are looking for.* By defining precisely what need a garment is to serve, you can more accurately pinpoint what you are looking for. Is the white blouse you are seeking for dressup or for casual wear? Are the shoes you are buying strictly for use with a tailored suit or will buying a slightly lower heel make them feasible also for wearing with your favorite wrap-around skirt?

2. *Know the alternatives.* As you shop, ask yourself, "What can I substitute if this item is not available?" Take note of the alternatives while you are in each store. Then after visiting five or six stores without successfully locating the item you sought, you will know which store to return to in order to acquire the best alternative.

3. *Plan ahead.* It's better to start thinking about buying shoes when you see the thin spot in your daughter's sneakers instead of waiting until the day her toes come poking through. By keeping a constant inventory of your family's wardrobe, you can start to look for needed items before something turns into a "have-to" situation.

4. *Shop cooperatively.* Your shopping time is cut considerably if you know before you walk into a store that what you need is there. Work out a cooperative plan with a few of your friends. While one of them is buying her son's western boots, she can ask if the store has your son's size and color in the jogging shoes you have been seeking. While you are buying your husband a brown wallet for his birthday, notice whether the store also carries the black trifold style one of your friends wants to buy. A bargain network can help everybody save money. Have an agreement with your friends that whoever finds bargains on anything that all of you buy frequently will immediately telephone the rest of the group with the news. This makes it possible for all of you to cover more territory in less time.

5. *Know quality.* There was a time when price was the primary indicator of

quality, but this is no longer true. As a seamstress, I was amazed when I examined some of the poor-quality, high-priced garments my customers brought to me for alteration work. Price alone is not the determining factor in choosing quality garments. Quality is a combination of fabric choice, appropriate design, ample cut, and skilled construction techniques.

Judging Quality

Do you sew? If you do, then perhaps, like me, you are aware of the inferior quality of some ready-made garments. It is disappointing to pay a hefty price for a piece of clothing, only to have the hem come undone with the first washing or the neckline facings poke out because they were not properly sewn down. Here are some guidelines for buying quality clothing for the family.

1. *Is the fabric suitable for the pattern?* Home sewing enthusiasts are not the only ones who make the mistake of matching the wrong fabric and pattern. Sometimes clothing designers do this too, and the result is a lowering of the overall quality of the garment.

2. *Is the fabric cut well?* It is possible to sew up a ripped seam but it is not possible for any seamstress to correct the poor fit of a badly cut garment. No matter how beautiful a design might be or how appealing a bargain price might seem, a garment is not a good buy if it is not cut well. The garment must be cut with the grain of the fabric or it will never hang properly at the hemline. In addition, the sleeves should not bind when the arms are lifted, the waistline should be precisely at the waist, and the skirt should not crawl up when you walk. For long sleeves, proper fit means that the sleeves cover the wristbone. For skirts, particularly bias cut ones, proper fit means an even hem and a grain line that does not cause the skirt to sag at the hipline.

3. *Is the garment constructed well?* Ample seam allowances used to be one of the marks of quality; but now even some of the better-known clothing manufacturers are starting to skimp on seam allowances. It is advisable, however, to buy garments with a half-inch or more of seam allowance when you can find them at a price you can afford, because otherwise no alterations will be possible if you gain a few pounds or if the garment shrinks when it is washed.

Another construction point to check is the stitching. Seams should be sewn with about twelve stitches to the inch. If a garment has less than that, it is not going to hold together well, and you will constantly be restitching ripped places. Give a tug on the back seam of trousers and slacks if these are going to be bought to fit snugly. If so, choose a brand that features stretch stitches that give under pressure; this saves a lot of embarrassment in the long run. Stay away from garments that are sewn with colorless nylon thread. It is scratchy against the skin and, while it doesn't break easily, it does tend to come unsewn.

Zippers and other fasteners are important too. When buying men's trousers choose those with metal zippers rather than nylon ones. After a few washings, the nylon ones tend to separate while the garment is being worn. It is getting more and more difficult to find women's garments with metal zippers. But whenever you do have a choice, the metal ones are the most durable.

When inspecting trousers, be particularly choosy about pockets. Look for pockets that are made of sturdy material, even if you are buying a suit rather than a pair of casual slacks. Men carry almost as much weight in their pockets—even when they are dressed up—as we carry in our purses, so those pockets need to be durable. Learn to recognize those that contain rayon (it ravels) or dacron (it "pills"). Check, too, for ample belt loops. Nothing detracts from a man's well-dressed appearance faster than does a gap between his belt and his waistband.

4. *Is the style a basic one or a faddish one?* The woman who wants to get the

most for her clothing dollar will avoid the clothing fads that come and go. Quality clothing should be virtually timeless. Just because some of the Paris designers are putting spangles and feathers on their five-thousand-dollar dresses does not mean that those dresses have quality as far as lasting wearability is concerned. A basic garment of good quality construction should be as stylish next year as it is this year.

—From Edith Flowers Kilgo, *Handbook for Christian Homemakers.* Grand Rapids: Baker Book, 1982.

FOR FURTHER READING:

Jackson, Carole. *Color Me Beautiful.* Washington: Acropolis, 1980.

Neff, Mariam. *Discover Your Worth.* Wheaton, Ill.: Victor Books, 1979.

Wallace, Joanne. *Dress With Style.* Old Tappan, N.J.: Revell, 1983.

Wilhelmina. *The New You.* New York: Simon & Schuster, 1978.

COMMITMENT

COMMITMENT MUST issue in action. Until something is done, commitment is not complete. Faith becomes saving only with confession and obedience; love becomes marriage only with the exchange of vows and life lived together.

Moving life in the direction of the choice is the essence of commitment. The archetype is faithful Abraham: "By faith Abraham obeyed . . . sojourned . . . offered" (*see* Hebrews 11:8, 9, 17). It is on the basis of faith that choice becomes commitment; by faith, decision is translated into action.

Faith has become a fuzzy concept. It is commonly confused with a warm and possibly worshipful feeling. But biblical faith is not a feeling. It is an activity. It is a confidence that allows one to take the risk of commitment: not an unfounded confidence, it should be pointed out. For while faith is, at times, "a leap in the dark"—it is not a leap into darkness without light, nor is it essentially irrational. It is based on a reasonable assurance that what we hope for may be.

The moment of the actual exercise of faith, or making of a commitment, is a moment of intense conflict. The person who is considering the step is most aware of an overwhelming sense of risk. "If I do this, what about the other alternative that I am hereby rejecting?"

I remember the day that a minister friend

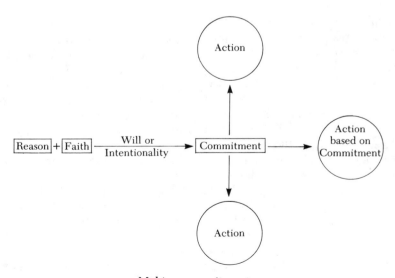

Making commitment

of ours signed his membership card for the political party that my husband was representing in an election. He had long supported another party, but in support of Cam's candidacy, he made the new commitment. Under the blue fluorescence of our kitchen light, he looked at his new membership card before slipping it into his wallet. "Dear Lord," he whispered, ashen faced. "I hope that this is not the end of all that I hold dear."

That is what the moment of commitment always feels like: the end of all that I hold dear, and the hope that it is not. The moment of commitment is always a moment when the risks appear huge. This awareness of risk may last for many months, as described by Saint Augustine in his *Confessions*. The sense of risk begins to subside at the moment at which commitment is made—never before. Thus, making a commitment requires a decisive moment which, though illumined by hope, is fraught with risk and a sense of intense peril.

.   .   .   .   .

Every commitment is a sort of gamble. But for the person experiencing the acute sense of risk that comes at the moment of making a decisive commitment, there is a dual risk: Not only the risk of exercising faith and making a commitment, but the equally acute risk of *not* exercising faith and making a commitment. It is what Sheldon Vanauken describes so well as the "gap behind"—the sense that one cannot draw back from the risk that is to be taken, except at even greater risk. The human adult must constantly choose to take risks, for there is no risk-free living that is worthwhile.

Commitment is not irrational. It would be foolish to trust a foothold you have not properly tested, or to marry a person you have not adequately assessed, or to trust a message you have not investigated. But commitment requires more than reason. It requires the act of faith: that shifting of weight, that trusting of oneself. And then, as commitment is

made—and the rope does hold on its mountain hook—the sense of risk fades and hope grows.

—From Maxine Hancock, *The Forever Principle.* Old Tappan, N.J.: Revell, 1980.

FOR FURTHER READING:

Elliot, Elisabeth. *Discipline: The Glad Surrender.* Old Tappan, N.J.: Revell, 1982.
Getz, Gene A. *The Measure of a Woman.* Ventura, Calif.: Regal, 1977.
Ghezzi, Bert. *Getting Free.* Ann Arbor: Servant, 1982.
Murphey, Cecil B. *Press On: A Disciple's Guide to Spiritual Growth.* Ann Arbor: Servant, 1983.

Checklists

From the scars of past mistakes and burnouts, I developed a checklist to help keep curbs on the use of my time and talents.

SPIRITUAL CHECKLIST:

1. Are my priorities in order? God, husband, family, Christian and community service. Are there any weak spots at this time? Where?
2. Private Devotions: Did I substitute public or family devotions in place of the intimate one-on-one with the Lord today? This week?
3. When I prayed, did I allow times of silence? Did I run through my prayer list and then run on about my own business? Did I try to hide from God, using the excuse, "I just didn't have time to even pray today"?
4. When asked to make a commitment for the church or community, did I try to avoid giving an immediate answer? Did I promise myself to pray during a given period of time *before* giving my answer?
5. If I had my mind partly made up when asked to participate, did I make known to God that I'd be willing to have *my* preferences changed or rerouted if *his* will so desired?

ATTITUDE CHECKLIST:

1. Do I think of myself more highly than I ought? "I bid every one among you not to think of himself more highly than he ought . . ." (Romans 12:3, RSV).
2. Am I willing to believe I can be expendable?
3. Am I keeping my eye peeled for pride when any activity or project might puff up my ego?

PHYSICAL CHECKLIST:

1. Do I have any physical symptoms that indicate I'm overextending myself (i.e. sickness, chronic run-down feelings, headaches without medical explanation, the desire to nap excessively)?
2. Do I have any vitamin deficiencies contributing to these feelings?

INTERPERSONAL CHECKLIST:

1. Do I find I'm unable to listen to an individual without allowing my thoughts and eyes to dart around the room, as if I need or want to be doing something else?
2. Am I persistently short-tempered with loved ones?

THOUGHT-LIFE CHECKLIST:

1. Do I find I can't control my daydreaming?
2. Do certain thoughts consume my waking hours and distract me excessively when I try to go to sleep at night?

CALENDAR CHECKLIST:

1. Are there any obvious imbalances observable by checking my calendar? (Consider that Little League doesn't last forever; likewise Christmas and Easter . . . don't be too hard on yourself if the crunch of activity will be over soon.)

2. When was the last time I checked my calendar *thoroughly?* (Watch out . . . it sneaks up on you.)

ACTION:

1. Maintain sense of humor at any cost.
2. Get rest!
3. Squeeze out five or ten minutes (it *is* possible) to lie down with pillows under your knees to relax each afternoon.
4. Change your daily pace by interspersing "surprises" (i.e., take your husband to lunch—be a mystery lunch guest on his business calendar; take a warm bath in the afternoon while sipping a cool beverage; buy a bouquet of flowers for yourself; visit a museum).
5. *Plan* a vacation . . . don't wait for one to happen. (Look forward to rest!)
6. Take a sabbatical rest (it's biblical).
7. When you see commitments are obviously excessive, set a two-week limit during which you will try to:

   a. Delegate some jobs to others who need to develop gifts and talents in those areas where you are becoming "muscle-bound."
   b. Eliminate those activities which are simply "wants" rather than "needs."
   c. Maintain those activities that really cannot be done by someone else (i.e., nursing a baby!).

8. Be willing to work slowly. Instant solutions and hasty decisions often remove symptoms, but underlying causes remain to bubble up later.
9. Take credit as well as the blame when it is due. Stop playing "Adam," by blaming others for your failures.
10. After admitting infallibility is impossible, choose to get on with the business of living. *Stop looking back at past failures.* (That's a tough one.)

—From Nyla Jane Witmore, *I Was an Over Committed Christian.* Wheaton, Ill.: Tyndale, 1979. (Out of print but available through author.)

COMMUNICATION

Principles of Communication

1. *Listen more—talk less. Most of us talk too much and listen too little.* James said it loudly and clearly: "Dear brothers, don't ever forget that it is best to listen much, speak little, and not become angry" (James 1:19).

. . . . .

Why don't people talk? Here are some of the reasons that I have heard some people give:

1. Because you don't give me a chance.
2. Because you don't really listen.
3. Because you come through as not really caring what I say, what I feel.
4. Because you would become defensive.
5. Because I am afraid you will think less of me.
6. Because you make me feel so stupid.
7. Because I just don't trust you that much.
8. Because you act like you know all the answers.
9. Because you always have to be right.
10. Because I'm afraid you won't accept me as I am.

Seek first to understand, not to be understood. Have you ever said: "He doesn't understand me"; "She doesn't understand me." I can tell you from personal experience that as long as a man is exclusively preoccupied with being understood by his wife, he will be overrun with self-pity and trapped in his own miserable self. I have a sneaking idea that women sometimes become just as self-centered and consequently make themselves just as miserable.

One of the smartest prayers you can pray is this: "Lord, grant that I may seek more to understand than to be understood . . ."

2. *Don't allow trivial things to break down your communication with other members of your family.* In the play, *Philadelphia, Here I Come,* a success in Britain and on Broadway, one sees the pathetic and heartbreaking attempt of a father and son to break through the silence and habits of years. On the eve of the son's departure from Ireland for America, neither father nor son can sleep. Late at night they go to the kitchen for a snack and are surprised to meet each other there. They search for words, but can't find them; they plunge into painful silences. Nonverbal communication to the audience indicates how hard they are trying to get the barriers down and communicate during these last hours together before their final separation.

And then, as if he were inspired, the father begins to talk about when the son was ten years of age and they went fishing together. Through sharing the recollection of this happy memory the long standing barriers begin to drop and at long last father and son are enjoying communication with one another.

The boy said, "You know, that was one of the best times of my life, Dad. I'll never forget that little red boat, and the good times we had together fishing."

"No," contradicts the father, " 'twas not a red boat; 'twas a blue one." The son said, "It was a red boat!" "No," said the father, "it was a blue boat!" And the argument is on.

Tragedy ensues as each contends for his memory of the insignificant detail to be accepted as correct. Stubbornness on both sides brings back the separation and alienation and the curtain falls on the spectacle of two lonely people, unwilling to remove the barriers that isolate them from each other.

What trivial things often separate family members: edgemanship, wanting to be right, and clinging selfishly to one's position. How tragic that we allow such little things to become barriers between us and stop communication. All because we have to be so proud, so stubborn, so right. Suppose you do win the argument. But if you have created a gulf and each person is alone and lonely, everyone loses. The way always to win is never to allow the trivial to create gulfs in your family. Make togetherness your aim—and whatever you do, don't allow trivial things to erect barriers between you and your loved ones.

Exercise tongue control. In the book of James in the New Testament, the tongue is compared to the rudder of a ship; although the rudder is a small part of the ship, it turns the ship in any direction and determines its destiny. What husbands and wives say to each other can either help or hinder, heal or scar, build up or tear down.

Don't settle for anything less than complete control of your own tongue. Only a fool rattles off anything that comes into his mind. (See Proverbs 29:20.) First Peter 3:10 says it like it is: "If you want a happy, good life, keep control of your tongue, and guard your lips. . . ." Controlling your own tongue is not easy to accomplish in your own strength. You can do this only with the Spirit of Christ living in full control within you. Let God have his complete way with you.

Don't nag. Nagging is constantly harping or hassling your mate for one reason or another. A technical definition is critical faulting, but whatever it is called, it irritates and frustrates marriage partners—the "nagger" as well as the "naggee." Solomon said in the Old Testament, "A nagging wife annoys like a constant dripping" (Proverbs 19:13).

3. *Never stop expressing yourself—just learn to do it better.* Prolonged silence is not golden; it is a cruel weapon. Phyllis McGinley penned these words: "Words can sting like anything, but silence breaks the heart." When communication is broken off, things are at their worst. I have known husbands and wives who would go for days without speaking to each other. At the breakfast table the father would say, "Johnny, tell your mother to pass the bacon." They wouldn't talk to one another day after day after day. That is horrible. It's destructive. It hurts. How it hurts every member of the family. Whatever you do, don't stop talking to each other.

The Bible gives us some great advice. It tells us to settle our differences on the same day they arrive. "Let not the sun go down upon your wrath" (Ephesians 4:26 KJV). Keep talking and listening until you work out your differences and arrive at a mutual point of understanding.

Say what you mean. One of the key problems in communicating is making yourself understood. Sometimes we think we have said it, when we haven't. What you meant to say, what you actually said, and what the other person heard are often three very different things. This illustrates why it often takes extra effort to clearly communicate your exact meaning to others. The old proverb, "Say what you mean and mean what you say," is a most worthy goal. So let's work at it.

Question to ask: "Am I saying what I really mean?" A wife criticizes her husband as he sits at the dinner table hidden behind his newspaper. She says, "I wish you wouldn't slurp your coffee." What she means is, "I feel hurt when you hide in the newspaper instead of talking to me." Be straightforward; learn to say it like it is, gently if necessary, but clearly. The Bible says, "There is a right time for everything . . . a time to be quiet; a time to speak up . . ." (Ecclesiastes 3:1, 7).

Learn to speak the truth in love.

. . . . .

To speak the truth in love is to learn to report honestly and openly your own ideas and feelings, "This is the way I feel." "This is my viewpoint." "I don't know why this bothers me, but it does." Don't blame the other person or make him to be all wrong, and yourself all right.

No one has the right to be another's judge—that's playing God. Who but God can read the intentions and motives of another? "Judge not, that ye be not judged," Jesus said (Matthew 7:1 KJV). Leave the judging to God.

Say it with love.

. . . . .

4. *For the greatest in family communication, together converse with God.* How sad it is that all too many homes are depriving

themselves of the tremendous joy that Jesus wants them to have simply because they neglect praying together. It is sharing with God through family prayer that opens the door to greater sharing between members of a household.

Hearts open to God invariably open to each other.

—From Dale E. Galloway, *We're Making Our Home a Happy Place.* Wheaton, Ill.: Tyndale, 1976.

Nonverbal Communications

Words, important as they are—even with their emotional overtones—are not the whole story. So much is said sublingually. When it comes to feelings, the most powerful conveyances can be nonverbal: posture, gestures, facial expressions, voice inflections—even the cadence of the words themselves. I know of at least two ways to say, "Did you close the door?" There is a language deeper than words—more primitive than syntax and vocabulary. A wink can say more than a thousand words. A yawn can terminate a party. A sigh can signal a romance. A tear can reveal a broken heart.

. . . . .

Certain actions mean different things to different people, too. Often we say one thing with our words then proceed to contradict with our behavior. It is all part of this complicated process called understanding.

What does it mean when Jack comes home from work and Jill is still in her bathrobe? It could mean a lot of things. What does it mean if Jack stops off for a few beers before he comes home? Nothing? Everything? What does it mean when the little woman suddenly decides to go to the beauty parlor and "get the works." Is she depressed and wants an emotional lift? (Julia gets blue if she thinks her hair looks dowdy.) Is she hinting for a night out on the town? Or is she trying to say, "I'm just as pretty as your secretary"? Who knows what that combination of torture chamber and Swedish massage is

designed to do! But it's a wise husband who tries to figure it out.

Why did he leave his dirty socks on the bathroom floor? Is he just absent-minded? Did his mother always pick them up, and he assumes that his wife is just like good old Mom? (Maybe she actually enjoys mothering him, and they have a kind of a thing going.) Or does he know that socks on the floor will make his wife as mad as hops? By leaving them there, he can smack her one without even raising his voice or lifting a finger.

Psychodrama—a method of therapy—takes bodily manifestations very seriously as meaningful communication. For example: A man sits leaning back, with his arms folded and his legs tightly crossed. His barriers are up. He is defensive. He doesn't want to get involved. The counselor accepts this action as communication and helps the man talk about it. Or a sophisticated woman sits completely relaxed, it seems, smiling and composed. But her right hand tightly squeezes a tiny handkerchief. That small fist, half-hidden between her body and the chair, gives the scarcely perceptible signal that she may be the most anxious person in the room. The therapist, who is trained to spot such nonverbal signs, may ask her to "be her hand." He asks her to let her whole body and personality reflect the feelings of her hand. She may temporarily deny that she is at all anxious or afraid, claiming either that she was not really squeezing her handkerchief, or that it is a meaningless little habit. But with some encouragement, she may be enabled to act out her fright, or she may be able to say in words what her hand has been saying all along.

The intelligent couple learns to interpret fairly accurately the nonspoken signals in their marriage relationship. They even try to use them to good advantage.

—From Richard B. Wilke, *Tell Me Again, I'm Listening.* Nashville: Abingdon, 1973.

The Memo Method

The next time you are frustrated by your mate, take a separate sheet of paper and write the word PROBLEM in the upper left-hand corner. Then, in as clear and concise a manner as possible, state the problem. Try to limit it to one or two sentences.

"I cannot stand your drinking anymore," or "You never back me up when it comes to disciplining the children," or "You are always correcting me and I'm supposed to take that calmly, but if I correct you once, you become very defensive." These are examples of typical problems.

Once the problem has been stated, start another paragraph and write the word CAUSES in the left-hand margin. Under the heading CAUSES list all the reasons why you think your mate acts in the way that disturbs you. For example, some responses you may list for the last problem mentioned above ("You are always correcting me and I'm supposed to take that calmly, but if I correct you once, you become very defensive") might be:

1. "You are overly sensitive and think you have to be perfect. For that reason, when I criticize you in a normal way, you cannot stand it."
2. "Your parents have always criticized you, and when I do, you think I'm putting you down just like they did."
3. "You've had a couple of failures in your life recently and I think you have become very touchy over them. As a result, you have become needlessly sensitive about having *anybody* find fault with you."

After CAUSES comes the most important step of all—the proposed SOLUTIONS. Write the word SOLUTIONS in the left-hand margin and again list the possibilities that you feel will clear up the problem. In this case, we might suggest the following:

1. "Stop and realize, honey, you are a worthwhile being even if you have your failures."
2. "I hope you don't mind if I remind you when you get in this mood that I am not your mother (or your father). I am your wife (or husband) and love you very much. Let me suggest a good book you can read that will show you what a worthwhile person you are, although you

have some faults. Maybe some of our friends know of a good book that will help us in this matter."
3. "If this problem persists, I would recommend that you seek professional counseling. In the final analysis, it is nothing less than an inferiority complex and I am sure it can be helped. Even when you think I am wrong to criticize you, try to remind yourself that I have a right to be mistaken. Everyone has a right to be wrong. I do not feel I am mistaken by making these comments, so grant me the right to my opinion although it is different from your opinion."

The plaintiff could go on proposing possible solutions until the subject is thoroughly covered.

Next, the defendant is encouraged to take a sheet of paper and make the same sort of analysis the plaintiff has made. The defendant should write out the problem as he or she sees it, and write out causes and solutions in an identical manner, but from his or her point of view.

After studying each other's papers, both should sit down over a cup of coffee when the mood is particularly calm and discuss what each has written. In most cases the discussion will proceed in a rational and open manner and the issue can be managed.

If satisfaction is not derived from the post-memo session, then each can write an additional memo concerning the new matters brought to light during the conference.

And so it can go on for years and years with numerous memos passing back and forth, each partner calmly presenting and defending and perhaps modifying his or her case. These memos can be kept as a running diary of tribulations and growth in the family experience. At some future time the couple can sit back and review their memos and realize that although their marriage had its ups and downs, they overcame significant difficulties which at one time terribly concerned them.

—From Paul A. Hauck, Ph.D., and Edmund S. Kean, M.D., *Marriage and the Memo Method.* Philadelphia: Westminster, 1975.

FOR FURTHER READING:

Hancock, Maxine. *People in Process*. Old Tappan, N.J.: Revell, 1978.

MacDonald, Gordon. *Magnificent Marriage*. Wheaton, Ill.: Tyndale, 1976.

Powell, John S. *Why Am I Afraid to Tell You Who I Am?* Allen, Tex.: Argus, 1970.

Wright, H. Norman. *Communication: Key to Your Marriage*. Ventura, Calif.: Regal, 1974.

COMPETITION

I MUST CONFESS that I was surprised at myself. It was a warm, sunny day in July and for the first time my neighbor was trying out his new underground sprinkler system. Sparkling in the summer sun, the cascading droplets of water reflected a rainbow of colors as they fell to the parched ground below. I was not conscious of any feeling of jealousy, but I did wonder how our thirsty lawn could possibly compare to the green expanse which was sure to persist next door. Our old hose could never water the grass like my neighbor's automatic sprinkler system. Suddenly I became aware of an inner competition with my neighbor over something as insignificant as the color of our lawns.

Competition is like that. It isn't always rational. It creeps up on us without warning, and at times it can pervade our whole way of thinking. Everyone expects that athletes will learn to compete, strive to surpass others, and train to win. But competition is not limited to sports. It characterizes the business world, it is basic to the military, it is at the core of politics, it is a way of life for students, and it can even dominate the home. Children, who compete in school, music, and Little League, often bring their anxieties home where the tension persists, and sometimes explodes—to the surprise of innocent siblings or busy mothers. Husbands, working wives, and other employed family members compete in society and sometimes find it difficult to tame their tensions when the work day is over. Few households are free of competition between brothers and sisters, and certainly many married couples find themselves competing with one another.

Competition is so common in our culture that it once was considered to be an inborn human instinct. We now know that it is learned, but it comes so early that few if any of us reach adulthood without that urge to win over others. At times we find ourselves competing with relatives, friends, fellow workers, church members, and neighbors, with whom we compare our homes, our children, our successes, and even the quality of our lawns.

Competition isn't all bad, of course. It can motivate, keep us alert, give opportunity for people to discover their gifts and abilities, provide enjoyment, and add zest to activities which otherwise might be dull or unpleasant. Spurred on by competition, many people learn more, accomplish greater things, develop skills, and reach levels of success which they might never achieve otherwise. Although some people seem to thrive on competition (and others do not), probably all of us have grown because of the competitive spirit which dominates our society and pervades our lives.

But competition can also destroy. Pro basketball's Bob Cousy called competition "the killer instinct"—a devastating force which can spread like cancer, compelling people to drive themselves unmercifully, to subject themselves to sustained and severe pressure, and to act unscrupulously in order to win. Competition is able to divide us, drain away our peace of mind, build tension, and wear us down physically.

Several years ago, for example, two San Francisco cardiologists wrote a thought-provoking and widely acclaimed book which they titled, *Type A Behavior and Your Heart*. Type A people, the book suggests, are aggressive, impatient, work-dominated individuals who have "deep-seated insecurity," a lot of hidden anger, and *an excessive competitive drive*. Sometimes these people work too much, drink too much, eat too much, and relax too little. They are the people most prone to have heart attacks. For them, competition can lead to physical collapse.

The destructive effect of competition has been described even more dramatically by a psychiatrist who wrote about the patients who are always running to succeed but who rarely are satisfied. Afraid to slow down, they push on in a never-ending chase. They seem to be "engaged in a marathon race, their eager faces distorted by strain, their eyes focused not upon their goal, but upon each other, with a mixture of hate, envy, and admiration." This description might be slightly overdrawn, but it dramatically shows the harmful power of competition.

If this existed only in the athletic world many of us could overlook it, but competition affects all of us and its destructive power is impossible to ignore.

It is important, therefore, to develop what someone has called a "competition tolerance"—that ability to live with competition and to help others do the same, without giving in to its smothering power. There are several ways in which this might be done.

1. *Commit It to God.* This is not a simplistic, easy answer. It is a realistic starting point whereby we ask God to help us face the competition which is a fact of life in our society.

Psychologist Robert Goldenson has written that "there is no more complex question in the field of psychology than that of competition." Surely, then, we need to seek God's constant wisdom as we face this issue in ourselves and others.

2. *Reduce Competition in the Home.* I have a student who coaches the local "midget" hockey team. "The kids are fun to work with," my friend said recently, "but some of the parents are impossible. They pressure the young players to succeed and heap scorn and criticism upon any son who does not do well." These parents are teaching Type A behavior to their children, and putting them under tremendous pressure to compete and win.

Surely the home should not harbor such attitudes. Instead, it should be a haven from the pressure cooker competition of our cul-

ture. When children constantly are pushed to succeed, compared unfavorably with others, urged to compete, and criticized for failure, a competitive atmosphere pervades the family. As every parent is aware, no two children have the same abilities, interests, or personalities, even when they grow up in the same home. In our house, therefore, we try not to contrast report cards, musical skills, or athletic abilities. We don't always succeed, of course, but we attempt to emphasize the individual abilities of each person, and resist making comparisons between the children. Although they make comparisons among themselves, we try to emphasize each person's unique gifts, helping family members to accept and realistically evaluate their strengths and weaknesses.

This applies to adults as well as children. Tension is increased when critical comments between husband and wife are intended to "put down" each other and when one's mate is compared unfavorably to relatives or friends. In such an atmosphere, the family members learn to compete at home and there is no haven from the competitive pressures of the society.

3. *Divorce Competition From the Self-Concept.* Very often we determine our worth in terms of how well we succeed in competition with others. People who fail quickly get the idea that they are "no good" and this brings feelings of inferiority sometimes accompanied by bitterness, withdrawal, negativism, a tendency to criticize, self-pity, and at times futile attempts to keep on trying to win. Sometimes parents attempt to boost their sagging egos by pushing their children to accomplish what they themselves failed to achieve. This creates tension for everyone.

Frequently, we should remind ourselves and each other that every person is loved by God. He created us, sent his son to die for us, adopted us as his children, and gives each of us gifts and abilities. In God's sight we are all valuable, even when we fail. The Creator is not concerned about our looks, intellect, strength, status, or ability to win a competition with someone else. He wants us to run the race of life and to win, not by beating out others, but by serving Christ with the abilities and gifts which we have been given.

Perhaps one of the saddest commentaries on the church today is that we Christians have fallen into a mindset which emphasizes cut-throat competition and equates self-worth with winning the status, power, money, and prestige which others do not possess. We have forgotten that God made each of us unique and gave us gifts, responsibilities, and opportunities which are important to him, even though they may not be valued by the society around us.

4. *Rethink Our View of Success.* Recently I was invited to give a series of lectures at a college in another part of the country. As I rode to the campus from the airport, my host described the speakers who had come in previous years. "They were brilliant speakers," I was informed, "capable, informed, and outstanding in their ability to communicate." As this conversation continued I felt less and less adequate. Surely I could never live up to the standards of those who had come before, and I began to ponder how it would be possible to get back to the airport and flee for home. It was important for me to be successful as a visiting lecturer on that campus, but I was so busy comparing myself to others that I had forgotten my own uniqueness and God-given strengths.

Later, as I waited to be introduced, I began to see my task in a new perspective. "I am here to do the best I can," I told myself. "I have prepared carefully and even if I fail, the world will not end, God and my family will still love me, and life will go on." Quickly I relaxed and was able to give my speeches without worrying about whether or not these talks were better or worse than those that had preceded me.

Have you ever noticed how much we compete with others in our minds? So often we compare ourselves to someone who appears to be a better parent, a more capable hostess, a more charming personality, a more dedicated Christian, or superior in our field of work. Rarely do we realize that these people who seem so capable probably are insecure like us and also might be competing mentally as well—perhaps even with us.

The apostle Paul once discovered that the Christians in Corinth had divided into denominational factions and were competing with each other in an attitude of jealousy and strife. These attitudes concerned Paul but he appeared to have no concern about who was the most successful Christian leader. "What difference does it make?" he asked. We are all God's servants, each with unique abilities, working as a team, and not trying to compete with one another.

In an age when people appear to be driven by the need to succeed and by a desire to win over others, we need to remember the words of Jesus. To really be successful in God's eyes, he told his disciples, we should be servants, helping and encouraging one another instead of competing.

5. *Compete Against Ourselves, Not Against Others.* This, of course, is difficult to do in practice but it reduces tension and makes life a lot more pleasant.

When my wife and I entertain, we find that our dinner parties often are followed by a late-night "post-mortem" while we do the dishes together. We discuss the guest list, the food, the table setting, and other details of the evening—not in an effort to compare ourselves to others, but in a desire to determine how we can do better next time. We compete against our own past record, pleased when we make progress, and especially analytical when we are less successful.

This attitude of competing against ourselves can enter every aspect of our lives. I hope this article will be better than the last one I wrote, but not as good as the next one. I want my spiritual life to be better now than it was last year, and even better next year. As each new year dawns I want to be a better husband and father than I was the year before. Such an attitude motivates me, but prevents the bitterness and destructive "put-downs" which can come when I spend time comparing myself to others and worrying about winning.

6. *Learn the Value of Cooperation.* The Bible is a book which emphasizes mutual caring, burden-bearing, and support. Within its pages we are instructed to help one another, not in a spirit of competition, but in an attitude of teamwork and cooperation.

In this age of competition, teamwork is not easy. Most of us have to work constantly at developing our competition tolerance. We have to resist the pressures to win over others in a spirit of intolerance or insensitivity. The place to start counteracting competition is with prayer and with an evaluation of our attitudes and values.

I'm even learning to develop these attitudes with my neighbor. I still don't have an underground sprinkler system, and probably never will. At times his grass is greener than mine, but we work together on our lawns, share responsibility in caring for a little piece of village property, and exchange pleasant comments as we work alongside each other during the warm summer months. This is more healthy, and more biblical, than competing. And it makes life a lot more pleasant.

—GARY R. COLLINS, chairman of the Division of Pastoral Counseling and Psychology at Trinity Evangelical Divinity School in Deerfield, Illinois.

FOR FURTHER READING:

Ahlem, Lloyd H. *How to Cope: With Conflict, Crisis and Change.* Ventura, Calif.: Regal, 1978.

Lederer, William J., and Don D. Jackson. *The Mirages of Marriage.* New York: Norton, 1968.

Scanzoni, John. *Love and Negotiate: Creative Conflict in Marriage.* Waco, Tex.: Word Books, 1979.

COMPLIMENTS

ACCORDING TO a study conducted at Colorado State University, two out of three people feel uncomfortable when paid a compliment. Half of the 245 subjects surveyed felt obligated to return the compliments or reciprocate in some fashion. Thirty percent

felt they would appear conceited if they failed to neutralize the compliments gracefully, and twenty percent suspected that ulterior motives lay behind the praise.

"Compliments often give rise to uneasiness, defensiveness, and cynicism," according to Professor Ronny Turner, who conducted the survey. There was a tendency, upon receiving a verbal compliment, to say, "Oh, you say such nice things"; "I had lots of help"; "It was really nothing"; "It would have been better if . . ."; "I was lucky"; or wait for the compliments to be followed by criticism. Other typical responses from the majority were, "I can't take all the credit"; "Anyone could have done it"; "This old thing? I've had it for years."

There is a basic psychological law to this effect: We tend to act in harmony with our self-image. If our self-image (self-respect, self-love, self-worth) is weak, a compliment may be out of harmony with the way we perceive ourselves, in which case we tend to reject it.

What *can* one say, then, that does not seem conceited, nor yet self-abasing? Self-accepting people respond with neither "Oh, I thought my performance was awful!" or "Yes, I agree I was pretty wonderful." Instead, a simple "Thank you" suffices. By practicing that, one can overcome any mild embarrassment when praise is offered.

—From Cecil G. Osborne, *The Art of Learning to Love Yourself.* Grand Rapids: Zondervan, 1976.

FOR FURTHER READING:

Leman, Kevin. *Sex Begins in the Kitchen.* Ventura, Calif.: Regal, 1981.

Shedd, Charlie W. *Letters to Karen.* Nashville: Abingdon, 1965.

Wood, Leland Foster. *Harmony in Marriage.* Old Tappan, N.J.: Revell, 1979.

CONFLICT

WHAT EXACTLY is conflict? For some the word conjures up scenes of battlegrounds and warfare. This is one of the meanings of conflict, but the meaning with which this chapter is concerned is, according to Webster, "Disagreement, emotional tension resulting from incompatible inner needs or drives."

That definition is a challenge for every married couple. How can they handle their disagreements—the tensions that come when the needs and drives of one spouse are at cross-purposes with the other? How do they keep cross-purposes from becoming crossed swords?

Every married couple needs to know how to deal with conflict in a creative, constructive way.

Objectivity, flexibility, willingness to compromise (Is squeezing the toothpaste tube at the bottom rather than in the middle *really* one of the big issues of life?) and the willingness to let the other person be himself, all need to be developed if couples are to enjoy a satisfying and growing marriage relationship.

DON'T AVOID CONFLICT WITH THE SILENT TREATMENT

Some people use the "silent treatment" as a means of avoiding controversy. They use silence as a weapon to control, frustrate or manipulate their spouse. Or sometimes the husband or wife takes the pathway of silence because it seems to be the least painful. Perhaps one spouse is silent now because in the past the other spouse was not a ready listener. Also, there's always the possibility of a deep hurt that is keeping one marriage partner silent.

But silence never pays off in the long run. "Silence is golden" so the saying goes, but it can also be yellow! Don't hide behind silence because you are afraid to deal with the issue at hand.

Marriage counselors estimate that at least one half of the cases they see involve a silent husband. Men have a tendency to avoid conflict in discussion. Ironically, the issues they avoid are often the ones that indicate where

adjustments and changes need to be made—and fast.

Here is a typical pattern that results in the use of silence. When married partners are not communicating because one of them is silent, both of them experience frustration and a rising sense of futility, all of which compounds the silence problem. The more the communicative person tries to talk, the farther the silent person draws into his hostile shell. The person who is trying to talk then feels increasingly useless, inadequate and hurt. The talkative spouse may try shouting, or even violence, in an attempt to drive the silent mate from his refuge. But this is futile because it does nothing more than to drive the silent spouse into deeper silence. When you say to a silent person, "Why don't you talk to me?" or "Please say something—why can't we communicate?" or similar pleas, it usually does nothing more than reinforce that person's silence!

How, then, do you encourage the silent person to talk? First, you have to let the silent partner choose the time to speak. Then, when this person does speak, you must communicate in every way you can that you're willing to listen without judging what is said; that you are willing to accept feelings and frustrations. The silent person must find that you really do listen and care. If you create an acceptant, unthreatening climate, the silent spouse will in all likelihood start talking and then communication can begin or be reestablished.

DON'T SAVE "EMOTIONAL TRADING STAMPS"

Always watch yourself to make sure you're not saving up hostility yourself. A husband or wife, for example, could easily save up a lot of hostility when trying to deal with a mate who is dealing out the silent treatment (discussed above). But the worst method of dealing with feelings or irritation or frustration is to deny them and bottle them up. Feelings must be expressed. They shouldn't be allowed to accumulate.

Some individuals, however, deal with

their emotions like trading stamps. They save up each little irritation as though it were a stamp. They accumulate many stamps and finally, when something happens that is the last straw they blow up and "cash in" with all of their pent up irritations and frustrations. Their emotional trading-stamp book becomes full, and they decide that now is the time to trade it in. In this way they think "they get something back" for all of their trouble. They "redeem their trading stamps," so to speak, and tell themselves, "Well, now at least I feel better."

Are you an emotional stamp saver? If you suspect that you are, now is the time to start doing something about it. It is much better to release your emotions as they *arise*. God created all of us to feel deeply, but we must express what we feel. Our expressions should, and can be, done in a healthy way.

Much of the arguing, quarreling, fighting that occurs between married couples turns into sadistic, emotionally crippling sessions. How do *you* handle your disagreements?

A crucial question is how you handle anger—those strong, even passionate, feelings of displeasure that well up within. How does your anger handle you?

Suppose your spouse acts negatively toward you or even gets angry with you. Ask yourself these questions:

Am I really being hurt or affected by this?

Will counter-anger, even if it's justified and rational, really help here?

Is getting angry the most effective thing I can do?

What will my anger accomplish?

How do I respond to or answer another person who is angry? Whatever you do, do not tell the other person, "Now don't get angry." When you say that, it has exactly the opposite effect! Instead, try saying as sincerely as you can, "I'm sorry something is making you angry. If it's me, I apologize. What can I do to help?" This suggestion is effective at home, at work—just about anywhere. Strangely enough it sounds vaguely familiar—"like something from the Bible." Solomon, who had quite a bit of marital ex-

perience, once wrote. *A soft answer turns away wrath* (Prov. 15:1, *Amplified*).

—From H. Norman Wright, *Communication: Key to Your Marriage.* Ventura, Calif.: Regal, 1974.

Resolving Family Conflicts

Every family has problems and conflicts. Struggles consist of relating to each other, of satisfactorily working out everyday routines, of meeting each person's needs. There are problems with children at different ages and stages—involving money, health, friends, responsibilities, tragedies, accidents, death, etc.

Surveys point out that successful families have problems identical to those of unhappy families involved in open conflict. The difference is that happy families learn to work through their conflicts as they surface. They learn to face the situation honestly. They try to resolve their differences and arrive at a satisfactory solution for all. They're interested in harmony in the home.

When family problems arise in your home, do you tend to blame someone else? Do you try to resolve conflicts with angry words, physical attacks, or the silent treatment? None of these really are solutions. They only create more problems and conflicts.

The key to resolving family conflicts lies in the husband-wife relationship. How do Dad and Mom face their problems? If they are able to resolve their differences in a good way, they are supplying a positive example for their children to follow.

Henry would "burn up" every time he came home to a littered-up house. His wife, June, knew this. At first she reacted negatively. After all, what did it matter—some magazines and a book or two on the floor, a pair of slippers in the middle of the room, a table full of clothes that needed to be folded. At least they were clean. He should appreciate that!

June always defended herself: "I don't think our house is a mess. You ought to see my sister's house!" They'd end up arguing, followed by the silent treatment. After several months, Henry stayed away more and more with excuses such as "I have extra work at the office," or "The fellows want me to go out with them."

Fortunately, June realized what was happening. She really did want to have a home he'd be happy to come to. So one evening when both of them were in a good mood she asked him directly, "Honey, are you staying away because you can't stand an untidy house?"

To June's straightforward confrontation, Henry responded honestly, "I'm afraid so." He then proceeded to discuss his feelings. June expressed hers also and admitted her I-don't-care attitude. Henry admitted he was too much of a perfectionist. They both asked forgiveness and pledged their willingness to cooperate with each other. Their love for and desire to please each other were greater than personal preferences.

That was the beginning of a change. June needed help to know how to keep house. A close friend gave her some simple, helpful tips: Have a place for books and magazines and return them when you're through reading for the day. After you kick off your shoes, put them in a corner or under the couch. June put a table in the laundry room where she could dump the clean clothes that needed folding. She also planned a daily schedule. She was glad she did. She needed this experience before the children came—when it was even more difficult to keep a tidy home. Henry became more cooperative. He helped her when he could.

Several guidelines helped Henry and June resolve their conflicts. Any couple can use these guidelines in their own particular conflicts and struggles toward compatibility. They are also applicable in resolving conflicts between them and a child, or any other person.

1. Admit there is a conflict.
2. Look at the problem when both are in a good mood, if possible.
3. Honestly share feelings about the situation.
4. Stick with the issue at hand. Don't dig into the past or start attacking each other.
5. Lower your voice.
6. Find a positive approach for yourself rather than for your spouse.
7. Be patient through the struggle of changing behavior patterns.
8. Cooperate with each other through the problem.
9. Be interested in the happiness and welfare of each other.
10. Affirm your love for each other.

For some couples, guidelines aren't sufficient. They may need to confide in another person—a trusted friend or a pastor—in order to arrive at a satisfactory solution.

If a couple cannot reach agreement on the issue after honestly sharing feelings and needs, one may find the solution by giving in 100 percent in supporting the other's wishes. Love is the basis for resolving conflicts. Love cares. Love wants to please, not demand. Love doesn't limit either husband or wife to the fifty-fifty basis: "I gave in last time. It's your turn now!" That's law, not love!

I believe God intended the home to be the laboratory of life. There the child *learns* how to live with others. Brothers and sisters and parents form a little community, a miniature world, where together they practice the lessons of life. When there are no good models, where there are only bitter quarrels and fights, couples often separate and the children scatter and may become delinquents. Children need models to show them *how* to work through conflicts.

—From Ella May Miller, *The Peacemakers*. Old Tappan, N.J.: Revell, 1977.

FOR FURTHER READING:

Augsburger, David. *Caring Enough to Confront*. Ventura, Calif.: Regal, 1981.

Bird, Joseph and Lois. *To Live As a Family*. Garden City, N.Y.: Doubleday, 1982.

Davis, Creath. *How to Win in a Crisis*. Grand Rapids: Zondervan, 1976.

MacDonald, Gordon. *Magnificent Marriage.* Wheaton, Ill.: Tyndale, 1976.

Wilke, Richard B. *Tell Me Again, I'm Listening.* Nashville: Abingdon, 1973.

COOKING

COOKING GIVES women a greater opportunity to shape their family members' lives than any other area of homemaking. A gleaming bathroom won't see the family through the morning, but a nutritious breakfast will. A freshly polished floor won't influence anybody's outlook on life, but the consumption of either sugar or protein will. A lovingly sewn slipcover won't change anybody's health, but well-planned meals can mean fewer visits to the doctor and dentist.

The power a homemaker holds when she takes charge of a kitchen is tremendous. Food preparation is much more than just filling empty stomachs. Proper food promotes physical, mental, and spiritual well being. Perhaps the most memorable example is found in the story of Daniel and his three friends. These young men chose to eat good wholesome food instead of the rich delicacies from the king's table. The result? "And at the end of ten days their countenances appeared fairer and fatter in flesh than all the children which did eat the portion of the king's meat" (Daniel 1:15).

Ironically, some Christians seem to have the idea that the body doesn't matter much at all. The body is only the "container" for the soul, they say. Paul, however, had a different opinion of the worth of the body. He said that the body of a Christian is a temple of the Holy Spirit (1 Corinthians 6:19), and that alone is reason enough to take good care of ourselves.

The business of taking good care of the body is not something outrageously impossible to do. Rather it is just what is *reasonable.* Paul, in Romans 12:1, says, "I beseech you therefore, brethren, by the mercies of God, that ye present your bodies a living sacrifice, holy, acceptable unto God, which is your reasonable service."

Back to School?

Would you apply for a typist's job without first learning to type? Would you be able to do an efficient job as a teacher without first getting an education? Of course, such ideas are ridiculous, but every day a similar ridiculous thing is happening in many kitchens. Homemakers who don't know anything about nutrition are preparing meals for families and are inadvertently shaping lives— many times in directions in which they should not go.

Nutrition information comes about in different ways. We study the basic food groups for a day or two in a high school home economics course or we simply cook as our mothers did, and, if the food is nutritious, it is merely by accident. Some of us learn to cook by color. We like a meal to look appealing, so we add a colorful vegetable or a green salad. Yet none of this constitutes a real education in nutrition. Education usually comes about when a family member is diagnosed as being diabetic, hyperactive, or obese. It is a little frightening to get a crash course in nutrition in order to save somebody's life, yet every day some homemaker is having to rethink her menus because of the threat of high blood pressure or too much cholesterol.

The wise homemaker learns about good nutrition and then puts it into practice *before* sickness forces her to learn. And the learning really isn't all that difficult. The Government Printing Office has most of the information you will need in the *Handbook of Basic Food Values.* (Write to the Superintendent of Documents, Washington, D.C. 20402 for your copy.)

—From Edith Flowers Kilgo, *Handbook for Christian Homemakers.* Grand Rapids: Baker Book, 1982.

FOR FURTHER READING:

Kerr, Graham. *The Love Feast.* New York: Simon & Schuster, 1978.

Lappé, Frances Moore. *Diet for a Small Planet.* New York: Ballantine, 1980.

COUNSELING

THE TERM *counselor* is gradually becoming an umbrella term covering everything from those who give intensive psychotherapy to others who offer gentle advice. Some are referred to as counselors though they never chose the title and do not particularly want it.

Thus social workers, nurses, psychiatrists, psychologists, welfare workers, school guidance counselors and a host of other professionals who are consulted about personal problems have come to be known as counselors. Training courses in counseling are multiplying and graduates may be referred to as pastoral counselors, marriage counselors or family counselors, according to the nature of the training they have received.

Because the training of counselors varies widely their skills will likewise vary, some having special skills that others lack. Psychiatrists and psychologists, for example, will have a better working knowledge of the central nervous system than say pastoral counselors whose expertise lies in biblical and doctrinal knowledge. Even more important . . . the experience, the personalities and the attitudes of counselors vary to affect their usefulness.

There are thus two kinds of information one should seek about counselors: first, about their training and theoretical orientation and second, about their personality. Both kinds of information are important, and if one kind is more important than the other, I would say (though many professional colleagues would disagree with me) that it is their personalities, their length of experience, their degree of interest in each client, their capacity for warmth, their objectivity and freedom from prejudice. As to the different kinds of counselors and the training they receive, sketches of some of them follow below.

1. *Pastors.* Some pastors give time to counseling even though they have had no special training. Others take special courses from seminaries or from seminaries in conjunction with university behavioral science departments. Their training may include a theoretical review of different psychological schools along with some practical supervision of clients they counsel during their training. It may lead to a doctoral degree and even postdoctoral work. Usually the training places special emphasis on marital and premarital counseling. Some pastoral counselors are trained to administer psychological tests to people they seek to help.

2. *Psychologists.* Psychologists are specialists in human behavior whose primary interest is in normal rather than abnormal behavior. Many psychologists devote themselves to research, studying animals to gain clues about human behavior or else studying undergraduates, the species of human they have the greatest access to. They could be referred to as *nonclinical* psychologists.

Other psychologists are trained to administer tests, tests that attempt to evaluate personality, intelligence and potential problem areas. Increasing numbers of psychologists are interested in counseling which they may refer to as psychotherapy. (The term *psychotherapy* was originally coined by psychoanalysts to refer to a modified form of psychoanalysis. Nowadays *psychotherapy* can mean whatever the user of the term wants it to mean and is often used synonymously with counseling.)

Psychologists who administer tests and those who give counsel both refer to themselves as *clinical* psychologists. Their theoretical orientations may vary widely. I meet psychologists whose views are psychoanalytic, others who are followers of Piaget, others who are essentially humanists, still others who adhere to one of the many behaviorist schools and some who are interested in Gestalt psychology, to mention only a few. Christian psychologists who have thought carefully about psychological theories in relation to a biblical view of human nature are in a position to make use of the insights from various schools without adopting the underlying philosophies associated with them.

Clinical psychologists differ also according to the ages of the clients who interest them. Thus there are child psychologists, adolescent psychologists and so on. Or again, psychologists may take a special interest in group psychotherapy, in family therapy or in T groups.

3. *Psychiatrists.* Psychiatrists are physicians who have specialized in mental illness. Unlike psychologists they have a greater tendency to focus on abnormal rather than normal behavior. As a psychiatrist myself, I believe our greatest usefulness lies in the diagnosis and the treatment of the graver forms of emotional disturbance. However, psychiatrists vary as much in interests, activities and beliefs as do psychologists. In many medical schools and universities psychologists and psychiatrists work together in departments of human behavior.

Perhaps the most significant difference between the two is that in most areas in the Western Hemisphere only psychiatrists, because they are physicians, are permitted to prescribe medication. It is possible that economic and political factors will gradually force psychiatrists back into the role of medical consultants, but at present many psychiatrists prefer to spend a great deal of their time giving psychotherapy or counseling.

While all psychiatrists are physicians specializing in mental illness, psychoanalysts are psychiatrists who have undergone psychoanalysis themselves and have taken training from a recognized training analyst. (Psychoanalysis is a school of thought which originated with Sigmund Freud and which now has many forms.) Outside North America one may practice as a psychoanalyst without being a physician since psychoanalysis does not involve administering medication.

4. *Social Workers.* Psychologists, psychiatrists, education and pastoral counselors may all be engaged in giving counsel of varying kinds and depths, sometimes referring to the counsel as psychotherapy. Social workers, too, whose role used to be conceived as that of giving direction to people whose distress called for social help, are now increasingly engaged in general and marital counseling and psychotherapy. Their training may include both theoretical and clinical exposure to psychological theories and to counseling practice.

5. *Nonprofessional Groups.* It should be clear by now that while I have a healthy regard for good training and proper qualifications I have an even greater respect for experience, intuitive perceptiveness and a capacity for warmth. This being the case I would not hesitate at times to recommend the help of nonprofessional agencies. . . .

6. *School Guidance Centers.* Sometimes help is offered to children via school systems. Many school systems enjoy the resources of child guidance centers staffed by social workers, psychologists, speech therapists, education specialists and psychiatrists. Once teachers see that a child has problems, especially ones that guidance counselors in the school are unable to handle, the school may request (with or without the parents' knowledge and consent) help from the guidance center.

In most cases the system is beneficial and works for the child's good. Almost invariably the guidance center will contact parents who will be interviewed by a member of the center's staff in order to get more information about the child's problem.

Christian parents are sometimes uneasy about the kind of help the center offers, help which may range from speech therapy to psychoanalytic psychotherapy. They face a choice between accepting what the center has to offer (usually without any charge) and opting for private help for which they will have to pay.

It is hard for me to give guidelines which are equally valid in all parts of the [country]. Generally, where speech difficulties and dyslexias are concerned, parents do well to accept help from the guidance center. Problems are more likely to arise where the help involves family therapy or the treatment of emotional and behavioral disorders. Here everything will depend on the background and personality of the therapist concerned. If parents are uneasy, however, they still face the problem of where to find suitable help in the community.

CHOOSING FROM THE POTPOURRI

To the onlookers it must seem confusing. Increasing numbers of professions are getting into the act of helping people by listening to them and making wise and helpful comments. Unhappily there are rivalries not only between the distinct professions but among various groups within each profession. Thus an analytically oriented psychiatrist will feel more akin to an analytically oriented social worker than to a fellow psychiatrist who leans more toward behavioral psychology.

How then can a troubled parent select from the potpourri of professions, qualifications, theoretical orientations and personalities the person most likely to be of help? Let me make a few suggestions.

1. *Your Child Must Want Help.* With younger children the rule does not necessarily hold. You can win a younger child over and influence him or her for good. But the older children grow, the more important is the rule that they must want help if they are to get it. By the time children are in their late teens, no experts are going to set matters right unless the help is warmly welcomed and eagerly made use of.

Many parents bring me rebellious teenagers with the plea, "Please change her, doctor!" But I can't change anyone who doesn't want to be changed. It is quite another matter if the teen-ager says, "I don't know why I act the way I do and I want to change. Please help me." But such a desire is a sine qua non for professional help. And if the root of the trouble lies in fouled up communications in the family as a whole, then the members of the family must likewise recognize that they are involved in the problem and be eager to work at it.

Professionals are not magicians. At best they can assess accurately and give valuable pointers. Don't consult them unless those with problems are prepared to resolve them.

2. *Check With a Family Physician or a Pastor.* If you already know of a competent Christian counselor, consult him. But if not, your family doctor may have an idea whether it is medical help or nonmedical help you need. Your minister as well as your physician will have a more adequate grasp of community resources than you and be able to point to the particular person who can best help. They may also know which of the local professionals or clinics, while not themselves Christian, are sympathetic toward the faith of their clients.

3. *Do Not Refuse Help Because It Comes From a Non-Christian.* I can sympathize with those of my correspondents who will not contemplate help from a non-Christian. I can fully undertand that a Christian will have more confidence in a fellow believer. Yet from my vantage within the profession, having talked with scores of my colleagues about their own faith and the faith of their patients, I know that many of them have genuine respect for a faith they do not share. They would regard it as a gross breach of professional ethics to do or say anything that would undermine Christian (or any other) faith. I wish I could make the same claim for all my colleagues, but I cannot.

There is something else you should think of. We have a proverb: The looker-on sees most of the game. We fool ourselves as Christians into believing that non-Christians are unable to understand our words and actions. While this may be true some of the time, non-Christians see through us a good deal of the time precisely because they look at us with worldly-wise eyes. We close our minds at many points to the conviction of the Holy Spirit to such a degree that he has to use a non-Christian mouthpiece to point out where we are fooling ourselves.

4. *Be More Concerned About the Person Than the Qualifications.* This point bears

repetition. All the qualifications in the world are not worth as much as experience. If one of my own children needed help I would (if the choice lay between the two) choose a warm, firm, understanding and experienced social worker—even one without a degree—rather than a brilliant psychiatrist recently qualified from the best school in the country. I would also choose a competent and experienced non-Christian over an inexperienced Christian.

—From John White, *Parents in Pain*. Downers Grove, Ill.: InterVarsity Press, 1979.

CREDIT

"DON'T YOU know? Every woman, married or single must establish her own credit rating."

"Why?"

"If your husband left for some reason and all your credit ratings were in his name, where would you be?"

"Home—and lonely," I mused.

. . . . .

How to Get a Good Credit Rating

First of all, in case you're saying, "Okay, maybe I should have a credit rating, but what is it," I'll tell you. A credit rating is a record of your past spending habits and paying performance. Creditors use it to check on whether or not you can meet your obligations. Proof of your ability to pay enhances your chances for a loan.

At this point you may want to check to see if you are already on record. Perhaps you had established credit before you married. If so, have them change your name or add your married name to your maiden name. This credit check on yourself will probably cost you about five dollars and can be accomplished by calling a credit rating agency. TRW Credit Data is one that has offices throughout the United States.

If you find you really don't exist, at least

on the computer's readout and feel the need to be somebody, take these steps.

1. Apply for credit at a department store in your name only. Use your name, Rose Ann Turner, not Mrs. John. This type of credit is easiest to get. However, I feel I must caution you. If a credit card in your hands turns into a super-powered money eater, move on to suggestions three and four.

2. If you and your husband already have several credit cards, write to one or two of the creditors and ask them to issue a separate account in your name. This new credit card of your very own should be used sparingly. Make occasional small purchases and always pay off the bill at the end of each month to avoid interest charges.

3. The next time you need to purchase a larger item, such as a washer, dryer, television, or microwave, charge it on a ninety-day-same-as-cash loan. Many retail stores offer this service to customers. You can have three months to pay it off with no interest. Secure the loan in your name. Avoid debt. Save the money and make payments from savings.

4. Open your own checking or savings account. Some women I know have a separate checking account for household expenses. Talk with your husband about the pros and cons of such an arrangement. And, be careful the bank charges don't eat all your money. By having your own account the bank can serve as a handy reference for a loan officer. You can also ask to have your banking record appear on your credit rating.

Using Credit

In the credit game there are rules as well as a financial lingo that you will want to learn before you play. Here are some rules that may help.

1. Be aware of and ready to fulfill your responsibility in repaying the loan. Know when the payments are due and how much

they will be. Also be aware that the creditor can tack on a late charge. Of course the loan company won't mind if you're a few days late, they'll just demand five dollars a day or more in late charges.

2. Know the legal lingo. While I can't take the space here to write you a dictionary of financial terms, I will give you explanations as I use them. If before signing a contract you come across a term you don't understand, ask someone; or if you're embarrassed, excuse yourself to the ladies' room and look it up in your dictionary. Better yet, ask to take a copy of the contract home with you so you can study it at your leisure and perhaps ask a trusted and experienced friend.

One woman I know of nearly lost her home because she signed on the line without full understanding of the contract terms. The contract called for a balloon payment at the end of five years. She thought at the time it was a strange request, shrugged it off as a quirk, and forgot it.

Five years later she got a letter threatening to foreclose if she couldn't come up with the balloon payment of $40,000. The "balloon" payment was the whole balance she owed on the house. Although she managed to secure a bank loan, she could have saved herself much grief by knowing the rules first.

3. Realize that the lending institutions don't loan you money out of the goodness of their hearts, but because they make money on interest rates, and fees. Consequently you are doing them a favor by letting them loan you money. I'm not telling you this so you can gain a sense of superiority, only so you won't feel lowly and intimidated.

4. Anytime you use a credit card you are borrowing money. If you pay off the balance in full each month you pay no interest and in fact will be using that institution's money for free.

5. Credit expands your buying power when used within the guidelines of your budget. It can ease the discomfort of expending large amounts of cash by allowing you to pay over a period of time. However, when you use that power as the pot at the end of the rainbow and if most of your transactions are made on credit—you're probably in big trouble.

6. The more money you have, the easier it is to get a loan. Does that make sense? It's like the old saying "Them that has gets." How true. The easiest loans to obtain at the lowest interest rates are those which are fully secured. In other words, if you want to borrow $10,000 and you have $10,000 in a savings account, the bank will loan you the money. They usually charge about 1 percent more than what you would be receiving in interest on the saved money. The $10,000 in your savings account is frozen by the bank until you've paid off your loan. It is used as collateral. I know, you're thinking, *That doesn't make any sense either. Why would anyone need to borrow money they already have?* Don't ask me. I really couldn't tell you. I think it's one of those strange rules someone made up when the board of directors were out to lunch.

7. The game is over for you when you fail to meet your financial responsibilities.

8. The credit game is a dangerous one. If you're not careful it can plunge you into a case of the Credit Card Crazies.

Surviving the Credit Card Crazies

In a world of plastic money that's as good as cash, it's easy to get ourselves overextended. The line we walk between safety and disaster in credit card use is as fine as the one between sanity and mindlessness. In fact, the way we behave toward spending money depends a lot on our mind control. How much control do you have? Have you developed a case of the "crazies"? Here's a quiz that will give you the answer.

	Yes	No
• Do you have six or more credit cards?	☐	☐
• Do you use three or more of those cards on a regular basis?	☐	☐
• Do you worry about whether or not you'll be able to make your credit card payments at the end of each month?	☐	☐
• Have you been operating in the red for two or more months in a row?	☐	☐
• Do you feel a pang of guilt when you pull out a card to pay for an item?	☐	☐
• Do you often charge, knowing you don't have funds in the bank to cover that amount?	☐	☐
• Do you buy small items on credit that you wouldn't buy or couldn't buy if you had to use cash?	☐	☐
• Do you often pay only the minimum required balance on your charge statement?	☐	☐
• Do you receive notices of late payments?	☐	☐
• Does more than 20 percent of your income go for paying of credit card or installment loans?	☐	☐
• Do you buy on credit to lift you out of the "I ain't got no money" blues?	☐	☐
• Do you ever charge as a revenge tactic against the husband who says no?	☐	☐

Positive answers to six or more means you've developed a full-blown case of the Credit Card Crazies. Three to five affirmatives leaves you mildly afflicted. One to two yes answers means exposure to the disease and in order to survive I suggest you immunize against further attack. Here are some guidelines that can nurse you back to sanity and help you sidestep further complications.

1. Use cash or your checkbook whenever possible.

2. Reduce the number of credit cards you carry with you. If you can remain disciplined and immune and never charge more than you can pay off at the end of the month, go ahead and keep your favorite cards. If you are crazed with an out-of-control budget, even one card can mean disaster. For complete protection against the crazies, leave the cards at home. In severe cases of the crazies the only cure is surgery. Cut those plastic money munchers into guitar picks for your budding musician, or slip the tiny plastic chips in the garbage.

3. Refrain from buying when depressed. Do you ever experience mood swings? I do. In fact, the days just before my period I usually feel about as low as an alto with a cold. I think, *Maybe if I buy a little something just for me* . . . At times like these my sales resistance is low and advertisers can make me believe anything. I'd like to take my "so-worldly, so-welcome" MasterCard and fly off to the Riviera, or slip into a designer sack from Saks. Instead I should be praying, "Lord, lead me not into the temptation to charge."

4. If shopping really does lift your spirits, do it; only don't spend any money. If you just gasped and said, "I can't," relax, I'll tell you how. Leave your credit cards and checkbook *and* cash at home. Try on all the clothes you want. Be extravagant, you can afford it. Whenever you find the perfect dress, hat, shoes, bag, fur coat, or whatever, ask the clerk to hold it for you for an hour or so. Have your fling. When it's over go home. List all those must-have items, if you can remember them, and rationally consider each one. Is it something you need? Can your budget handle the expense? If you decide the item needs you as much as you need it, call the store and ask them to hold it for you until you can come back.

5. Pay your entire bill each month. I have devised a method of doing this that is entirely pain free. Even the usually agoniz-

ing procedure of writing a check to pay the bill quiets into a dull ache. I list each charge as I make it in my checkbook and subtract it from the balance. Beside each entry I indicate which card was used. For example MC means MasterCard and AMX stands for American Express. At the end of each month I mark each entry with a yellow marker. I then add them up and subtract them from my total cash supply so I can balance the check statement. The amount I have deducted for charges will cover my bills and there's no chance of my not having enough money to pay it all off. I find this method cuts down on credit card use because, if I don't have the money in my checking account I won't buy.

Another method that works for a friend of mine is this. Keep a small diary or notebook in your purse. In it write each of your charge cards by name and set a limit. When you've reached your limit stop charging. Keeping track of your day-to-day charges makes you painfully aware of where your money goes.

7.　Pay off your debts as soon as possible. If you have allowed your credit card bills to zoom out of control, see about getting a consumer loan (at less interest) to pay your smaller bills off. If you must take this step to get yourself out of debt, then by all means, stop using the credit cards. The Credit Card Crazies can be much like alcoholism. If you have the disease, you must give up the habit "cold turkey" or you'll fall back into the same trap.

Although the Crazies doesn't destroy your body like alcohol or drugs and you probably won't die from an overdose, your budget could. You stand the chance of facing bankruptcy. In either case, you lose.

8.　If you feel overwhelmed by your debts and can't get yourself out of debt, seek professional help. Many cities offer programs with counseling services.

9.　Consider the following thoughts while you decide whether credit cards and installment loans are for you.

Proverbs 22:7 ". . . the borrower is the slave of the lender." (RSV)

First John 2:15, "Do not love the world or the things in the world." (RSV)

Romans 13:8, "Owe no one anything, except to love one another . . ." (RSV)

I'm not trying to convict you or convince you that credit is an evil influence. Used for the right purpose and with deliberate control it can make us better stewards of the money God allows us. Used wrongly, credit can control us.

—From Patricia H. Rushford, *From Money Mess to Money Management.* Old Tappan, N.J.: Revell, 1984.

FOR FURTHER READING:

Dayton, Howard L., Jr. *Your Money: Frustration or Freedom?* Wheaton, Ill.: Tyndale, 1979.

Fooshee, George, Jr. *You Can Be Financially Free.* Old Tappan, N.J.: Revell, 1976.

D

DATING

How to Meet Men

"Women are like elephants to me," W. C. Fields once joked. "I like to look at them, but I wouldn't want to own one." While you may not appreciate his sense of humor, Fields touches on a truth which every woman ought to consider. The women men like to look at aren't necessarily the ones they want to live with, or even meet.

There are two places to meet elephants. You can see them at the circus where they are painted up and trained and made to act just so. Or you can make the trip to their natural habitat in Africa and watch as they revel in their freedom while enjoying elephanthood. The elephant at the circus puts on an impressive show but is disappointingly shallow when you get to know it as an elephant. It's not nearly as easy to get close to a wild elephant, but once you do you'll be overwhelmed by its authenticity. You'll take pictures and then tell your friends, "Now *there's* a real elephant!"

It's best to meet men in their natural habitat, too. But to do so doesn't require that you join a safari, hire a guide, or scramble over dusty trails in a jeep for weeks on end. At least, not for most men. But if we get the impression you're going to gun us down, you can be sure we'll run for the hills.

The best strategy for getting next to elusive, undomesticated single men is the method used by nature photographers: patience. Don't stalk them relentlessly. Rather, observe habits, find out migration patterns, locate favorite water holes, and see if you can't find out why and how they live as they do. This requires careful observation.

The first thing you'll notice is that the typical American male has an apartment or owns his own home and returns each evening year-round, with only a few exceptions. He feels right at home here and will likely welcome visitors—especially if they show up bearing symbols of neighborly goodwill such as homemade food of any kind. One way to a man's heart is through his stomach.

Usually no visitors show up in the evening, so he pursues other activities such as gloomily watching television, quietly reading a book or magazine, carefully fixing something around the house, tinkering with his car, or patiently engaging in a favorite hobby. Some listen to music or write letters. A growing number trot out the back door for a daily six-mile run or spend a couple of hours on the tennis courts or at the racquet ball club.

All of these activities have value in their own right and may be practiced regularly. You might consider developing similar interests yourself. They are not only enjoyable and rewarding, they also provide opportunities and places to meet men. Knowledge in these areas also provides you with common ground for conversation once you've met. For example, a friend of mine at Michigan State University started spending his lunch hour at the pool; and he reported that it was the most refreshing part of his day, especially since he met Carol there. Now he has lunch with her one day a week after their swim.

To a large extent, the activities men engage in are substitutes for human companionship. Generally, a man will enthusiastically include you in his plans or else make room for you in his weekly or monthly schedule—but it might require a bit of initiative on your part. If you have not developed an interest that the two of you can enjoy together, you won't thrive on each other's company. In fact, you'll probably never meet.

Here's another strategy. Some men have jobs in offices where they make important decisions and attend stuffy conferences and deal with pages full of either numbers or words. The term "luncheon meeting" is familiar to this type of man. He won't mind at all if you ask him out to lunch—especially if it's just to relax and enjoy each other's company. Unless he is overweight, the most nonthreatening environment for him, next to his home, is a restaurant. If you ask him out you should also offer to pick up the tab; but, of course, he will probably insist on paying at least his half of the bill. Chivalry is not that dead!

If he has a job running machines or screwing nuts onto bolts or doing janitorial work or painting buildings or washing windows, he might feel out of place in a restaurant at noon, but would probably appreciate being invited over to your place for an evening meal.

Today there is absolutely nothing wrong about women initiating relationships. If you call him up and say you really want to attend a play or movie or concert or whatever, but don't like the idea of going alone, there's a good chance he'll be more than happy to accompany you. Unless he can't stand plays, or movies, or concerts, or whatever. The other possibility is that he already has something planned for that evening, in which case he'll say he is really sorry, but how about another time? If he really is sorry, you can expect to hear from him in the near future—unless he's terribly busy. If that's the case, the reason may be that he's working two jobs to get out of a tight financial situation. But more than likely he has intentionally made himself busy in order to avoid relationships. If that seems to be the case, let him alone—at least for now. We are all in the process of growing, changing, and adjusting to new situations in life. Although he appears to want to be left alone for the time being, in six months he may come to realize that he would value your friendship highly.

You may notice that on a Sunday morning some men will put on a jacket and tie, tuck a Bible under their arms, and set out for the neighborhood place of worship. These men are especially fascinating; and if they suspect that you share their ideas and beliefs about the Creator, the world itself, and the people who live here, they may be even more receptive to the idea of friendship with you. Worship with them, discuss the Word with them, sing with them. Find out what companionship is really all about. A young lady I know started her own home Bible study and has more men coming over each week than she knows what to do with! Nice guys, too!

Every man is different from every other man. And no two women are exactly alike either. So it is impossible to give you specific things to do to meet a certain man—except that in the beginning you must identify one interest that you both have in common and then participate in this event together. The relationship will grow from there.

Maybe you have the patience of Job, have done everything I've suggested for meeting men in their own environments, and still feel like a dismal failure. If so, ask yourself why. It's possible that you're expecting too much from the relationship. Do you tell yourself each time you meet a man: *Ah, this is the one!* Even if this is the way you feel, don't try to lock him up for keeps. The nature photographer within you would suggest letting him roam—thus introducing you to others in the process of your relationship. This doesn't mean you should exploit your friends; just enjoy them for what they are. They will be rewarding in their own right and will also lead to still other friendships.

One example will explain what I mean. My friend Reneé got married; since we work together we continued as friends, and I also became friends with her husband, Kirk. Then, one day she told me about Becky, another friend she wanted me to meet.

Three months later I finally mustered the

courage to ask Becky out. We had a great time. And, though I soon realized there was no romantic interest between us, we continued to enjoy each other's company. Then one day Becky invited me to a party at her place where I met Debbi, Cindy, Cathy, Sandy, and Joan. They are all nice girls; and, since I try not to be too selfish, a few months later I had Becky and her batch of friends over to my place where they got acquainted with my buddies Wendall, Doug, Tim, John, and Dave. It works both ways!

It has been said that success in business and in getting a job depends more on who you know than on what you know. The same is true in relationships. Treasure the friends you have; they will lead you to still others. (I can hardly wait till next Friday. That's when my friend Mark's new wife, Denise, will introduce me to her former college roommate Sue.)

One other thing: To avoid white-elephant relationships, be yourself. Meet men as you are, not as you think they expect you to be. In the long run most men are more impressed by women who are secure within their own identities than by any circus act they may be able to pull together. Accepting yourself as you are enables you to accept the men you meet as they are. The result can be good friendships—and many of them.

—Dan Runyon, "How to Meet Men," *Christian Single,* February 1983.

Dating for the Formerly Married

For most people, dating again and thinking of remarriage is natural. But there are, especially for the Christian, wrong times and wrong motives for the dating. Here are a few:

1. Don't date to show up your ex. Don't date to retaliate. Date for you.
2. Don't date to prove yourself. You have nothing to prove. You're a unique, lovable child of God.
3. Don't date merely to avoid loneliness. Date because you have something to offer in companionship and because you really want to.
4. Don't date to make yourself anything.

When a marriage ends, the persons involved often suffer from a self-hate feeling. You are a worthwhile person. Learn to like yourself first. Then begin dating.

You're ready to date people again. And it's hard. You feel like a teenager, very self-conscious, unsure of yourself. When you do go out, your voice sounds nervous even to you. Your hands are clammy. You find yourself tightening up because you want to do everything right. If you can remember back during your teen years, you're going through the stage of self-assurance. It'll get easier.

One tendency is to look at every datable person as a potential marriage partner. Try not to get involved in that game. Accept the dates for what they are right now. Don't project into the future. You may be so starved for appreciation that anyone who finds you attractive seems like the greatest person in the world. But remember, you felt that way about the first two or three people you dated as a teenager, too!

Maybe you don't know *how* to start dating again. Think about these ideas.

1. Get out and do things besides your job. Find activities you enjoy for their own sake. Investigate needlepoint. Or a course in mechanics. Attend lectures. If you're a woman and you go to activities where only women attend, go anyway. First, because you're going for your own sake. Second, because even there you might get introduced to someone who introduces you to somebody else.

2. Some have tried the computer services that they find in newspaper ads. You don't need it; you're not that desperate. There are twenty women applicants for every man. There are better ways.

3. You take the initiative. If you find a person you're interested in, plan a dinner party. Invite friends, several friends. Also invite that new person you're interested in.

4. Let your friends provide dates. But make certain you want them to. Some people are natural matchmakers and yearn to see everyone married.

5. Pray about dating. One advantage of the Christian: We know that God cares about every need that we have. God can send the right person into your life.

Dating plays a significant role in our modern culture. It's the stage when a man and a woman look each other over. They ask themselves, "Do I want to spend the rest of my life with this person?"

Both as a Christian and a formerly married, it also provides an opportunity to face the dating game realistically. You can brush the stars out of your eyes. You know that marriage, as wonderful as it may be, isn't all romance, tender words, and fireworks. As you see flaws in the other, you think more seriously about making final commitments. As a Christian, you exercise caution, allowing the inner impulses of the Holy Spirit to guide.

Because you know that the Lord wants only the best for your life, you allow the Holy Spirit to lead you in the direction he wants. You don't have to be satisfied with just any eligible person who crosses your path.

Some fine Christians frown upon divorce, and consider remarriage unthinkable. I don't share that opinion. When God forgives the sins you committed in the breakup of your marriage, he forgave you as surely as if he cleansed you from murder, adultery, or stealing. You're now free. You're God's child. I also believe that God may even now have someone special, reserved for you.

Won't that be a wonderful combination—two special, unique, lovable children of God marrying each other? In the meantime, you can enjoy life, take pleasure in your friendships, and experience more of God's presence.

—CECIL MURPHEY

FOR FURTHER READING:

Chapman, Gary. *Toward a Growing Marriage.* Chicago: Moody, 1979.

Florio, Anthony. *Two to Get Ready.* Old Tappan, N.J.: Revell, 1974; Victor Books, 1978.

Nelson, Elof G. *Your Life Together.* Richmond: John Knox, 1967.

DAUGHTER-MOTHER RELATIONSHIPS

Better Communication

Maybe you're the kind of woman who grew up sharing your deepest secrets with your mother. Or maybe you respected and loved your mother but never really talked to her on an equal basis.

In any case, many women find that as adults, talking—really talking—to their mothers is difficult. Separated by miles and diversity of experiences, mothers and daughters sometimes drift apart and find themselves communicating on a surface, how's-the-weather level.

But it's never too late to improve communication with your mother. Here are some basic guidelines to remember which will help you and your mother learn more about each other and improve your relationship.

1. *Ask for Advice.* Remember how much your mother loved to make suggestions while you were growing up? Everyone likes to feel that her opinion is important—especially mothers. And who knows more about you than the woman who lived with you for so many years? Learn to be open to your mother's suggestions on dressing, working, and raising your children. You don't have to follow her advice, but listening with an open mind and asking for her opinion is a sure way of opening communication channels.

2. *Help Her Feel Important.* Once the children have left home, many women feel unneeded and suffer from self-doubt about their value in society. During this time, more than ever, your mother needs to feel important—especially in your eyes.

Send her a card or flowers for no special reason, just to let her know you're thinking about her. Tell her why she's important to you with specific examples of traits or habits she instilled in you as a child. Tell her what you've always admired about her. (And do it all sincerely!)

137

3. *Remember Together.* If you live near your mother, plan a nostalgia evening. Bring out the old photo albums or home movies, pop some popcorn, and remember together. If you're miles away, send your mother clippings or cards that remind you of childhood experiences. Or send a postcard that simply says, "Remember when we baked fudge together and ate it all by ourselves?" Let your mother know that your memories of childhood are important to you.

4. *Share a New Interest.* If you live near your mother, sign up for a community class together in Chinese cooking or chair caning. If you're further apart, send your mother a book you just read and then call her and talk about it together. Consider doing a Bible study with your mother, even across the country. Study the same book of the Bible or use the same study guide. Write or call each other to share your insights. And commit to pray for each other every day. You may find that God is teaching you both some valuable new lessons.

5. *Dream Together.* No matter what her age, your mother has dreams for the future just as you do. Encourage each other to dream. Talk about your secret hopes, share your wildest dreams, and plan together. Maybe you've both wanted to travel and your dreaming will lead to a mother/daughter trip. Maybe you'd both like to be model-thin and you can plan a diet together.

Whatever the case, remember to encourage your mother to stretch and grow as a woman. Together you can challenge each other as perhaps no one else can.

—From Dale Hanson Bourke, "How to Talk to Your Mother," *Today's Christian Woman*, Winter 1980.

When a Mother Is a Friend

Birth begins the relationship as the mother simply transforms her ideas, teachings and disciplines to her dependent, helpless, and ignorant infant. As the daughter begins to exert her first signs of independence, the relationship increases in complexity. The baby exhibits her first signs of individualism within a few years as she grows into a young girl and eventually into a woman. During the process, the daughter extends her awareness of her own identity and needs, and she learns to meet those needs herself. This growth process varies from mother to mother and daughter to daughter. The degrees of freedom and discipline, as the daughter matures, differ greatly from family to family. But no matter how and when the shift occurs, the time comes when the mother and daughter are on the same level. The mother eventually chooses to no longer exert discipline over her daughter. If the maturation process progresses in the proper way at the right time, the mother and the daughter come to a point where they can relate to each other woman to woman, as friends.

The timing is crucial. I believe mothers make a big mistake when they give daughters the freedom to govern their own lives too early, before they have the wisdom and expertise to do so. Obviously the mother's ability to discern when to give her daughter freedom is a sensitive issue that each mother must settle within herself. But most high-school girls are not mature enough to live without parental boundaries such as curfews, which movies they can see, which parties they can attend. Mothers who think they are being buddies to daughters by allowing them to grow up in their own way or whenever they want to are actually playing with fire. The results are dangerous: First, the mother exposes her daughter to the risk of making an irreparable mistake that may cause her undue misery; second, chances are that the final relationship between the mother and daughter will never reach the full potential it could have had if the mother had acted more courageously in her role as disciplinarian.

It takes courage to say *no!* Afraid they won't be liked by their children, parents have been known to retreat from their disciplinary responsibilities, hoping to gain love. This results not in the love and admiration they desire, but in a lack of respect and much needed guidance.

THE FREEDOM OF FRIENDSHIP

Today mother and I share a deep, intimate friendship. Yet we do not limit our friendships to each other. Both of us have many other friends, and each relationship is as different as the personalities concerned.

The freedom to give ourselves to each other and to our friends results from our sense of personal self-acceptance. Security is essential in promoting healthy friendships between mothers and daughters. The lack of it not only drives a mother to a premature relinquishment of her responsibilities as her daughter's disciplinarian; it can also cause a mother to hold her child back in the process of maturation. Some mothers try to keep their daughters as little girls all their lives. Perhaps they fear that if they let them go, their girls will pass them by. Mothers can become jealous of their daughters, and jealousy is a natural by-product of insecurity.

True friends do not allow jealousy to destroy their relationship. A healthy spirit of competition may exist, but the green-eyed monster cannot come between friends, for it is more akin to hate than to love.

HOPE FOR THE FUTURE

If attaining a friendship with your mother or daughter sounds just short of impossible, remember this; when I ask the majority of my friends to describe their mothers in one word, the choice is almost unanimous: *friend!* Eventually most mothers and daughters reach the point in their lives when they are able to overcome past hurts, fears, and frustrations and are able to say, "She is my friend." This is God's plan for mothers and daughters. We need meaningful friendships as women.

So if you're a mother with a teenage daughter who gives no indication of affection toward you, don't dismay. Your relationship will bloom in time. And if you're a teenage girl who thinks your mother is the strictest ever, be glad she cares enough about you to be involved. The day will come when you will have the freedom you long for, though I hope it will not descend upon you before you are ready to handle its responsibilities.

No matter what your relationship seems like today, it is not the same as it was yesterday, nor will it be the same tomorrow. Give your friendship room to grow. Allow your mother or your daughter space for changes. Relish *all* your friendships.

For when we each, mothers and daughters, grow as individuals, we will be able to bring more and more to our friendship. Through my friendship with my husband, my sisters, my colleagues, as well as others, I contribute richly to the friendship I enjoy with my mother.

—From Sheila Schuller Coleman, *Between Mother and Daughter*. Old Tappan, N.J.: Revell, 1982.

DAY-CARE CENTERS AND PRESCHOOL

IF PARENTS ACCEPT the reality that each preschool child requires constant individual attention and daily routines which overburdened mothers or working parents cannot always supply, then quality day-care centers can contribute greatly to strengthening family life. They can fulfill the needs of both the children and the family.

A day-care center is as good as the caretaker who works there. She must earn the trust of her charges by being sensitive to their moods, feelings, and needs. She must always be conscious of how the children respond to what she does with them.

Parental participation is fundamental to a successful operation. Parents and teachers need to exchange information about the child's behavior, his likes and dislikes, and his health on a regular basis.

We have learned at least two things from Head Start: remedial programs must begin before the child is three years of age and the parents must be involved in these programs. A day-care center that provides the child with a good initial learning experience and social stimulation is offering an opportunity that many children would not receive from their mothers. Even if the mother were at home and had the time available, chances are she would not have the educational background to offer her child the stimulation he needs.

Should a mother feel guilty about wanting to send her toddler to a day-care center? Is a day-care center as good as home care? Is day care *only* for working mothers? Dr. Bruno Bettelheim, a distinguished child psychiatrist, disagrees. "I feel that it is too narrow to think of Day-Care Centers merely for mothers who have to work or as therapeutic centers for underprivileged children. Day Care can do a vital job for *all* mothers and *all* children. There is no doubt that mother is the most important person for a child but we are aware of too intense a mother-child attachment. . . . We need to find a better balance between home care and day care. . . . A child feels much better about himself and the world if he spends part of the day in a planned setting that exists only for him."

The real difficulty with day-care centers is not that they separate mother and child, but that there are so few good ones. The modern mother has considerable need for time by herself. If she has her own time, she can more easily and happily relate to her child. A child, too, needs to go his own way.

Syracuse University has set up a day-care center for children beginning at six months of age. The center began as an experiment to show how "culturally determined mental retardation" could be prevented among children from disadvantaged areas. It deliberately tried to stimulate the child's intellectual development by offering a highly individualized type of care. The experiment proved that the children thrive and that their IQ score increased with time

(rather than the reverse, which usually happens with these children).

The study also demonstrated that early day-care experience with its attendant separation from the mother does not lead to emotional insecurity. Conversely, inadequate day care may be harmful and nothing is worse than a series of caretakers. A child needs one person to identify with as the mothering figure.

Educators agree that in addition to complying with local safety regulations, a good day-care center should have a cheerful environment, good equipment, and well-trained, loving teachers, as well as:

1. Forty to fifty square feet of indoor space per child.
2. One hundred square feet of enclosed outdoor space per child.
3. A nourishing lunch and frequent snacks available.
4. A place to nap with privacy and a cot for each child.
5. Medical attention at the center, as well as home care when the child is too sick to attend class.
6. Diapers and changing tables.
7. Furniture and toilet facilities adapted to the child's height.
8. Two to three adults available to each group of eight to ten children.
9. Ample storage space for the child's clothes and toys.
10. Mandatory parent participation.

Day Care and Early Education, an informative magazine presenting a broad range of topics to the concerned working mother, is available by writing 2852 Broadway, New York, N.Y. 10025.

Private industry is beginning to enter the day-care field, realizing that providing day care increases their available work force and aids in retaining their employees. Day-care facilities cut down on expensive absenteeism and permit a woman to work full time instead of part time. Without day-care centers, many mothers could not work and as a result would be on welfare.

140

Providing good day-care service is expensive, but what better opportunity do we have for offering children of low-income families educational and health facilities where they are most needed?

The federal government makes funds available to state public welfare agencies under Title IV of the Social Security Act. Other funds may be obtained from state and local public welfare agencies.

PRINCETON CENTER FOR INFANCY POINT OF VIEW

Children who are taught how to learn, to use their senses to their best advantage, and to express themselves in their early years are more likely to function successfully in any classroom. In fact, day-care services should be available to all families so a child can have experiences that supplement the ones provided by the home. Our children are our best investment and richest resources!

HOW TO SELECT A PRESCHOOL

In selecting a preschool, parents are sometimes bewildered by the variety of different programs available, as well as the differences in methods, materials, and goals. Many preschools have no "formal information sheets" describing their educational philosophies, so the astute parent must visit the various programs and observe the classes in session. Before making a final selection, you should discuss the program in detail with the teacher. You should not hesitate to ask questions. It is much better to ask questions than to enroll your child in a program you are not comfortable with.

MATCHING A PRESCHOOL PROGRAM TO YOUR CHILD

First of all, the preschool program you select for your child should not conflict greatly with your own philosophy of child rearing. If you tend to be a "permissive" parent, you probably would not choose to enroll your child in a structured preschool program. If you encourage independence, self-discipline, and responsibility, you probably would be unhappy to have your child in a very "permissive" or "anything-is-okay" school. Similarly, you must consider your child's personality and tendencies.

Also, you should consider the number of children in the class, their ages, and the child-adult ratio. How much individual attention does your child need? Most nursery schools use chronological age grouping while many Montessori schools use mixed-age grouping.

In evaluating a preschool, you should look carefully at its program. Is there a daily routine followed by allotted time periods for free play, snack, story time, rest time, etc. or is most of the time unstructured?

Does the teacher insist that all the children join the group during certain activities—group singing, story time or snack time? What is included in the *content* of the curriculum? (Are there science experiments, nature study, animals, pre-reading and pre-math activities, etc?) Can you judge how much pre-planning takes place? How many new projects are planned and how many trips are taken? Is the program organized into units (farms, community workers, foods, etc.)? Does the program incorporate special events and special visitors?

Are there special teachers to enrich the program (music, science, art, foreign language)? What is the music program: singing, rhythm instruments, Montessori sensory training, Orff and Kodály music methods? What is the structure of the program, formal or informal, i.e., do the teachers instruct the class as a whole? Is a great deal of spontaneous learning taking place?

What are the opportunities for group interaction and for dramatic and social play? This varies with the goals of the particular preschool. Are there opportunities for individual play and concentration? How is snack time handled, as a group social time (everyone altogether) or individually at any time during the preschool day, as in many Montessori programs? How is rest time handled and moving from one activity to the next?

What *values* are stressed in the program: sharing, co-operation, cleanliness, routines, etc.? Are the children encouraged to learn to do things for themselves? Finally, are fathers encouraged to become involved in the program in any way?

THE STAFF

It is important that you feel some rapport with your child's potential teachers. You should feel comfortable with the way the teachers are handling the children. You should feel satisfied with their "education approach" and their competency.

Do they in any way seem "overwhelmed" by the classroom situation? What are their methods of "discipline," of modifying the unacceptable behavior of a child? How well do they handle disputes among the children?

Do the teachers interact with the children as individuals or is the majority of their time spent dealing with small groups of children? Are teachers tuned in to the "room as a whole," as well as individual children? Are they warm without "smothering" them with affection? Are they genuine with the children? How do the children respond to the staff?

DISCIPLINE AND BEHAVIOR

What kinds of behavior are encouraged and what are the limits on a child's behavior? How is discipline handled and how effective does it seem? How much pressure is put on the child "conforming," joining the group, and learning to "get along" with the group? Does the teacher allow for a child's individuality? How are the children helped to grow? Do the teachers encourage the children to learn to do things by and for themselves? Do the teachers genuinely listen to the children when they are talking or are

they busy "getting something ready" for the next project?

How do the children interact with one another?

ATMOSPHERE

How would you describe the atmosphere in the classroom? Is it chaotic, spontaneous, controlled or stilted? Do the children seem happy? Do you feel their social, cognitive, and affective needs are being met? Do the children seem bored, restless, or overstimulated by the program?

PHYSICAL EQUIPMENT AND SURROUNDINGS

Look carefully at the physical surroundings. Are they clean and inviting? Are the children learning to handle the equipment with respect or are they behaving destructively? Are the books and puzzles accessible and attractive? Are the children encouraged to clean up after themselves; to put their own toys, books, and materials back on the shelves? Is there enough of a *variety* of stimulating materials accessible to meet the changing interests of the children? Are the materials varied during the school year?

Outdoors, is the equipment safe, supervised, adequately spaced, and attractive? Are the children able to move freely from indoors to out or does the group as a whole have an "indoor time" and an "outdoor time"?

Indoors and outdoors, is there opportunity for sand play, water play, and other "messy" activities? Is there a variety of art materials available at all times or only during art "lessons"? Are the art "projects" appropriate for the preschool child or are they teacher-designed to "take home and impress mama and papa"? Is there enough physical space inside, as well as some indoor provision for rainy day, large-muscle exercise and play?

What is the physical arrangement of the room? Are there activity areas: a doll corner, a housekeeping corner, an art area, a place for water and sand play, toys, blocks, puzzles, a workbench, a comfortable book corner, records, child-sized tables and chairs?

No two preschool programs will ever be exactly alike. The most important variable is the teacher. You should feel she is genuinely enjoying her work with young children. You should see whether she acts as a caretaker or as a sensitive person who enters into the play life of the group and enhances the learning. The second most important variable is the physical space and equipment.

—From The Princeton Center for Infancy, *The Parenting Advisor*. Garden City, N.Y.: Anchor Books/Doubleday, 1978.

FOR FURTHER READING:

Reynolds, Jean K., ed. *How to Choose and Use Child Care*. Nashville: Broadman Press, 1980.

Sauerman, Thomas H., and Schomaker, Linda, eds. *Starting a Church-Sponsored Weekday Preschool Program: A Manual of Guidance*. Philadelphia: Fortress Press, 1980.

DEATH

Death for the Christian

Most of us know what it means to be stunned by the sudden passing of a dedicated friend, a godly pastor, a devout missionary, or a saintly mother. We have stood at the open grave with hot tears coursing down our cheeks and have asked in utter bewilderment, "Why, O God, why?"

The death of the righteous is no accident. Do you think that the God whose watchful vigil notes the sparrow's fall and who knows the number of hairs on our heads would turn His back on one of His children in the hour of peril? With Him there are no accidents, no tragedies, and no catastrophes as far as His children are concerned.

Paul, who lived most of his Christian life on the brink of death, expressed triumphant certainty about life. He testified, "To me, to live is Christ and to die is gain" (Philippians 1:21). His strong, unshakeable faith took trouble, persecution, pain, thwarted plans, and broken dreams in stride.

He never bristled in questioning cynicism and asked, "Why, Lord?" He knew beyond the shadow of a doubt that his life was being fashioned into the image and likeness of his Savior; and despite the discomfort, he never flinched in the process.

PAUL KNEW FOR SURE

Things didn't always work out according to his own plans and ideas, but Paul did not murmur or question. His assurance was this: "We know that in all things God works for the good of those who love him, who have been called according to his purpose" (Romans 8:28).

When his tired, bruised body began to weaken under the load, he said in triumph, "We know that if the earthly tent we live in is destroyed, we have a building from God, an eternal house in heaven, not built by human hands" (2 Corinthians 5:1).

The world called him foolish for his belief that men could become partakers of eternal life through faith. But he jutted out his chin and said exultantly, "I know whom I have believed, and am convinced that he is able to guard what I have entrusted to him for that day" (2 Timothy 1:12).

Every one of these triumphant affirmations rings with the note of hope and the assurance of life immortal. Though the Christian has no immunity from death and no claim to perpetual life on this planet, death is to him a friend rather than a foe, the beginning rather than the end, another step on the pathway to heaven rather than a leap into a dark unknown.

For many people, the corrosive acids of materialistic science have eroded away their faith in everlasting life. But let's face it— Einstein's equation $E = MC^2$ is no satisfactory substitute for Faith + Commitment = Hope.

Paul believed in Christ and committed his all to Christ. The result was that he *knew*

143

Christ was able to keep him forever. Strong faith and living hope are the result of unconditional commitment to Jesus Christ.

CHRISTIANS HAVE A GLORIOUS HOPE

One of the bonuses of being a Christian is the glorious hope that extends out beyond the grave into the glory of God's tomorrow.

The Bible opens with a tragedy and ends in a triumph.

In Genesis we see the devastation of sin and death, but in the Revelation we glimpse God's glorious victory over sin and death. Revelation 14:13 says, " 'Blessed are the dead who die in the Lord from now on.' 'Yes,' says the Spirit, 'they will rest from their labor, for their deeds will follow them.' "

But what is the basis of the Christian's hope of eternal life? Is our hope of life after death merely wishful thinking or blind optimism? Can we have any certainty that there is life after death and that some day those who know Christ will go to be with Him throughout eternity?

Yes! There is one great fact which gives the Christian assurance in the face of death: the *resurrection of Jesus Christ.* It is the physical, bodily resurrection of Christ that gives us confidence and hope. Because Christ rose from the dead, we know beyond doubt that death is not the end, but is merely the transition to eternal life.

Never forget that the resurrection of Christ is in many ways the central event of all history. Paul said, "If Christ has not been raised, your faith is futile; you are still in your sins. . . . If only for this life we have hope in Christ, we are to be pitied more than all men. But Christ has indeed been raised from the dead" (1 Corinthians 15:17–20). The resurrection of Christ makes all the differences! Because He rose from the dead, we *know* that He was in fact the Son of God who came to save us through His death on the cross, as He claimed.

Because Christ rose from the dead, we *know* that sin and death and Satan have been

decisively defeated. And because Christ rose from the dead, we *know* there is life after death, and that if we belong to Him we need not fear death or hell. Jesus said, "I am the resurrection and the life. He who believes in me will live, even though he dies; and whoever lives and believes in me will never die" (John 11:25,26). He also promised, "In my Father's house are many rooms; if it were not so, I would have told you. I am going there to prepare a place for you. And if I go and prepare a place for you, I will come back and take you to be with me that you also may be where I am" (John 14:2,3). We know these words are true, because Jesus died on the cross and rose again from the dead. What a glorious hope we have because of Jesus' resurrection!

> No eye has seen,
>   no ear has heard,
>   no mind has conceived
>   what God has prepared for those
>   who love him
>   (1 Corinthians 2:9)

Our confidence in the future is based firmly on the fact of what God has done for us in Christ. No matter what our situation may be, we need never despair because Christ is alive. "Now if we died with Christ, we believe that we will also live with him. . . . For the wages of sin is death, but the gift of God is eternal life in Christ Jesus our Lord" (Romans 6:8,23).

DEATH TO THE CHRISTIAN: A CORONATION

Death is said in the Bible to be a *coronation* for the Christian. The picture is that of a prince who, after his struggles and conquests in an alien land, comes to his native country and court to be crowned and honored for his deed.

I have attended a coronation, and the pomp and grandeur is magnificent. It expands my imagination to limitless heights to begin to comprehend what our coronation in heaven will be like!

The Bible says that as long as we are here

on earth, we are pilgrims and strangers in a foreign land. This world is not our home; our citizenship is in heaven. To him who is faithful, Christ will give a crown of life.

Paul said, "Now there is in store for me the crown of righteousness, which the Lord, the righteous Judge, will award to me on that day—and not only to me, but also to all who have longed for his appearing" (2 Timothy 4:8).

Death is the Christian's coronation, the end of conflict and the beginning of glory in heaven.

DEATH IS A REST FROM LABOR

The Bible also speaks of death, for a Christian, as a rest from labor. The Bible says, "Blessed *are* the dead which die in the Lord . . . that they may rest from their labours" (Revelation 14:13 KJV). It is as if the Lord of the harvest says to the weary laborer, "You have been faithful in your task, come and sit in the sheltered porch of my palace and rest from your labors—enter now into the joy of your Lord."

God's saints do not enjoy much rest here on earth. They are ceaselessly busy for the Lord. Some of them accomplish more in a few years than others do in a lifetime. But their labor and toil will some day come to an end. The Bible says, "There remains . . . a Sabbath-rest for the people of God" (Hebrews 4:9). That rest cannot begin until the angel of death takes them by the hand and leads them into the glorious presence of their Lord.

The apostle Paul declared, "We are confident, I say, and would prefer to be away from the body and at home with the Lord" (2 Corinthians 5:8).

DEATH A DEPARTURE

The Bible speaks of death as a *departure*. When Paul approached the valley of the shadow of death he did not shudder with fear; rather he announced with a note of triumph, "the time has come for my departure" (2 Timothy 4:6).

The word *departure* literally means to pull up anchor and to set sail. Everything which happens prior to death is a preparation for the final voyage. Death marks the beginning, not the end. It is a solemn, decisive step in our journey to God.

Many times I have said farewell to my wife as I have departed for some distant country to proclaim the gospel. Separation always brings a tinge of sadness, but we part from one another in the sure hope that we shall meet again. In the meantime the flame of love burns brightly in her heart and in mine.

So is the hope of the believing Christian as he stands at the grave of a loved one who is with the Lord. He knows that the separation is not forever. It is a glorious truth that those who are in Christ never see each other for the last time. We say good-bye to our loved ones only until the day breaks and the shadows flee away. It is not really "good-bye" but (as the French say) *"au revoir"*—till we meet again.

DEATH A TRANSITION

In addition, the Bible speaks of the death of a Christian as a *transition*. Paul wrote, "Now we know that if the earthly tent we live in is destroyed, we have a building from God, an eternal house in heaven, not built by human hands" (2 Corinthians 5:1). The word *tabernacle* in the KJV means "tent" or "temporary abode."

To the Christian death is the exchanging of a tent for a building. Here we are as pilgrims or sojourners, living in a frail, flimsy home, subject to disease, pain, and peril. But at death we exchange this crumbling, disintegrating tent or body for a house not made with hands, eternal in the heavens. The wandering wayfarer comes into his own at death and is given the title to a home which will never deteriorate, for it is eternal.

DEATH AN EXODUS

Death is also said in the Bible to be an *exodus* for the Christian. We speak of being deceased as though it were the end of everything, but the word *decease* literally means "exodus" or "going out." The imagery is that of the children of Israel leaving Egypt and their former life of bondage, slavery and hardship for the Promised Land.

So death to the Christian is an exodus from the limitations, the burdens, and the bondage of this life. Victor Hugo once said, "When I go down to the grave, I can say like so many others that I have finished my day's work; but I cannot say that I have finished my life. Another day's work will begin the next morning. The tomb is not a blind alley—it is a thoroughfare. It closes with the twilight to open with the dawn."

Death therefore is not only a going out. It is also a going in. As the Easter hymn puts it, "Jesus lives! henceforth is death but the gate of life immortal."

A PLACE PREPARED

Do you think that the God who has provided so amply for living has made no provision for dying? Bear this in mind: the hope of eternal life rests solely and exclusively upon your faith in Jesus Christ! Make no mistake about that.

Before He told His disciples about the many "mansions" or resting places, and before He gave them the hope of heaven, Jesus said, "Trust in God; trust also in me." Then He went on to tell them, "I am going there to prepare a place for you," and He gave them the added assurance, "I am the way and the truth and the life. No one comes to the Father except through me" (John 14:1–6).

Eternal life is by and through the Lord Jesus Christ. To put it in the Bible's exact words, here is the secret of the blessed hope: "Whoever believes in the Son has eternal life, but whoever rejects the Son will not see life" (John 3:36).

When a true believer dies, he goes straight into the presence of Christ. He goes to heaven to spend eternity with God. By terrible contrast, the person who rejects God's offer of pardon is separated from God, a place that Jesus called hell.

—From Billy Graham, *Till Armageddon*, copyright © 1981 by Billy Graham, pp. 198–206; used by permission of Word Books, Publisher, Waco, Texas 76796.

FOR FURTHER READING:

Brooks, D. P. *Dealing with Death—a Christian Perspective*. Nashville: Broadman, 1974.
Kübler-Ross, Elisabeth. *On Death and Dying*. New York: Macmillan, 1969.
Murphey, Cecil B. *Comforting Those Who Grieve*. Atlanta: John Knox, 1979.
Westberg, Granger E. *Good Grief*. Philadelphia: Fortress, 1971.

DELAYED MOTHERHOOD

FRIGHTENING, isn't it? Or perhaps others have told you it is.

You feel bewildered and confused. Or you don't feel certain about the decision you've made or are about to make.

You are acutely aware that you face a major decision when you consider having a child (or another child) when you are over thirty years of age. Undoubtedly you have heard all the myths and rumors, as well as the facts, that accompany this decision, but you probably have not been able to sort them out in your head. You think you want a baby, but you worry:

"Won't I appear ridiculous as an older mother or father?"

"Will the baby be retarded or have a birth defect?"

"How can I give a teenager the energy he'll demand, if I'm over fifty at the time?"

"Won't a child be embarrassed by having older parents when all his friends' parents are younger?"

"Am I too set in my ways to let a child intrude into my life?"

"How do I keep my friends when I change my life to one that is more child-centered?"

One final and major question: "Am I very different from younger parents because I'm over thirty?"

We think you are—in very positive ways.

. . . . .

As a mature individual you have a chance to plan. You can think through problems and devise solutions; you have been doing that for some time in your work and in your personal life. You also, as a mature individual, know that you do not *have* to have that child. Conceiving a child or carrying a child is *your* choice. If you do become a parent, therefore, you will *want* and thus love that child, which gives the child a better than average chance of success.

One of your immediate concerns will be whether you will find others of your age and interests who can join your circle of friends when you become an after-thirty parent. You will not have to look too far to find them, because the number of people facing the same situation grows each year. In 1977, for instance, there were 593,301 births to mothers over thirty; one out of every six births occurred to an over-thirty woman; and one out of every three new fathers was over thirty. This number of births to mature parents was 5½ percent greater in 1977 than in 1976. The figure is significant because birth rates have been decreasing steadily since 1970. The first sign of an increasing trend in births occurred in 1977, and was noted specifically in the 30–35-year-old parent group.

But are after-thirty parents *your* kind of people? How do they compare to you and the way you live? Let us look at what the census has to say about a typical after-thirty parent. (Each of these examples is documented in or interpreted from scientific population reports issued by the National Bureau of the Census.)

• Chances are that you married later than your parents did. The average age of marriage in 1978 was 24.2 for men and 21.8 for women; this is almost exactly one year later for marriage than in 1970. But these figures do not tell the whole story. If you tally the number of single persons between the ages of twenty and thirty, you discover some startling facts. The number of single persons between twenty and thirty has increased about 10 percent between 1970 and 1977, but the married rate after thirty years is about the same. *This indicates that marriage is being deferred as a growing social trend.* Many hundreds of thousands of people are waiting to a later age to get married and start a family.

• You probably have more education than the average member of the population. Many of you waited to put that task behind you before you started a family. In 1977, the figures show that almost 43 percent of all those new mothers over thirty had more than a high-school education, and 25 percent of them had a minimum of a college degree. The number of advanced college degrees among mature mothers is on the rise. The after-thirty fathers had even more advanced educational credentials. Add wisdom to the potential maturity you can offer a child.

• Both of you are probably working. You waited to start a career. The 1977 data show that the husband is the family's sole earner in only 26 percent of married couple families. In fact, when both spouses are earners, the median age for wives is thirty-seven years of age and for husbands forty. Of these couples, 22 percent have one child and another 21 percent have two children. Only 42 percent have no children.

• You probably live in a metropolitan area—at least that is what the statistics say.

• As a couple, your salaries are comparable, suggesting a mutual concern for career and financial security. One of your motivations for waiting was that you wanted to be able to afford a child.

• You make a substantial family income. Now you can add to your nuclear family without a great deal of personal sacrifice.

• You have seriously considered divorce at some time or another. If you actually went through the process of a previous divorce, you remarried in your early thirties. A new marriage . . . a new child.

This typical picture is, of course, only a statistical composite, not the *real* you or your mate. There is no need to find your counterpart within these numbers, which represent a whole spectrum of people, nor is there a safe haven in merely knowing that you are not very different from other after-thirty potential parents.

What can you learn from these statistics? Literally millions of people have decided to become parents after thirty, people who are well educated, secure, and wise. They have adjusted well to children—so well in fact that many of them have had several children as after-thirty parents. Some of you readers are considering parenthood for the first time; many other after-thirty readers have older children and are now pausing and wondering about the pros and cons of having another as mature people. Children of after-thirty parents thrive because they are wanted and loved; they are not pawns in a marriage. The youngsters are planned and they are needed. Whole patterns of living are altered in order to make room for the new members of the family, but without interrupting careers or life goals.

· · · · ·

In other words, you *can* do an excellent job of parenting after thirty, probably even better than when you were younger.

· · · · ·

You have the motivation, the capacity, and the qualities of maturity, wisdom, and forethought.

—From Murray M. Kappelman, M.D., and Paul R. Ackerman, Ph.D., *Parents After Thirty.* New York: Rawson, Wade, 1980.

FOR FURTHER READING:

McCauley, Carole Spearin. *Pregnancy After 35.* New York: Dutton, 1976.

DEPRESSION

How do you get rid of depression? The first step is to *rule out any physical reason*, which means having a complete examination by a physician. Consider your sleeping and eating habits. If none of these is the cause, ask yourself: What am I doing that is causing me to be depressed? How and about what am I thinking that could be making me depressed?

Severe depression brought on by improper self-concepts and thought patterns may require therapy and, for some, hospitalization. If a person is depressed he should always seek assistance from someone, whether it be a physician, a qualified pastor, or a counselor.

Many people who experience depression periodically or continuously could reverse the process by restructuring their thought pattern. The first step is to *recognize and identify the thoughts that you express to yourself.* When an event occurs and a person experiences depression, he fails to realize that there is more than just this particular stimulus and response. Between the two there is a thought or a value judgment that he is making about himself, whom he views as the real culprit. Perhaps this was one of the characteristics of the type of imagination God reacted against in Genesis 6:5 AMPLIFIED where we read, *The Lord saw that the wickedness of man was great in the earth, and that every imagination and intention of all human thinking was only evil continually.*

A woman drops a dish, breaks it and feels depressed. Between the act and the depression was the thought, "I am so clumsy. I cannot be trusted even to pick up a dish." It was that type of thinking that elicited the depression. The more you identify your thoughts the more you can question and determine the validity of the thought. You may discover a pattern to these thoughts—a negative view of yourself, deprivation, or a false view of the future.

A second step is to *realize that many of these thoughts are automatic.* Sometimes we put these thoughts into our minds but in many cases they are involuntary. The severely depressed person is invaded by these thoughts and has little resistance to them. But for the person who is less ill it is possible to recognize that these thoughts are involuntary and they are *not the result of deliberation or reasoning.* They are almost an obsession. By reasoning and consideration the rational thinking process *can* overrule and put events into the proper perspective. A detachment toward our thoughts will help in transforming them.

A third step is to *distinguish between ideas and facts.* Simply because a person thinks something does not make it true nor does it mean that he should believe it. A person's thoughts do not always represent reality and they should be validated before they are accepted. A high-school girl thought her girl friends no longer liked or accepted her. Before accepting this as true, however, she was told to check out her observations and consider other reasons for the reaction of the girl friends. She also considered other hypotheses to account for the apparent situation and learned how to view the events differently. By doing this she found out that her initial thoughts were invalid.

But what if she had found them to be valid? What then? At that point she might again cloud her thinking by degrading herself and believing that the situation would never change. Instead she should investigate the reasons for the rejection, attempt to correct and rectify the problem, and discover new girl friends. She should also realize that all of us experience rejection, whether right or wrong, from time to time. But life does

not come to a halt because of it. An important part of the process involves checking the accuracy and thoroughness of our first observation. Jumping to conclusions and first impressions are not always accurate. They need to be questioned.

The fourth step is often difficult but is very important. *After discovering that a particular thought is not true, state precisely why it is inaccurate or invalid.* Putting the reasons into words helps in three ways. It reduces the frequency of the ideas coming back again, the intensity of the idea is decreased, and finally, the feeling or mood that the idea generates is lessened.

To help even more it is important to identify specifically the kind of faulty thinking you engage in. Generalizations? Do you magnify the problem? Jump to conclusions? Learn to say, "Hey, I'm jumping to a conclusion again," or, "I exaggerated again. That isn't true." Strange as it seems, it is important for the person (when he is alone) to say this aloud and hear his own voice expressing it.

Another method is to consider alternative explanations to the events. Did you interpret the situation correctly or could there be another explanation?

Some people become depressed because they concentrate upon failures, losses, or difficulties in the past. By concentrating on them they allow themselves to be controlled and limited by the past. But to be miserable now because of something that occurred (or so you thought) in the past does not make sense. It is really a waste of energy that could be directed toward some constructive action.

Another problem of letting the past depress us is the failure and inactivity it imposes upon us for the present. "It is always wrong to mortgage the present by the past," says Martyn Lloyd-Jones, and "... to allow the past to act as a brake upon the present." If you are really sorry about what happened in the past and feel that things were wasted, wouldn't it be better to force yourself to

149

move ahead now and make up for it in the future?

The example of Elijah in 1 Kings 18 and 19 vividly illustrates both the cause and the cure of one man's depression. The depression came after his triumph upon Mount Carmel and the event that triggered it was the threat of Jezebel (*see* verse 19:2). Jezebel was greatly angered by Elijah's victory and threatened him with the same fate to which he had subjected the prophets of Baal. Many despondencies can be traced to a single action or word. The problem is not the deed or the word but the person's own subjective interpretation and reaction to it. James Vold in his article "God's Cure for Emotional Depression" depicted the results of this depression and then God's answer. The following is an adaptation.

The tortures of depression are depicted very clearly (1 Kings 19:3, 4, 10, 14). Elijah's depressed mood caused him to leave his familiar surroundings and faithful servant. This discontent with ordinary associations and friends is the companion of depression.

Secondly, Elijah prayed for death. Disgust with life and a longing for suicide seem to accompany the gloom of despondency. Elijah wasn't the only one who felt this way.

And Moses heard the people weeping throughout their families, every man at the door of his tent; and the anger of the Lord blazed hotly, and in the eyes of Moses it was evil. And Moses said to the Lord. Why have You dealt ill with Your servants? And why have I not found favor in Your sight, that You lay the burden of all this people on me? Have I conceived all this people? Have I brought them forth, that You should say to me, Carry them in your bosom, as a nursing father carries the sucking child, to the land which You swore to their fathers [to give them]? Where should I get meat to give to all these people? For they weep before me and say, Give us meat, that we may eat. I am not able to carry all these people

alone, because the burden is too heavy for me. And if this is the way You deal with me, kill me, I pray You, at once and be granting me a favor, and let me not see my wretchedness [in the failure of all my efforts].

Numbers 11:10–15 AMPLIFIED

Moses complained to God, "Why me? Why do I have to have this burden?" He also felt that he was carrying around the entire burden himself (verse 14). His feelings of inferiority are also revealed (verse 15). Many people who feel inferior are reluctant to relinquish their authority or tasks to others and yet the amount of work they must do is overwhelming. God gave a very simple answer. He divided up the labor by appointing seventy men of the elders of Israel. This is an important lesson for us to learn—to allow others to help and to face our inferiority feelings and deal with them realistically.

Elijah reached the depths of depression when he started to argue with God. This action reveals another effect of depression. It causes a loss of personal confidence in the promises of God. This lack of confidence in God is often accompanied by the belief that God is considered both unwise and unfair. Elijah was not flippant or sarcastic in his conversation with God. He was very perplexed.

Fourth, Elijah thought of himself as alone. He suffered from what men call megalomania, "an excessive concept of one's own importance." Depression shrinks one's outlook until life is limited to self. A person is persuaded that the whole world is against him. This view leads to self-pity with a total loss of perspective.

There were many ways in which God ministered to Elijah and his depression. The first phase of treatment was physical. Elijah asked for death (1 Kings 19:4) but God gave him the essentials of life (verse 6). Bread and water were delivered by an angel. The provision here was a proper diet and sufficient sleep. Proper food and rest are essential to psychological and physical health. Many problems have seemed less insoluble after a sleep. Any individual with a tendency to emotional exhaustion needs to guard against excessive weariness and improper eating habits.

The second aspect of the treatment for Elijah was psychological and spiritual. Elijah was given the opportunity to "get everything off his chest." Elijah's reply to God's question of "Why are you here?" was simple. "I am despondent and have in a sense deserted my post of duty . . . (another accomplice of depression, the resignation from responsibility) because I have been zealous for God and forsaken by Him. I am all alone and my life is in danger because of my faithfulness" (see 1 Kings 19:10). These words express a question as to God's dealings with him; they presuppose total loneliness and they also attribute to the people of Israel a murderous desire on their part.

God did not forsake him and He showed Elijah that Israel wasn't trying to kill him. Jezebel was the only one. There were seven thousand others who were faithful, too. God, in His time, answered Elijah and showed him that his confession was not accurate. Elijah is a good example of a person who misinterprets a situation and sees only certain elements of it. He made misconceptions concerning himself, others, and God. This in itself was enough to bring on the depression. It can bring on depression for us, too! God revealed to Elijah His purpose, and this explanation helped him to regain the proper perspective. Often our perspective is changed by opening ourselves to God and His plans.

If you are depressed, ask yourself these questions and apply to each the principles discussed in this chapter.

1. What are your eating and sleeping habits?
2. When was the last time you had a complete physical exam by a physician?
3. Are you taking any medications or drugs which might be building up in your system?
4. Do you have any disease or illness at the present time which might contribute to depression?
5. Have you evaluated the kind of depression you have, based on the information you have just read?
6. Have you evaluated your pattern of thinking as suggested in this chapter and the chapter on your thought-life?
7. Are you following your normal routine of life or are you withdrawing by staying in bed longer, staying away from your friends, avoiding regular activities? If so, it is important to force yourself to stay active while following the other principles suggested for dealing with depression.
8. Do you spend time studying and reflecting upon the Word of God? Do you have a consistent time of talking and listening to God?

—From H. Norman Wright, *The Christian Use of Emotional Power.* Old Tappan, N.J.: Revell, 1974.

Depression and Menopause

About one in ten women experience severe depression during menopause. Though physical changes do play a part in these depressions, Pauline Bart feels that we often become depressed simply because we are middle-aged. We have no clear or important role to play in our society. Very little if anything is expected of us. We have no status. But at the same time, our life span has lengthened, we have twenty or thirty good years ahead of us. If we have had children, we end our childbearing years sooner than we did in the past, and we are left with a lot of time on our hands and space in our lives. For there are no clear societal norms which give us a useful place in our children's lives. Often we are in their way after they leave home. If we have overprotected them or expected them to live out and fulfil our own lives for us, we are both angered by their leave-taking and saddened by our loss. Often, not understanding that we feel anger, unable to direct it toward our children or unable to express it in any way, we turn it inward onto ourselves and become severely and heavily depressed.

We are faced with other real losses. Some of us feel deeply saddened by the end of our ability to bear children. We are losing our youth. And if in general we feel unfulfilled personally, we may be bitter about not having achieved happiness yet.

If we are already working during menopause and middle age, we are less likely to suffer certain forms of depression, though heavy work can take its physical toll on us.

There are many legitimate reasons for our depression. We have to recognize that its causes are not so much personal as social; that is, our society does not recognize us as necessary or valuable members. More research needs to be done on both the physical and social causes of our depression. And we must try to provide discussion and work groups for ourselves and others to understand better our own feelings and capabilities, to share them, and to move out of depression into new and worthwhile lives.

—From The Boston Women's Health Book Collective, *Our Bodies, Ourselves.* New York: Simon & Schuster, 1973.

FOR FURTHER READING:

LaHaye, Tim. *How to Win Over Depression.* Grand Rapids: Zondervan, 1974.

Markell, Jan. *Overcoming Stress.* Wheaton, Ill.: Victor Books, 1982.

Wright, H. Norman. *The Christian Use of Emotional Power.* Old Tappan, N.J.: Revell, 1974.

DEVOTIONS

How to Start

God never gets in a rut, so be prepared for the unexpected. In addition to your King James Version of the Bible, get hold of a version that talks your language; buy a paperback if you're short of cash. There are many good translations and paraphrases available, and they make God's thoughts easier to understand than at any time since Christ was here among His disciples. Compare your new version with King James—read from both.

Look for a thought that's new to you. God wants to help you find a verse, phrase, or challenge that's going to help you during the day. You will never run out of material, believe it or not. Read a paragraph at a time, a thought-provoking sentence, or even a whole chapter—not always a set number of verses. Read a whole book at one sitting once in a while. Follow a list of devotional readings or follow a plan of your own. Do what works for *you.* They're your devotions—and private—so be as independent of other people as you feel you must. Let God direct you.

Mull over your new thought during the day at odd moments, all day long; or all night long, if that's your shift. You'll tingle frequently for these are God's thoughts for our modern world and He's personalizing them for you. Buckminster Fuller, one of today's best thinkers and a top-grade scientist, thinks through and rewords the Lord's Prayer *each night.* He's been doing it for years, he says, and he still tingles as God shows him new insights in the familiar words of the prayer Christ gave His disciples.

Regular Station Stops for Faster Starts

A regular schedule of servicing works as well for Christians as it does for autos. God adjusts your valves, or something like that, when you read His Word and talk with Him. So, do it regularly.

The disciples talked with Christ, as they did with each other, and they did much of their learning while they walked from one place to another. Why shouldn't you? They learned to do what He wanted by taking instructions from Christ and then practicing in real life. You can, too. Paul wrote many letters, talked to many people about Christ, and as he wrote and talked, he learned from God. You will, too.

Peter insisted on sticking his neck out and was always impatient to get on with the job—or the comment. He made mistakes, but he learned from his mistakes, so you're in good company if you do the same thing.

As you make your devotional station stops, God will help you see more of His will, and you'll adjust with a great deal less shock than if you wait until you need a major overhaul because of neglect.

STAY AWAKE

Not many will admit it, but a lot of people fall asleep praying. So it's possible that a little discomfort might *help you pray* better. Prayer is essential! Christ needed it for Himself—often. And He recommended it many times to His followers.

Good prayer is private: "When you pray, enter your inner room" (Matthew 6:6, NASB). So find an effective way to take your inner room with you. Pastors pray while they're driving from one appointment to another (*most* of them keep their eyes open!). Housewives pray while they're doing housework and tending the kids. Astronauts pray while they're orbiting. And so on.

Moving around doesn't guarantee you're praying right though, even if you do stay awake. You can muddle things up whether you're vertical, horizontal, or bent, if you try hard enough. The old folks used to say, "An idle mind is the devil's workshop." Right! A mind running at idling speed or out of gear is a good staging area for little demons, too. So, be a genius; focus your mind!

When God wants to speak to you, tune in carefully. He may come on in bursts and want your undivided attention for several seconds or several minutes. Afterward you can mull it all over and decide what it means. And what to do about it. Or, God's Word may just *seep!* But He'll come through to you if you're willing to listen, that's for sure.

Turn up your hearing aid, for God seldom shouts. In the best verse on private devotions in the New Testament (Matthew 6:6, again), Christ suggests not only that you get away

from distractions, but also that you concentrate on God.

EVERY DAY?

Sometimes devotional periods seem to get in the way of what we want right now. Let's face it honestly, we're not all that pious by nature. But devotions are essential in the same way that food is essential. Even food's a bother, too, sometimes, but we manage to eat regularly—and some of us do a little munching on the side.

When Jesus talked with the woman at the well in Samaria, He'd had a long, hard walk, but He put spiritual need ahead of His physical need and *He ended up so refreshed He didn't want food!* (John 4:27–34) He put His spiritual side first because He wanted to. He felt better for doing it and so will you. Witnessing, healing, and praying were vital *re-creations* for Christ; believe it or not, as a Christian you're put together the same way.

If the disciples neglected their moments with Christ (devotions), they goofed. Their problems after the crucifixion are examples (John 21:2–7). And when they seemed to be unhooked in general, it turns out that they hadn't been as close to the Master as they should have been (John 20:25, 21:12; Luke 24:21, 25–27). They quarreled, sought preference, and even had to be lectured by Christ. Did you ever miss devotions and have a day like that?

—From Harland A. Hill, *Cure Your Devotional Blahs.* Wheaton, Ill.: Victor Books, 1974.

Family Devotions

The purpose of family devotions is that the Lord God may speak a personal word to each of you each day for the living of that day. Then each day can be an exciting adventure with the Maker of the universe! You can be caught up in His great plans and draw upon His power. It is just as important that you continually communicate with Him as it is to talk to your parents and brothers and sisters if you have them. God wants to talk to you about your school, your work, your play, your friends, your thoughts. He is personally interested in everything that affects you because He has given Himself for you so that you can freely give yourself back to Him. Try every day to hear some word from His Book that relates to what you are now doing.

If you are going to have a happy home, each member must be open and honest with each other member. None of us will be perfect until we see the Lord face-to-face, so now all of us want to be growing and changing. Of course, outside your home you will stand up for each other, but inside, in the presence of the Lord who understands us all, we must face reality—things as they are, our weaknesses as well as our strengths. Since there are reasons for everything we do, try to understand each other, help each other, and pray for each other, that each of you may become what you want to be. If you hide in your shell or put on a mask to protect what you don't like about yourself, you become unreal, a phony, hurting rather than helping yourself. It's a wonderful feeling to be free and transparent before God and before men. So be free to rejoice over what God does for you and also free to say *I'm sorry* when you do wrong.

Each member of the family should bring his or her own Bible to family devotions. If possible each of you should work in a different version so that you can often read a verse from various versions to give it depth of meaning. Younger children will find it easier to read the paraphrased Living Bible and the New Testament's Good News For Modern Man. It would also be helpful, though not essential, to have handy a chalkboard and chalk to make notes as you go along.

Though Father or Mother leads devotions, all of you should be ready to take your part. God gives younger people as well as older people insight into His higher ways. Parents can learn from children as well as children from parents. If you have your own questions about a subject in addition to the questions asked in the book, don't hesitate to ask

them. Home devotions focus on our daily lives, just as they are, difficulties as well as joys. See if you can grow stronger in some way every day.

—From Lois E. LeBar, *Family Devotions With School-Age Children*. Old Tappan, N.J.: Revell, 1973.

DIVORCE

ON JANUARY 11, 1976, I woke up and the spot next to me in the bed was already empty. I could hear my husband moving around in the other room, shuffling boxes. I heard drawers sliding open and shut, the quick crumple of newspaper, and the rip of tape. He was packing.

I got up and went to watch him. He never once glanced my way. The small pile of boxes in the corner of our living room grew a little bigger. The doorbell buzzed, and his friend came in to help carry his things out. I stood there with a cup of cold coffee in my hand, staring out the picture window. The door clicked shut. It wasn't official yet. But I knew. The marriage was over.

In the months of incredible pain that followed, I kept asking, *Why? What happened?* At the time, I thought I was unusual, that no one else's experience was quite like mine. But as I searched for clues, any shred of information to answer the questions that plagued me, I encountered many others in my situation—men, women, ranging in age from their twenties to their fifties—all of them Christians. And I found that we had much to talk about and much in common.

Like me, those I confided in were concerned that other Christians develop empathy for the divorced person. Like me, they had known the hurt of rejection from God's people—the very people they thought would understand most. Like me, they had felt the sharp sting of spoken and unspoken judgment: "Well, if only you hadn't been so (check one) weak, immature, unspiritual, emotional, etc., etc., you'd still be married." Like me, they had wanted to retort in kind, but instead, some of them quietly shrugged their shoulders and walked away from the church. In some cases, from the Church.

And, like me, they still don't know how to explain that after most of the dust has settled, they are beginning to see how God has used their divorce for the better.

The following is part of what we've learned—myself and these others who shared with me. We hope this will help our fellow Christians better understand how a marriage—even a Christian one—could break up and what happens to a person when it does.

Why?

Why? Why does divorce happen? The question haunts us all. It disturbs us when we look at the divorce statistics. It hurts us when we see those statistics personalized in the divorce of a friend or relative. And it worries us to think that our own marriage could end up as one of those statistics, too.

Unfortunately, there is no simple answer to the questions of why some marriages break up while others survive. But I think a variety of contributing factors can be named that are common to many of the divorces we are seeing today.

I am not talking about the "reasons" many divorced people will give you if you talk to them right after their divorce. "We fought all the time." "She was a spendthrift." "He never took an interest in the kids." These tend to be merely the symptoms, immediate causes, the ones that the person in his pained state can deal with at the moment. The involvement of a third party, for example, is a popular "reason" for divorce. However, such an involvement is usually a symptom of the rift that has already occurred. What is the cause of that rift? That is the real reason for their divorce.

The following are some of the reasons marriages fail:

FAILURE TO BE FRIENDS

If two people are not friends, they are missing a critical binding element in a marital relationship. According to a survey of nearly 2,000 people by psychologist Joel D. Block, companionship was the aspect of marriage that people ranked as most important—ahead of sexual satisfaction, material things, the opportunity to have children, and the security of having someone to turn to for problem-solving.

Yet, tragically, many people never thought to look for the same qualities in a spouse that they would have looked for in a friend. Maybe they were too young and thought that romantic love or physical attractiveness was all that mattered. But one day they wake up and discover that the spouse doesn't have the qualities of a friend—and that they are not, in fact, friends.

This realization usually takes about eight to ten years, Block discovered. And that, he points out, is about the time in a marriage when most divorces occur. "If it is a time when many people join the ranks of the formerly married, this occurs not so much because the passion left the union," says Block, "but, more crucially, because they no longer feel they have anything in common, little to be friends about. . . ."

Sometimes it takes even longer for a person to realize that friendship is the frustratingly absent element in his marriage. A middle-aged man whose marriage of eighteen years recently ended, put it this way: "In the end, our communication totally broke down. I couldn't sit down and just talk with her the way I could with the kids. I just didn't have a relationship with her, or she with me, and we were at a complete stand-off."

Sometimes people start out as friends and end up as strangers without realizing what's happening. He pursues business, she pursues child-rearing, and the shared parts of their lives that help bind the friendship disappear. And then, sometimes so does the marriage. "While he was busy with his job, I spent so much time alone—bringing up the children, making decisions, running the house—that after awhile it didn't even dawn on me to include him," said one divorced mother of three.

Christians are as prone to this drifting apart as are other couples. It's just that the sphere of over-involvement sometimes differs. For some couples, it's the job, or the pursuit of material goods. Many Christians can add another area of over-involvement—the nightly round of church activities. "I realized our marriage was in serious trouble the day I sat down with the calendar and saw that out of a month, Jim and I had one night together," said a devoted church woman who is now divorced. Friendship takes time together. The litany of warning about hyperactive churchgoers has been chanted again and again. Yet couples still fall into the trap of church involvement at the expense of family.

Split Values

Shared values, though a critical factor in friendship, is so important that I have given it a separate heading. Shared values—the beliefs that are important to us—is a foundation stone for marriage. When a couple goes in different directions in their values, their relationship is likely to go in different directions, too, whether the value disagreement is over how to spend money or leisure time, or how to raise children.

This is particularly true when one partner's values become increasingly Christian and the other's become decreasingly so. Scripture warns against being "unequally yoked with an unbeliever," yet many Christians find themselves in this position *after* marriage—and sometimes even after many years. "When I married him, my husband was the model Christian. I don't know—maybe that should have warned me . . ." says a twenty-nine-year-old, pressing her fingers into her forehead. "But no—he *was* sincere. I still have his Bible and sometimes I look through it—at the underlinings and the notes and all—and I think, 'How could he . . . ?' " She stares into the corner for a minute, then goes on. "Well, we were both disillusioned somewhat with the church, and were groping around for a while. I came out of it

to a renewed faith. He never did, but went further into a non-Christian value system until he finally left God—and me."

Unhealthy Adversary Roles

"Is it possible to have a healthy, constructive relationship with anyone of the opposite sex?" asks Gretchen Cryer in her musical, "I'm Getting My Act Together." For Cryer, who sees men and women as hopelessly locked into adversary roles, the answer is a resounding no. For too many couples, who are in fact locked into those roles, Cryer is right.

Consider the stereotypes. He thinks he is supposed to be strong, tough, unemotional, independent. She thinks she is supposed to be needy, emotional, dependent. As Anthony Campolo, sociologist at Eastern College, has so eloquently pointed out, these stereotypes are the two halves of a whole person. A whole person has both strengths and needs, is both dependent and independent. Christ exemplifies the whole person, says Campolo, because he was able to live out the two halves. For example, he could show both strength, as in the Temple incident in Matthew 21, as well as tender emotion, as when he wept at Lazarus's tomb.

Now consider the couple trying to live out the stereotype. At best, you have two half-people, and a phony complementariness—one based on artificial distinctions rather than actual interaction between two personalities.

And often these artificial roles develop into an adversary relationship. What happens when she has strengths, and must suppress them because he can't handle the idea of a strong woman? What happens when he has needs, and must go hurting because he can't tell her about them—and because she would look down on him if he did? "One of the biggest killers of my marriage was my belief that the husband should be perfect and have no needs," a thirty-year-old woman told me.

"That creates a tremendous strain on a

guy," pointed out a man of the same generation. "I was under that strain in my marriage, and I couldn't handle it. For a marriage to work, there has to be equal sharing and the recognition that neither person has it all together. They *both* need each other."

FAILURE IN YOUR RELATIONSHIP WITH PARENTS

"I married to escape my parents, because I disliked them and couldn't get along with them," stated one woman, who soon discovered that she had brought her own poor relationship skills right with her from one household to another. People, especially young people, often don't see the connection between their inability to get along with their parents and their inability to get along with their spouses. Actually, there is every connection.

Consider a man whose mother has always done everything for him, never crossed him, given him everything he wanted. One woman married such a man—and it wasn't long before she realized he expected her to treat him just as his mother had. "The marriage worked as long as I went along with his whims," she commented. "I put him through school, let him buy all the 'toys' he wanted—from guns to scuba diving equipment." Three degrees, four children, and innumerable toys later, she could no longer put up with his latest whim—a mistress—and a divorce was filed.

On the other hand, learning better ways to relate to one's parents will almost certainly strengthen and improve a marital relationship. One woman had a tendency to totally withdraw when she had a disagreement with her parents. She had practiced this negative behavior from childhood on and carried it right into her first marriage, where it helped destroy the relationship because her side of a story was never aired. But as a result of counseling she began to learn to express her point of view to her parents. When she remarried she discovered that this newly developed ability carried over into the relationship with her husband, too. "I'm able to tell him when I disagree instead of pulling into my shell and letting my views and needs go unspoken," she said, "and the marriage is stronger for it."

FALSE EXPECTATIONS OF MARRIAGE

Our romance-laden society has fostered the happily-ever-after idea of marriage. Those of us who grew up watching Cinderella dream of the day her prince would come are perhaps particularly vulnerable to a sugarcoated view of matrimonial bliss. Outwardly we laugh at such pipe-dreams of perfection, yet the media keeps perpetuating them because inwardly we still believe in them; and couples continue to be disappointed when their relationship (or, more precisely, their mate) doesn't measure up.

BUT WHAT ABOUT CHRISTIANS?

Having said all that, we still hear those who cry, "Yes, that may help explain the breakup of so many secular marriages. But why are so many *Christians'* marriages breaking up?" To which we can simply point to the same reasons and say, "Because Christians are human, too."

And, like the rest of society, Christians are finding divorce more permissible today. But we should not take the view of today's society, that divorce is *always* permissible, nor of yesterday's society, that it is *never* permissible. Christ acknowledged that because of the "hardness" of people's hearts, there may be some instances when divorce will occur (Matthew 5:32, 19:3–9).

What pressures does the Christian young person face when contemplating marriage? Have we subtly and unconsciously contributed to the problem of rising divorces among middle-aged persons?

I think many Christian young people rush to the marriage altar because they have been taught that this is the road to acceptance and legitimacy within the church body. They have heard the jokes about singleness as being "the gift nobody wants." They get the clear impression that the only people who count are the married ones.

But the Bible teaches something entirely different about singleness and marriage. One state is not considered better than another. Each is a gift. Christ was not in such a hurry to get people married off. He said they ought to think hard before they entered matrimony, because it was to be an irrevocable contract (Matthew 19:4–8). Paul even went so far as to suggest that he felt singleness was preferable to marriage (1 Corinthians 7:7,8, 32–35).

Perhaps another reason many Christians have overstressed marriage is because they think it is the only safe container for the "dangerous problem" of sexuality. They actually fear the single person, whose sexuality, they feel, is uncontained—dangerous, highly explosive. Yet, this, too, is unbiblical and insulting to the single person who has willed that his sexuality be contained by his chaste spirit and the indwelling Holy Spirit. The will to remain chaste—or faithful—is the only safe container for sexuality, not marriage, as too many Christian married people have discovered.

Another reason I believe we see many divorces among Christians, especially those in the middle years, is our tendency to be inflexible. Over the years we come to see everything in life as a fixed truth (or untruth), and we forget that we are always learners, always struggling toward a clearer understanding of truth. We lose the ability to dialogue and change, not only in matters of doctrine, but in relationships. Yet marriage is above all a living relationship in which we are to grow and change. There is nothing static about a marriage (unless it is already dead).

What Happens After Divorce?

When all the causes, reasons, and explanations are given, there still remains something mysterious about divorce. How can two people who loved each other enough to wed and bed and even rear children now decide they do not want to be together anymore? No one has the complete answer.

What is perhaps clearer is what happens to an individual in the process of and after divorce. Psychologists have delineated several stages the person will go through, much like the stages of grief over the death of a loved one that Elisabeth Kübler-Ross defined. And for all the mystery and pain, several things must happen during these stages for a person to survive a divorce and to live a whole life again.

The process a divorced person goes through involves three stages, according to psychologists Kenneth Kressel and Morton Deutsch. Their research included in-depth interviews with twenty-one highly experienced therapists whose combined practices involved hundreds of cases.

The three stages are the decision period itself, mourning, and the time of "reequilibration." Or, as Jim Smoke puts it in lay terms in his book, *Growing Through Divorce*, "shock, mourning, and growth."

Let's look more closely at each of the three stages.

Stage 1—The Decision Period

"The decision to divorce is firmly made by at least one partner," state Kressel and Deutsch of the onset of this stage. But, they point out, this is closely followed by an attack of separation anxiety—which can lead to the "marital flip-flop" as both partners take turns pushing for and opposing the divorce.

It is at this point that some marriages can be saved, as both parties struggle with their vacillating feelings. And yet Smoke, who served as minister to single adults at Garden Grove Community Church, warns against encouraging false hope. "Without hope, life in general would be dry as dust," he said, "but hope has to be coupled with realism. Realism looks at a situation as it exists, not as you would like it to exist . . . Just hoping a marriage will come back together by itself is like wishing on a chicken bone. Each person must evaluate for herself whether the relationship has died or whether there is enough life to hold out some hope." If a fellow Christian sees that a divorcing person's marriage really has died, the wisest and most Christian thing to do is to help accept that, not prolong his agony by falsely encouraging him to hang on.

Besides shock and denial, other characteristic reactions at this stage include a frenzied social pace and the need to tell all and tell everyone. At the same time I was going through this stage, a close friend of mine was, too. She used to embarrass me by her constant talk about how her husband had left her. Then I realized I was doing the same thing. This kind of self-exposure is uncharacteristic of me. Normally, I am fairly reserved. But for this time in my life, I needed to talk about my personal life in order to work out my pain. It was a kind of self-therapy. I found a group of Christians who understood my need to do that and kept listening empathetically to my story over and over again.

This uncharacteristic behavior of mine brings up an important point. As far as anyone who didn't know me very well could have told, I lived up perfectly to the reputation divorced people have for being unstable. Many Christians, I fear, view divorced people as having personality disorders. But the divorced *person* is not necessarily unstable. His *situation* is. Throughout the process of divorce, say Kressel and Deutsch, we can view the divorced person as being "buffeted by strong emotional forces over which [he] has little control." On such a wildly tossing ship, even the most stable or mature person would behave in some unusual ways.

STAGE 2—MOURNING

After several months of praying that my ex-husband would come back, it began to become apparent to me that it wasn't going to happen. Gradually, the hope of Stage 1 changed to mourning—and I had entered Stage 2. There were many nights when I would cry myself to sleep and cry myself awake again in the morning. Kressel and Deutsch note that this stage is characterized by "an acute sense of failure and diminished self-worth, loneliness and depression. Mourning a spouse lost through divorce is in some respects more difficult than mourning a dead spouse, since the partner in divorce is still alive. . . ."

A person may vent his or her frustration at a former spouse—either in person or, if he or she isn't around, at someone else. This signals a "return to equilibrium and an upswing in self-regard," says Kressel and Deutsch. Christian friends might want to help the divorced person channel his anger in a constructive manner—like shouting in an empty room, or even looking for a new, more interesting job. But they shouldn't condemn the anger itself. It is a healthy feeling, and often a justified one.

STAGE 3—REEQUILIBRATION

"This is a period of heightened self-growth and diminished dwelling on the marriage," comment Kressel and Deutsch. It is marked by the ever increasing intensity of acceptance of one fact: The marriage is *over*.

This complete, total, unequivocal acceptance is difficult to reach. The hold of the old is insidious—especially when a total break is impossible because of children involved. The idea of being "friends now" is suspect—it suggests an unconscious wish to hang on to the marriage.

Besides having accepted the finality of his divorce, the person who comes out healthy from the divorce has also gotten himself, his ex-spouse, and his former marriage into perspective. He can remember the good and bad times in the marriage. He can evaluate it for what it was. He can see the strengths and weaknesses of both himself and his former spouse, and he can accept and acknowledge the ways in which *both* parties contributed to the divorce. In addition, I believe a Christian can come out of a divorce with his view of God revitalized and his faith in God strengthened.

It has been several years since my divorce. And in those years I have learned and grown a tremendous amount. I have found answers to some of my questions and the ones to which I found no answers, I've learned to accept. And the divorce has helped me see my life as a Christian in a whole new way.

First, experiencing a divorce de-Pharisaized me. I used to be the first to point a finger and say, "Tsk, tsk" when a fellow Christian fell short. Now I know what it feels like to be on the other end of the finger. I hope I am now more understanding and tolerant.

Suffering through a divorce also humanized me. I was mortal after all. Calamity had befallen me, just like any other human being on earth. Furthermore, I was capable of the whole gamut of human emotions, including rage, hate, and the desire for vengeance—and God still accepted me. He loved me even when I was imperfect.

My failed marriage also helped correct my view of God. It seemed that he was not in the business of protecting my personal kingdom. He was in the business of building his kingdom—however best that might be done. He had never promised me a rose garden. But he did promise to be with me through the thorns. And he kept that promise.

It seems sad that it took a divorce for God to teach me these things, yet because of that I feel better able to minister to members of the Body who are hurting. For I know now that no matter how drastically our lives may be shattered—by divorce or other difficulties—God is able to put the pieces together again. I only wish that more of us would be willing to become channels of God's healing, restoring love to our hurting brothers and sisters.

—Kristine Miller Tomasik. Reprinted by permission of the author.

Effect on Children

Many couples endure marriage "for the sake of the children." But which is harder on the children, divorce or staying together?

A whole field of evidence now being compiled indicates that the divorce itself need not have a long-term adverse effect on children. At the time of divorce, very young children show distinctive behavioral changes such as reverting to bed-wetting, thumb-sucking, and troublesome sleeping. But within a year they have usually overcome those reversions, especially if they receive love from the custodial parent. However, when the custodial parent is overwhelmed and controlled by his/her own needs, the children reflect this and show problems in their development.

While experts concur that children feel the initial pain of their parents' divorce, often intensely, most of them recover rapidly.

The single most important factor in prolonging the children's adjustment appears to be the amount of bitterness between the couple. If they seethe with anger and express it frequently to the offspring, they not only do damage to themselves but can cause serious problems to the normal development of their children.

During the divorce and custody proceedings (and even afterward) children often become pawns in the game. Parents attempt to bribe, threaten, or demand their loyalty. One parent may encourage the child to spy against the other.

And what about the children? They're human. Realizing their situation, they're bright enough to take advantage of it. Jimmy used to say to his father when he didn't get his way, "If you don't give it to me, I'll go back to Momma. She'll let me go skating every Saturday." They become experts in setting one parent against the other.

For the Christian divorcee, the best advice from those who have been through it, goes like this: As much as possible, do nothing and say nothing against your ex. That's not always easy, especially when the ex deliberately seems to frustrate your plans or interfere with the child-care agreement.

Here are a few practical tips on handling the children.

1. *Tell the Truth.* Children generally know when you're lying or trying to hold back. They don't need to know everything (and shouldn't), but they do need to know basic facts.

2. *Expect to Feel Ambivalent About the Children.* For the custodial parent, a heavy weight often hangs on them. At times you may think or perhaps even say out loud, "If I didn't have children to tie me down, I could ..." With almost the next breath you'll probably add, "But my children enrich my life. The problems are worth it, just to have them."

Those feelings are natural. Most custodial parents go through it. Try to accept those feelings as normal.

3. *Having Custody Doesn't Prevent Loneliness.* "At least I have my son," one mother recalls saying shortly after the marital breakup. "For the first few weeks we had so many adjustments to make, I didn't think about being lonely. But after awhile, it got to me. I had almost no adult companionship. I wanted to talk about anything adult—recipes, books, morality, theology. But how much of that can you do with a five-year-old?"

4. *Being the Custodial Parent Means No Other Parent There to Undercut Authority.* In family stress, one parent tends to allow the youngsters to break the rules the other has set. If you have custody, you set the rules and you enforce them. (When they visit the other parent and the rules change, they still need to know what to expect when with you.)

5. *You'll Never Have Enough Time With Your Children.* If you're the custodial parent, it generally means you're also working. One mother said, "In trying to be both mother and father, you never have enough time for your children. You're too busy doing things for them—especially when they're young. But you have so little time to hold them, to love them, or simply to listen."

6. *Allow the Children to Express Their Emotions Over the Divorce*—both at the time they hear about it and later. They have a right to their moods and depressions just as the parents do. If they scream and say they hate you, allow it. Let them use any nondestructive outlet. And let them know it's okay to feel the way they do.

7. *Tell Your Children They Didn't Cause the Divorce.* Many children blame themselves. "I was naughty and Daddy left" or "I'm not nice and my parents split up." The feelings of guilt are never logical. But the child may need assurance that he or she was not the factor in the divorce.

8. *Explain the Future to the Children.* As much as possible let them know where they'll live, what will happen in school. Tell them of the lowered standard of living. Also let them know how often they can expect to see the other parent. Most of all, give them a sense of security and help them feel that life is under control.

9. *Don't Allow the Children to Play the "Parent Trap" Game.* Don't encourage them to plot ways to get mother and father back together. When the divorce becomes final, don't hold up the possibility of reconciliation. If there is a possibility (and not merely a vague hope), be honest there, too.

10. *Don't Get Overly Concerned About the Broken-Home Image.* As stated earlier, one-parent families can be as happy and healthy as two-parent families. In fact, when children grow up in an atmosphere of being loved and feeling secure, the actual circumstances make little difference.

11. *Be a Parent, Not a Buddy, and Not a Brother or Sister.* Your children can develop friendships. They can't easily find parents. They need authority figures to set the limits for their behavior.

12. *Don't Expect Too Much From the Children.* Don't make the oldest the house-

keeper or a surrogate mate. Or don't go to the opposite extreme of being overly protective and sheltering. Don't give your children the picture of "You and me against the world."

13. *If Your Children Show Serious Behavioral or Emotional Problems, Get Help.* Single parents often wonder, Will my son turn into a homosexual if he's only around females? Or will my daughter become promiscuous? If this troubles you, get help. If you're a mother, find surrogate fathers for your son.

14. *As a Christian Parent, Remember Your Responsibilities Before God.* Most believers either have their children baptized or dedicated. That presentation of children is also a covenant with God. As a parent you promise your faithfulness to teach your children about him. Even though your marriage has dissolved and you may personally be in heavy turmoil, keep the children's lives as natural as possible.

Keep involved in your congregation.

If you're not already doing so, I suggest you pray for and with your children every day. Let them know your concern.

Have a daily Bible reading plan. Those few minutes communicate to your children that you consider God an important aspect of life.

15. *Most Important, Let the Children Know You Love Them.* You can show your love in hundreds of ways. Take time to listen to the children when they want to talk. If you can't stop then, why not say, "Sammy, I'm very busy right now, but as soon as I finish, I'll sit down and we'll talk." Then keep that promise.

Let them know where you are. They may never need to call, but it gives them a sense of security to know that you can be reached if they need you. That includes when you go out on dates, too.

Don't hesitate to tell them that you love them. Especially in the months after the divorce, the children need to hear that often.

Don't assume they know because you pay the bills or take them places. They need to have it expressed.

We need to experience human love, too.

—CECIL MURPHEY

FOR FURTHER READING:

Rogers, Dale Evans. *Woman.* Old Tappan, N.J.: Revell, 1980.

Smoke, Jim. *Growing Through Divorce.* Eugene, Ore.: Harvest House, 1976.

Smoke, Jim. *Suddenly Single.* Old Tappan, N.J.: Revell, 1982.

DRUGS

IN GENERAL, there has been for the past decade a tolerance toward the use of marijuana in particular and drugs in general. Never before has society so changed its mind and attitude about a dangerous (or, at least, potentially dangerous) drug such as marijuana. We have gone from a *tough* stand against it in the sixties to a *tolerance* of it in the seventies and the prospects of its *legalization* in the eighties!

NEEDED: KNOWLEDGE AND ACTION

Since we have not been able to depend on the government to protect our children from marijuana (either by stepped-up detention of the smuggling trade or enforcement of the laws), as concerned parents we must prepare a moral and spiritual defense against it.

The first step is to *get the facts!* It is important to become as knowledgeable about its dangers as possible, yet at the same time not panic or overreact if and when a teenager is found to be trying it. Given the choice between overreaction and inaction, I would rather see the former. But it does not have to be either. Parents all across the country are waking up and getting involved in trying to get the facts about drugs.

The next step is to *do something!* Parents

must do something *before* drugs break out and, of course, must know what to do when the child is already experimenting or is a regular user.

There are nearly a thousand different parent groups nationwide that have banded together to fight back against drug abuse. Their impact is being felt. This is an encouraging sign.

Most of all, we have to teach our youth *before the fact rather than just react after the act.* Our youth need inner mechanisms and inner controls against the temptation to experiment with marijuana (since this is usually the lead-in to other more potent drugs) and other artificial "highs" in general (such as booze). In the final analysis, it is the inner legislation of the heart that acts as a policeman or deterrent to help us and our kids to keep away from forbidden fruit. When there is no market for drugs, the supply dries up.

We need a moral and spiritual "renewal" to hit our schools, communities, and churches. Kids need to see that "straight" is the only life-style that guarantees a future survival. We need to pray for, work for, and support a new generation of kids who are made aware of what drugs have done to their older brothers and sisters and to a past generation—and begin a campaign for abstinence. The best way to fight fire is with fire. Kids take drugs because of its availability and the peer pressure resulting from its widespread use. One of the most effective deterrents is counter peer pressure. If even a small group of kids or students in a school make a pledge to "keep off the grass," it can have a remarkable effect on other kids. If the market is wiped out, drugs will be wiped out. This is getting to the source at the other end. There is little hope of cutting off the supply of marijuana where it's grown, but it can be cut off at the other end—where it normally is smoked. No sales—no smoke!

What if prevention fails? What if our children refuse to accept preventative measures or the Christian-Judeo standards that teach, preach, and practice against it. Worse, what if parents discover the teenager has gone beyond experimentation and has become a chronic user or is even taking other hard drugs?

It takes a very mature parent to face the trauma of drug addiction in the home. There are no easy answers or easy steps to solve the problem. Some children get worse before the situation can ever get better. The parents are often helpless, when their son or daughter runs away, gets immersed in the drug scene, or ends up in a hospital or jail.

This does not mean something cannot and should not be done. No matter what, parents must always try to "do something." They must always be ready and willing to help when the addict wants that help. It is Mom's and Dad's reaction to drug abuse and drug addiction in the home that is often the key to helping the youth if and when he or she is ready for that help.

When it comes to marijuana, the parent can begin by acquiring as much knowledge about the drug as possible. Neither ignorance nor emotional overreaction to a child's pot smoking will help matters. We must face the reality of raising kids in the eighties. Drugs, especially marijuana, are probably here to stay. All kids—Christian or non-Christian—churchgoing or nonchurchgoing—have to face the drug issue.

Therefore, all parents must work out a strategy to protect their kids. Drug abuse today often has little to do with the failure of parents to raise their kids properly. It has more to do with the failure of society to deal with drug abuse. It is a symptom of our times. The best of homes and the best of parents can raise a child with the highest of standards, meeting the child's emotional and spiritual needs, only to see the grown youth get involved in the abuse of drugs when at school or away at college.

While we must deal with the results of those who have already abused drugs, efforts must be concentrated on the upcoming generation.

FAILURE OF EDUCATION PROGRAMS

We have tragically assumed that drug-education and prevention programs do not

Common Drugs of Abuse

CATEGORY	1 Drugs	2 Sample trade or other names	3 Medical uses	4 Dependence Physical	Psycho- logical
CANNABIS	Marijuana	Pot, grass, reefer, sinsemilla	Under investigation	Unknown	Moderate
	Tetrahydrocannabinol	THC			
	Hashish	Hash	None		
	Hash oil	Hash oil			
DEPRESSANTS	Alcohol	Liquor, beer, wine	None	High	High
	Barbiturates	Secobarbital, Amobarbital, Butisol, Tuinal	Anesthetic, anti-convulsant, sedative, hypnotic	High-moderate	High-moderate
	Methaqualone	Quaalude, Sopor, Parest	Sedative, hypnotic	High	High
	Tranquilizers	Valium, Librium, Equanil, Miltown	Anti-anxiety, anti-convulsant, sedative	Moderate to low	Moderate
STIMULANTS	Cocaine	Coke, flake, snow	Local anesthetic	Possible	High
	Amphetamines	Biphetamine, Dexedrine	Hyperactivity, narcolepsy		
	Nicotine	Tobacco, cigars, cigarettes	None	High	High
	Caffeine	Coffee, tea, cola drinks, No-Doz		Low	Low
HALLUCINOGENS	LSD	Acid	None	None	Degree unknown
	Mescaline and peyote	Button, Cactus			
	Phencyclidine	PCP, angel dust	Veterinary anesthetic	Unknown	High
	Psilocybin-psilocin	Mushrooms	None	None	Degree unknown
INHALANTS	Nitrous oxide	Whippets, laughing gas	Anesthetic	Possible	Moderate
	Butyl nitrite	Locker Room, Rush	None		
	Amyl nitrite	Poppers, snappers	Heart stimulant		
	Chlorohydrocarbons	Aerosol paint, cleaning fluid	None		
	Hydrocarbons	Aerosol propellants gasoline, glue, paint thinner	None		
NARCOTICS	Opium	Paregoric	Antidiarrheal, pain relief	High	High
	Morphine	Morphine, Pectoral Syrup	Pain relief, cough medicine		
	Codeine	Codeine, Empirin Compound with Codeine, Robitussin A-C		Moderate	Moderate
	Heroin	Horse, smack	Under investigation	High	High
	Methadone	Dolophine, Methadose	Heroin substitute, pain relief		

164

5 Effects in hours	6 Possible effects	7 Effects of overdose	8 Withdrawal symptoms
2-4	Euphoria, relaxed inhibitions, increase in heart and pulse rate, reddening of the eyes, increased appetite, disoriented behavior	Anxiety, paranoia, loss of concentration, slower movements, time distortion	Insomnia, hyperactivity, and decreased appetite occasionally reported
1-12 1-16 4-8	Slurred speech, disorientation, drunken behavior	Shallow respiration, cold and clammy skin, dilated pupils, weak and rapid pulse, coma, possible death	Anxiety, insomnia, tremors, delirium, convulsions, possible death
½-2 2-4	Increased alertness, excitation, euphoria, increase in pulse rate and blood pressure, insomnia, loss of appetite	Agitation, increase in body temperature, hallucinations, convulsions, possible death, tremors Agitation, increase in pulse rate and blood pressure, loss of appetite, insomnia	Apathy, long periods of sleep, irritability, depression
18-12 Variable 6	Illusions and hallucinations, poor perception of time and distance	Drug effects becoming longer and more intense, psychosis	Withdrawal symptoms not reported
Up to ½ hr.	Excitement, euphoria, giddiness, loss of inhibitions, aggressiveness, delusions, depression, drowsiness, headache, nausea	Loss of memory, confusion, unsteady gait, erratic heart beat and pulse, possible death	Insomnia, decreased appetite, depression, irritability, headache
3-6 12-24	Euphoria, drowsiness, respiratory depression, constricted pupils, nausea	Slow and shallow breathing, clammy skin, convulsions, coma, possible death	Watery eyes, runny nose, yawning, loss of appetite, irritability, tremors, panic, chills and sweating, cramps, nausea

Source: National Institute on Drug Abuse

work. Since the first outbreak of drugs among the middle-class in the sixties, there has been a flood of materials, programs, and proposals to solve the problem. Before this (and when the problem was confined primarily to the inner city and the ghettos), it was virtually ignored. When the drug-abuse circle widened, we were unprepared for it. Many parents refused to believe when it began happening in lily-white America. When the full impact of drug abuse was finally recognized, crash programs of all sorts were instituted. Schools began drug-education classes. Community prevention programs were launched, as well as rehabilitation programs established.

What good such programs did or what effect these programs and materials had on prevention to stop further drug abuse is suspect. They probably had few positive results, primarily because the programs came too late. Some people say they had no effect at all. The fear then was that drug-education programs might make kids even more curious about drugs and thus they would go out and try them as a result. Most drug-education programs were one-shot deals containing misinformation and scare tactics that turned most kids off.

If the publishing of drug materials, lectures, films, rap sessions, and the presentation of drug-educated programs did anything, they made us aware that there *was* a problem. And there still is. But now, with the public tolerance towards drugs, plus funding cutbacks for school and community drug-education programs, we have not been able to keep current on the data on hand that should be taught to students in the schools and made available to parents and families. Drug abuse, with marijuana leading the way, seems to have become another vice and abuse added to our social ills that is here to stay. Like crime, pornography, prostitution, and homosexuality—marijuana has been added to the acceptable moral ways of society that too many feel we're just going to have to "live with."

We may not be able to stop the moral landslide of drug abuse completely—probably far from it. But we can at least let our kids know our opposition to it. In the process, it is possible to save the minds and lives of thousands of our youth and our younger children who will inevitably follow the path we set for them. I can't change the alcoholic laws in our country, but I can preach and promote a moral philosophy against its use and abuse which will list voluntary abstinence. We must do no less in respect to the use and abuse of marijuana.

This does not mean we should give up trying to prevent its legalization or that we cannot pressure our schools and legislators to enforce the present laws against its abuse. We can! We all know that governmental bodies respond to the pressure groups in our society.

Many parent groups and neighborhood action groups need to serve notice to federal, state and local governments that they are not going to tolerate drug abuse. When they do, we will begin to see a reversal of present trends which have created a generation of pot smokers.

—From Don Wilkerson, *Marijuana.* Old Tappan, N.J.: Revell, 1983.

E

EDUCATION

Obtaining a College Degree at Home

Have you ever found yourself wishing that you had gone to college or that you had not dropped out of college? Many women share this longing for more education, but wonder how it will fit in with marriage, motherhood, and career.

Because lack of time is the biggest hindrance for many adults, educators have taken a second look at traditional college programs. Now it is possible to obtain a college degree in a variety of ways, not all of which involve actual on-campus study. Using such tools as CLEP tests, credit for life experience, independent study, correspondence courses, and the University Without Walls program, a student can now go to college without actually *going* to college.

Of course, the logical question about the use of these methods is whether or not the degree acquired is actually an authentic one. The answer is yes, provided the college or university through which the program is administered is accredited.

A degree acquired through off-campus study is called an external degree, meaning, of course, a degree that is acquired away from the college. However, within this rather broad definition are many differences. In some cases, it is theoretically possible to obtain enough credits for a degree without ever going to classes at all—although this would be a rare case. Other colleges will allow only residents of that particular state to participate in the external degree program. Others accept a liberal amount of credits from such sources as life experience

study, but then require a certain number of quarters or semesters of actual residency at the college before a degree can be awarded. Still others will grant credits for non-traditional study but only to students who have already acquired as much as two years of college credit in a classroom.

Any woman interested in these non-traditional methods will need to explore the options available to her, based on the individual requirements of the college she has chosen. Not all colleges accept all kinds of non-traditional studies so it's best to find out first before beginning any actual program.

For the woman who has never attended college, a good starting point might be the College Level Examination Program. These tests enable a person to prove her knowledge in a particular subject area and are the equivalent of taking a particular college course. CLEP tests are given at colleges around the country on a monthly basis, so regardless of where you live there's probably a testing center within driving distance. The cost of each examination is $20—quite a bargain when you consider how much it would cost to take the actual college course.

Another alternative to classroom study is credit for life experience. To acquire credit in this way you must put together a life experience portfolio, detailing experiences you feel have given you learning equivalent to that in a typical class of the same subject. For instance, if you've taught Sunday School, served as PTA president, and been a member of Toastmistress, you might feel that these activities entitle you to credit for a speech course.

167

Correspondence courses are another means by which off-campus credits can sometimes be acquired. Many universities allow students to take courses by mail for at least a portion of the credit required for a degree, and a handful of colleges will allow you to complete an entire course of study in this way. However, most colleges do limit their correspondence program, either by establishing certain prerequisites to be taken on campus, or by limiting the number of credits to be accumulated through study by mail.

One of the innovative methods being used for external degree programs involves a means of independent study known as the University Without Walls. Through this program such things as CLEP tests, credit for life experience, previous college study, etc., start the student off with as many credits as possible. (Individual participating schools have varying policies as to kinds of credit and amount of credit they deem acceptable.) Then, once a student's scholastic standing is assessed, she is ready to embark on a personalized program of study. Courses are put together as learning contracts drawn up between student and instructor. These courses allow for individual circumstances and are highly flexible. The requirements for acceptable completion of the course will vary, but in most instances there is either no time limit or a generous one—as much as two years per course.

To further increase a woman's opportunity for acquiring a college degree, some colleges allow credits for television "classes." These programs usually are broadcast at some outrageous time, such as five o'clock in the morning, but even that may still be more convenient than regular on-campus study. Credit for television study is usually quite restricted, so don't expect to acquire more than a few credits in this manner.

With all these new methods available, it's becoming easier for adults to go back to college. But, it would be a mistake to assume that because these programs are flexible,

they require less work than traditional programs. Colleges don't give away degrees—you have to earn them. In many cases, a student will find herself working harder in correspondence courses or independent study or in the preparing of a life experience portfolio than she would if she had been able to attend classes on campus.

To learn more about opportunities for going to college at home, check these resources:

• The Council for the Advancement of Experiential Learning (CAEL) maintains a file of colleges which grant credit for life experience. You can receive free information about participating institutions in your state by calling toll free, 800-638-7813.

• *Catalyst*, 14 East 60th Street, New York, N.Y. 10022, will send you, upon request, a free listing of resource centers which provide counseling for women in the areas of further education and career choices.

• The Educational Testing Service, Princeton, N.J. 08541, offers a workbook to help in preparing a life experience portfolio, called *How to Get College Credit for What You Have Learned as a Homemaker and Volunteer.* (It also contains the *Catalyst* listing of resource centers.)

Several book publishing companies also offer informative books about off-campus study. *National Directory of External Degree Programs*, by Alfred W. Munzert, Ph.D. is available from Hawthorn Books, Inc., 260 Madison Avenue, New York, N.Y. 10016. *Guide to Independent Study Through Correspondence* is available from Peterson's Guides, Box 978, Edison, N.J. 08817.

—EDITH FLOWERS KILGO, author of *Money in the Cookie Jar; Money Management;* and *Handbook for Christian Homemakers.*

FOR FURTHER READING:

Gundry, Patricia. *The Complete Woman.* Garden City, N.Y.: Doubleday, 1981.

Ward, Patricia, and Martha Stout. *Christian Women at Work.* Grand Rapids: Zondervan, 1981.

EMOTIONS

EMOTIONS are a mixed blessing. They are responsible for many of man's finest and greatest achievements. They are also responsible for some of the greatest tragedies in our world.

We usually talk about emotions in terms of how we *feel*. I *feel* angry. I *feel* disgusted. I *feel* depressed. Although the words *emotion* and *feeling* are often used interchangeably, there *are* differences between them. Perhaps we could define *feeling* as experiences of mild intensity, and *emotion* as those which move us strongly.

Emotions may arise from either external or internal stimulation—a condition in the body or a thought in the mind. Technically, emotion may be defined as: an acute disturbance or upset of the individual which is revealed in behavior and in conscious experience as well as through widespread changes in the functioning of viscera (smooth muscles, glands, heart and lungs) and which is initiated by factors within a psychological situation.

Several elements are involved in an emotion. It is usually sudden in onset, temporary, and disrupts, disturbs or disorganizes the total person. An emotional reaction to a stimulus involves both past reactions to a similar stimulus and the individual's present psychological condition. It also involves behavior, for we usually observe certain types of behavior in an emotional reaction. Because the intellect is involved in emotional experiences, conscious experience is present. The physical part of the body is also involved because of the various organs which are affected.

Emotions produce chemical and neurological changes within the body. They produce energy which mobilizes a person and keeps him alive and functioning. When you experience fear, energy becomes available which helps you run away from danger. Anger can provide you with the energy you need to survive by fighting for your life. The maternal feelings of a mother provide the love that infants need to survive.

Emotions are similar to reflex action. In a given situation you will feel a particular emotion. If you touch the cornea of your eye with a handkerchief your eyelid will blink. There is no way you can stop that reflex from happening. When the eye is touched, certain nerve cells are activated and a message is sent to your brain. Other nerves are put into action until the message arrives back at the eye and the eyelid blinks. Once the cornea is touched, the eyelid blinks automatically.

Our emotions are quite similar. If you stub your toe your immediate reaction is to get upset or angry. You may say to yourself, "I won't get upset! I won't get mad! I won't!" But if your toe hurts badly enough you will still get upset. You cannot prevent the emotion, but you can control what you do with that emotion.

Sometimes we experience a strong emotion and are not aware of it. Fear may manifest itself as tenseness. Anger might manifest itself as hurt feelings, depression, fear, or insomnia. At other times we may be afraid or angry and not know why we feel that way.

Each day we experience stimuli that trigger emotional reactions. It is even possible for the memory of a past event to arouse an emotion. When this emotional energy is aroused it must be directed into the proper outlet. If it is not, it does not disappear. If anything, it will increase until it overflows. Emotions that are not expressed through healthy outlets such as play, work, and talking about our feelings, usually end up directed toward certain organs of the body.

Emotions are aroused when a person makes a value judgment. This judgment is usually made on the basis of sensory appeal or repulsion and rational evaluation. For example, something you like may provide you with great pleasure and satisfaction but, from a rational standpoint, it might be bad for you. A chocolate candy bar may be very desirable to the diabetic but if he eats it he knows he will suffer the consequences. A college student may want to skip his classes and go to the beach, but if he gives in to that desire he may flunk his examinations.

If it were possible to look into a person's

169

mind we would find a process occurring of which the person may not even be aware. An emotional reaction is preceded by knowledge, evaluation, and finally, judgment. But these occur so rapidly and even unconsciously that you might not be aware of them happening at all. After the judgment has been made the emotional reaction follows with the appropriate muscular and glandular changes which are a part of emotional activity.

Emotions involve reactions and experiences which come about as we adjust to life situations. They are tied to intellectual functions because a person first has to perceive and understand something about a situation before his emotions come into play.

The meaning of any situation is gradually built up during a person's lifetime because of innumerable experiences with similar situations. If a person has five bad experiences with dogs, one after another, naturally a fear response is gradually reinforced.

Why do some people react differently than others? Are they *more emotional* or are some people *less emotional?* Is there a normal way people should react? Each person reacts emotionally because of the influences and experiences of his own childhood and background. Some individuals feel great intensities of emotions and react with intense joy or disappointment. And then we run into the person who seems to be insulated from such depth of feeling.

Differences of emotional expression can sometimes be attributed to constitutional makeup. Some babies almost immediately are more excitable than others. Their nervous systems seem to be more sensitive. Early training also plays a part. Some children are taught to deny and hide their emotions, others are encouraged to express them. Transient factors such as fatigue, illness, and alcohol can affect emotional response. Brain damage will also cause variations.

Still another factor is a person's frame of reference. The feelings a person has and the way he expresses and controls them depend on his basic beliefs and attitudes about what is true, right, and possible. He actually reacts to a situation according to his own needs.

Finally, a person's cultural background and environment will affect his emotional reaction. If you live in a highly competitive, hostile society you will probably reflect that with a lack of love and sympathy.

The intensity of an emotion depends not only on how attractive or repulsive or dangerous we judge a situation to be, but also on how important this attraction is for us and how much we would mind having to put up with the negative features. We *can* order and regulate the intensity of an emotion if we consider the emotional situation in its relation to the goal we determined. This can result in a significant reduction in the degree of its appeal or repulsion.

There is a balance wherein two different people can react differently and still be considered normal. Outside of that norm, however, emotional reactions can be considered out of balance. A very superficial reaction may indicate a protective type of rigid lifestyle.

While we usually are not able to control an emotional response to a particular stimulus, we *can* control how we will express that emotion. If you feel hate, you do not have to act hateful. When you stub your toe you can choose how you will react. You can kick whatever you hit, say "ouch," swear, or hop about on one foot. If you walk into a strange yard and a mountain lion starts coming toward you, you will naturally feel fear. You can choose to run, climb a tree, yell for help, or pick up a stick and run toward the animal. But you will still be afraid initially.

If you always react a particular way to certain stimuli, you may feel it is impossible to react differently. Even if you do react out of a habit pattern, you can choose to react differently and try a new pattern. If the channels of a dam are opened, allowing the water to flow out, nothing will hold back that water. But the water can be controlled and diverted into different stream beds. In similar fashion you can divert your emotional energy into healthy and useful channels.

—From H. Norman Wright, *The Christian Use of Emotional Power*. Old Tappan, N.J.: Revell, 1974.

FOR FURTHER READING:

LaHaye, Tim and Bev. *Spirit-Controlled Family Living*. Old Tappan, N.J.: Revell, 1978.
McMillen, S.I., M.D. *None of These Diseases*. Old Tappan, N.J.: Revell, 1963, 1984.
Wright, H. Norman. *The Christian Use of Emotional Power*. Old Tappan, N.J.: Revell, 1974.

EMPTY NEST

AFTER A LIFETIME of raising children, the elderly spend their later years either alone or with their mate. Unfortunately, these times of potential fulfillment are often overshadowed by neglect. A great deal has been written about how the elderly suffer in isolation, cut off from others. The time has come to recognize that everyone suffers from being cut off from them!

Loneliness is prevalent among "senior citizens," primarily because mandatory retirement has become synonymous with having no place in life. Those with vitality haven't bought into the myth that "old age is a disease." Instead, they have a continued goal and a way of being useful. A kind of energy cuts through loneliness when you can affirm that you have a place.

One man volunteered how he combated our "throw-away" society. "I reviewed my whole life history," he said, "and I discovered that many of the experiences I'd had could be useful. Especially with the renewed interest in 'roots,' I learned a new way of contributing. I've been invited to give an oral history course at my church to children of elementary school age. It will be quite exciting to talk about their heritage in terms of experiences I've had!"

This fellow is, unfortunately, the excep-

tion. Too many think "old" means unnecessary and unused. Another woman, a widow in her seventies, talked about her lonely moments. "For me, loneliness is a seldom occurrence. When my husband died, I was left with this huge house. I really didn't want to move nor did I want to live with my children. They have their own lives to live and as long as I can care for myself, I want to. Anyway, I don't want anyone to treat me like a dependent child. So I rented some of my rooms to four college kids. They were struggling through school and needed a place to stay, and I'm on a fixed income. So they pay modest rent, and we share in the cooking. When we can, we eat together and we get to know each other's friends. It's marvelous! It's easier to have an extended family with people who aren't your real family. You don't get caught up in an emotional tug-of-war. These college kids are really stimulating, and I think I have something to offer them in return."

What is missed by isolating the elderly is what comes with the wisdom of age. Not nostalgia or a return to the good old days, some of which weren't so good; rather, the elderly offer wisdom that only experience can teach. The last years of life can be the prime time for investigating the ultimate meaning of life. But so little discussion centers around a theology that stresses the values and significance of aging.

We assume that God is old, and that His wisdom represents the ages, but what about a theology of aging?

Not everyone has the extended families of the people mentioned above. Over half of the elderly are single and alone. Some have friends; others do not. Some can travel to visit relatives; others are too impoverished even to take a bus to a friend's house. Those who are not widowed may be confined to their homes. They've seen their neighbors die or move away, their ministers called to other churches, and their friends become physically ill.

Loneliness is accented in the life-styles of the elderly. Being old means different things to different people. How someone living beyond retirement is treated is a large factor in the blanket of loneliness that covers so many. Just look at the plight of some of those who have survived generations. The elderly know what it is to see their meager pensions and savings buy less and less. They know the loneliness of forced isolation as cars become too costly to maintain or too difficult to handle. They wait for family too busy to visit, for a bus that doesn't come, for a doctor who won't make house calls, for the day they lose more independence through disease, illness, or inability to move around.

For many, being old means nursing homes if they live in the city, and isolation if they live in a rural area. And for many, being elderly is being forgotten, except during election time. It's a time when they may not be touched by another human being, and that results in being imprisoned by loneliness.

Yes, many of the elderly are lonely and are treated like second-class citizens. Yet, the elderly, just as the young and middle-aged, want independence. Help, yes, but only when it's needed and not a fostering of patriarchal dependence just because age has signaled forced retirement from careers.

Becoming old is a transitional period in which you face, and must adapt to, disruptive changes. Certainly, if you're active, well-adjusted, and confident during mid-life, you'll carry those characteristics with you. But, you still have losses to deal with. For one thing, you're forced to retire from the work role that has added focus to your life. Even if your skills and ability are unchanged, you're separated from the mainstream of society and labeled "dependent."

As one man tearfully recalled, "All of a sudden I was a has-been. I got my gold watch and was turned away. Not having meaningful work has dampened my zest for living. There's no way to maintain self-esteem when one day I'm a productive engineer, and the next day I sit on my back porch and chase blue jays from the garden. I feel like I'm just waiting to die, or everyone else is, at least!"

The elderly person's self-image is affected by multiple losses of role, status, income, and health. And, as friends, family, and neighbors die or move, they discover that they're isolated at a time when they need emotional support. The fear and loneliness of such a plight often encourages withdrawal from community activities, which in turn increases isolation. Being caught in this cycle is a troublesome problem for numerous people.

Yet even the healthy and energetic must fight the stereotypes. In a society that rewards and is built for the young, many live with insensitivity toward the people whose ingenuity built this country. The fact is, many elderly people are capable of work, intellectual growth, and creative use of leisure time. You wouldn't think that was the case, however. Just look at advertising which focuses on the elderly; it centers around people unable to perform on their own behalf. The advertising reflects the mainstream public image we have of elderly people.

The elderly make up a large segment of American society. Many live in "rest homes." (Again, the subtle stereotype that the elderly spend their last days unproductively!) They eat together, share, fight, and talk as a family unit. Yet, another family form places the elderly, middle-aged, and the young together. This form is the church. The elderly generally place a high priority on relationships, regardless of age. Children and teenagers are valued as much as adults. Couples, the elderly, single-parent families, blended families (where two divorced or widowed partners have married each other), and traditional families are represented. The "family of faith" can provide a community to minister during turning points.

—From Nancy Potts, *Loneliness: Living Between the Times*. Wheaton, Ill.: Victor Books, 1978.

FOR FURTHER READING:

Bird, Joseph and Lois. *To Live As a Family*. Garden City, N.Y.: Doubleday, 1982.

Chafin, Kenneth. *Is There a Family in the House?* Waco, Tex.: Word Books, 1978.

ENGAGEMENT

THERE IS A RIGHT TIME for exclusive friendship, and to my mind this is not far short of engagement. The learning about the opposite sex, the looking round, is almost over and now begins the task of discovering whether you really love each other, and whether your interests and outlook harmonize well enough for full committal to each other.

The difficulty often arises because engagement is misunderstood and misused. It is meant to be a preparation for marriage. Only in exceptional circumstances should it be long, because it *is* the time when closer physical contact is inevitable, and for those who are determined to keep sexual union for marriage the strain of doing so should not be prolonged.

This is where the misuse comes in. Young people in a hurry imagine that announcing an engagement will make their exclusive friendship more acceptable to their elders. And some undoubtedly assume that it legitimizes sexual intercourse, by lifting it out of the level of "promiscuity." Does it?

Another point about engagement (in its true sense) is that it can provide a last-ditch escape if that should be necessary. Ideally it should not; but if an engaged fellow and girl become finally aware of something that would wreck their marriage, it would be better to face it honestly at the time than to regret for the rest of their lives that they didn't.

Broken engagements are often unhappy, but human beings are resilient and usually not only recover themselves, but are able to retain their respect for the other partner. But can we ever really know who is the right partner? Isn't it all a colossal gamble, or a gigantic game of blind man's buff? There seem to be so many unknown factors that trip us up, and then mock us when we've made the wrong choice. Christians have a great advantage here, because the Christ they have chosen to follow has promised to guide them in their decisions. This is meant to be taken seriously and applied to the whole of life, including all decisions great or small. And few could be greater than the choice of a marriage partner.

I do not mean to imply that Christians do not make mistakes here. But when Christians make mistakes it is hardly fair to blame Christ. His offer of guidance is not withdrawn, and the last thing he wants is for any of us to make a mess of our lives. But Christians are human too, and can yield to pressure, whether it comes from outside or from their own emotions. They can temporarily set some other desire ahead of their love of Jesus Christ, and then turn a blind eye to the guidance he is giving. But it is equally true to say that no mistake is beyond his forgiveness for those who are really sorry; and when they have accepted the lessons to be learned from the mistake, they may experience his over-ruling to put them on their feet again. No Christian need live in defeat.

As the cynics are fond of saying, when you leave school you either become a student, or work. But the appealing thing about both employment or higher education is the new taste of freedom that comes to you—freedom from the previous restrictions of school, home and parents. True enough, there have always been ways of getting around these restrictions, and many young people are aided and abetted in this by parents who have copped out. Sadly in many cases the parents concerned have little value system of their own left. They are therefore reluctant, or unable, to give moral guidance to those to whom they owe it—their own children.

—From Branse Burbridge, *The Sex Thing*. Wheaton, Ill.: Shaw Publishers; London: Hodder & Stoughton, 1972.

FOR FURTHER READING:

Lewis, Kay Oliver, *The Christian Wedding Handbook*. Old Tappan, N.J.: Revell, 1981.

Mason, Robert L., Jr. and Caroline L. Jacobs. *How to Choose the Wrong Marriage Partner and Live Unhappily Ever After*. Atlanta: John Knox, 1979.

Vaughn, Ruth. *To Be a Girl, To Be a Woman*. Old Tappan, N.J.: Revell, 1983.

ESCAPISM

ESCAPISM is a modern way of life! Society is immersed in this method of problem-avoidance. Because escapism has permeated our daily life, its pervasive effects are heightened; our commitments, our values, and ultimately our mission in life is subtly eroded and corroded with cowardice.

Tell me, is this not today's world? Perhaps Peer Gynt lives in your block, in your house! Think for a few minutes—how do realtors advertise a new housing development? Every time we turn on the radio we hear, "It's a place to escape from it all!" "Come to Escape Country!"

Retreat has become the hallmark of the suburbs; it is a hallmark of our way of life. We retreat to where we live; we draw our curtains around ourselves and wish to push all others out.

. . . . .

History and psychology both warn us what happens when there is an increase in comfort and a decrease in discipline; the result is always a softening of character. Anytime there is a growth of affluence and a corresponding lessening of demand, you can bet that this combination will not produce strong, tenacious, tough people.

This phenomenon has a great deal to say about how you and I raise our children. It has a lot to say about what we put into our children, and with what we confront them. What a danger it is to have their thinking infected! Without realizing it, we raise them to be people whose style of life is avoidance rather than engagement. There is escapism in our families!

Bamboozled, Boozed, and Bored!

We just do not meet life very well at all. The statistics demonstrate this very clearly. Hearing some of the facts on the radio, I wrote the statistics down because I could not believe they were true—that we have had to meet life that artificially! Last year in the United States over *300 million* prescriptions were written for tranquilizers! That represents something over *50 billion* tablets! Think about it! Three hundred million prescriptions to artificially deal with life because we can't face it head-on!

In the United States today are nearly 7 million alcoholics and over 12 million dependent drinkers. A large chunk of that problem has occurred because people have not learned to adjust to life. What makes Alcoholics Anonymous so powerful? Through their twelve-step program, people are taught how to face reality and to engage themselves in life again. They learn how to face life honestly rather than by retreating.

. . . . .

Here Are Two Answers!

Since avoidance and evasion are so unacceptable, what must I do with life so that it will not reduce me to a straw man? There are several things I need to know.

The first is that most of us retreat because we have not found an adequate foundation on which to stand. Our retreat is symbolic of our fearfulness about the adequacy of our life's base.

This is true for Christians too. You and I may be very much within the church, and we may very strongly affirm Jesus Christ as Lord, but we still may not have found that Jesus Christ is the ultimately secure foundation on which our lives can stand.

Many of us live a long time without discovering that Jesus is final security. The first thing that allows me to stand up against "the way it is" is the personal realization that deep within my being my God is able.

—From Robert L. Wise, *Your Churning Place.* Ventura, Calif.: Regal, 1977.

ESTROGEN

ESTROGEN is the general term for the female sex hormones, which are produced chiefly in the ovaries. There are a number of different kinds of estrogens (pronounced es'tro-jenz), including *estrone*, estriol, and estradiol. Estrogens are the substances that are responsible for the maturation of a woman's sexual organs, the development of her breasts, and her rounded form and high voice.

Estrogens are secreted in particular abundance during ovulation. They stimulate the uterus to prepare for pregnancy, causing a thickening of the lining and enrichment of the blood supply. If conception occurs, the estrogens also stimulate growth of the milk glands.

Estrogens are produced synthetically and used in the treatment of numerous female disorders, among them painful menstruation (dysmenorrhea). They are also used to alleviate the symptoms, both physical and emotional, of the menopause.

—From *Family Health Guide and Medical Encyclopedia* prepared in association with Benjamin F. Miller, M.D. New York: Reader's Digest Association, 1970.

FOR FURTHER READING:

Lamb, Lawrence E., M.D. *Stay Youthful and Fit*. New York: Harper & Row, 1974.
Padus, Emrika. *The Woman's Encyclopedia of Health and Natural Healing*. Emmaus, Pa.: Rodale, 1981.
Penner, Clifford and Joyce. *The Gift of Sex*. Waco, Tex.: Word Books, 1981.

EXERCISE

WHAT YOU ARE about to read could add ten or more years to your earthly life, if you desire that enough to apply these concepts and actions to yourself. With the exception of being inflicted with cancer or a few other relatively rare conditions, a body that is in a good state of physical fitness can resist and postpone death from many causes for a long time. Certainly death from most diseases associated with the heart, blood vessels, or lungs can be staved off for many years. Even if you don't desire to live longer, the quality of your life, long or short, will be greatly enhanced by exercising to fitness.

Front-page headlines in the *New York Times* reported on November 28, 1977, from Miami Beach: "Study of 17,000 Men Indicates Vigorous Sports Protects Heart." The occasion was the annual convention of the American Heart Association. Finally, what had been suspected for years had been proven by documented statistics on death and disease. These were compiled over a ten-year period from records of thousands of men involved in all levels of physical activity, from the completely sedentary to the athlete. The study showed that these men, all Harvard alumni, had had fewer heart attacks the more active they had been, and that strenuous, regular, leisure-time physical exertion produced a "definite protective effect." These principles are equally true for women.

Of particular interest was the finding that small amounts of activity required in "light" sports, such as bowling, baseball, golf, and so forth, which require little energy output, had no protective effect. On the other hand, those men who were regularly involved in brisk walking, climbing stairs, jogging, swimming, tennis, squash, or handball had far lower incidences of both fatal and nonfatal heart attacks. It seems that a minimum of three hours per week, with the expenditure of 2,000 calories each week, was the level to aim for. Those alumni who expended fewer than 2,000 calories per week (300 per day) above their normal daily routine had a 64 percent higher risk of heart attack than their more energetic classmates.

Also put to rest in the study was the oft-heard opinion that those who are able to exercise strenuously are those who are more fit or more athletic to begin with. The exact opposite was discovered. Men who had been athletes while at Harvard were not protected in later years if they had failed to remain physically active. Conversely, men who had not been athletes in college had a reduced risk of heart disease if they had started exercising after graduating. Most gratifying of all was the finding that the protective effect of exercise was even of significance in men who had such high-risk factors as high blood pressure, overweight, cigarette smoking, previous inactivity, and family history of heart disease.

Why is it that regular exercise is so protective? The basic answer is that rhythmic and vigorous contraction and relaxation of the muscles and heart (also a muscle) during a long enough period of time lead to increases in their blood supply. Both the size and the number of blood vessels over a period of time are increased as a result of regular activity. In the case of the heart, the increase in the internal diameter of the coronary artery and its branches reduces the likelihood of a heart attack occurring. Also, the increased number of these branches significantly improves chances of recovery if an attack should strike.

Also increased during exercise are body temperature, heart and respiration rates, oxygen consumption and sweating. All these physiological effects lead in turn to these well-recognized signs of physical fitness:

1. Better cardiovascular efficiency
2. Lower blood pressure
3. Lower serum cholesterol and triglycerides
4. Higher ratio of high-density lipoproteins
5. Increased coronary circulation
6. Reduction of excess body fat
7. Increased muscle size and strength (enabling the heart, for example, to pump more blood per beat)
8. Increased ability to consume oxygen

Exercise physiologists can measure oxygen consumption by collecting and analyzing the expired air of someone walking or jogging on a treadmill. Between 40 and 50 milliliters of oxygen consumed per kilogram of body weight indicates good to excellent conditioning. Below 40 indicates poor shape, above 60 is found in the superathlete. If you can run one and one half miles in twelve

minutes, this would mean an oxygen consumption of 42 milliliters per kilogram, which is fairly good conditioning. If you can do one and three quarter miles in twelve minutes, you will have consumed just over 50 milliliters per kilogram, which means you are in very good shape.

Now for ourselves, before we even start an exercise or get-fit program, we need to evaluate how unfit we are, because the worse shape we're in, the lower the level of activity must be at the start, and the slower must be the initial rate of progress. Too much too quickly could be dangerous.

First, if you are over thirty-five, have a physical examination which should include a stress EKG. This test will pick up as many as 95 percent of patients with coronary-artery disease, or the imminent potential for a heart attack, as contrasted with only 15 percent using a resting EKG. Then, if your doctor says your heart and general condition are okay, try, over a few weeks, to build up from walking to jogging, gradually increasing the distance and pace. Increase slowly. Slow down or stop when you get out of breath or if you feel any ache or pain across the front of your chest. This pain is called angina and indicates too much load on the heart.

When you feel ready, take a stopwatch with you to a measured track at your local high school, YMCA, or YWCA. See how far you can walk/jog/run in twelve minutes. This simple test which you can give yourself was developed by Dr. Kenneth Cooper of Dallas, Texas, a leading authority on exercise physiology. To avoid overexertion, try the talk test. Go with someone while you jog. If shortness of breath prevents conversation while you are running, slow down, you're overdoing it. Don't be impatient. Getting fit takes several weeks, with gradual escalation of pace and distance. Stop at once if you have any pain in the chest.

If you are under fifty years of age, you should be able to cover one and one half miles in those twelve minutes, if you're in reasonable shape. Men over fifty should be able to do one and one quarter miles; women under thirty, one and one third miles; over thirty, one and one fifth miles in twelve minutes.

Another very simple test of fitness is the measurement of resting pulse rates. Resting means having been totally relaxed for at least fifteen to twenty minutes. The average unfit American has a resting heart rate of 72 beats per minute in males, up to 80 in women. A male with a pulse over 80 is in poor shape; for women, over 85 is also poor. By contrast, in response to a good conditioning program the heart will enlarge and increase its volume of blood pumped per beat. This will reduce the number of beats needed to circulate the blood. A man or woman in excellent shape can expect the rate to drop into the 50s or even 40s. Mine is in the 40s; many top athletes' pulses are in the 30s.

Studies done at Northwestern University on 1,300 men revealed three times as many sudden deaths in those with resting heart rates of over 90 as in those with rates under 70. Another measure of fitness is that of the ability of the heart rate to return to less than 100 within ten minutes of severe exercise. This is the medical definition of being in good shape.

If you are only fifteen pounds overweight, your heart may have to beat up to ten times more per minute. If you smoke twenty cigarettes per day as well, or if you are thirty to fifty pounds overweight, your heart rate may be increased by as much as twenty extra beats per minute. That's almost thirty thousand more beats per day, over 10 million extra beats per year. No wonder life expectancy is reduced!

Once you've tested yourself and discovered how fit or unfit you are, what about creating a weekly program for yourself? Not everyone enjoys walking or jogging. Many prefer bicycling, swimming, or some competitive ball game (individual, not team). Although daily participation in a sport is ideal, three nonconsecutive days each week is a good second best for frequency. As little as three consecutive days of immobility can lead to significant loss of muscle mass and strength.

—From O. Quentin, Hyder, M.D., *Shape Up.* Old Tappan, N.J.: Revell, 1979.

Types of Exercise

Aerobic exercises are the more vigorous types of activity designed to improve the organs and systems which help the body to process oxygen—the heart, lungs and blood vessels. These exercises, which include running, jogging, bicycle riding and swimming, help your lungs to process more air with less effort. This in turn strengthens your heart and increases your endurance capacity. The key to aerobic exercise is continuous activity without rest periods. It is often referred to as long slow distance (LSD) activity.

Anerobic exercise includes activity of short, intense duration followed by a period of recovery. Such activities as tennis, handball, and sprinting are examples of anerobic exercise. These activities require a sudden and high demand on the heart and lungs.

Isometric exercises are strength-building activities which involve no actual movement. This kind of exercise is accompanied by pitting muscle groups against one another or against unyielding objects. This is usually done for a period of 10 to 15 seconds at maximum effort. Due to the limited movement, isometrics provide little functional strength development and in some cases, may limit joint range of motion. Furthermore, many doctors believe that elevation in thoracic pressure may cause dizziness and fainting in some individuals. Isometric activity may be harmful to some individuals and is not recommended by the President's Council on Physical Fitness and Sports.

Isotonic exercises are strength-building exercises which require using muscles through a full range of motion. Such activities as weight lifting, push-ups, sit-ups, and pull-ups

177

are all examples of isotonic exercises. This kind of strength work is important in maintaining muscle mass, body portions and sound posture.

Q. What is the simplest and most effective way to exercise?

A. Walking is a superior form of exercise because it is available everywhere and requires no special training or equipment. Persons can achieve an adequate level of fitness by walking 20 miles per week as briskly as possible. Begin gradually at a pace that is comfortable for you and work up to this goal. You can work it into your daily routine by avoiding elevators and climbing stairs when possible, walking to the local stores instead of driving and taking a daily brisk walk after lunch. You will find as you increase your mileage that you can invent pleasant ways to keep your body in motion—and you'll feel better!

Q. What are some of the benefits I could expect from a good exercise program?

A. Regular exercise benefits you in many ways:

- It improves blood circulation throughout the body. Lungs, heart and other organs and muscles work together more efficiently.
- There is evidence that it helps to counteract the unhealthy effects of cholesterol in one's diet.
- It helps an individual handle stress, so he or she can do more and not tire so easily. It bolsters enthusiasm and optimism and can enhance personal appearance.
- It is good for psychological well-being; it is a tension release and helps relaxation and sleep.
- Along with a balanced diet, it helps control weight.

—From *Exercise* (Stay Well Series). New York: Metropolitan Life Insurance Company, 1979.

FOR FURTHER READING:

Kounovsky, Nicholas. *The Joy of Feeling Fit.* New York: Dutton, 1971.

Krafft, Dr. Jim. *Flab: The Answer Book.* Old Tappan, N.J.: Revell, 1983.

Morehouse, Laurence E. and Leonard Gross. *Total Fitness in Thirty Minutes a Week.* New York: Simon & Schuster, 1975.

F

FATIGUE

Organic Causes

The specific illnesses or diseases which can cause fatigue are legion. Almost every conceivable disease can cause, as a symptom, fatigue. The index pages of a several-thousand-page medical book would be an incomplete listing. Despite the fact that fatigue is one of the most common complaints a physician hears, less than 10 percent of patients seeking medical assistance have any organic illness actually causing their fatigue. Even of this 10 percent, many times only a portion of the fatigue they experience is due to the disease.

Some of the more common diseases that produce fatigue are *infections, endocrine disorders,* and *anemia.* Most *infections* are fairly acute and make their presence quite obvious, but occasionally a smoldering infection can persist for months without localized symptoms severe enough for one to seek medical attention. With modern-day drugs and medical attention this is much less common than it used to be and can be fairly well excluded as a factor by a good physical, chest X ray, and some urine and blood tests.

Metabolic, nutritional, and *endocrine disorders* are often implicated as the cause for fatigue. Patients and doctors commonly blame an individual's fatigue on one of these. *Hypothyroidism* (low thyroid) heads this list. However, it is a greatly overdiagnosed disease, and, in my experience, only a small percent of the patients that I see who are taking thyroid medication really need it.

There are at least four reasons why hypothyroidism has been overdiagnosed in the past. First, our tests were not as precise, leaving many borderline situations for the physician's best judgment as to whether or not the patient had a thyroid problem. When this fact was coupled with complaints of fatigue and overweight, two of the most common symptoms seen both in society in general and patients with hypothyroidism, it is no wonder the combination led to an overdiagnosis of this disease. Also, patients want answers and they are much more willing to accept a disease as the cause than to receive no answer or a long discussion regarding fatigue, obesity, and other problems. Lastly, the doctor often finds it easier to give the patient a prescription and tell him this will help, instead of going into a detailed discussion regarding many other possible explanations for the patient's problem.

Fortunately, when small amounts of thyroid are taken, a normal thyroid gland will compensate by proportionately decreasing its output of thyroid so that the patient remains in a normal thyroid state. Occasionally, however, we see a person who has excessive amounts of thyroid being given him, often to help him lose weight or to give him an extra spurt of energy. The symptoms of excessive thyroid commonly are weight loss, irritability, nervousness, palpitations, diarrhea, and sweating. However, lest we generalize too much, there are some patients who desperately must have thyroid to function normally. So be careful not to prematurely and wrongly judge either a person who is on thyroid medication or his physician.

Another problem called *reactive hypogly-*

cemia occurs occasionally and definitely can cause fatigue and several other symptoms. When a susceptible person eats a large amount of carbohydrates (that is, starches or sugars), at a fairly predictable time after eating these foods—usually two to five hours—he will experience nervousness, pounding of the heart, sweating, irritability, and hunger. Also, he may experience fatigue. Usually these symptoms will last for only fifteen to thirty minutes and then the body will compensate through reserve mechanisms by overcoming the drop in blood sugar which has resulted. Many times the person learns that by eating a candy bar or drinking a coke, he recovers more quickly.

Reactive hypoglycemia, in my opinion, is much more common than hypothyroidism. However, again we must be careful not to overdiagnose this symptom complex. Reactive hypoglycemia can easily be diagnosed by either obtaining a blood-sugar test at the time of the symptoms, or by having the patient take a five-hour glucose-tolerance test. During the test the patient is given a large sugar meal and then his blood sugar is checked periodically over a five-hour period. The doctor must find concurrently both a low blood sugar and the symptoms described, or at least some of them, to make the diagnosis of reactive hypoglycemia. The treatment is rather simple. A diet high in protein content and low in carbohydrates is usually all that is necessary. In rare instances, six meals a day are necessary. Most of these people have no further problem with hypoglycemia as long as they follow their diet. However, there is the rare person who will later develop diabetes, so blood sugars probably should be checked once a year.

Anemia is another and somewhat frequent cause of fatigue, especially in the menstruating woman. This can easily be checked by a laboratory. Some reports suggest that some women who do not have anemia but who have decreased iron storage in the bone marrow actually feel better taking small amounts of iron. If this is necessary, the very inexpensive ferrous-sulphate form of iron is almost always adequate.

Another common source of fatigue in our modern society is *birth-control pills.* This usually is very easy to diagnose because of the relationship between taking this medication and the onset of fatigue. Stopping the "pill" for several months may be necessary to clarify the point.

A woman may be slightly more subject to fatigue during certain periods of change in her life, such as *menstrual periods, pregnancy,* and *menopause.* She must boldly accept these changes. An understanding husband is extremely helpful. Let me quickly add, however, that menopausal symptoms are very real, affecting some more than others. Nevertheless, it often becomes the scapegoat for psychological and spiritual problems. Estrogens can help and should be used in normal doses in most cases, particularly if the patient is having symptoms. However, estrogens will not resolve the more deep-seated emotional problems.

Nutritional inadequacies are often blamed for fatigue, especially by companies profiting from this philosophy, or by doctors or patients who are unwilling to search in depth for the underlying causes. Though many in the United States do not eat as ideal a diet as they should, seldom are malnutrition or vitamin deficiency a problem if they have any regular intake of the basic food classes which include cereals, fruits, vegetables, meat, fish, poultry, and dairy products. Only if there is some coexistent disease will a person be malnourished even though he eats from these various classes regularly. Though additional vitamins seldom hurt, they usually provide an excess of the basic needs of the body and are excreted in the waste products. It is possible, however, to take too much of some vitamins. Excessive amounts of vitamins A and D can cause, in part, irritability, headaches, loss of hair, decalcification of bone, loss of appetite, an elevated calcium, and other toxic effects on the system.

These are days when we hear a lot from proponents of various diets. Some of this may have its place. The emphasis to maintain an ideal weight is good and also to decrease our total cholesterol and saturated fat intake. Too much cholesterol is related to increased incidents of heart and vascular disease. Many of the other somewhat fad diets are much more questionable, especially if generalized for all individuals. We emphasized above a high protein, low carbohydrate diet for people with reactive hypoglycemia. We also encourage this for diabetes or certain people with an excessive amount of some fats in the blood (technically called triglycerides). One might add to this list individuals who are trying to lose weight but, beyond this, it is questionable if this diet should be followed by the general population.

Probably the greatest nutritional problem in our modern society is too much nutrition. *Obesity* has reached epidemic proportions. It takes a tremendous toll in morbidity and mortality—it decreases the quality and length of life in untold millions. Many diseases are either caused by or adversely affected by it. A partial list includes heart disease, hypertension, diabetes, hyperlipidemia (elevated fats), and arthritis, to say nothing of the tremendous emotional disability affecting every thought and act of the overweight person.

Obesity also causes fatigue. Part of this fatigue is due to "post-prandial fatigue" which to some extent occurs in all of us after we eat. This is due to blood going to the gastrointestinal tract and the chemical processes of digestion and metabolism. Latin Americans take advantage of this during the heat of the day and have a siesta. College students sometimes yield to the temptation to nap during their one o'clock classes, especially if the room is dark and a movie is being shown or the lecturer is boring. The point is, we all experience some of this—but the obese person experiences more. Also he finds that it is a lot bigger job to move around numerous pounds of extra adipose (fat) to say nothing of the emotional drain. At any rate—obesity is a definite cause of fatigue.

There are other rare and somewhat interesting diseases which cause fatigue as the major symptom, such as *myasthenia gravis,* where, upon repeated use of a given muscle, weakness progresses eventually to the point of inability to use that muscle. This particularly occurs with ocular (eye) muscles but can first appear elsewhere and eventually may become generalized. Drugs are available for the treatment of this disease, but care must be exercised so that it is not overdiagnosed as it is a relatively uncommon illness.

Another rare illness is *familiar periodic paralysis* where discreet episodes of marked weakness occur. Again, this is of medical interest but, in the general population, seldom the cause of fatigue. This is not even a primer on the diseases that can cause fatigue.

To a certain degree, organic fatigue is present all the time and is increased with all work activity as the day passes. It is present when doing both enjoyable as well as mundane activities. If you have any question about the possibility of organic diseases causing your fatigue, see a competent physician for a thorough evaluation. If, after you have seen a physician, you question whether or not he's gotten to the bottom of your problem, ask for a consultation with another doctor. No physician worth his salt objects to your asking for another opinion if you do it in an appropriate manner. If, however, the second physician doesn't agree with your diagnosis, you'd better question your diagnosis. A doctor evaluating fatigue usually looks mainly for organic causes.

Constitutional Causes

Normal variations occur in almost every aspect of life. There are blondes and brunettes, tall people and short people, varying IQ's, and different physiques. Some individuals, unfortunately, face numerous medical problems. Others live to be one hundred without seeing a physician.

There are also tremendous variations in the constitutional energy levels from one person to another and the rapidity in which fatigue develops. My wife and I see this in our children. Our boy is eight; he wakes up almost instantly and needs less sleep than our girl, who is three years older. She rises later than he, often taking a good thirty minutes to wake up in the morning. They both seem perfectly normal and well-adjusted, but their constitutional makeup is different.

Some individuals need eight hours of sleep a night and others do very well on five or six. To some degree this may be altered. I find that though I enjoy eight hours of sleep a night, I usually can function quite well if I get six or seven. However, if I consistently get much below six hours, the warning signs develop before many days pass. Some people find that if they take a nap in the late afternoon, say for a half hour, they can stay up a full extra hour in the evening.

Be honest and realistic about yourself. A person with an IQ of 60 will never be able to keep up educationally with someone whose IQ is 140. And there are some who will never be able to keep up the energetic pace of others about him. Fortunately, God knows better than we do our energy capacity and needs and never requires of us more than He knows that we are capable of achieving. We, then, must accept ourselves as God has made us—with varying capabilities. We must be careful about comparing ourselves with others (*see* 2 Corinthians 10:12) and remember that many about us may be more tired than we think.

Physical Causes

Any activity or combination of activities which are engaged in too long or too strenuously will cause fatigue. These activities may be entirely normal in their own right. Here we are differentiating between fatigue caused by normal activities and fatigue whose primary cause is faulty attitudes or thought patterns.

Overwork is probably one of the greatest problem areas for dedicated, sincere Christians today. We too often are characterized by busyness and frantic activity resulting in fatigue and weariness instead of love, joy,

compassion, and interest in others without ulterior motives.

Elijah in 1 Kings 18 and 19 is an excellent example of this problem. You will recall he was God's faithful prophet. He stood up against King Ahab who repeatedly threatened and sought his life. Elijah offered his sacrifice to God upon an altar saturated with water, and God sent fire down upon it to verify that He was the only true God and that Elijah was His servant. Elijah, then, had all of Baal's four-hundred-fifty prophets killed and subsequently prayed rain down from heaven. After such manifestations of God's power and presence, a woman, Jezebel, threatened him. Poor old Elijah became afraid, fled, and sank into depression so severe he wanted to die.

What caused this depression? There are several factors involved. For one thing, there had been a famine and drought, and in the long run that may have weakened the prophet. Also, God had told Elijah to go talk to threatening King Ahab. Instead, Elijah imposed on a friend, Obadiah, to go ahead of him to the king. One cannot determine from the Bible whether or not this was in God's plan, or whether the manipulation involved sapped Elijah of some of his energy. We find, also, that the prophet was totally unaware of many others who loved and served his God. He felt alone, saying, "I, even I only, am left; and they seek my life" (1 Kings 19:14). He then proceeded to compare himself with others saying, "I am no better than my [Baal-worshiping] fathers" (19:4). And to top it all off, he forgot God's obvious hand of blessing upon him and the miracles performed by his own hand. The last straw was the intimidation of a woman, causing Elijah to feel worthless and want to die.

How many of these things or others not recorded led up to his fatigue and depression, we don't know. However, we do know that God did not reprimand him for his lack of faith, or possibly many other legitimate areas of criticism. God's profound diagnosis was simple: "Elijah, you need rest and food" (*see* 19:5). Then he went in the strength of the Lord, and sometime later heard God speak in a "still small voice." Though God had business to do with Elijah, He had time to let him first eat and rest. There is no doubt that God could have given him instant nourishment and refreshment, but He didn't choose to use supernatural powers to remedy this natural need. The supernatural power involved to perform miracles was absolutely necessary to vindicate God's power before the nonbelieving generation. But it wasn't in God's plan and therefore was not to be expected or sought for Elijah's personal needs at this time, which were to be met by the normal, natural, God-given means—food and rest.

So it is with our activities. If God wanted to give us supernatural means to overcome His laws of nature—He certainly could. Instead, I believe He wants to give us strength and wisdom to live within His laws of nature. He could give us twenty-five hours a day to finish the many tasks that need to be done. However, the way human nature is we would soon need twenty-six and then twenty-seven hours in the day, and the basic problem would never be solved.

Or God could totally refresh the Christian after one hour of sleep and give us all bottomless pocketbooks so that we wouldn't have to "waste" time working for food and clothing. Think of all the extra time we would have to work in the fields that are "white to harvest." While He is at it, would it be too much to expect Him to increase our natural capabilities so that the learning and maturing process could be quickened? Then our life could be freed from many seemingly mundane activities so our productiveness for Christ could be increased. (I'm being facetious to emphasize my point.)

At special but probably infrequent times, God may choose to override His natural laws and give us supernatural energy. But for the most part God has not chosen to change any of the natural laws for the Christian when his spiritual rebirth occurs. Therefore we must learn and be willing to live under these natural (including physical, psychological, and spiritual) laws until we receive our resurrected bodies.

We must realize and accept the fact that we have as much and as little time as every other person has each day. This is exactly the right amount of time to complete every task He has ordained for us as long as we don't squander that time by self-centered activities. We often try and make up for squandered time by attempting to squeeze out of our lives extra energy to compensate. This leads to fatigue and abusing our bodies, His temple. Such abuse can be a form of yielding to temptation as much as it would have been if Christ had cast Himself down from the pinnacle in "faith" that the angels would protect Him from physical harm.

God has promised us all the riches of glory—but not necessarily now and in the manner that we dictate. It seems to me many Christians expect unrealistic special privileges and favors from God. After all, we think, if God controls the universe and extends such wonderful gifts as His Son, salvation, forgiveness, and so on, He can also prevent sickness, regardless of how I take care of my body, or whether I follow the doctor's advice, or miss sleep, etc. Certainly He can; but He usually chooses not to. That is, He expects us to live under the same natural laws as our non-Christian friends as long as we occupy this mortal body. Therefore, we must stop looking on Him as a magic charm that should make us immune to everyday problems and natural laws. Instead, we must follow Him moment by moment in obedience, utilizing our innate ability as well as His spiritual strength to deal with every natural and spiritual battle we face.

—From Dwight L. Carlson, M.D. *How to Win Over Fatigue.* Old Tappan, N.J.: Revell, 1974.

FOR FURTHER READING:

LaHaye, Tim. *How to Win Over Depression.* Grand Rapids: Zondervan, 1974.

Padus, Emrika. *The Woman's Encyclopedia of Health and Natural Healing.* Emmaus, Pa: Rodale, 1981.

Schuller, Robert H. *Self Esteem.* Waco, Tex.: Word Books, 1982.

FEAR

THERE ARE several inner conflicts that can plunder and rob a woman of her natural beauty.

The chief criminal of these inner conflicts is FEAR.

A woman can be beautifully coiffured, expertly made up, and properly groomed; yet, if fear has vandalized her soul, then her face, her walk, and her words will betray her. Nothing she can do will disguise the disastrous results of fear.

In one of my mother's notebooks I found these descriptive lines:

> Where Worry is a mouse,
> a small scampering thing with sharp tiny feet,
> that scurries over our souls—
> Fear is a roaring lion,
> with huge paws, extended claws and teeth
> that slash us into strips.

I've seen this lion at work, tearing, maiming, roaring, and paralyzing all movement, not only in my life but in the lives of many women. We are all at one time or another the lion's victim.

A tense young woman nervously understates, "I'm afraid my marriage is over."

A bank teller honestly faces up to a fact when she says, "My only fear is the fear of death."

A distraught young wife, biting at the edge of what was once a fingernail says, "My husband has been out of work for months; we may have to go into bankruptcy. There is no financial security left any more and I'm afraid. I'm scared to death."

A wife, barely able to control her ravaged emotions, trembles as she blurts out, "My worst fears have come true. What I've suspected for years is now confirmed. My husband says he's never loved me, that he's 'gay,' a practicing homosexual, and he's leaving me. What will I do? I'm so afraid."

A mother, admitting a fear that has become a reality for the first time, whispers, "My son is on drugs. I am filled with fear."

A young bride thinks it's silly of her, yet she confesses, "Every time Ron is even a little late from work, I just know he has been in an accident, is hurt, or worse—is dead."

An older woman remembers her childhood and reminisces, "If I came home from school and nobody was there, I'd always be scared to death that the Lord had come back and I'd been left behind."

A teen-age girl, twisting with the weight of an enormous guilt, stammers, "I'm afraid I'm going to have a baby."

These fears have been expressed to me—brought into the open where we could examine them. But for every shared fear, there are probably many unspoken fears, hidden fears, even unacknowledged fears, that lie just under the surface of many a woman's face.

All of these women, with their different fears, shared the same look. The same panic and the same destruction was written across their faces. Fear is powerful. It is a panic in the blood, and it attacks the heart.

David wrote, "My heart is in anguish within me. Stark fear overpowers me" (Psalms 55:4). Fear can cause complete blockage to one's normal, rational thinking and it is an emotion which can paralyze all movement. David expertly diagnosed fear when he wrote, "I am losing all hope; I am paralyzed with fear" (Psalms 143:4).

It is entirely possible to be a child of God (or even the King of Israel) and experience the stark power of fear. I do not want to give the impression that Christians should never have any fear. That's simply not true. We are all susceptible to fear that flashes its lightning at us.

When a doctor says to me, "Mrs. Landorf, I don't mean to alarm you; however, we have found . . ."

I'll tell you *I am alarmed*—before he even finishes the sentence! That I am struck with fear is a fact of life. But I will not be paralyzed by this fear if I remember God can be trusted.

Eugenia Price, writing in *Just As I Am*, states:

> I grow afraid, just as you do. But my fear, even of the death of a loved one

184

(most difficult of all for me), lives and grows only as long as I turn to other people with it; only as long as I try to overcome it myself. It is cast out (the unhealthy, destructive fear—not the circumstance) when I deliberately remember Jesus.

The woman who lets the roaring lion of fear take over in her world will show this fear first in her walk and arm movements; then in her face. Consider this hypothetical Christian woman. She has just heard her doctor diagnose her problem as "breast cancer." She cannot move. Her previous anxiety and general feeling of apprehension has now changed to fear. She is in a stunned, paralyzed position. She denies the truth of it even as she listens to her concerned doctor. When she finally tries to leave his office, she finds she's severely limited in her ability to walk. She has become rather uncoordinated and the simple act of walking across a room has become a monumental chore. She reaches for the door handle but misses on the first try.

Still in shock, she finds herself becoming rigid and harsh. She drives home and tries to pull herself together to tell her family. If the fear is great enough she will wait hours or days. In any case, by the time she has regained enough courage to tell them, the family already knows something is seriously wrong. After that her every waking moment is filled with fearful thoughts. She forgets Jesus. She allows herself to be mauled by the lion of fear. She eventually closes her mind against surgery or refuses to change her opinion about some other treatment. Her mind seems to refuse to think logically or move in any direction.

If her fear is of a less serious threat than cancer, if she fears driving on the freeway or flying in a jet, she will not get into a car and she will not board a jet. Her whole life hardens into a steel-reinforced rut.

Seneca makes the wife of Hercules say of Lyches, "His mind is like he walks." When fear grips our lives, every move reflects it.

One of the first ingredients of beauty and graciousness in a woman is a cool, relaxed, prepared look. The woman of true beauty usually looks as if she can calmly handle anything from a house afire to a spilt glass of milk on her carpeting.

This prerequisite of charm is completely obliterated by the lion of fear.

Then, look at what fear does to a woman's face.

Just as fear restricts any relaxed movement and paralyzes the mind and body, it also hardens facial expressions into frozen masks. If a woman's fear is great, she rarely finds anything to smile about, and all others see is a cold, rather sterile countenance. Nothing makes it light up in expectation and nothing softens the almost-a-frown expression. And nothing ages a face quite so fast as fear.

Perhaps none of the fears I've already mentioned have attacked you, but here are some other fears women have disclosed to me. Some are major threats; others are rather trivial; but all are real fears. Do some of these sound distressingly familiar?

The fear of . . .

1. Wondering what others (my husband, mother-in-law, neighbor, boss, peers) will say or think.
2. Traveling, driving, or flying alone.
3. Discovering cancer in any degree or quantity.
4. Dying.
5. Being a widow.
6. Losing a child either to drugs, alcohol, or disease.
7. Not having anyone left to love or need you.
8. Suspecting your husband is having an extramarital affair.
9. Failing (at marriage, raising children, on the job, or with some responsibility).
10. Being disappointed in people *again*.
11. Bankruptcy.
12. Seeing a live snake, lizard, and/or spiders.
13. Growing old ungracefully.
14. Being left alone and isolated from family and friends.
15. Pregnancy.

16. Being caught in an immoral or illegal act.
17. Being physically or sexually inadequate in marriage.
18. Dealing with problems or conflicts.
19. Change.
20. Making a decision.

—From Joyce Landorf, *The Fragrance of Beauty.* Wheaton, Ill.: Victor Books, 1973.

Overcoming Fear

Here are some ways to overcome fear:

1. Determine what it is you are afraid of. Pinpoint it. Examine it. Look at it for exactly what it is. Discover exactly what you must deal with.
2. Discover your reasons for being afraid of this or that. Ask for God's wisdom to help you see exactly when and where this fear or inhibition started. If you're not certain you know the reason or reasons, then get expert counseling.
3. Get your fear out in the open. Drag it out where you can attack it. Often a surprisingly small thing has tried to frighten you.
4. Fill your mind full of faith facts. Fear and faith cannot coexist. Your mind must choose one or the other. The Bible tells you that God is not the author of fear, so you don't have to accept unreasonable fear. You will choose faith.
5. Do your best. Decide to leave all results to the Lord. After all, "If God be for us, who can be against us?"
6. Learn to stand up to your fear and dare it to do its worst. Actually, most fear springs from your own imagination. As Mark Twain said, "I'm an old man and have known many troubles, but most of them never happened."
7. Sometimes your fear is based on fact. When that happens, you can overcome. God will help you release the spiritual and mental strength you need. "Yea, though I walk through the valley of the shadow of death, I will fear no evil: for thou art with me; thy rod and thy staff

they comfort me" (Psalms 23:4 KJV). The word *comfort* means "with strength." Pray! Praise! And God will replace your fear with supernatural strength.

When I take dominion over my life—mind, body, and spirit—I can decide to weed out those things which are detrimental to my best interests. I can take charge of myself. I can decide to quit losing and start winning, for a change.

—From Charlotte Hale Allen, *Full-Time Living.* Old Tappan, N.J.: Revell, 1978.

FOR FURTHER READING:

Hauck, Paul A., and Edmund S. Kean. *Marriage and the Memo Method.* Philadelphia: Westminster, 1975.
LaHaye, Tim. *How to Win Over Depression.* Grand Rapids: Zondervan, 1974.
LaHaye, Tim & Bev. *Spirit-Controlled Family Living.* Old Tappan, N.J.: Revell, 1978.

FEELINGS

ALTHOUGH God has created us to experience the full gamut of feelings, it is important to realize that we can choose not to act on our feelings. This would be a terrible world if we all went around acting out our feelings. In psychological terms we refer to the libidinous forces that are running around our body as the "Id." The id is the portion of the personality that drives us to act on impulse.

Just imagine what would happen if we all acted on impulse. For example, what do you do when you are in a restaurant and all of a sudden feelings of sexual arousal come over you? I realize that you really could act on your emotions right then, but you'd sure never go back to that restaurant again, would you? And I'm sure your mate would never want to go out to dinner with you again.

. . . . .

Many times people who act out their feelings in an unrestrained way choose to cop-out by saying, "I'm sorry, but that's just the way I am." That's putting up an invisible shield around himself. It's a way of saying, "I refuse to change. I'm going to dominate and control by not becoming part of it." How sad!

If you feel angry, like punching someone or spitting on them or something equally antisocial, you don't *have* to act on your emotions. What's important is that you realize how you feel and that you express those feelings in an acceptable manner. Now, suppose that in a restaurant a waitress is discourteous. You may feel very put out and you may have to weigh the possibility of expressing this anger to the waitress or to the manager. There might be times when it would be best not to express the feeling verbally, for example if there are several people dining with you. But you still have the right to express how you feel by not leaving her a tip. However, such is not the case in your marital relationship. It is usually best to express the feeling—again in a non-violent, socially acceptable way—rather than tucking it away. By expressing those feelings we become more solidly bonded than just "two ships that pass in the night."

Paul told the Ephesians to "not let the sun go down while you are still angry (4:26)." In other words, don't go to bed with unexpressed feelings toward your mate. Let him know the feelings you are experiencing, even if you don't choose to act on them.

Feelings Draw You Closer, Judgments Push You Apart

One of the reasons we have difficulty understanding our own and our mate's feelings is that we layer the feelings with judgments, opinions, values and sheer surface-level type of communication. When we do try to get close to expressing feelings, we tend to blame those feelings on other people. "You made me really mad." "She makes me so angry, I could scream!" Or even, "You made me love you." Statements such as these are examples of how we project another person as the source of our anger or other emotion.

The fact is, *our feelings are made, manufactured and distributed by our own self!* Anger, joy, happiness, fear—every emotion comes from within us. No one else can make us angry. No one else can make us happy. These emotions grow from our own depths.

Try to begin expressing yourself with "I" statements rather than "you" statements. Instead of saying, "You make me so angry!" say, "I feel very angry when you say things like that." H. Norman Wright, in his book, *The Pillars of Marriage*, says that "there are four main ways to describe feelings verbally: (1) Identify or name the feeling. 'I feel angry'; 'I feel sad'; 'I feel good about you.' (2) Use similes and metaphors. . . . 'I feel squelched'; 'I felt like a cool breeze going through the air.' (3) Report the type of action your feelings urge you to do. 'I feel like hugging you'; 'I wish I could hit you.' (4) Use figures of speech, such as, 'The sun is smiling on me today'; 'I feel like a dark cloud is following me around today.' "

Learning to express your feelings, recognizing that nobody but your own self is responsible for your feelings, will help you to stop being judgmental. It is important to make a commitment to not offend each other by being judgmental. It is important that you accept each other as you really are. Think how fulfilling it would be if you could tell your mate your frustrations, your deep love and hidden concerns and know that your mate would not judge or condemn those feelings. You might soften the sharing of your feelings by saying, "I'm not sure why I'm feeling this, but right now I'm feeling hurt, I'm feeling angry, I feel revengeful, I feel left out." Whatever that feeling might be, try to express it.

One way to discover if you are judging the *person* rather than the *act* is to see if you include "that" in your statement. If you preface your feeling with the word "that" then it is a *judgment* and not a *feeling*. "I feel *that* you are always finding fault with me." That's an opinion or judgment, not a feeling. In order for your emotion communication to be *effective* you must not put the other person on the defensive, which is exactly what the

187

little word "that" does. Instead try, "I feel very hurt inside when golf is more important *every* Sunday than I am."

A very serious problem in being judgmental of a person is that we tend to harbor our judgments, bringing them up long after the fact. I call this activity "bone-digging." Long after the situation is over, after the dust has settled, if true emotions and feelings have never been expressed, the "bone-digger" digs up those bones of long-gone emotions. Such an exercise is rarely productive. Only during therapy does it pay to be a bone-digger. If there is a need to go back and examine a relationship, if there are some old bones back there that are still causing problems today, then it is imperative that we dig them up, examine them, talk about our feelings, then bury them once and for all. "Old bones" are often deep hurts or imagined injustices that we have tried to bury but which resurface to hinder the growth of a successful relationship.

If your marital relationship is not based upon openness and honesty, then chances are your relationship will be adolescent-like, where all the manifestations of adolescence—jealousy, accusations, bantering back and forth, pouting, getting mad, leaving in a huff, running to your room or home to mother—are evident. Those kinds of behaviors will be found in relationships that are stagnant, non-growing.

.   .   .   .   .

Sharing our feelings with each other is not a one-shot deal. It's a continual process of unraveling the mystery of each of us to the other. Every day we're changing, we're perceiving different things. We have different attitudes and we must talk over these changes.

Begin today to share your feelings. Listen for the words that might indicate that you are blaming someone else for your feelings. If and when that happens, realize it, express it, retreat, gather your thoughts and feelings

again and then go forward. It's not going to be a rose garden. It's not going to be a 180-degree difference; but if you begin to plod through the various thoughts and feelings you have, you'll find that your relationship experiences a new high, a new awareness of a love that once was, or should be. *Acceptance* is what happens after you have shared your feelings.

—From Dr. Kevin Leman, *Sex Begins in the Kitchen*. Ventura, Calif.: Regal, 1981.

Acknowledging/Admitting/Accepting

Acknowledging, admitting, accepting (notice the progression) is the most valuable step. If we could have accepted ourselves in general to begin with, we wouldn't have "feeling" problems. If you feel good about life, about yourself and your relationships, acceptance is pure pleasure.

Willingness to meet *all* negative feelings without threat or fear or self-condemnation is essential. Paralysis will set in immediately after the first listening if the information you've uncovered or discovered isn't a "welcome guest" in your mind. This acknowledgment frees us to make decisions. I don't have to slow up the process, the approaching solution, with feelings of guilt. The more quickly we can accept what we hear, the more will be revealed to us. If we turn aside in nonacceptance, we simply block the way to further progress.

Since I'm dependent on a process over which I don't have all the control (the reservoir is deep, much of it below the level of our consciousness), acceptance allows me to relax, to be unhurried. Life is too pressing always to hold these negative feelings and unsolved puzzles in conscious tension. If we have accepted them, yet can't immediately discover all we need to know about them, we can learn to wait. I've discovered that my mind has a kind of shelf on which I can lay unsolved problems. I think a principle exists within us that tends toward healing if we don't fight it with nonacceptance, and the healing process continues in between our active efforts to seek solutions.

. . . . .

Acceptance of negatives is hard. I will share an experience of my own that is difficult to disclose because I'm still working through the terrible feelings it brought. In a class at church we were led through the last night of Jesus' life, from his first trial to his crucifixion. The teacher of this class, a scientist, gave a carefully researched and unemotional step-by-step walk through those hours. Three or four times I was moved to tears, which doesn't happen to me very often. At the climax of the cross there came swiftly into my mind this thought: "I hope someone is noticing how this moves me." It makes my heart pound and my throat tighten to repeat it, so deep is my disappointment in myself. I got a glimpse of self-abhorrence. That morning I immediately thrust it aside and have kept pushing since. Perhaps right now, by writing it down, I am made to face it more fully. You think I'm making too much of it? You think I shouldn't have shared it with you? Perhaps you're thinking, "How could she?" For me to accept those feelings, an unpleasant reality about myself, isn't easy, but I'm doing it because it hasn't changed God's opinion of me at all.

Even when we approach being judgment-free, acceptance of another's pain is difficult. Dear friends of ours have a daughter who may very well have a progressive, awful disease. When her mother tells me about it, although I love her and want very much to help, I don't really want to hear. I think: "The doctors surely haven't diagnosed it correctly," or "It's obviously too soon to know," or "You must be exaggerating." I am too sensitive to feelings to say these things out loud; how terrible it would be if I did say them. Although I wouldn't be judging my friend's feelings, I would be making other judgments over which she has no control and I would only add to her pain. My problem is that I don't *want* her to feel bad, nor her

husband, nor any members of her family, least of all her daughter.

Deciding/Choosing a Way/Acting

We sometimes find that with the step of acknowledgment and acceptance the process is complete. As I suggested earlier, nothing more may be necessary than to live with new freedom. My discoveries about myself have often in themselves been final kinds of things, not requiring decision or action. That is true of the experience I described about resolving a large difficulty. I am grateful to God.

One decision is to do nothing. Settled indecision is always a decision.

Pencil and paper help. To list possible courses of action and see them in black and white is confrontive and clarifying.

To decide well you must know what pleases God. You had better study your Bible. There are hundreds of good Bible studies available. It is hard work. To live on spoonfeeding from the preacher is one of the dangerous results of wanting to feel good. Generally it feels pretty good to sit and listen effortlessly.

Our daughter keeps asking, "Have you mentioned the 'think machine'?" Sometimes at our house we remind each other to "Put it through the 'think machine.'" Often a little reasoning goes a long way. It was easy to get past my irritation in the traffic jam by simply reasoning that only tension could result from my continued irritation (and all the big things tension brings, headaches, and so forth). I decided to sing—it's always safe in a car! Major decisions take more time to think through.

The helping person is invaluable at this point. The heavy feelings of sorrow or temptation or fear are out in the open where they can be looked at; their power is somewhat dispelled and the thinking process can be activated. Be careful with whom you share. If it's someone to whom you really feel the need to say, "Please don't tell anyone," it's probably because you know that person is a

FEELINGS · FEMALE/MALE

poor risk. (Sometimes, though, I say that to a true confidant only to reassure myself that my "secret" is safe.) If you're sharing a temptation, it's probably better not to share it with someone involved in your temptation unless it's a person of great integrity. If you're tempted to tamper with the funds, the president of the company is probably not the best person to tell. If you're tempted by your neighbor's wife or husband, probably neither of them is your best choice for sharing. Of course I'm assuming in all the matter of sharing that you really want to be rid of the thing.

Growth can be stopped if decision isn't carried out. The courage, the determination that may be necessary is the price of new growth. The decision to do something, particularly if it involves meeting someone eyeball to eyeball (a confession, for instance), can immediately give rise to more uncomfortable feelings, even acute ones. If you've arrived at your decision scripturally, thoughtfully, with integrity, I know nothing helpful short of plowing ahead with what you've decided to do. Having decided, does it ever feel better to try to forget it? Probably not. God promises even the right words in hard places.

Deciding seems to me the most complicated and farreaching step in the process. It puts feet on the first two steps (when decision is necessary), and produces both inward and outward fruit. It's also the step that brings us into the battle between sin and righteousness.

The word *honest* keeps coming to my mind. "Honesty" is sometimes paraded in a foolish way, as when you feel righteously honest about telling Mrs. Brown her wig is atrocious, or brag that all of your life is an open book to everybody. Real honesty recognizes all that we are. It puts names on "bad" feelings as well as "good" ones. It accepts (however sadly or grudgingly at first) that they belong to us. It acts in light of God's standards. It keeps on making necessary efforts. "And for that [seed] in the good soil, they are those who, hearing the word, hold it fast in an honest and good heart, and bring

forth fruit with patience [perseverance]" (Luke 8:15).

—From Joan Jacobs, *Feelings*. Wheaton, Ill.: Tyndale, 1976.

FOR FURTHER READING:

Elliot, Elisabeth. *Discipline: The Glad Surrender*. Old Tappan, N.J.: Revell, 1982.
Wright, H. Norman. *The Christian Use of Emotional Power*. Old Tappan, N.J.: Revell, 1974.

FEMALE/MALE

Separate, But Equal

I happen to believe that a woman is entitled to equal pay for equal qualifications and performance. There have been inequities in this department, and I realize this. However, if I were considering hiring a man or a woman who were equally qualified for a job, and the man had a family with a nonworking wife, while the woman applicant was single, or had no children to support, I would be inclined to hire the man who needed to support his family. I don't think this is sexual discrimination.

If the man were single and the woman a single parent, I would tend to hire the woman, because of the needs of the children.

Women, we aren't all the same. Some women are born homemakers, domestically inclined and oriented. They should be lauded, not demeaned. Their occupation is tremendously demanding, but probably the most rewarding of all. Her works "praise her in the gates of the city" (*see* Proverbs 31:31). The most important works are her children, who come after her. To nurture and shape a young life to meet confidently the challenges of a swiftly changing world is, to me, the ultimate of achievement for a woman or a man. Whoops, did I say *man*, too? Is this a role reversal? I don't believe so. I see nothing wrong with a man helping with the children and the housework, particularly if both parents work outside the home. It's pretty difficult for me to understand a man opting to completely reverse his role, being the homemaker, while his wife goes out to work, unless, of course, he is disabled. However there may be exceptions to that rule, also.

Children are just as much a part of the man as the woman; the male image, as well as the female, is crucial for the full development of the children.

When it comes to the home and the children, I do not believe that a tally sheet should be kept on the things a man and a woman do within the family. As for women, we are not less than man, we are part of man and man is part of us.

Woman is the feminine of man. We were not only created to be man's helper, but also his complement. Throughout history men, either through pride or moral perversion, have mistreated women. The ancient world was predominantly a man's world. But in the nation of Israel, the Jews held women in high esteem.

However, it was Christ who truly set women free, who gave them a status equal with man, but separate from manliness. It has been Christianity which has freed women from second-class citizenship. All the laws, regulations, and ordinances which are being introduced into our society today could be eliminated, if women only realized that man-made rules are not going to give us the satisfaction, joy, and inner peace which we desire. Women, lay aside your banners and quiet your shouting voices. Listen to the quiet, assuring voice of Jesus Christ.

And He said to the woman, "Your faith has saved you; go in peace."

Luke 7:50

—From Dale Evans Rogers, *Woman*. Old Tappan, N.J.: Revell, 1980.

Masculine and Feminine

Do the women's liberationists want to be liberated from being women? No, they would say, they want to be liberated from society's stereotypes of what women are

supposed to be. There are, according to their theorists, no fundamental differences between men and women. It is all a matter of conditioning. Some very interesting facts have been uncovered by scientists which feminists will have to treat very gingerly for they show that it is not merely society which determines how the sexes will behave. There are strong biological reasons (a matter of hormones) why the male has always dominated and will continue to dominate in every society. The idea of matriarchy is mythical, I've learned, for not one that can be documented has ever existed. Doesn't it seem strange that male dominance has been universal if it's purely social conditioning? One would expect to see at least a few examples of societies where women rather than men held the positions of highest status. (The existence of reigning queens proves nothing, since they have their position by heritage, not by achievement, choice, or election.) Isn't it really much easier to believe that the feelings of men and women throughout history bear a direct relationship to some innate prerequisite? For a scientist that prerequisite may be biological and/or emotional (the least suggestion that there might be an emotional as well as a physical difference between males and females is for some women horrifying) but for you and me the prerequisite lies further back.

It was God who made us different, and He did it on purpose. Recent scientific research is illuminating, and as has happened before, corroborates ancient truth which mankind has always recognized. God created male and female, the male to call forth, to lead, initiate and rule, and the female to respond, follow, adapt, submit. Even if we held to a different theory of origin the physical structure of the female would tell us that woman was made to receive, to bear, to be acted upon, to complement, to nourish.

.   .   .   .   .

There is a fundamental and to me quite puzzling omission in most "feminist" discussion—the failure to talk at all about femininity. Perhaps it is because the elements of rule, submission, and union are part and parcel of femininity itself and of far more lasting and universal importance than any culturally defined notion. To get at this the place to start, obviously, is the body itself.

A human being comprises body, mind, and spirit. Any doctor will attest to the effect the mind may have on the body. Any psychiatrist knows that his patient's psychological problems may have physical effects. Any minister admits that what appears to be a spiritual issue may turn out to have physical and mental dimensions as well. No one can define the boundaries of mind, body, and spirit. Yet we are asked to assume nowadays that sexuality, most potent and undeniable of all human characteristics, is a purely physical matter with no metaphysical significance whatever.

Some early heresies which plagued the Church urged Christians to bypass matter. Some said it was in and of itself only evil. Some denied even its reality. Some appealed to the spiritual nature of man as alone worthy of attention—the body was to be ignored altogether. But this is a dangerous business, this departmentalizing. The Bible tells us to bring all—body, mind, spirit—under obedience.

Yours is the body of a woman. What does it signify? Is there invisible meaning in its visible signs—the softness, the smoothness, the lighter bone and muscle structure, the breasts, the womb? Are they utterly unrelated to what you yourself are? Isn't your identity intimately bound up with these material forms? Does the idea of you ... contain the idea of, let's say, "strapping" or "husky"? How can we bypass matter in our search for understanding the personality? There is a strange unreality in those who would do so, an unwillingness to deal with the most obvious facts of all.

Every normal woman is equipped to be a mother. Certainly not every woman in the world is destined to make use of the physical equipment but surely motherhood, in a deeper sense, is the essence of womanhood. The body of every normal woman prepares

itself repeatedly to receive and to bear. Motherhood requires self-giving, sacrifice, suffering. It is a going down into death in order to give life, a great human analogy of a great spiritual principle (Paul wrote, "Death worketh in us but life in you"). Womanhood is a call. It is a vocation to which we respond under God, glad if it means the literal bearing of children, thankful as well for all that it means in a much wider sense, that in which every woman, married or single, fruitful or barren, may participate—the unconditional response exemplified for all time in Mary the virgin, and the willingness to enter into suffering, to receive, to carry, to give life, to nurture and to care for others. The strength to answer this call is given us as we look up toward the Love that created us, remembering that it was that Love that first, most literally, *imagined* sexuality, that made us at the very beginning real men and real women. As we conform to that Love's demands we shall become more humble, more dependent—on Him and on one another—and even (dare I say it?) more splendid.

—From Elisabeth Elliot, *Let Me Be a Woman.* Wheaton, Ill.: Tyndale, 1976.

Sexual Differences

An effort has been underway for the past few years to prove that men and women are identical, except for the ability to bear children. Radical feminists have vigorously (and foolishly) asserted that the only distinction between the sexes is culturally and environmentally produced. Nothing could be farther from the truth; males and females differ biochemically, anatomically, and emotionally. In truth, they are unique in every cell of their bodies, for men carry a different chromosomal pattern than women. There is also considerable evidence to indicate that the hypothalamic region, located just above the pituitary gland in the mid-brain, is "wired" very uniquely for each of the sexes. Thus, the hypothalamus (known as the seat of the emotions) provides women with a different psychological frame of reference than that of men. Further, female sexual desire tends to be somewhat cyclical, correlated with the menstrual calendar, whereas males are acyclical. These and other features account for the undeniable fact that masculine and feminine expressions of sexuality are far from identical. Failure to understand this uniqueness can produce a continual source of marital frustration and guilt. Two of the more consequential differences in sexual appetite are worthy of particular note.

First, men are primarily excited by *visual* stimulation. They are turned on by feminine nudity or peek-a-boo glimpses of semi-nudity. (Phyllis Diller said she had the first peek-a-boo dress: men would "peek" at her, and then they would "boo"!) Women, by contrast, are much less visually oriented than men. Sure, they are interested in attractive masculine bodies, but the physiological mechanism of sex is not triggered typically by what they see; woman are stimulated primarily by the sense of touch. Thus, we encounter the first source of disagreement in the bedroom: he wants her to appear unclothed in a lighted room, and she wants him to caress her in the dark.

Second (and much more important), men are not very discriminating in regard to the person living within an exciting body. A man can walk down a street and be stimulated by a scantily clad female who shimmies past him, even though he knows nothing about her personality or values or mental capabilities. He is attracted by her body itself. Likewise, he can become almost as excited over a photograph of an unknown nude model as he can in a face-to-face encounter with someone he loves. In essence, the sheer biological power of sexual desire in a male is largely focused on the physical body of an attractive female. Hence, there is some validity to the complaint by women that they have been used as "sex objects" by men. This explains why female prostitutes outnumber males by a wide margin and why few women try to "rape" men. It explains why a roomful of toothless old men can get a large charge from watching a burlesque dancer "take it all off." It reflects the fact that masculine

self-esteem is more motivated by a desire to "conquer" a woman than in becoming the object of her romantic love. These are not very flattering characteristics of male sexuality, but they are well documented in the professional literature. All of these factors stem from a basic difference in sexual appetites of males and females.

Women are much more discriminating in their sexual interests. They less commonly become excited by observing a good-looking charmer, or by the photograph of a hairy model; rather, their desire is usually focused on a *particular* individual whom they respect or admire. A woman is stimulated by the romantic aura which surrounds her man, and by his character and personality. She yields to the man who appeals to her emotionally as well as physically. Obviously, there are exceptions to these characteristic desires, but the fact remains: sex for men is a more physical thing; sex for women is a deeply emotional experience.

Now, so what? How can this sexual distinction interfere with a marital relationship where genuine love is evident? Simply this: unless a woman feels a certain closeness to her husband at a particular time—unless she believes he respects her as a person—she may be unable to enjoy a sexual encounter with him. A man can come home from work in a bad mood, spend the evening slaving over his desk or in his garage, watch the eleven o'clock news in silence, and finally hop into bed for a brief nighttime romp. The fact that he and his wife have had no tender moments in the entire evening does not inhibit his sexual desire significantly. He sees her on her way to bed in her clingy nightgown and that is enough to throw his switch. But his wife is not so easily moved. She waited for him all day, and when he came home and hardly even greeted her, she felt disappointment and rejection. His continuing coolness and self-preoccupation put a padlock on her desires; therefore, she may find it impossible to respond to him later in the evening. Let me go one step further: when a woman makes love in the absence of romantic closeness, she feels like a prostitute. Instead of participating in a mutually exciting interchange between lovers, she feels used. In a sense, her husband has exploited her body to gratify himself. Thus, she may either refuse to submit to his request, or else she will yield with reluctance and resentment. The inability to explain this frustration is, I believe, a continual source of agitation to women.

If I had the power to communicate only one message to every family in America, I would specify the importance of romantic love to every aspect of feminine existence. It provides the foundation for a woman's self-esteem, her joy in living, and her sexual responsiveness. Therefore, the vast number of men who are involved in bored, tired marriages—and find themselves locked out of the bedroom—should know where the trouble possibly lies. Real love can melt an iceberg.

THE VARIABILITY IN DESIRE

Men and women also differ significantly in their manifestations of sexual desire. Recent research seems to indicate that the intensity of pleasure and excitation at the time of orgasm in women and ejaculation in men is about the same for both sexes, although the pathway to that climax takes a different route. Most men can become excited more quickly than women. They may reach a point of finality before their mates get their minds off the evening meal and what the kids will wear tomorrow morning. It is a wise man who recognizes this feminine inertia, and brings his wife along at her own pace. But thousands of women will end this day in frustration because their impatient husbands will race through intercourse like

they are going to a fire. And then when the moment of supreme pleasure is over, the men will be overcome with sleep and their wives will stare at the ceiling and listen to the sounds of the night. There's nothing thrilling about that.

. . . . .

When sexual response is blocked, males experience an *accumulating* physiological pressure which demands release. The prostate gland, a small sac containing semen, gradually fills to capacity; as it reaches this maximum level, hormonal influences sensitize the man to all sexual stimuli. Whereas a particular woman would be of little interest to him when he is satisfied, he may be eroticized just to be in her presence when he is in a state of deprivation. A wife may find it difficult to comprehend this accumulating aspect of her husband's sexual appetite, since her needs are typically less urgent and pressing. Thus, she should recognize that his desire is dictated by definite biochemical forces within his body, and if she loves him, she will seek to satisfy those needs as meaningfully and as regularly as possible. I'm not denying that women have definite sexual needs which seek gratification; rather, I am merely explaining that abstinence is usually more difficult for men to tolerate.

Getting back to the variability in sexual appetites, not only do men and women differ, but enormous differences occur *between women*. Human nature is infinitely complex, and that complexity is expressed in a wide variety of sexual desires, particularly in the feminine gender. To put it graphically, female sexuality (and most other human characteristics) is probably "normally distributed." See the graph illustrated below:

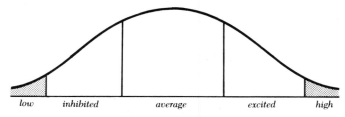

| low | inhibited | average | excited | high |

FEMALE SEXUAL DESIRE

The greatest number of women are represented by the center region of the curve, reflecting an "average" degree of sexual interest. The shaded area at the left reflects about two percent of the adult feminine population who have the least desire; they have been called frigid, cold, and unresponsive. The shaded area at the right symbolizes a comparable two percent at the maximum end of the distribution; this small group is composed of extremely sensual women who have been labeled "oversexed," nymphomaniacs, and less flattering descriptions. In between these divergent positions are ninety-six percent of the female population who are less extreme in sexual responses.

I have presented this diagram in order to discuss the often frustrated women who are represented by the lower half of this distribution. It is estimated that 20 to 25 percent of the adult females in our society exist in an "inhibited" zone, reflecting lukewarm or expressly negative attitudes toward sex. They rarely (if ever) experience orgasms and view intercourse as a marital duty and a chore to be endured. The bedroom holds no promise of the breathless thrills and chills so widely advertised. It is well worth our time to seek an understanding of these women, who often suffer constant mental anguish and anxiety.

First, why are some women less sensual than others? Adult attitudes toward sexual relations are largely conditioned during childhood and adolescence. It is surprising to observe how many otherwise well-adjusted people still think of married sex as dirty, animalistic, or evil. Such a person who has been taught a one-sided, negative approach to sex during the formative years may find it impossible to release these carefully constructive inhibitions, on the wedding night. The marriage ceremony is simply insufficient to reorient one's attitude from "Thou shalt not" to "Thou shalt—regularly and with great passion!" That mental turnabout is not easily achieved.

But I want to emphasize another factor: Not all differences in intensity of the sex drive can be traced to errors in childhood instruction. Human beings differ in practically every characteristic. Our feet come in different sizes; our teeth are shaped differently; some folks eat more than others, and some are taller than their peers. We are unequal creatures. Accordingly, we differ in sexual appetites. Our intellectual "computers" are clearly programmed differently through the process of genetic inheritance. Some of us "hunger and thirst" after our sexuality, while others take it much more casually. My point is that we should learn to accept ourselves sexually, as well as physically and emotionally. This does not mean that we shouldn't try to improve the quality of our sex lives, but it does mean that we should stop struggling to achieve the impossible—trying to set off an atomic bomb with a matchstick! As long as a husband and wife are satisfied with each other, it doesn't matter what *Cosmopolitan* magazine says their inadequacies happen to be. Sex has become a statistical monster. "The average couple has intercourse three times a week! Oh No! What's wrong with us? Are we undersexed?" A husband worries if his genitalia are of "average" size, while his wife contemplates her insufficient bust line. We are tyrannized by the great, new "sexual freedom" which has beset us. I hereby make a proposal: let's keep sex in its proper place; sure it is important, but it should serve us and not the other way around!

How does a sexually unresponsive woman feel? It is certain that she is keenly aware of the erotic explosion which burns throughout her society. While her grandmother could have hidden her private inhibitions behind the protection of verbal taboo, today's woman is reminded of her inadequacy almost hourly. Radio, television, books, magazines, and movies make her think that the entire human race plunges into orgies of sexual ecstasy every night of the year. An inhibited wife can easily get the notion that the rest of America lives on Libido Lane in beautiful downtown Passion Park while she resides on the lonely side of

Blizzard Boulevard. This unparalleled emphasis on genital gymnastics creates emotional pressure in enormous proportions. How frightening to feel sexless in a day of universal sensuality!

Sexual misfires—those icy bedroom encounters which leave both partners unsatisfied and frustrated—tend to be self-perpetuating. Unless each orgasm is accompanied by roman candles, skyrockets, and "The Stars and Stripes Forever," the fear of failure begins to gnaw on body and soul. Every disappointing experience is likely to interfere with the ability to relax and enjoy the next episode, which puts double stress on all those which follow. It is easy to see how this chain reaction of anxieties can assassinate whatever minimal desire was there in the first place. Then when sex finally loses its appeal, great emotions sweep down on the unresponsive lover. A woman who finds no pleasure in intercourse usually feels like a failure as a wife; she fears she may not be able to "hold" her husband who faces flirtatious alternatives at the office. She experiences incredible guilt for her inability to respond, and inevitably her self-esteem gets clobbered in the process.

—From Dr. James Dobson, *What Wives Wish Their Husbands Knew About Women.* Wheaton, Ill.: Tyndale, 1975.

FOR FURTHER READING:

Smalley, Gary. *For Better or for Best.* Grand Rapids: Zondervan, 1982.

FIGHTING

HERE ARE OUR "Seven Official Rules for a Good, Clean Fight." We signed them in our souls as affirmations, and we'll give them to you here just as we've enjoyed them for twenty-five years.

1. *Before we begin we must* both *agree that the time is right.* There is an eager lit-

tle beaver in nearly everyone which likes to get right on with it when something is needling inside. Then we have other days when it takes all our strength just to go on breathing.

A wise woman learns to purr with the kittens sometimes when she would prefer to scratch with the cats. If he's suffering from "battle fatigue" at the office, this is not a good time. The smart man also learns how to command "Arms Rest!" even if his spleen is ready for venting. Since women have hard days with the children and weeks when they're not up to their best, he too must practice self-control. That little word *"both"* in this rule grows more important as you study it.

You can also learn to read each other's signs that the time is drawing near for getting on with it.

．　．　．　．　．

2. *We will remember that our only battle aim is a deeper understanding of each other.* There are several important gun labels for conversational warfare between husbands and wives who really do care.

"Humility and honesty" will be the theme of a later letter but you'll need these now. Neither of you is "all St. George" and neither of you is "all the dragon."

"Patience" is another requirement. Without it you could tear up more in an hour than it might take weeks to repair.

"Mercy," "Grace," and "Telling the truth in love" should be in your hearts as you shout, "Ready-aim-fire!"

If either of you is to hit the bull's eye you must never forget this: Your main aim is to improve your marriage by deeper understanding!

3. *We will check our weapons often to be sure they're not deadly.* This follows naturally on the heels of what we've been saying. "The battle unto death" may be all right in its place but its place is not in the home.

Here you are shooting down troubles, not firing for funerals!

So be especially careful of the words you hurl when the smoke gets in your eyes.

. . . . .

Even the mildest criticism is best handed over softly. When it is hurled in rage it may bring retorts which might add nothing and take away much.

We all have within us a defense mechanism which comes roaring out of its corner when we are censored! Some men learn much from their women about self-control. If you remain master of your tongue, even when he doesn't, he may emerge from this battle with a new respect for a wonderful wife who knows what not to say when!

Another weapon to lay aside permanently is the overused phrases which have become so tiresome that they automatically bring bad reactions. One successful couple I know says that they have agreed to delete "never" and "always" from their battle vocabulary. "You are *never* home on time!" Or "You *always* put the children first!" ignite fuses for them which lead to trouble. So they have wisely decided to eliminate these triggering words. You'll soon learn your own "loaded" phrases and do as they've done.

Now comes a paradox! We have said that there are times when no answer is the best answer. But at other times it may be worse to *say nothing* than to *say something!* The utter absence of any utterance from the lady he loves may be one of the loudest noises a man ever heard if he's dying for her to break her silence!

So study rule three and use it smartly. The swords you swing on this "battle of the bridge" must be cut of the stuff which bends and gives. Your cannon balls should be more like snowballs than great balls of fire.

4. *We will lower our voices instead of raising them.* This is the one rule of our seven which was built into our courtship before we were married. It came, as so many

good things of our love, from out of your mother's quiet. In my stormy background we "hollered" when our ire was up, and the volume went higher with the increasing ire.

. . . . .

5. *We will never quarrel in public nor reveal private matters.* We belonged to a group in one of our churches which included a pair of bloodhounds. These were "people bloodhounds," a husband-wife pair who were constantly nosing about for each other's negligibles.

. . . . .

There is one more subpoint to our rule. This is our agreement that we will never fire at each other publicly when we are *not* together. I have known very few men who could readily forgive their wives for criticizing and complaining behind their backs.

6. *We will discuss an armistice whenever either of us calls "halt."* Notice the wording, "We will *discuss* an armistice!" Some men are quitters by nature, and some women run up the white flag too soon! With us it requires a unanimous vote of two before we finally sign the truce. Sometimes silence is not golden. It may be a pale shade of yellow.

If you agree to these rules, then a sense of fair play is an absolute must all the way through to the end. Without good sportsmanship on both sides you can't have the kind of "good, clean fight" which our rule-label bears.

Yet, as we have seen, some things in marriage can go either way. Some men want to stay up all night and push the adversary around!

How *can* you end it if you want to quit and he wants to continue? Here is one move for cease-fire which seldom fails for us. It goes like this—"I'm *beginning* to see what you meant! But I'll need some time to think this over. *Please, let's make up now so I can consider awhile how you could be right!*" (He could be, you know!)

If this doesn't get through, your marriage may be sicker than you think! Perhaps you need help from experts outside to go far down inside and settle more serious problems than rules such as these could ever cure.

7. *When we have come to terms we will put it away until we* both *agree it needs more discussing.* A healthy union requires that you never forget some things and never remember others. Wedlock must have its lock boxes. In some of these you put certain items and throw the key away. Others you keep for later opening.

Did you notice that "both" in this rule also? If one "eyeball" glowers unduly at the "wait-a-whiles" you will do well to talk it over and maybe take out the problem for review.

One of the most infinite understandings in any husband-wife relationship is that *you can still love each other even if there are things you don't exactly like around here!*

—From Charlie W. Shedd, *Letters to Karen.* Nashville: Abingdon, 1965.

FOR FURTHER READING:

Wilke, Richard B. *Tell Me Again, I'm Listening.* Nashville: Abingdon, 1973.

Wright, H. Norman. *Communication: Key to Your Marriage.* Ventura, Calif.: Regal, 1974.

FINANCIAL SECURITY

EVERY WOMAN needs a way to support herself financially. It doesn't matter if you are rich, beautiful, and charming and the world is at your feet. All that could change. You need to be self-sufficient financially. The greatest hardship women alone face is lack of money.

Any woman can find herself alone. We grow up thinking that will not happen, and I hope it will not happen to you. But it might. We buy insurance hoping we will never need it, but are wise enough to buy it any-

way. Even if you intend to be a homemaker supported by a husband, get a trade for yourself.

If you are already married and without a trade, go get one. It is possible to go to school at night or by correspondence, to teach yourself, or persuade someone else to train you. Even if it takes you years of part-time work to learn your trade, do not neglect to start after it. Even if you never need or want to use it, please get it.

There is another reason besides financial security for you to be able to support yourself, several reasons in fact. One is that it is good for your own self-esteem. Housewifery calls for many skills. It is actually a job that demands the ability of a corporation executive with skills in all branches of the company. But our society and many of the families in it do not highly value the housewife's contributions. She is seen as the woman of all work, as the servant of the family. It is good for you to know that if you needed to or wanted to, you could go out and earn with the best of them.

Another reason it is important for you to have earning potential is that, men being human, they sometimes are heavy-handed with a woman who is dependent on them financially. Sometimes the heavy-handedness is subtle: you tend to feel bad about wanting more money for this or that, or you do a little extra for him that you do not expect for yourself because you don't bring in any money. With some men it isn't subtle at all. They will demand haughtily, "What did you spend it all on? You want more!" Some are glad to lord it over the dependent wife.

It's amazing what a little financial clout will do. You don't even have to flaunt it. If the people who live with you realize that you can make it very well without them, they definitely invest more effort in making sure you want to make it with them. This is nothing against men. It is merely the facts of financial life. Power corrupts and financial power tends to corrupt the one who has it all. So equalize the possibilities.

While you are looking for a way to make

sure you can support yourself, please be kind to yourself. Don't settle for what you know you can get without any hassle. Instead, go after what you really want. It may take longer, but it will wear much better with time. Ask yourself what you like to do so much that you would do it for free. Then get a job or qualifications for one in that field. Why not get paid for doing what you like?

Women who are already in a job or career field but not happy there should analyze the situation and see if they can switch to something they like better. Both men and women tend to stick with jobs they hate because they are already trained for them or have seniority or retirement benefits. Or they simply fear change. It's your life and if you are not happy with your job, you are throwing away pieces of your life every time you go to work. Life is a day at a time, an hour at a time. Don't waste it piece by piece in a situation that you can change.

Educational opportunities are opening up for adults in colleges and other training institutions in ways that were unheard of a few years ago. We are going to become a nation of older, not younger, people in the future. Because of this, colleges will have to go to educating people who are out of their teens and twenties if they hope to stay in business. Go back to school, they will welcome you there. It is never too late.

Besides getting the skills to support yourself, project the future of those skills. Will you have to retire at a certain age? Are there auxiliary fields you can enter from the one you are interested in? Does the field you want to try for offer enough variety and opportunity that you will not be boxed in? We found that we, as a family, had less mobility than we would have liked because my husband's job is specialized to the point that he cannot work just anywhere he would like to live. So think about where your job will place you and if its restrictions are likely to bother you before you invest too heavily in it.

—From Patricia Gundry, *The Complete Woman.* Garden City, N.Y.: Doubleday, 1981.

FORGIVENESS

Apologizing

"Love is never having to say you're sorry."

Don't you believe it. It's a widely quoted line from a best seller. It's also been heard by millions who saw the movie.

But there's one outstanding thing wrong with it. It isn't true.

Sure, there are some lovers who might buy it. But the great ones know something else. Not far behind the three little words "I love you" are four more, "I'm sorry. Forgive me."

Some men simply can't apologize or won't. Roger may be one of these, but if he is, it probably isn't your fault. Something happened long before he met you to cauterize his apologizer. I know many women who have agonized a long time with such characters, and some forever.

But there are at least two things you might keep in mind. One is you can tell him you're sorry even if it is mostly his fault. Another is that you can give him a chance to express his regrets even if he can't say them.

That's what Ruth did.

Mike is a traveling salesman. Very much a man, but very much hung up some ways. Because he couldn't unbend enough to express his regret, she did an interesting thing. One week when he took off on Monday, she wrote him a note. She packed it in his bag where he'd be sure to find it. She told him how much she cared about their relationship. She was sorry for whatever she'd done wrong. Would he please forgive her for any part she played in their problem right now? (She told me, not him, she couldn't even think of one place where she was at fault in this particular fracas.) Then she wished him a good trip and told him she'd be praying for him and for them.

If a man found a note like this and still couldn't apologize, what would he do? He might do what Mike did. He stopped at the florist and bought her a dozen red roses. No, he's still never said, "I'm sorry. Forgive me." But she got the message.

Ruth is a wise woman. She did two things

any wise woman can do with any fuss under any circumstance. She let him know she was sorry things weren't going well between them. And she gave him a chance to say the same thing his way.

If a man ever did feel like talking, he'd know one thing for sure. A woman like Ruth might be one fine place to begin.

—From Charlie W. Shedd, *Talk to Me.* Garden City, N.Y.: Doubleday, 1975.

Confession

True confession is painful. If it is not painful, it is not likely to be very effective. There is no particular pain involved in saying, "I find it difficult to forgive." These are generalizations and, very largely, evasions; for they could be said of almost any human being on earth. It is just another way of saying, "I am not all I ought to be, just like everyone else."

As stated before, there is within us a tension between the need to conceal and the need to reveal. The truth of our guilt demands expression. We need to tell someone, but we fear their condemnation or judgment and rejection. It is common, therefore, to feel great reluctance in facing our true guilt.

. . . . .

"A saint is one who sins less and less and confesses more and more," as has often been said. There is never a time when we can cease to confess. Long after the sins of the flesh are confessed, there remain all of the corrosive sins of the spirit: pride, envy, greed, avarice, lust, jealousy. And if one is almost certain that he has mastered the sins of the spirit and is quietly congratulating himself on this worthy achievement, he is horrified to discover the sin of pride operating with new vigor!

Must we always struggle, never winning, never reaching the goal line? The answer is an unqualified yes. The struggle here never ends, but with every step of the earthly pilgrimage there is a new sense of inner peace

and quiet, the growing sense of a Presence working with and within us. "For God is at work in you." We are not alone in our struggle, we are not condemned by our failures. Though we fall a thousand times, if we rise again and continue to follow the Light, we are accepted and forgiven. There is no limit to His love and His forgiveness.

See how gently Jesus reproves the spiritual shortcomings of the twelve. When rejected by the inhabitants of a village, James and John asked, "Lord, do you want us to bid fire come down from heaven and consume them?" I am not certain that Jesus smiled, but I think He did, as He said, "You do not know what manner of spirit you are of." In other words, "You are not to play God, and besides, why all this hostility?" Later He referred to those two as "sons of thunder," humorously, I think, but with telling effect. He dealt with their intense hostility, but did not condemn or reject them. When the same disciples asked if they might be seated one on the right and the other on the left when He came into His kingdom, there was no condemnation of their colossal pride. He simply told them that what they asked was not His to give. The other ten disciples were indignant, but Jesus was understanding and patient with James' and John's spiritual blindness and egomania.

And there was Peter's unconsidered protestation of loyalty and fidelity: "Even if I must die with you, I will not deny you." A bit later we hear him denying vehemently that he knows Jesus at all. The cock crows, and Jesus turns and looks at him. I am sure that it was not a look of condemnation—"I told you that you wouldn't hold out. See how weak you are?"—but rather a glance of infinite love and compassion and forgiveness, for this was His nature.

Jesus regards us in the same manner, and Jesus is the manifestation of God. "If you have seen me you have seen God," He declared. So, in His compassion and forgiveness we see the nature of God, for God is like Jesus.

One basic difficulty is not that we are reluctant to confess to God but that we are unable to believe *deeply* that God could really forgive us instantly, without qualification. We find it almost incredible that God could give unconditional love, especially in view of all our previous failures. "But I've done this again and again," said one man to me. "How could God ever forgive anyone as weak and faulty as I?" I said, "You are supposing that God is no better than you. You have trouble forgiving others, especially after they have let you down numerous times, and you imagine that God is like you, able to forgive one or two failures, but not fifty. God is better than you, my friend. His love is infinite."

How, specifically, does one confess so as to receive inward assurance of forgiveness at the feeling level? What does one say? How much and how often must one confess? Far more important than that is what we have just been considering: our concept of God and His nature; for it matters little what we say or how we confess if we do not have the overwhelming conviction that God *does* forgive instantly and willingly, that He does not condemn us. If our concept of God is adequate, our prayer of contrition will be adequate. If we have a weak concept of God and His love, we will never feel fully forgiven. But assuming that one is able to believe—and feel deeply—that God is anxious to forgive, how does one go about confessing so as to have a sense of cleansing? There are many steps and many ways, but here are some of them.

First, one does not rush into the presence of God and blurt out a request for pardon, or any other kind of petition, without suitable preparation. Not that our haste and crudeness can offend God. He is beyond that. But we need the preparatory period. Begin first with a time of meditation. This is a part of prayer. Think about the nature of God. Affirm what you know to be true about Him. "God's love is limitless, therefore He forgives to a limitless degree. Nothing I have ever done is so bad that He loves me less. Nothing good I have ever done is sufficient to cause Him to love me more. His love is a fixed and unchanging factor. I do not increase his love for me by any good deed, nor do I decrease it by my failures. Because He loves me I can ask for and receive instant forgiveness. It is promised that "If we confess our sins, he is faithful and just, and will forgive our sins and cleanse us from all unrighteousness." I believe this about God. This affirmative type of meditation is one aspect of prayer.

Second, let the confession be utterly, ruthlessly honest. A young woman told me that she and her husband had been so beset with financial troubles that they were half out of their minds with worry. Creditors telephoned and came to the door in a steady stream. There were threats of suits. She had prayed for a solution but no answer had come.

One night she went out and walked for miles, and finally she said, "God I hate you! I've asked for help and you didn't give it. I hate you!"

This was an honest confession, and a genuine prayer! God knew how she felt before she told Him, and what she did in that moment was to admit to herself and to God what she had never admitted before. Her tirade against God lasted some time, and finally, emotionally exhausted, she returned home.

She gave up praying for a miraculous deluge of money that would solve their problems. Instead she said, "God, if you want something done, you'll have to do it. I give up." This was a real prayer, a prayer of abandonment. No one would say that it was the highest form of prayer, but its very honesty had merit, and in abandoning her struggle she was, for the first time, turning it over to God. She had given up her childish prayer for a quick, easy miracle, and faced her true feelings.

Weak and human though it was, it was an honest prayer, and honesty with self and with God is the starting point. It is the absolutely essential first step. If we will not be honest with ourselves, how can we be honest with God? And if we cannot be honest with Him about our true feelings, how can He help us? Within a week she had a sudden "inspiration," which she knew was guidance.

It provided temporary relief, and in a matter of months the entire problem was solved. More important, she and her husband grew spiritually in the process.

—From Cecil G. Osborne, *The Art of Understanding Yourself.* Grand Rapids: Zondervan, 1967.

FOR FURTHER READING:

Cornwall, Judson. *Let Us Enjoy Forgiveness.* Old Tappan, N.J.: Revell, 1978.

Evans, Colleen Townsend. *Start Living: The Miracle of Forgiving.* Garden City, N.Y.: Doubleday, 1978.

Landorf, Joyce. *The Fragrance of Beauty.* Wheaton, Ill.: Victor Books, 1973.

Small, Dwight Hervey. *Your Marriage Is God's Affair.* Old Tappan, N.J.: Revell, 1979.

FORNICATION

IS THERE A DIFFERENCE between adultery and fornication?

The Bible uses the terms *adultery* and *fornication* interchangeably in some places and separately in others. Some people try to distinguish between them, suggesting that adultery is infidelity on the part of married people and fornication involves intercourse between the unmarried or when one is unmarried. We can't see that it makes any difference. Both are forbidden and condemned in the Bible, which states that "they which [continually] do such things shall not inherit the kingdom of God" (Galatians 5:19–21; cf. 1 Corinthians 6:9).

—From Tim and Beverly LaHaye, *The Act of Marriage.* Grand Rapids: Zondervan, 1976.

FRAGRANCE*

PERFUME HAS a magic way of completing your personality and adding the final dainty touch to your grooming. What perfume to choose? That's easy. Select only those that you really like. Experiment by trying the samples at the toilet-goods counters. Put them on your skin so that you will know how they react with your body chemistry. A first love in the bottle might turn out to be a lu-lu on your skin. Buy small bottles and then use them. Don't save your perfume for some vague, special occasion.

WHERE TO APPLY

Rub it on your shoulders, in the bend of your elbows, in the deep V of your blouse. The warmth of your skin will cause the aura of your perfume to float about you—oh, so subtly. Keep a vial in your bag so that you can renew its witchery away from home.

There are three concentrations of perfume and you should learn to use them all. *Lightest is cologne*—wonderful as an all-over body rub. It can be sprayed on, or rubbed on in the form of a "stick." These cooling fragrances are wonderful for warm weather. *Toilet water is stronger.* Spray it on your lingerie or use it as a refresher on your throat and palms. Finally, there is the enchanting concentrate, *perfume*, most potent and lasting of all.

Christian Dior has said, "Femininity is inconceivable without the association of fragrance. When I recall a charming woman, her fragrance is an inseparable part of the memory."

WHICH IS YOUR TYPE?

FLOWER FRAGRANCE   This is the scent of one flower only. It is charming and appropriate in the spring and summertime. Seems best suited to the "feminine" personality.

BOUQUET FRAGRANCE   The flower bouquets in general have a wearability that's hard to equal. They are year-rounders, never-failers, like pearls. There's one blended, undoubtedly, just for you.

WOODSY FRAGRANCE   Some of the most well-liked, best-selling perfumes in

*Reprinted from *A Womans Guide to Business and Social Success* by permission of the Milady Publishing Corporation, 3839 White Plains Road, Bronx, NY 10467.

America are woods, leaves, grass blends. Wonderful for the out-door, all-around good sport type.

FRUIT FRAGRANCE Offers a sunny, ripe warmth. It's fascinating mixed with flowers. Seems most appropriate on the "young matron" type.

SPICE FRAGRANCE Is intended to awaken the senses. It is sharp and clean-cut. Probably a favorite of several personality types for daytime wear. If anything it seems youthful and alive.

ORIENTAL FRAGRANCE Not for children. It is sultry and clinging. Wonderful for after-five wear on the sophisticated, voluptuous and exotic types.

MODERN FRAGRANCE Is concocted of just the right ingredients to give it a special brand of "chic." Obviously, intended for the busy "modern" woman.

HAVE YOUR SCENTS MAKE SENSE

You are now aware that some perfumes should not be worn to work. Just as you change from day dress to date dress when the evening shadows fall, so should you change your perfume. In fact, the best sense perfume can make is that it be worn when, where and on whom it will be appropriate and enchanting. Here are five suggestions:

1. Take lots of time in selecting the proper scent. Put it on your skin and wait a few minutes to give your own skin chemistry a chance to react with the perfume, then you'll be able to honestly judge.
2. Wear a single scent and carry it through from bath oil to cologne.
3. Change your perfume from daytime to date time. Some scents are too cloying for business wear.
4. Collect a wardrobe of scents to fit the mood, the season and the "types" you want to be.

5. Perfume evaporates, so once you have opened the bottle, use it or re-seal with paraffin.

—From *A Womans Guide to Business and Social Success* by permission of the Milady Publishing Corp., 3839 White Plains Rd., Bronx, NY 10467.

FOR FURTHER READING:

Pierre, Clara. *Looking Good.* New York: Reader's Digest Press, 1976.
Wallace, Joanne. *The Image of Loveliness.* Old Tappan, N.J.: Revell, 1978.
Wallace, Joanne. *Dress With Style.* Old Tappan, N.J.: Revell, 1983.
Wilhelmina. *The New You.* New York: Simon & Schuster, 1978.

FRIENDSHIP

Male/Female

"I've never had a male friend before," she said. "Not ever." And she was 54.

"Think of what you've missed," I said. I meant it, too.

Like many, she grew up in a generation where men and women fell in love, married, sometimes divorced, or committed acts of unfaithfulness, but never, never had friends of the opposite sex.

"Just think where friendship with a man could lead," a friend once advised her.

That insidious remark suggests that any time one male and one female spend enough time together, the end is inevitable: sexual gratification.

Some women have had this idea so ingrained in them that they avoid male companionship in their jobs. Some men have been so brainwashed, they seem to feel it's their duty to make aggressive passes or at least leer at every female.

Such people miss much of the joy of life because they hide in compartmentalized worlds of the stereotypes. Men always take aggressive steps. Women entice but never initiate. They treat each other as objects rather than persons.

I write that last statement because each potential relationship with a person of the opposite gender raises questions and causes hesitations. Something clicks in their minds and says that only one thing can come out of a male-female relationship—and it's *NOT* platonic!

Instead we can choose to look at people as people—individuals—everyone different. Then we can choose our friends on the basis of people with whom we feel a kinship.

For example, Shirley and Don became close friends. As singles they met in the same church, dated a few times, but mostly they simply liked being together. When I came on the scene, Shirley explained the relationship.

Later, I married Shirley, and three years later still, Don married a lovely girl. But the friendship between Shirley and Don continued until we moved overseas and they moved to another state and we lost contact.

Why can't we have friends of the opposite sex? It seems almost silly to ask the question. Since childhood I have always had friends of both sexes and no one ever made me feel I did anything wrong. That is, no one did until I got involved in the church. The church, like much of society around us, reflects attitudes and fears of their members.

I have a feeling that Jesus caused many lifted eyebrows in His dealings with women. We know from the story in John, Chapter 4, that His disciples were amazed to find Him talking to a woman in public. It simply wasn't done in those days. But Jesus did it.

Jesus not only had 12 disciples whom He called friends (John 15:14), but right along with those men, female disciples such as Joanna and Mary Magdalene seemed to be part of His followers. From the story in Luke 10, it appears Jesus had a meal alone with two women.

We know they had a brother named Lazarus, but he's not mentioned in that account and may not have been home. What a scandal it could have caused—Jesus eating in the home of two unattached females!

In the years I have been a professing Christian, I have experienced the joy of fe-

male friendship—and male as well. No one has ever accused me of improper behavior. I eat lunch with a woman because I like *HER*, not because my pulse races for her body.

I don't pick my friends because they are masculine or because they come from a particular age group, educational background or race. I select my friends because they are people I instinctively like.

As I ponder this question of friendship, I like to think I'm living within the range of the ideal the apostle Paul set forth when he wrote, "There is neither Jew nor Greek, there is neither slave nor free, there is neither male nor female; for you are all one in Christ Jesus" Galatians 3:28 RSV.

—CECIL MURPHEY

How to Help a Dependent Friend

Are you going down for the third time? Has another's burden become your own? Perhaps you need to gently untangle the relationship. Here are some ideas:

1. *Examine Your Motives.* Perhaps unconsciously you have been encouraging your friend to depend on you. You may actually depend on her dependence! After all, it does feel good to be needed. If this is the case, confess it to your friend. Together discuss ways both of you can develop a more healthy friendship, for both of your sakes.

2. *Limit the Time You Spend With Your Friend.* Talk to her frankly about your other responsibilities: "Jane, I'm committed to our relationship, but I must spend time with my family and my other friends, too. And I need some time to myself so I can be the kind of friend I want to be. How about only getting together on Friday mornings before my tennis lesson?"

3. *If Your Friend Is Facing a Serious Crisis, Firmly Suggest She Get Professional Help.* Perhaps you can say to her, "Jane, I'm willing to listen to you, but I really feel helpless when it comes to suggesting what

you should do. I know a psychologist who might be able to give you the insight that I can't. Would you like his phone number?"

4. *Try to Get Your Friend Involved in Group Activities.* You have been a willing "ear" and your friend has focused her emotional energy on you. But other Christians may be willing to listen and help, too. Plan an informal get-together and introduce your friend to others.

5. *Pray for Her.* If your friend is dealing with difficult problems, the best thing you can do is pray. Help your friend to depend on the Lord by praying for her and with her.

—Kelsey Menehan, "How to Help a Dependent Friend," *Today's Christian Woman*, Fall 1982.

FOR FURTHER READING:

Anderson, Colena M. *Friendship's Bright Shinings.* Grand Rapids: Zondervan, 1976.

Hauck, Paul A., and Edmund S. Kean. *Marriage and the Memo Method.* Philadelphia: Westminster, 1975.

McGinnis, Alan Loy. *The Friendship Factor.* Minneapolis: Augsburg, 1979.

FRIGIDITY

IN ORDER FOR TWO PEOPLE to get together sexually, they must make a choice to do so. People usually choose what they desire. Thus, if people do not particularly desire sex, they are less likely to choose to get involved in a sexual experience.

This lack of desire, or lack of interest, is one of the most common of the sexual difficulties. To maintain interest in sex, a person must gain some satisfaction from sexual encounters. Lack of satisfaction leads to lack of interest. And lack of interest leads to lack of sex—unless the person chooses to be involved in sex because of a sense of duty, or habit, or a desire to please one's partner.

In this section we look at various situa-

tions that lead to lack of interest, and discuss some ways to solve this most perplexing and elusive problem.

The Uninterested Woman

In the past, the woman who is not interested in sexual activity was often called "frigid." In more recent years, particularly since the Masters and Johnson studies, we have tried to use this term less and less. "Frigid" is a critical and judgmental term, whereas we prefer to be supportive. In addition, the term has been so misused that it has come to mean almost any kind of sexual problem that a woman might have—problems with interest, arousal, or release. For this reason, we normally choose not to refer to any woman as being frigid, but rather to define her problems more precisely.

Good sexual feelings are often referred to as erotic feelings. Erotic feelings are usually a combination of physical and emotional sensations. The woman who lacks interest or desire is sometimes one who experiences little or no physical arousal and almost no emotional pleasure in sex. She does not experience the sexual act as a way of giving or receiving love. Usually she is not eager for a sexual experience except to please her partner. In terms of the actual physical signs of arousal, such as lubrication or nipple erection, she may have some slight sensations of pleasure, but these are usually far outweighed by the resistant emotional feelings that go with them.

We might ask, then, why a woman would engage in an activity that has so little positive and so much negative in it for her. We might compare it to going to the dentist. Sorry, dentists! People go to the dentist even though they hate having their teeth drilled, because they recognize that the consequences of not doing so will be harmful. They are willing to subject themselves to the distasteful experience of the dentist's drill for the long-term benefit of controlling tooth decay. Similarly, a woman usually has some understandable reasons for putting up with sex even though it is a negative ordeal for her. The main reason is to carry out her duty as a wife; she feels she must meet her partner's needs to maintain the integrity of her marriage. If she is a Christian, she may see this not only as a marital duty but also as a Christian duty.

Other women who don't enjoy sex prefer to avoid it rather than perform their duty. But they are not usually very direct. Few women will just say, "Hey, I hate sex, so forget it, buddy." Rather, they will find more subtle ways to get around it. The standard excuse is the headache. Even though there are many jokes about it, such a physical complaint is often used to avoid contact. Another way women avoid sex is to develop a busy schedule. The woman goes to bed or gets up later or earlier than her husband, and thus avoids being around when he might be sexually interested. A third common ploy is to initiate a hassle around the time when a sexual encounter might take place. Many couples report that they have their biggest fights at the times when sexual involvement would be most likely. After a while, the man may, without realizing it, slip into the pattern too.

Let's look at some specific reasons why a woman might be uninterested in sex.

One reason why a woman might avoid sex is that she does not experience her partner as warm and caring about her needs for sexual pleasure. As we have already said, it is essential for a woman in any sexual experience to feel loved and cared for, to feel some tenderness, some concern for her thoughts and feelings and her current situation. Without this atmosphere she is not likely to allow

herself to be intimate and emotionally vulnerable. If that emotional support is regularly lacking, she will be regularly uninterested.

Closely connected with the lack of emotional satisfaction is a lack of interest due to problems with arousal or release. If the woman does not become aroused during sexual pleasuring, does not go from the excitement phase to the plateau phase, does not experience lubrication and clitoral and genital engorgement or response, any interest she may have had in sex will wane. Even if she experiences arousal, consistent failure to reach a climax will eventually squelch her interest in sex. It's no fun to have your body and your feelings prepared for an orgasm over and over again, and then to experience only frustration. This causes such intense discomfort that it's no wonder a woman's interest fades away.

The graph for the woman who often becomes aroused without release is shown below. At one point her experience would be charted by line 1, in time it resembles line 4.

When a woman does not experience satisfaction even though there is arousal, over a period of time the arousal is likely to diminish. You will notice that the bottom line on the graph is almost a straight line. The way it usually goes is something like this: a new bride is delighted and excited about being involved with her partner, and finds herself becoming very aroused. She may have felt a similar arousal during hugging and kissing before marriage. However, when she has no orgasmic response, and hence feels no satisfaction, the arousal takes her nowhere. Be-

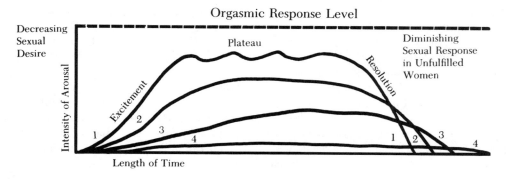

Orgasmic Response Level

cause of what this does to her, she begins to slow down.

You will notice on the graph that it takes a little longer for her to get aroused and she does not become quite as aroused. Then as time goes on, arousal takes even longer and is even less intense. It also takes longer for her to return to her unstimulated state. This is usually a period of discomfort. Finally, she experiences almost no arousal and hence no desire. She goes nowhere in the whole experience.

This flattening out of the curve will often occur between the fifth and tenth years of marriage. The timing is sometimes related to other events in life, such as having children and being occupied with heavy responsibilities. The pattern is certainly reversible, but the woman may need some professional help. If you are in this sort of situation, and you want to reverse it, you must identify yourself as being in this pattern. You and your partner must communicate with one another about your understanding of how this developed and the fact that you want to do something about it.

The pattern may have been caused by the fact that the man ejaculated prematurely, not allowing enough time for the woman to respond with an orgasm. Or it may have come about because the woman could never allow herself to experience an orgasm, so she was left hanging in her preorgasmic state regardless of how long the man could maintain his erection. Whatever the original cause, the pattern must be reversed if you are going to feel any sexual desire.

Another major cause of decreasing sexual interest in the woman is the boredom that may set in because of mechanical or goal-oriented sexual activity. By this we mean that a woman's interest is not likely to be maintained if the couple has adopted a standard routine for love-making—what we've talked about as the three-push-button approach—the woman is passive while the man goes through the standard procedure like an airplane pilot checking to see if the airplane is ready for flight. If a man follows this kind of procedure and the woman does

not go after variation or creativity, then it is not likely that her interest will be maintained. By goal-oriented activity, we mean sexual activity that is always aimed at having an orgasm rather than having as a goal the expression of love and care and affection, the joy and delight present in the relationship. Lack of interest is likely to develop after a couple has functioned together under these circumstances for some period of time.

Another major cause for lack of interest in women is emotional ambivalence. A woman may find herself being intensely responsive, but she cannot accept this response as part of herself. Something in her training or her upbringing, some fear, an experience in her past, or a general discomfort with pleasure interferes with her enjoyment of sex. She will probably not want an activity that causes her inner turmoil. Because of this conflict, some women will cut off their natural and God-given sexual responses. As a result of cutting off their sexual feelings, they will experience less pleasure, and when they experience less pleasure, they will lose interest. They end up in the same place as those who have little or no intensity in their arousal to begin with.

Other women enjoy full, intense arousal and response once they are actually sexually involved. Nevertheless, those good erotic feelings of arousal and release do not lead to future interest or initiation. The conflict about allowing those good feelings seems to block the desire. Their graph might look like [that on page 208].

There is no interest or desire, in fact continual resistance. It takes a long time to get into the experience. Arousal may be slow. But once they are aroused, the arousal is intense and the release fairly rapid. Resolution follows rather naturally.

There are other psychological reasons for lack of interest. These include anxiety or depression. Any continuous tension or stress can also reduce desire. Sometimes the causes are much deeper; these are unconscious barriers. Helen Singer Kaplan, a sex researcher and therapist, has cited unconscious reasons such as fear of success, fear of intimacy, oedi-

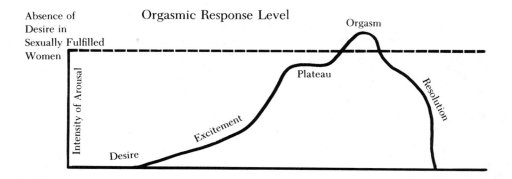

pal conflicts, deep long-term anger, and other interwoven, complicated psychological problems.

—From Clifford and Joyce Penner, *The Gift of Sex*, copyright © 1981, pp. 195–200; used by permission of Word Books, Publisher, Waco, Texas 76796.

FOR FURTHER READING:

LaHaye, Tim and Beverly. *The Act of Marriage*. Grand Rapids: Zondervan, 1976.

Wheat, Ed, M.D., and Gaye Wheat. *Intended for Pleasure*, Rev. ed. Old Tappan, N.J.: Revell, 1981.

G

GOALS

A YOUNG MOTHER once called me and told me in detail just how miserable her life was. Her husband constantly criticized her. Her young children would not mind. Life was boring. There was never enough money.

Betty wanted sympathy. But I didn't give her sympathy—not because I didn't feel sorry for her, but rather because I really wanted to help.

"Betty," I asked, "have you set any goals for your life?"

"Goals? Why, of course. I wish we could move out of this apartment into a house with a yard. I would like to have some new clothes. But more than anything else, I want my family to be happy."

"And how do you expect to reach these goals?" I asked.

"Why, I don't know," she replied vaguely. "Those are just . . . dreams."

How many times had I heard other women express their desires in much the same way! They thought they knew just exactly what they wanted, but they did not know how to get it. *They didn't have goals but only dreams*—fairy-tale wishes requiring a magic wand to turn ugly frogs into princes.

Proverbs doesn't have a magic wand. But it does have advice that will work miracles, if we will but use it.

> I would have you learn this great fact: that a life of doing right is the wisest life there is. If you live that kind of life, you'll not limp or stumble as you run. Carry out my instructions: don't forget them, for they will lead you to real living.
>
> Proverbs 4:11–13

Real living. Reality. These key words mean that you are not expecting perfection—of yourself or of others. We must all learn to live in reality. If you would have your dreams come true, you must first figure out exactly what a life of doing right is—for you. In other words, you must set your goals.

Yes, God wants you to see your dreams come true. You can open yourself up to the gift of life and joy that He wants to give to you, if you are willing to plan and to work for it.

The best way is to remember that *a goal is the target for your behavior*—then take aim! Aim your behavior right at the bull's eye. If a goal is the target, then to reach that goal you must make your behavior consistent with your goal.

You don't have to change everything all at once. Set your goal. Make a commitment to that goal. Then ask for God's help in achieving it, and let your heart follow.

The only way in which anyone can change his attitudes or his behavior is to work on them, one area at a time.

For example, since Betty wishes for a new house, she can set a goal of making money for a down payment. She can then start aiming for behavior at that goal by doing part-time work. Perhaps she longs for new clothes. If so, she can set a goal of learning how to sew. The wish for a happy family might be met by setting a goal of reading inspirational books, or of obtaining family counseling.

There is little to be gained by falling into the trap of trying to achieve goals by wishing something would happen. That's only dreaming. Ten little words can help you set the right kind of goals:

IF IT IS TO BE, IT IS UP TO ME.

Everything we do every day is either aimed at our goals, or it is not. Many miserable people try doing what feels good at the time, instead of disciplining themselves to work on their behavior. "Feelings" are not reliable. You don't always feel like doing everything that is essential for your happiness and success. You may not "feel" in love with your husband when you are annoyed with him, but you may have to discipline yourself to be understanding and loving, if your goal is a closer relationship.

You may not feel overjoyed when you answer the phone and learn that a friend has a problem and wants to take up precious moments of your time. But if your goal is to serve God by serving others, you will take the time to listen with interest.

If we make a commitment of the will and of the heart to work toward a certain goal, then duty and discipline will carry us through to success.

A word of warning, however: Sometimes dedicated people fail to change their behavior because they have overlooked two important points in the setting of goals:

1. It is important to set realistic goals.
2. Goals must be clearly defined. Goals that are too vague are seldom reached.

Realistic Goals. If you set a goal that will be impossible for you to reach, you will automatically fail. Such a failure makes you feel worse about yourself than if you had never tried. I once asked a group of high-school seniors what goals they had set for their lives, and their answers were very revealing.

"I plan to be a lawyer," said the first.

"I'm going to become a master photographer," the second replied.

The third student shrugged realistically. "I just want to pass my exams for now," he admitted. His goal was limited, but for him it was the best goal he could possibly set. He was a borderline student. If he decided to set

a realistic goal of passing his exams, he could easily adapt himself to meet the requirements by studying hard. For him to set a goal of trying to be a doctor would have been unrealistic. He did not have the grades in past work which would get him accepted in a college premed course. Such a long-range and ambitious goal would only have frustrated him and destroyed his motivation for trying to pass the senior exams. He would have failed, ending up with a poor attitude about himself.

Goals that are too vague. Betty said she wanted a happy family, but she could not say specifically how she could change her behavior to make herself and her family happier. Her goal was too vague. A more specific goal for Betty might have been to learn to control her tongue, instead of nagging at her family in order that they might be happier.

Many women have idealistic goals of wanting to help others, or to serve God in another way. These are wonderful desires; however, they need to be specific in order to be considered goals. One way might be to start a Bible study in the home. Another might be to do part-time work and earn extra money for a worthwhile cause, or to donate time and services wherever needed. I like the advice written in the margin of an elderly missionary woman's Bible:

You ask me what is the will of God
And I will answer true.
It is the nearest thing that should be done
That God can do through you.

When dreams come true at last, there is life and joy! We are happier when we are achieving goals than when we are merely waiting and wishing for ugly frogs to turn into princes!

Every person wants to believe that his life counts for something. How wonderful that it is possible to make our lives count with the aid of our Source Book, the Bible! In it God has provided just what we need.

Many people have not been taught to have goals. Many live dull, humdrum existences. Because they have never been encouraged to have dreams, they feel life is meaningless. They have never learned the secret of turning their wishes into realistic and attainable goals by simply changing their attitudes and their behavior—one step at a time!

Think big! Attempt great things.
Believe big! And you'll get big results.
Don't sweat the small stuff.

Proverbs tells us that a life of doing right is the wisest life there is. If we set goals and commit ourselves to achieving them, then ask God to bless our efforts, we can make our dreams and wishes come true!

How to Set Goals

Have two goals: wisdom—that is, knowing and doing right—and common sense. Don't let them slip away, for they fill you with living energy, and are a feather in your cap.

Proverbs 3:21, 22

We can learn to know what is right by studying the Bible and by attending worship. We can learn to do right by setting goals to change our behavior—and by leaning on God's strength. If we learn to practice this kind of wisdom, then Proverbs promises abundant energy, which will help us accomplish more than we ever believed possible.

On page 212 is a chart which has proved helpful to many. I suggest that you take the time to fill it in and then refer to it frequently. I think you will find that it will be helpful to you, too!

What you write on *your* chart will be entirely different from what I would write on mine. Setting goals is a highly individual matter. Each of us has different problems, needs, and desires, as well as different tastes.

It is important, however, for you to consider each goal carefully. After doing so, write down your thoughts as to what your goals should be and what the possible obstacles might be to reaching each goal. Finally, write down the possible solutions to each obstacle. In the TIME FRAME column, write down a date when you expect to begin working on each goal (as well as a date when you

want to attain it). Check your progress weekly and note your findings in the PROGRESS REPORT column. Don't forget to include in the POSSIBLE REWARDS column the benefits you will receive from attaining each goal. To stimulate thinking about how to fill in your goal sheet, let's look at each of the areas to be considered.

Intellectual Goals. Perhaps you might wish to begin reading some inspirational books or study information necessary for your job. If so, write it down under possible goals. The possible obstacles might be that you are a slow reader, or that you have vision problems. Perhaps you have little or no time for reading. Perhaps you need new glasses. You could set aside some time each day for reading. The possible rewards are that you may become a more interesting, fulfilled person, or one who is more knowledgeable on the job.

Emotional Goals. You might want to heighten your appreciation of your loved ones, or of the beauty around you. A recovered alcoholic once told me that he had never been able to fully realize the loveliness of his wife, his home, his children—even his yard. Each time he had taken a drink, his awareness of the beauty that should have stirred his emotions was dulled. Drugs, too, can dull awareness. But so can the fact that you are too busy to notice—or too tired—or too worried.

One of the greatest enemies of womankind is fatigue. It clouds our decisions and erodes our dispositions. Everything looks different to us when we are rested and refreshed.

A word about worry. Worry is the biggest waste in the world. It accomplishes exactly nothing. Worry never robs tomorrow of its sorrow. It only saps today of its strength.

If either of these conditions is an obstacle for you, the solution might be to become more organized, or to use your time more efficiently. And if you find that resentments and irritations are taking the place of gratitude and appreciation in your life, you might

HAPPINESS IS ACHIEVING WORTHWHILE GOALS

Area of Life	Possible Goals	Possible Obstacles	Possible Solutions	Time Frame	Possible Rewards	Progress Report
INTELLECTUAL						
EMOTIONAL						
PHYSICAL						
SPIRITUAL						
SOCIAL						
FAMILY						
FINANCIAL						
BUSINESS-CAREER						

"A GOAL IS THE TARGET OF YOUR BEHAVIOR."

find it helpful to start thanking God each day for the source of the irritation: your husband, your home, your children, the family automobile. The possible rewards are greater happiness for you and for others as you find your own attitudes changing to those of gratitude and appreciation.

Physical Goals. Perhaps you would like to lose weight and the big obstacle is food, or having to cook for your family, or having to eat out as you travel to work. There are many possible solutions: You might change the eating habits of your family; resist buying snack foods; start reading books on nutrition; learn about food supplements and salt substitutes. Start eating a breakfast heavy in protein. I have to plan a period of fifteen minutes of stretching and breathing exercises every day. It takes discipline! Of course, our main goal should be glowing good health! You'll find the rewards will be obvious in your mirror!

Spiritual Goals. Do you long to know God better? to have more time to spend with Him? to have such a strong relationship to Jesus Christ that you feel Him working in your life and overcoming the character defects that you recognize in yourself? If so, set

a goal to intensify your relationship with God.

The possible obstacles may be that you are just too busy, or perhaps you are concerned that if you insist on having a prayer time every morning, your family will think you are a fanatic. Perhaps you are afraid that you will lose friends. The possible solutions are to spend more time with other Christians so that your behavior will not be adversely influenced by non-Christians. Read your Bible daily. Join a Bible-study group, or start one. Pray every morning and learn to replace doubt and frustration with faith and prayers.

What are the possible rewards of enhancing your spiritual life? You will be blessed. You'll have a victorious life and be better able to function. You will be filled with more energy, and you'll be calmer and more serene, even on the more trying days!

Social Goals. All of us need friends, but friends don't just happen. We have to cultivate relationships. In doing this, you might decide that you are going to be more sensitive to the needs of the other people you know. More specifically, you might find that you will want to express your gratitude to the people who regularly perform essential services for you—services that are normally taken for granted. I have found that a small gift and a personal note of recognition and thanks mean a great deal to the people who do important things for me, such as taking away my trash, and it always inspires them to do a better job.

The obstacles to your social goals may be many. Maybe you are just too busy to take the time to think of others. Possibly you just do not see people such as waitresses and busboys as real people with real concerns and needs. Perhaps your mind is on other things, or you are too shy to reach out to others.

The solution might be to begin by doing simple, thoughtful things such as writing little notes to people who don't get much mail. The rewards? You will have more friends and you'll have the satisfaction of bringing joy to others.

Family Goals.   We all want to have a close, happy family. Perhaps your goal in this area might be to learn to have more patience with others. You might also improve the quality of your time together by having family devotions.

The possible obstacles might be that you find it hard to get the whole family together at one time, because everyone is busy and on a different schedule. Perhaps there is not enough time. Possible solutions could be to watch less television or to otherwise utilize your time better. You might make a trip to the supermarket do double duty by taking one of your children with you and giving that child your undivided attention for a time. And on the rare moments when you are alone with your husband, pay attention to him and let him know that he is loved and appreciated. The rewards will be greater happiness for your entire family.

Financial Goals.   You may want to have a better house—to be free of debt—to contribute to the Lord's work. The possible obstacles to these goals might be your recklessness with charge accounts. If you are unable to use credit wisely and with restraint, a good solution might be to destroy them and start

paying cash. You will be rewarded with peace of mind, as you will find yourself getting free of debt. Remember that the most uncomfortable place to live is just beyond your income!

Business Goals.   If all your goals are worthwhile and are being met satisfactorily, you are likely to find that you are achieving your goals in business, providing they are worthy, specific, timely, and realistic.

> Wisdom is the main pursuit of sensible men, but a fool's goals are at the ends of the earth!
>
> Proverbs 17:24

Wisdom is a necessary factor in the selection of prudent goals, and God has promised to give wisdom. The Bible tells us that He will give wisdom liberally to those who ask for it. What a wonderful thing to know that we can have the wisdom from above, just for the asking!

As we seek the wisdom of God when we set specific and attainable goals, as we gradually conform ourselves to God's pattern for our lives and start chipping away at the barriers that stand between ourselves and what we desire to achieve with God's help, we are amazed to find that our lives have begun to change in dramatic ways. We become more productive, more successful, happier. It seems that we can see miracles being wrought right before our eyes!

But God is in the miracle business, and we are co-laborers with Him. As we seek to apply His heavenly principles to our lives, we cannot help but be successful!

—From Mary C. Crowley, *Women Who Win.* Old Tappan, N.J.: Revell, 1979.

FOR FURTHER READING:

Bright, Vonette Zachary. *For Such a Time as This.* Old Tappan, N.J.: Revell, 1976.

Lakein, Alan. *How to Get Control of Your Time and Your Life.* N.Y.: Wyden, 1973.

Tchividjian, Gigi. *A Woman's Quest for Serenity.* Old Tappan, N.J.: Revell, 1981.

GOSSIP

ACCORDING TO the dictionary, gossip is passing on (to person after person) facts, rumors, or behind-the-scenes information of an intimate, personal, or sensational nature. Gossip is different from lying, though sometimes it includes telling lies or exaggerated half-truths.

But is it gossiping when we simply tell the truth about another person who might not happen to be present? Not necessarily. There are times when it may be right and proper to gather information in order to make an intelligent decision.

In Matthew 10, when Jesus sends out the Twelve, he tells them, "And whatever town or village you enter, *find out who is worthy in it,* and stay with him until you depart." In the same way, a job reference form is not forcing someone to gossip when it asks semi-private questions about a potential employee.

I wondered a couple of years ago whether I was gossiping when a possible tenant for the vacant apartment above mine asked me about the landlord. Though I did say several negative things about my landlord, I decided that it was not gossip, since the person needed information to make a decision, and I was presenting verifiable facts.

Above all, gossip is about other people, and when we gossip, we take advantage of other people in some way. How is this so?

People have an insatiable desire to know about other people. This desire isn't bad in itself; it's what we do with that desire that matters. For the most part, people are the stuff life is made of. To avoid other people is to miss out on life itself, and to avoid talking with and about other people might be nearly as bad.

But when we gossip, we do more than just talk about someone else. We move into a vast gray area where motives and truth become unclear. What turns our everyday conversation into gossip? Consider a few characteristics, and ask yourself the accompanying questions:

Gossip involves unnecessary information. Just because I think Mary talks too much, do I have the right to tell everyone else so? Do I need to give others the freedom to decide that for themselves?

Gossip involves careless words. Should I tell a juicy story even if I'm not sure I have the facts correct? What could happen if someone retold my story and distorted it further?

Gossip may tell more than the whole story. Maybe I've told the facts, but have I added my own opinions about what happened to the point that they are indistinguishable from the facts? Have I exaggerated the facts in any way? Have I sensationalized the events by trying to arouse inappropriate emotion or judgment?

Gossip may tell less than the whole story. Have I omitted some of the facts and therefore left the wrong impression? Have I told a story I knew so little about that it left too much to the listener's (and my own) imagination?

Gossip takes place behind someone's back. Even if Margaret has told me all about the problems she's having with her husband, would she approve of my telling others about them? Would it be better to wait until I get her permission before I speak? Have I alienated myself from Margaret by breaking her confidence?

Gossip may arise from ulterior motives. Am I telling this story to impress someone, or to show him/her that I'm "on the inside" of a situation? Am I trying to get even with someone I don't like? Do I want others to feel just as angry at this person as I do? Do I have some underlying feelings about this person that I may not be aware of?

Gossip usually makes life more complicated. Will I be able to tell this story to anyone, or only to selected people? Why? Do I feel uncomfortable around the person I've told others about? What might happen if people who shouldn't know this information find out about it? Can I be sure that people will keep the information I've told them confidential?

It isn't hard to see that gossip can quickly damage our own and others' reputations. But if this is so, why does gossip come so easily?

We often catch ourselves in the act—"I shouldn't say this, but"—but we go ahead and say it anyway.

We gossip for many reasons, some of them conscious, some unconscious. No one can say which reason is used more often, but here are some general possibilities.

First, sometimes we gossip because we're afraid to confront a specific person directly. Let's look at an example. Linda often felt dumb around Joyce, whom she taught Sunday school with. Joyce sometimes ridiculed Linda right in front of their class of third graders for petty mistakes she made. Unfortunately, Linda was so afraid that she'd hurt Joyce's feelings by speaking up that she just avoided Joyce altogether, and instead told some of the other women at church how "bossy" and "negative" Joyce was with "everyone."

Joyce, on the other hand, simply didn't realize that she was bothering Linda, though she should have known that her behavior was out of place. She was just a forceful person who set high standards for herself and sometimes imposed them on others. Linda didn't realize that she might do a lot more good by telling her feelings to Joyce directly. Chances were good that Joyce would have said, "Oh really? I didn't realize I came on so strong. I'm sorry I made you feel that way." The problem could have been worked out. Even if Joyce didn't change, Linda would have been honest with Joyce (and herself) and would have avoided the gossiping.

Another reason we gossip is to compensate for our own (conscious or unconscious) feelings of inadequacy or failure. Sometimes we think that by putting others down we make ourselves look better. We may especially need this ego-boost if we are feeling unsure of our own worth.

This category of gossip can include a variety of motives. For example, we may talk about someone else's mistake or problem just to call attention to the fact that "*I* would have handled it better," or "I'm glad *I* don't have *that* problem." Or the gossip might stem from outright jealousy or envy, also by-products of low self-esteem.

A third reason, related to the second, is that we may gossip because that's the deepest we can get in our conversations with other people. It's always easier to talk about other people than to talk about ourselves—our own joys and hurts and dreams. We may feel that it's too great a risk to be vulnerable with our friends, so we protect ourselves by talking about others instead.

Why does the risk of being vulnerable seem so great? Because it means exposing the *real* truth about ourselves—what we feel inside—and many of us don't like ourselves on the inside. Besides, if we let others see us as we really are, they might reject us—or so we think. Telling the truth about ourselves can be much more difficult than telling the truth (or even half-truths) about others. It's much easier to gossip.

Do you see how we can substitute gossip for being a real person? That's what all three of the above reasons boil down to. Of course, we're not always sure of what underlies our tendency to gossip. Perhaps we can make ourselves more aware of our motives by asking some of the questions listed earlier. But whether we're aware of our reasons or not, we are still responsible to God for the things we say. Let's take a minute to see what the Bible says about gossip.

In Romans 1:26–31 Paul lists gossips among those whom God gave up to "a base mind and to improper conduct" (v. 28). In fact, gossips are mentioned in the same list as murderers, homosexuals, and haters of God. That list should dispel the notion that gossip is one of the "lesser sins," along with telling an occasional white lie, procrastinating, overeating, or running a stop sign when no one's looking.

God does not see it that way. No sin is worse than another in his eyes. All sin is serious to him. "For whoever keeps the whole law but fails in one point has become guilty of all of it," writes James (2:10).

While in God's eyes gossip is no worse than any other sin, it may be one of the most difficult sins to conquer. Gossip seems to come up again and again in Scripture. The Old and New Testaments condemn gossips and idle talkers on a regular basis. Read through the book of Proverbs sometime and take note of how many references there are to the tongue, mouth, lips, or speaking:

"A fool takes no pleasure in understanding, but only in expressing his opinion. . . . A fool's lips bring strife, and his mouth invites a flogging. A fool's mouth is his ruin, and his lips are a snare to himself" (Proverbs 18:2, 6–7).

Jesus reiterates the concern for pure speech in Matthew 12:36–37: "I tell you, on the day of judgment men will render account for every careless word they utter; for by your words you will be justified, and by your words you will be condemned."

Here Jesus seems to be telling us that the words we utter are an extremely important part of our total behavior on earth, and that God watches the words we say very carefully. If God watches our words carefully, then so should we.

In James we again see the importance of our words: "We all make mistakes in all kinds of ways, but the man who can claim that he never says the wrong thing can consider himself perfect, for if he can control his tongue he can control every other part of his personality!" (James 3:2 PHILLIPS; see also Proverbs 13:3; 21:23). This verse can help us not only to see how important our manner of speech is to God, it can also help us to bring other areas of our life under the Holy Spirit's control.

If we know of undisciplined areas of our lives—our thoughts, our use of time or money, our eating habits—we should check to see if we're in control of our tongue. The two may go hand in hand.

How can we keep ourselves from gossiping? Here are a few suggestions. First, pray for the Holy Spirit's help. Each morning commit to God all the words you will say that day and ask him to keep them pure.

Second, search the Scriptures for teaching on how Christians are to handle their speech. There is a wealth of material on the subject. Examine the words of Jesus to see how he kept them under control. A study of

the Proverbs dealing with speech or the tongue will also be rewarding.

Derek Kidner, in his commentary on Proverbs (InterVarsity Press), notes four marks of the righteous person's words: They will be *honest*, they will be *few*, they will be *calm*, and they will be *apt*. Can we say that we follow even these four principles?

Third, avoid people who themselves gossip (Proverbs 20:19). This does not necessarily mean that you should have nothing to do with them, but that you should flee from the idle conversations that begin so easily. T.N. Tiemeyer says, "When tempted to gossip, breathe through your nose."

Fourth, be honest with yourself and open with other people. In other words, admit to yourself why you want to gossip about someone else. Choose instead to go directly to that person if you have underlying feelings you need to express. If someone comes to you with gossip, go first to the person spoken of and find out if it's true, and if he or she wants you to talk about it with others.

Fifth, since the mouth speaks out of the abundance of the heart (Matthew 12:34), let us fill our hearts with those things which are true, honorable, just, pure, lovely, gracious, excellent, and worthy of praise (Philippians 4:8). Then our attitudes, motives, and thoughts will be pure, and as a result our speech will be godly and self-controlled.

—VERNE BECKER, associate editor of *Campus Life* magazine.

FOR FURTHER READING:

Gundry, Patricia. *The Complete Woman.* Garden City, N.Y.: Doubleday, 1981.

Schlink, Basilea. *You Will Never Be the Same.* Minneapolis: Bethany House, 1972.

GRANDPARENTS

Helpful Hints for Those About to Become Grandparents

1. Be willing to help after the birth of the baby—if asked.

216

2. The new parents are grown-up adults, not children. They can make their own decisions. They don't need parental interference or intervention, unless they ask for it.

3. Don't compete with the other grandparents by buying expensive presents or monopolizing the parents' time.

4. Our children have a different perspective from ours. They don't do things as we did. Because they are adults, they have chosen their life-style.

5. When visiting, remember you are a guest in that home (or when they visit you, remember they are guests).

6. You'll love the new grandchild because babies are easy to love. Don't neglect the parents, especially the new mother, who needs help and consideration.

7. Disposable diapers are just as respectable as cloth. Pacifiers won't disfigure a child or destroy his/her character. All this says is that if your grandchild starts out life differently than your children did, it will do no irreparable damage.

8. Babies don't need extra-warm bundling (as many of us were taught).

9. Breast-feeding can be an emotional subject. Find out for yourself the pros and cons, but let the parents decide for themselves.

10. Don't be afraid to say "I don't know," whether you're talking about a two-month-old infant's sudden rash or why Melinda cried out in her sleep.

11. Pray much for the new child, for the new parents, for yourself. Ask God to make this a happy period for all of you.

Helpful Hints on Being a Grandparent

1. Enjoy this time of life. It's a new stage of your own development. You've earned the right to enjoy the little ones.

2. Be loving and available grandparents, as much as your schedule and life-style permit. But don't be the ubiquitous kind (always underfoot) and constantly offering advice that sounds like marching orders.

3. Learn to listen. Let the grandchild find you as a source of someone who cares, whom he/she can talk to, and yet won't pump for family information.

4. Pray daily for your children and your grandchildren.

5. About giving advice: *don't.* They'll love you for it.

6. Being a grandparent doesn't mean you're over the hill or too old for sex. Grandparents can still be great lovers.

7. Make your home a warm, welcome place which the grandchildren look forward to visiting and are reluctant to leave.

8. As grandparents, we have much to teach—values, attitudes, knowledge. But we can also learn to see life anew through the eyes of the young.

9. When you criticize a child, you're criticizing the parent; when you compliment the child, you're complimenting the parent. That means that most parents (unconsciously) view their offspring as extensions of themselves.

10. Conflicts will occur—even though we love our children and grandchildren. Acknowledge and deal with the conflicts, asking forgiveness when appropriate. Most of all, keep the relationship open.

11. Children aren't miniature adults. When we talk to them, let's use words and concepts on their level.

12. When we grandparents have the responsibility to discipline grandchildren, we need to do it lovingly but firmly. Why not reward children for doing right while minimizing their wrongs? Above all, teach them about God's forgiveness by the way we accept and forgive others.

13. Some *don'ts* to minimize the roadblocks in relationships: Don't urge children to deny their feelings. Don't offer easy solutions and glib answers to life. Don't lecture or moralize. Don't threaten punishment. Don't play psychiatrist.

14. We'll never be *perfect* grandparents; no one ever is. By loving and depending on

Jesus Christ for daily strength, we can be *very good* grandparents!

15. Don't stop growing as an individual. Being a grandparent is a new stage of life—not the final one.

—From Cecil B. Murphey, *Devotions for Grandparents.* Old Tappan, N.J.: Revell, 1983.

FOR FURTHER READING:

Berven, Ken. *I Love Being Married to a Grandma.* Nashville: Nelson, 1978.

Shedd, Charlie W. *Grandparents.* Garden City, N.Y.: Doubleday, 1976.

GRIEF

GRIEF IS THE RESPONSE of emotional pain to great loss. To lose anyone or anything of real significance produces grief. The loss may occur as a result of death, divorce, children's leaving home, moving, from the loss of a job, of reputation, security, money, or one of the senses, such as sight. We need to remember that the greater the emotional investment in the person or object lost, the more intense the pain. For our purposes here we focus on death; but the same reactions can be observed in other grief-filled situations.

. . . . .

It takes time for the wound to heal. But the healing can make us stronger, more sensitive, and appreciative of life and of the people who love us.

Let us turn our attention to the different reactions we will, in all probability, experience in grief. The first is *shock:* "How can this be?" It will seem unreal. It's hard to register the reality of the loss. We will be numb and may appear dazed, confused, or stoic. We simply need a little time at this stage for the reality of our situation to sink in.

Emotional release usually follows the shock. It is not "Christian" to choke back the tears. The great men of faith wept over loss, and so did the Lord Himself. It is healthy and needful to cry. Give your feelings expression! Healing comes faster when you do.

Feelings of hostility and guilt may be present in our grief. It hurts so bad that we may become very critical of everyone and everything related to our loss. This may include the doctors and nurses, family members, and even God Himself. "Why would God permit such a thing to happen?" we often ask. While we may not find an adequate explanation, we can know a God who cares for us so deeply that He too participates in our suffering. He allows us to work through our hostile feelings without rejecting us or withdrawing His love. One indication that we have worked through our grief is the realization that we can trust God beyond our understanding of Him or the events of life.

Guilt is a painful part of grief. "Why didn't we do more? Why did we do some of the things we did?" The tendency is to distort reality. We need to remember that we may be reading too much out of our present grief reaction back into our prior relationship with the deceased.

The mistakes we made can be faced and committed to the living Christ. His forgiveness is readily available. Now the tough task of forgiving ourselves must be undertaken for freedom to come.

Depression and withdrawal are common to the grief process. We may feel that no one else has ever grieved as we are grieving, and that no one really cares, not even God. It is dark; all hope seems to disappear. Recognizing this as a normal part of our dealing with grief can keep us from becoming panic-stricken over what is to become of us. This too will pass—if we let it!

Great loneliness and the loss of meaning are common and normal. The people we love are a vital part of us. When they die, a part of us dies too. What seemed important before may lose its importance, and we are left with a sense of emptiness. The person we intended to share our life with continually is gone, and no one can take his place. The loneliness will seem unbearable! But others have experienced the same and have survived. You can survive too. Even Christ experienced the agony of aloneness on the cross when He cried out, "My God, my God, why hast thou forsaken me?" Jesus has promised to be present with us and never to leave us comfortless. He does not take the place of another person in our lives: no one can. But He can take His own place as Lord and bring unbelievable resources into our lives to heal and even give our loss meaning.

Anxiety and fear are also normal. "What am I going to do?" becomes a focal question. We may have never considered life without the one we lost. For a time we will be disoriented. This is normal, because facing the unknown always creates its share of anxiety. Fear also relates to the future dimension of grief. The death of someone close makes us keenly aware of the fact that we too will die.

There are some definite steps we can take to bring about healing in our times of grief. First, *we need to express our emotions.* Holding everything in only hinders our recovery. Talking with a family member, a friend, or a minister about both our negative and positive feelings will do wonders for us. As already mentioned, there may be feelings of anger, guilt, anxiety, or fear. Talking about these feelings diminishes them and serves as a kind of confession that opens the way for the positive feelings of love and gratitude, even joy, to return.

It helps to talk about the deceased to recall events experienced with him. This helps you face the reality of your loss, release your emotions, and affirm the life of the deceased, whose influence and contribution to your own life will never die. The memory of the deceased will remain and even enrich your life further as you learn to let them go.

Verdell's mother did a beautiful thing prior to her husband's funeral. She gathered her children and their spouses around the casket and talked openly of her great loss. Then she prayed and gave thanks for the forty rich years they had together. The final act of her prayer was to give him up to God. She later said that in that moment she experienced a "letting go" of Eldred. It's hard, but we must let go of the person if we are to experience healing. It takes time to turn loose, but if we are moving in that direction, we can count on the resources of the living Christ to enable us to allow our beloved to rest in peace.

Death can make us aware of the unlimited resources of faith in a way that nothing else can. To be without a solid faith in Jesus Christ is to find death the loneliest experience of life. With Christ we discover the truth of His statement, "I will not leave you comfortless: I will come to you." This does not mean that there will be no pain or struggle. It does mean that nowhere in all the world is the pain felt as keenly and as deeply as it is in the heart of God. He is in it with us and will help us when no one else can.

A relationship with Christ brings hope, and without hope we would all die in despair. This world is not the whole story. There is life beyond death, and the prospect of being reunited someday with the one we have lost brings joy indeed. The older we get, the more we should realize that the balance of our investment is shifting from this world to the next. This realization will not only help us accept the loss of a loved one, but will lessen the anxiety and fear in facing our own death.

Finally, give yourself some time for the wound to heal. Don't push yourself too fast. In the death of your beloved, you have lost a significant person who was an important part of your life. It takes time to recuperate, and the amount of time varies with the individual. It is imperative that each person work through his own anguish completely.

Unresolved grief is destructive. Therefore deal honestly with your feelings; allow others to walk with you in your sorrow; hold firmly to your faith in the God whose death and life can enable you to move beyond every loss into the fuller hope that is yours in Him. Then you will know the meaning of the Scripture, "Grieve not as those who have no hope."

—From Creath Davis, *How to Win in a Crisis.* Grand Rapids: Zondervan, 1976.

FOR FURTHER READING:

Graham, Billy. *Till Armageddon*. Waco, Tex.: Word Books, 1981.

Murphey, Cecil B. *Comforting Those Who Grieve*. Atlanta: John Knox, 1979.

GROOMING

I FEEL IT IS MY Christian duty to be at least as careful in my personal grooming, if not more so, than before my conversion. You may have dry hair and my habits may not be workable for you. But shampooing my hair twice a week is as much a part of my spiritual life as my daily quiet time.

A Christian woman in a baggy skirt and a blouse that isn't fresh is a bad witness, no matter what else she does. If you can't afford frequent dry cleaning bills, then buy clothing which is washable. If you can't go to the hairdresser often, then have your hair styled so you can handle it yourself. I don't visit my hairdresser once between permanents. She has styled my hair so that I can shampoo and set it myself without benefit of one single bobby pin!

Americans have been accused of over-bathing. Sometimes when I am pressed into the middle of a crowd of people after a meeting, I think this is an unjust accusation! I think I'm too tired for a shower sometimes, too, but I always feel rested and refreshed after I take it. Just the nervous tension alone in the average twentieth century woman's life is adequate reason for a daily bath. And if your best friend won't tell you, I'll tell you that there are excellent deodorants on the market. And they are not on the market to keep TV stations in operation, they are on the market for us to use—regularly. Women, I must say, are not as adept at offending in this way as men. At least this has been my experience in crowds. But we all need to remember, as Christians, that we not only "present our bodies" unto the Lord, we present them to those who don't yet know Him, too! No matter how many Bible verses you

can quote, no matter how well you have all your points assembled for winning a person to Jesus Christ, if you offend that person's finer senses, you may slam the door of the Kingdom in his or her face.

A few good poems and thousands of bad ones have been written about a woman's hands. About the touch of a woman. It can be a soothing, creative experience. Or it can feel like a brush with a piece of number two sandpaper. I know all about detergents in the dishpan. No wonder they cut grease on dishes and skillets so quickly, look what they do to the natural oils in our hands! Mine show it immediately. But, no reason to blame detergents. Make more frequent use of your hand lotion. Keep a bottle at the kitchen sink and keep using it. I know what housework and packing and unpacking heavy suitcases from a car can do to fingernails, too. But this is no excuse for poorly groomed nails on a woman's hands. Any leading manufacturer of nail polish also manufactures nail cream. And the ads are true which claim that extra-heavy portions of protein in gelatin form prevent breaking nails. Typing as much as I do, I am speaking from experience when I speak of broken nails.

My eyes go involuntarily to two points of a woman's anatomy when I meet her. Her hands and her teeth. Glamorous, long, regularly formed nails and white even rows of teeth are found only rarely except in the ads for toothpaste and nail polish. But teeth can be clean and nails can be clean and both can, and must be, regularly cared for if we are to be good for the reputation of Jesus Christ in our daily contacts.

Quite sometime ago I learned that after thirty minutes of talking, the human throat dries out to such an extent that the breath is bad as a consequence. As regular a part of the mysterious contents of my purse as a comb, is a bottle of breath sweetener or a roll of mints. No one is safe from offending in this way. The slightest tip one way or another in our body chemistry, from fatigue, overeating, or overtalking can cause halitosis. And quite often lack of proper dental care causes it. The use of dental floss and a rubber massage tip on your toothbrush helps wonderfully.

I am very much aware that you already know these things. I am not writing this book for bush women. I am writing it for you. And I am writing as I am in this chapter more as a reminder that we owe careful grooming to the Lord as part of obedience. Polish your shoes, clean your galoshes, shampoo your hair, care for your skin and nails and teeth, and bathe frequently to the glory of God! All of these things, too, can be meaningful sacraments if we really love Christ.

Adornment

I am marching now, right into what some of you may not even know is a battlefield among women. Christian women, that is. I know I am suspect with many groups and will be more so, no doubt, because of what I am going to say here about woman's *adornment* if she is a Christian.

And before I begin to say it, I want you to know that I know the particular verses in the Bible which many sincere people feel prohibit a Christian woman from adorning herself at all. I fully respect this thinking. I respect the willingness of these persons to be "different." Being different isn't an easy thing for most of us. And I also want to express in print my gratitude to the dozen or more people who have written to me (a few quite kindly!) about the fact that I do use a moderate amount of make-up and I do wear small earrings and I do occasionally wear a ring. I am well aware that my critics are oftentimes the unpaid guardians of my soul. And I pray about every letter that comes, in which I am criticized for any reason.

I am thinking now of several genuine Christian women whom I love and whose lives show their love of Christ. These women don't wear make-up at all. Some never have. Others have gotten "guidance" to stop wearing it. This "guidance" I respect deeply. I simply have never gotten it. In no way do I intend this to be an argument for wearing make-up and jewelry as a Christian.

I am stating my beliefs and my reasons for holding them. You are free to take them or leave them. One dear friend of mine, who feels "led" not to wear earrings herself, had humor enough to send me a lovely pair for my birthday last year! Women are a strange lot. On this the men will agree. And I think we should, too. With our humors in full operation.

Most of the persons who write me (kindly or unkindly) quote Peter on the subject. I have before me as I write two translations of 1 Peter 3:3, 4. One is the King James translation and the other is the contemporary and fine Berkeley translation. Here they are:

King James: "Whose adorning let it not be that outward adorning of plaiting the hair, and of wearing gold, or of putting on of apparel; But let it be the hidden man of the heart, in that which is not corruptible, even the ornament of a meek and quiet spirit, which is in the sight of God of great price."

Berkeley: "Your adornment should not be on the outside—braided hair, putting on gold trinkets, or wearing attractive dresses; *instead*, the inner personality of the heart with the imperishable qualities of a gentle and quiet spirit, something of surpassing value in God's sight."

The italics used in printing the word "instead" in the Berkeley version are mine. This, to me, is the key. It is not so clearly said in the King James version, but it is still there in meaning. In other words, this does not necessarily mean that women are not to adorn themselves at all. As I see it, and as many other Christians see it (including Dr. Verkuyl who edited the Berkeley version), it simply means that our most noticeable adornment as Christian women must be *inward!* If any make-up and jewelry and extremely cut clothes call more attention to me outwardly than does my Christian spirit, then I am wrong.

Christians of either sex are not to call attention to themselves primarily. Jesus Christ lived a normal, unobtrusive life on earth. He dressed the way other people dressed. He did not make eccentric use of His religion. He moved easily and naturally among the people whom He had come to save. He did not draw away from them at all. He did not compromise His holiness for one minute, but neither did He do anything that made Him appear odd or peculiar.

At the time of my conversion, I wore much too much make-up. Heavy, overdrawn mouth, eye shadow, mascara, and very, very dark pancake make-up on my face. No one told me to stop. My heart just wasn't in calling attention to me any longer. I toned it all down. Way down. I'm not against discriminate use of it, but I have large eyes and didn't really need eye shadow anyway, so I dropped that altogether. All excess seemed to drop away. And for the first time in my entire life I found myself hating to call attention to me. This, in fact, was one of the first strong inner impulses which the Lord used in convicting me because I was so much overweight. Overweight women call attention to themselves. Heavily made-up women call attention to themselves. Women dripping with large, glassy jewelry call attention to themselves. And, by the same token, in the twentieth century, women devoid of any color in their faces also call attention to themselves.

It is the inner life which must glow and attract. Dr. Verkuyl, in one of his excellent footnotes in the Berkeley translation says of the oft-quoted 1 Peter 3:3, 4: "(Adornments) not forbidden; Sara and Rebekah wore them; but minor in comparison with Christian character traits."

I want to say once more, however, that no one should take my word for this. For that matter, not even Dr. Verkuyl's. Go to the Lord. And if you honestly believe He is telling you to leave off all adornment, then by all means leave it off. Some women in certain groups seem to feel that it is all right to wear jeweled pins, but not earrings. Others that it is all right to wear necklaces, but not earrings. Earrings have it hard. Why, I don't know. They're usually made up about the same as necklaces and brooches, but they are much discriminated against in certain groups. There are even some who feel they should not wear their wedding rings. This,

too, is a personal matter. But Jesus apparently didn't disapprove of rings. In the prodigal son story (which Jesus made up) He is attempting to show us what the Father's heart is really like. Attempting to convince us that our heavenly Father is capable of making merry when one of His loved ones comes home. And one of the ways in which He illustrates this point is to say that the father in the story called to his servants ordering them to "put a ring on his finger." But again, I am not arguing for the wearing of jewelry or any other adornment. I am simply attempting to force us as women to look at what the Bible says is the *central issue:* our very inner natures themselves. Let not your main adornment be outward—let it be inward.

—From Eugenia Price, *Woman to Woman.* Grand Rapids: Zondervan, 1959.

Hints for Success

Look neat, look successful, be an asset to your profession!

1. Don't let there be a clash in your image: look the same each day. The average person doesn't feel comfortable with drastic changes, so change your colors and/or fabrics, but not your general look (unless it needs improving!).
2. Bathe daily and always use deodorant or antiperspirant.
3. Use breath spray, mouthwash, or sugarless breath mints often.
4. Don't wear an excessive amount of perfume. None may be best.
5. Refuse to wear anything too tight, too low, too clinging, or that is see-through. Such items do not belong in the business profession.
6. Clean and press clothing often between wearings. Double-check often for body odor or spots. Remember that fluorescent lighting can bring out many spots in clothing.
7. Do not wear white shirts or blouses more than once without washing. Cuffs and collars are noticed first.

8. Check your undergarments to see that they are mended. Undergarments should not be visible when one is standing, sitting, or bending over. Double-check to see that your undergarment straps are secure and will not drop out on your arm. Never wear colored undergarments with light-colored clothing. Choose skin color for work.

9. If pants are worn, be sure you check fore and aft! Bikini panty lines should never be seen. And no polka dots under white slacks!

10. Be sure your slip is neither too long nor too short.

11. No thigh-high slits in skirts, dresses, or wraps that gap open where you sit.

12. Don't be careless about little things. Sew on buttons and snaps. Stitch up loose hems.

13. Check yourself in a full-length mirror before going to work. Be certain that no hem is hanging below your coat.

14. Do not wear jewelry that dangles, clatters, or distracts.

15. Underarms and legs should be clean-shaven.

16. Check to see that your nylons are not bagging at ankles or knees. Wash them out after each wearing.

17. If you are wearing a knitted dress, you may want to wear control-top panty hose to avoid bulges.

18. Never go without hose when dealing with the public. If you get a run, change to a new pair. Wise working women keep that spare pair handy for such emergencies.

19. Keep shoes polished and heels in repair.

20. Rotate shoes on successive days. This helps banish foot odor.

21. Apply makeup carefully and be sure there is no makeup line at the chin.

22. Hair is the frame of your face. Shampoo often (no dandruff on clothing). Get a good haircut every six weeks. Hair should be of moderate length (no hair below shoulders, and avoid short styles that might be considered mannish). Consult hair charts for colors most flattering to you.

23. Hands should always be well manicured. Nails should not be extremely long or too brightly polished.

24. Glasses can add an authoritative look. Choose plastic frames in grays or browns to flatter your natural coloring. Avoid wire rims. Consult a glasses chart and choose frames in a style to complement your facial shape. Select a frame color no darker than your hair (lighter is best).

—From Joanne Wallace, *Dress With Style*. Old Tappan, N.J.: Revell, 1983.

FOR FURTHER READING:

Jackson, Carole. *Color Me Beautiful*. Washington: Acropolis, 1980.

Wallace, Joanne, *The Image of Loveliness*. Old Tappan, N.J.: Revell, 1978.

GROWTH

PERSONAL GROWTH is a continual process. One never graduates from the school of life. There is always more to learn, and the more we learn, the more enriched our lives become, and the more interesting we are to those about us.

Any observing person knows that a woman's life is crammed with petty details. These often usurp her time and prevent her from doing many of the things that she would otherwise enjoy. She seems destined to detail—there's a stitch to be sewed, a cake to be baked, a dress to be pressed. As a mother, she must nurse a wounded knee, prod a poky piano practicer, or serve as referee when young wills clash. Small things to be sure—but so time consuming. These daily duties *are* demanding, yet they need not deter your personal growth. Nothing can keep you from personal development without your permission. If you are not satisfied to remain static, if you are unwilling to bury your God-given talents, then, where there's a will there's a way. Growth does not necessarily need to take place under ideal conditions. You may live in uninspiring circumstances, or be surrounded by somewhat uninteresting people, yet you can be the exception to the rule. Stately pines often grow on a rocky ledge. If you wait for the "perfect time," it will never come. Growth is a result of attitude. Determine that you will not be the same tomorrow as you are today, then pray and persist in your purpose.

Growth seldom happens in a dramatic way, dramatic as it may be when you look back. It is a way of life, a day-by-day experience growing out of dedication to a purpose. Women such as Clara Barton, Florence Nightingale, Carrie Jacobs Bond, Marie Curie, Evangeline Booth, Frances Siewert and multitudes of others have carried the banner of purpose and have won. You may not reach the public pinnacle they have; but you can be a blessing and an inspiration to your children and your friends. You will be happier and more satisfied because you have enriched your environment and developed your potential. But most of all, you will have fulfilled God's plan for your life. He wants His *best* for you.

Mental Stimulation

Thumb back through the pages of your experience and re-read a chapter in your childhood. You are in elementary school. The teacher throws out a question and immediately several hands shoot up. It's the same ones who consistently wave their hands in response to teacher's questions. These are the "smart kids," and, interestingly enough, mostly girls. The boys, because of their later development, will have their opportunity to shine later on.

What happens to all those "smart little girls" when they grow up? Not many of them will become doctors or lawyers like their male counterparts. Some will become teachers or office workers. But the majority of these bright girls will grow up to be mothers and homemakers. Many of them will become leaders in the community. They have keen minds that demand a challenge; with-

out it, they become the victims of frustration and boredom.

You are an intelligent being. God has given you an inquiring mind. Yet, unless you are satisfying its demand for mental stimulation, you will become stale and uninteresting.

Intelligence is not a quality chiefly cornered by the male sex or by a few gifted women. Every person has intellectual qualities. Unfortunately, some women become so involved in the daily routine of the home or office that they squelch their intellectuality. The important factor is not merely what you learn, but also your own attitude toward self-development. When you see the value of continued growth, the circumstances around you can become stepping stones. Much of the knowledge you assimilate in life is gained in an informal manner. When you learn to sharpen your powers of discernment and train yourself to be more observant, a whole new world will unfold before you. Even the commonplace will take on new meaning.

The alert woman recognizes opportunities for mental stimulation in many forms. Even helping your youngster with his school work can be a real source of learning to *you*. Times have changed since you were in the classroom. With the increased knowledge of our scientific society, textbooks are outdated in just a few years. So your children are learning many things that were not even known until recently. Although you won't be filling a classroom seat, you do have the opportunity to learn as you help your children.

Don't wait for your husband to give you the signal to grow. You may even have to lead the way. He may not realize how intellectually stifling your situation is for you. He may be in a job where he must read and talk with others, or where he has the opportunity of taking business trips and meeting interesting people. Be that as it may, you have a responsibility to yourself, as well as to your husband. So while he is growing in his experience, take the initiative to grow in your own right.

Intellectual growth is rewarding for its own sake, but it also has its by-products. You gain in confidence and self-respect, the world becomes a more fascinating place, and you become a more interesting person.

The Reading Habit

Today, interesting books are piled high almost everywhere you look. Yet, despite this open road to the printed page, many people spend little time reading. This is especially true of women.

"I don't have time," said one homemaker. "My days are so full with caring for the children, doing home chores, committee meetings, taking the older children to and from various activities, and a multitude of other things, that I don't have a free moment to myself. After dinner there's dishes, getting the younger ones into bed, and taking care of a dozen other jobs. By the time everything quiets down I'm so weary I can't concentrate. So I just turn on the TV for a little relaxation before I go to bed."

It is obvious why *that* woman does not do more reading. And there are many others like her. Even magazines are often not much more than skimmed through.

—From Clyde M. Narramore, *A Woman's World*. Grand Rapids: Zondervan, 1963.

FOR FURTHER READING:

Elliot, Elisabeth. *Discipline: The Glad Surrender*. Old Tappan, N.J.: Revell, 1982.

Landorf, Joyce. *The Fragrance of Beauty*. Wheaton, Ill.: Victor Books, 1973.

Murphey, Cecil B. *Press On: A Disciple's Guide to Spiritual Growth*. Ann Arbor: Servant, 1983.

Price, Eugenia. *Woman to Woman*. Grand Rapids: Zondervan, 1959.

GUIDANCE

FOR THE PAST TWO YEARS I've been asking a lot of questions about guidance. I started questioning as I read the success stories of people who prayed. These people received miraculous answers (and I don't oppose miracles!). But always?

I've often wanted to ask about their not-so-startling answers. What about the times they prayed and life blew up in their faces?

Other questions troubled me. Does God continually desire our instant achievement? Does he will for us to go from one delirious mountaintop experience to the next? Is it only the devil who drags us into the low spots in life?

While no specific Bible verses answer those kinds of questions, reading the biblical accounts of the lives of the great saints at least indicates how God works in the lives of his people.

What about King David—called the apple of God's eye—who prayed often for guidance? ("Evening and morning and at noon I utter my complaint and moan, and he will hear my voice," Psalms 55:17, among others.) Yet that same praying man spent much of his adult life fleeing the wrath of King Saul.

Paul's impressive revelations, which excelled those of ordinary believers, led him onward—but onward to suffering, shipwreck, imprisonment, and attempts on his life.

What about Moses? Joseph? Jeremiah? Hosea?

In our Western world, on the other hand, God has particularly blessed us with high standards of living, relative comfort, easy mobility, and religious freedom. As a result, many of us seem to have the subconscious idea that if God leads us we'll not have problems or setbacks.

Then, when setbacks do hit us, confusion takes over and we wail, "Why me, God? Why me?"

And if we're going to get it all together with God, if we're going to understand guidance, we have to begin with God—not ourselves.

Starting with God doesn't mean all the answers will be clear to us. He's a supernatural God. He's also elusive at times. Just when we've nearly figured out all his operating principles, we realize that there's more to

God we don't yet understand. But there are some things we know about God that can help us understand how he leads us. When we pray for guidance, the answers may become more satisfying if we bear in mind four facts:

1. *God Wills for Us to Mature.* We often mature after first stumbling. For instance, Jesus warned Peter of his three-time denial. He could have said, "Peter, I want you to be careful. I'm going to be betrayed by Judas and, when you see me standing before Pilate, you'll be asked by onlookers if you're one of my followers. You'll be tempted to deny you even know me. I'm telling you now so that you can fortify yourself."

Jesus did warn Peter. But the disciple never really heard the Master's warning. And he failed in the crucial hour.

But Peter also matured through that ordeal. He learned he was fallible. He realized that, as much as he loved Jesus, he could still yield to the impulse of saving himself first.

2. *God Wants Us to Overcome.* Interestingly, although this concept appears all through the Bible (e.g., 1 Corinthians 15:57; Revelation 2:7), we still seek God for directions to keep us out of harm, danger, or testing. Then we tend to become angry with God if anything breaks up our pleasant lifestyles.

Overcoming can happen only when we fight and win! Overcoming applies to those swept into battle, but it holds no meaning for people who sit at the sidelines and continually pray for God to take them away from problems and remove all their difficulties.

In the early 1970s I became pastor of a church in a changing community. Formerly the home of comfortable, middle-class whites, it was rapidly becoming a black community with only a smattering of whites left. During that transitional period, our congregation began moving out, some losing money on their property. Since many had no one to whom they could lash out in anger, I, their pastor, often received the brunt of it. Others accused me of manipulating to make it an integrated church, whether they liked it or not. Some of the most religious people in the congregation said some unreligious things.

I'm years past that experience—and it was one of the most painful times in my life. Yet today, looking back, I believe myself to be a stronger person and a more effective Christian leader because of having struggled through the situation in that church.

Five times during the last year I was there (We finally accepted our inability as a white congregation to minister to a black community, and turned the property over to a black church.) pulpit committees approached me about filling their vacant pastorates. Two offers tempted me, but I felt I had to stay with the people.

The last months proved to be the most painful. It was like sitting at the bedside of a dying patient, mourning and yet unable to do anything except hold the patient's hand. Yet, by God's grace, I came out of the ordeal stronger and more committed to Christ. It was a battle I had to fight in order to be an overcomer.

3. *God Wants Us to Strengthen Others.* In order to do that we need to experience personal growth. We have to endure suffering first.

I learned that fact firsthand. For years, I had preached funeral sermons, talked to the lonely, and offered comfort. It was my duty as a minister, and I had done the best I knew how. Then, within a period of eighteen months, four members of my immediate family (including both parents) died. And I grieved.

As a result of my own heartache, I became more understanding and sensitive toward others going through periods of grief. I believe that's part of what the apostle Paul means in 2 Corinthians 1:3–4, when he refers to the "God of all comfort, who comforts us in all our affliction, so that we may be able to comfort those who are in any affliction, with the comfort with which we ourselves are comforted by God."

4. *God Wants Us to Be Like Jesus Christ.* Romans 8:29 says, "For those whom he foreknew he also predestined to be conformed to the image of his Son." Hebrews 5:8–9 reads, "Although he was a Son, he learned obedience through what he suffered; and being made perfect he became the source of eternal salvation to all who obey him."

God sent Jesus to save. But he saved after being persecuted. He experienced betrayal by a disciple, rejection by others, misunderstanding by all—and then he made the supreme sacrifice at Calvary.

Jesus never escaped the hardships. He knew he had to wear a martyr's crown before receiving the king's diadem.

Thinking of Jesus makes me wonder if God really guides us to escape hardship . . . always.

Perhaps getting it together with God means obedience. It holds no guarantee of ease, prosperity, or blessing. It does promise peace, eternal life, and God's presence. That's what Jesus had. That's all the apostle Paul asked for.

When I talk about God's will *for me,* I can rely on four things:

1. *God's Will Is Never Capricious.* That means God has a plan. The apostle Paul wrote, "He chose us in him before the foundation of the world, that we should be holy and blameless before him" (Ephesians 1:4). God formulated the plan that includes each of us. And he's not making any pencil changes. Somehow, despite our doing things wrong and stupidly, God's blueprint remains unchanged.

2. *God's Plan Is Loving.* We can perceive God's love around us in the world he has created. Many people can quickly acknowledge his loving plan for humanity. Those same folks quote verses such as "For God so loved the world." They readily acknowledge that God loves people. But the fact that he loves *them* specifically—that's hard for some to accept.

The Old Testament tells that Moses in-

vited his father-in-law to join the Israelites on their trip out of Egypt into the promised land. He said, "Come with us and we will do you good." That's the operational plan of God. He always works toward making us better, healthier, and happier.

Our Father has no great need or desire to punish us. He's not out to trick us, trip us up, or catch us.

In the Old Testament we read of God punishing his people, and some portions sound awful. But the stories never *begin* with the chastisement. They start with God's pleading with the people through his prophets, begging them to return to him. Only afterwards does he say, "I'm wearied with you. You haven't repented; now you'll have to endure the consequences."

3. *God's Guidance Always Brings Glory to Himself.* When God wills an event to happen, it's going to be good. People will recognize a little more of the greatness of God himself.

I've been pastor of the Riverdale Presbyterian Church for five years. One thing that keeps me excited about serving the Lord in this particular congregation is the spiritual growth. I can look at almost any phase of our congregational life—the sharing groups, the prayer fellowships, the choir, the youth. Adult classes that didn't even exist five years ago are now filled with people. Looking over the leadership of our congregation, I realize many of them weren't even members when I first came. Others, who have been here a long time, have only recently moved into their leadership positions. People are exercising their spiritual gifts, giving themselves to the life of the congregation.

And where does all this lead? It brings glory to God. I've heard more praising the Lord in the last two years than ever before. We're maturing, but we're also recognizing that God is the one carrying out the maturing process.

4. *God's Guidance Has Our Ultimate Happiness in View.* I have to insert the

word *ultimate.* That's the only way we can understand when God shouts "No!" Immediate circumstances may look as though our comfortable worlds have been bombarded with insurmountable forces. But that's only for the present. That's not the long view.

What's God's will for me?

When we look at our situations from an objective viewpoint, when we understand God's working principles, we can rejoice. Ultimately, there's only good ahead for us—because God is good. He only wants the best for his people, and his best means making them perfect.

—From Cecil B. Murphey, *Getting There From Here,* copyright © 1981, pp. 11–15, 19–21; used by permission of Word Books, Publisher, Waco, Texas 76796.

Checklist

Christ once told his disciples, "I have still many things to say to you, but you are not able to bear them *nor* to take them upon you *nor* to grasp them now" (John 16:12 AMPLIFIED). . . .

Regardless of your degree of maturity as a Christian, let me briefly reiterate the basics in our living God's will. The first step, obviously, is that you have accepted Jesus Christ as your personal Savior through faith. The second step is to confess and appropriately deal with any known sin that the Holy Spirit reveals to you. The third step is to start feeding on God's Word, the Bible. If you are not familiar with it, I would suggest that you start reading in the New Testament. Read the Gospel of Mark or John and then read through the New Testament. Absorb what you can, and what you don't understand put aside for the time being. Try to read the Scriptures daily. Spend some time each day in prayer, asking God to direct you. Get to know some Christians who really want to know and please God and have fellowship with them. As you do these simple things God will reveal more and more of his will to you.

CHECKLIST TO CONSIDER BEFORE MAKING ANY MAJOR DECISION IN YOUR LIFE

Below is a summary of the steps for knowing God's will in a particular matter. They are arranged in the form of a checklist to help alert you to factors that might need to be dealt with before God will reveal his will to you.

The matter you want to know God's will in is:

_____

_____

Step 1: **Be obedient to his already revealed will**
    A. Have you accepted Jesus Christ as your personal Savior? Yes___ No___
    B. Is there any known sin in your life? No___ Yes___
    C. Are you being obedient to God's will to the extent to which it is now revealed? Yes___ No___

Step 2: **Be open to any means or results**
    A. Are you willing to follow God's will when he reveals it to you, regardless of what his will is or what it might cost you? Yes___ No___
    B. Are you open to any means he might choose to lead you, whether supernatural-miraculous or some less dramatic means? Yes___ No___

Step 3: **God's Word: the cornerstone of guidance**
    A. Do you have an adequate intake of God's Word? Yes___ No___

B. Are you familiar with what the Scriptures really say about the issue for which you are seeking guidance? Yes___ No___

Step 4: **Prayer**

A. Do you have a daily prayer time when you seek God's will and have fellowship with him? Yes___ No___

B. Have you specifically asked God's will regarding the matter for which you are seeking his guidance? Yes___ No___

C. Are you too busy to adequately meditate and wait on him? No___ Yes___

Step 5: **The Holy Spirit**

A. Have you acknowledged the presence and function of the Holy Spirit in your life? Yes___ No___

B. Does the Holy Spirit now fill your life? Yes___ No___

Step 6: **Counsel**

A. Do you consistently have fellowship with other Christians and hear God's Word proclaimed? Yes___ No___

B. Is there any possibility of a medical problem for which you should obtain help? No___ Yes___

C. Should you specifically seek the counsel of another, whether a minister, Christian friend, professional counsellor, etc.? No___ Yes___

Step 7: **Providential circumstances**

A. Have you adequately considered the providential circumstances that are available to you? Yes___ No___

Step 8: **Evaluation**

A. Are you tired? No___ Yes___

B. Have you specifically evaluated the reasons for and against the decision you are considering and your underlying motives (preferably on paper)? Yes___ No___

C. Have you considered the needs of the world around you? Yes___ No___

D. Have you considered your own abilities? Yes___ No___

E. Have you considered your own desires and whether or not they are possible within God's will? Yes___ No___

F. Will your decision harm your body or hurt others? No___ Yes___

G. Will it hinder your spiritual growth, walk with Christ, or testimony? No___ Yes___

H. Will it hinder the spiritual growth of others? No___ Yes___

I. Is it the choice that is most pleasing to God? Yes___ No___

J. Is it the best and wisest choice using your enlightened judgment? Yes___ No___

K. Have you prayerfully evaluated the matter alone, without unnecessary time pressure?   Yes___ No___

Prayerfully consider all of the above points—especially any responses in the right-hand column. These responses may indicate some action you need to take before you will be able to come to a conclusion about God's will in the matter.

List any steps that should be taken before you conclude what God's will is in the matter.

_____

Is there anything else he wants you to do or consider?

_____

Step 9: **The decision: to wait or to act**
Should you postpone the decision as to what God's will is in the matter?_____
Should you decide but wait for its fulfilment?

_____

You already know God's will but not his timing; therefore, must you patiently wait his time?

_____

Or should you now come to a deliberate decision on what his will is? If so, what is that decision?

_____

Step 10: **The stamp of approval: God's peace**
Having determined God's will in the matter, do you have a deep, inward peace about the decision? As time passes and you continue to reflect and pray about the decision, do you have an increasing assurance from him that the decision was the right one? If so, proceed accordingly.

—From Dwight L. Carlson, *Finding God's Will.* Old Tappan, N.J.: Revell, 1976.

FOR FURTHER READING:

Dobson, James. *Emotions, Can You Trust Them?* Ventura, Calif.: Regal, 1980.

GUILT

Unresolved Guilt

I repeatedly encounter Christian believers who have not resolved their guilt proneness, or who have developed an exaggerated guilt mechanism, not all of which is spiritually healthy.

It is true that spiritual guilt, when acknowledged, can cause a valid state of psychological guilt. However, this form of guilt does not have the same irrational quality that much neurotic guilt has. It is more constructive, reparative, and amenable in forgiveness than neurotic guilt.

For example, let us suppose that one has perfectionist tendencies. A perfectionist is someone who cannot avoid doing anything without making impossible, unrealistic demands on himself. Some of us have perfectionistic *traits*, in that we must tidy up behind us because we cannot stand to see anything dirty or disorganized. These traits are not necessarily unhealthy. The true perfectionist, however, has a built-in system of self-punishment which is applied whenever he feels that he has not measured up to the standards of performance set for himself. Such people may feel that the right thing to do is to be out of bed by at least 6:00 A.M. If for some reason they oversleep, they will punish themselves by self-criticism or depression for the remainder of the day. If, in addition, they believe that God wants them to be out of bed by that early hour, they could easily interpret their guiltiness as God's speaking to them. Such guiltiness does not easily respond to forgiveness. It demands punishment as the only way to relief.

It is possible, of course, for ministers and evangelists unwittingly to utilize psychological mechanisms for creating a state of guilt in their listeners. This misuse has long been the cause of concern in Christian psychological circles, as it can give rise to spurious conversions and commitments which, in turn, can hamper further spiritual development in the individual concerned.

For me, the most significant thing about guilt is the frequency with which it triggers other emotional reactions or is triggered by them. It is probably the most common chain emotion. We might get angry at our children and shout at them and then are almost immediately moved by a reaction of feeling guilty. We feel sorry for what we have done and then try to reduce our guilt. The net result of this is a large swing from shouting and anger to placating and reconciling—all very unsettling to our children.

Or we might become depressed by something. As soon as we are aware of our depression we feel guilty and react because of this guilt with a further sense of loss, thus deepening the depression.

Guilt and Anger

Guilt can trigger anger very easily. I might come home from work, having forgotten to stop and buy something my wife has asked me to get. As I walk in the front door and see my wife, I remember what it was I should have purchased. I feel guilty, but rather than admit my guilt I react by getting angry: "You always ask me to get something for you when you know I am busy. You know I've got more important things to think about." By attacking her, I both alleviate my guilt feelings and at the same time prevent her from attacking me for my forgetfulness.

Many a wife has probably been trapped by that helpless look on her husband's face as he peers into his sock drawer and finds it empty. "You should have told me you were near the end of your socks," she protests in anger. "You knew very well that Mother was coming to visit and that I would not have time to do the wash on my usual day." Why the anger? Because she feels guilty. A little voice tells her that she could have prevented this by just a little forethought, but she didn't. She also knew that her mother was coming and could have planned accordingly, but she didn't—so she feels guilty and anger is triggered.

Two Types of Conscience

Can you let your conscience be your guide? Not always. You may be on shaky ground whenever you use your conscience to help you make a decision or guide your behavior. Conscience is usually helpful, but—since it can be so easily distorted and is merely the reflection of an internalized overstrict parent we need to be cautious.

Conscience can also be warped in another direction. It can be underdeveloped and inadequate to guide us because it lacks any sensitivity. When someone is brought up in an atmosphere of neglect, there is invariably no parent to internalize.

Conscience can be a problem in both extremes. On the one hand it may be overdeveloped and dominate our personality, causing us to make extreme demands on ourselves. We then respond to irrational ideas as to what is the right behavior for a given situation. We impose moral standards on ourselves more out of the fear of the consequences than because of any genuine concern for morality and tend to feel guilty almost all the time about everything we do. It becomes impossible to assert ourselves and stand up for very basic rights without feeling guilty, since we cannot say no to a request and have great difficulty confronting someone who is hurting us. These are the sorts of problems which develop when our conscience dominates us.

On the other hand, it is possible to suffer from an inadequately developed conscience. In this case we experience very little anxiety when we cause pain to others. It is possible to engage in behaviors that most people consider to be immoral and yet feel no tension. While we may conform to the standards of behavior of those around us, we do so in order to "keep the peace" or be accepted, rather than out of a sense of what we believe to be right or wrong. It becomes commonplace to make the same mistake over and over again and not benefit from the experience. We seldom really feel sorry for what we do and resent any effort anyone may make to punish us. In its extreme form this lack of conscience is called a "conduct disorder," as it frequently causes the person to be in trouble with authority figures or the law.

A Normal Conscience

Obviously, somewhere between these two extremes there is a region that we can describe as normal. A normal conscience exists when there is enough concern about the welfare of others that a tension is created whenever their rights are infringed. Such concern is not dominated by an exaggerated feeling of worthlessness about oneself, nor are the basic beliefs that underlie the conscience totally unfounded or irrational. The person with a normal conscience understands why something is right or wrong and does not experience condemnation of himself without an adequate basis in reality. For instance, one who *accidentally* fails to stop at a traffic signal—and then continues to feel depressed throughout the remainder of the day because of guilt—is failing to make some allowance for human imperfection. The person who *deliberately* drives through a traffic signal because he is in a hurry deserves to feel guilty afterwards. However, if the resulting guilt feeling is unduly prolonged, even this latter person may lack the capacity to forgive himself and to benefit from such an experience by making sure that he does not do it again.

In summary, therefore, I would say that a normal, healthy, and well-balanced conscience has the following qualities:

1. A normal conscience is concerned with "morality" (the correct source of moral attitudes) and not with "moralism" (the preoccupation with right behaviors). Moralism is more concerned about the appearance of the behavior than with the reason for it. What our parents teach us is usually mere moralism. Their underlying message is: "Do it this way and you will please me." Later in life we still do things just to please our internalized parent without knowing *why* we do it. When the behavior is wrong, therefore, we feel guilty even if a truly moral principle has not been violated. True morality, on the other hand, knows why something is wrong. Because it endangers the lives of others, it is bad to go through a red traffic light without stopping. Throwing off the moralisms of our upbringing and developing a well-balanced morality are necessary steps toward developing the freedom to experience our emotions in a healthy way.

As Christians, it is very easy to become

engrossed in moralisms. We can become preoccupied with behaving the "right" way, with no understanding of the underlying moral issues. By contrast, the Gospel is more concerned with morality than with moralism. Righteousness has to do with the *source* of right behavior. If the source is moral, the behavior will be righteous. If the source is not moral, no matter how perfect is our behavior by outward standards, it will not be righteous.

2.   A healthy conscience should be flexible not rigid, and it should be sensitive yet sensible. It should alert us to wrong just as pain alerts us to disease, but it should not proceed to punish us unnecessarily for what we have done. A well-balanced conscience should allow us to weigh all the factors involved in the wrongdoing, so that we can have an honest understanding of the limits of our responsibility. Could we have avoided what happened? Were there factors beyond our control? Was it really our fault? Can we easily rectify the wrong? A healthy conscience permits us to ask this sort of question. An overbearing conscience condemns us without mercy and will allow no mitigating factors. This should not be confused with a tendency to make excuses for what we have done wrong. These excuses are often dishonest and are designed to buy off our conscience with deception. If we are really guilty, we should feel guilty. What we then do with the guilt is the most important question.

3.   A well-balanced conscience does not engage in excessive self-blaming, self-condemnation, or self-punishment. If we allow our conscience to do this, we only destroy the learning value of the failure experience. "Failures are to grow by," but we keep wanting to use them to punish ourselves— and this is self-obstructive. If we hurt someone with sharp words, we should learn from the experience not to do it again. If we have fallen prey to some immoral behavior, we should also learn from that experience. Guilt should serve as a warning sign that something is wrong—not as a self-punishment device. If we become preoccupied with self-blame and self-punishment, we will not be able to utilize the failure as a learning experience.

4.   A normal conscience knows how to obtain and accept forgiveness, whether this forgiveness is from other people or from God. In fact, we cannot stop self-punishment until we know how to obtain forgiveness. We must learn to trade our self-punishment for God's forgiveness. If someone we have harmed will not forgive us, we then receive that forgiveness from God. We must not let our failures continue to cast a dark shadow of guilt across our freedom and happiness, since we can receive the ultimate in all forgiveness. To punish oneself is to make a mockery of the Cross. Christ wanted to carry responsibility for all our failures, so why not let Him do His work completely?

Neurotic Guilt

While it takes an overdeveloped conscience to create neurotic guilt, not everyone with a supersensitive conscience is neurotic. The difference between having a demanding conscience and having guilt which is neurotic is in the *degree* and *quality* of the guilt. Your guilt can be labeled as "neurotic" when it has the following qualities:

- You have a strong sense of your own evil.
- You feel guilty nearly all the time without adequate justification.
- You keep labeling yourself as "bad."
- Your guilt reactions last a long time.
- Your guilt is triggered by imagined wrongs, and then you cannot stop the guilt.
- Your guilt reactions to little wrongs are extreme.
- Your guilt so incapacitates you that you cannot relate to anyone and want to be alone.
- Your guilt causes you to want to take

extreme actions (such as suicide) to remedy your wrongs.

- You cannot stop remembering all your past misdeeds.

Neurotic guilt can even be caused by imagined violations. I know someone who often fantasizes that he is punishing those who have harmed him. When he is finished mutilating them, an intense guilt overtakes him. Despite the fact that no actual harm has been caused to anyone, he responds with guilt more appropriate to real harm. Naturally, his problem is much more serious than the disturbed guilt mechanism.

While many of my readers will not experience guilt to this extreme, there may be more subtle traps of neurotic quality that imprison them. Perhaps you recognize one of the following self-talk statements: "I *must* do this," "I *should* do that," or "I've just *got to!*" It's just possible that you are being controlled and manipulated by what you think others will say, or you have an exaggerated fear that you will not please everybody. Whenever you break one of the rules, you feel terrible and engage in self-condemnation. While some "shoulds" in life are necessary, they are mainly arbitrary and irrational and need careful evaluation before you respond to them. Strangely, when they are legitimate, they never feel like "shoulds." I should support and care for my family—but I hardly ever feel it is a "should." I'm only too glad to do it. The irrational "shoulds" we lay on ourselves make prisons for us without our realizing it. Fortunately, we hold the key to unlocking this prison and can, with careful thought and attention to the principles I am enunciating here, free ourselves from neurotic guilt. If we can't, professional help should be sought from someone we feel we can trust.

Some Important Determiners of Guilt

Developing and maintaining a healthy conscience and appropriate guilt response are not things that happen automatically. These attitudes require constant cultivation.

You can pass through your childhood unscathed and then find that you fall prey in early adulthood (or any later stage of your life, for that matter) to influences that increase your guilt proneness.

In Christian circles there are three important determiners of an aggravated conscience. These are:

1. An inadequate God concept.
2. An inadequate sin concept.
3. An inadequate forgiveness concept.

Anyone reared in an environment where these inadequate concepts are propagated will find himself prone to guilt problems in later life. The influence of belief systems erected around these inadequacies can be great enough to affect someone even in later life.

I was introduced to such a system shortly after my conversion at age eighteen and was subjected to many erroneous ideas related to these concepts. As a result I experienced a marked increase in my guilt proneness which lasted for nearly five years, before I became aware of what was happening. Rather than finding my early Christian experience to be happy and fulfilling, it became burdensome and depressing. Looking back now, I regret that there wasn't someone to correct my erroneous ideas. At least two of my close friends who were converted at the same time fell victim to these erroneous ideas and were so depressed by the experience that they gave up their commitments. As far as I know, they have not returned to the Christian faith since then.

1. *An inadequate God concept.* We hardly ever pause to reflect on the concept of God which we have constructed in our minds. We assume that everyone else has the same idea about who God is. I have researched the variability of concepts of God among different Christian groups for some years now, and this has confirmed my contention that Christians show marked differences in their understanding of the nature of God. I have examined the concept of God as seen by missionary groups, ministers, and lay

people of various denominations and found that people, even within the same church group, have markedly different ideas. Women have a different concept from men. Marked differences are found with age, and, of course, different cultures produce quite different ideas about the nature of God. The net result is that we all end up in adult life seeing God slightly differently. This difference is not always important, but there are some extreme ideas which can influence our emotional health.

Your God Is Too Small by J. B. Phillips is a most imporant book on this topic. The author warns us to be careful about the image that we form of God. If our understanding of God is that He is nothing more than a form of policeman, or if God is seen as harsh and punitive, we may experience considerable guilt proneness. As I have worked in therapy with people who have developed an inadequate God concept, it has become obvious that they have frequently merely internalized images of their parents, usually the father. If he has been harsh and punitive, they tend to see God this way.

2. *An inadequate sin concept.* Guilt problems can also arise when we do not have a clear understanding of the nature of sin. Our conscience can bother us even when no sin has been committed. We feel guilty about so many things, and few of them can be classified as sin. Frequently, guilt over social rules and mores is only relevant to one culture and not another, yet we label break-ing these rules as "sin." We can easily make our consciences into a god.

3. *An inadequate forgiveness concept.* Forgiveness is the genius of Christianity. No other religious belief system places it as central as the Gospel does. What else is the Cross about? God knew when He created us that we would need forgiveness. It is for *our* benefit. I have a sneaking suspicion that most Christians have the irrational idea lurking in the back of their minds that perhaps God needs to forgive us more than we need His forgiveness. It's true that He *wants* to forgive us more than we are willing to receive it, but does He *need* to give us forgiveness? When we have sinned or our conscience is bothering us, we believe that somehow He needs us to ask for forgiveness, as if He benefited in some way from it. No, it's the other way around. God has provided forgiveness because *we* need it. This is the only way we can deal with our consciences, whether they are healthy or not.

—From Archibald D. Hart, *Feeling Free.* Old Tappan, N.J.: Revell, 1979.

FOR FURTHER READING:

Osborne, Cecil G. *The Art of Understanding Yourself.* Grand Rapids: Zondervan, 1967.

Schlink, Basilea. *You Will Never Be the Same.* Minneapolis: Bethany House, 1972.

Wise, Robert L. *Your Churning Place.* Ventura, Calif.: Regal, 1977.

H

HABITS

WHY IS IT so hard to make changes in our lives that we know are desirable? It's because we are chained to established behavior and thought patterns by one of the most powerful linkages in the world: the force of habit. The great psychologist, William James, once wrote that repeated actions or repeated thoughts wear a kind of psychic groove in our minds, a groove that gets deeper with every repetition. And the deeper it becomes, the harder it is for the mind to get free.

But it can be done! The Bible says that with God's help, and the right kind of faith and determination, nothing is impossible. So this year, instead of worrying about January's failures, why not make one determined February resolution and really mean it? Why not say to yourself, "During the remainder of [the year] I'm going to work at and finally master the good habit of breaking bad habits"? Make that a promise to yourself—then nail it down with the powerful phrase: "So help me God!"

A bad habit is a problem; to get rid of it you must develop and use problem-solving techniques. Wishing won't do it. You have to be calm, cool, logical, alert—and determined.

So here are some procedures that will help anyone who wants to liberate himself or herself from thought or behavior patterns that need changing. Over the years they've helped me.

First, take responsibility for your bad habits. The Lord didn't put them into you. You put them into yourself. But He will help

you get rid of them if you ask Him sincerely; you can be sure He has no use for such things.

Next, believe you can get rid of them. Not instantly, perhaps, and not all at one time. But one by one. Within a reasonable time-span. The reason most New Year's resolutions fall by the wayside is that the resolvers don't really believe that they can keep them. They don't expect to keep them. They just vaguely hope to keep them. And that's not enough.

You must begin by sending a clear, unmistakable signal to your unconscious mind. "As a man thinketh *in his heart*," says the Bible, "so is he" (Proverbs 23:7). That word "heart," I feel sure, means the unconscious mind. To break a bad habit, then, your conscious desire to escape from it must be stronger than your unconscious wish or tendency to stay in that same old groove. If you send a halfhearted message to your unconscious mind suggesting that it might be nice to stop doing this or that, it will brush you aside and go right on its accustomed (habitual) way. No, you have to build up in your conscious mind a motivation so strong that your unconscious mind will go along with it.

Constant repetition of a specific goal or objective will eventually sink down into the unconscious mind. You can write down your habit-breaking goal on half a dozen three-by-five cards, paste one on your bathroom mirror, keep one in your pocket, have another in your desk drawer at the office, make sure one is on your bedside table where you can start the good habit of reading it last thing before you go to sleep at night. Each time you do read it, add those words: "So help me God!" Sooner or later—probably sooner—your unconscious mind is going to get the message. And when it does, when your "heart" is changed, you will change.

Another way to strengthen your motivation is to make a list of the bad habits you know you have. Then ask yourself how these traits affect other people's opinions of you. A bad habit almost always sends out a signal about the possessor of it. Usually a negative signal. Right or wrong, a nail-biter gives the impression that he is nervous and unsure of himself. The habitual name-dropper, that he has an inferiority complex. The person who is always late, that he is selfish and inconsiderate. The procrastinator, that he can't be trusted with anything that needs to be done efficiently. The user of profanity, that he has no respect for God or other people's sensibilities. Bad habits really do handicap people. That's why they're bad!

So take your list and study it carefully. Which of these disagreeable traits is doing you the most harm? Single out that one as your first target. Then go after it.

And don't visualize a struggle against tremendous odds. Visualize the victory! If you're a nail-biter, *see* yourself with attractive hands, with well-cared-for nails. If you're overweight and inactive, *see* yourself slim and energetic. Images held firmly in the mind have an almost miraculous way of becoming realities. So don't see yourself fighting to break that bad habit; see yourself triumphant because you *have* broken it!

Some bad habits may be so ingrained that you're not even aware of them. In such cases, enlisting the aid of friends or family may help. I knew one woman who was totally addicted to that verbal crutch, the phrase "you know." She could seldom complete a sentence without using it, to the boredom and irritation of her hearers. Finally she asked her family to keep count, promising to donate 10¢ to her church for every lapse. The very first day her brother's tally added up to $9.30. And he was only *one* of the counters!

Today, except for an occasional lapse, she's "you know"-free.

Sometimes deliberately adopting a good habit will drive out a bad one. I once counseled a man who had problems that he was well aware of. One was stinginess; he really was a tightwad, the result of a childhood spent on the edge of poverty. He asked me how he could break this unpleasant habit. "If I tell you, will you do it?" I asked him. He promised he would. "Then try tithing," I told him. "For three months, give ten percent of all your income to church or charity."

"Before or after taxes?" he moaned. "Before!" I said firmly. I knew that once he began tithing he would never stop, because tithing activates a law of abundance, and people who tithe faithfully invariably wind up with more than they had before. So he did tithe, and his habit of stinginess, if not completely broken, was at least severely dented.

Finally, in your assault on a bad habit, call on your religion, because it will come to your aid. Take worry, for example, the most universal of all bad habits. And one of the most damaging, because it can start with one specific worry and spread until it colors the whole personality. The real antidote for worry is not optimism or self-confidence or even positive thinking—it's trust. Trust in the goodness of a loving God and in His promises to us. "Fear thou not, for I am with thee" (Isaiah 41:10); "If God be for us, who can be against us?" (Romans 8:31). The mightiest force in the universe is God. What thought can be more sustaining than that?

So when you take aim at a bad habit, pray every morning and every night that God will help and strengthen you. He doesn't want you to have bad habits. He sent you into this world without any bad habits at all. And He gave us all a perfect model to try to imitate: Jesus Christ.

Pray to Him. He'll be listening.

—From Norman Vincent Peale, "The Good Habit of Breaking Bad Habits," *Guideposts,* February 1983.

HAIR

Style and Cut

Unfortunately, by the time many women reach forty-plus, their frame has become a "menopause bob." And with it, has gone most of the crowning glory and femininity that an ageless face needs for softness in order to look and feel fabulous.

What is this phenomenon that happens to women as they near the middle years? I'm not sure. There seems to be an unwritten rule that is secretly transmitted to every woman over thirty-five: "You should never wear long hair again—it must be short, neat and controlled."

But, "nothing could be farther from the truth. The proof is that the world's most glamorous ageless women, with a few exceptions, prefer longer hairstyles. Their hair is voluminous, luxuriant, a veritable mane . . . they all have a quality of elegant disarray." Touchable hair is one of our most feminine physical qualities. Hair is sexy. Female country-western singers have always known this. No menopause bobs for them!

I'm not talking about hair that reaches past your shoulders. That can be as aging as the menopause bob. If you prefer to wear your hair longer it should be swept off your face. Gravity tends to pull the face down; that's why we need to keep our hair on the "up" side.

Long hair or longish hair should have some kind of movement—layering, soft curls, waves. Some of the outstanding forty-plus-and-looking-fabulous women, still have fullness and movement in their hairstyles.

Another consideration in finding the right style to look fabulous at forty-plus is the shape of your face. It's essential to consider whether your face is square, round, diamond shaped, or pear-shaped. Some women are lucky enough to have a perfect oval. But if your face is other than an oval, select a hairstyle in which the fullness of your hair softens angular corners, too-strong jaws, receding chins, or low foreheads, advises Joanne Wallace in her book *The Image of Loveliness.*

Many women use a center part, but it can be hazardous to your beauty since it cuts facial features in half, rather than creating an overall look that flows together. It also forces you to try to style both sides of your hair exactly the same. That is virtually impossible because of the natural way hair grows. My own hairdresser, Kathleen Harlan, cautions that since no one has a perfectly symmetrical face, a center part only accentuates those differences.

Kathleen, though not yet forty-plus, is well on her way to developing an ageless attitude, so she will be looking and feeling as fabulous then as she does now.

As styles director for *Hair With Interest* shops in Milwaukie, Oregon, looking fabulous is Kathleen's business, and she knows that arriving at the proper cut is perhaps more important than style. She believes that a precision cut is what enables a woman to achieve a style without effort. Just what is a precision cut? It is when the stylist works with the unique growth pattern of your hair while she is cutting it.

If hair is cut properly, it should just fall into place nicely. But when hair has been cut improperly, you have hassles, because you are trying to work against the natural growth pattern. It makes me think of trying to iron out a porcupine—an impossible task!

Besides being a battle of the hairs, the wrong style can also create an immediate impression of inflexibility, repression, or sexlessness—none of which is part of the ageless-attitude agenda.

When selecting a style, remember that many things must be considered, such as your hair's texture, location of cowlicks, and even the direction of hair growth. If you have communicated with your stylist (a must!), she'll know the feeling or look you want and will do everything she can to find a happy solution for you.

Do be realistic about your request. If you have thin hair, you aren't going to get a beautiful, long, windblown look. So don't expect miracles!

Another thing to consider is your life-style. If you swim or are physically active, you might want a shorter cut that is flattering but easy to blow dry. Many women with longer hair no longer swim because hair care is too time consuming. If your style is restraining your physical activities, it's defeating its purpose in your life.

If you're in doubt about the cut that will help you look and feel more fabulous now that you're forty-plus, look at the magazines and notebooks full of hairstyles at a beauty shop. You can browse through at your leisure. Just take time to go in before you make an appointment. You might even take advantage of that time to talk with, and watch, the stylist who will be working with you. Watching her will give you a clue about the quality of work to expect.

One more thing to remember—many hair stylists do not have an ageless attitude. They may not think being forty-plus is fabulous at all, and they may try to talk you into a menopause bob. Go with determination and caution. Don't allow anyone to deter you from a new ageless hairstyle once you've decided to let go of the old look.

Hair Care and Health

Cut and style are important, but without healthy hair, no style can do you justice. Your hair is another reason to maintain good physical health.

Healthy hair reflects a healthy body—it's that simple. Pregnancy, hormones, anesthesia, and surgery all have their effect on the condition of your hair. If you've had surgery within six months to a year, a permanent may not take properly.

It's always wise to tell your hairdresser about the condition of your health and any medication you may be taking, before having color applied or a perm.

Illness, medication, and poor nutrition can affect your hair's growth, texture, thickness, and sheen. Sunlight, heated and air-conditioned rooms, extreme cold weather, chlorinated water in swimming pools, all dry your hair, as do blow dryers.

To counteract all these drying influences, conditioning is a must. Some hairdressers suggest having three different good-quality shampoos and conditioners in your bathroom. Each time you wash your hair, use a different product so your hair won't become resistant to the beneficial effects of any one.

To Dye or Not to Dye

And now, on to the fascinating world of color again. To dye or not to dye is the question many women ask at forty-plus, when we find more silver threads among the gold than not. But today, no one need be gray, except by choice.

One alternative to gray is frosting (sometimes referred to as aluminizing or foil wrap). Softly, a frost blends in natural gray with blonde. Since natural-color hair always has many highlights of different colors, a frosting leaves the same effect.

But stay away from harsh tinting and dyeing, warns Kathleen Harlan. It looks dated, colored, and unnatural. A tint will scream out, "Hey, everybody—I've covered my gray!" By contrast a frost gently blends the gray all together, subtly.

There are two ways to have your hair frosted. One is painful. The other is a pleasure. I have experienced both and prefer the foil-weaving method.

The old-fashioned, painful way is done with a tight rubber covering that fits your head like a bathing-cap and has several tiny holes. The hair is pulled through the holes with something like a crochet hook, just a few strands at a time. It's hurtful and time-consuming if you have longer hair. I've sat for hours while the tears rolled down my cheeks, promising myself I'd never subject myself to that torture again. It was truly a blessing when I moved to another town, and a new hairdresser suggested the foil-weaving method.

Weaving is a relatively new method of color application. (It can also be used for a reverse frost—light to dark.) Your hair is woven, creating indistinct sections. The sections that are colored become blended, eliminating streaks or stripes.

—From *Ruby MacDonald's Forty Plus and Feeling Fabulous Book.* Old Tappan, N.J.: Revell, 1982.

Wigs

When considering an investment in a wig, by all means do so intelligently. Don't buy anything just because it's cheap. I have found there are very few bargains in life. The few times I have tried to save a few pennies, I have had to sacrifice quality somewhere along the line.

Some guidelines on what to look for when shopping for synthetic wigs:

1. Try to examine the wig in the daylight. If it picks up unnatural colors such as pinks, purples, or greens, put it back on the counter.
2. Check the wig carefully for natural luster. Avoid anything that is too dull or too bright.
3. The fiber should feel soft and similar to human hair. It's not for you if it is slick like the hair they put on dolls.
4. Even the best synthetic can be damaged in the dyeing and curl-baking process. This results in bristly hair. A good way to check this is to use a brush to see how the hair behaves. The best wigs move well and handle easily in every direction.
5. No matter how adventuresome you feel, always pick a wig that matches your skin coloring. Blonds may "have more fun," but not if they're unattractive. Create a new image if you want to, but please stay within the bounds of reality and good taste.

Most synthetic wigs have their curl baked in and need no resetting. Natural-hair types, however, *do* require attention. Use a setting lotion made specially for wigs and hairpieces. When wigs are made of real hair, a squirt of water is all that's necessary before you use each plastic roller. I set my own hairpieces by securing them to a wig stand;

inexpensive ones of Styrofoam are to be found in most stores. Heated rollers can be used on a hairpiece, but I've found that if you utilize them too often, the hair becomes dry. Of course, there are no natural oils to remedy this. Should this happen to your hairpiece, you might give it a light touch of a cream dressing or spray conditioner—but *go easy, please.* You can spoil it for all times with too heavy a hand.

To remove surface dirt, brush the piece gently with a wig brush or one with soft bristles. The wig can be styled with this brush, too. If your hairpiece should become snarled, untangle it with a wide-toothed comb or a very large hairpin, working carefully from the ends or tips of the hair toward the base.

Don't wash a hairpiece of real hair. You can dry-clean it yourself with a special solution, but if you value its beauty, it's worth having it cleaned professionally. You can wash your synthetic pieces with shampoo and cold water very easily and with good results. Hold the piece by the base and lightly swish it through the suds. Rinse. Pat dry with towels, and hang it by the front to dry. You can put it in a mesh laundry bag to prevent snarls while it's being washed. If the wig base should get wet, put it on a block and don't comb the hair until the base is dry. The block will prevent it from shrinking.

A synthetic hairpiece cannot be recolored. Real hairpieces shouldn't be dyed either, but a rinse can be put on by a professional hairdresser or colorist. Don't try to do this yourself.

Keep hairpieces pinned to a wig stand. They should be kept away from heat and bright lights, because the hair will oxidize and change color. Keep the stand in a tall covered box, or tie a silk scarf around it loosely. It can be stored in a roomy plastic bag if you wish.

Other reminders:

1. Avoid permanents or straightening on hairpieces.
2. Don't use regular hair spray on them.
3. Make certain your hairpieces match your basic hair color.

In putting on a fall, switch or wiglet, make two or three pin curls of your own hair and crisscross them with bobby pins in the place to which you want to attach the hairpiece. Now slide the little comb attached to the piece under the pin curls and you're all set.

One of the most important factors in getting a soignée effect when you're putting on a wig—stretch or any other kind—is what you do with your own hair. I still think it is best to wind up your own hair neatly in pin curls and make one or two pin curls crisscrossed with bobby pins just a little past your front hairline to keep the wig from slipping. You can cover your head with a nylon stocking, but I find that isn't very comfortable. If you have long hair, pull your hair back and divide it into three strands. Twist each strand and pull it as flat as possible to your scalp. This eliminates any large bumps. Keep some hair out to make a small pin curl on each side of the temple and on top of your head so that the wig can be secured by the small combs usually attached to the front; or you can stick a hairpin carefully through the net to hold the wig in place. Now you are ready for the styling.

If the wig has bangs or soft curls that cover your forehead, you don't have to worry about your hairline. If you want to cover the hairline of the wig, do everything mentioned above, but leave a quarter inch of your own hair out around the hairline. This should be enough to brush over the wig line. If it's not, then try again, leaving more of your own hair showing. Don't overdo, however, for that can spoil the naturalness.

I have found that whether it's a short or long hairpiece you want to wear, a slight combing of your own hair over the front and sides makes the entire styling more attractive.

For ten years now I have been doing my own wigs and pieces, and I've become quite adept. Still, once every three cleanings, I take them all into my hairdresser. He uses little trade secrets or a new style I hadn't even thought of that keeps my wigs and hairpieces fresh and fashionable. I advise you to follow my lead.

If you haven't thought of owning and wearing a wig, fall or other hairpiece until now, I hope I've convinced you that they are fun, great timesavers and really worth trying.

A good crop of fresh, clean hair, any length, and a supply of becoming wigs and hairpieces allow you to be your most attractive, well-groomed self for all occasions. Whether the events are planned well in advance or take place on a moment's notice, *you* are always ready.

—From Wilhelmina, *The New You.* New York: Simon & Schuster, 1978.

FOR FURTHER READING:

Gundry, Patricia. *The Complete Woman.* Garden City, N.Y.: Doubleday, 1981.

Wallace, Joanne. *The Image of Loveliness.* Old Tappan, N.J.: Revell, 1978.

HEADACHES

MOST HEADACHES can be categorized in one of several distinct patterns. These include: (1) *tension headaches;* (2) *dilation headaches* (migraine, cluster, hypertensive, fever, hunger, hangover, and toxic poisoning); and (3) *traction* or *inflammatory headaches* (infection or diseases of the eye, ear, nose, throat, sinus, teeth, or jaw; and mass lesions as in tumors and cerebral hemorrhage). It is very possible to have a combination of two types of headaches simultaneously or sequentially.

1. **Tension Headaches.** The most common headache (about 90 percent) is the tension or muscle-contraction headache. Three times as many women get tension headaches as do men. Forty percent of tension-headache sufferers have a family history of headaches.

In tension headaches, the muscles of the head, neck, and scalp tighten, and the blood vessels constrict, causing pain. The headache is the brain's way of saying, "Relax! Give the muscles a rest, and let the blood flow normally."

Tension headaches can occur on both

sides of the head, in the forehead, at the back of the head, or in the jaw area. The head usually feels as though you have a band around it, which is being tightened. The head can also feel as if there is a pressure within which might cause an explosion. Tension headaches do not usually throb; they will more likely ache, and there may be tenderness of the scalp and neck. There may be a burning or tingling sensation. Nausea, although not usually common, can occur, especially if the pain becomes severe. A tension headache usually lasts a few hours, but it can last longer.

Tension headaches can develop in anticipation of an unpleasant occurrence, during an emotional upset or conflict, after a stressful or fatiguing event, or from poor posture. Worrying about getting a headache can even cause a headache. Other specific influences include squinting in bright light, holding a telephone with your shoulder, typing or sewing for too long, wrinkling your forehead while worrying, and wearing high heels.

The emotions generally associated with tension headaches include worry, anxiety, fear, pent-up anger, and/or depression. Sometimes the headache provides a useful excuse to avoid a task or to get help. Experiencing tension headaches can often lead to insomnia, tiredness, irritability, and eating disorders.

Almost all tension headaches can be alleviated and/or prevented by following [certain] exercises, including relaxation, pressure-point massage, and changing your thinking processes. In addition, taking a leisurely hot bath often helps relieve a tension headache. Although medication is rarely necessary, circumstances might warrant an occasional aspirin. Additionally, counseling may be appropriate to learn skills of conflict resolution, stress management, and other coping skills and goal setting.

2. **Dilation Headaches.** In these headaches, the blood vessels swell (dilate), inflame, and exert pressure on the nerves around them, causing pain. Headaches of this type include *migraine, cluster, hypertensive, fever, hun-*

ger, hangover, and *toxic poisoning.* With dilation headaches, the brain is saying, "Make changes so that the blood vessels can return to their normal size."

Symptoms of Migraine Headaches. The pain often localizes on one side of the head. The temple area is usually tender. Migraine sufferers experience intense throbbing and constant pain, and the neck may become stiff and achy. The pain is generally so severe that the sufferer cannot carry on normal activities. The migraine is sometimes accompanied by nausea or vomiting and a loss in appetite. Bending over makes a migraine worse. The headache may last a few hours, although it often lasts a full day or longer. When the attack is over, the victim will feel exhausted for hours or days.

Occurrence of Migraines. The migraine occurs most often after a stressful situation, such as following a vacation, or on the morning after a trauma of the day before. It can wake the person up in the middle of the night. Migraines can, however, also occur during the stress itself.

A migraine can be triggered by something as simple as rays of sunlight, physical exercise, sitting in a stuffy or smoky room, or watching television in a dark room. It can also come after eating certain foods, such as milk products, chocolate, wheat, nuts, citrus fruits, spicy food, pork, or alcohol. Migraines can also be brought on by going without eating for an extended period, as is true when one oversleeps or fasts. They can also be triggered by withdrawing from caffeine. Weather changes or high altitudes can cause a migraine in some persons.

Effect of Drugs and Chemicals. Drugs which can stimulate a migraine include reserpine, nitroglycerin, estrogen, and too much ergotamine. Even car exhaust and certain odors can trigger an attack. Migraine headaches can occur from changes in hormonal levels, such as during ovulation, menstruation, pregnancy, and menopause, or as a side effect of birth-control pills. Ironically, some women who usually get migraines become free of them during pregnancy.

It is estimated that about 70 percent of

242

migraine sufferers have a family history of such pain, indicating the possibility of a hereditary predisposition and/or an environmental influence. As children, most migraine sufferers experienced headaches, nausea, and/or car sickness.

Personality Traits of the Migraine Sufferer. Traits associated with migraines include being meticulous, compulsive, and perfectionistic. Migraine sufferers often are ambitious, hardworking, and conscientious; they become overly concerned with setting and meeting goals. They are usually highly energetic and often very intelligent. Delays and failures trouble them deeply. They are usually demanding of themselves and others, eager to please, and sensitive to criticism. Not all migraine sufferers have these personality traits, nor do all individuals with these traits have migraines. In some cases, these personality traits can be abandoned fairly easily by acknowledging their counterproductiveness. In other cases, it might be necessary to enlist the help of a therapist, because the personality traits and habit patterns may be very deeply ingrained and attached to issues of self-acceptance.

Types of Migraines. There are two kinds of migraines: the *common* and the *classic.* The common migraine accounts for about 80 percent of all migraines and affects men and women equally. More women are affected by the classic migraine, and its symptoms are usually on one side of the head (while the common migraine can be on both sides). Unlike the common migraine, the frequency of classical migraines diminishes as a person gets older since, with aging, there is a general loss of elasticity of artery walls.

If you are a common-migraine sufferer, your warning phase, if any, will be a generalized vague, uneasy, or irritable feeling.

If you are a classic-migraine sufferer, you will have a warning of from ten to thirty minutes, during which time the blood vessels constrict. The preheadache symptoms usually occur on the opposite side of the head from where the throbbing will occur later. You may see streaks of light, zigzagging lines, blotches of darkness, blurring,

or other visual distortions. Your speech may become slurred and/or indistinct. Numbness or tingling may occur in your hands and feet. You might experience nausea or tremors and will probably feel weak, tired, confused, restless, and irritable. It is best to lie down and relax in a dark room as soon as possible when the warning comes.

The dilation and inflammation phase is similar for both the classic and the common migraine. The blood vessels in your head become larger, the tissues around the blood vessels become inflamed and chemical irritants collect. The headache throbs with increasing severity. You feel tense, short-tempered, and confused. Your voice becomes low, perhaps even inaudible. You may accumulate fluid in your ankles and face. You may experience heavy perspiration, increased urination, constipation, and/or diarrhea. Sounds and bright light become especially irritating. During this phase, it is best to cool your forehead and warm your hands and feet to help reverse the dilation of the arteries in your head. Since the pain seems unbearable during this phase, medication may be necessary.

Later—sometimes after a full day—a dull, steady headache replaces the intense pain. During this time, you may suffer from a stiff neck, tenderness, exhaustion, and tension.

Cluster Headaches. Another dilation headache, with pain as unbearable as the migraine, is the cluster headache. Ninety percent of cluster headaches occur in men, and these men usually range in age from twenty to forty.

The excruciating pain of a cluster headache occurs behind one cheek and eye and stretches to the back of the head and neck. Sometimes it pierces the other side of the head. If you suffer from a cluster headache, you may experience tearing, heavy perspiration, or nasal congestion. The headache usually throbs and aches, and it reaches its intensity very quickly. The pain often feels like a knife stabbing in your head.

Cluster headaches can occur in the middle of the night every night during the period of the attacks. The headaches can occur several times in a single day, or daily over a period of time up to two months. They then disappear for months or even years. The headaches often occur in the spring and/or fall. Usually a cluster headache lasts between ten minutes and four hours. Occasionally the headache can last continuously for a long period of time. Alcohol, nicotine, histamines, or nitroglycerin often trigger these headaches.

The cluster-headache sufferer may share the personality traits which are often true of migraine sufferers. Vigorous exercise, such as running, swimming, tennis, or lifting weights, can reduce these headaches.

Hypertensive Headaches. Another dilation headache is the hypertensive headache, caused by elevated blood pressure. This headache normally starts in the morning and diminishes on its own during the day. It produces blurred vision, drowsiness, and even confusion. When the blood pressure goes down, the headache decreases.

Miscellaneous Dilation Headaches. Other dilation headaches include those resulting from fever, hunger, environmental conditions, strenuous sexual activity, a head injury, exhaustive exercise, overconsumption of alcohol, and poisons, such as carbon monoxide. Although the causes of these headaches are different, the response of the blood vessels is similar to that for migraine and cluster headaches. The intensity, however, of these miscellaneous headaches is usually less.

3. **Traction and Inflammatory Headaches.** These headaches are stimulated by organic diseases or infections, such as meningitis, strokes, phlebitis, arthritis, or neuralgia. Other headaches may be associated with inflammation in specific areas, such as eyes, ears, nose, throat, sinus, teeth, or jaws. Although rare, headaches can also occur within the brain itself, such as from mass lesions, including tumors and cerebral hemorrhages. In these cases, specific medical treatment should be sought for the underlying disease or infection.

Sinus Headaches. An example of an inflammation headache is the sinus headache, which results from increased pressure, caused by inflammation of the mucous membranes in the sinus cavity. A stuffy nose and sometimes a fever may accompany the pain. If the pain is in the forehead area, it is worse in the morning; if it is in the cheek area, it usually gets worse in the afternoon and diminishes at night. Sinus pain is usually dull and aching. It often occurs more in cold weather, after drinking alcohol, during the menstrual cycle, during sexual excitement, or as a result of an allergy attack or cold. The pain becomes worse when bending over, coughing, sneezing, or lifting a heavy object. Nausea or vomiting are seldom present. Many people label tension or dilation headaches as sinus headaches, and therefore treat them incorrectly.

Allergy Headaches. Very similar to sinus headaches are allergy headaches, caused by reaction to such environmental conditions as pollen and molds. Nasal congestion and watery eyes usually accompany an allergy headache.

Eyestrain Headaches. Another traction headache can occur from eyestrain and is therefore located behind the eyes. It may come after prolonged reading, reading at an improper distance, watching television in a dark room, or reading in poor light. If these headaches persist after altering the conditions, then your eyes need to be examined.

Jaw-related Headaches. A final traction headache may be associated with the jaw or temporomandibular joint. Pain resulting from this problem usually occurs in front of or behind the ears. Your temple area may also be tender, and you experience pain when you chew. You may experience a clicking sound when you open your jaw. This ache can result from clenching or grinding your teeth, or having a poor bite because of teeth or bone structure. If these aches persist, consult an orthodontist, who can often make an adjustment (which is sometimes as simple as grinding or capping).

Remember that your headache may come from several sources and may appear only under overlapping conditions, such as stress, nutritional imbalance, infection, and exhaustion. It is, therefore, important to become aware of all the potential causes for your headaches, and try to correct as many as possible.

—From Joan Miller, Ph.D., *Headaches: The Answer Book.* Old Tappan, N.J.: Revell, 1983.

FOR FURTHER READING:

McMillen, S. I., M.D. *None of These Diseases.* Old Tappan, N.J.: Revell, 1963, 1984.
Miller, Joan, Ph.D. *Headaches: The Answer Book.* Old Tappan, N.J.: Revell, 1983.

HOBBIES

HOBBIES ARE chosen in different ways—or, hobbies choose persons in different ways, if you prefer. What has been an avocation before retirement may become a hobby that is close to a second vocation in retirement. What has been a vocation in life may become an eagerly pursued hobby in retirement. More frequently, however, the hobby that claims an individual in retirement is a new interest, at least an interest that one was unable to follow earlier for lack of time and freedom.

That is the case with one of my favorite hobbies, reading. The two careers that claimed most of my professional life, ministry and teaching, demanded that I read much. However, my reading in retirement is quite different. The content of the reading is different and my purpose is not the same. Earlier, I read to keep "intellectually respectable" in my chosen field of work. Now, my reading is for enjoyment, pure and simple. If I do not find pleasure in the reading, the book is usually put down.

Recently, I discovered a new author. Why I had missed her for so long, I do not know. Having made the discovery, I sought to rectify my shortcomings without delay. What a treat! A half hundred books bear her name as author. One entire winter and a large part of spring were brightened by her stimulating characters and intriguing plots. The reading gave me new friends, as real as the neighbor next door. It gave me sheer delight and, make no mistake at this point, *delight*, pleasure, is an essential of successful living. The reading put truth and virtue into flesh and blood and I saw those two principles in action. In my reading I received inspiration. I saw men and women face hardship and disappointment with courage and fortitude until I dared believe that I could act in such a way if called upon to do so!

.   .   .   .   .

Travel stands high on my list of hobbies. Travel is costly and that has to be considered by most retirees. Drawing heavily upon my own observation and experience, let me suggest this. It does not cost as much to travel at home as it does to travel abroad. And, very few of us have reaped the full benefit of travels at home. And, if there is something or someone of significance in the next state, county, or town, it may be as important that you travel there as that you go to Europe next summer.

As for traveling at home, it, too, is costly. However, there are considerations. The time, the place, the mode of travel have much to do with prices. Those of us who are retired are doing a great percentage of the traveling these days. Our business is important; we are catered to; reductions are freely offered. There are many ways to economize.

.   .   .   .   .

It has been observed that the happiest people are those who touch life at the greatest number of points. My own life is enriched by having a number of hobbies. The field is wide: auctions, autograph collecting, baking, bird watching, animals, coin collecting, hiding-out, drawing, painting, fishing, stamp collecting, writing, window-shopping.

.   .   .   .   .

A hobby a day may not keep the doctor away from your retirement domicile but it is a better and more potent medicine than that proverbial apple!

—From J. Winston Pearce, *Ten Good Things I Know About Retirement.* Nashville: Broadman, 1982.

FOR FURTHER READING:

Pearce, J. Winston. *Ten Good Things I Know About Retirement.* Nashville: Broadman, 1982.

HOME

. . . HOWARD HENDRICKS, renowned lecturer on the home, often says, "Heaven help the home!" The woman, he maintains, must be the magnet in the home "to draw the husband home at the close of day and children home at the close of play." Each home needs that kind of magnetism if it is to provide the necessary warmth and stability for all its members.

It is true that many women work outside the home, either part-time or full-time. They come home at the end of the day and still have lots of work awaiting them there. Many advocates for Women's Lib are saying that it is just impossible for a working woman to make the effort that is required to create a loving atmosphere in the home.

Many women have discovered, however, that a loving atmosphere does not depend on the amount of time involved, but rather on the depth of the commitment to the family structure.

> It is better to live in a corner of an attic than in a beautiful house with a cranky, quarrelsome woman.
>
> Proverbs 25:24

In the marriage ceremony, couples pledge to love each other " 'till death us do part." And all too often the death that occurs is the death of the relationship rather than an actual physical death. How easy it is for today's beautiful bride to become tomorrow's nagging wife—unless she has a commitment.

Many things in life tend to tarnish and must be polished frequently in order to stay new and shiny. Love, too, needs to be constantly shined and polished, protected and nourished, lest it grow dim and lose its lustre.

It is difficult to build a strong family life for Satan's greatest attacks today are on the home. To quote Edith Schaeffer, wife of Dr. Francis Schaeffer of L'Abri, "We are endeavoring to preserve an endangered species—the family!"

It is not impossible, however, to build a good home. *The first prerequisite is a right relationship with God,* for our relationship with our Heavenly Father directly affects all others. This relationship, above all, must be genuine and vital, for nothing grieves our Father more than when we merely go through the motions. He wants to be real to us.

Jesus said, "The Father and I are one." He spent time with His Father in a close personal relationship, always drawing aside and seeking communion with God. We need that personal, individual time to commune with our Father, just as Jesus did, and we must follow our Savior's example.

Our second priority of commitment is to our husbands. Strange, that after children come they so often grab first place, then grow up and go away leaving two strangers who—thanks to those children—no longer know each other! The husband-wife commitment must always supersede that of commitment to the children. If this is not the case, nobody will be secure—not even the children.

Sometimes, after several years of marriage, a woman will say, "Well, I just don't love him any more." William James of Harvard University, the most famous psychologist in America at the turn of the century, used to say, "It is easier to act your way into feeling, than to feel your way into acting."

When love fades, it is always because actions are following feelings and it should be the other way around. So if you don't feel love any more, *act as if you did.* Behave as you did on your honeymoon, as you did on the first day of your marriage, or even when you were dating. And if you keep on *acting as if,* the feeling of love will return!

Love is much more than mere feeling. It is commitment. It is necessary for us to have a real commitment to marriage, home, the job—even if we don't feel like it at times. It is a fact of life that most of the work in the world is done by people who do not "feel" like it. If we keep on doing the things that make marriage work and stop worrying about our feelings, we will soon be surprised and happy to realize that, somewhere along the way, we began to feel like it!

Often we make the mistake of thinking that we can change our husbands, but we must remember that only God can change people. It is our job to make our husbands happy, and God's job to make them good. Remember, when you took your wedding vows you said, "I do,"—not "I will *re-do.*" As Billy Graham's lovely wife, Ruth says, "Don't marry a man you are not willing to adjust to." If, however, you are already married, as most of us are, then be willing to adjust. After all, why should he do all the adjusting?

Third on the list of priorities is *our relationship with our children.* The successful parent works himself out of the job, but never out of the relationship. Remember that the kindest thing you can ever do for your children is to teach them to be independent of you—but dependent on the Lord.

One of the best gifts we can ever give our children is our time. We must be sensitive to their need for our time and attention, and we must aid them in building self-confidence and in developing a good self-image. When our school system teaches the Theory of Evolution as fact, and our children hear that they are descended from primates, how can they possibly have a good self-image? How different they become when they learn that they are indeed created in God's image and likeness! How wonderful for them to know that they are special, that God has a plan for their lives! It is so vital that every boy and girl feel like somebody—and *be* somebody!

Fourth on the list of commitments is *our relationship with special people* or, as Morris Shieks calls them, "the significant others." These would be the people, relatives and friends, who are special in your life. My grandmother always urged me to expose my children to exciting, attractive Christian adults outside the family. Most children do not always listen to the members of their own family, and they need someone else to keep them balanced. They need role models outside the family to emulate.

And finally is our commitment to everyone else with whom we are involved in daily lives. These are the people whom Jesus referred to when He told us to love our neighbor as ourselves. It is interesting that Jesus suggested here that we definitely are supposed to love ourselves. And loving ourselves means nothing more than having a good self-image, *liking* and *respecting* ourselves. If we do not first love ourselves, then we can never be free of ourselves.

Unfortunately, not all women love themselves. Many do not have a good self-image and do not feel like winners. Many tend to think of themselves only as extensions of their husbands, and not as separate individuals.

Every woman is a "somebody," and she needs to think of herself as a distinct individual and not just as her husband's wife. Others, too, will then think of her in that way. Deborah in the Book of Judges in the Bible, the great heroine of the Israelites, was the wife of a man named Lappidoth. She was not called Mrs. Lappidoth, however; she was known as the mother of Israel!

Remember, to God *you* are a person. God knows your name and He never mistakes you in a crowd! If God thinks of you as a special individual, don't you think you should be one?

Heaven help the home! May God protect the home from all the enemies that assail it—from without and from within. The threats to the home from outside are great, but the ones that attack it from within are just as deadly.

—From Mary C. Crowley, *Women Who Win.* Old Tappan, N.J.: Revell, 1979.

FOR FURTHER READING:

    Kilgo, Edith Flowers. *Handbook for Christian Homemakers*. Baker Book, 1982.
    MacDonald, Gordon. *The Effective Father*. Wheaton, Ill.: Tyndale, 1977.

HOME BUSINESSES

BASICALLY, ALL types of work fall into three categories: teaching, selling, and service. Yet under each classification there are endless possibilities and variations. You may even have a home business which simultaneously covers more than one category.

Betty James, of Doraville, Georgia, enjoyed her hobby of decorative painting so much that she soon had a house full of beautiful accessories. Friends who admired her work began asking Betty to paint articles for them, too. They brought her such things as old bread trays, umbrella stands, and even coal scuttles. Skillfully, Betty transformed the cast-offs into beautiful, one-of-a-kind accent pieces. She had performed a service.

As Betty's interest in decorative painting grew, she began selling some of her creations. These were items she had acquired, refurbished, and adorned with colorfully painted designs or scenes. Her home business had then branched out into the selling category, too.

Betty's skill increased as she produced more and more of her work. Consequently, other women often admired her finished products. Time after time she heard the remark, "Oh, I'd love to learn how to do that!" Again Betty made a transition. Now her home business includes teaching decorative painting to others.

While it's helpful to categorize types of home businesses in order to see the options available, it's also essential to keep an open mind regarding various possibilities for developing the business in more than one area. Had Betty James simply limited herself to one rigid category, she would have totally bypassed two other equally lucrative possibilities.

SELLING AS A HOME BUSINESS

Selling is possibly the most popular type of home business. The reason is simple. Many women develop a home business as a direct result of a hobby they love or a skill they already possess. If a woman enjoys her work, she will produce considerable output. After awhile the family cannot use any more hand-knitted sweaters, woven baskets, or blackberry jam. Consequently, in order to continue production, something must be done with the surplus. Selling comes about as a logical alternative. Then the creative woman has the continued pleasure of making her specialty, yet no longer has the guilty feeling of having overdone a good thing. Of course, the money is an incentive, too. After all, she reasons, selling an item for five dollars will keep her in raw materials sufficient to make eight more of the same object.

Even homemakers who are not remotely creative can find a profitable career in selling. If you haven't the slightest desire to make rag dolls or crocheted doilies, you can still have a home business in the selling field. There are innumerable items you can buy and resell for a profit if selling interests you, but creating does not.

Selling requires more face-to-face contact with more people than does either teaching or performing a service. Performing a service, such as making a dress for someone, involves meeting people, but in different circumstances. You'll usually meet the customer, work out the details of the service to be performed, do the job, and then report back to the one who hired you. This is one-to-one contact, but on a more prolonged basis and in a situation where you have a chance to get to know your customer. Selling may not always offer that advantage. While you may develop a stream of repeat customers, many selling jobs will be on a one-time basis only.

Because you may have only a brief time to present both yourself and your product, an easy-going manner of dealing with customers is essential. If meeting strangers puts butterflies in your stomach, selling might not be the right career for you. A successful career in selling depends on presenting both yourself and your products in a positive manner. You may be offering the world's most useful gadget for sale, but unless you can properly deal with people, success will be limited.

Selling usually involves considerably more paper work than does either teaching or service jobs, so a good bookkeeping system is essential. If you perform a service, such as typing manuscripts, your bookkeeping will be limited to keeping records of expenditures such as paper and supplies, and income received. A home business which involves selling requires more bookkeeping effort. You must record expenses for raw material, advertising, and mileage. You may also have postage expense. Additionally, you must collect a sales tax if your product is sold retail, and, of course, accurate records must be kept on the sales tax. If you sell wholesale in quantity lots, you may get involved with credit and billing, too. Nevertheless, don't let all the paper work scare you away from a career in selling. Even if you failed high school math, there's no need to panic. Your bookkeeping doesn't have to meet professional standards; it merely has to be accurate.

SERVICE JOBS

Service jobs offer a great deal of flexibility. First, you have the advantage of not having to cope with a large inventory of items. Most service jobs will involve simply you and perhaps one piece of equipment, such as a sewing machine, typewriter, or weaving loom. These may entail a considerable cash outlay in the beginning, but after the initial expense of acquiring your necessary equipment, most service jobs don't require large investments.

In my case, with a home sewing business, the purchase of the sewing machine was the only really big dent in my budget. After that, such things as keeping my scissors sharpened and giving the sewing machine an occasional oiling were about the only expenditures I

had. These costs, plus the cost of the tiny amount of electricity used, were so small, I practically ignored them when tallying operational expenses.

Service jobs offer perhaps the greatest opportunity for building repeat business. If your business is poodle grooming and you are reasonably competent at the task, the same customers will need you again and again. Selling a tangible object such as a basket or a piece of pottery does not offer you this advantage. No matter how much a customer likes your product, she'll eventually get all of it she needs. Not so with a service—Fido will go right on needing your grooming services year after year.

Another advantage of service jobs is that if you are housebound because of small children, a physical handicap, or the lack of a car, you can still get your work done. While selling will involve occasional trips to buy supplies or to make deliveries to your customers, with a service job customers come to you.

You may find that customers enjoy watching you perform your service, too. If you can talk while you work, a service job can be a perfect opportunity for socializing while you get paid. Also, people appreciate your work more when they know how much effort went into the task. A customer who watches you hand-quilt only a small portion of her quilt top in an hour's time and sees how slowly the work goes, is less likely to quibble over prices. Then, too, customers are impressed when they see you re-do a job in order to get it exactly right for them. When I was sewing for others, I always insisted that customers try on finished garments before paying for them and taking them home. If the fit wasn't just right, I made the necessary adjustments right then. Certainly, the corrections took time, but the good will created was well worth the effort. Customers will come back again and again once they see that you take pride in your work.

Bookkeeping for a service job will mostly involve keeping an accurate record of income. Unless your service is one such as Betty James's, which involves the purchase of paint, you won't have much expense to record.

The biggest pitfall in a service business is failure to get payment from the customer. If you're selling a product, theoretically, you can march over to the nonpayer's house and ask to have the goods returned, but once a service job is done you must collect payment immediately, or you may never see any money at all.

TEACHING

Teaching is both selling and service. The salable product is knowledge and the service is giving it to others. Therefore, since teaching is a form of selling, enthusiasm is a necessary partner to knowledge. You can't "sell" someone else on the joys of creating jewelry unless you're "sold" on it yourself.

A mention of teaching makes most people think of college degrees and children. However, children aren't the only ones benefiting from the home business of teaching, and most of the courses being taught don't require college degrees. As a matter of fact, you can be so uneducated that you can neither read nor write, yet if you have a unique skill that's in demand, you can teach.

Teaching can consist of any subject from herb gathering to making corn husk dolls. A look at the courses offered by your local recreation center, community college, or YWCA will give you an idea of the subjects in which potential students are interested. In my community the junior college offers such things as photography, tax preparation, will preparation, creative writing, canning and freezing techniques, how to make Christmas decorations, and even how to become a clown or a magician! Evidently these subjects continue to attract students year after year because in the three years I've been on the mailing list the subjects offered have changed very little. Take a look at what is being offered in your community. Chances are you're qualified to teach at least one subject which is already a proven winner.

If standing in front of a crowd makes your

knees go wobbly with fright, you can still find a way to teach. Try tutoring on a one-to-one basis. Anything that can be taught on a classroom basis can be taught equally well to only one student at a time. The main difference is that you won't make as much money. In order to realize a decent hourly wage you'll have to charge each student considerably more than you would in a classroom situation.

The biggest disadvantage to teaching may be that it intrudes into your privacy. For some reason, students in an informal classroom are much more likely to call the teacher on the telephone or to drop in for an unannounced visit. They don't really mean to intrude, but when they don't understand something you're teaching, they expect you to bail them out of their troubles. You might partially eliminate this problem by making yourself available to answer questions immediately after class.

Bookkeeping is not difficult when you are teaching. Unless you are also selling raw materials to your students (a highly profitable business—often more profitable than the classes are) your bookkeeping will consist mainly of entering into your records the fees received and deducting the cost of any demonstration materials.

BUT WHICH SHALL I CHOOSE?

With all the possibilities available to you in each of the three categories, are you wondering how you'll ever make a decision on the one that's right for you?

Let's take another look at your personal needs and interests. Have you determined how many hours per week you want to spend on your business? Obviously, if time is severely limited, your choice will have to be either teaching or performing a service. It's difficult to produce a product and make sales calls on a schedule limited to a few hours each week.

Have you also taken into account your temperament? If your patience is limited, try something besides tutoring or doing detailed work. If your shyness is extreme, find something which won't constantly bring you into contact with strangers.

LOOKING FOR A BUSINESS

Make a list of all your talents, skills, work experiences, and hobbies. Even if you are not especially proficient in a particular area, put that skill down on your list. For instance, if you play the piano fairly well, even though you've not had extensive training, put piano playing on your list. You might not have the ability to teach concert playing techniques, but you might be able to reach first-year students or even adults who wish to learn just enough music to be able to sing in the church choir. List everything you can think of that has any possibilities at all as a money-maker.

As you complete your list of capabilities, you may be wondering how a group of unrelated skills could possibly lead to finding a home business. Yet the list is probably not as unrelated as it at first appears to be.

Let's suppose your list looks something like this:

1. sewing ability
2. management ability
3. enjoyment of meeting new friends
4. quilt-making as a hobby

Do you see a pattern emerging from these seemingly unconnected items? With a list like this you could exercise your talents in several ways. You might find it suitable to open a small shop in your home to sell quilting supplies to other quilters. If there is no room for a shop, perhaps making quilts to be sold on consignment might be the answer. If meeting people is a pleasure, you might enjoy taking a booth in arts and crafts fairs to provide yourself with an opportunity to make new acquaintances while bringing in extra income. However, if all forms of selling are uninteresting to you, a service job might be appealing. Many potential customers would like to find a qualified quilter to finish their own hand-pieced quilt tops. Then to

carry your range of qualifications to all possible fields, you might decide this list of skills and interests points in the direction of teaching.

Look at your own list in this way and soon you will see a definite pattern emerging from seemingly unrelated components.

—From Edith Flowers Kilgo, *Money in the Cookie Jar.* Grand Rapids: Baker Book, 1980.

FOR FURTHER READING:

Crowley, Mary C. *Women Who Win.* Old Tappan, N.J.: Revell, 1979.

HOMOSEXUALITY

THE COMMONEST deviation [in sex experience] is homosexuality: sex attraction towards members of the same sex. The term applies to both sexes, though another term, "lesbianism," has come to be used for women, after a Mediterranean people whose women supposedly practiced it extensively. By its emphasis on sex, modern society leads young people to think that they should be highly sexed, and that if they are not, they are latent homosexuals. This of course is quite untrue: we vary considerably in our feelings. But some, whose sexual feelings are not strong, are thus tormented by a very real, but groundless, fear of abnormality.

It is important to recognize the distinction between the condition and the practice. Until recently our law regarded the practice of homosexuality as a criminal offense; but this was felt to be too harsh on those whose tendencies were homosexual through no fault of their own, or who were psychologically unable to regain normality. As to practice, the law now says, "If responsible adults choose to have homosexual relations together, that's their affair." The law does, however, protect children, and regards pederasty (which literally means loving a boy) as a serious offense.

For this is how it very often begins. An early experience of seduction by an older person may initiate a child into homosexual practice. But this is not the only cause. Stable homes and families should bring children through all the stages that result in normal sex. But unfortunately today so many homes are broken or family relationships unhappy that this does not always happen, and a child may be left with some fixation on his or her own sex, or with a fear connected with the opposite sex. A great deal can be done nowadays to help, though it must be admitted that the cases like these where personality has been damaged are the most difficult.

Others have heard about homosexuality, and in their curiosity have found someone to try it out with. Or perhaps they have been obliged to live for a period of time deprived of the companionship of the opposite sex. These usually revert to heterosexuality (normal male/female relationships) when normal contacts are resumed.

It's vital for a homosexual to get the right kind of help. A boy once came to my home to see me about a spiritual problem. We sat down in the living room and I asked him to tell me what the trouble was. He seemed excessively anxious that we should not be interrupted and asked if we could go to another room, so we went to my office den. We settled, and started again. Then he asked me if I knew anything about homosexuality. I probed a little: what particular aspect did he mean? Then he said, "It's very difficult to explain; I'd have to *show* you, for you to understand. . . ." I was no help to him; he needed a skill which I didn't possess. I'm not sure even now if I was being conned, but I thought so because he didn't seem interested in being put in touch with a trained person with the right skill to help him. He was looking for a new partner.

I am happy to say that I know people who through therapy have been really lifted into normality, as far as I can tell. Some are happily married. I know of others for whom in spite of treatment this is not so. Perhaps they had been more deeply affected in the first place. Nevertheless they have been helped to come to terms with their problem. . . .

Every homosexual knows in spite of ra-

tionalization, that his approach to sex is abnormal. But not all want to be helped. Thank God for those who do. There are many who have no intention of seeking help and their practice is a danger to society. This is the kind of homosexuality which is so rightly condemned in the Bible.

The most famous example in the Old Testament is the city of Sodom, of which God said, "their sin is very grave." It may seem inconceivable to us that a whole city could be characterized by it; but when two strangers visited Lot in Sodom, the writer of Genesis 19 tells us how "the men of the city, the men of Sodom, both young and old, to the last man, surrounded the house," clamoring for the visitors. Judgment fell on them from God.

No less severe is the punishment Paul speaks of in Romans 1:26: "God gave them up to dishonorable passions; their women pervert the natural use of their sex by unnatural acts. In the same way the men give up natural sex relations with women and burn with passion for each other . . . as a result they receive in themselves the punishment they deserve for their wrong-doing."

It is clearly the *wilfulness* of the activity that makes it sin. That it can be put right is equally clear from the experience of the Corinthians, to whom Paul wrote listing evildoers, none of whom could possibly inherit the kingdom of God. The list included homosexual perverts. "Some of you were like that," wrote Paul, "but you have been cleansed from sin: . . . you have been put right with God . . ." (1 Corinthians 6:11). The sin was gone. That did not necessarily mean that their homosexual tendencies had disappeared (though God's healing and redemptive power has often worked here too). But now that they were Christians, their approach to the matter would be entirely different.

—From Branse Burbridge, *The Sex Thing*. Wheaton, Ill.: Shaw Publishers; London: Hodder & Stoughton, 1972.

FOR FURTHER READING:

Kirk, Jerry. *The Homosexual Crisis in the Mainline Church*. Nashville: Nelson, 1978.

LaHaye, Tim and Beverly. *The Act of Marriage*. Grand Rapids: Zondervan, 1976.

Williams, Don. *The Bond That Breaks: Will Homosexuality Split the Church?* Los Angeles: Bim, Inc., 1978.

HONESTY

WHATEVER WAY we look at it, being "real" is exactly what Christ wants us to be. Could I go so far as to suggest that ultimately your ability to be real depends on whether you allow Him to be in control of your life? How else can you be totally self-accepting? How else can you cut through your self-dishonesty and see your true self? How else can you determine your true value and bring yourself to the place of being willing and able to forgive yourself?

It is God, His Word, and His Spirit that create in us the desire to be honest with ourselves and show us where we can change and where we need to be self-accepting. It is God who gives us the ability and resources to change. He gives us a new perspective on ourselves as well as a new valuing of others, since we can now see them through His eyes. He gives us a reason to be forgiving. It is His humility, as demonstrated in Christ, that keeps our failures in perspective and prevents us from finding fault in others, merely to diminish the importance of our own inadequacies. God sets us on the way to becoming real by doing two important things for us:

He frees us. Romans 6:18 KJV says "Being then made *free* from sin, ye became the servants of righteousness" (italics added). This freedom to be real is crucial. What good is discovering your true self, as Dr. Carl Rogers advocates—including the experiencing of your feelings and the removal of your masks—if when you have found yourself, you still don't like what you see? You are then imprisoned by what you have found.

Even if you are no longer afraid of yourself, you are still not free. The beauty of the Gospel message is that when you have explored every ounce of your being, when all the dark corners have been illuminated and the total picture becomes clear, you are *set free* to become a new creation. You don't have to settle for the old. Trade it, if you will, for the new creation which God can offer you.

He transforms us. Romans 12:1, 2 makes this clear. The transformation takes place "by the renewing of your mind." Even as a psychologist I doubt if I could explain all that is implied in this "renewing" of the mind. I know that it can mean a major upheaval and that our values can change drastically. Suddenly we can tell the essentials of life from the nonessentials, so that we don't have to clutter up our emotions with reactions to that which is trivia in God's sight. We establish new priorities so that we change "I ought to" into "I want to," and each unnecessary "I've got to" in life becomes secondary to "What does *God* want me to?" We also have a clearer understanding of our obligations to others.

So, when you are freed and transformed you have laid the essential foundations for becoming real. You now have the potential for becoming all the things that Carl Rogers and others have so clearly identified as being the essence of reality:

- Genuinely authentic
- Openly transparent
- Acceptingly tolerant
- Comfortably understanding
- Empathically responsive
- Honestly integrated
- Flexibly adaptable

If you examine these qualities closely, you will see that they are all aspects of the fruits of the Spirit. The tragedy seems to be that Dr. Rogers and other psychotherapists have clients more willing to develop these quali-

253

ties than the Holy Spirit has obedient and pliable disciples.

—From Archibald D. Hart, *Feeling Free.* Old Tappan, N.J.: Revell, 1979.

FOR FURTHER READING:

Allen, Charles L. *Life More Abundant.* Old Tappan, N.J.: Revell, 1968.

Jacobs, Joan. *Feelings.* Wheaton, Ill.: Tyndale, 1976.

Powell, John S. *Why Am I Afraid to Tell You Who I Am?* Allen, Tex.: Argus, 1970.

Williams, Margery. *The Velveteen Rabbit.* Garden City, N.Y.: Doubleday.

HOSPITALITY

What Is Hospitality Like?

—an open door where they take you in
—a place where you are listened to and not "put down"
—a hospice where there is shelter
—the holy of holies where the presence of Christ is shared
—a couch where "reality checks" take place
—a party where people celebrate
—a hospital where healing takes place
—a home where you can be yourself
—a cozy ski lodge where friendships are made
—a bench at the park where you can reflect and reminisce
—a sanctuary where the sacrament of communion happens
—a camp where you are cared for, and people give themselves to you
—a little nook where you can live without fear, and experience community

What Hospitality Is *Not* Necessarily Like . . .

Words easily lose their deepest meanings and, thus, their strengths. One example is the word "fellowship." Christians tend to consider every encounter as fellowship even when it is destructive or superficial. Hospitality has suffered from a similar misuse. Sweet, plastic smiles, back-slapping, safe conversations, and comfortableness are not necessarily synonymous with hospitality.

Henri Nouwen, in his book *Reaching Out* describes what hospitality is like by tracing the meaning of the word in different languages.

In the German, the word for hospitality is *Gastfreundschaft* which means "the freedom of the guest."

Nouwen talks about the relationship of freedom to hospitality. He argues that hospitality is creating a free and friendly space for people. I agree that part of hosting is to allow the guest room or space for God to do as he pleases in his life. And I agree that it is one of the most difficult tasks to do. When people with different backgrounds, values, and goals get close to me, they touch many of my insecurities in a very short time. To give them space and freedom is hard work.

Hospitality is opening our lives to people. It is a way of ministering to an impersonal, lonely, fast-moving, fearful, technological society. The old reformer John Calvin once prayed, "O God . . . My heart I give Thee, eagerly and sincerely." That is the way it is with hospitality. We open our hearts to God and as we do so, we open our hearts to our brother. We become willing to take risks, be inconvenienced, and give of ourselves.

A number of theological questions are tied together. Who is God? Who is my neighbor? Am I my brother's keeper? The scriptures refuse to let these questions be separated. It is not possible to love God and hate (ignore) our brother, declares John the apostle.

Hospitality is developing the *attitude of a servant.* In John 13, Jesus puts on "the apron" and serves the disciples. It was not beneath his dignity to take the basin and towel, get down on his knees, and dirty his hands to serve others.

.   .   .   .   .

So, is the Lord calling us to allow our floors to get dirty and our furniture worn and dishes broken in our obedience to host people for his glory? It is obvious that hospitality is more than just throwing a party. Sometimes it means weeping with a friend, or staying up late listening to his story. It is not simply a quick prayer for someone, but, like old Abraham, we may be called on to share our tent, food, family, friends.

Helpful Hints

KEEP IT SIMPLE

In entertaining—we need to keep it simple. Gourmet meals are not essential. Meals do not need to be expensive and they do not have to take a great amount of time and energy to prepare. Perhaps you can invite people to a dessert only. Or, it can be delicious soup which is bought from a nearby delicatessen. Or, it can be a do-it-yourself salad bar luncheon for our weight-conscious generation. Simplifying your food preparation will give you more time to focus on your guests.

LET YOUR NEW FRIENDS PARTICIPATE

If someone volunteers to help, let them bring a dessert or help with one or two things when they arrive. That might be a bridge-builder to friendship that cannot be accomplished in a more formal sit-down conversation. If someone is willing to clear the table, or wash a dish or two, why not let them? It can help them feel more deeply involved in the event. It can be a means of affirmation for what they have done. It can help you keep your entertainment expenses down.

ACCENT THE UNIQUENESS OF YOUR APARTMENT OR HOME

What drew you to the place where you are living? Was it the entry way? an extra big family room? a kitchen with a spectacular view? a balcony? a big yard? What have you done to make those things extra special? Can you share that with friends? Have you visited that very old home in the inner city that is filled with antiques? Or visited a home with a large picture window looking out on a massive oak tree? The uniqueness of such places are more apparent, but everyone can learn to make their hospitality more interesting by accenting the unique features of their abodes.

SET HOSPITALITY GOALS FOR YOURSELF

Perhaps you will begin to aim for a once-a-month occasion to extend yourself to new persons. Plan it into your budget. You might even put something in your cooker before church, praying that you will meet a guest. Pray that God will bring someone into your life whom you can befriend in the name of Christ.

Another helpful hint that a number of people have shared with me is to always have on hand the ingredients for a favorite dish which can be fixed easily and quickly. In my bachelor days, a friend taught me how to make spaghetti sauce in thirty minutes with just hamburger and tomato soup and a few spices from the cabinet. It doesn't taste like a professional chef's sauce, but it passes for a good meal. And, of course, I prepare it with dramatic fanfare. I put on a chef's hat, line up all the ingredients, make lots of noise, and add many extra movements, and have great fun. The novelty of seeing me cook the one meal I do three times a year adds to the occasion. This meal is not only fun, it is inexpensive. Spaghetti is also one of the few meals that is a favorite of everyone in our family. What simple, inexpensive meal can you have ready for a spur-of-the-moment occasion?

My father's hobby was trout fishing in the streams of Lake Superior. Our freezer always had a couple of five-to-eight pound trout. As company came, the big fish was taken out and thawed and filled with lots of butter. To company, ours was the home of frequent delicious fish dinners. And they heard the story of the fish that was caught, rather than the one that got away.

Janelle is a mother of two small children, teaching two art classes, and selling her paintings commercially. She was also making and selling stained glass windows. In between times she led a Bible study and visited people in their homes on a regular basis. Somehow, she still managed to have numerous groups of people new to our community into her home for dinner parties. I interviewed her and this is what I learned.

1. Clean the house the day before. If you take on scrubbing, washing and ironing, cupboard arranging, grocery shopping, plus cooking in the same day, you'll be too tired to enjoy the evening. *The enjoyment has to outweigh the effort.*

2. Make a list of things to do with a corresponding time schedule—

   a) prepare the main course   4:00 p.m.
   b) set the table   5:00 p.m.
   c) potatoes in the oven   5:30 p.m.
   d) salad   5:45 p.m.
   e) change clothes   6:00 p.m.
   f) heat the bread   6:16 p.m.
   g) greet the guests   6:30 p.m.

3. Determine your goal beforehand. Why are you reaching out to these people? If married, it helps for it to be a common goal with your spouse.

4. Accept people where they are on that particular evening. If they want to engage in intellectual conversation, fine. If they want to crack jokes and laugh and release tensions, okay. If they prefer to be quiet and reflective, let them.

—From Bruce Rowlison, *Creative Hospitality.* Campbell, Calif.: Green Leaf, 1981.

Hospitality Notebook

When guests arrive unexpectedly, you can easily forget about the simplest recipes or where the guest towels are kept. Write all your guest information down and keep it in a "company" notebook. Include sections on:

Meals—List all the ingredients for several complete menus for two, four, and six guests. Write down all timing instructions like "begin roast at 4 p.m., casserole at 4:30, and pie at 5:00 for dinner at 5:45." Write out adjusted ingredients for each number of guests. Help yourself do as little thinking as possible. With the additional pressure of unexpected company (and the probability of someone chatting with you as you prepare dinner) you don't want to be reworking recipes or timing four different dishes.

Decorations—Along with the menus, write out the placemats, candles, and serving dishes that accompany the meal. Not only will it help you get organized, but it also makes it easy to have extra hands take over just when you need them.

Entertainment—Make a list of easy excursions for day trips as well as ideas for evening entertainment. Include such vital information as where the Scrabble board is kept and telephone numbers for local museums.

Preferences—Keep notes on family and friends' preferences, including food allergies, favorites, etc. In the excitement of the moment it's easy to forget your best friend's mushroom allergy.

Company Helps—If the notebook has a pocket, use it to hold a map of the area, a map of your neighborhood with specific directions to your house, a list of phone numbers where you can be reached during the day (if guests are sightseeing while you go to work), plus an extra key so guests can come and go. Aided by maps, a key, and your telephone number, guests can explore the area and entertain themselves during the day.

—From Dale Hanson Bourke, "Start a Hospitality Notebook," *Today's Christian Woman,* Fall 1982.

Breaking Into a New Neighborhood

"Bring six cookies to our apartment drop-in," the invitation read. We invited people in each of the twelve units and half showed up. It was the beginning of community. In that group, as the years passed, a woman decided to give God another chance. Another person announced, "I just found out this afternoon that I have leukemia." An elderly person protested, "You wouldn't really want someone as old as me. I'm not any fun." (She came with a whole box of cookies!)

Then we moved into a house in a new city, and I panicked. I was sure people who lived in houses wouldn't be as friendly as people in an apartment building. We would be too young, too old, and (when I'm honest about my worries) too Christian to be liked.

But God took care of my feelings by dumping the biggest snowstorm in Chicago's history right on top of the party I was planning for out-of-town guests. No one could come, so I invited the neighbors. The first man I asked said, "No thanks. There is no way we could find a babysitter." My husband quipped, "We were only inviting you because of your kids. We don't have any, and we think it's selfish of you not to share." We all laughed, the family came, and my new feelings of community were born.

Some community break-in ideas just happen—like our snow party. Others have to be worked at. Here are some ideas to start you thinking. Adjust them to fit your own situation.

Drop-In Dessert. Don't be disappointed if only a few people come. One of our drop-ins brought three women. Only three, and we had a wonderful time!

Plan the drop-in on an off evening. Thursday was good for us. Most people don't want to give up prime time for developing new friendships. Start realistically—right where people are.

Plan something for people to do at the first drop-in, especially if the people don't know each other. I like to have people make name tags from a pile of material scraps, construction paper, pins, tape, and other junk.

Ask people to bring something to the drop-in: six cookies, cheese, or a favorite Jello concoction. People feel more commit-

ted to an evening's success when they have contributed something.

Walk. Take an evening walk through your community. Say hello to people. We have a front porch—the perfect spot from which to yell to passing neighbors and dogs.

Do Something. Offer to do something for a neighbor—before he asks. Vacation times are perfect times for you to offer a feeling of security to homeowners or apartment dwellers. "Could I pick up your mail?" "Do you want me to park my car in your drive from time to time?" "I'd be happy to make sure no one leaves an ad clipped to your front door."

One of our neighbors turns on our back lights when we're not home. That has built a bond of trust between us; we feel a little less vulnerable in our city location.

Join. Join neighborhood organizations. Ours is the Northeast Neighbors Association. We are currently fighting to keep the city from putting a main road straight through our tree-filled community. Nothing like a good fight to bring people together!

Decorate. Decorate your front door for the seasons. Christmas is easy. We've hung huge red flowers for Valentine's Day. Easter would not be difficult to do. It sets your house apart, and signals people that you're fun and creative. It gives people a reason to say hello to you.

Kids. Make a big deal out of your neighbor's kids. Learn their names. Know their hobbies. Admire their pets. Ask questions that encourage them to give intelligent answers. Play their games. It's hard for adults not to like you when you like their kids.

Needs. Watch for special needs, and bring your Christian love and wisdom into the situation. When one couple's son was left by his wife, my coffee pot was on for the parents. My husband and I care; we hurt with them. We can't take away the problem, but we can surround the problem with love.

Fill the Car. Some of the older people in most communities don't have cars. So fill up yours when you go somewhere special. When we go to the circus, why shouldn't the retired man next door come along? When we want to try a new restaurant, why shouldn't we make room for the widow raising two children? These special events rarely cost more than five dollars, a small price to pay for community.

Pray. Pray for your neighbors by name. Or if you don't know the name, pray by location. If God wants you involved, he'll figure out a way. Just keep your eyes open so you'll recognize the opportunities when he presents them.

—MARLENE D. LEFEVER. Used by permission of the author.

FOR FURTHER READING:

Kilgo, Edith Flowers. *Handbook for Christian Homemakers.* Grand Rapids: Baker Book, 1982.

Neff, Mariam. *Discover Your Worth.* Wheaton, Ill.: Victor Books, 1979.

HOUSEKEEPING

How To Cope

Let's find out just exactly what we are going to do about that dirty word, *housework.* Everybody gets twenty-four hours a day to work, eat, sleep, and relax. Since that's the limit we have to work with, the challenge comes in putting as much as possible into those twenty-four hours while maintaining a cheerful and lovable disposition.

First, decide what your housekeeping priorities are. You are the only person who can do this; what is right for someone else may not necessarily be right for you. Your own personal standards of what constitutes a

clean house are the only guidelines you need follow. There's no magic formula for keeping house, however, in ten years of conducting home businesses while keeping a clean (or at times semi-clean!) house, I've found a method which works well for me.

I can't tolerate dirty dishes, unmade beds, clutter, dirty laundry, or obvious dirt. That means that in order to keep my personality lovable I must daily make my bed, wash the dishes, pick up clutter, do the laundry, and take out the garbage. These things are the absolute necessities of housekeeping as far as I'm concerned. Depending on your own personal approach to housecleaning, you probably think I'm either a compulsive housekeeper or a slob. That's the point! Everyone has to set her own standards.

After deciding what your housekeeping priorities are, the next step is to set up a schedule. Although my own schedule is far from perfect, it works reasonably well for me. Since I've already mentioned my idiosyncracies regarding daily chores, you're probably wondering how I handle the bigger nondaily tasks.

GETTING ORGANIZED

For me, Monday is not a good day for writing, but it's just right for cleaning house. Why? If your family is like mine and all of them were at home during the weekend, you may have noticed things usually aren't spic and span by Monday morning. This is especially true if your weekends, like ours, are filled with church activities and leisure pursuits. Since I don't do any unnecessary cleaning other than bed making, dish washing, and so on during weekends, Monday morning finds my house looking as if it needs my undivided attention. Therefore, I devote my Mondays exclusively to housecleaning and fill my hours with such tasks as vacuuming, polishing furniture, scrubbing walls, cleaning closets, and taking on any other house job that needs doing. Admittedly, Monday is my least favorite day of the week, but after all the chores are done I have the satisfaction of knowing the house is thoroughly clean, and I can do something besides clean house for the next few days.

Tuesday, Wednesday, and Thursday are the days I stay at my typewriter. I cook breakfast, pack lunches, wash a load of laundry, make my bed, and wash and dry dishes before I drive Karen to school. Then as soon as I get home I put the clothes in the dryer and plan what I'll cook for supper. With these two chores accomplished, I head straight for the typewriter and stay there the rest of the time Karen is in school. I stop work only long enough to take the clothes out of the dryer, to eat lunch, and to go to the mailbox. This gives me six hours a day for my work. I've found that eighteen hours a week is an adequate amount of work time for me.

Friday is designated as my "goof off" day. Actually, there's no goofing off involved, but it makes me feel better to think of Fridays that way. Friday is the day I buy groceries, run errands, shop, go to the beauty shop (once every six months, that is!), or go to the dentist. As every homemaker knows, a wife who stays home automatically inherits the task of errand running, so rather than grieve and fret over it, I just set aside a day specifically for that purpose.

In addition to running errands on Fridays, I try to vacuum the house (just floors—the walls, drapes, and furniture get attention only on Mondays), dust, and in general get the house looking presentable for the weekend. Of course, with all those things to do, plus all the errands to run, I don't have time to cook, so Friday is the night we go out to eat. If your family is in the habit of going out to eat one night a week, you, too, might find it helpful to schedule your dining out time for a day when it will benefit your schedule the most.

TIME FOR CHURCH AND FAMILY

What about weekends? For us, Saturday and Sunday are reserved for family and church activities with an occasional civic or school function thrown in, too. Weekend activities are always those that our whole family can participate in. Sometimes our only Saturday activity is planting a garden or washing the car or going to the library, but whatever the event is, we choose something the three of us can share.

Sunday is for us a church day and a day for relaxing. My Sunday housework is minimal, just bed-making, cooking, and dishwashing. I believe the "recharge" I get from a day of rest will, in the long run, be of more benefit to me than any amount of work I might do on that day.

This is my way of taking care of my housekeeping responsibilities while conducting a home business. All of my ideas might not work for you, but they can serve as a starting point in your own planning. Do whatever fits you and your family best. Just be consistent and stay with a schedule that works. It's the only way you can successfully run a home business without having the home business run you.

—From Edith Flowers Kilgo, *Money in the Cookie Jar.* Grand Rapids: Baker Book, 1980.

The Illusion of a Clean House

Have you ever tried to define what you mean when you say your house is clean? Does it mean it is freshly waxed, polished, scrubbed, vacuumed, and tidied? Or does it mean that everything is in order and apparent dirt or clutter is not showing?

At one time or another most of us have used both of these measuring sticks as a definition of *clean.* The problem is in the way we apply them. *My* house must be waxed, polished, scrubbed, vacuumed, and tidied in order to merit my approval as clean, but if I visit *your* house I see clean as the absence of anything to detract from the order of the house. I don't stop to find out if your house is waxed, polished, scrubbed, and so on. All I notice is that it is clutter-free and that the coffee table doesn't have a layer of dust on it. If it meets this test, I will probably think of it as clean, because I won't be peering beneath the bed to look for dust balls and I won't be opening cabinet doors to look for untidiness.

All of us tend to set higher standards for clean for ourselves than we do for others. While you won't think less of your friend for having newspapers lying on the sofa when you arrive for a visit, you would undoubtedly see yourself as slovenly if the same thing were to happen when she came to visit you.

A great deal of what visitors see as a clean house is merely an illusion. Without lifting a vacuum cleaner or a mop, a clever home-maker can, in an emergency situation, create the illusion of cleanliness just by putting things in order. Of course, it helps to be effi-ciently organized to start with so that in times of emergency "cleaning" can be done quickly. Here are a few of the things which can make a house appear clean even during emergencies or sicknesses when it is not pos-sible to do a thorough job.

1. *Get Rid of the Clutter.* If all homes were run with the precision and efficiency advocated by home management experts, we would never encounter the problem of clut-ter, because all family members would put away everything without being told. But be-cause all of us are tired or lazy at times, a certain amount of clutter will develop even in the most smoothly running home. There-fore, when time is short and everything seems to be going wrong, I start by getting rid of the clutter and, having won that bat-tle, I am encouraged to work quickly at the next task. If time is really short, it may not be possible to put away the clutter. When my father was in the hospital I stayed day and night at his bedside and I went home only long enough to rest briefly, cook a meal, or wash some clothes. I couldn't take time to put everything in its proper place so I would walk quickly through the house and gather the misplaced items into a laundry basket and tuck it away out of sight. The house was not clean in the truest sense of the word, but with five minutes of effort I had the house presentable. A week later I retrieved and put away those misplaced items.

2. *Do the Obvious Things First.* Other than clutter, what are the two most obvious

signs of lack of housekeeping? You probably answered "dirty dishes and unmade beds." No matter how clean the rest of the house might be, if these two things are left undone, the effect created will be one of untidiness. For that reason, these two things are high on my list of priorities even during times when my schedule is upset. When the clutter is gone, the dishes are clean, and the beds are made, visitors won't be nearly as aware of other housekeeping shortcomings. Then if after these chores are done you have addi-tional minutes, concentrate on such things as cleaning the bathroom, taking out the gar-bage, and dusting at least the flat surfaces of the living room furniture. With these things done, you can skim by with the illusion of a clean house until your situation improves enough to make thorough cleaning possible.

3. *Detract From Housekeeping Faults.* Most teen-age girls are especially concerned with their looks and work hard at projecting the best possible image. Accordingly, one of the first things a girl learns is to dress in such a manner as to emphasize her good points and to downplay her bad ones. The same thing is true in housekeeping. It isn't possible to have all good points, so learn to empha-size what is good instead of emphasizing what isn't. If a friend telephones to say that she will be at your house in ten minutes, what can you do? Eliminating clutter and putting away the dishes will mean that you will have no time left to vacuum the living room rug. Yet you fear the rug will be imme-diately noticeable. The solution? Try de-tracting from the rug's appearance. The bowl of daisies you picked for the bedroom can be quickly transferred to the living room, and your guest most likely will look repeatedly at the blossoms and may not even remember the color of your rug much less that it needed to be vacuumed. Household conversation pieces also work well for this purpose.

4. *Don't Apologize.* I have been in many, many homes while working with our church visitation committee and have had the op-portunity to see many homemakers as hos-

tesses. Although I deliberately try not to notice housekeeping flaws, some of these homemakers make it difficult for me. While I could move a stack of newspapers, sit down on the sofa, and forget the incident, most of them won't let me. Because of their embarrassment, they apologize for the mess and then make both themselves and me more aware of it by mentioning it. Offering excuses—or even good reasons—doesn't help either. I have been in homes that looked clean enough to me until the homemaker started pointing out cobwebs in the corner and dustballs under the couch. This is not part of hospitality and is not at all necessary. Most people who come to visit you do so because they are your friends and they really don't see as much of your house as you might think they do. (If you don't believe this, try describing the color and pattern of the sofa in the last home you visited.)

5. *Be at Ease in Your Own Home.* I can remember when the term "gracious hostess" was the absolute tops in complimentary phrases. What does it mean to be gracious? It doesn't have anything to do with how many rooms a homemaker has in her home or how clean those rooms are or how much the main dish cost or how many kinds of homemade chip dip are on the table. Rather, it describes a woman who not only can make others feel at home in her house, but makes herself feel at home there too. There is no quicker way I know—other than hiring a team of house cleaners—to make your house appear clean than to do the other things I have mentioned and then relax.

Being hospitable is somewhat easier than is being gracious. A homemaker who is hospitable makes her guests feel welcome— even if it kills her. A gracious homemaker makes her guests and herself feel relaxed. She is secure in knowing she has done her best—even if doing her best didn't include finishing all the chores she had set for herself.

—From Edith Flowers Kilgo, *Handbook for Christian Homemakers.* Grand Rapids: Baker Book, 1982.

FOR FURTHER READING:

Kilgo, Edith Flowers. *Handbook for Christian Homemakers.* Grand Rapids: Baker Book, 1982.
Kilgo, Edith Flowers. *Money in the Cookie Jar.* Grand Rapids: Baker Book, 1980.

HYSTERECTOMY

OPERATIVE REMOVAL of the uterus is known as hysterectomy. A hysterectomy is the most common major surgical procedure in gynecology. The operation may be performed alone or in conjunction with additional surgery on the tubes or ovaries, or as part of repair of the anterior or posterior vaginal walls. This operation may be done by either the abdominal or vaginal route.

The uterus is the organ known familiarly as the womb, because its function is to nourish and protect the fertilized ovum throughout the forty weeks of gestation, and then to expel the baby by its contractions.

The uterus is a hollow, thick-walled, muscular organ resting in the pelvis between the urinary bladder, in front, and the rectum, behind. This organ is roughly pear-shaped and, in the adult woman, about three inches long. The uterine tubes open on either side of its broad portion, and the small end, the cervix, opens into the vagina. In comparison with the size of the whole uterus, the cavity is a small, triangular-shaped area lined with velvety endometrium. The uterus is balanced in the pelvis by ligaments, which pass from the sides of the uterus to the pelvic wall.

When the uterus is removed, a woman's reproductive life is over. Pregnancy is impossible. The desirability of pregnancy should be of serious consideration. If a choice can be made in the operation to be performed, this decision is based on possible future effects on the patient.

Removal of the uterus inhibits future menstruation. Most women look forward to being relieved of menstruation but others look on the loss of menstruation as the end of youth and the beginning of old age.

261

Premature menopause ensues if the ovaries are also removed with the uterus. This does not present a problem to the women at or near the climacteric. And for the younger woman, simple harmless hormones, estrogens, can be prescribed to be taken by mouth. These eliminate the hot flashes and nervousness associated with the "change of life."

Interference with the normal sex functions is sometimes caused by a hysterectomy, since the vagina may be shortened. This encumbrance seldom follows an abdominal hysterectomy but does frequently occur in a vaginal hysterectomy. Regardless, many women find that their sexual life is more enjoyable with the cessation of menstruation, possibly because the fear of pregnancy is eliminated.

The most common reason for a hysterectomy is the presence of fibroid tumors, leiomyo-fibromata.

Fibroids are quite common in women. Approximately one out of five women has a fibroid and the incidence is higher in the Negro race. Fibroids are clusters of knots of fibrous tissue and usually are no more significant than warts on the skin. Although they seldom become malignant, the possibility does exist. Because fibroids are dependent on estrogens, they seldom continue to grow after the menopause. They are often multiple.

Fibroids are a reason for hysterectomy if they are the cause of profuse menstruation which incapacitates the woman and keeps her anemic; if they are so large that they produce difficulties because of their size (fibroids up to 80 pounds have been reported); if they are growing rapidly; or if they are painful or become twisted on the pedicles.

Myomectomy is an operation in which the fibroid is dissected out from the uterus, leaving the body of the uterus intact. This procedure is done in a young woman who is anxious to have children when the fibroid is either the cause of her sterility or would interfere with the growth of the fetus. Fibroids may cause spontaneous abortions.

Pregnancy may occur in a uterus that contains fibroids, and it often does, with the baby going to term and being delivered without difficulty.

Chronic bilateral inflammatory disease of the tubes and ovaries, or of the ovaries alone, may be a reason for hysterectomy and removal of the tubes and ovaries, salpingo-oophorectomy. Surgery is not done in the acute or subacute stages. Moreover, if sufficient and specific antibiotics are given early in the acute stage, surgery may be entirely avoided. However, if the tubes are so involved, together with the ovaries, that they should be excised, then the uterus also should be removed. In the absence of ovarian function, a uterus is a liability if it remains. If the tubes and ovaries are removed, the uterus has no function and often causes tenderness and discomfort. It may become the seat of cancer or tumor later so that another operation may be inevitable.

A hysterectomy may comprise a part of any surgical procedure in which all of the ovarian tissue must be removed.

Endometriosis of the uterus, inflammation of the lining of the uterus and ovaries, may require a hysterectomy and salpingo-oophorectomy. However, with the development of oral hormones, which prevent ovulation, this operation now is seldom necessary.

Cancer of the cervix. Hysterectomy may be done in the early stages of cancer. With the aid of "Pap" smears, more cases of cervical cancer are being found early enough, before the cancer has spread to the ligaments, so that more hysterectomies are being performed for cancer of the cervix. Radiation, followed by hysterectomy, may be done in cases still early, but extending beyond the confines of the cervix. Every case of cancer of the cervix must be evaluated by the gynecologist or team as to the kind of cancer, its extent, and its rate of growth before the decision is made whether to use radiation or surgery for that particular growth.

Cancer of the endometrium, lining of the uterus, within the body of the uterus, is usually treated by hysterectomy. At the time of the curettage, if the tissue is definitely cancerous, the cavity is sometimes filled with small metal tubes containing radium or cobalt which remain in for a specified time, forty-eight to seventy-two hours; and the hysterectomy is performed four to six weeks later.

Cancer of the ovaries is treated by the removal of both ovaries and tubes, together with complete hysterectomy. The same is true of cancer of either Fallopian tube.

Uterine prolapse, fallen womb, is a reason for vaginal hysterectomy. Vaginal hysterectomy is also done to repair extensive childbirth trauma which is manifest in the form of a large projection of urinary bladder into the wall, prolapse of the bladder, and bulging of the rectum into the vagina. Removal of the uterus disposes of the prolapse but with its excision, a better approximation of uterine and fascial supports can be obtained.

Uterine bleeding, from any cause, which cannot be controlled by other methods of treatment, is an indication for hysterectomy.

Cesarean hysterectomy may be performed at the time of a Cesarean section for various conditions which may be present, related to either childbearing or to situations in the pelvis.

The Operation

In abdominal hysterectomy, the uterus is removed through an incision in the abdominal wall. One of two types of operative procedure may be used, the midline operation extending from the pubic bone up toward the umbilicus, and the curved transverse incision below the hair line, extending up on both sides toward the hipbones. The midline incision is preferable in most cases because it requires less time to perform, permits better exposure, and heals faster. However, the scar of the transverse incision is concealed by the hair, which is the chief advantage of this procedure. The gynecologist decides which operation should be done.

After the organs are exposed, the technique depends upon whether or not the ovaries are to be retained and further, the

extent of the tissue to be removed. In a woman past the menopause, the ovaries are usually removed since they are functionless and may be the site of cancer later in life. If the operation is done because of cancer, a wide dissection is made to remove all the tissue in which secondary extension to the glands may be present. The urinary bladder is separated from the uterus, and the ureters, coming from the kidneys to the bladder, are identified so that they will not be injured. The ligaments connected to the uterus are divided and the blood vessels are clamped and tied. The cervix is seldom retained unless some special reason is determined for its retention. The vagina is cut from around the cervix and the uterus. Then, with or without the tubes and ovaries, they are removed together.

An appendectomy, removal of the appendix, is often performed at the same time as a hysterectomy.

The abdomen is closed in layers and the skin may be closed by clips or removable sutures.

An anesthetic is always essential. It may be of an inhalation type or, more usually, a low spinal injection.

Vaginal hysterectomy, which is usually performed for a prolapsed uterus and for repair operations, is popular with some surgeons, who use it routinely except for especially large tumors. The vaginal hysterectomy requires greater skill by the surgeon. This procedure has the disadvantage of not allowing for exploration of the abdominal organs at the time of the operation, and is quite difficult if adhesions are present.

—From Anna Mantel Fishbein, ed., *Modern Woman's Medical Encyclopedia*. Garden City, N.Y.: Doubleday, 1966.

FOR FURTHER READING:

Fishbein, Anna Mantel, ed. *Modern Woman's Medical Encyclopedia*. Garden City, N.Y.: Doubleday, 1966.

17 Women Doctors, with D. S. Thompson, M.D., as consulting editor. *Everywoman's Health*. Garden City, N.Y.: Doubleday, 1980.

I

IDENTITY

WHENEVER I reach a point at which I begin to wonder who I am and whether what I'm doing is worth it, the Lord seems to answer my unexpressed questions.

One morning when Roy was out of town I attended church via television. My hungry soul was fed abundantly, as I listened to Chuck Smith of Cavalry Chapel, Costa Mesa, California, say, "We hear much talk about 'finding ourselves,' who we are . . . and all of the other nebulous phrases we apply in our search for personal identity. . . ." Then he looked straight into the eye of the camera and stated this strong truth: "Instead of worrying about who we are and finding ourselves, we must first find God." He explained that when we find Him we will find our true selves in Him. Wow! I was all alone in the house, with only the animals to hear me. I shouted, "Hallelujah!"

By God's grace, I endeavor to explain to the folks the essential and eternal meaning of "finding yourself" every time I witness or do a gospel concert.

BEYOND THE LOOKING GLASS

To "find yourself" on a strictly humanistic basis is almost always a disappointing experience. Women are getting caught up in so many pursuits today that lead to dead ends on a street going nowhere. I was listening to a radio-talk show the other night when the interviewer, a woman who openly admitted she was "agnostic," was questioning her guests about their involvement with "Krishna Consciousness." Before the inter-

view was over the talk-show hostess admitted that she was searching for a "deeper meaning in her life," and thought that a "religious experience" via the application of the meditative processes of Krishna Consciousness could be the answer to her need.

Oh, my, how I wish I could have been on that program! I know "experiences" are not the answer to meaning in life. Many women are trying to make a career or a job fill the gap in their personal identity crises. Others cram their lives with social or community projects, or concentrate on physical fitness. We try this and that, bouncing from one activity to another, discarding this avenue because it has flaws, and looking for another path.

The relentless need to *be* somebody bogs down when nothing seems to satisfy. The truth of the matter is, in my humble opinion, that we are unable to change the inherent weakness in our natures because of original sin in our flesh. Hey, don't tune me out yet, if you happen to be one who scoffs at original sin. I don't believe the Bible teaches that we come into this life all good and pure, and then the world pollutes us. Because Eve yielded to temptation of Satan and ate the forbidden fruit, fellowship was broken with Almighty God, and that nasty little three letter word *sin* became man's plight. I'm so happy God loved us so much that He provided a way for our sins to be forgiven.

If God didn't care about us, He would have left us to flap around like a bird with its wings clipped. We'd never get off the ground. He could have said, "You folks down there are so smart, you'll just have to find your own way to take care of your sin and guilt."

Without God our efforts to find ourselves are so puny.

Identity Through Marriage

For some women, the search to find themselves narrows to the hunt for a husband. When a woman believes she must be a Mrs. to be complete as an individual, she may settle for less than God's best for her life.

Almighty God puts a spiritual searchlight in us women, and He intends for us to use it to find Him. Saint Paul said, "Follow me, as I follow Christ" (*see* 1 Corinthians 11:1). If we find ourselves in a conversion, born-again experience in Jesus Christ and we are married to unbelievers, our allegiance, according to my understanding, is first to God. We are to obey our husbands in the Lord. If he disparages our faith, we must stand firm in Jesus, not allowing anything or anybody to draw us from our beliefs. Jesus said that in heaven there is no marrying, nor giving in marriage, but we are as angels (Matthew 22:30). We must never lose sight of this truth. Loving our husbands to the exclusion of loving Christ is never the ultimate answer to our emptiness, even though a good marriage seems to be completely fulfilling.

In the first and last analysis, our allegiance is to God, through Jesus Christ.

—From Dale Evans Rogers, *Woman.* Old Tappan, N.J.: Revell, 1980.

FOR FURTHER READING:

Ruby MacDonald's Forty Plus and Feeling Fabulous Book. Old Tappan, N.J.: Revell, 1982.
Elliot, Elisabeth. *Let Me Be a Woman.* Wheaton, Ill.: Tyndale, 1976.

INFERTILITY

DOCTORS DEFINE infertility as failure to conceive after one year of regular intercourse without the use of contraceptives. Infertility should not be confused with sterility, which is an absolute inability to reproduce. Infertility simply means the failure to achieve pregnancy within a specified period of time.

Studies have shown that 66 percent of pregnancies occur within three months of the initiation of unprotected intercourse. Within six months of such continued exposure, 75 percent of the women have become pregnant, and by the end of one year about 80 percent of the women have conceived. The remaining couples may want to seek help. Examination and counsel by their own physician might be all that is necessary.

The essentials of fertility are normal ovulation, unobstructed fallopian tubes, and normal semen. These factors must be present for pregnancy to occur:

1. The husband must be able to produce a normal number of healthy, motile (or mobile) sperm cells.
2. The sperm cells must be able to be discharged through the urethra during ejaculation.
3. These sperm cells must be deposited in the female, so that they reach the cervix, penetrate the cervical mucus, and ascend through the uterus to the fallopian tube. This must occur at the proper time in the menstrual cycle for the ovum to become fertilized.
4. The wife must produce a normal, fertilizable ovum which must leave the ovary, enter the fallopian tube, and become fertilized.
5. Once conception has taken place, the fertilized ovum must begin to divide. After four days this tiny cluster of cells should drift down the fallopian tube and move into the uterus, where it becomes implanted in a properly developed lining membrane, and there undergoes normal development.

If a couple are unable to achieve pregnancy, it is because a breakdown has occurred in one or more of these essential factors. Infertility is usually not the result of defects in only one partner, but the result of several factors, often minor, in both partners. In seeking help, both husband and wife should begin by having a complete physical examination, asking their doctor to search for any condition that might keep them from having a baby.

The physical examination of the wife includes a routine pelvic examination, with special attention to possible fibroids, polycystic (enlarged) ovaries, and vaginal and cervical infection. The hymen may even be intact, indicating that semen has never been deposited at the cervix.

It is possible for infectious organisms to produce substances that injure the husband's sperm as soon as the semen enters the vagina. The cervix of the uterus may be obstructed by thick or heavy mucus. Tumors in the uterus (fibroids) or an inflamed lining membrane could be the problem. An improper tilt or position of the uterus can be a barrier to the path of the sperm. The tube where ovum and sperm meet can be blocked by mucus or obstructed by scar tissue from an earlier infection. The ovum itself may not mature properly because of an endocrine disturbance.

During a physical examination of the husband, any of these problems may be easily detected: undescended testicle, very small or atrophic testicle, varicocele, or prostatitis.

A testicle will not be able to produce sperm if it has not descended into the scrotum by the age of puberty. (Generally one should try to surgically correct an undescended testicle by the age of five years.)

A varicocele is any unusual dilation of the veins in the scrotum above the testicle. Almost always (85 percent of the time) it appears only on the left side, and is often detected only when the man is in a standing position. It is seen as a bluish, irregular swelling above the testicle in the upper part of the scrotum. The condition is similar to varicose veins found in the legs. This does not always produce infertility; many men with varicocele have normal semen quality. If a man with a varicocele has a decreased sperm count and lowered sperm mobility, significant improvement occurs 80 percent of the time when the varicocele is removed.

Prostatitis and epididymitis (infection of the area where sperm is stored) pose a threat to fertility, possibly due to a chemical alteration of the seminal fluid, or to obstruction of the genital ducts by scarring.

Fertility is often influenced by one's general health, so the physician will look for any kind of chronic infection, malnutrition, anemia, or a metabolic problem. We know that endocrine disturbance, particularly hypothyroidism and deficiencies in the hormones from the pituitary, adrenal, and reproductive glands can definitely affect fertility. Vitamin A is needed to maintain the production of the sperm. B complex vitamins are essential to pituitary function. Vitamin C (ascorbic acid) is thought to be involved in preventing sperm destruction. So both husband and wife will be encouraged to follow the basic rules of good health, with a balanced diet, as well as adequate exercise and rest.

The physical examination of husband and wife may be only the beginning of the physician's search to help the couple. Obviously, it is no simple matter to pinpoint the cause or causes of infertility.

Although infertility has traditionally been regarded as a female problem, it is traceable to the male in 30 percent of childless couples. In an additional 20 percent, the male is a contributing factor. (The Bible long ago recognized the possibility of the barren male: "Thou shalt be blessed above all people; there shall not be male or female barren among you . . . ." [Deuteronomy 7:14].) If the couple must be referred to a specialist, the husband will be studied first, since his evaluation is less time-consuming and less expensive.

However, infertility is always viewed as a couple problem, and each couple is thought of as a "reproductive unit." The family doctor will attempt to rule out other obstacles to conception before the husband is referred for a full fertility workup.

For instance, has the couple tried for *one full year* to have a child? The length of time is important in diagnosing infertility. How frequent has their intercourse been? Once every two weeks sometimes is not often enough to determine infertility. Have they been using any kind of artificial lubricant during intercourse? Some lubricating jellies are spermicidal. So is petroleum jelly (Vaseline). And any cream or jelly, even K-Y Jelly, will interfere with the mobility of the sperm. The use of artificial lubricants, particularly those that kill the sperm, will cause temporary infertility, but the situations can be easily remedied.

Has the wife been douching before intercourse for the purpose of cleanliness? This will have an undesirable effect upon the male sperm, changing the normal acidity of the vagina, so that normal sperm function and mobility are altered. Was the wife using oral contraceptives prior to the start of unprotected intercourse? (There is now strong evidence that after long-term use of the pill, the return to normal ovulation may be quite slow.)

The doctor will turn his attention to sexual dysfunction as a possible cause of infertility. Is there in reality an impotence problem? Or retrograde ejaculation, where the man feels that he is ejaculating, but the semen goes into the bladder, rather than through the penis?

The husband's occupational history must be considered, as well as his recent emotional and psychological history. Diminished fertility often results from strong physical or emotional stress, or from a buildup of psychological tensions. Fortunately, fertility seems to often be restored when the stress is reduced.

Certain environmental agents, such as heat and radiation, may contribute to male infertility. One important function of the scrotum is to keep the testes about 2.2 degrees cooler than the abdominal cavity. But the husband may be inadvertently heating the scrotum to body temperature level by wearing tight bikini or jockey-type underwear, or by the taking of long, hot tub baths. In primitive tribal rites, the men sit in a cold stream before having intercourse! Heat can reduce the sperm count enough to cause temporary infertility, but by wearing loose-fitting clothing for a few weeks, a normal sperm count will be restored.

Radiation exposure, either medical or occupational, may be the source of infertility. The germinal cells of the testes are extremely sensitive to this. However, depending upon the dosage of radiation, fertility may be restored.

A particular medication may be at fault. Most of the anticancer drugs inhibit the production of sperm, as do certain cortisone drugs, antimalarial compounds, diuretics, nitrofurantoins (used to treat urinary infections), and some drugs used in treating depression. Taking testosterone will tend to shut off production of the hormone which, in the male, stimulates cell function and development. It has even been considered as a male contraceptive!

A past infection may be the hidden cause of infertility. For example, mononucleosis or a prolonged fever can cause temporary male infertility, but this will not show up for three months or so. Also, response of the sperm count to therapy cannot be expected for at least three months. This three-month time frame should always be kept in mind. It takes the testes seventy-two days to produce the sperm, and another ten to fifteen days are required for the sperm to travel a circuitous route to the seminal vesicles.

If all the family doctor's lines of inquiry prove to be unproductive, the husband will need to go to a urologist or fertility clinic for semen analysis. Semen is analyzed for sperm numbers, mobility, and shape and form, as well as volume of seminal fluid. Sperm count may be highly variable when different samples are taken from the same man. Sperm mobility is estimated in terms of the speed of forward progression. Sperm shape and form is highly variable, and a 100 percent normal sample is never seen. Deformities are found in up to 15 percent of the sperm of fertile men. If more than 60 to 70 percent of the sperm are deformed, the chances of fertility are considered remote. Satisfactory mobility and normal shape are actually more important than the sperm count itself. In other words, the issue is quality, not just quantity.

In years past, normality was defined as 60 million or more sperm per ml (about one-quarter teaspoon) of semen. Today, even if there are as few as 30 million sperm per ml, the patient can be considered fertile if mobility, form, and structure are normal.

The *average* volume of semen ejaculated is 3.5 ml, or a little more than three-quarters of a teaspoonful. The couple wanting to conceive should remember that multiple ejaculations (four times within forty-eight hours, for instance) will definitely reduce both the sperm count and the semen volume.

If the average volume of semen has a normal sperm count, about 210 million sperm cells will be ejaculated during the usual sexual intercourse. This may sound like a great many, but from among this entire group of sperm, only 50 to 60 percent are fully mobile. As the sperm begin a progression toward the point of fertilization in the outer third of the fallopian tube, there is a considerable loss of mobile sperm. The vaginal secretions alone will destroy a large percentage of sperm, and the remaining sperm will be reduced in number, as they travel toward their ultimate destination at the membrane covering the tiny ovum. In the final act of fertilization, a certain number of sperm must attach to this membrane and activate the membrane, so that finally *one* sperm may enter and fertilize. You can see that millions of moving sperm are necessary for fertilization, even though only one sperm ultimately connects.

Some recent research has indicated that conception is even possible with as few as 20 million sperm per ml by using specialized procedures to make the best use of the sperm that are produced.

Postcoital tests are routine in an infertility study. The test is performed at the time of ovulation, and involves microscopic examination of the cervical mucus a few hours after sexual intercourse. This allows a direct look at the moving sperm to determine how their mobility is affected by the cervical mucus.

If the infertility has been caused by an acidity in the mucus that immobilizes sperm transportation, the woman should douche with a sodium bicarbonate solution (one tablespoon baking soda in one quart of luke-warm water) thirty to sixty minutes before intercourse. This will greatly improve the chances of sperm survival. Women with vaginitis need the sodium bicarbonate douching because it not only neutralizes the acidity, but also removes the excess discharge, allowing many more sperm to move into the cervix.

Because most of the sperm are in the first three or four drops of semen, the technique of coital withdrawal may be effective when the male has a low sperm count. This is done by a deep penetration of the penis, as the first few drops of semen are released, and then an immediate withdrawal from the vagina in order to leave only the most concentrated semen at the mouth of the cervix.

Sometimes artificial insemination, using the husband's semen, is recommended. The physician places a freshly obtained specimen of the husband's semen at the mouth of the cervix on the expected day of ovulation. Again, the first three or four drops of fresh concentrated semen are used. This process will be repeated two or three times during the fertile period each month. If it is carried out for six consecutive months, conception will occur for approximately 50 percent of the couples with infertility due to a low sperm count.

Here are some simple procedures to follow in having intercourse, which will greatly increase the chances of becoming pregnant, if no physical abnormalities exist.

1. The wife lies on her back, her legs pulled back against her chest with her hips upon two pillows.

2. The husband makes the deepest possible penetration as he begins ejaculation. Then he stops all thrusting until ejaculation is finished, and immediately withdraws the penis. Because 60 percent to 75 percent of the sperm are in the first three or four drops of semen, it is desirable to have this semen as

undisturbed as possible. Additional thrusting would bring the sperm in contact with the acid vaginal secretions, which are unfavorable for their survival. Sperm usually survive well in the cervical mucus.

3. The wife stays for one hour in this position with hips elevated on the two pillows. She then removes the pillows and remains for one more hour flat on her back.

4. The couple should have intercourse every thirty to thirty-six hours during the three days each month when she may be fertile. (Every twenty-four hours is too often!) There is evidence that the ovum must be fertilized within twenty-four hours of the time of ovulation.

5. There should be no intercourse for the three or four days before the calculated fertile period to allow the husband to accumulate the maximum number of sperm.

6. The husband has the maximum number of healthy sperm when he ejaculates regularly, at least every four days. More than four days of abstinence will decrease the number of sperm.

If a doctor finds the wife's uterus is tipped backward (retroverted), a completely different intercourse position should be used for conception. She should get on her hands and knees, then place her chest on the bed. The husband should insert the penis from the male-behind position. He should make the deepest possible penetration as he begins his ejaculation; then, stop all thrusting until ejaculation is finished and immediately withdraw the penis. Though this will be a tiring position to maintain, the wife should remain in her knee-chest position for one hour after the husband's ejaculation. Whether she achieves orgasm has no bearing on the probability of conception.

Even when no specific cause is found for the infertility problem, certain forms of medical therapy can be initiated. There may be repeated tests, observations, and treatment. Much energy, money, and time may be invested by the couple with no guarantee that a solution will be found. In the best fer-

tility clinics, conception in 30 to 40 percent of the patients is considered quite good.

—From Ed Wheat, M.D., and Gaye Wheat, *Intended for Pleasure, Rev. ed.* Old Tappan, N.J.: Revell, 1981.

FOR FURTHER READING:

Padus, Emrika. *The Woman's Encyclopedia of Health and Natural Healing.* Emmaus, Pa.: Rodale, 1981.

Penner, Clifford and Joyce. *The Gift of Sex.* Waco, Tex.: Word Books, 1981.

The Diagram Group. *Woman's Body.* New York: Simon & Schuster, 1981.

17 Women Doctors, with D.S.Thompson, M.D., as consulting editor. *Everywoman's Health.* Garden City, N.Y.: Doubleday, 1980.

IN-LAWS

INTERFERING IN-LAWS, well-meaning friends, and nosy relatives: this is the phalanx that newlyweds often have to break or circumvent. It is a formidable force to face, and only the united front of husband and wife can protect the privacy of marriage.

It is difficult enough for newlyweds to adjust to each other's habits and life-styles without having to carry the albatross of their families around their necks. Ideally husband and wife owe their first loyalty to each other. Yet love and respect for parents, and memories of protected childhood, cannot be put aside easily, nor should they be. Basically there is no competition between those two emotions: love for the mate and love for parents. Still, sometimes a not-so-silent struggle goes on between in-laws and a newly acquired mate. It results in an emotional tug-of-war which, to say the least, can be nerve-racking. Accusations such as, "Your mother keeps interfering" or "Yours is not much better, always insinuating I was not good enough for you," are commonplace. An endless stream of accusations, many of them fabricated in the heat of the argument, obscure

269

the true facts. It is time then to sit down and write the memo.

If, for instance, the problem is that you find yourself always going to your mate's relatives for the holidays or on vacations and you dislike this, then by all means say so. Your partner is not going to know what you really feel unless you talk up about it fairly strongly. You needn't do it in an angry way, but you should do it in no uncertain terms. Do not feel guilty about insisting upon your mate's loyalty. You have a right to expect to be number one and not play second fiddle to parents and relatives.

One major reason why a marriage partner will put the first family before the second is the feeling of guilt and obligation toward parents. That means that he or she feels uneasy for denying them their wishes and putting the mate in first place. Perhaps the mother-in-law cannot fully accept the fact that her son is married and has new obligations. She expects the same devotion from him that he gave her when he was still unmarried. The husband and son who has not broken the tie to his family to a reasonable degree will be very uncomfortable about disappointing his mother. He will try to pacify her—a mistake that is bound to multiply in due course. As we mentioned before, we should not feel responsible for other people's disturbances. It is his mother, in this case, who has the problem. She will have to work on growing up and realizing that her son has another family.

If she indirectly makes him feel sorry for her and guilty for her loneliness, she practices emotional blackmail. When a family controls a member of a marriage it often does so through this means. In effect the family is saying, "You are responsible for our unhappy state of mind."

Here is a wealth of material that a husband and wife could discuss or put down in writing if speaking to each other causes too much of an emotional involvement. If you can bring the right interpretation to light and let the marriage partner see how this situation looks to you, the offending behavior may change. By your calm written message

and simple explanation your mate will gain insight into what is disturbing you.

I recall the case of the very pretty wife who rejected her brother-in-law, making her husband quite angry with this attitude. Later it was established that the brother had attempted to fondle her in a most unbrotherly fashion. Her desire to avoid an unpleasant situation almost caused a bitter separation between husband and wife. It is not necessary to be approved of by everyone. As long as you are not being hated by someone, you have reason to feel secure. It is time that we realize how much more serious it is to be hated than not to meet approval. This sort of rejection is harmless unless we allow it to affect our egos, but hatred can be quite serious and lead even to bodily injury. Therefore, the difficulties you have with the in-laws or the misunderstandings with your family that develop after marriage may well be irritating, but they are not usually vital issues to your ultimate well-being.

—From Paul A. Hauck, Ph.D., and Edmund S. Kean, M.D., *Marriage and the Memo Method.* Philadelphia: Westminster, 1975.

Establish Bylaws on In-Laws

It was my privilege the other day to have lunch with an old friend. In the course of the conversation, my friend shared with me that for several months now, he and his wife have been separated. In the past several weeks he has made the discovery that both of them had been programmed by their own relatives to stay away from each other and encouraged to go ahead and get a divorce.

With moist eyes, my friend related that in a long overdue face-to-face conversation with his wife, they discovered that they still loved each other deeply. To be sure, the relatives were motivated by what they believed was best for their particular relative. I looked at my friend and said, "If you are going to make a success of your marriage, this is what you've got to do. Establish some bylaws on in-laws." Here they are:

1. Be loyal first of all to your mate. Do not allow any relative or anyone else to come

between you. Your love and loyalty to each other is first and foremost.

2. From this day forward, neither of the marriage partners will make any negative remark about the other to any of the relatives.

3. Neither of you will listen to or allow any relative to make any negative comment about the mate that you have chosen to live with. If it happens, you will kindly ask them to stop, and refuse to listen.

4. Honor and respect your husband's or wife's relatives simply because you love your mate.

The Bible puts the solution to outside interference from in-laws in this nutshell: "If you love someone you will be loyal to him no matter what the cost. You will always believe in him, always expect the best of him, and always stand your ground in defending him" (1 Corinthians 13:7). Put this kind of love into action and it will wipe out your problem.

—From Dale E. Galloway, *We're Making Our Home a Happy Place.* Wheaton, Ill.: Tyndale, 1976.

FOR FURTHER READING:

Fritze, J.A. *The Essence of Marriage.* Grand Rapids: Zondervan, 1969.

Galloway, Dale E. *We're Making Our Home a Happy Place.* Wheaton, Ill.: Tyndale, 1976.

INSOMNIA

SLEEPING MEDICATIONS are among the most commonly used drugs—both over the counter and by prescription. Plus, when you take into account the number of tranquilizers taken to ease the daytime worries that people lose sleep over, insomnia adds up to some eye-opening profits for the drug companies. In fact, more than 25 million prescriptions for sleeping potions are written annually in the United States—with women being the number one consumers!

Trouble is, although many people depend on sleeping pills to cure them of insomnia, the drugs offer no cure.

"Some of the most important aggravators of insomnia are drugs used to treat the problem," says Thomas D. Borkovec, Ph.D., professor of psychology at Pennsylvania State University. "Most of the sleep-inducing drugs lose their effect and disrupt the stages of sleep eventually."

Studies conducted at Penn State indicate that sleeping pills can bring on chronic insomnia if used for more than two weeks. As pills lose their effectiveness, the user tends to increase the dosage, which causes a spiraling effect. Anthony Kales, M.D., of the Hershey Medical Center in Hershey, Pennsylvania, found that when 10 participants in a sleep experiment were taken off sleeping medications, they experienced intense and vivid dreams and frequent nightmares.

THE REBOUND EFFECT OF SLEEPING PILLS

"Sleeping medications suppress the amount of the REM [rapid eye movement] stage of sleep in which dreams occur," explains Dr. Borkovec. "When a person is taken off the drugs, a REM rebound results. The person has very vivid and often horrifying dreams and the experience is much like that of an alcoholic having delirium tremens. A person often will continue taking the sleeping medications just to avoid the rebounds, which are most severe the first or second night. They diminish over the next four- or five-day period."

People who believe a little nightcap is just the ticket for dreamland should consider a different travel agency. Alcohol may send them off to dreamland, but it also shortens their stay.

"Alcohol affects sleep very adversely and should be avoided at bedtime," says Charles Pollak, M.D., co-director of the Sleep-Wake Disorders Center of Montefiore Hospital Medical Center in the Bronx. "When alcohol is first taken, it acts as a sedative. But then it metabolizes during sleep, causing a with-drawal effect. The person is aroused by it and will not sleep restfully as a result."

While some people don't drink coffee be-cause they think the caffeine will keep them awake, others believe they won't be able to get to sleep without it. The fact is, coffee dis-rupts sleep, says Dr. Pollak. "People may think they tolerate it well, but the caffeine causes arousal and disturbs sleep patterns. The caffeine in teas and colas may have the same adverse effect," he adds.

Most of us know that a good bout of exer-cise during the day makes it easier to fall asleep at night. But did you know that when you exercise, the *quality* of the sleep you get changes for the better? It's true. What hap-pens is that the rhythm of your sleep changes so you spend relatively more time in a phase that sleep researchers call slow-wave sleep, or SWS. Slow-wave sleep is a very deep form of sleep which is also the most restorative, especially to the physical body. Samuel Dunkell, M.D., a New York psychoanalyst and author of the book, *Sleep Positions* (Wil-liam Morrow, 1977), told us that "strenuous exercise for half an hour three times a week increases SWS. But this should not be done too close to sleep, because after strenuous exercise, the body is very stimulated. Several hours before bedtime is fine."

Arthur J. Spielman, Ph.D., a clinical psy-chologist specializing in sleep disorders, added that exercise done in the morning has no effect on slow-wave sleep that night. So it looks like the best time to exercise—at least as far as sleeping goes—would be, for most people, between about 4 P.M. and 8 P.M.

But here is the really interesting thing. The exercise-for-better-sleep routine works much better in people who are physically fit. Research by an Australian scientist reported in 1978 revealed that when fit and unfit peo-ple were given exercise, the amount of slow-wave sleep increased in the fit people, but not in those who weren't. Curiously, the fit people had relatively more slow-wave sleep even on days when they weren't exercising. That indicates, perhaps, that their bodies

had become conditioned to restoring them-selves more effectively.

Don't think that exercise won't do you any good, just because you aren't fit. All it takes is a good solid half hour of rapid walking after dinner every day for a few weeks, and you'll be getting the benefits of SWS along with all the others that come with regular exercise.

Habits are something that are pretty much out of style these days. Nobody wants to be in a rut. But when it comes to sleeping, Monte Stahl, associate director of the Sleep Disorder Center at Presbyterian Hospital in Oklahoma City, Oklahoma, told us that "an irregular bedtime is disruptive to good sleep." So try to find a time at which you are naturally and pretty consistently tired. Then hit the hay with just as much promptness as you wake up.

An especially good idea came from Wilse B. Webb, Ph.D., psychologist at the Univer-sity of Florida in Gainesville. Dr. Webb told us the need for sleep varies greatly among in-dividuals, with each person having specific requirements for sleep just as for nutrition. With nutrition, a person who functions best at a body weight of 150, let's say, can *survive* by adapting to a weight of 130. But that per-son won't feel up to par; a certain vitality will be absent. The same goes for sleep re-quirements. The individual who needs nine hours of sleep may try to crowd all his or her sleep into seven hours, but will have a con-tinuous struggle to wake up and will fre-quently feel fatigued—if not downright rot-ten.

Moral: a woman who shortchanges herself on sleep may be cheating herself of her zest for living. Why cheat yourself of anything, let alone the enjoyment of life?

—From Emrika Padus, *The Woman's Encyclo-pedia of Health and Natural Healing.* Emmaus, Pa.: Rodale, 1981.

Thirty Ways to Help Us Sleep

1. Change what we can. Delete late-night television or disturbing novels.

2. Think pleasant thoughts. Create positive and peaceful images.
3. Prepare through prayer. Commend ourselves to God as the day's final act.
4. Include others. Share the day's last minutes with our loved ones.
5. Set things straight. Reconcile any hurt or oversight.
6. Watch our diets. Don't stuff ourselves with midnight snacks we can't digest.
7. Expect God's presence. Anticipate that God will stay in the bedroom with us through the night.
8. Get some exercise. Do something physical to get our bodies ready for sleep.
9. Get comfortable. Check the thermostat, the bed covers, the windows.
10. Stroke ourselves. Think of the good we accomplished today.
11. Focus on friends. Consider those who love us and pray for us.
12. Affirm our faith. Acknowledge we belong to God.
13. Read the Bible. Center on the great passages of petition.
14. Consider others. Intercede for people who need assurance of God's love.
15. Anticipate tomorrow. Rest in order to be fresh and alert.
16. Don't dread dreams. Receive dreams as part of God's revelation.
17. Use a technique. Try breathing exercises or body manipulation.
18. Encourage mysticism. Feel Jesus' presence until we see him.
19. Celebrate interruptions. Enjoy the surprises God sent today.
20. Claim serendipity. Look forward to the surprises God sends tomorrow.
21. Accept ourselves. What we do is important.
22. Anticipate growth. Tomorrow will be better than today.
23. Don't rush things. Wait on God to bless us in his time.
24. Be honest. Admit what keeps us awake and seek God's help.
25. Make a separation. Divide the day world from the sleep world.
26. Build a bridge. Ease ourselves from the day world into the sleep world.
27. Affirm our election. Know God chooses us for particular purposes.
28. Commune with Nature. Find a place where we see God's handiwork.
29. Don't be afraid. God never takes a vacation.
30. Worship last. Go to bed on the note of praise.

—From Phillip Barnhart, *Devotions for Insomniacs.* Old Tappan, N.J.: Revell, 1982.

FOR FURTHER READING:

The Diagram Group. *Man's Body.* New York: Simon & Schuster, 1981.

INSURANCE

LET'S ASSUME, at this point, that you have started planning your estate by attending a seminar, reading books, and/or seeing an estate planning specialist.

As you continue to plan, be sure to take definite steps toward securing adequate insurance.

You do know how essential it is to have *medical* insurance, do you not? Anyone who fails to carry hospital and doctor coverage is like the fellow who drives through a heavy rainstorm on the freeway without his windshield wipers on. He's taking a terrible chance. *Fire* insurance is just as important.

BUT THAT ISN'T ALL

One of the best investments you can make for the future security of loved ones, and which should be part of your estate planning, is *life insurance.* The costs certainly are justified.

SOMEONE'S LIFE MAY DEPEND ON IT

Perhaps it is because we can't quite believe that death will ever come to *us*, that we fail to realize that life insurance is vital, especially for those with families.

During the early part of this century, few people carried life insurance and the "poor farm" was a dreadful reality. Widows and dependents were often left struggling for their very existence. If they had lived in this day and age, welfare would have been offered, but their living still would not be one of complete comfort and pride. If they'd had life insurance, all of that would have been changed.

Let's assume your wisdom exceeds that of many, and you realize that you must provide for your family in this way. So, you may ask,

What Kind of Life Insurance Is Best? Books are written on this subject, extolling the virtues of one kind of coverage as opposed to another. There are policies available such as *high initial cost whole life* and *ordinary life,* or *low initial cost level* or *decreasing term life,* and a myriad of combinations in between and on both sides.

Although all types should be explored, one definite consideration should be Whole Life Insurance. For some, this type of insurance has been a form of forced savings. A whole life policy has a cash value that increases as premiums are paid and, as time passes, this cash value can be borrowed by the insured for any purpose. Many family emergencies have been met successfully by the availability of these funds. And, of course, there is money for your loved ones should you be taken in death.

Also, take a close look at Term Insurance. This is life insurance carried for a period of time, known as "The Term" and usually for a particular purpose such as providing added funds while the children are young or going to college, to protect a business transaction, and so forth. A term policy can provide for continuation or renewal for additional terms of time and if in force at the death of the insured, it pays the policy benefits. A term policy has no cash value, you cannot borrow on it, and if it's canceled or the term expires prior to death and is not renewed, the policy pays nothing.

Then there is the Decreasing Term Insurance which provides for high benefits at the start and gradually reduces the benefits over the years, again to fit your needs, as the children are grown and become independent, and as your estate grows in other areas. The great difference between whole life insurance and term life insurance is the initial out-of-pocket costs, so your insurance, which probably should be a combination of the above, should be tailored to meet your needs and fit your budget.

All insurance is not the same cost since there is a lot of real competition in this field for your dollar. Therefore, you can find some very good buys with a little shopping.

Some of the most common questions asked regarding this subject include the following:

Are the Proceeds From My Life Insurance Included in My Taxable Estate? If you retain ownership or incidents of ownership in the policy, such as the right to borrow on it, surrender it (the right to cancel it), or assign it to someone else (so they can receive the policy benefits), or the right to change the beneficiary, then, yes, the proceeds from the policy will be included in your taxable estate. This is a major reason why your insurance should be a part of your entire estate plan. There are certain exemptions from tax for insurance benefits in some states and these should be considered in your planning.

Should My Wife Have Any Life Insurance on Herself? Most men, probably in the interest of economy, neglect this area, to say the least. They reason that the husband is the wage earner and as such should be the one who is insured. Now that more women are moving into the labor market, that doesn't hold as true as it once did. Besides, as my wife pointed out to me, if she were to die and I had to hire some of the many things done in our home that are now being done by her, it would cost a lot of money. I now have a policy on her. You and your wife should discuss the extent of this need and provide enough insurance to cover it.

Should My Wife Own the Insurance on My Life? The advantages gained by the practice of having the wife own the insurance on the husband's life were eliminated by the unlimited marital tax exemption contained in the Economic Recovery Tax Act of 1981. In the past, before the Act, this process was used by some to keep property out of the insured's estate at the insured's death, thus reducing tax at the insured's death.

Under the new law a spouse who dies can give all insurances and whatever additional property he or she has to the survivor in life or at death and have no federal estate tax on the estate of the giver or first to die. But watch out for the tax on the death of the survivor.

Depending on the size of your estate, your estate planner may, however, show you how to save taxes by sheltering a part of the insurance through use of a tax-savings trust—thus keeping a part of the insurance proceeds out of the survivor's estate while paying no federal estate tax on the death of the insured.

What Happens to Life Insurance Proceeds If the Named Beneficiaries Are Minor Children? The proceeds are paid to a guardian for the child, who is appointed by the Court. Many problems face the guardian and children when insurance proceeds are payable to minor children.

Who Should Be the Beneficiary of My Life Insurance? This is a question that should be asked and answered in conjunction with a comprehensive estate plan for you under your circumstances. Generally, in the small estates, everything is to go to the surviving spouse, so the insurance should likewise be payable to the surviving spouse.

If there is an estate plan that provides for a trust to care for minor children, in the event both parents are dead, then the alternate beneficiary of the insurance should be the trust for the children. If the estate is medium or large and warrants estate splitting for tax savings, then the insurance benefits should be paid to conform to that estate splitting, tax saving plan.

If you have dependent children other than those living with you, as in a divorce, you may wish to have additional coverage, with a policy payable for their benefit upon your death.

Can I Serve Charity Through My Insurance? Yes. This is an area overlooked by many. You can name one or more charities as alternate or as primary beneficiary. Furthermore, if you no longer need the policy proceeds in your estate for use now, you can transfer ownership of the policy to the charity or charities. If the policy has cash loan value, the charity can draw this out and use it. In this case, you not only receive a charitable gift deduction, but any additional premiums you pay are tax deductible for you now. And, on your death, the charity receives the balance of the policy proceeds and none of it is included in your estate for tax purposes.

If your insurance man truly is knowledgeable in estate planning, he probably will introduce you to an attorney who is an expert in this field, as well, to complete any planning you do. And, if he is wise, he will hold any final decision on your part regarding life insurance until you and the attorney work out your affairs in a will and/or trusts which will work together with your insurance to serve you and yours in the best possible way.

—From George and Margaret Hardisty, *How to Plan Your Estate.* Lafayette, Calif.: Carodyn Publishers, 1983.

FOR FURTHER READING:

Dayton, Howard L., Jr. *Your Money: Frustration or Freedom?* Wheaton, Ill.: Tyndale, 1971.

Fooshee, George, Jr. *You Can Be Financially Free.* Old Tappan, N.J.: Revell, 1976.

INVESTMENTS

Prerequisites to Financial Investments:

Give at Least a Tithe to the Lord. "You must tithe all of your crops every year"

(Deuteronomy 14:22). Don't expect God to bless your financial investments if you are robbing Him of the tithes which are rightfully His.

Pay Off Your Debts. If you are investing money that rightfully is due others, then you really are investing money for others without their permission. The principle in the Scripture is to pay your debts first, before investing your money: "Don't withhold repayment of your debts. Don't say 'some other time,' if you can pay now" (Proverbs 3:27, 28).

Commit Your Financial Investments to God. Give up all your rights to your assets. Dedicate your investments to His glory, to be used for His purposes. He is trustworthy. While suffering in jail, Paul expressed his complete trust in Christ in this way: ". . . for I know the one in whom I trust, and I am sure that he is able to safely guard all that I have given him until the day of his return" (2 Timothy 1:12). And He is the best investment manager of all.

Why Invest Money?

To Plan Ahead. "A sensible man watches for problems ahead and prepares to meet them. The simpleton never looks, and suffers the consequences" (Proverbs 27:12).

I am appalled at the number of Christians who violate this principle. I know several who have seen that their youngsters were in a church that preached the gospel. They have tried to provide a fine home (in most cases, even cars during high school) for their children. However, when the time came for the youngster to attend college, no money had been set aside to pay for an education in a private Christian school or even to provide funds to leave home and attend a public institution. In every case I know of, it was not because of a lack of income on the part of the parents. The irony is that if the income of the parents had been low enough, the youngster would have been able to secure a scholarship or a tuition grant to help with

college expenses. The parents had placed more emphasis on "things" during the formative years than on laying aside money to provide for college expenses when that time arrived.

To Provide for Your Family in Time of Need. "But anyone who won't care for his own relatives when they need help, especially those living in his own family, has no right to say he is a Christian. Such a person is worse than the heathen" (1 Timothy 5:8).

A boy in our tenth-grade Sunday-school class has learned much already about providing for his own family. His father, through sharing the Word of God with him, taught him about tithing. While working as a busboy in a local cafe during high school, this boy earned $150 monthly. Every month he knew the joy of giving. He sent $5.00 to his church, $5.00 to his needy grandfather in Florida, and $5.00 to the Billy Graham Evangelistic Association. (He had told me that the Billy Graham television programs had a real ministry in his life.) This young man was already following God's commandments to care for his own family.

Statistics reveal that most men do not save money. As a result, they reach the sunset years of life with little or no income.

Providing for your family in time of need means saving now. A prudent plan for managing your income, so that a regular nest egg is built, should provide money for unforeseen emergencies, retirement living, and an inheritance for your children.

The enemy of the nest egg is procrastination. Note the excuses of those who always seem to put off saving money till later.

AGES 25–30: I can't save now. I'm just getting started and my income is low.

AGES 30–40: I can't save now. I have a young family to raise.

AGES 40–50: I can't save now. I have two children in college.

AGES 50–60: I can't save now. My wife and I want to enjoy life.

AGES 60–65: I can't save enough between

now and retirement time to make much difference.

AGES 65 AND OVER: I can't save now. I'm living with my son and his wife.

Mishandling our personal finances is grounds for disqualification for a church responsibility. Paul writes: "He must manage his own household well, keeping his children submissive and respectful in every way; for if a man does not know how to manage his own household, how can he care for God's church?" (1 Timothy 3:4, 5 RSV). The idea here is very clear. Mismanaging family finances disqualifies us for holding leadership positions in the church. No wonder many churches are in spiritual and financial trouble.

Investing our savings proves our faithfulness and provides for future contingencies, family emergencies, and inheritances for our children. God is pleased when we honor Him by saving and investing.

—From George Fooshee, Jr., *You Can Be Financially Free.* Old Tappan, N.J.: Revell, 1976.

Avoid Risky Investments

The desire to secure large, quick, and effortless returns is the primary reason for losing money through speculative investments.

There is another serious problem I [Solomon] have seen everywhere—savings are put into risky investments that turn sour, and soon there is nothing left to pass on to one's son. The man who speculates is soon back to where he began—with nothing. This, as I said, is a very serious problem, for all his hard work has been for nothing; he has been working for the wind. It is all swept away.
Ecclesiastes 5:13–15

Scripture clearly warns of avoiding risky investments; yet each year thousands of people lose money in highly speculative and sometimes fraudulent investments. How many times have you heard of "little old ladies" losing their life's savings on a get-rich-quick scheme? It is not uncommon.

To help you identify a potentially risky investment, I have listed eight benefits that often appear in such schemes.

1. The prospect of a large profit is "practically guaranteed."
2. The decision to invest must be made quickly. There will be no opportunity to thoroughly investigate the investment or the promoter who is selling the investment.
3. The promoter will have an "excellent track record," and he is doing you a "favor" by allowing you to invest with him.
4. The investment often will offer attractive tax deductions as an incentive.
5. You will know little or nothing about the particular investment.
6. Very little will be said about the risks of losing money.
7. The investment will require no effort on your part.
8. You are going to make a "handsome profit" quickly.

If any potential investment has one or more of these "benefits," it should trigger a red warning light in your mind and alert you to carefully and thoroughly investigate the investment before risking your money.

Before you participate in any investment, seek the wise counsel of those experienced in that particular investment media.

Be patient! I have never known anyone who made money in a hurry. Diligence, study, and counsel are prerequisites for improving your chances for successful investments and for avoiding risky ones.

—From Howard L. Dayton, Jr., *Your Money: Frustration or Freedom?* Wheaton, Ill.: Tyndale, 1979.

FOR FURTHER READING:

Dayton, Howard L., Jr. *Your Money: Frustration or Freedom?* Wheaton, Ill.: Tyndale, 1979.

Gundry, Patricia. *The Complete Woman.* Garden City, N.Y.: Doubleday, 1981.

McLean, Gordon. *Let God Manage Your Money.* Grand Rapids: Zondervan, 1977.

J

JEALOUSY

JEALOUSY can ruin a relationship, mangle a marriage, and make life miserable.

Jealousy is a mixture of attitude and behavior. The attitude is primarily suspicious. And the behavior is basically hostile.

Jealousy is born and lives in the less conscious regions of the personality. It is not immediately conscious or understandable. It's almost automatic.

And jealousy is not incurable. It can respond to self-monitoring and deliberate change. It can respond to professional help, too.

In male-female relationships, jealousy has many parts. Here are seven:

1. Suspicion—an attitude which looks for clues of unfaithfulness, and asks searching questions, and gives motives for behavior, and distorts facts, and refuses to be reasonable, and can't be wrong, and sees anyone, friend or stranger, as a potential threat.
2. Distrust—lack of confidence, and the refusal to depend upon and have faith in the person.
3. Resentment—bitterness and hostility expressed in silence, or words or action.
4. Fear—often unspoken and often unaware terror of the loss of the person.
5. Dependency—mostly unaware exaggerated need for the person, like an addiction.
6. Imitation—possible unconscious copying of attitude and behavior learned from parent of same sex.
7. Guilt—for having wanted to do or having done what the other person is accused of doing.

Well, what can a jealous person do? How can he help himself with this problem?

He can monitor his feelings and thoughts. He can consciously talk to himself about his attitude. He can doubt his view of the situation.

Here are some ways of doing it:

1. *Question your suspicion:* "Am I making up all these ideas? Am I seeing things that are not there? Am I over-reacting?"
2. *Look closely at your distrust:* "Do I trust anyone? Do I have confidence in anyone? Am I trustworthy?"
3. *See what your resentment does:* "Does it push the person further away from me? Is that what I want? Is it fair?"
4. *Face your fear:* "What am I afraid of losing? Does this fear control me? Is it realistic, or like a phobia?"
5. *Decipher your dependency:* "Is it excessive? Is it childish? Can I reduce it some?"
6. *Check for imitation:* "Am I doing just like my daddy did with my mom? Do I catch myself acting like he did? Can I break up the copying?"
7. *Give guilt a thought:* "Am I guilty of what I accuse her of doing? Do I want to do what I am suspicious of her doing? Is it really me who is unfaithful?"

If these suggestions don't help, then get professional help. Don't wait, and stay miserable. Both of you deserve a better life!

—HUGH BURNS, Th.M., psychotherapist, Clayton Professional Building, Riverdale, GA 30274.

JOURNAL

The Story of Your Life

Many women are discovering that a private journal is a safe, silent friend, a place for preserving memories and for pouring out hopes, fears, and frustrations. It can also aid in communicating with our deepest selves, and with God.

I started my own journal at a time when I didn't want or need the guilt of undertaking a new activity that wouldn't work out. I was therefore delighted to discover that journal writing is very much a "do your own thing" routine. There are no rules or regulations.

If you'd like to experiment with a journal, the following suggestions may help you keep the experience pleasurable—not just one more abandoned fad.

1. *Motivation.* If you decide to try keeping a journal, do it because you want to, not because somebody said it would be good for you. Believe that you deserve the chance to find out if this kind of writing works for you. Tell yourself: *I am important. I love myself enough to spend some time and energy on this subject.*

2. *Materials.* If a consumer agency were rating activities according to the value received for the money invested, a journal would surely be at the top of the list. All you need is a notebook to write in and something to write with. The luxury of a handmade, leather-bound notebook may be inhibiting to the beginner. It would probably be better to choose your first notebook from the five-and-dime store.

You might look over the notebooks at stationery and office supply stores or at artists' outlets. Heavy-duty school notebooks, hardbound record ledgers, or unlined sketchbooks are options. Some gift shops, department stores, and religious book houses carry soft and hardback notebooks for personal writings. Sometimes these books have titles such as "My Book," "Bits and Pieces of My Life," "Memories and Musings."

While ballpoint pens are adequate for writing grocery lists or signing the kids' report cards, when I write in my journal I indulge myself with a good fountain pen and old-fashioned, real ink. Sometimes I experiment with nibs of different widths or with different colors of ink. Once you find a pen you like, keep it with your notebook and only use it for journal writing.

3. *Place.* While you may want to vary your writing location from desk to bed to the lawn under a tree in your backyard, you should always keep your journal in the same place between writings. Unless you live in a highly curious household, you probably won't need to keep the notebook under lock and key, but it should be a bit off the beaten track. On the other hand, don't hide it under a three year accumulation of *National Geographics* or behind the canned peaches. If you have to work too hard to get at it each time, you may not bother.

4. *Subject Matter.* Perhaps at first you'll wonder what to write. Some of us still carry scars from school years, believing we're no good at compositions or organization of material. Immediately dissuade yourself of any negative notions about your ability. Anything is okay to write in your journal, and any way is okay to write it. No teacher is hanging over your shoulder with a blue pencil; no one cares whether your spelling and punctuation are correct. Write anything that seems important or interesting to you, and say it any way that makes sense to you.

Although anything goes in a private journal, you will probably discover that describing a dress or recording a menu will not help you gain any knowledge about yourself or others. It might be better to describe a communication skill you observed, especially one that you and your husband might try. Or ask yourself if you're more relaxed as a hostess, or a guest, than you used to be, or if you enjoyed the evening or pretended to out of a sense of duty.

Maybe you'll paste pressed leaves, clippings from periodicals, or cartoons that prompt ideas you want to explore in your journal. One day as I was grocery shopping, I saw pots and pots of hyacinths, a flower that has a special meaning for me. My entry that night was brief:

> Bargain
> Hyacinths in the store
> Cost $2.99
> I smelled them there
> For free.

Had I not written the image in my book, I'm sure the beauty, the heady scent that filled the produce department would have been forgotten long ago. Now, whenever I read those few words, I experience the hyacinths again.

5. *Spontaneity.* Like coloring books that subtly teach children to stay within the lines, diaries with consecutively dated sections of uniform length are limiting, and eventually self-defeating. What if you don't feel like writing exactly five lines on June 1, 2, and 3, but on June 4 you'd like to write several pages about your class reunion?

It's not necessary to write every day, and it's unrealistic to pretend you'll have precisely the same amount of material to record each time. Better to approach the journal after a long lapse with a sense of excitement and something significant to say than to write, robotlike, 365 days a year about the weather and highway fatalities.

Perhaps your entry will sometimes be one word: *Harried.* Or perhaps it will be a few lines explaining why you don't have time to write: *So beautiful outside I had to dig in the garden all day. Too busy (and too happy) to write.*

There is only one inviolate guideline in journal keeping: Always record the date at the beginning of each entry. Don't simply say "Wednesday" and proceed. Write the day, month, and year. You might even record the time so that later you can compare early morning entries with those made later in the day or night. You may come to some conclusions about your inner clock, mood, penmanship, and so on. When do you feel most vulnerable, peppy, eloquent, or optimistic?

6. *Purpose/Audience.* As you begin to write, ponder these questions:

Is the journal for your eyes alone?

Do you intend to leave the journal as a record for children or grandchildren after you're gone?

Are you writing for another purpose?

In order to maintain your journal's usefulness as a safety valve, a private place where you can pour out temporary anger, mutterings about the misdeeds of your mate or offspring, and other provocations, you must be sure no one else is going to see it. In such a case you may decide to destroy your notebooks after a time or to leave instructions with a lawyer or trusted family member for disposal of the writing—unread—after your death. This is an individual choice. Perhaps you'll feel that after all that time it doesn't really matter if others read it.

Another type of journal has an audience other than the writer, though it may be a future one. Some women use a journal as a means of exploring inner feelings about their children's early years. Imagine the thrill of receiving letters written by your mother at the time she discovered she was pregnant, on the day of your delivery, and as you grew, waxed in wisdom, and passed various milestones of life. The writer of this kind of journal, if she is to be credible, must be careful to include the entire variety of maternal emotions, not just the "nice" ones.

Another kind of record is kept by a woman I'll call Norma. She came by it almost accidentally while she was keeping a regular journal. From time to time she included a list of prayer concerns and titles of religious books she was reading. The prayers were family- and self-focused, and the reading, fairly elementary.

As Norma's prayer and study matured, her journal charted the growth of her faith. Tentatively, with several other women, she started a fellowship group. They used their individual journal entries to prompt sharing at their weekly meetings. They made a special effort to avoid bragging or adopting a "see-how-religious-I've-become" tone. In addition to sharing the high moments and instances when prayer was most effective, the women helped each other through dry spells and periods of doubt.

If you're wondering which kind of journal to start, perhaps the solution might be to keep several—either simultaneously or consecutively—as your needs change. Presently I'm writing in three: my regular all-purpose and extremely private journal, a notebook all "Marriage-Encountered" husbands and wives are encouraged to write in and to swap daily for dialogue and growth as a couple, and a thirteen-month diet record. (I'm planning to wear my wedding gown on my twenty-fifth anniversary and am jotting down specific encouragements and obstacles along the pound-dropping, flab-firming way.)

7. *Attitude.* If there were a twin rule linked to dating the entries in a journal, it would be about candor. Provided your journal is private, there is no reason for diluting or adulterating the content to spare the feelings of others.

Indeed, it may be precisely to spare the feelings of others that you privately write accusations, gossip, or uncharitable thoughts. While I have never regretted any rantings and ravings scribbled in my journal, no matter how unreasonable or petty they seemed later, I have often felt sorry for words I've said aloud, hastily or in anger, to people I love.

Out in the real world we're expected to be brave, mature, and rational. In a journal it's okay to be cowardly, childish, or downright mean and nasty. In this sense journal writing is very much like prayer. If we can come to the journal with our masks and pretences down, we'll be able to release some of our concerns and worries. *Here I am, God, warts and all. Maybe tomorrow I'll feel differently. But for the present, this is the way I am—the real me.*

Total honesty is important for several reasons. Particularly if your journal is to serve as an emotional barometer, it must calibrate the pressures you experience accurately.

Take the case of Eileen, who for years has struggled with depression. She calls herself during bad times "H and H" for "helpless and hopeless."

A year ago Eileen started keeping a journal. During the downs as well as the ups, she daily rated her moods on the scale of one to ten. One represented total immobilization and ten absolute euphoria. At first there were no fives, let alone tens. Though it was an effort just to pick up the pen and notebook, Eileen wrote as frankly as she could about her despair, inertia, emptiness.

"After years of seeing myself as a victim, I'm finally making progress," she says now. "I used to think my depressions would go on forever, and that each one was worse than the one before. But I've discovered that the spells have a beginning and an end. Best of all, they don't seem as incapacitating as they used to."

Eileen credits the journal with providing not only the evidence that her depression is decreasing, but also the vehicle that assisted in bringing about the change. "I still call myself 'H and H,' but now that stands for 'healthier and hopeful.' Verbalizing was what did it, and my three-dollar notebook was darn cheap therapy."

Just as Eileen didn't sugarcoat her journal entries to attempt to make her life seem happier than it really was at the time, all serious journal writers should be more concerned with candor than with eloquence. Ask yourself: Am I telling the truth? Is there a more accurate way of expressing what I really feel? If you are bored or restless, say so, baldly, without alibis; then ask why, and pursue that also.

I may be beginning to sound as if I thought all journal entries should be negative, but that isn't so. Though I often write when I'm discontented, I also use my journal to explore happiness and even dreams I'd hesitate to reveal to others.

8. *Anticipation.* Instead of dreading the writing, train yourself to be on the lookout for little gems of insight, adventures, and thoughts you itch to record. Aim for a sense

of wonder. Even when you can't get to your journal the instant you have an idea, a key word or phrase jotted on a piece of paper or in a small notebook carried in your purse will bring back the thought when you're ready to write. Strive to decipher and transcribe these entry triggers at least every two or three days, or their significance will fade.

In order to avoid writing out of a sense of guilt, learn to think of it as something you want to do. If you don't truly want to, just drop the project for awhile and don't reproach yourself.

9. *Hands Off.* Once an entry is made, let it stand—inviolate, unaltered and complete. If you appreciate the need to be honest in a journal, you'll see the value of never adding to, correcting, or worst of all, removing an entry, no matter how strange, distressing or embarrassing you may find it on later readings.

A journal is not only a steady valve, it is also an educational tool. Many people use a journal to learn about themselves. Even if you wonder about the sanity of the person who made the July 17 entry, don't give in to the temptation to rip that page out or to obliterate it. Some day those very paragraphs may provide the insight you need or at least you'll better understand why you wrote as you did. Just as some people contend that everything in life is a learning experience, so most journal writers come to believe there is no such thing as a valueless entry.

Allow a little time to pass. Try to understand and accept the person who made the disturbing entry.

10. *Periodic Review.* Especially if you make fairly regular entries, indulge yourself from time to time by browsing through what you've written. This practice will prompt new or revised ideas and may also reveal growth and changes you might otherwise be unaware of.

A mother of five realized that her journal was crammed with descriptions of overflowing diaper pails, flu epidemics complicated by ear infections, and rainy, shut-in winters. Though these were accurate descriptions of her life at that time, she decided she wanted to include other memories, too—for balance. She put in her journal the first artwork her middle child brought home from kindergarten, a clipping about the book fair she organized for the children's school, an affirming quotation from Ezra Pound, "What thou lovest well remains, the rest is dross."

Journal writing, while useful on many levels and for many purposes, is not a panacea. It won't bring about world peace, cure the common cold, or deflate the price of groceries, and it probably won't solve all *your* problems, either.

But many people do insist that keeping a journal has kept them sane and, in certain cases, saved their lives. If you're interested, try it for six months—no less—and see for yourself.

—Carol V. Amen. "How to Keep a Journal," copyright © 1980, Lutheran Church Women, Lutheran Church in America.

JOY

Joy is an inner attitude not dependent on situations and things. It is not a natural characteristic, but joy can become a habit. You can learn to be joyful. And joy shared increases joy. Some lines from an old song put it this way:

> Share your joys, do not withhold them.
> Each one shared will sweeter be.

You as an individual can create an atmosphere and feeling of joy by your attitudes and actions.

To help cultivate joy, try this experiment when you get out of bed tomorrow morning: The first thing you do is look in the mirror, smile, and say hello to yourself. That will get you off on a jolly note.

Some homemakers play joyful music in the early morning. Others sing songs of joy and gladness. Do you know what this does to you and to the entire family? It sets an atmosphere, a mood, for the entire day. Joy is contagious.

Joy floating into the home during those early-morning hours gives Mom and Dad and the children a good start for the day. Sure, there will be some difficult decisions you need to make, some incidents that could be irritating, but making up your mind to be happy gives a different dimension to daily living—both for you and for everyone else in your day.

Another guideline is to practice looking on the bright side. Joy is a positive approach to each situation. Look for a constructive approach, for glad thoughts, words, and actions. When you're depressed, fearful, uptight, worried, or sad, look to God. Claim one of His promises. This gives you peace with yourself, with God, and with others. Joy flows from such a heart.

A joy within cannot be hidden. It causes you to overcome moments of worry and depression by singing songs of praise and thankfulness, by repeating Scripture verses, or by reviewing pleasant memories. You can laugh, smile, sing, and think positively in the daily situations and relationships with the family, neighbors, or friends.

Another help in finding joy is to have purpose in life—to have goals beyond yourself and the present, to be "other" centered. This springs from an unselfish life and from a heart at peace with self.

Knowing the facts and the demands of what you're about to do also helps put joy in each day. Through the years, I've received many letters from homemakers who never learned the skills of homemaking. Their mothers never taught them and they never took time to learn. Now they are confronted daily with housekeeping chores, with caring for a husband and children. They are swamped with work. They're frustrated, nervous, and tired simply because they don't know how to cope.

However, from some of these same homemakers I received letters some months or years later. Surprisingly, they conveyed a completely new life, a new joy. What has happened? They've learned more about themselves and about each family member, and now can enjoy everything related to them. They've learned the basics of their homemaking profession and are more relaxed. They've also discovered Someone who is by their side, helping them to face every situation. That Someone is God—the Source of inner peace, the Source of that inner ability to face each day and each situation with joy.

They live with joy each day. They enjoy the little things in their world—a smile, sunshine, health, a breeze flowing through the windows, the child's first steps, each new word, the smudgy kiss, a wink. They enjoy their home, the familiar objects and furnishings. They enjoy the relationship with each family member.

Ignorance and the unknown bring frustration and fear in every area of our lives. A successful vocation depends largely on being aware of what's required and being prepared. This is true for a successful marriage and parenthood. However, there's no excuse if one wasn't fully prepared. Any person can learn from all the available literature and seminars, from those with experience, and from God.

Many persons fail to capture today and its joys because their thoughts are focused on memories or dreams. Many parents either live in the past or in the future—when the baby comes, when they didn't have any children, when the baby will talk or walk, or how nice it was when he was an infant. Dad can hardly wait till son is old enough to go fishing or to help him in his business. Mom dreams about the day when daughter will help in the home or when she will be a young girl bringing her friends and dates home.

Joy produces contentment. You're not coveting *things* someone else has, because your joy comes from within.

In a happy home there will be laughter. Laughter is like a tonic. It's often relief for pain. At times it can be better than medicine. It's health to the body. "A good laugh is sunshine in a house," said William Makepeace Thackeray.

Laughter needs to be developed, and we

should encourage it in the home—not laughter at each other's mistakes, at disappointments, or at physical defects, but laughter with each other as we pull out the humorous happening or make an observation.

A happy home experiences family fun. This also includes jokes—old ones as well as new ones. The family plays and laughs together while doing daily routine chores. Singing together or playing musical instruments adds joy. Sharing daily experiences around the supper table or at family council can also add to the atmosphere of joyful relationships.

Another aspect of joy in daily family living is having basic guidelines for behavior and responsibilities. There is a security in knowing the limits—what is allowed and what is not.

God is a God of order. He has given us natural, physical, moral, spiritual, and emotional laws. He's also given interpersonal laws which, if followed, help families resolve conflicts and enjoy life. If these laws are disobeyed, it spells trouble.

Joyful family living includes faith in God—a faith that brings God into daily thoughts, attitudes, and actions. "The joy of the Lord" is their strength. He, too, is the Source of love—the foundation on which to build joy in our lives. He helps us to be joyful through troubles, trials, and temptations. These are necessary for growth and maturity, and for strengthening our faith.

The psalmist says about God, "Thou wilt shew me the path of life: in thy presence is fulness of joy; at thy right hand there are pleasures for evermore" (Psalms 16:11 KJV).

A joyful family is a great advertisement for the Christian faith! The incident is told of a missionary family who had moved to a foreign country. One day a neighbor came over, politely introduced himself, and announced, "My family would like to join your church."

The astonished yet delighted missionary responded, "So you've heard the Gospel message?"

"No," he responded, "but we've heard the laughter in your home and observed the fun

you have together, and we know you have something we don't have."

Such a family will be familiar with Bible reading and memorization, and prayer. They'll attend church services together. Belonging to a larger group such as the church gives opportunity for fellowship with others and gives roots and meaning to life.

—From Ella May Miller, *The Peacemakers.* Old Tappan, N.J.: Revell, 1977.

FOR FURTHER READING:

Evans, Colleen Townsend. *A Deeper Joy.* Old Tappan, N.J.: Revell, 1982.

Murphey, Cecil B. *Put on a Happy Faith.* Chappaqua, N.Y.: Christian Herald, 1976.

Schlink, Basilea. *You Will Never Be the Same.* Minneapolis: Bethany House, 1972.

JUDGING

JUDGING OTHERS will bring the wrath of God down upon us. He will be against us, because this sin is especially satanic. Judging others and accusing them is what Satan does. He is the accuser. Judging is one of the manifestations of our pride, manipulated by Satan. In great presumptuousness we sit in judgment on everything that we see or hear about others, usually without knowing the background and the motives of their behaviour or mistakes. Judging is satanic poison in our hearts, which can bring us terrible judgment, if we persist in it. Jesus tells us this clearly by addressing those who judge with the words: "You hypocrites!" (Matthew 7:5). Jesus threatens the hypocrites, saying they will not enter His kingdom, but the kingdom of hell; they will go to the "father of lies." So the spirit of criticism, nourished by the accuser, is our greatest enemy. We have to hate it from the bottom of our hearts and not tolerate it in the slightest, unless we want to find ourselves in the kingdom of the accuser instead of with Jesus.

How can we attack this enemy? First, recognize the fact that we are full of criticism and stop trying to explain it away. We should no longer make excuses for ourselves by saying, "I have to tell others what they are doing wrong to prevent them from making a mess of things." In reality, however, we enjoy correcting others and reproaching them. Often the real source of our criticism is rebellion or annoyance, because someone did something against our wishes.

Therefore, we criticize him and accuse him. So in the light of God we have to ascertain that it is presumptuous to accuse others, to reproach them and especially to pronounce our verdicts in front of someone else. Then we will become guilty towards our neighbour, by getting others to be against him, and this could seriously harm him. When we search our consciences in our quiet time, we should ask ourselves: Where have I brought guilt upon myself by judging others and reproaching them? What has my spirit of criticism brought about? Perhaps it has even ruined people's lives. Have I harmed the souls of people at home or at work by reproaching them again and again and continually accusing them? If we—perhaps as a parent or educator—have filled our hearts with this satanic poison and sprayed it out at others, we have to admit that we are subject to God's condemnation, that we were Satan's servants.

What a terrible harvest we will reap! Our criticism will rob us of the most precious gift that Jesus has given us: forgiveness and the blotting out of our sins. Criticism provokes the wrath of God, who has forgiven us, as the parable of the unmerciful servant tells us. Although He had forgiven this servant, He delivers him to the jailers, because this servant would not forgive his fellow-servants (Matthew 18:32–34).

So it means that we have to make every effort to get free from this spirit of criticism and whole-heartedly repent. Here we must act according to Jesus' words, "If your eye causes you to sin, pluck it out!" (Mark 9:47). That means waging an intensive battle against the satanic sin of judging others. Jesus clearly shows us the way and we have

to follow it. Otherwise there will be no release. "First take the log out of your own eye!" (Matthew 7:5). Jesus is exhorting us: Stop giving your opinions about others and accusing them, before you become quiet in the presence of God and ask Him whether you are guilty of the same sin. Our sin of criticism usually begins when we neglect to do this. We do not follow Jesus' words; we criticize immediately without first becoming silent in the presence of God and humbling ourselves under our sin which is even greater. When we come into the light of God, we will usually find out that we have the same faults, perhaps even more dominantly and many other undesirable traits in addition. Then we will see that our guilt is like a log in contrast to our brother's splinter. We will be ashamed of our own sin and lose our presumptuous and indignant desire to criticize others.

Then we will be struck by what the Apostle Paul writes, "Therefore you have no excuse, O man, whoever you are, when you judge another; for in passing judgment upon him you condemn yourself, because you, the judge, are doing the very same things." (Romans 2:1). And further: "Why do you pass judgment on your brother? Or you, why do you despise your brother? For we shall all stand before the judgment seat of God"— and be judged for this sin (Romans 14:10).

So today we must choose a new way, a new place. Instead of sitting on the judgment throne above the others we must sit where we deserve to sit: in the defendant's box, where we can be judged and hear God's judgment on our sins. When we are willing to do this, God will no longer be against us and we will no longer be in the hand of the accuser. On the contrary, we will belong to our Lord Jesus, who had to let Himself be accused in five trials. He did this, although He was innocent. Shouldn't we, who are guilty, be able to take this place? If we earnestly begin to judge ourselves, we will ask people at home and at work to tell us the straight truth about ourselves. Humbled beneath this, we will be able to accept the reproaches of others, even when they are unjust. Then our lips and hearts will be silent and we will not be able to criticize others so quickly and judge them so harshly.

Jesus went the way of humble love. He humbled Himself in the dust and let Himself be judged. Now He had redeemed the members of His body to live this love, which covers up others' mistakes instead of criticizing, which forgives and tolerates instead of making reproaches, which bestows kindness instead of criticism.

This does not mean tolerating sin. But if we should ever have to pronounce judgment, we will do it quite clearly but with a humble and loving heart.

But whoever wages a war of life and death against his spirit of criticism will find that nothing sits so deeply in our Adam's nature as the spirit of criticism. It will not disappear overnight by making one commitment, "I want to let myself be judged and place my mouth in the dust." No, our blood is infected with it. There is only one Person who is stronger than our old Adam. It is Jesus Christ. His blood has greater power than the blood that we have inherited from our fathers. This blood of Jesus has complete power to free us, if we call upon it ever anew; in it there is really power to cleanse us from our sins, from the great sin of judging others, from hypocrisy, which makes us guilty and brings us into Satan's hands. In faith we must appropriate the redeeming power of this blood. This will only happen in an intensive fight against this sin, in a daily battle of faith and prayer. This includes speaking the "nevertheless" of faith in spite of the defeats we experience: "I am redeemed to love and to forgive!" Whoever is willing to endure in this battle in spite of his short-comings, believing in Jesus' redemption, will be freed from his great sin of judging others.

—From Basilea Schlink, *You Will Never Be the Same.* Published and copyright 1972, Bethany House Publishers, Minneapolis, Minnesota 55438.

FOR FURTHER READING:

Ghezzi, Bert. *The Angry Christian.* Ann Arbor: Servant, 1980.

Shedd, Charlie W. *Letters to Karen.* Nashville: Abingdon, 1965.

Stoop, David. *Self-Talk.* Old Tappan, N.J.: Revell, 1982.

L

LATCH-KEY CHILDREN

LATCH-KEY CHILDREN come home from school to an empty house every day. Either or both parents are still at work, or it is a single-parent family. Because these children wear or carry a house key, they have been given this name. No one knows how many children go home and care for themselves until an adult arrives. There may be as many as 8 million in the United States, and the number continues to grow. Precise figures will probably never be known because most parents (often guilt-ridden) urge their children not to tell others that they are alone.

What can parents do to make the best of their situation for latch-key children? Here are practical tips for parents to give their offspring.

1. Instruct children never to tell strangers they are alone.
2. Tell them not to say, when answering the phone, "My mother hasn't come home yet" or even "My mother isn't here." Instead, teach your child to say something such as "I'm sorry but she can't come to the phone just now. Would you like to leave a message?"
3. Give your child responsibilities. The nothing-to-do situation can result in endless television watching or the temptation to leave the house out of boredom.
4. Teach your child to cook—even simple meals. Or leave instructions to turn on the oven or plug in the crock pot.
5. Instruct your child on emergency strategies, such as a telephone number where you can be reached and the name of a nearby neighbor who can help if needed.

6. Instruct your child to keep the doors locked. If strangers come, the child must not let them in. Instead, he or she can say, "My mother's busy now and she says I can't let anyone in."
7. Most important of all, explain the situation to your child so that he or she understands why no one is home after school.

—CECIL MURPHEY

LEAVING HOME

THE YOUNG WOMAN experiences ambiguity concerning leaving home, for leaving implies loneliness, risk, and taking responsibility for oneself and one's body. Separation from the secure world-view makes one vulnerable and confused about how to make choices, what to do, what paths to follow, which relationships to pursue. The fear of freedom is connected in the life of every adolescent with making mistakes and the lack of approval from society. To know who I am, I must take my search seriously, and, though I am afraid, I must explore all elements of my life. Women in this society have not been taught that they too have a spiritual quest, that they shape and mold their self-identity. It is harder for a woman in our culture to trust her freedom, to actualize her powers and risk herself. On one level her fear comes from her sexual vulnerability. She *must* wrestle with the responsibility for her procreative potential. She must deal with her identity and how it relates to the expression

287

of her sexuality. Who am I? for a woman is not identical with her sexual role, but it cannot exclude a consideration of it and a decision about its potential expression.

The reality of female sexuality leads many young girls to respond to the ambiguity of the adolescent life-crisis by assuming a false identity. Identifying oneself with one's body is no longer a graceful option in our world but represents a demonic solution. Erikson calls it a "false ideology," a meaning system to which one turns to avoid the risks and confusion of the crisis stage. It is not a true resolution but represents being overwhelmed by the terrors of making choices, the fears of responsibility.

A young woman often turns to her sexuality to protect her from the implications of this identity crisis. She defines herself in terms of her attractiveness to boys and focuses all value in her need to be loved. Her sexual attractiveness thus becomes the totality of her identity, and she is unable to trust any other element of her personhood, either her physical, intellectual, or creative powers. She has no sense of self-worth but is defined from without by the response that men give her. Her sexuality is manipulative since it is expressed, not from self-love, but out of a desperate need to find identity in being loved. Her sexuality often seems to rule her, for she lacks any self-understanding and purpose except in the immediate moment.

What women really want, I hope, is to be whole, and in this wholeness a true identity and a sense of ultimate worth may be found. A woman's vulnerability in her sexuality often causes her to ignore her other creative aspects, her intellectual, artistic, and physical powers. Women are particularly prone to solve the crisis of adolescence by submerging themselves into another. Relationships with others *are* essential elements of a woman's self-discovery, but no one of them offers the solution to the question of her identity or an ultimate value by which she can define her life.

. . . . .

The young woman who embarks on her journey away from home with a healthy degree of confidence in her worth and a trust in her powers cannot be destroyed by the hardships and ambiguity. As she engages life in the many aspects it presents, she will discover a greater sense of worth and a greater ability to know what she wants. Taking responsibility for herself, financially as well as ethically, will give her a clearer sense of what is ultimately valuable for her and enhance her sense of trust in her own perceptions of reality. Intellectual challenge, financial survival, responsibility for sexual behavior, finding new friends and relationships, new tests of physical strengths, are all aspects of this creative experimentation in order to discover one's particular personal meaning structure. There will be failures, choices that lead nowhere, experiences which appear destructive and unproductive.

We cannot protect the individual from these failures; indeed it is necessary that she undergo them, for without some loss nothing new can be born.

—From Penelope Washbourn, *Becoming Woman.* New York: Harper & Row, 1977.

LIFE STAGES

IT IS REMARKABLE that we have no standard language for identifying the major seasons of the life cycle. Is there a valid and useful way to divide the total life cycle into several gross segments, each having its own distinctive character? We can probably agree without difficulty on an initial segment of some twenty years, a pre-adult phase embracing childhood and adolescence. There is also "old age," which starts at age sixty or sixty-five. Gerontology has thus far provided considerable information, though little understanding, about this time of life. But what about the adult years between twenty and sixty-five. Though everyday language provides terms such as "youth" and "middle age," there is little agreement regarding their definition and their place in the life cycle.

Our view of the life cycle is a product of our research. It is not an armchair speculation or assumption we made beforehand. We believe that the life cycle evolves through a sequence of eras each lasting roughly twenty-five years. The eras are partially overlapping, so that a new one is getting under way as the previous one is being terminated. The sequence goes as follows:

1. Childhood and adolescence: age 0–22
2. Early adulthood: age 17–45
3. Middle adulthood: age 40–65
4. Late adulthood: age 60–?

An era is a "time of life" in the broadest sense. Although important changes go on within it, each era has its own distinctive and unifying qualities, which have to do with the *character of living*. In studying the character of living, we take account of biological, psychological and social aspects, but do not focus on any one of these to the exclusion of the others. An era is thus not a stage in biological development, in personality development or in career development. It is much broader and more inclusive than a developmental stage or period. The sequence of eras constitutes the macro-structure of the life cycle. It provides a framework within which developmental periods and concrete processes of everyday living take place. The eras are analogous to the acts of a play, the major divisions of a novel, or the gross segments into which a biographer divides the life of his subject. The developmental periods give a finer picture of the dramatic events and the details of living; the eras give an overview of the life cycle as a whole.

The main focus of our study, as I have mentioned, is on the years from the late teens to the late forties. On the basis of this study, we identify early and middle adulthood as separate eras in the life cycle. Early adulthood comes to an end in a man's forties, when the character of living once more un-

dergoes a fundamental change and middle adulthood begins to emerge. One of the most important—and most controversial—contributions of this study is the demarcation between early and middle adulthood as clearly defined eras.

I have set forth a specific age at which each era begins, and another at which it ends. This is not to say, however, that a bell rings at precisely the same point for everyone, demarcating the eras as though they were rounds in a boxing match or classes in a highly regulated school. Life is never that standardized. There is an average or most frequent age for the onset and completion of every era. There is also a range of variation around the average. The variation is contained, however, within fairly narrow limits—probably not more than five or six years. The discovery of age-linked eras is another unexpected finding of our study. This finding goes against the conventional assumption that development does not occur in adulthood or, if it does, that its pace varies tremendously and has almost no connection to age. On the contrary, it seems to be closely age-linked.

The move from one era to the next is neither simple nor brief. It requires a basic change in the fabric of one's life, and this takes more than a day, a month or even a year. The transition between eras consistently takes four or five years—not less than three and rarely more than six. This transition is the work of a developmental period that links the eras and provides some continuity between them. A developmental transition creates a boundary zone in which a man terminates the outgoing era and initiates the incoming one.

Though pre-adulthood ends at roughly age twenty-two, early adulthood begins several years earlier, usually at seventeen. The span from seventeen to twenty-two is thus a "zone of overlap," a period in which the old era is being completed and the new one is starting. This period is the Early Adult Transition. It bridges the two eras and is part of both. Likewise, the Mid-life Transition extends from roughly forty to forty-five. It serves to terminate early adulthood and to initiate middle adulthood. There is a subsequent transition in the early sixties, we believe, and perhaps another at about eighty.

—From Daniel J. Levinson, et al., *The Seasons of a Man's Life.* New York: Knopf, 1978.

Life Stages of Women

The general pattern of the life-cycle applies to both men and women, but the rhythms of the male and female cycles differ. The differences are related to the physiology and social roles of the sexes. [Gail] Sheehy has categorized the paths which women typically choose to follow. These life patterns, established in the twenties also affect the transitions of the later years. The *care-givers* marry young and envisage their lifework as centered in the home. *Either-or women* feel compelled to choose between work and marriage. Those who marry postpone their career until later; others put off marriage or childbearing or both in order to get established in a career. *Integrators* try to combine marriage, motherhood, and work during their twenties. The *never-married* are women who will remain single, often playing nurturing roles in helping professions such as nursing or unconsciously serving as "office wife" to a male boss. Finally, *transients* are women who never settle down in their twenties, but wander from job to job, emotional attachment to emotional attachment, place to place. Of course, Sheehy's categories are merely suggestive of life patterns; they are not definite. In real life, people cannot be pigeonholed so neatly.

Change and growth are so basic to adult experience that no woman can automatically view herself as "locked into" a single role or career for her entire life. The courage to change is both active and passive; it is the courage to face and accept changes within ourselves and others and the courage to take risks to change the direction of our lives and work.

IDENTITY, WORK, AND GOD'S PLAN FOR OUR LIVES

Erik Erikson has indicated that in the healthy personality a sense of inner identity begins to emerge as the individual leaves adolescence and enters adulthood. "Identity" connotes several things: a conscious sense of being a unique individual, a feeling of continuity of the self and a striving to maintain this continuity, an integrated "I," and a feeling of belonging or solidarity. During the transitions of adulthood that "I" is still in the process of becoming integrated or complete, and at times we may feel that our sense of identity has become confused or lost as we try to discover new sides of our personality, or launch out in new directions.

Christians struggle, just like non-Christians, to find their authentic "I." Women in particular have had to learn the lesson of acceptance by Christ and responsibility for self, both keys to a healthy concept of the self. Identity is so intertwined with the life-cycle and the choices we make in our twenties that our job can be an important and valuable way by which we establish our identity and self-esteem.

An additional factor in the attitude of Christian women toward their identity and their work is their understanding of the sovereignty of God. One of the most quoted clichés in Christian circles today is "God has a plan for your life." The New Testament unmistakably indicates that there is a divine purpose for each life, a purpose related both to redemption and to spiritual vocation. Jesus speaks of the fulfillment of the divine purpose as the central factor of his life. "My food . . . is to do the will of him who sent me and to finish his work" (John 4:34). Paul comments, "It is God who works in you to will and act according to his good purpose" (Philippians 2:13), implying that the Holy Spirit is constantly empowering us to be obedient to the will of God. And in the well-known passage on predestination in Ephesians 1:3–14, Paul develops a theology of the sovereignty of God by which God wills or chooses that we should be redeemed and adopted as children in the divine family.

Nowhere does biblical teaching indicate that the purpose or will of God is a blueprint to which no alterations or additions can be made. In reality, God's will unfolds for us just as our personality or identity unfolds in time. Being open to change and finding the courage to change, while being conscious of remaining in God's will, are signs of spiritual, as well as psychological, maturity. Paul Tournier has described the essence of life as movement. Grace is not extended to us in a rigid, fixed way; it is granted within the natural dynamic of the life process. God's purpose and his grace may lead us to dramatic moments of choice, but the stuff of life is made up of imperceptible, gradual change leading us to those choices.

. . . .

THE TWENTIES

Marisa was engaged and looking forward to her marriage when she talked with us. Although her concerns are representative of many women in their twenties, she is refreshingly flexible about her future roles and future work. She teaches government and history in a Catholic high school in a working-class area near Boston. Her fiancé is a journalist and a nurse. Marisa views her identity as quite distinct from her work. "I have never been a very career-oriented person. My teaching is an outgrowth of my Christian commitment and my sense of needing a ministry which uses my gifts. I never felt that my career was something that was walled off and that had to go on no matter what. I could stop teaching high-school students. I could have children. I could have a part-time, or maybe even a volunteer job where I teach something to someone, and that would be fine with me. I don't need to be professional or even to be paid to feel that I have a career.

"I have a friend who is definitely career-oriented. For her to be 'out of the market,'

and out of the struggle of being on top and being known professionally, would be death. Her identity is very tied up with that; mine is not." Marisa continued by explaining that her future husband, although committed to being an artist, was not career-oriented either. "He has a strong sense that family comes first. I can see Michael and me sharing a lot of home responsibilities. I think he will be with the kids as much as I will be with the kids. He feels that the man should be doing that. He doesn't have this rigidity about roles."

We found that the relative importance of work to the self-esteem and identity of individual women varied tremendously according to background, personality, and where they were in the life-cycle. For example, Marisa was about to enter a stage where her primary role would be within the home. Although she expected to work outside the home in the future, having a career was relatively unimportant to her. Barbara, on the other hand, faced a struggle over the issues of career and marriage. She is in her twenties, married, and has two sons, aged five and four. She never envisaged herself as staying home with small children, even on a temporary basis. "I never liked to baby-sit. I never liked to cook. I had never been shopping until I got married. It took me about two hours to do our first week's shopping. I just didn't have the interest. . . . I was really frightened about having no identity, and I saw being a mother as having no identity. The reason that we decided to have children was that two couples we knew who had children remained very active in a lot of things and really enjoyed their children and had their children be a part of things."

. . . .

Since the accepted social pattern has been for women to marry in their late teens or early twenties, those who remain single face a number of transitions which set them apart from the "norms" of society. Beth is twenty-two, a graduate student in mathematics, and a teaching assistant. She is from a rural coal-mining area of Pennsylvania where few women go to college and almost everyone stays in "the valley," marries, and raises a family. "The small town that I come from is such that very few of the women have had college education, and the ones that have are mostly teachers in the high school. A lot of my friends got married right after high school and stayed right in my hometown. Most of the people who have gone away from there have come back and are teaching high school or performing some other traditional role. Very few women have gone on to graduate school, and many of the other women in the town don't understand why I'm going on and why I'm interested in pursuing my education."

. . . .

Thirty-Five and Beyond

Gail Sheehy calls age thirty-five the "crossroads" for women, the age when all sorts of unexpected questions force themselves into our consciousness. It is the age when most women send their last child off to school. It is the time when single women take urgent steps to try to marry or else become reconciled to singleness. The end of the childbearing years begins to loom ahead. Women return to work; career women change their careers; wives run away; marriages begin to dissolve. Although men go through a mid-life crisis in their forties, and women may go through a transition connected with menopause in the late forties, thirty-five seems to be the age when women must begin to think of themselves in new terms. In our interviews, we noticed that this shift in consciousness occurred anywhere between thirty-five and fifty. Sheehy adds that women who have gone through the post-thirty-five transition period are the possessors of significant levels of energy. Once childbearing is behind, women seem able to focus themselves and their energy in a more single-minded way than they did when they were younger.

The transition at thirty-five also occurs because women frequently marry before their identities are firm; they have to sort out who they are in their middle years rather than in their early twenties.

. . . .

Fulfilling Postponed Dreams

For some women, the desire to do something more with their life once their last child has started off to school is accompanied by a great struggle as to what that "something" ought to be. We've already seen some of the steps people can take to determine their gifts and begin to use them. Our unmonitored fantasies and dreams constitute a clue about work that we often overlook. *If nothing were stopping you, what would you like to be doing?* Women can and do take steps to fulfill such dreams.

Pat Gundry always wanted to write. She says now that she is not sure whether to describe herself as a "housewife who writes or a writer who housewives." Pat had no formal training as a writer and until her last child started off to school she was a full-time housewife. Once, when her children were small, she had signed up for a correspondence course, but she couldn't follow through with her plans because of her duties at home. She read, painted, gardened, and played the guitar as her children grew older. Writing, however, "eats at you. It tickles you until you finally give in to the urge."

One day at the public library Pat found a book on determining goals and achieving them by concentrating on a single one. Her goal was to write. She bought an old typewriter with a bent key (which she straightened) and set up a little office in her basement. On the morning that her last child set off for his first full day at school, she began to write every day. She read books from the public library on writing, and she "practiced." In the five years since she has been working as a free-lance writer, Pat has completed, and published, three books.

A great user of the resources of the public

library, Pat recommended that other women, puzzled as to what they might do with their lives, should read books on determining goals. In the course of the conversation, she made several useful suggestions for women who want to make changes:

1. "Don't look for pie in the sky by and by. Live your life now today."
2. "Examine your latent abilities which are there waiting to be used."
3. "Be courageous enough to get help." Find out what training you need and get it.
4. "Remember, you don't have to leave home to find worthwhile work."
5. "Read things on assertiveness. Women always think they're less than they are."

. . . . .

RETURNING TO SCHOOL AND TO WORK

Emily Greenspan recently wrote an article for the *New York Times Magazine* entitled "Work Begins at 35." Her research among women in general emphasized that those who return to work after being out of the job market have low expectations and are riddled by anxiety as they enter a climate of competition. The same reactions occur when women go back to school for training in a new field. Being a Christian in no way eliminated the anxiety of the women to whom we talked, although their faith did give them a coping mechanism.

A nurse in her forties who returned to hospital work after an absence of many years confided, "I was so nervous. I didn't sleep for a week. . . . And it was hard to get back, but once I had been in it a couple of weeks, I wondered why I was so nervous. The only thing that gives you confidence is doing it, and it doesn't come overnight, either. I'm just starting to feel comfortable there, and it's been about six months."

A woman with prior business experience went back to school to obtain her license in real estate. "I was very much up on the business world before, and then all those years elapsed. I used to tell my husband, 'I really don't feel like I want to go back to school.' It's terrible. You feel reluctant, and I think—I'm sure—it's because you don't have confidence. You aren't sure how you will fit in. But I've found real estate to be a great career, and it's a good career for women who do have some age on them."

Sometimes the Christian woman's stress is increased by her ethical and moral values. Margaret told us of a position which she obtained through an employment agency and then quickly turned down. "I'd heard all these wild stories about American businesses: I had one experience in particular where an employment agency set up an interview for me. I actually went and interviewed and got the job. Then the man at the employment agency called me and asked me to come in and see him. He said, 'I don't think you realize the reputation of this company. I've felt guilty about sending you there.' Then I said, 'What are you talking about?' He said, 'Everybody who works there needs to be available for cocktail hours and weekend visits and this kind of stuff.' I began to realize what he was saying, and I thought truly his warning was the Lord protecting me."

—From Patricia Ward and Martha Stout, *Christian Women at Work.* Grand Rapids: Zondervan, 1981.

LONELINESS

THERE ARE two types of the human condition called loneliness: one is the loneliness borne of existence; the other is borne of the experience of life. The loneliness of existence begins at birth. Not as the result of something a person does, but as a condition of being alive. The original awareness of separation from God, from others, and from one's-self has its origin in the Christian understanding of sin.

Times of Loneliness

Many situations trigger feelings of loss and loneliness. Learning to deal with the little griefs better enables us to face and move through major losses when they occur. Acknowledging the uncelebrated rites of passage can help us to face ourselves and to be alert to some of the triggers for loneliness. Here is a selection of predictable experiences which are passages of living. Naturally, your response to any one of these may be different than someone else's, depending on the circumstances in your life.

Parents give birth to a child. The occasion is one of celebration. But when parents realize how much a baby alters their lifestyle, they may feel a gnawing loneliness tugging at them. Energy, time, attention, and freedom are changed in the midst of celebrating a new addition to the family.

The birth of another child. This occasion makes additional demands on the parents, and on the children already in the family, who often wonder if they're loved as much, since so much attention is given to the new baby.

Childhood disability or illness. This triggers parents' feelings of helplessness to prevent the pain of their child. Hospitalization can be agony for the child as well as for parents separated from him by doctors, nurses, rules, and clinical apparatus. Lack of control over events breeds loneliness.

The first child enters school. Parents may have feelings of separation even while they are excited about new learning experiences. They may sense a loss of total influence on their child's life. The peer group and teachers begin a never-ending influence, and there's no going back to infancy.

Further education. Each movement from day-care center to kindergarten to elementary school to middle school to high school to college is a link in a chain of more independence. Parents may feel gratitude that their children are becoming adults but, at the same time, an awareness dawns that child-rearing days will end.

Marriage. The marriage relationship's first face with reality triggers loneliness if expectations for marriage and the image you had of your spouse are not all that you thought. Facing loneliness and disappoint-ment can be the first steps toward negotiating a realistic, healthy relationship.

Loss of friendships. Friendships change through geographic distance, loss of common ties, or misunderstanding.

Job loss. Being out of work can be lonely, regardless of the reason.

Moving. A move to another city is considered to be one of the most traumatic changes in people's lives. Children must reestablish themselves. A husband may be immersed in a new job while his wife is alone, sorting out her new identity in unfamiliar surroundings.

Birthdays. The age marked by an adult's birthday isn't as significant as the meaning it has for him.

Major illness. Illness brings an awareness of the lack of control one has over life and death.

Unfilled dreams. These prompt a first awareness of what might have been if other choices had been made.

First dates of children. To parents, these are announcements that their children will make their own lives. Parents wonder if they'll be ready, if they have done all they can do in preparation, and if the children will repeat or avoid the mistakes they made.

Death of a pet. The death of a pet often highlights loneliness, even for adults.

Great expectations. Loneliness comes when you feel misunderstood or expectations in a relationship aren't met.

Gossip. The first time you're aware that you're the recipient of the latest gossip is a startlingly lonely moment.

Career changes. Changes of careers plunge many into loneliness.

Self-perception. Loneliness comes when you first realize that how you view yourself is different from how others see you.

Early achievers. Those who reach career/financial/social goals early in life question, "Where to from here?"

Leadership. Loneliness is inherent in leadership and decision-making positions.

Empty-nest syndrome. This starts when the children are grown. You and your spouse are a family alone for the first time in over twenty years. Some prepare for the change and greet the transition with anticipation. Others are shocked by the impact, and fear they no longer have anything in common with their mate. Children marry, and/or become involved with their careers. Reestablishing relationships on an adult level is difficult if you're a parent who has lived your life through your children. You're on your *own* now!

Divorce. Divorce involves enormous grief, loss, and loneliness.

Grandparents. If you become a grandparent, you notice your children spend more time with *their* children than with you. Christmas celebrations may now move to their houses. Perhaps a joyful occasion, but underlying is an awareness that life goes on.

Death of friends. Good friends die sooner than you expected.

Physical changes. Such changes prompt the recognition of additional limitations. The desire to prove youthfulness to yourself or other people, to recapture dreams, or to reevaluate how you spent your time may accompany the aging process.

A realization of age. This happens the first time you hear someone refer to "the old people" and realize that you're one of them.

A dream house. Loneliness can occur when you move to a dream house or apartment and realize that it doesn't solve all your problems.

Singleness. Loneliness may be a problem if you do not marry, and have to deal with disappointment and the expectations of other people, as well as your own.

Childlessness. Remaining childless for any reason other than by choice can be devastating.

After a year. The year anniversary of the death of a loved one is solitary.

Anniversaries. If you feel you have nothing to celebrate, anniversaries can be lonely.

Terminal illness. Loneliness can come from being with someone who is terminally ill. You can care, but that doesn't remove the pain.

Evaluation of faith. The first major evaluation of your faith, and each subsequent one, underscores that you are human. Not every question will have answers nor can you control all the events of your life.

Retirement. This could involve financial, home, or location changes, depending on circumstances.

Certainly, additional experiences activate loneliness. Looking at old scrapbooks; entering a dark, empty house; getting lost on the freeway—all are examples of situations which drive you into the lonely part of yourself.

The list at first glance may cause you to think of life as a continual time of loss and loneliness. Granted, life *is* problem-solving. Recognizing the stages of life and learning to deal with the potential loneliness, frees you to experience the joy, hope, and fulfillment in life. That's the paradox of looking into your identity as a solitary individual. By looking inward, you have a greater capacity to relate upward and outward.

NO ONE IS IMMUNE

Many people assume that loneliness happens only to other people and that success, marriage, financial security, or "something" else is an antidote to being lonely. Biblical truth, however, reveals that no one is immune to loneliness. Not in Bible times, nor in the twentieth century.

Numerous examples could be explored, but one of the most powerful expressions is evidenced in the lives of two very different people—Jesus and Judas. We often presume that since those in public life are surrounded by people, they're spared from lonely anguish. However, anyone who holds a position of responsibility or expresses strong convictions must contemplate the lonely nature of existence.

Matthew wrote that Judas returned the thirty silver pieces to the high priest after Jesus' death. According to his words, he'd condemned an innocent man. Judas, the traitor, threw the money down in the temple and later hanged himself (Matthew 27:3–5). His misery and remorse drove him to self-destruction. Judas was exposed to condemnation and rejection on all sides. The chief priests didn't trust him; they used him. His fellow disciples condemned him. He knew misunderstanding and grief, but Judas also made his choices and lived with their consequences. The One who could have forgiven him was the One he helped execute. Although he could have sought forgiveness, he chose suicide instead. Few can bear the constant torment of condemnation, regardless of the rightness or wrongness of the crusade. With no one was Judas acceptable or welcome, least of all to himself.

Jesus was no stranger to loneliness either. His cause and purpose did not spare Him from the weight of suffering. He went to the Mount of Olives with His disciples to pray, for the time of His crucifixion was near (Luke 22:39–51). He prayed that if there was any way to accomplish God's purpose without facing the coming events, God would "take this cup away." The gentle Messiah returned from prayer to find His disciples asleep, and to the loneliness of being misunderstood, mistrusted, receiving physical and verbal insults, and of being betrayed by a kiss. Jesus could understand loneliness because He'd lived with it throughout His life. Search the Scriptures to discover that He had His own struggles. From birth to physical death, He realized that no one but the Father could completely understand Him.

Jesus and Judas were two men with different purposes: One came to save the world, the other to become a traitor. Both were crusaders but for different goals; both felt deserted. Neither was understood by the people closest to him; each grieved; each had choices about how to handle the terror in loneliness. One discovered you can't destroy another without doing the same to yourself. The other chose to follow the way of the cross and life eternal.

The Prophet Isaiah and John the Baptist echo the words, "Prepare ye the way" (Isaiah 40:3; Matthew 3:3). Learning to live with the little griefs helps to prepare us to deal with the ultimate, more painful ones. Jesus was prepared. He prayed and grieved

when friends died; He felt pain for unbelievers. He knew the meaning of rejection. His whole life was preparation, so that at the final moment He was able to face the next rite of passage.

—From Nancy Potts, *Loneliness: Living Between the Times.* Wheaton, Ill.: Victor Books, 1978.

FOR FURTHER READING:

Clarkson, Margaret. *So You're Single.* Wheaton, Ill.: Shaw, 1978.

Hulme, William E. *Creative Loneliness.* Minneapolis: Augsburg, 1977.

Smoke, Jim. *Suddenly Single.* Old Tappan, N.J.: Revell, 1982.

LOVE

Romantic

BELIEFS ABOUT LOVE

Item 1: "Love at first sight" occurs between some people—true or false?

Though some readers will disagree with me, love at first sight is a physical and emotional impossibility. Why? Because love is not simply a feeling of romantic excitement; it goes beyond intense sexual attraction; it exceeds the thrill at having "captured" a highly desirable social prize. These are emotions that are unleashed at first sight, but they *do not constitute love.* I wish the whole world knew that fact. These temporary feelings differ from love in that they place the spotlight on the one experiencing them. "What is happening to *Me*? This is the most fantastic thing *I've* ever been through! *I* think *I* am in love!"

You see, these emotions are selfish in the sense that they are motivated by our own gratification. They have little to do with the new lover. Such a person has not fallen in love with another person; *he has fallen in love with love!* And there is an enormous difference between the two.

. . . .

Did you know that the idea of marriage based on romantic affection is a very recent development in human affairs? Prior to A.D. 1200, weddings were arranged by the families of the bride and groom, and it never occurred to anyone that they were supposed to "fall in love." In fact, the concept of romantic love was actually popularized by William Shakespeare. There are times when I wish the old Englishman was here to help us straighten out the mess that he initiated.

Real love, in contrast to popular notions, is an expression of the deepest appreciation for another human being; it is an intense awareness of his or her needs and longings for the past, present and future. It is unselfish and giving and caring. And believe me these are not attitudes one "falls" into at first sight, as though he were tumbling into a ditch.

Item 2: It is easy to distinguish real love from infatuation—true or false?

The answer is, again, false. That wild ride at the start of a romantic adventure bears all the earmarks of a lifetime trip. Just try to tell a starry-eyed sixteen-year-old dreamer that he is not really in love—that he's merely infatuated. He'll whip out his guitar and sing you a song. "Young luv, true luv. Filled with real emo-shun. Young luv, true luv. Filled with true devoshun!" He knows what he feels, and he feels great. But he'd better enjoy the roller-coaster ride while it lasts, because it has a predictable end point.

I must stress this fact with the greatest emphasis. The exhilaration of infatuation is *never* a permanent condition. Period! If you expect to live on the top of that mountain, year after year, you can forget it! Emotions swing from high to low to high in cyclical rhythm, and since romantic excitement is an emotion, it too will certainly oscillate. If the thrill of sexual encounter is identified as genuine love, then disillusionment and disappointment are already knocking at the door.

How many vulnerable young couples "fall in love with love" on the first date—and lock themselves into marriage before the natural swing of their emotions has even progressed through the first dip? They then wake up one morning without that neat feeling and conclude that love has died. In reality, it was never there in the first place. They were fooled by an emotional "high."

. . . .

If genuine love is rooted in a commitment of the will, how can one know when it arrives? How can it be distinguished from temporary infatuation? How can the feeling be interpreted if it is unreliable and inconstant?

There is only one answer to those questions: *it takes time.* The best advice I can give a couple contemplating marriage (or any other important decision) is this: make *no* important, life-shaping decisions quickly or impulsively, and when in doubt, stall for time. That's not a bad suggestion for all of us to apply.

Item 3: People who sincerely love each other will not fight and argue—true or false?

I doubt if this third item actually requires an answer. Some marital conflict is as inevitable as the sunrise, even in loving marriages. There is a difference, however, between healthy and unhealthy combat, depending on the way the disagreement is handled. In an unstable marriage, anger is usually hurled directly at the partner. Hostile, person-centered "you messages" strike at the heart of one's self-worth and produce intensive internal upheaval.

Item 4: God selects one particular person for each of us to marry, and He will guide us together—true or false?

Anyone who believes that God guarantees a successful marriage to every Christian is in for a shock. This is not to say that He is disinterested in the choice of a mate, or that He will not answer a specific request for guidance on this all-important decision. Certainly, His will should be sought in such a critical matter, and I consulted Him repeatedly before proposing to my wife.

However, I do not believe that God performs a routine matchmaking service for everyone who worships Him. He has given us judgment, common sense and discretionary powers, and He expects us to exercise these abilities in matters matrimonial. Those who believe otherwise are likely to enter marriage glibly, thinking, "God would have stopped us if He didn't approve." To such confident people I can only say, "Lotsa luck."

Item 5: If a man and woman genuinely love each other, then hardships and troubles will have little or no effect on their relationship—true or false?

Another common misconception about the meaning of "true love" is that it inevitably stands like the rock of Gibraltar against the storms of life. Many people apparently believe that love is destined to conquer all. The Beatles endorsed this notion with their song, "All we need is love, love, love is all we need." Unfortunately, we need a bit more.

.   .   .   .

Item 6: It is better to marry the wrong person than to remain single and lonely throughout life—true or false?

Again, the answer is false. Generally speaking, it is less painful to be searching for an end to loneliness than to be embroiled in the emotional combat of a sour marriage. Yet the threat of being an "old maid" (a term I detest) causes many girls to grab the first train that rambles down the marital track. And too often, it offers a one-way ticket to disaster.

The fear of never finding a mate can cause a single person to ignore his better judgment and compromise his own standards. A young woman, particularly, may argue with herself in this manner. "John isn't a Christian, but maybe I can influence him after we're married. He drinks too much, but that's probably because he's young and carefree. And we

don't have much in common, but I'm sure we'll learn to love each other more as time passes. Besides, what could be worse than living alone?"

This kind of rationalization is based on a desperate hope for a matrimonial miracle, but storybook endings are uncommon events in everyday life. When one plunges into marriage despite the obvious warning flags, he is gambling with the remaining years of his earthly existence.

For those readers who are single today, *please* believe me when I say that a bad marriage is among the most miserable experiences on earth! It is filled with rejection and hurt feelings and hatred and screaming and broken children and sleepless nights. Certainly, a solitary walk as a single person can be a meaningful and fulfilling life; at least, it does not involve "a house divided against itself."

Item 7: It is not harmful to have sexual intercourse before marriage, if the couple has a meaningful relationship—true or false?

This item represents *the* most dangerous of the popular misconceptions about romantic love, not only for individuals but for our future as a nation. During the past 15 years we have witnessed the tragic disintegration of our sexual mores and traditional concepts of morality. Responding to a steady onslaught by the entertainment industry and by the media, our people have begun to believe that premarital intercourse is a noble experience, extramarital encounters are healthy, homosexuality is acceptable, and bisexuality is even better. These views— labeled as "the new morality"—reflect the sexual stupidity of the age in which we live, yet they are believed and applied by millions of American citizens.

.   .   .   .

Mankind has known intuitively for at least fifty centuries that indiscriminate sexual activity represents both an individual and a corporate threat to survival. And history bears it out. Anthropologist J.D. Unwin conducted an exhaustive study of the eighty-eight civilizations which have existed in the history of the world. Each culture has reflected a similar life cycle, beginning with a strict code of sexual conduct and ending with the demand for complete "freedom" to express individual passion. Unwin reports that *every* society which extended sexual permissiveness to its people was soon to perish. There have been no exceptions.

Why do you suppose the reproductive urge within us is so relevant to cultural survival? It is because the energy which holds a people together is sexual in nature! The physical attraction between men and women causes them to establish a family and invest themselves in its development. It encourages them to work and save and toil to insure the survival of their families. Their sexual energy provides the impetus for the raising of healthy children and for the transfer of values from one generation to the next.

Sexual drives urge a man to work when he would rather play. They cause a woman to save when she would rather spend. In short, the sexual aspect of our nature—when released exclusively within the family—produces stability and responsibility that would not otherwise occur. When a nation is composed of millions of devoted, responsible family units, the entire society is stable, responsible and resilient.

If sexual energy within the family is the key to a healthy society, then its release outside those boundaries is potentially catastrophic. The very force that binds a people together then becomes the agent for its own destruction.

Item 8: If a couple is genuinely in love, that condition is permanent—lasting a lifetime—true or false?

Love, even genuine love, is a fragile thing. It must be maintained and protected if it is to survive. Love can perish when a husband works seven days a week, when there is no time for romantic activity, when he and his wife forget how to talk to each other.

. . . .

Where does your marriage rank on your hierarchy of values? Does it get the leftovers and scraps from your busy schedule or is it something of great worth to be preserved and supported? It can die if left untended.

Item 9: Short courtships (six months or less) are best—true or false?

The answer to this question is incorporated in the reply to the second item regarding infatuation. Short courtships require impulsive decisions about lifetime commitments, and that is risky business, at best.

Item 10: Teenagers are more capable of genuine love than are older people—true or false?

If this item were true, then we would be hard pressed to explain why half the teenage marriages end in divorce in the first five years. To the contrary, the kind of love I have been describing—unselfish, giving, caring commitment—requires a sizeable dose of maturity to make it work. And maturity is a partial thing in most teenagers. Adolescent romance is an exciting part of growing up, but it seldom meets the criteria for the deeper relationships of which successful marriages are composed.

All ten items on this brief questionnaire are false, for they represent the ten most common misconceptions about the meaning of romantic love.

—From Dr. James Dobson, *Emotions: Can You Trust Them?* Ventura, Calif.: Regal, 1980.

DEPENDENCY

Getting hooked on a person is similar to getting hooked on a drug. And it can be as hard to let go of a person, as it is to give up a drug. But it can be done.

How does a person get addicted to another person? It starts with a strong sense of emptiness and lack of meaning and purpose to one's life. As one person said: "Until he came along I just existed. I didn't know what I wanted out of life. I just floated along day in and day out."

Next, there is a sudden, surprising, exciting experience with a particular person. She said: "It just happened! He swept me off my feet. I have never felt that good before in my life. I fell in love with him. I couldn't help it. He's everything I've always wanted. I think about him all the time. I call him every day. My whole life is different. I feel wonderful!"

Next, dependency develops. Friendships are neglected. Everything begins to center around the new person. Obsession occurs. A small world is created only big enough for the two of them. "All I think about," she said, "is him, and what he's doing at this very moment, and when I will see him again. I just can't be with him enough. The FEELING is what I want, of being close to him, and being loved and cared for, and feeling complete. Nothing else matters. He's everything to me. He's my whole life!" (She is addicted to the FEELING of fullness. She dreads the emptiness.)

What kind of person gets addicted to another person? It can happen to any of us who feel empty inside, and have no sense of direction or purpose, and yearn for companionship.

And addiction is even more likely to occur if a person tends to be overly dependent, lacking in self-confidence, and does not have many close friends or social activities.

And the addictive-prone person seems to come out of one of two kinds of family backgrounds.

He may come from a family where he was ignored or neglected, left on his own, and never had anyone he could depend on. He had to learn early to take care of himself. Underneath his self-made-manness is still the little boy who yearns to be taken care of and cared for.

Or, she may have come from an overly protective family where she was told what to do, never learned to think for herself, was never on her own, was sheltered from responsibility, and was encouraged to find a good man, marry and be taken care of.

What can an addicted person do? First, face the fact. Admit to yourself that you are hooked. *Second,* decide if you want to break the habit and change your life. *Third,* if you decide to become unhooked, then begin to do things that increase your self confidence. Get back with your friends. Be with people. Develop your abilities and talents. Take a class. Pick up a hobby. Join a club. Be a volunteer. Do things that don't depend on the person you are addicted to. *Fourth,* expect to be miserable from time to time. That's part of withdrawal. You won't feel good all the time. Your sleep will be affected. So will your moods. But, it gets better, not worse. *Fifth,* guard against impulsively running back to him/her because of your pain. It's especially bad on weekends and late at night. Put it off till the next day, then reconsider. *Sixth,* be proud of your handling of the withdrawal. Brag on yourself to friends. *Seventh,* deliberately restrict your time with the person you are addicted to. If possible, see him/her only in the company of other people. *Eighth,* don't expect much help from the person you are addicted to. He/she is getting something out of the addiction, too. *Ninth,* find ways to reward yourself for moving from addiction to affirmation. *Tenth,* don't discard the person you are addicted to. Instead, get to know the real person, the humanness, the weaknesses too, and hopes and fears, aims and ambitions, ordinariness and uniqueness. You may find that as you move away from "I need you, therefore, I love you," you will say to that person, "I love you, therefore, I need you!"

—HUGH BURNS, Th.M., psychotherapist, Clayton Professional Building, Riverdale, GA 30274.

Let Yourself Be Loved

All I said to her was, "I like your outfit." I said it casually and had started on to some other topic when she interrupted me.

"Oh, this old thing. I've had it for years. It's really outdated. And I don't have the right shoes to wear with it and . . ."

Good grief! I only wanted to pay her a

simple compliment in passing, and she turned it into a discussion. She seemed unable to say "Thank you" and accept a compliment and leave it at that.

She has a problem, of course, and many of us have touches of it. If we don't like ourselves, we can't let others like us. It affects our relationships in varying degrees and often more than we are aware of.

Deep psychological problems often take a long time to work out, but therapists often suggest small exercises to get started. Like calisthenics, if we keep doing these, we'll gradually see a difference.

1. *Accept compliments graciously* (and pay them sincerely). Forget that false humility. If you find yourself starting to protest when someone pays you a compliment, even wondering if they are putting you on, just say "Thank you" and keep quiet. You *do* have a lot going for you, you know, and your friends, if they really are friends, will occasionally bring them up.

2. *Let people know who you are.* In other words, open up. Share a little of yourself. People can't love you unless they know you.

This doesn't mean that you pour out your deepest thoughts in an avalanche of emotion to any casual acquaintance.

Pulling the mask back a little bit and letting people see us as we are, warts and all, is not the same as letting *everything* hang out at all times. People do, however, want to share your joys, fears, worries, hurts, satisfactions, etc.

3. *Put yourself where you can be loved.* This is an old high school story, but it happens to many young men and women. Today I smile at it. Then it wasn't so funny.

She was popular. I was practically unheard of (so I thought). She had friends on the football team. I was too skinny for that, but I did manage to place in a cross country race. She lived in an upper-class part of town. I didn't have two nickels to rub together.

I wanted to ask her out, but I was afraid she'd say no.

That summer I got a job in a produce store, only to find that her father owned it. She worked there, too, that summer, and between the cauliflower and the zucchini we got to know each other. From there on it was all peaches.

Sometimes we must put ourselves in a place where we can be loved because we're afraid of being hurt. Loving is risking. We don't have to take the risks, of course. We can avoid them—not pursue relationships, not show any signs of interest or affection, not get too close to other people just as we don't let them get too close to us.

I guess it all comes down to the fact that you can't let yourself be loved, unless you love yourself. And that would make a great title for a country-western song.

—Ron Wilson, "Let Yourself Be Loved," *Today's Christian Woman*, Spring 1982.

Love for Husband

Paul also got down to the heart of the matter in his remarks to Christian husbands. He exhorted them to love their wives "just as Christ loved the church" (Ephesians 5:25; Colossians 3:19). Peter added another dimension, "Husbands, in the same way be considerate as you live with your wives and treat them with respect as the weaker partner and as heirs with you of the gracious gift of life, so that nothing will hinder your prayers" (1 Peter 3:7). Both Paul's and Peter's remarks represent the "bottom line" in solving many problems for a Christian wife. When a Christian husband loves his wife as Christ really loved the Church, normally his wife will respond at the behavioral as well as at the feeling level. But when he doesn't, frequently greater anxiety and resentment are created which almost invariably reflect themselves in negative behavior.

But this "formula," ideal as it is, does not always solve problems. It is basic, but not always the quick and easy solution. The formula is always foundational in helping a couple overcome their problems, but we must be prepared to go further. So consequently, Paul also dealt with the problem from another perspective, offering some additional suggestions for overcoming negative feelings. This, I believe, is Paul's focus when he exhorted Timothy to teach the older women to behave in a certain way in order that they might be able to "train younger women *to love their husbands.*"

In the phrase, "to *love* their husbands," the Greek word translated "love" is not the most common word for love in the New Testament. *Agapao* and *agape* are used most to refer to love that acts in a proper way, a love that does the right thing no matter what our feelings. Christ demonstrated this love most significantly when He went to the cross and suffered for mankind, even though, at the feeling level, His desire was to escape this pain and agony (see Matthew 26:38, 39). In spite of His painful ambivalence and His agony of soul, He asked that God's will be done. It is this kind of love a Christian man is to demonstrate towards his wife (see Ephesians 5:25; Colossians 3:19). It is this kind of love we are to have towards our neighbors, both Christians and non-Christians.

But the Greek word used by Paul in Titus 2:4 refers to a *phileo* love, often used to describe the "emotional" dimensions of love. *Phileo* involves "friendship." It expresses "delight" in doing something. It refers to doing something with "pleasure." This is why *agapao* is not used in the Bible to describe "sexual love," particularly sexual responsibility. "Sexual love" involves emotions and you cannot command a person to "feel" a certain way towards someone else. You *can* command a person to *do something* in spite of feelings. (Thus the Bible says, "Husbands, *love* your wives," or more dramatically, it says, "*Love* your enemies.") But you cannot force a person to *feel positive* when he *feels negative.* Thus Paul worded the statement very carefully to Titus; older women were to "train the younger women to love their husbands." The word "train" that Paul used here and the context in which he used it implies a process. It was to be a process of learning, a process of coming to the place where wives felt "friendly" toward their husbands; where they felt "warm" and "se-

cure" in their husbands' presence; where they had a deep sense of "trust" and "emotional commitment" toward them. And this, of course, would be a new experience for many first-century wives, for a number of marriages had never included this dimension before.

Paul made it very clear in this passage that this training process involved older women. They were to be "reverent in the way they lived"; they were "not to be slanderers or addicted to much wine"; rather, they were to "teach what is good." And *"then,"* wrote Paul, they can *train* the younger women to "love their husbands." Putting it another way, these younger women needed a model, an example, a pattern. They needed to "see" and "experience" older women demonstrating loyalty, affection, and commitment to their own husbands. They needed to learn *how* to love.

—From Gene A. Getz, *The Measure of a Woman.* Ventura, Calif.: Regal, 1977.

Love for Children

How can a woman learn "to love her children"? What practical suggestions and guidelines are there for developing this capacity?

1. *Realize that negative feelings under certain circumstances are normal, even for mature Christian women.* The pressures of family life, particularly when children are young, are very real. Life with small children in the home is wall to wall, literally involving twenty-four hours a day. At no other time and in no other situation will there be as much physical and emotional drain on a mother. And this is complicated and intensified by the fact that this is a new role for her. Innately she takes her responsibility very seriously and, as a Christian, her natural sense of responsibility becomes even more acute through her knowledge of biblical expectations. There is no more threatening thought to a young woman than the prospect of being a failure as a mother. And most face

this mental obsession sometime during the early years of motherhood.

We must also realize that physical strain has a tendency to make a person vulnerable to emotional difficulties. Furthermore, emotional stress invariably leads to feelings of resentment. And for a Christian particularly, hostile emotions lead to guilt and depression, which in turn creates a vicious cycle leading to more guilt and recurring depression.

Every young woman must understand these pressures and the natural tendency toward resentment. To have periodic negative emotions and feel resentment toward young children in the home is normal. Generally it does not mean a "lack of real love" for the child, any more than experiencing periodic negative emotions toward her husband means she doesn't really love him. To understand these emotions and why they are occurring helps a person to accept the feelings, and to avoid the nagging guilt which inevitably makes the problem worse.

It goes without saying, though it *must* be said, that a young husband *must* understand his wife's struggles in this area. If he is threatened, feels rejected, and becomes insensitive, and then vents his own emotional frustration on her, he will only compound her anxiety and depression. She must have a listening ear from the one who is closest to her.

2. *Young women need help from older women.* This is why Paul told Titus to "teach the *older women*" to "train the *younger women*." And this is why he emphasized the older woman's example in this process. Young women need mature adult models. And they need insight that is helpful, not harmful.

Unfortunately, some older women forget what it was like to go through these early years of motherhood. And some develop an idealism that is far removed from reality. Rather than easing the burden of anxiety and guilt by letting the young woman know they experienced the same emotions, they accentuate the problem by telling them "not to feel that way," and by giving the impression

that mature people don't have these problems.

First of all, you cannot change a person's feelings by telling them *not to feel that way.* And second, it doesn't help to give the impression these feelings are abnormal. And third, it is dishonest for an older woman to give the impression she never had these difficulties when indeed she really did.

Note: If you happen to be an older woman who never experienced negative feelings towards your small children, you are the exception, not the rule. If indeed you did not have these feelings, there were probably some very significant reasons why this was true: a very understanding husband, unusual help from someone else in carrying out the process, a completely different environment and cultural milieu, etc. If you are going to be a good counselor you must understand why your experience deviated from the norm.

3. *Realize more than ever that cultural trends can be devastating to family life.* Nancy, of course, is a good example of this. She was basically happy and contented with her role until she began to associate with women who convinced her she was "unfulfilled." And indeed, she began to *feel* unfulfilled. The more she read the writings of "unhappy" women, the more she identified with their plight and the more she began to *feel* like them.

The women's liberation movement, of course, is only one trend in our culture that has made devastating inroads into the average American family. Combined with this are the trends of secularism, materialism, sensualism, and existentialism. Everywhere a woman turns she is bombarded with a value system that is eating away at what God ordained to be a very fulfilling and rewarding life-style.

4. *Develop a biblical perspective on motherhood.* The Bible clearly teaches that children are a "gift of the Lord" (Psalms 127:3 NASB), and personally, I believe the Scriptures teach that having children is one of God's major plans for women to experi-

ence fulfillment. Thus Paul, when discussing the effects of the fall on woman's status in life (see 1 Timothy 2:11–15), wrote something that is rather difficult to understand out of context. He said, "But woman will be kept safe through childbirth, if they continue in faith, love and holiness with propriety" (1 Timothy 2:15).

What Paul meant by this statement has been the subject of a lot of discussion. Obviously, he did not mean a woman finds eternal salvation through producing children. This would be totally contradictory to the whole of Scripture. Rather it seems he is saying that a woman, though she has been affected negatively by the fall, being the first one to sin and though she must recognize man's authority in her life, yet, her most significant fulfillment will come by being a good wife and mother.

If she turns her life totally over to God, she can be "saved" from the competitive problems in a male-dominated culture— men whose male egos are also desperately affected by sin in the world. She will be "saved" from the loneliness and frustration that often accompany a career. She will be "saved" from the pressures of a rat-race culture, having someone who will understand and help her find fulfillment.

We must hurry to add, of course, that this doesn't mean a woman cannot be fulfilled without having children or a husband. In fact, Paul commends singlehood for those who feel led this way. The point is that many in today's world are attempting to communicate that having children, being a wife and mother can *never* lead to fulfillment. This, of course, is in direct contradiction to the Scriptures and runs counter to God's principles.

5. *Realize however, that culture does create new problems for women.* We cannot ignore culture. Young girls in our society are taught to be professionally oriented throughout their academic experiences. The concept of parenting takes a decided backseat to the excitement of a professional career.

Psychologically, most women are geared

in a direction other than what God intended. And this means that all of us, both men and women, must understand the influence culture has on our personalities. To simply "put a woman down" or "to put her in her place" may accentuate her problem. She needs to *understand* her problem. She must realize her tendency is to act the way she has been subtly conditioned to act. Together, a husband and wife must face the reality of this problem and, within the context of Christian principles, work toward a satisfactory solution.

—From Gene A. Getz, *The Measure of a Woman.* Ventura, Calif.: Regal, 1977.

How to Convey Love to Children

Let's consider how to convey love to a child. As you remember, children are emotional beings who communicate emotionally. In addition, children (and the younger, the more so) use behavior to translate their feelings to us. It's easy to tell how a child is feeling and what frame of mind he's in simply by watching him. Likewise, children have an uncanny ability to recognize our feelings by our behavior, an ability most people lose as they reach adulthood.

On many occasions my sixteen-year-old daughter has asked me such questions as, "What are you mad at, Daddy?" when I'm not even consciously aware that I'm feeling a certain way. But when I stop and think about it, she's absolutely right.

Children are that way. They can so finely sense how you are feeling by the way you act. So if we want them to know how we feel *about them,* that we love them, *we must act like we love them,* "Dear children, let us not love with words or tongue but with actions and in truth" (1 John 3:18 NIV).

The purpose [here] is to examine how parents can put their feelings of love into action. Only in this way can they convey their love to their child so that he will feel loved, completely accepted, and respected, and able to love and respect himself. Only then will parents be able to help their children to love others unconditionally, especially their future spouses and children.

Before we launch into discoveries of how to love a child, there must be one presupposition. It must be assumed that parents love their child. That is, it must be assumed that parents are willing to apply what they learn. There is a difference between having a vague feeling of warmth toward a child, and caring enough about him to sacrifice whatever is needed for his best interest. It is rather pointless to continue reading . . . if you are not willing to seriously contemplate what it says, understand it, and apply its contents. Otherwise, it would be easy to read it superficially and to disown the information as simplistic and unrealistic.

Conveying love to a child can be broadly classified into four areas: eye contact, physical contact, focused attention, and discipline. Each area is just as crucial as the other. Many parents (and authorities) will focus on one or two areas and neglect the others. The area most overemphasized today, to the exclusion of the rest, is discipline. I see many children of Christian parents who are well-disciplined but feel unloved. In many of these cases the parents have unfortunately confused discipline with punishment, as though the two are synonymous. This is understandable when one reads books and articles and attends seminars on the subject. I frequently read or hear authorities tell parents to use the rod and physically pinch their child with no mention of loving him. There is no mention of how to help a child feel good toward himself, his parents, or others. No mention of how to make a child happy.

Every day I see the results of this approach to childrearing. These children are well-behaved when they are quite young, although usually overly quiet, somewhat sullen, and withdrawn. They lack the spontaneity, curiosity, and childish exuberance of a love-nurtured child. And these children usually become behavior problems as they approach and enter adolescence because they lack a strong emotional bond with their parents.

So we parents must focus on all areas of loving our child.

POSSESSIVENESS

Possessiveness is a tendency of parents to encourage a child to be too dependent on his parents. Paul Tournier, famed Swiss counselor, deals with the subject quite well in his article, "The Meaning of Possessiveness." He states that when a child is small, dependency is "obvious and almost complete." But if this dependence does not diminish as a child grows older, it becomes an obstacle to a child's emotional development. Many parents try to keep their children in a state of dependence upon them. Dr. Tournier states that they do this "by suggestion or by emotional blackmail," or else by using their authority and insisting upon obedience. The child is theirs. They have rights over him because he belongs to them. Such parents are termed *possessive*. These parents tend to treat their child as an object or property to be possessed or owned, and not as a person who needs to grow in his own right and to become gradually independent and self-reliant.

A child must have respect from his parents to be himself. This does not, of course, mean no limit-setting or being permissive. (Every child needs guidance and discipline.) It means to encourage a child to think, to be spontaneous, to realize he is a separate person who must assume more and more responsibility for himself.

If we parents disregard a child's right to gradually become independent, one of two things will happen. He may become overly dependent on us and overly submissive, failing to learn how to live in his world. He may become easy prey to strong-willed, authoritative personalities or groups such as the Moonies; or there will be deterioration of our relationship with a child as he gets older. He will become more resistant to our guidance.

Again, as Dr. Tournier suggests, we should "possess as if not possessing." Such is the great message of the Bible. Man can never truly possess anything. He is but the steward of the goods that God entrusts to him, for "the earth is the Lord's, and everything in it" (1 Corinthians 10:26 NIV).

Of course there is some possessiveness in every parent. But we must take care to (1) identify it within ourselves, (2) separate it from true concern for a child's total welfare, especially concerning his need to become self-reliant, (3) be as continuously aware of it as we can, (4) resist its influence.

—From Dr. Ross Campbell, *How to Really Love Your Child*. Wheaton, Ill.: Victor Books, 1977.

FOR FURTHER READING:

MacDonald, Gordon. *Magnificent Marriage*. Wheaton, Ill.: Tyndale, 1976.

Martin, Ralph. *Husbands, Wives, Parents, Children*. Ann Arbor: Servant, 1978.

M

MAKEUP

PROPERLY APPLIED, makeup can be almost as effective as a fairy godmother's wand in transforming "plain Janes" into irresistibly attractive women. In fact, seventeenth-century Englishmen were so aware of this fact that Parliament passed a law to protect men from being unfairly enticed into marrying plain women posing as ravishing beauties.

The law states: "All women, of whatever age, rank, profession or degree whether virgins, maids or widows, shall not . . . impose upon, seduce and betray into matrimony any of His Majesty's subjects by scents, paints, cosmetics, artificial teeth, false hair, Spanish Wool, iron stays, hoops, high-heel shoes, bolstered hips; and shall incur the penalty of the Law in force against witchcraft and like misdemeanors, and that marriage upon conviction shall stand null and void."

If women didn't wear makeup today, it's quite possible that modern politicians might want to pass a law *requiring* its use! After all, life is so much more fun when we can all look more attractive and feel confident. And as the wise old farmer said to his wife in regard to her use of cosmetics, "If the barn needs painting—paint it!"

Don't be afraid to use makeup. You don't have to apologize for enhancing your appearance. In fact, once you learn to use it properly, and others see the subtle but positive effect makeup has on you, they may be encouraged to experiment.

Let me emphasize the "natural look" in makeup, for a well-made-up face is never overdone. Your face should look as fresh and lovely as a dazzling rainbow, but as soft and subtle as a spring bouquet.

Basic Cosmetics and Their Use

Foundation—should match the deepest tone in the skin. (Most women have at least seven, so choose carefully!) A foundation that is too light makes the face look heavier and puffy.

Blush—if applied correctly, may be used to highlight eyes and ovalize the face. But it is very important to choose one that matches your skin tone and shade. If you apply blush too close to the nose, you "lengthen" it. If you place it too low, you make your face appear to sag. If you place it too close to the eye socket, you emphasize wrinkles. Be sure to angle the blush upward on the face. You may also place a light touch of rouge on your temple, forehead and chin to add warmth and sparkle.

Powder—use a translucent product that will not change the shade of your foundation. Avoid chalky looks by using natural or organic powder. Dust powder over your entire face, then dampen a natural sea sponge and lightly pat your entire face to set makeup and avoid a powdered look.

Liner—use only in a thin line or a slightly smudged line, which adds color only to the base of the lashes. A brown shade is softer and more feminine than black. Use a pencil and start with the center of the eye, moving out in a soft, not definite, line. The purpose of the liner is to make your lashes look longer and fuller.

Shadow—a deeper shade on the lid, fading into a softened color reaching up to the brow. Different shades come and go in the fashion world, so be open to experimentation. Get professional advice to help you select the best colors and techniques for you. But again, remember that eye makeup should only bring out the beauty of your eyes—and never be overdone.

Eyebrows—visualize two straight lines running perpendicularly from your tear ducts to the top of your head. If any hairs lie between these two lines, tweeze them out. To determine where the eyebrow should end, place a pencil on your face so that it lines up with the tip of your nose and the corner of your eye and extends beyond it. The eyebrow should arch over the eye and end at the pencil. You may tweeze below the brows for a neat look, but never tweeze above. Remember, if you arch your eyebrows too high, you will look perpetually surprised; if you leave them too low, you will have a scolding demeanor.

Curler—make sure all eyelashes are under the bar and press, holding ten seconds. Then bring the curler farther out on the lash and press again. Try for a sweep, not a tight curl. Apply mascara after curling.

False lashes—if you must add them, they should look natural. Eyelashes must be cut to fit one's eye.

Mascara—use brown rather than black for a softer, more feminine appearance. Apply to the base of your lashes in a rolling motion. Let it dry for a few seconds, then apply a second coat to the tips. Use mascara on the bottom lashes, too.

Lipstick—should complement complexion, harmonize with clothing. A shade that is too light makes the nostrils appear large and the face puffy. Apply by brush for a more finished look that will remain on the lips longer.

—From Joanne Wallace, *The Image of Loveliness.* Old Tappan, N.J.: Revell, 1978.

Eye Makeup[*]

Eyes are a beautiful, expressive part of a woman's face, and it is appropriate to accentuate their beauty. Yet many women make their worst errors in this effort. The object of eye shadow, for example, is to enhance the shape and color of your eye. You want people to say, "Look at the girl with the pretty blue eyes," rather than, "Look at the girl with the blue eye shadow!" *Never* let anyone tell you to make up your eyes to match your dress. That defeats the whole purpose of eye makeup.

Eyebrows

Eyebrows should be plucked to follow the natural shape of the eye. Flat eyes usually are accompanied by flat eyebrows. Clean up the eyebrow area, but don't try to create a fake arch. Average to round eyes usually have arched eyebrows, and in that case plucking the arch area makes the brow attractive. Eyebrows growing toward the lid serve only to make the eye look smaller, so do pluck, but do it judiciously. Take a pencil and hold it against the outside of the nose and across the tear duct. The tip of the pencil will point to the place where your brow should begin. Now run the pencil from the nose to the crease at the outside of the eye to see where the brow should end. Pluck out the excess or feather in the missing area with an eyebrow pencil. Do not pluck brows so that they become too thin.

If you need an eyebrow pencil, choose a color based on your brow and hair color. Try it out on your forehead. Winters and Summers need charcoal, brown, or blonde tones that have absolutely no red in them (even if the hair has red highlights). They should look for grayish or taupe tones. Autumns and Springs are the opposite and should look for golden blonde, reddish brown, or dark brown eyebrow pencils.

[*] Reprinted with permission from COLOR ME BEAUTIFUL by Carole Jackson, copyright © 1980 by Acropolis Books Ltd., 2400 17th St., NW, Washington, DC 20009, $14.95.

EYE SHADOWS

Eye shadows come in powders, creams, liquids, and crayons. Use whichever you personally find easiest to apply. I find powders the easiest to control, but they may accentuate crepiness on dry or aging skin. If you prefer crayons, be sure you use a creamy one that spreads easily. You don't want to stretch the skin around your eye area.

Eyes are of three general types: deep-set (with little or no lid showing), average (with some lid showing), and prominent or sunken (with most of the lid showing). Eye shadows can bring out or recess certain eye areas. A light shadow brings out an area; a dark shadow makes it recede. Each eye needs to be treated individually, but here are some basic guidelines.

For purposes of illustration, we will divide the eye into three areas from top to bottom: the underbrow, the orbital bone, and the lid. Some women need a highlighter shadow on the underbrow, a second shadow on the orbital bone, and a third on the lid. Others have eyes that have room for only two shades, a pale highlighter on the underbrow and a color or darker neutral on the lid, brought slightly up onto the orbital bone.

Underbrow. A highlighter on the underbrow is a light neutral color that serves to open the eye and clarify the skin, eliminating pink or tired brown tones around the eye area. Applying the highlighter from the brow to the lid gives you a good, clear base for the whole eye area.

Lid. On the lid, it's best to use a color that blends with your own eye color, but in a considerably softer shade. I do not recommend an eyelid color that contrasts with your eyes. Having tested contrasting colors extensively, I find that they simply are not flattering and do not achieve the goal of making the eyes look their prettiest. Brown eyes are a slight exception. Brown eye shadow, while good on many brown-eyed Autumns and Springs, makes Winters and Summers look tired and drab. These brown-eyed types can use

smoked mauve, plum, or navy to bring out their eye color—these provide a complement rather than a contrast.

A person with prominent or sunken eyes must stick to neutrals, rather than colors, on the lid. These might be brown, gray, smoked navy, or smoked plum, depending on the person's season and eye color. Any color-color is glaring and calls attention to the lid rather than minimizing it. For such eyes, apply the highlighter in the crease and the dark neutral on the lid just near the lashes, leaving the rest of the lid as is.

Orbital Bone. For most eyes, it's best to use a dark to medium neutral on the orbital bone. This neutral can also be brought down onto the outer third of the eyelid to widen the eyes a bit. A deep-set eye, with no lid showing when the eye is open, is the exception; it is sometimes effective to bring the eyelid color onto the bone area, lightly. Just a hint of muted color on the bone will bring out the color of the eye. If it is too bright, mix it with a neutral.

The lighter your skin, the lighter you apply everything. "Dark," "medium," and "light" mean relative to you. Blend with a cotton ball or your fingertip. Remember, eye shadow means shadow, not bright color. Even color is used here to create a "shadow" effect for a natural look.

If you wear glasses all the time, you may apply eye makeup a little more heavily than other people, but be careful not to overdo it.

FALSE EYELASHES

False eyelashes can be fun for the dramatic or romantic type woman. The most natural are the clusters that you apply individually. Use five or six clusters for each eye, applying short ones on the ends and medium-length ones in the middle positions. Many beauty shops will put these lashes on for you, though it is relatively easy to do yourself. These lashes stay on in the shower and last for a few weeks.

The strip styles look natural if the false lashes are thin, merely enhancing your own. These, too, should be shorter on the ends, longer in the middle. Lashes that are long at the outer edge will make your eyes look droopy.

EYELINER

Eyeliner is not for everyone. Many eyes, especially deep-set or average types, look smaller when eyeliner is applied to the upper lid. But with the advent of smudgy pencils or crayons the line can be softened with your fingertip to serve as a deep eye shadow. It is effective on deep-set and average eyes to use a touch of crayon on the outer third of the upper lid.

The prominent eyelid needs eyeliner, in a neutral color, smudged along the upper lid close to the lashes. This helps make the eye recede.

All eyeliners should be a neutral or smoky version of your eye color—never a bright color. The exception is liner for the eye that is so deep-set that the lid does not show at all. In this case you may use a crayon liner in the same color as the lid eye shadow, applied thinly at the base of the lashes, then blended with your finger. This color will barely show when the eye is open and will help bring out your eye color. The woman with deep-set eyes, as I mentioned previously, can bring her lid color lightly onto the orbital bone. Both of these techniques will "open" her eye and enhance her eye color.

All eyes except prominent ones can have the outer two-thirds of the lower lid underlined in a neutral color.

—From Carole Jackson, *Color Me Beautiful.* Washington: Acropolis, 1980.

FOR FURTHER READING:

Jones, Candy. *Finishing Touches.* New York: Harper & Brothers, 1961.

Pierre, Clara. *Looking Good.* New York: Reader's Digest Press, 1976.

Wallace, Joanne. *Dress With Style.* Old Tappan, N.J.: Revell, 1983.

Wallace, Joanne. *The Image of Loveliness.* Old Tappan, N.J.: Revell, 1978.

Wilhelmina, *The New You: How to Maximize Your Total Appearance.* New York: Simon & Schuster, 1978.

MAMMOGRAPHY

ONCE A [breast] lump is palpable, it has already been growing for a while, which is why routine mammographies are so important. They can detect a lump usually long before you can. It's a low-radiation X ray, capable of showing early changes in breast architecture and 90 percent of the time distinguishing a benign tumor from a malignant one. It's such a sensitive tool that it can detect cancer too small to be seen by surgeons in tissues actually removed during a biopsy. However, a substantial number of lumps have been found by examination when mammography has been negative. Obviously neither mode of screening for breast cancer is as good as the two together. It can catch the cancer while it's still minimal, before it has invaded surrounding tissue (metastasized), and women undergoing mastectomy for minimal breast cancer have an excellent chance of being completely cured.

Ten percent of the time the mammography cannot distinguish between a benign and a malignant lesion, and at this state a surgeon is normally consulted to try to aspirate the lump. Aspirating means taking fluid out, and if this decompresses the lump or if the aspirated fluid contains no malignant cells, nothing further is required except follow-up examinations every three to six months. If the lump is solid or yields very little fluid, or if the fluid contains malignant cells, the entire mass will have to be removed (called a biopsy) and examined under a microscope.

The newest recommendation of the National Institutes of Health is that all women over fifty should have annual mammograms, and that all women over thirty-five should have at least one. It should probably be performed more often on women who are at higher risk—if they have a family history of it, for example, or if they've never been pregnant. Remember, you should have *both* a physical exam and a mammography regularly, not just one or the other.

—From Barbara Edelstein, M.D., *The Woman Doctor's Medical Guide for Women.* New York: Morrow, 1982.

MANIPULATION

EVERY WOMAN alive knows how to play games. We keep our motives a secret, say no when we mean yes, and seductively use our power to get our way, manipulating husbands, sons, and bosses into giving us what we want by making it look as if they had the idea all along. But it is deceptive and dishonest. It is also sin. When the wicked witch on the inside, dresses up as the charming belle on the outside, we act like Scarlett O'Hara—the antithesis of what God means for us to be as women.

Many authorities on women believe this manipulative form of power comes from centuries of powerlessness. They suggest when women have more power of our own in the world, we will not use it underhandedly—that when we recognize our own power, we will stop trying to live our lives through our husbands and sons, driving them to fulfill our ambitions instead of their own. There is some truth here. But I think the problem lies deeper than this.

A basic core of selfishness and egocentricity resides in all of us, no matter how much or how little power we have. The Bible calls it our sin nature; psychology calls it our shadow or our id; anthropologists speak of our survival animal instinct. But whatever you want to call it, we must deal with it. We must decide what we will do with our power, how we will use it; and who it will serve.

We've all met the women who serve from a sense of duty, instead of from the heart. They often sigh deeply, somewhere in the back of the kitchen. Their attitude seems to be, "I'm going to serve you, if it kills me, which it probably will, so you'd better appreciate it properly!" These martyrs make everybody feel guilty and then wonder why everyone leaves as soon as possible. After all, "Look what I do for them! How ungrateful they are!"

There are those of us who serve manipulatively. Rushing in to help, unasked, we brush off efficient hands in smug satisfaction and smile sweetly as our attitude says, "Now that I have done all this for you, I expect you to do something for me." We ingratiate ourselves to others in order to control them and then feel abandoned and unloved when we don't get what we want in return.

Some also selfishly help individuals who should be helping themselves, because helping meets a need to be needed. The zealous woman of this sort only feels good when she helps, so she may "mother" her husband in an overly solicitous way that undermines his manhood or never gives someone else a chance to be in charge. How much of this kind of helping is done in the name of Christianity!

Or there are the *smother mothers*, who instead of encouraging new growth, smother with their comfort, like a feather bed on a hot summer night. "I don't want you to be hurt by life," they say, "so I won't let you live it. I want you to be comfortable, and life isn't always comfortable, so I will protect you from it." In their well-meaning way, they stifle maturity, clipping grownup wings, which are meant to be used for flying; meeting needs that no longer need meeting; still shoving the worm down the throats of those who should be out finding worms or mates or nests of their own.

Or finally there are the *god mothers*, who play God in the lives of those around them. All-knowing, all-loving, all-sufficient, they naturally see exactly what is best for everyone, and expect others to follow their directions, all the while praising them and giving adoration for all they do. Instead of challenging others to seek God's purpose for their lives and letting Him be God, they usurp His position and then wonder why those they love never seem to want a relationship with God for themselves.

How often we fall into one or more of these ugly categories. There have been times I have been every one of them. We have a responsibility to come to terms with this shadowy side of ourselves, if we want to have the positive side of our power at our disposal. Robert Johnson says, in his marvelous little book *She*, that women have two valuable items: a lamp, with which we can shed

311

the light of our insight, and a knife, with which we can impale with those deadly looks and devastating remarks we all use at times, skewering the very ones we love with an angry flow of words. Choosing whether we use the lamp or the knife in any situation is one of a woman's greatest responsibilities, and it is a choice we all face many times each day.

Perhaps the most vulnerable time for any of us is when we first recognize our power. If we have long had feelings of low self-esteem, as many women have at this point we can become prideful and dangerously inflated. It is not an accident that Jesus was propelled by the Holy Spirit into the wilderness, where Satan tempted Him and the Father tested Him, immediately after He was empowered for His unique mission here on earth. Upon first recognizing our power as God's women, we, too, can expect to be tested and tempted, tried in a refiner's fire to see how we will come through. And the wicked witch will be there, whispering in our ears, "Use the power for yourself. You deserve it." But improperly used power will turn us into the kind of helpers who become hindrances and into mothers who devour.

—From Barbara Rice, *The Power of a Woman's Love.* Old Tappan, N.J.: Revell, 1983.

MARRIAGE

THE PROMISE at the beginning of marriage is a statement of hope that the common process of growth may begin and that the other may be a witness and aid to that journey. A wedding does not *make* people married. Marriage itself is not a state or a new identity one achieves on a certain day. Marriage is rather a possibility, a potential, a hoped-for reality begun on a certain day but unrealized for many years. Marriage itself *is* the process through which the individuals within it gradually achieve ever-deepening forms of self-acceptance and personal growth through daily interaction. The hoped-for moments of grace which reveal to

the partners their common commitment are symbolic occasions that provide the two with a shared understanding of the meaning of life, the uniqueness of their individualities, and the singular value of their mutual bond.

The act of marrying for a woman is then a crisis that continues. The dangers of formulating a restrictive understanding of marriage and identity within it and of looking to marriage for a false identity are very real. The rituals that our culture uses to symbolize the nature of marriage fail to articulate a proper view of the necessary death and rebirth and the graceful possibilities of that relationship and of growth within it. No other event involves a woman in such a great risk since it is within the context of that relationship that the experience of her female sexuality in pregnancy and childbirth may be carried out and the further life-crises of parenthood, maturity, and old age must be negotiated. The hope for a marriage is that it may provide, not only a context for increased personal trust and growth and self-understanding, but that it may in itself be creative in its power to reveal a sense of the mystery of life, our aloneness and togetherness in face of it, and the continual element of dying and being reborn that constitutes the very wonder of it all.

—From Penelope Washbourn, *Becoming Woman.* New York: Harper & Row, 1977.

Preparation

ARE YOU MATURE ENOUGH?

The implication here is that maturity usually, but not always, increases with age and experience. The more mature a person is the more successful his marriage is likely to be. Just what do we mean by mature? The dictionary definition doesn't quite fit our context in this discussion: "fully developed," "ripe" are given as synonyms. But maturity in the sense that we are thinking of is a relative thing. We may be mature enough at age six to enter school and attend to some of our needs like eating, dressing, etc., but we are not mature enough at that age to understand the high-school curriculum or to exercise complete control over all of our needs. Maturing is a process involving growth and, except in the physical sense, few if any of us ever achieve complete maturity on all levels of our personality.

But we do recognize that marriage requires a level of maturity that includes willingness to assume responsibility for our own actions, for our own welfare, plus the welfare of a mate and children. It includes vocational readiness, the ability to earn a living that will provide adequately for one's family. In some circumstances the parents of college-student married couples agree to pay their expenses until graduation. This situation requires a level of maturity that will enable both young people to strike a fine balance in their attitudes towards their helping parents. They need an appropriate appreciation for the valuable contribution their parents are making and a constant awareness that such help doesn't bind them to the dictates of their parents. Unfortunately, many parents do not give help without invisible strings attached—conditions that may threaten a cutoff of funds if the young couple does not comply. Such family situations can cause deep resentments in grown children and their parents, and add deep and divisive emotional burdens to a young marriage.

A young person contemplating marriage ought to be mature enough to recognize his or her reasons for wanting to marry and to judge correctly whether those reasons are adequate. A girl who rushes into marriage to escape an unhappy homelife isn't acting responsibly. After marrying, the probability is that there will be two unhappy individuals. Or the couple who do not love each other, who have nothing in common, whose dispositions clash, who come from totally different backgrounds frequently marry when the girl finds she is pregnant. They marry "for the sake of the child" and condemn that child to emotional crippling. This is immature reasoning and irresponsible behavior.

Becoming mature enough to marry ought also to include learning the motivations for your actions and how to control your behavior. The person who lives at the mercy of his instincts is a menace to himself and others.

A very young couple have not lived long enough to experience many of the situations that alone can teach them mature responses. The learning process is, to some extent, a trial-and-error proposition. We are confronted with situations for which at times there are no correct or incorrect answers. Sometimes we respond wisely, at other times not so wisely, but we begin to amass a data bank of information based on the consequences of the actions we took. Reason alone would indicate that the more practice you acquire in decision-making, through situations confronted, the greater will be the resources for capable decision-making when the need arises. So when parents, or pastors, or professional counselors advise against early marriage or teen marriage, the reason may not be merely because you are too young, but that you are not yet mature enough to handle all that is implied in the marriage relationship.

MARRIAGE MEANS RESPONSIBILITY

What do we mean by this phrase, "all that is implied in the marriage relationship"? In spite of the impression given by advertisers, TV, movies, and popular fiction, you won't spend most of your married life in bed or sitting on a couch holding hands. The greater part of your life together won't be spent surfing, either, or walking hand in hand through a field of flowers. Your wife won't look great in a bathing suit forever. Your husband may go without a shave or leave his dirty socks on the floor. And there may be times when you'd like to give your children back.

Children? But you may be planning to marry in your teens, grow up together (there's no satisfactory way of doing this without putting enormous strain on the marriage), and avoid having a family until you've outgrown your immaturity and are ready for parenthood—a plan I hear frequently when I am asked to counsel with teen-age couples. In spite of the Pill and the best intentions, brides *do* get pregnant, and successful parenthood requires more than the ability to procreate, to prepare a formula, and to change diapers.

When you bring into the world another human being, you have given life to more than a physical organism, you have created an individual who will become the sum total of his genetic inheritance, plus his interpersonal relationships and his own will. But beyond this, he will also be a living soul, one who will have the opportunity to accept eternal life through his relationship with Jesus Christ, or who will forfeit that experience and be separated eternally from God, through his unwillingness to believe. The sexual relationship of a man and woman carries with it the possibility, if not the probability, of this kind of responsibility. If you aren't mature enough to assume the role of a parent, then you are not mature enough for marriage.

Danger Signs

Like red lights, blinking danger signs mean *STOP*, then proceed with caution (if at all!). It is better to take this brief test before you become engaged so that if definite danger signs turn up you will have time to do something about them before committing yourself officially to marriage plans. If you are already engaged and encounter danger signs, then by all means delay your wedding plans until you can straighten out the problem areas that you or your partner have. Like icebergs, the negative traits may be hidden from you, and just the tips show what is going on beneath a supposedly mature exterior.

1. A general uneasy feeling about the relationship. Lack of inner peace. A nagging, aching, disturbing feeling inside that says, "Something is wrong." Don't

ignore that feeling. It may be your own temporarily numbed common sense, or it may be God's Spirit trying to communicate something to you. More than a few clients have admitted to me that they knew the marriage was a mistake even as they were walking down the aisle.

2. Frequent arguments. Never sure how the date will end. More fighting than fun.

3. Avoiding discussing sensitive subjects because you're afraid of hurting your partner's feelings or starting an argument. You find yourself thinking, "I'd better not talk about this." Perhaps subjects like: "I wish he'd show me more affection, I wish he wouldn't treat his mother so mean. I wonder why he always has a temper tantrum when he gets a flat. Can't he control it better? I wish he would shower more often."

"She makes a pig of herself when there's a box of candy anywhere in sight—don't you suppose she cares about getting fat? I wish she'd read a book once in a while. Why can't we ever talk about something interesting instead of just superficial topics?"

4. Getting more involved physically. You resolve to limit the acceleration of your physical intimacy, but find that on each new date you start again at the place where you left off. Sometimes couples get involved physically as a way to avoid arguments. Just one of the reasons for this being a danger sign is that your relationship may remain on the physical level only, throughout your courtship and marriage. After you're married you may not like the personality that goes along with the body.

5. If you find yourself always doing what your partner wants you to do. Constantly giving in, being accommodating. This could indicate a selfish, domineering partner and/or a serious insecurity on your part.

6. If you detect serious emotional disturbances such as extreme fears, extreme shyness, bizarre behavior, irrational

anger, inflicting physical injury, inability to demonstrate affection.

7. If you feel you are staying in the relationship through fear. For example, if thoughts like these go through your mind: "I wish I could get out of dating him, but I'm afraid of what he might do to me. Or he might commit suicide. I feel trapped and I couldn't stand the guilt if something happened."

8. If your partner is constantly complaining about apparently unreal aches and pains and going from doctor to doctor.

9. If your partner continually makes excuses for not finding a job. If he or she borrows money from you frequently. The partner who evades responsibility and who can't manage his money wisely will be a poor marriage risk.

10. If your partner is overly jealous, suspicious, questions your word all the time, feels that everyone is against him.

11. If the one you date is a perfectionist and is constantly critical. This kind of a person often creates a tense unhealthy atmosphere.

12. Treats you contemptuously. Uses biting sarcasm.

13. Parents and other significant people are strongly against your marriage. Consider their reasons before you make a final decision.

14. Lack of spiritual harmony.

15. Few areas of common interest.

16. Inability to accept constructive criticism. Doesn't apologize when he is wrong.

DANGER SIGNS THAT WOULD INDICATE THE NEED FOR PROFESSIONAL COUNSELING

1. Undue jealousy, suspicion, distrust.
2. Constant chip-on-the-shoulder attitude.
3. Temper tantrums.
4. Unresolved anger, resentment. Vindictiveness.
5. Physically abusive.
6. Objects to or is distant to any kind of romantic involvement.
7. Severe mood swings. High elation followed by depression.

8. Constantly negative attitude. Pessimistic.
9. Suspicious of everyone. Suspects some sort of plotting against him.
10. Speaks of suicide and the meaningless of life.

—From Anthony Florio, *Two to Get Ready.* Wheaton, Ill.: Victor Books, 1978. Available through the Saddle River Counseling and Educational Center, 188 E. Saddle River Rd., Saddle River, N.J. 07458.

Roles

In 1982 the Equal Rights Amendment (ERA) was defeated because the needed 36 states didn't ratify the change in our Constitution. Christians argued on both sides of the issue.

Even with the failure of ERA the issue has not been settled. Nor will it be settled for a long time. One thing is clear, however, marriage roles and our view of husband-wife relationships have changed in recent years. Today we have moved toward a more equalitarian position. Even among the most conservative, the theological stance has moderated. For instance, among those who point out the apostle Paul's use of *submission* for women and *headship* for men, just as quickly affirm that those words don't mean servitude and suppression for women and autocratic control by men.

Theologians of earlier days took a less-gentle approach.

Martin Luther, in his *Table-Talk* said, "Men have broad and large chests, and small narrow hips, and more understanding than women, who have but small and narrow chests, and broad hips, to the end that they should remain at home, sit still, keep house, and bear and bring up children." (DCCXXV, 1569).

Charles Hodges, in his commentary on Ephesians (1856), wrote,

"The apostle, therefore, says, wives are to be obedient to their husbands, because the husband is the head of the wife, even as Christ is the head of the church. The ground of the obligation, therefore, as it exists in nature, is the eminency of the husband; his superiority in those attributes which enable and entitle him to command. He is larger, stronger, bolder; has more of those mental and moral qualities which are required in a leader. This is just as plain from history as that iron is heavier than water. . . . This superiority of the man, in the respects mentioned, thus taught in the Scripture, founded in nature, and proved by all experience, cannot be denied or disregarded without destroying society and degrading both men and women; making the one effeminate and the other masculine."

I wonder how many today would agree with the obvious interpretation of male *superiority?*

As in most critical issues, devout Christians have based their arguments on biblical texts. Their interpretations have spanned the spectrum.

In various passages God sets a pattern of authority. He declares the husband head of the wife as Christ is head of the church (*see* especially Ephesians 5:21–33, but also Colossians 3:18–19). Abraham is also Sarah's master (1 Peter 3:1–7). Thus, scripture says that a wife submits to her husband. The children are the third link in this divine chain of command (*see* Ephesians 6:1), so that human authority in the Christian home, given by God, starts with the husband as the head with the wife submissive to him, and the children submissive to both.

This position further declares that God's chain of command in marriage has no cultural considerations and is based on God's eternal principles.

Today, most conservatives would agree that certain cultural situations existed. After all, women had few rights. But that does not change the principle, they argue.

An often-used illustration involved Paul's injunction to "greet one another with a holy kiss." (*See* Romans 16:16; 1 Corinthians 16:20; 2 Corinthians 13:12.) Today most of us do not kiss upon meeting. That's the cultural aspect. But we do greet each other. A kiss symbolized a warm and affectionate

greeting. The principle, then, is to greet each other warmly.

—From Cecil Murphey, *The Encyclopedia of Christian Marriage.* Old Tappan, N.J.: Revell, 1983.

Improving

It has been said that when two people marry, they become one, but the question often is, which one? Visualize two solar systems trying to occupy the same space at the same time; two suns vying for center with planets orbiting around each. The result would be chaos and collision. The same is true of a home with conflicting centers and different interests whirling around each. In some homes such a situation is solved by everyone yielding center place to one. Then the home centers around the mother or father or a child. Peace reigns, but the price is frustration and humiliation. This kind of peace is not the Christian answer.

In Christian marriage Christ is the center, and husband, wife, and children can find their proper orbit around Him.

Let us express this mathematically. In a marriage without Jesus Christ, 1 plus 1 equals 2. Where there are children, 1 plus 1 plus 1 plus 1 equals 4, and four centers in a home are hell!

The Bible says about marriage, "These two shall become one." Mathematically this means that 1 plus 1 equals 1. This sounds ridiculous in the science of mathematics, but it makes wonderful sense in the metaphysics of matrimony!

One attractive young couple came to realize that their budget was their biggest problem. Each felt that their tight budget and growing debts were the result of the other's irresponsibility and poor management. The subject was explosive and neither dared bring it up knowing the violent consequences. The wife expressed her rebellion by going on a periodic clothes buying spree, while the husband bought model trains.

When they admitted as new Christians that Christ could help them decide how they should spend their income, they were able in a short time to discuss their finances without anger, live within their income, and slowly begin to come out of debt. They set a time each week to go over the budget, and to remind them who had the final word, they always placed an empty chair at the head of the table.

Human love presupposes marriage to one's ideal. As disillusionment comes, the marriage breaks down. Christian love is not blind, but it has its eyes wide open. It does not vanish when the other's faults appear. A Christian marriage involves seeing and understanding the other person as he really is and loving him just that way.

Christ's plan for two people who are married and who live their lives in Him is that the wonderful glow of the courtship and honeymoon will not only last but deepen. True romance may not begin until we find this plan.

I can think of a couple married thirty years who are discovering Christian marriage after a lifetime of bickering and fighting. Today they are living in the glow of what it means truly to love each other. They are grandparents and also have young children of their own who share this new love in the home.

It all began with a conversation in which the wife expressed her life-long complaint. Her husband was hard to live with and touchy. He sulked and was unreasonable. He was extremely stubborn. Above all, *she* was active in her church and her husband was not. She wanted to know how to make her husband a Christian!

It was pointed out that if she were really a Christian, her only obligation was to make her husband happy, not good. This was a new thought. She saw that in spite of all of her church work, perhaps she had never let Jesus Christ become the center in her life.

One day she made a list of all the things she knew should be different in her life. Then she prayed, asking God to come into her life and change all these things. She discovered a wonderful new peace.

Five days later her husband, amazed by the wonderful change that had come over his wife, asked if the same thing could happen to him. He honestly faced the things that were wrong in his life and he prayed, asking Christ to forgive him and to change him and to take over his life. The marriage was transformed.

There is no way for God to change a marriage and leave the people involved unchanged. C. S. Lewis has said, "No clever arrangement of bad eggs ever made a good omelet." We waste too many of our prayers praying for the other person to change, when some really honest prayer for ourselves may do wonders.

Not long ago a woman came to her minister, begging him to tell her what to do with her alcoholic husband. She had taken all the abuse and humiliation and poverty she felt she could stand as the result of his drinking. Her minister asked her what she had done to try to change him. She said she had begged him, argued with him, shamed him, preached at him, read the Bible to him, threatened him, and prayed for him for years.

"Have any of these seemed to work?" the minister asked.

"No!" said the woman. "They have not."

"There is one thing you haven't tried. Why don't you pray for *yourself*, instead of your husband, and ask God to change all the things in your life that you know are wrong?"

The woman tried it and it worked. Her husband stopped drinking. He no longer had to escape.

Anyone can discover a Christian marriage who will sincerely pray the prayer, "Lord, change this marriage beginning with *me.*"

—From Bruce Larson, *Dare to Live Now!* Grand Rapids: Zondervan, 1965.

FOR FURTHER READING:

Augsburger, David W. *Cherishable: Love and Marriage.* Scottdale, Pa.: Herald Press, 1971.

Small, Dwight Hervey. *Your Marriage Is God's Affair.* Old Tappan, N.J.: Revell, 1979.

MASTECTOMY

ONCE [breast] malignancy has been established, you'll have to face the controversy about the best surgical procedure to remove it. The original operation was the disfiguring Halsted procedure, or radical mastectomy. This was conceived in 1894 and is virtually unchanged today. It evolved from the idea that breast cancer proceeds in an orderly, stepwise fashion from the original tumor to the lymph nodes to distant sites. Therefore, everything within range of the tumor was systematically removed—breasts, lymph nodes, chest muscles, the works.

The most common method of treatment today is the *modified* radical mastectomy, which is similar to the original except the chest muscles aren't removed. Recently there has been a movement toward preserving the breasts; surgeons remove the lump (a procedure called, appropriately enough, a lumpectomy) and the auxiliary nodes but leave the connective tissue. Then they radiate the breast to try to kill remaining cancer cells (if any) and to give better cosmetic, functional, and psychological results than one would have with surgery. This radiation is called adjuvant therapy, which means preventive treatment when there is no evidence of spread. Chemotherapy (the use of one or several chemicals) and hormone therapy are beginning to show promise as adjuvants with surgery.

Spurred by the idea that surgeons seek to "defeminize" their patients without consent, a very vocal group of lumpectomy enthusiasts has emerged. You're most likely to benefit from this limited surgical removal with radiation therapy if you're a young woman with minimal breast cancer anxious for the best cosmetic results. In some cases, however, a lump with clear margins removed may constitute as great a deformity as losing the entire breast.

It's a shame that so little surgical progress has been made in this disease since 1894, especially since the organ, while useless except for nursing, has such important sexual overtones in our society. To be fair, surgeons have worked very hard to cure and control the disease itself, and the partial mastectomy has been possible only in the past twenty years with the sophistication of radiotherapy. This is a local treatment, like surgery—although doctors can safely radiate a larger area than surgeons can remove—and it preserves the function of the tissues being treated. It's impossible, however, for doctors to measure the amount of tumor foci that might remain after radiation; and it's possible that normal cells may be altered by the radiation and, hence, become cancerous themselves.

One exciting development for women who have had major breast surgery and, two years later, no recurrence of the cancer, is breast augmentation. This sophisticated technique of reconstruction has become so refined that it's no longer a cosmetic tragedy to have a breast removed. And breasts, alas, are cosmetically very important to a lot of women (not to mention men).

Personally, I have trouble relating to the intense feelings most women have about their breasts. Part of their worry, I'm sure, is how their husbands will feel: "Will I be as sexually attractive? Will he be repelled?" It's too bad females have to be slaves to the masculine ego in matters vital to health. I certainly wouldn't want to have my breasts amputated, but I've never attached much importance to them—cosmetic or otherwise. Although the loss of one breast might be a shock to the other breast, those appendages of fat and connective tissues are not the seat of your femininity. If you have breast cancer, there are more important things to worry about than the loss of a breast. It won't affect your sexuality in the least, and if your husband is unhappy, that's *his* problem. Don't let it bother *you;* recent studies suggest that a positive, optimistic attitude plays a role in preventing further outbreaks of cancer.

—From Barbara Edelstein, M.D., *The Woman Doctor's Medical Guide for Women.* New York: Morrow, 1982.

FOR FURTHER READING:

LaHaye, Tim and Beverly. *The Act of Marriage.* Grand Rapids: Zondervan, 1976.

Padus, Emrika. *The Woman's Encyclopedia of Health and Natural Healing.* Emmaus, Pa.: Rodale, 1981.

MASTURBATION

MASTURBATION is deliberate and conscious self-stimulation so as to produce sexual excitement with the goal of orgasm. Whether or not the goal is achieved depends upon age and other factors, but it is certainly the ultimate aim of the sexual arousal. Masturbation can be observed in small children, but the chief period for it is during adolescence and early young adulthood. Without doubt it is the major sexual activity of teenagers.

Hulme quotes the old joke, "Ninety-nine out of a hundred teenage boys and girls masturbate and the other one's a liar." Just how widespread is it? For obvious reasons it is not possible to state with complete accuracy, but data derived from questioning thousands of people in clinical survey leaves no doubt that it is an extremely common practice among both males and females of all ages. The Sex Information and Education Council of the United States (SIECUS) says that about 90 percent for males and above 60 percent for females, over a period of time, is a realistic figure. Most experienced counselors would confirm similarly high percentages on the basis of their own records.

Is Masturbation Sinful?

Let me now try to set forth my own conclusions on the subject, which are based on counseling uncountable numbers of people.

1. *There is no clear and direct word on masturbation anywhere in Scripture.* The two passages used in ancient times, Genesis 38:8–11 and 1 Corinthians 6:9,10, have nothing to do with it. Onan's sin was his failure to obey the ancient Hebrew law by practicing *coitus interruptus,* and was not masturbation. The King James Version term "abusers of themselves," in the Corinthian list, was a mistranslation and is now correctly rendered "homosexuals" in all modern versions.

When we know how almost universal and ancient masturbation is (it is mentioned in the *Egyptian Book of the Dead,* circa 1550–950 B.C.), and when every other sexual sin such as fornication, adultery, homosexuality, bestiality are listed and clearly condemned, why is it—if it is always a sin—nowhere mentioned in the Bible? I realize the argument from silence is dangerous, but in the case of something so widespread and well known it would seem to be conspicuous by its absence.

2. *From a scientific and medical standpoint we now know that there is no mental or physical harm in masturbating;* so there are no moral arguments for health reasons. All this means that we will have to use other related Christian principles in determining its rightness or wrongness.

3. *Therefore, I believe that the act of masturbation in itself is neither good nor evil.* What, then, determines this? Two basic Christian principles. First, *the thought-life.* When masturbation is accompanied by sexual fantasies, it clearly comes under the condemnation of Christ's words about "mental adultery" in Matthew 5:27, 28, and is a sin. According to SIECUS, it is usually accompanied by such fantasies in three-fourths of males and half of females. However, I agree with Miles that the experience is possible without fantasy or lust, so that it cannot simply be taken for granted that it is always a lustful and thus a sinful act.

Second, *the social and relational life.* When masturbation, with or without lust, becomes an emotional substitute for proper interpersonal relationships, when it is used as a means of escaping from the pressures of loneliness, frustration, and depression, then there is no question that it is harmful to the person and therefore wrong from a Christian viewpoint.

Years of counseling has forced me to distinguish between masturbation as a temporary and occasional means of relieving normal sexual buildup (almost an inevitable part of normal growing up, particularly for teenage boys) and masturbation as a compulsive, enslaving habit which feeds, and is in turn fed by, deeper emotional hang-ups. Some of these would include an inability to relate to any person—especially those of the opposite sex—depression, deep-seated resentments, and the inability to find normal ways of coping with frustration and anxiety. In this case masturbation is really only a symptom for deeper problems which are far more serious and damaging than it is. In my experience some of the worst cases of the latter kind are among married persons. It can, in a Christian, unfortunately become the peg upon which he hangs his guilts and anxieties that keep him from actually getting to the real problem. Parents, pastors, and Christian counselors must learn to discern the difference between the various types.

Dealing With Masturbation

May I suggest what I have discovered to be some practical ways of dealing with masturbation:

1. *Do not try a direct, frontal spiritual attack.* My main quarrel against this is that instead of lessening the problem, it usually makes it worse. Nothing provokes masturbation more than to create anxiety about it. Try to get the person's mind off his guilt and anxiety by explaining to him that it is one of those gray areas where rightness or wrongness depends on other factors. Usually he has already tried prayer and Scripture reading with the only result that he feels worse than ever for breaking his promises to God. His prayers are often doing more harm than good, for they are totally negative. Words of reassurance about God's accepting love, his faithfulness even when we fail, and teaching the person how to pray positively ("Thank

you, Lord, for loving me and healing me and helping me with all my problems") will break the vicious circle of guilt and despair.

2. *Get his mind onto his social life and his interpersonal relationships.* Often he is a lone wolf and needs to break out of himself. "Socialize, don't fantasize" is another good suggestion. Persons who do this find within a matter of a few months that the compulsive nature of masturbation has been broken, reduced to a minor and only occasional means of relieving sexual tensions which finally may be abandoned altogether. The true joys of making friends, finding companionship, or of a dating relationship have filled the need formerly filled by a poor substitute. He no longer masturbates because he doesn't need to. He has grown up, matured, and "put away childish things."

My wife and I brought up our three children on the basis of this attitude towards masturbation. Where there is openness of communication on the subject of sex, including masturbation, we can testify that it will be simply an incidental part of growing up and not become a major problem. As one of my teenagers said to me one day when we were talking about it, "Don't worry, Dad; it's sure no big deal with me!" I think that sums up my view. It's high time we stop making such a "big deal" out of masturbation and give it the well-deserved unimportance it merits.

—From David A. Seamands, "Is Masturbation Sinful?" in *For Families Only*, J. Allan Petersen, ed. Wheaton, Ill.: Tyndale, 1977.

FOR FURTHER READING:

Fix, Janet. *For Singles Only.* Old Tappan, N.J.: Revell, 1978.

Ketterman, Grace H., M.D., *How to Teach Your Child About Sex.* Old Tappan, N.J.: Revell, 1981.

MEDDLING

PROVERBS 20:3b indicates that "every fool will be meddling," which surely invites the uncomfortable conversion: everyone who meddles is a fool. Proverbs 26:17 states: "He that passeth by, and meddleth with strife not belonging to him, is like one that taketh a dog by the ears." Yet the Good Samaritan took risks of equal potential and in so doing set an example we are urged to follow. That his action, which exemplifies the highest form of helpfulness, can possibly fit the definition of meddling gives some indication of the difficulty we encounter in distinguishing between the two.

So what *is* meddling, anyway?

Meddling is rearranging people's drawers—or people's lives. It's telling others what they should think, say, or wear—even if they don't ask. It's making them feel less than they are or could be—less capable of coping, less confident in decision-making, less attractive, less worthwhile. It's an initiation or perpetuation of chronic dependence. An invasion of privacy. A diminution of self-esteem, of personal or group pride. An erosion of motivation. A mutilation of relationships of every type. It's shabby and unsavory and uncomfortable—and much, much easier to recognize *after* the fact.

Few people set out to meddle. Most really want to help and feel sincerely that they have some basics and background for helping.

But it's a thin line we walk between "bearing one another's burdens"—a commission that, as Christians, we couldn't avoid if we wanted to—and meddling. It's a line which varies with situations, with individuals, with emotional factors which constantly fluctuate. No matter how perceptive our antennae of instinct, no matter how carefully we "read" each situation, the chances are great that we're going to blunder at times, stumbling "with the best of intentions" across that boundary.

I blundered a few weeks ago when I offered condolences to Anne, a woman I knew slightly and respected a great deal. The mother of Susan, one of my students, Anne had been expecting a baby late in life. I'd experienced the fallout of the entire family's happiness through Susan's glowing anticipa-

tion. One day, though, crestfallen, Susan confided that they'd lost the baby. Remembering our own two sorrows, one of them a miscarriage, I sympathized with Susan and—some time later in the grocery store—with Anne.

If I'd simply said that I was sorry, she might have been able to handle it. But my empathy carried me onto dangerous ground without my sensing it until it was too late; until she was crying; until she was explaining that there'd been reason to suspect an abnormality; and that, with great personal pain, they'd decided on an abortion.

Once the meddling's been accomplished, once that line has been crossed, communication which had seemed simple can splinter, developing new facets, offering a whole new mine-field of conversational hazards.

On that particular day, between the meat counter and the frozen raspberries, I triggered at least three of them, and I left the checkout line feeling both awkward and cruel.

I meddled with even harsher results—though with motives just as rooted in love—when one of my best friends became severely depressed. At least, that time, I had company. Ellen—bright, vivacious, talented and beautiful—possessed an enviable corps of friends. We closed about her protectively, offering endless compassion, reassurances of our caring, invitations and gifts and nonstop yes-man-ship to everything she said. Our greatest disservice to her, it developed, was in accepting her interpretation of reality, in joining her (however carefully, *certainly* not wanting to meddle) in condemnation of her family's apparent lack of love: *yes, her husband should spend more time with her; yes, her oldest son had, indeed, been heartless; yes, her daughters were acting selfishly; yes, they should certainly be concerned that she was experiencing pain; yes, yes, yes.*

My daughter's fiancé, who was studying psychology, suggested tentatively that we were wrong. But I knew that we weren't. We were motivated by love. We were "just trying to help."

It may have helped a little, in that she

knew that we loved her. It must have hindered a lot. How large a part we played in the lengthening of her depression, how much we contributed to the fact that one depression led to another, and another, we can never know.

Am I too harsh in judging our blunders? An expression of compassion, however ill-fitting, is still a hand of helpfulness extended. We all blunder (meddle) often as we "love one another." Perhaps the only unforgivables are those motivated by vindictiveness or empowered by a Pharisee complex or by a stubborn certainty that "we know best."

An example of the latter attitude was Dorothy and Joe's insistence that their prospective son-in-law build a home on their gift of acreage. His reluctance was viewed with suspicion (was he trying to warp their close relationship with their only daughter?); with annoyance (he couldn't afford to indulge in rainbow-chasing when he was taking on family responsibilities. What could Colorado, Texas, or Alaska offer that he couldn't find living where they had always lived, working where Joe would be glad to give him a job?); and with reasoning (why throw $200 to $500 a month down the rent drain? With the lot free, that money would go a long way toward a down payment on a house . . . and they would, of course, live with Dorothy and Joe while they built . . .).

Two years later, viewing the wreckage, they comforted themselves with the knowledge that it wasn't their fault that the marriage had folded, that their daughter no longer called or wrote. They had done their best to help.

Meddling comes most easily, most naturally, when we're dealing with our own children, perhaps because we have such emotional stake in their lives, and because we lack the objectivity possible with someone else's children. We want to give so much, help so much, share so much, spare so much. The mother of one of my high school students wanted to pass on, in a chunk, the journalistic expertise she'd gleaned the hard way over the years. And so when her son enthusiastically produced the first chapter of what

was to have been a novel, she carefully blue-pencilled each small error in grammar or form. The novel promptly aborted. She was meddling, but well-intentioned. Which doesn't really help that much in the area of dying dreams.

Nor do good intentions help when I realize, five seconds after I've done it, that I've meddled in the lives of my own children. I'm learning, though. I'm learning that when Robin asks for advice, she doesn't really want my advice. She merely wants more input, so that she may sift through all available alternatives—my suggestions no more weighty than any of the others—to make her own decisions. (I've matured beyond the certainty that she asks my opinion only to turn in the opposite direction.)

It's easy to meddle in the lives of others close to us, too, and difficult to sense the line of demarcation where helping ends.

Connie was convinced that she was helping when she appeared at her widowed mother's home one Christmas week, had the faltering old stove hauled away, and superintended the installation of a microwave.

"But I really don't want . . . ." protested her mother.

Connie interrupted with a hug. "I want life to be easier for you, Mom. I can afford it now."

"Then why not just have the burners fixed. . . ."

"Mom, please! I *want* to do this! I love you!"

Far into the evening, long after Connie had returned, smug and happy, to her own life and her own microwave, her mother sat, slumped and listless, tears dripping into her aproned lap, as she remembered hundreds of pies, thousands of cookies, multitudes of rolls and bread loaves nursed to golden crispness in an oven she had understood and loved.

When my husband, disturbed by my chronic over-involvement, prepares dinner alone or runs some of my school materials to the printer while I begin more layouts, that's helping. And I'm sure that he feels he's still helping when he says something like: "You're going to have to let somebody else do this next year; you're killing yourself. . . ." But he's not. He's meddling. I recognize his right to say *something*. After all, my over-involvement robs him of something important to both of us—our time together. It inconveniences him in terms of chronic clutter, fractured schedules, trips to the printer, etc. It involves him by osmosis, by proximity, whether he chooses to be involved or not. But when he seems to be making an edict concerning my job, that translates as meddling, however minor.

So it's not just a matter of the geographical areas of our lives which may be affected; meddling is also a matter of degree and delivery. Truly Christian helping is not imparted as though it came down from Mt. Sinai. We haven't the credentials for edicts; we haven't all the "right answers" for any situation, even for ourselves, so how can we presume to offer snap-of-the-finger solutions to others? Helpfulness which is too high-powered, too certain of its omniscience, deteriorates easily into meddling.

There are those bonus times, of course, when someone sets out to meddle, and winds up helping. My paternal grandmother was good at this. A wiry little woman, strong physically and verbally, she was against more things than she was for, and her resistance ignited counterresistance, so that rather than dying because of her disapproval, our dreams firmed. And so my brother became a pilot for a time and I became an art teacher and my sister studied music.

But it was Mother who benefited most from Grandma's against-ness. We'd been in an automobile accident. Only Mother was injured, but she'd suffered a bad pelvic break, and her hospital stay was complicated by pneumonia. Three months later, when Grandma came to visit, Mother was still on crutches, and it was spring.

In the past, Grandma had often decreed that Mother shouldn't have such a large garden (over a quarter of an acre, including flowers which she cut for a church basket each Sunday during the growing season). On this occasion, Grandma pursed her lips and said with finality. "Well, you won't be planting a garden *this* year!"

Mother began her planting the next week, on crutches. Later, as the rows required cultivation, she parked her crutches by the catalpa tree and limp-ouched her way behind the small gasoline-powered cultivator, one row after another.

Her recovery was complete—and Grandma never knew what a help she had been.

Mother's German stubbornness has responded in the same way to the more recent meddling of well-meaning friends and relatives who have urged her (since she's growing older, since her arthritis is worsening) to give up sewing for the VA hospital and the Cancer Society. But Mother firms her expression, asks, "Why don't they mind their own business?" and works away at projects which have held boredom and arthritis at bay for years.

Why do we feel the need to meddle? Is it a dissatisfaction with our own lives and accomplishments which impels us to probe into the lives of others to have some lasting (hopefully beneficial) effect on them? One of my husband's close friends is a doctor who yearned to be a musician but studied medicine to please his mother. Another entered the ministry under "loving pressure" but finds his fulfillment in testing cars for a major manufacturer.

Are we afraid that those we love will be hurt? Grandma might well have feared our venturing into areas she had never known, and so suspected.

Do we feel that we need to draw firm lines which will keep society from crumbling beneath our feet? Surely those early Christians who fought Paul concerning circumcision for Gentiles felt that one loosened law would lessen all, and that the strong flame so newly ignited would be snuffed out in anarchy.

Do we fear for our own altered lives, like Dorothy and Joe, and so manipulate the lives of others in an effort to preserve what we have cherished?

Do we want to share what we have learned from experience (as the journalist mother of my student) and what we have learned from pain (as when I injured Anne) or do we sometimes see ourselves as in-residence experts whose advice *must* be followed?

Do we want to spare those we love, and so run interference—like the Disciples, realizing how Jesus spent himself on others, yearning to spare him the "unnecessary" clamor of small, active children?

Whatever our motivation (or motivations) we need to watch for those danger signals which trigger meddling, and to recognize when it has happened, if only through its results.

If I find myself probing for additional details merely for self-gratification rather than simply offering a supportive shoulder and ear, it's probably meddling.

If I find myself prefacing my remarks with: "Maybe I shouldn't say this . . ." (chances are, I shouldn't); "Perhaps it's none of my business . . ." (chances are, it isn't); "Don't you think you should . . ."; "Why don't you . . ."; "If I were you, I'd . . ."; I'm probably meddling.

Helpfulness is usually less verbal than meddling. There's more listening. Sometimes all a person really needs is to bounce his thoughts against a good listener, while listening himself. Helpfulness is more responsive, less strident, less officious, less sure of itself. It's more flexible, more willing to be convinced, and more accepting. (However unacceptable the actions, the person is *never* unacceptable in the eyes of God, nor in our eyes, if we truly want to help.)

Perhaps helpfulness becomes most vividly meddling in the following ways:

1. *It's meddling when it wounds, rather than incises with the promise of greater healing.* There are times within our relationships when something pain-producing must be said. Ignorance is not *always* bliss; sometimes people must be forewarned. At such a time, it's important to examine motives with brutal honesty. Is there no other, kinder way? Is there any hint of vengefulness ("she has this coming") or pleasure? Our own pain at the telling should be as honest and intense

as the hearer's can possibly be at the hearing. And the cut must be made carefully, like a surgeon's, slowly testing reaction, minimizing pain, allowing the person himself (or herself) to react, to question, to formulate, to suggest.

2. *It's meddling when it kills or mangles someone's "impossible dream."* It's so easy to do this with our children. We want them to learn to live in a world that *is*, to have graspable goals. We want to shelter them from having their dreams shattered, as ours have been shattered, and in the sheltering, we shatter them ourselves. "Honey, there are so few people who can make a living in music (or art, or spaceflight, or treasure-hunting). It would be a nice hobby, though, once you find what you *really* want to do with your life." Or, "But lion taming's so *dangerous!* I'd never sleep a wink, if I knew that you were about to be ripped into bite-sized bits in a circus tent somewhere." Or, "Yes, it *does* sound exciting! But aren't you too tall (or short, or clumsy, or whatever)." Why not, instead, play the game of "Let's Pretend" for a time—not to the point of buying the first lion—but in dreaming along, perhaps sharing some of our own impossible dreams?

3. *It's meddling if it probes, raises cloudy doubts or diminishes hopes.* Helpfulness clarifies (or tries to) and undergirds, giving positive thoughts toward a better situation.

4. *It's meddling if it violates the sanctity of privacy,* whether physical (as the condition of dresser drawers) or emotional ("How can you possibly *feel* that way—after all Aunt Sarah's done for you?"). Better to try to understand which of Aunt Sarah's characteristics might be abrasive or unpleasant to a child and move to ease the friction.

5. *It's meddling when it cheats someone of a decision-making process which could, should, and would have taken place without interference.* I know of a mother who reserved the reception hall for her daughter's wedding before the prospective bride and groom had even discussed where, when, or *if* a reception figured in their plans.

6. *It's meddling when it betrays, inhibits,*

limits, or lacerates self-confidence. Or causes schisms or strains in relationships. Or makes someone feel less than he/she already does. Or causes suspicion or dissent.

When meddling can cause such damage, when it's so easy to fall into, mightn't it be more sensible, even perhaps kinder, to give up on helping altogether?

No.

Because we follow Christ, we have his commission to help one another. Because we are Christians, we have a need within ourselves to be of help. No self-centered activity can ever produce that particular essence of happiness which comes from helping others.

But because we are human, and thus not infallible, the trick is to be alert, sensitive, perceptive, cautious, prayerful, and as slow to action as we are to wrath. Or even slower.

No one, except perhaps a very young child, would reach out in haste to "help" a butterfly from its cocoon. We'd know that if anything meddled with the natural process, the butterfly would be a poor and crippled parody of what it might have been. Instead, we stand patiently, scarcely breathing, awed by what God's creative power and planning can do.

In the same way, we must be patient, allowing helping to happen in a healing way.

There's a great deal of humility involved in true Christian helpfulness, and a great deal of love. And if we're fair to everyone involved, we'll need a great deal of self-forgiveness for those occasions when we do blunder—as we all will—across that indefinable dividing line.

—Evelyn Minshull

FOR FURTHER READING:

Schlink, Basilea. *You Will Never Be the Same.* Minneapolis: Bethany House, 1972.

MEDITATION

WE HEAR A LOT about meditation these days. People learn eagerly to sit in just the right position—toes curled up over their thighs, hands at rest in the lotus position, palms up, shoulders relaxed, breathing deeply, pulling in their abdomens, exhaling in exactly the proper rhythm. Perhaps it will come soon. "Meditation." Some learn to slow down their heartbeat and triumphantly announce that it came to such a slow rate it was negligible. Others help along the arrival of meditation by taking some sort of powdered chemical substance into the stomach. Yet others smoke with what they feel is correct puffing of various plant substances, and with clouded eyes and minds wait for the great meditation to commence. Mystical, cloudy, floating, unreal—separated from earthly sequence of logical thought, separated from understanding and answers to questions, separated from verbalized explanations—modern meditation drifts in ebb and flow with no defining framework. Blurred, misty, with no sharp lines is this meditation. A student in an American seminary writes a friend firmly, "Don't mention the word *prayer* to me anymore. We don't pray. We meditate. Often we find it is necessary to smoke pot to meditate properly." A pastor in Sweden selects certain nights of the month to teach the accompanying bodily positions for Transcendental Meditation. A church opens its doors in an eastern American city for serious lectures on this subject. Meditation—a mélange of mystical, mythical, baseless peace—a state separated from the interruptions of reality—a state in which one can float into an "experience" of some vague sort.

What is the word *meditation* supposed to mean to us, as those who have come into communication with the Living God through the One Way He has opened up into His presence? What does the Bible teach us—born-again children in the family of the Living God—about meditation? *Is* there a difference? Are we in danger of being drawn into something false without understanding the difference?

We need to look at a few verses to see. Psalms 119:97: "O how love I thy law! it is my meditation all the day." Here is no special position in which to put the body, for this meditation is taking place all the day, during the time in which normal daily life is being lived. Here is no empty mind, no slowed-down pulse—but a mind filled with the content of God's law. What is being referred to as "thy law"? Not the Ten Commandments in stark outline, but the full verbalized richness of the Scripture's explanation of the commands of God. Oh, how I love the Scriptures, the true Word of God, as I read it and think about it and come to fresh understanding day by day. Never do I come to the end of the possibility of meditating upon *that*. Sentence by sentence, phrase by phrase, idea after idea, and understanding after understanding drop into the fertile, tilled ground of my mind, and, as I dwell in conscious thought, the seeds of God's law and God's teaching burst and send forth shoots of green understanding that I can put into words of my own. All the day long, as I walk in fields or city streets, as I sit at the typewriter or make a bed with fresh sheets, as I converse with professors or tiny eager human beings wanting to learn—three-year-olds with endless questions—as I work in a lab or scrub a floor all day long in office or factory, I can meditate upon the law, the Word of God which my eyes have read or my ears have heard or my fingers have felt in Braille. This meditation has a base, a changeless base which is as meaningful as it was centuries ago—and as true.

Then on to verse 99: "I have more understanding than all my teachers: for thy testimonies are my meditation." *How* can I have more understanding as a child, as a primary-school or high-school person or a university student? By meditating upon the testimonies of God! The Bible is the place where we can have enough content to give us understanding which is complete in being true. What we meditate upon—as we read day by day and think about what we read—gives us understanding beyond whatever of man's knowledge we are being taught which may cut across this understanding. We understand with our minds full of things to understand. We do not understand with empty,

vague, drifting feelings changing with the weather. A foggy day brings depressed feelings—but the facts being thought about and dwelt upon in one's mind are not affected by weather changes. The admonition to meditate during a lifetime upon the content of God's Word is not an airy, fairy thing, nor a thing which is reserved for older and more brilliant times of life. Listen to Paul's admonition to Timothy in 2 Timothy 3:14–16 "But continue thou in the things which thou hast learned and hast been *assured* of, knowing of whom thou hast learned them. . . . From a child thou hast known the holy scriptures. . . . All scripture is given by inspiration of God, and is profitable . . . for instruction in righteousness." Yes, meditation—with the content of the Bible in one's mind in order to understand further—is possible from childhood to old age, and can give understanding of what really is true in the universe and in oneself, beyond any human teacher.

Yes, all the day and throughout the days of my life, I am to meditate at certain times of need—even in the wee hours when others are sleeping. "Mine eyes prevent the night watches, that I might meditate in thy word." Here in Psalms 119:148 we are given the picture of one being unable to sleep and using that time to meditate *in* the Word of God. In comfortable bed with the bedside light on, in the hospital ward with pain or fears making sleep impossible, in long times of waiting for news when sleep will not come, in prison where cold floor and hideous odors drive sleep away, we can and must meditate in the Word of God, the Bible— His true truth which gives us what we need to know for comfort and direction. God is communicating to us as we think for periods of time upon what He has given in written form. It is in this way that our help comes from Him time after time.

In Psalms 63:6, 7 David makes this more vivid to our understanding: "When I remember thee upon my bed, and meditate on thee in the night watches. Because thou hast been my help, therefore in the shadow of thy wings will I rejoice." Here, if we follow David in our times of worry about violent death, rise and fall of governments, taxes larger than our incomes, we meditate rather than worry. Meditate upon God. But God is not just a word, a misty idea of our own—we have His Word telling us who He is. We read of His Creation and power, we read of all He has done in centuries gone by, and we can meditate upon Him and the help He has been through the ages, and the help He has been to us individually, too. And the reality of being in the protective shadow of His wings becomes so clear that before the time is over a real rejoicing follows. How seek comfort in the "white hours of night worries"? By meditating in the Word of the One who we suddenly remember is really *there*.

—From Edith Schaeffer, *A Way of Seeing*. Old Tappan, N.J.: Revell, 1977.

MENOPAUSE

MENOPAUSE is defined as the period of cessation of menstruation, occurring naturally between the ages of forty-five and fifty. Menopause involves the gradual decline of the working of our ovaries. Our ovaries can begin to produce less estrogen starting even in our late twenties. But most of us do not actually begin to notice *signs* of menopause until our late thirties or early forties. In other words, menopause is a long process which ends with the complete cessation of menstruation and of our ability to conceive and bear children. Our bodies have to adjust to these changes in ovarian and hormonal function. The length of time and the quality of this adjustment will vary from woman to woman. Removal of both ovaries (as in a total hysterectomy) before the age of natural menopause will bring on menopause symptoms.

. . . . .

The popular image of the typical menopausal woman is negative—she is exhausted, haggard, irritable, . . . unsexy, impossible to live with, driving her husband to seek other women's company, irrationally depressed, unwillingly suffering a "change" that marks the end of her active (re)productive life. Our idea of menopause has been shaped by ads like the one in a current medical magazine that pictures a harassed middle-aged man standing by a drab and tired-looking woman. The drug advertised is "For the menopausal symptoms that bother him most." Menopause is presented as an affliction to us that makes us an affliction to our friends and families.

In our youth-oriented culture, menopause for many people marks a descent into uncool middle and old age. In a society that equates our sexuality with our ability to have children, menopause is wrongly thought to mean the end of our sexuality, of our responsiveness to men, of pleasure in bed. In a society that considers babies to be our major contribution, menopause, often coinciding with our children's leaving home, marks the end of our only important job, the end of our reason for existing. Menopause is called "the change" and all the implications are that life goes downhill from there. ("The words 'change of life' must have had a catastrophically destructive effect on countless women," writes one friend. "I'm not willing to suspect it's such a change.")

These views are being changed by women . . . who value themselves as more than baby machines, who move into middle age as a welcome time in which they can pursue other kinds of work, who make careful use of the drugs available to minimize menopausal discomforts, who learn about ways that good diet, rest and exercise can help to prevent problems with menopause. Not everyone finds menopause physically easy, but we are learning that if we feel good about ourselves and what we are doing at that time in our lives, we will tend not to be so depressed and bothered during menopause. And if we know what menopause is and what to expect, we will be less mystified and alarmed by our body changes. And for many of us, the freedom to talk openly with our family or friends about what we are experiencing promises to make menopause a less trying, tense and difficult time. It also seems important that our awareness of how men feel about themselves during their forties and fifties will help to prevent possible difficulties in our relationships with the men in our lives. (As they reevaluate their own lives during middle age, many men are faced with the fact that they will not "advance" further in their careers or that their lives will not be as they had hoped, and many fear a loss of virility and the approach of old age.)

Because almost all of us at some point during menopause will go to a doctor about physical symptoms, it will be really important to us to insist on good medical care and advice. Many women up until now have been adversely affected by their doctors' own ignorance and carelessness. One woman told us that she went from doctor to doctor asking why she was so tired all the time—not one of them suggested she was going through menopause. Another woman, feeling tired, went to her doctor and complained that she couldn't do as much as she was accustomed to doing. Her doctor said, "Well, after all, you *are* getting old." Used to bowing to his authority, she accepted his verdict and resigned herself to her loss of energy. Pitifully little research has been done into symptoms and cures for symptoms of a physical experience more universally shared by women even than childbirth.

What Is Menopause?

In order to understand how menstruation eventually ceases, it is helpful to know what causes it. . . . The following is a simplified explanation of how the normal hormonal process of menstruation changes as menopause occurs.

As we get older, our ovaries become less and less able to respond to the ovary-stimu-

lating hormones from our pituitary, which formerly caused the regular maturing and releasing of ova. Since progressively fewer ova are being released, the cyclic production of progesterone is interrupted, and this in turn causes estrogen levels to fall below the amount necessary to start endometrial bleeding (menstruation). The pituitary, without the usual cyclic feedback of estrogen and progesterone, generally overreacts, producing excessive amounts of those hormones that stimulate the ovaries. The result is a hormone imbalance, occurring to different degrees in different women. The most important feature of this hormone imbalance is a decrease in the amount of estrogen to which a woman's system has been accustomed.

This estrogen decrease is thought to be the major factor in many of the problems we might experience during menopause. However, the interrelation of all the hormones, and their relation to our physical and mental health, are extremely complex, and to say that all symptoms of menopause are caused by a lack of sufficient estrogen would be inaccurate. Some doctors have gone so far as to declare menopause "an estrogen-deficiency disease," which they claim can be "cured." Most others are more conservative but agree that many of the symptoms can be alleviated in some women by readjusting the body's estrogen level.

If your estrogen level is low, your whole endocrine system is affected. Depending on your individual hormonal and glandular make-up you might have symptoms that may be alleviated by estrogen-replacement therapy. However, if for any reason your doctor feels it would be better to keep your estrogen level low (for example, to permit the shrinkage of any possible tumors stimulated by estrogen), you may feel that taking estrogen is a bad idea. In any event, there is some estrogen secreted by some other glands—the adrenals, for example—and a woman's body may produce enough estrogen from sources other than the ovaries so that she will not experience low-estrogen symptoms, even though her estrogen production is lower than her original level.

An average natural menopause occurs around age forty-seven, although natural menopause may start as early as thirty-five or as late as sixty. The following factors can cause early onset of menopause: removal of ovaries, or infection destroying them or interfering with their blood supply; excessive exposure to radiation; very poor health; prolonged nursing of a baby; disorders of the endocrine glands; hypothyroidism, with serious obesity; having babies too close together; frequent abortions or miscarriages; very cold climates; hard manual labor or excessive output of energy. The claim that the earlier menstruation starts the later it will stop is apparently not substantiated by fact. Women who have late menopause are generally very healthy, although perfectly healthy women can experience menopause any time between thirty-five and sixty.

Ovarian function starts to taper off at age twenty-seven or thirty, but you probably won't notice anything happening until you are in your forties, at which time menstrual bleeding may become shorter and then longer; then this stage may be followed by irregular or skipping or lengthening of periods. In a few cases menstruation occurs regularly until one month when it just stops forever. Most women, however, will taper off in both amount and duration of flow, and will experience irregular and progressively more widely spaced periods for a time of two to three years. Some excessive bleeding is quite common during this time and need not be a cause for worry. However, if you have extremely profuse or prolonged bleeding, or if you bleed between the dates when you think your periods should be coming, you should see a doctor, because you may have a benign or malignant growth. Your breasts may increase in size or become tender, and at this time cystic mastitis (nonmalignant breast growths) or similar conditions may develop or become more serious. It is a good idea to keep a record of exactly what hap-

pens after you first notice irregularity in your menses; the information can be useful in determining treatment, if you should need it.

The removal of ovaries by themselves or in combination with other parts of the reproductive system, as in a hysterectomy, will cause early menopause. When ovaries are removed, your body must adjust to a lower level of estrogen, and this brings on all the low-estrogen symptoms associated with menopause. If you have any choice in the matter, hang onto your ovaries as long as you can—don't let anyone remove them as part and parcel of a hysterectomy unless s/he has proved to you that it is absolutely necessary for your health. One ovary is better than none. Ovaries continue to secrete small amounts of estrogen after menopause, and this is useful for strong bones and other parts of your body.

—From The Boston Women's Health Book Collective, *Our Bodies, Ourselves*. New York: Simon & Schuster, 1973.

Needs of Woman

The need of modern woman to find a symbolic framework for this fundamental stage of life is acute. She needs a new basis for self-understanding outside her earlier interpretation of her sexuality. The issue facing her is whether she can find new purpose, new identity, new worth, a new self-concept, and a new sense of ultimate meaning as she passes into middle age. The crisis is more than a physiological adjustment to declining hormone levels. A woman must come to terms with herself and the meaning of life on a radical level. Perhaps the reason this crisis is so difficult and has so many aspects is that it foreshadows the end, death itself, the last crisis. The end of a woman's fertile years intimates the decline of the whole body and signifies a gradual approach toward the end of its powers in death. Menopause unmistakably marks the slowing of the whole system before we are ready for it. In midlife we are still strong; we are often healthy, and yet one element of our body's creative powers is now over and forces us to recognize our gradual movement toward death.

. . . . .

To discover new depths of self-understanding requires first of all a recognition of the nature of the crisis. The physiological symptoms of menopause and any effects that they have on mood may be helped by chemical means. The problem is that the woman finds it difficult to distinguish what part of the depression is caused by changes in her life situation and what part is a result of hormonal imbalance. Separating the physiological from the psychological factors is indeed impossible. As in all other life-crises there *is* a distinct physiological process at work. In some women it has marked effects; in others, almost none. In fact, women who have felt very well during pregnancy may be "estrogen sensitive" and experience more depression postpartum and during menopause. To recognize the nature of the crisis in both its physiological and its emotional forms is essential for a graceful resolution. Hormonal therapy, if proved safe, may indeed ease the physical changes, but the personal issues need to be recognized in all their implications for a new life-pattern.

Something dies at menopause; the fertile female potential is over. For this there needs to be mourning as well as thankfulness. The ability to experience a new body, free from menses, free from the fears of unwanted pregnancy, depends, I believe, on acknowledging and grieving for what is no longer—the end of one stage of life. All the joys and sorrows, hopes and disappointments, connected with the experience of one's sexuality in its procreative function need expression. Acknowledging this sorrow and expressing it without guilt to oneself and to others will eventually enable new hope to emerge. The new self cannot grow until the process of mourning and grief has been completed.

—From Penelope Washbourn, *Becoming Woman*. New York: Harper & Row, 1977.

Problems

According to many doctors, 20 percent of all women experience no problems during menopause. Ten to 15 percent have severe symptoms, including nervous breakdown or severe depression, and the other 65 to 70 percent experience a few symptoms in varying degrees. These include the following:

1. Tendency to gain weight with a redistribution of fat
2. Tiredness
3. Sleeplessness
4. Temporary lessening of desire for sex
5. Depression, mild to severe
6. Vaginitis, itching, irritation
7. Headaches
8. Leg cramps
9. Dizziness
10. Heart palpitations
11. Aches and pains
12. Opening leading to the bladder and part of bladder becomes thinner, sometimes making it difficult to empty the bladder (can cause bladder infections).
13. Gradual thinning and drying of vaginal tissues due to estrogen reduction (can make sexual intercourse painful unless lubricant is used)
14. Loss of fatty tissues from the external vaginal folds, which gradually become smaller as do the internal folds; vaginal walls may become relaxed from loss of muscle tone.
15. Hot flashes: wavelike sensations of heat that move up to the chest and to the head, frequently followed by profuse perspiration. Flashes may last a few seconds or as long as thirty minutes to an hour and are more frequent and disturbing at night.
16. Breasts have tendency to become smaller and flabbier from decrease in fat cells.
17. Psychological changes, including anxiety, increased tension, mood depression, and irritability
18. Osteoporosis (bone loss)

That's the bad news. But it's really not as grim as it seems. You're not going to experience all the symptoms at once—and you may not experience any of them, other than the stopping of your monthly flow. But it's helpful to know the signs so they won't interfere with your being Forty-Plus and Feeling Fabulous. Besides trying to keep your ageless attitude, the important thing is to be prepared.

—From *Ruby MacDonald's Forty Plus and Feeling Fabulous Book.* Old Tappan, N.J.: Revell, 1982.

FOR FURTHER READING:

Dobson, James. *What Wives Wish Their Husbands Knew About Women.* Wheaton, Ill.: Tyndale, 1975.

Landorf, Joyce. *Changepoints.* Old Tappan, N.J.: Revell, 1981.

Ruby MacDonald's Forty Plus and Feeling Fabulous Book. Old Tappan, N.J.: Revell, 1982.

MENSTRUATION

ESTROGEN in girls brings about many more changes than in boys. It stimulates the continuing growth of breasts to the full size each girl's genes and chromosomes planned for her to have. It is unfortunate that today's Western society has equated sexual desirability and even femininity with large breasts. Many flat-chested girls suffer real mental anguish because they believe they compare unfavorably with other girls. The small-breasted woman is just as lovely, just as feminine, and just as able to nurse her children as those who are more generously endowed. Teenagers need to be reassured and taught to accept themselves just as they are, physically as well as in all other ways. If they have learned the self-esteem we've been considering up to now, you can see how much easier it is to add the acceptance of their physical appearance as a teenager.

In the ovaries and the uterus, estrogen interacts with several other hormones to cause ovulation and menstruation. Ovulation is the process in which a microscopic egg (ovum) which has lain sleeping in the ovary begins to grow and is pushed out of its tiny pocket into the body cavity in the pelvis. Normally it is sucked up at once by the soft, waving motions of the fimbria into one of the Fallopian tubes, then moved gently into the womb.

While the ovary has been busy producing the ovum, the womb has been at work building up a velvety lining, rich with little blood vessels and nourishing fluid. If the egg is united with a sperm while it is in the Fallopian tube or the womb, it will rest on this soft uterine lining and then nestle in to begin the long process of becoming a baby. If it is not fertilized by the male sperm, it will die in a day or two and later will pass out of the womb along with some blood, serum, and tissue that were waiting for it. This is called menstruation. Many years ago, I was told, a medical student described the process as "the weeping of a disappointed womb." While this is picturesque language for the womb, it doesn't always describe the feeling of the woman!

The process of ovulation takes place about once every four weeks. Usually this happens midway between menstrual periods, though it may be as early as one week after or as late as a week before the period. While the average menstrual cycle is twenty-eight days, many women have shorter or longer ones. The period of menstruation may last from three days or less to a week or more. Not only do these facts vary from woman to woman but occasionally within a person as well. This does not necessarily mean there is anything wrong.

A change in schedule, moving, emotional upsets, physical illnesses, and many other factors may influence the delicate and intricate processes that are responsible for women's menstrual periods. Furthermore, it may take many months, or even years, for a young woman to settle into her individual cycle. It is important to know this to avoid worry and to realize the importance of being sexually responsible. Many girls believe that ovulation does not take place in the early months of their menstrual periods. While ovulation is irregular at first, it does frequently occur from the very first period, and as soon as ovulation begins, pregnancy can take place. I have seen several pregnant young girls who did not know this significant fact!

The signs of trouble with a girl's menstruation need to be noted. For these, a physician should be consulted. 1. A total irregularity of periods continuing two years after menarche (the first period). 2. Excessive bleeding—using more than one regular box of pads or tampons (and soaking them) per period. 3. Bleeding between regular periods. 4. Severe pain, cramping, and especially a tendency to faint during a period. Usually these symptoms do not indicate serious trouble, but a physical evaluation by a competent doctor can reassure both the girl and her parents.

An almost universal problem related to menstrual periods is the physical pain that accompanies them. In Genesis, we are told that as a result of Eve's disobedience to God's orders against eating the fruit of the tree of knowledge of good and evil, she would have to bear her young in sorrow and pain. Today, a slang expression for menstruation is "the curse." Many girls exaggerate this discomfort and some even take advantage of it to gain an extra day in bed, but there is no doubt that it is an uncomfortable and even miserable time for some.

As part of the hormone cycle that is responsible for menstrual periods, for a week or more before their periods women store up fluid in their bodies' tissues. This may amount to several pounds and will, in most women, produce a feeling of physical heaviness and emotional tension. They cry easily, feel gloomy, have headaches and a tendency to be explosively angry. Unfortunately, many women today deny this process because they feel it means they are in some way inferior to men. Instead of denying them, women need to be aware of these physical differences in order to take good care of their bodies.

Besides the fluid accumulation, there are other factors that cause menstrual cramps or discomfort. One of these is the increased size

of blood vessels in the pelvic area. Sometimes constipation may add to the sense of pelvic pressure. General fatigue or mild infections such as colds or flu are likely to affect the degree of discomfort.

A relatively new discovery shows that severe menstrual cramps are associated with the level of still another hormonelike substance called "prostaglandin." While this discovery is new and the treatment is experimental, there is great promise of real relief from the few truly severe cases of menstrual misery caused by this.

The use of pads and tampons to absorb the menstrual flow is historic. For several decades, schools have shown films and led discussions for preadolescent girls and their mothers. These are wonderful opportunities for parents to teach, guide, and share in this important event in their daughters' lives. A mother's sharing of the memories and feelings of her own puberty can draw her daughter close in a bond of understanding. This is the time for a mother to invite her child into the world of womanhood and begin teaching her how to become a beautiful woman. By accepting the fact of her daughter's new, though incomplete, adulthood many of the troublesome mother-daughter conflicts of the teen years can be avoided.

Finally, the use of tampons needs to be discussed. The widespread mass-media advertising campaigns leave little privacy to today's woman, so various sanitary supplies are well known. Tampons are specially made devices that fit into the vagina and absorb the menstrual flow directly from the womb. They are convenient, comfortable, and allow more freedom than do pads in activities such as swimming. Some people believe, however, that they cannot be used by a young woman who is a virgin.

Let me explain that in girls there is a protective membrane that partially covers the opening to the vagina. It is called the "hymen" and protects a child from getting dirt or germs into the genital area. Normally, there is an opening in this that adequately allows for the flow of the menstrual discharge and is usually big enough to easily insert a tampon. Some mothers have found their daughters using these without their knowledge and panic, thinking the girl has had sexual intercourse and broken the hymen. This is not necessarily true. It is possible for the hymen to tear through strenuous activities or minor injuries. On the other hand, in less than 10 percent of women, the hymen is so tough and the opening so small that tampons cannot be used. Such young women may need to consult a physician regarding possible treatment for this condition.

Newspapers have widely publicized a rare but occasionally fatal disease called "toxic shock syndrome," which may occur during menstruation. Gynecologists believe the evidence relating this syndrome to the use of tampons is as yet inconclusive. It would be wise for each woman to consult her doctor on this subject.

—From Grace H. Ketterman, M.D., *How to Teach Your Child About Sex*. Old Tappan, N.J.: Revell, 1981.

FOR FURTHER READING:

Dobson, James. *What Wives Wish Their Husbands Knew About Women*. Wheaton, Ill.: Tyndale, 1975.

17 Women Doctors, with D. S. Thompson, M.D., as consulting editor, *Everywoman's Health*. Garden City, N.Y.: Doubleday, 1980.

Washbourn, Penelope. *Becoming Woman*. New York: Harper & Row, 1977.

METABOLISM

HAVE YOU ever heard an overweight person envy a skinny friend because his *metabolism* lets him eat more and still stay thin? Whatever this thing called metabolism is, all fat persons wish theirs would let them eat the same way and not get fat.

Metabolism is simply the process by which food is changed into the chemicals your body can use for energy or to form body tissues. Doctors dispute whether overweight causes a faulty metabolism or whether a faulty metabolism causes overweight. The truth is probably somewhere in between.

Nevertheless, overweight persons have a disturbed metabolism. Their metabolism simply doesn't convert food into energy the way it should. It converts it into excess body fat instead.

There are several kinds of body metabolism. There is the basal metabolic rate, the part that is governed by the thyroid gland. But we also speak, for example, of salt-and-water metabolism, protein metabolism, fat metabolism—all describing the processes by which your body handles these substances.

The category that seems to make the most trouble for the overweight person is his carbohydrate metabolism. Because *insulin* plays such a vital role in your metabolism, you need to understand how carbohydrates affect its production, and what that, in turn, does to you.

Insulin is the hormone manufactured in cells within the pancreas. Its principal function is to act upon the carbohydrates in the bloodstream, which are in the form of glucose, and chemically deliver it to the body's tissues to be used as energy or to be converted into fat deposits for later use as energy. If there is a surplus of glucose in the bloodstream at any given time, it means that the body doesn't require any more fuel for energy at that moment, and thus the glucose is converted into stored energy or fat.

It doesn't take anyone too smart to figure out that the secret to not having glucose stored up as body fat is to have only enough in the bloodstream, at any given moment, to meet the energy needs.

—From Jim Tear and Jan Houghton Lindsey, *Fed Up With Fat*. Old Tappan, N.J.: Revell, 1978.

MID-LIFE

IN HER late thirties, Helen was a successful business woman who, it appeared, had everything. "I read all about the male mid-life crisis," she told me, "and I'm feeling the same restlessness you describe. I don't know who I am or what's happening to me."

Then for an hour she poured out her frustration, anger, sense of uselessness, and boredom. Amid tears she talked of being so unmotivated she wasn't doing anything at home or at work. She was simply surviving, an empty life, without purpose.

I had heard it before, strong conflicting feelings such as:

"I just want to be left alone. I can't stand people. I feel critical about everything and everybody."

"I'm tired of being home alone all day and night."

"I'm sick and tired of always doing what other people want me to!"

"Tough situations that wouldn't have been a problem at all to me a few years ago now overwhelm me. I can barely handle life."

"I've made up my mind it's time for me to have a little fun. I've sacrificed long enough for my family."

If you haven't experienced it yourself, you've probably watched someone else go through it. A woman in her thirties or forties may not understand what is happening to her. She is changing physically. Her roles and emotions are changing and cultural changes pressure her. For some reason—either she has avoided it or she's been too occupied with life—she has arrived at mid-life without having planned for it. She always knew that some day her children would go off to school and to work, get married, and start their own families, but she never thought those events would come so quickly. Single and childless women face similar mid-life adjustments. For them, life seems to be passing by without the experience of marriage and children. The mid-life career woman may begin to face stiff competition from younger women at work or in other relationships.

MATURITY WITHOUT ANSWERS

What does a woman do now that she is middle-aged? She may sense quiet desperation, but not know how to change her thinking and lifestyle to deal with the gnawing anxieties inside. The only relief may be an occasional social diversion. For many women, entering mid-life is a jolting experience, much like what happens when you grab a faulty appliance cord with wet hands.

The author of *The Prime of Ms. America: The American Woman at 40* explains it: "The role comes upon each of us suddenly, unexpectedly. We have lived . . . structured lives, for the most part, in which we knew what we wanted and what was expected of us. And now, suddenly, with the beginning of middle years, we face an identity crisis for which nothing in our past has prepared us and for which nothing in our society can provide guidelines. . . . The loss of youth, strength—age etching its marks on our faces and bodies; dread about menopause; death of parents; loss through death and separation of friends and family; dissatisfactions in our marriages; the 'forty-year syndrome' in our husbands; our children growing up, preparing to leave. And then the empty nest, the empty hours."

THE QUIET NEST

By the late thirties a woman may feel a strong need to re-evaluate her life. By this time, she may have been married fifteen years, and her last child has gone off to school. She isn't experiencing the *empty* nest when children move out of the home, but the *quiet* nest when everyone is away from home all day. Although she's still a mother, the hours are *deafeningly quiet* and she thinks, "Is life really meaningful? Has it passed me by?"

At the same time, her husband is becoming more and more successful at work. Her children are involved in school and moving toward their own careers. Suddenly she feels left out, unimportant, and insignificant. Has being a mother really amounted to anything? Now what about the rest of her life? If she has never married, she may wonder desperately if she ever will. And if she does, will she have childbearing years left?

Singles Are Not Spared

The single career woman in her mid or late thirties was maturing at a time when the feminist movement was new and oftentimes radical. Feminists' principles were often interpreted to mean that an independent, self-actualized, and liberated woman should avoid getting trapped into being "nothing but a housewife." Many of these women now complain that they feel cheated because they were led to believe the way to personal fulfillment was only through a career. In fact they feel just as cheated as their thirty-five to forty-five-year-old counterparts who were made to feel guilty because they chose to be only wives and mothers.

Round Two

A second major stress period comes in the late forties or early fifties when the average woman experiences menopause. This time of life brings emotional changes, quite often before the actual physical changes begin.

Often during this time, a woman may fear losing her husband. He may be in his own mid-life transition and he, too, may be asking, "Who am I? What shall I do with the rest of my life? With whom do I want to live my life?"

When her husband is in mid-life crisis, a woman may try to force him to love her and be responsible again. Struggling with a marriage that is about to come apart is not fun. A woman may find herself becoming "clutchy" and possessive with her husband in order to sustain the relationship.

Or a woman may fear losing her sexual vitality and get involved in an affair to reassure herself that she is still sexually attractive. Hurt by her husband's lack of understanding, she looks for attention from other men.

One woman slumped in the chair in my office and blurted out, "I'm in an affair! I met Tom here at church. We were both singing in the choir and ... we just started talking to each other. Nothing more than

that at first. Then one night after practice, the whole choir went out for coffee. Afterwards ..." she spoke slowly as if carefully choosing her words, "he and I just sort of stood around in the parking lot, talking to each other. I can't explain to you how it felt ... how good it felt! Someone was listening to *me*. ... It was exhilarating. I felt like a real, live person. Before I realized it, we had been talking in that parking lot for three hours. You must understand that that time met a very deep need in my life.

"I don't know why I got involved. I know it was wrong. I can't understand what's happening to me. I'm a grown woman, thirty-eight years old." Tears were coming slowly down her cheeks as she tried to explain the tearing conflict raging inside her. "I have a husband who loves me. I have teen-age children, yet I am acting like a teen-ager myself!"

Empty Nest

In the early years of the mid-life transition, a mother will probably experience loneliness because of the quiet nest. But later on, she may experience a deeper sense of separation as her children leave home for college, work, or marriage. If she never had children, she may feel sorry she missed the mothering experience, and she knows it is too late now.

Mid-life is unique because several drastic changes happen in a few short years. The last child has gone off to school. The mid-life woman may try to re-enter a career or begin one for the first time. Her husband may be ignoring her because of his own drive to succeed or his own mid-life crisis. She is aware of her physical aging. She is intimidated by the youth culture that implies a middle-aged woman is a disposable commodity. In a few short years, she will see her children leave home and marry. Then, before long she'll be a grandmother.

These are her own changes she must deal with. But in addition, she may face the trauma of her children's teen years and the potentially dangerous mid-life crisis of her husband. She may have to handle the anxiety of parents who need her. She may see her friends struggling with personal problems or shaky marriages. These are perilous years for a mid-life woman. Years that could alter everything—her home, her career, her personality.

WHAT CAN SHE DO?

Rather than avoid the many areas with which she is wrestling, the mid-life woman needs to allow her personality to grow in these various dimensions.

First, during her mid-years she will probably ask a number of questions such as "Who am I?"; "Why am I married or single?"; "What is the meaning of life?"; "What is the meaning of *my* life?" Many of these questions relate to the deep value structure within her. She needs to talk with friends about these questions and quietly reflect with God before she comes to any final answers. Re-evaluation requires time, reflection, new information, and discussion. Reading books and magazine articles on self-image and mid-life also helps.

Second, the various roles of her life are changing. Her children don't need her quite as much, and she may want to start a career. Or if she has never married, she may sense an urgency to have a family and her career may seem less important now. Previously, she had looked to the older generation for leadership. Now the younger generation looks to her. She must assume the role of parenting the older generation as well as leading the younger generation. Understanding the role changes is important, but *accepting* her changing relationships is crucial to a successful transition during the mid-years. A woman might ease the process for herself and others by getting a Sunday School class, small group, or fellowship group to talk about mid-life role changes.

Third, by mid-life, husbands and wives are usually the least satisfied in their marriages. If a woman understands this and spends her energy and time working on it, then her marriage will be rich, satisfying, and secure in the future. Extra-marital relationships, although temporarily scintillating, do not provide the long-range security and meaning for which she is looking and will only add guilt to the problems she already has. She must try in a new or deeper way to understand the needs of her husband and to meet those needs. For example, she could tell him how good he looks to her or that she appreciates all the stress he handles at work to provide for the family.

Fourth, her body is getting older. Her weight is shifting from her limbs to the torso of her body and it's not only because she ate that banana split. It's a part of the biological aging process. The structure of her skin is also changing, and no creams or soaps are going to change that, no matter what the manufacturers claim. If her self-image has been wrapped up in her body rather than who she is as a person, this will be a time of great stress. She needs to begin developing the other aspects of her personality not related to her body, such as her ability to be an understanding friend and companion. Going back to school might help. Or looking for new ways to minister to people may shift her sense of identity away from her body and toward her mind and relationships with others.

A FRIENDLY CAUTION

Women tend to become more assertive in mid-life and sometimes downright aggressive. She needs to be careful that this aggression does not drive a wedge between her and her husband, her children, her friends, or her work associates. Channeling that potential aggression will help her become a dynamic leader in the community, the church, and business.

No woman is alone in her mid-life struggle. Both women and men in their mid-years experience a time of reevaluation and readjustment. Some call it "shifting gears." After this transition, what comes next will perhaps be the most profitable, productive, and happy era of her life. She will have a stronger sense of who she is and what God has gifted her to do. With her new strength and security, she can move into relationships and ministries that are significant and satisfying.

But during the rough times, it's good for her to remember her transition has not caught God by surprise. He says, "I want you to trust me in your times of trouble, so I can rescue you, and you can give me glory" (Psalms 50:15 TLB). He loves her and will continue to help her through this time.

—JIM AND SALLY CONWAY, professors at Talbot Theological Seminary, La Mirada, CA, authors of *Women in Mid-Life Crisis, Men in Mid-Life Crisis,* and *You and Your Husband's Mid-Life Crisis.* Reprinted by permission from *Today's Christian Woman,* Summer 1981.

FOR FURTHER READING:

Lee, Robert, and Marjorie Casebier. *The Spouse Gap,* Nashville: Abingdon, 1971.

MacDonald, Ruby. *Forty Plus and Feeling Fabulous.* Old Tappan, N.J.: Revell, 1982.

MISCARRIAGE

MISCARRIAGE is always an emotional event. There are different kinds of miscarriages at different times during pregnancy. If it happens early and the fetus is barely formed, you might be less affected than if it happens after the fourth or fifth month, once you have felt the fetus move within you and it has become real to you. But if you want a baby, even if it happens early, and especially if it has occurred once or several times before, it can be occasion for increased anguish and despair and can add to the tension involved in trying to conceive again. Many fears are increased, and you become more and more vulnerable and must work on building up defenses. If a miscarriage occurs in the fifth month or later, some women feel incredibly incomplete and find themselves waiting for something to happen; their time sense gets shaken up. This incompleteness can be felt even after an earlier miscarriage.

All of this is not to alarm, but to make women aware that miscarriage is a possibility during pregnancy (one in ten women mis-

carry) and can be very difficult to cope with. But anxieties can be lessened by your persistence both in learning reasons for your miscarriage and in being as much as possible aware and constantly in touch with your feelings and fears. It is also vitally helpful that you talk out these feelings, and very important that your friends not gloss over the event (because they feel so uncomfortable with it—and it can be hard to deal with), so that you are frustrated when you try to communicate your feelings. Often through talking both to the man involved and to empathetic friends you can sort out your own strong feelings and begin to know your anxieties.

If a woman is not fertile, the reasons for her infertility might be the reasons for miscarriage. (The man is less physiologically responsible for miscarriage than for infertility.) So, many of the tests performed for infertility are useful in determining why a woman will miscarry.

There are four general classes of causes for miscarriage: (1) defective egg or sperm; (2) faulty production of estrogen or progesterone; (3) anatomical illness or functional abnormalities, or general illness or infection; and (4) psychological reasons. Ten percent of women miscarry, and about 50 percent of the aborted fetuses are found to be abnormal. Some additional statistics: After a first miscarriage it's 85–90 percent sure that the next pregnancy will be all right; after a second there's a 50 percent chance; and after a third a 25 percent chance. A woman who has miscarried three times or more is sometimes called a habitual aborter. She should definitely have preventative (preconceptual) therapy and treatment.

Miscarriages are classified into stages or types. One miscarriage can pass through many stages.

Threatened abortion. There's a difference between bleeding and abortion bleeding. Some women when pregnant bleed slightly for a few months at about the time they are supposed to have their period. Sometimes as the blastocyst implants into the uterine lining there's slight bleeding. Sometimes the bleeding might be bright red. If this continues for several days, go to the doctor; he'll examine you for lesions. Early bleeding has no effect on fetal development. If bleeding does begin (slight brown staining, with little or no abdominal cramps), there is always uncertainty. The pregnancy might or might not continue. You will often be advised to go to bed until the bleeding has turned brown and then has stopped for twenty-four hours. Afterward you should not douche, be too active, or make love until the fourteenth week of pregnancy. Many women find the fact that there is no treatment hard to accept. And they find it extremely hard to accept the fact that if the bleeding continues for several days, it means almost definite miscarriage.

Inevitable.   Severe cramps, cervical effacement, and dilation occur, with strong bleeding and clots. There is no way to stop it.

Complete.   The uterus empties itself completely of the fetus, membranes, and the decidual lining of the uterus. During the first three weeks, spontaneous abortion is almost always complete. Sometimes then, and even later, it might feel like a really heavy period; sometimes you might not notice it at all, as it takes place around the time you expect your period. If the pregnancy is more advanced than three weeks, the doctor would very likely give you a D & C to be sure that every bit of membrane is out of the uterus. Unless it is completely emptied, the uterine muscles won't contract to compress the bleeding vessels and control the hemorrhage, and infection may occur.

Incomplete.   Varying amounts of tissue remain in the uterus, either attached or free. Mild to severe cramps, perhaps pain in a specific place. Must have a D & C.

Missed.   The fetus has died but remains in the uterus. Symptoms of pregnancy disappear, breasts get smaller, the uterus stops growing and gets smaller. Spontaneous abortion almost always occurs. There's a brown

spotting. Doctors usually wait until it begins by itself and then give a D & C.

Sometimes a woman's cervix has been injured and can't hold in the fetus. A simple operation can be performed to prevent her from losing her baby, usually during the pregnancy.

In general, if you have a history of miscarriage, you should be fully examined along the lines of the infertility investigation. If you have miscarried only once, that usually means that the egg or sperm is defective and paradoxically, it's a healthy thing for your body to get rid of an embryo or fetus that isn't growing well.

The positive side of a miscarriage, for someone who has thought herself infertile, is that it means you can get pregnant.

—From The Boston Women's Health Book Collective, *Our Bodies, Ourselves.* New York: Simon & Schuster, 1973.

FOR FURTHER READING:

Padus, Emrika. *The Woman's Encyclopedia of Health and Natural Healing.* Emmaus, Pa.: Rodale, 1981.

17 Women Doctors, with D. S. Thompson, M.D., as consulting editor, *Everywoman's Health.* Garden City, N.Y.: Doubleday, 1980.

MONEY

Banks

1.   *Did you know that if your checking or savings account does not show activity for a number of years the bank can legally terminate the account and hand the funds over to the state?*   Although the time span involved varies from state to state, all state laws carry this provision. Consequently, even if you are not able to save on a regular basis the safest thing to do is to make some kind of deposit or withdrawal at least once a year in order to demonstrate that the account is still active. Also, by doing this you can avoid maintenance fees which some banks are allowed to

assess on the account if it seems to be "dead."

Legally, before an account can be confiscated the bank is required to make a reasonable attempt to locate the account's owner. However, this procedure is not too effective. Most banks will not allow employees to look in the telephone book for a new address if mail is returned from your old one. The theory is that the person in the telephone book might have the same name as you do, and if someone else is contacted in error, she might show up and receive your money, thus putting the bank in legal jeopardy. Therefore, when you move, it's imperative that you notify all banks where you have any kind of accounts. (A recent news story stated that the Bank of America in California was unable to locate such notables as Bob Hope and Lucille Ball and turned their dormant accounts over to the state.)

However, if you should suddenly remember an old account you had previously forgotten, you can still claim what's left of it by writing to the comptroller's office in your state. No interest fees will have accrued since the time the account was turned over to the state, but at least you can retrieve what's left of the principal after the bank subtracted its maintenance fees.

2. *Did you know it is standard policy in many states for banks to freeze all joint accounts as soon as one co-owner of the account dies?* This means that you might not be able to withdraw funds from either a checking or savings account or you might not have access to a safe deposit box until the estate is settled. You may wonder how banks work so quickly in freezing accounts. They have an "obituary employee" whose job it is to go through local newspapers and check death notices first thing every morning. When she finds the name of a person with an account at the bank, that account is immediately sealed to prevent further activity until the bank is presented with appropriate legal papers. (The best way to avoid such a dilemma is to have a small emergency fund savings account in your name.)

3. *Did you know that safe deposit boxes*

might not be as burglar proof as you had supposed? In several instances bank vaults have been robbed and the contents of safe deposit boxes stolen. Surprisingly, in most states, the bank has no obligation to reimburse you for the value of the stolen goods! To lower the risk, make sure the bank you choose has the most secure safe deposit "room" in town and then check with the agent who wrote your home-owner's insurance policy to find out if you can acquire a policy rider to cover the replacement cost of your valuables should your safe deposit box be robbed. Most insurance companies will add this rider at a miniscule price.

4. *Did you know you can have a checking account without using checks?* As part of the Electronic Funds Transfer (EFT) systems, banks can now totally eliminate the "paper" involved in checking accounts if you authorize them to do so. Without setting foot in the bank you can arrange to have your paycheck directly deposited from your employer. Then, through the use of preauthorized payment arrangements, you can have regular bills such as your mortgage payment, utilities, and insurance paid directly by the bank. You never have to bother with check writing at all. To avoid check writing for one time expenses such as your son's new pair of shoes or your pet's visit to the veterinarian, you can use your EFT debit card. This piece of plastic looks like a credit card but when used it gives the bank the authority to deduct that amount of money from your account immediately, rather than billing you for it later.

5. *Did you know that your bank can help you avoid stock broker's fees when you transfer stock certificates to different names?* If you want to sell or give someone a stock certificate, simply go to your bank and, in the presence of one of the bank officers, sign the ownership over to the recipient. The bank official will compare your signature to that on bank records and guarantee your signature. Then you simply send the stock certificate to the bank listed on the certificate as the transfer agent, give them the complete name and address of the person to whom the

stock is being transferred, and specify the form in which the certificate will be registered (single ownership, joint tenancy, guardianship, etc.). Within about six weeks you'll receive your transferred stock certificate without having to pay a broker's fee.

—EDITH FLOWERS KILGO, author of *Money in the Cookie Jar; Money Management;* and *Handbook for Christian Homemakers.*

Debt

GETTING BACK IN THE BLACK

1. Consider the benefits of being debt free.
   - Reduce your expenses.
   - Delight your creditors.
   - Please God.
2. Set a goal to be debt free.
   - It's better to aim at something and miss it than to aim at nothing and hit it.
   - No one gets out of debt by accident.
3. Plan to give a percentage of each paycheck to God's work.
   - Learn now the joys of unselfish giving.
   - Prove for yourself the words of the Bible, "It is more blessed to give than to receive" (Acts 20:35).
   - Discover the truth of the promise of Jesus, "Give and it shall be given unto you" (Luke 6:38).
4. List all you owe. Get it all down—everything!
   - Loans.
   - Bills.
   - Amounts due friends and relatives.
   - Moral obligations.
   - Home mortgages.
5. List all you own.
   - Property such as your home.
   - Possessions such as cars, furniture, appliances.
   - Financial—bank accounts, savings, securities.
   - Life insurance cash values.
   - Present value of pension or profit-sharing plan.
   - Business interests.

6. Have a sale.
   - Get rid of items you can live without, especially items on which you owe money.
   - Most people have no idea of what they can do without until they try.
   - Forget what may be lost on items you sell.
   - Focus on the amount that can be applied to immediate debt reduction.
   - Consider getting along with one less car. If you own two, get rid of one. If you own one, consider getting rid of it.
7. Get on a cash basis.
   - Have a credit card cutting-up ceremony.
   - Schedule a close-all-charge-accounts day.
   - Follow the good advice in the Bible, "Make do with your pay" (Luke 3:14).
   - Add no new debts. You can't borrow your way out of debt.
8. Decide on a monthly debt-payment amount.
   - Squeeeeeze as much as you can from your monthly budget.
   - After the giving and taxes, pay your debts next.
   - Scale your living down to make do with the money that is left.
   - You can live on less than you think. Look around and see how many others live well on less than you have.
   - Memorize and live by this:
     > Use it up,
     > Wear it out,
     > Make it do,
     > Do without!

9. Find out how long it will take for you to be debt free.
   - Divide the money you owe by the monthly amount of your debt payment.
   - Answer = number of months to be debt free.
10. Chop your time goal in half.
    - That's right! Plan to be debt free twice as fast.
    - Paying debt twice as fast does not double your payment.

• To pay off $5,000 with sixteen percent interest in two and a half years instead of five, increases your monthly payment from $121.59 by $81.72 to $203.31.

11. Create income projects to match needed debt payment.

• Convert some family time to work projects.

• Consider doing for others such things as housecleaning, house sitting, pet care, plant care, child care, sewing, building, yard care, gift-making, gardening, tutoring, etc.

• Find family income projects. Note— eight hours of work a week at $3.50 will produce about $112 per month (before taxes). Sixteen hours—$224 to add to monthly debt payments.

• Worth it? You bet!

12. Write out a repayment schedule for every creditor.

• Divide the amount you owe by number of months of your project.

• Answer = monthly payment for each creditor.

• Develop a monthly pay-off schedule.

13. Send your repayment schedule to each creditor.

• Each creditor will be glad to see your plan.

• Invite him to tell you if the plan is not satisfactory.

• Tell him you'll contact him if something happens to make you late or cause you to miss a payment.

• Profit from the Biblical promise, "Reliable communication permits progress" (Proverbs 13:17).

14. Stick to your plan.

• Beginning a job without finishing it simply amounts to wasting your time.

• Concentrate on the goal—to be debt free.

• Focus on the Biblical promise, "Desire accomplished is sweet to the soul" (Proverbs 13:19).

—From George Fooshee, Jr., *You Can Be Financially Free.* Old Tappan, N.J.: Revell, 1976. As excerpted in *Today's Christian Woman,* Summer 1981.

Home Mortgages

Are you shopping for a house? If so, there's more to consider than just the size, price, and location. How about the mortgage? The financing of your dream house could be the most important financial decision you'll make in your lifetime. And wrong decisions could cost you thousands of dollars over the coming years.

With interest rates rising and dipping and then rising again, it seems unlikely we'll see those single digit interest rates we once took for granted. Consequently, many newlyweds and single parent families are being forced out of the housing market. As a result, inventive bankers and real estate salespeople have concocted new ways to finance a home. Here are your options:

Rollover mortgages. These loans, available through savings and loan institutions, are so named because every three to five years there is a "rollover" or renegotiation of interest rates. This means that your house payment—exclusive of escrow amounts—remains the same from one re-evaluation period to the next. Then at the end of the period the interest rate is changed to the prevailing rate. (This kind of mortgage is known also as a "floating mortgage" because your payments fluctuate in accordance with the ups and downs of the interest rates.)

As frightening as this concept might appear, there is a built-in safeguard that prevents the lender from raising the rate more than five percent over the original interest rate at the time of the mortgage contract. The drawback to this kind of financing is that the rising inflation and interest rates cannot be utilized in a positive manner. The amount of a house payment at a fixed rate will gradually decrease over the years, whereas the rollover mortgage will always keep house payments high in proportion to total income.

Shared appreciation mortgages. Now being test marketed in limited areas of the country, this means of financing a home offers a completely new concept in mortgages. The lender agrees to finance a home in the $50,-000 to $150,000 range at an interest rate about one-third below the current rate. Then, in return for his generosity, he owns one third of the equity in the house. This means that, should you decide to sell the house at some future date, the profit you receive from the sale would not be yours alone. Instead, if you got $21,000 for example, you'd return $7,000 to the banking institution which had issued the original mortgage.

Of course, if housing values went down, the lender would receive nothing; but since it's not likely this will happen, the mortgager stands to lose nothing in the transaction. And what about the homeowner? As one young wife put it, "This is the only way we could get the monthly payments on a house down low enough so as to make buying a home a possibility. I think it's better in the long run to own two thirds of something, rather than one hundred percent of nothing."

Ground leases. Have you ever thought about buying a home without buying the land it sits upon? Commercial buyers have done this for decades but now home owners have the same option. What this means is that the buyer pays for the house and can ultimately call it his own but he only rents the land and thus can never own it. As a result, the overall price of a house is lowered considerably, making it more affordable. The disadvantage, of course, is that even if the house mortgage is eventually paid off, you'll still have to make leasing payments as long as you reside in the house.

Graduated payments. Popular for years among church groups who are financing building programs, this plan is now available for individual homeowners who are financing a home through a lending institution. Since presumably most young married couples are more secure financially after about five years of marriage, this plan makes house payments fairly modest for the first year and then increases the payment each year up to the fifth year. The lender is able to work

with those whose current budget does not permit large house payments but whose financial future looks promising. After the fifth year, the mortgage payment stabilizes and there are no more increases.

Joint ownership. This is another variation of the shared appreciation mortgage. You sell a *share* of the house in return for a portion of the down payment price. The shareholder would participate *only* in the raising of the needed down payment, but as a consequence would be guaranteed up to fifty percent of the equity when the house is sold. This does not mean that the interest rates or the monthly payments would be affected in any way. But the home buyer benefits because he or she doesn't have to raise the entire down payment.

In addition to these creative means of financing a house, prospective home owners have still other options in circumventing the high interest rate dilemma.

Urban homesteading. Did you know it is possible to buy a house for only one dollar? Yes, there is a "catch" to it, but for those who are financially unable to cope with current mortgage rates, the "catch" may be preferable to going houseless.

Urban homesteading works like this: City governments that are encouraging renovation of inner city property frequently offer downtown homes for sale for one dollar. Then the new homeowner is required to bring what was previously condemned property up to current city standards. This *is* costly—but not as costly as buying an equivalent amount of floor space elsewhere. As a further enticement, mortgage rates for this kind of house buying are lower. The Department of Housing and Urban Development now offers a Rehabilitation Mortgage Insurance program which guarantees these mortgages up to $67,500. For more information, write to Urban Homestead Division, Community Planning and Development, HUD, 451 Seventh Street, SW, Washington, D.C. 20410.

One of the major factors these days in

home buying is the working wife. Because of the added income she contributes, many families are now able to afford a more expensive house. Yet for many years lenders refused to take the wife's paycheck into consideration when calculating the mortgage loan a family could safely handle. Now, because of the Equal Opportunity Act, lenders are required to calculate the wife's earning power, too.

Yet, even with two working members of the family, many still find it impossible to save up the lump sum needed for a down payment. An alternative that is often considered is the second mortgage. Ideally, the second mortgage should constitute considerably less than half of the needed down payment, and the loan should be for as short a term as can be reasonably managed. Sometimes the seller will agree to finance a second mortgage at a rate somewhat lower than the going interest rate for primary mortgages; so there's no harm in asking. However, the lending institution which is financing the first mortgage must do so with complete knowledge of the existence of the second mortgage.

[If, after looking into other methods] available for financing your house, you still find yourself facing a traditional type of lending situation with a high interest rate, there is still one other alternative. Try to persuade your lender to write into the contract that you may pay off the mortgage early without a penalty. This means that, should future interest rates drop, you can then acquire a new loan to pay off the old high interest loan and can consequently lower your monthly payments. Even if you do have to pay a slight penalty, it still might be worthwhile to refinance your mortgage at a later date. Even an interest rate drop of one percent can substantially alter what you'll be paying over a period of thirty years.

After finding your dream house and deciding on the mortgage method you prefer, there's still one more fee to consider before all the papers are signed. This fee is called "points," and it is a one-time assessment of about one percent—sometimes a bit more—of the purchase price of the house. This method of squeezing a bit of extra interest into the price is completely legal. Lenders use it to offset their lack of profit when money is tight and they themselves must borrow money at a rate nearly the same as what they are going to charge you. Sometimes points are paid by the buyer. Other times they are paid by the seller or are divided between the two. Obviously, it is to your advantage to try to arrange a loan that includes points payment by the seller.

Another change in the mortgage market is forty-year mortgages gradually replacing thirty-year mortgages. This tactic, coupled with an easing of down payment requirements, will probably make it possible for many more families to enter the housing market. With savings and loan institutions now authorized to finance up to ninety percent of the cost of a house instead of the eighty percent formerly allowed, a lower down payment will be possible, too. With financing stretched out over more years, even high interest rates will not necessarily put two-income families out of the housing market.

If you've gone so far as to look at a possible house to buy you probably already know about FHA (Federal Housing Administration) mortgages and VA (Veteran's Administration) mortgages. These two government agencies are the guarantors on most of the houses being financed in this country. When a mortgage is secured through either an FHA or a VA loan, the government, in effect, is standing behind your ability to pay for your house. Then, should you default on your payment, the lending institution cannot lose money. FHA or VA steps in to repossess the house and make good on the loan to your lender. FHA and VA loans are most beneficial to buyers who could never afford conventional financing which involves larger down payments and shorter repayment times. (The larger the down payment a lender gets in the beginning the more secure he feels about the loan, because a borrower is less likely to default when a large chunk of cash is already tied up in a house or when fifteen or fewer years are needed in repaying the mortgage.)

For more information about buying a house, The Consumer Information Center, Pueblo, Colorado 81009, offers many free or low cost pamphlets.

—EDITH FLOWERS KILGO, author of *Money in the Cookie Jar; Money Management;* and *Handbook for Christian Homemakers.*

FOR FURTHER READING:

Fooshee, George, Jr. *You Can Be Financially Free.* Old Tappan, N.J.: Revell, 1976.

MUGGING

LAST WEEK two women were mugged in a local hospital parking lot. Constant reports come in of women being mugged and their purse snatched. Police departments in many metropolitan areas now offer courses and/or advice to women on what to do about this growing crime. What can you do to increase your safety if you must travel alone?

1. Be alert. When you're on the streets alone walk rapidly and keep aware of your surroundings and of other people. Muggers try to catch their victims by surprise.
2. If possible, use a purse with a shoulder strap. Wear it with the catch next to your body. Use your arm to press the purse against your hip and hold on to the strap so that if an attempt is made to grab your purse, you can hold on to your possession. Purse snatching occurs within seconds. Don't wear a purse hanging from your elbow. A snatcher can break your arm as he makes off with your purse.
3. Leave your charge cards at home unless you plan to use them. Carry keys and money somewhere else on your person, particularly in a place not easily accessible (such as an inside pocket).
4. During the day, stay close to buildings while walking. Many purse snatchers ride by on bicycles or in cars. At night, however, walk close to the curb and away from buildings—especially unlighted ones and away from dark streets or empty lots.
5. Don't be afraid of noise. If you are attacked by a mugger (or suspect you are about to be mugged), scream, "Help! Police!" Some women wear a whistle around their necks when they have to be out at night. Noise is the greatest deterrent you can offer because it can draw the attention of others.
6. Don't carry a weapon unless you're proficient in its use and intend to use it. Weapons can be taken from you and used against you. Even chemical sprays can be blown back at you by the wind.
7. Remain calm if you're attacked by a mugger. Give the mugger whatever he demands and don't fight.
8. Try to get a look at your attacker, especially noting his height, weight, age, distinguishing characteristics, speech patterns, movements, clothes—anything unusual. It's better to identify an individual with certainty than to have vague impressions of several people.
9. Call the police as soon as you can.
10. Pray before you go out, asking God to give you peace, wisdom, and protection.

—SHIRLEY AND CECIL MURPHEY

N

NAGGING

ALL THE dirty words in man talk aren't four letters. Any way you spell it, nagging gives off "bad vibes" to the male. Maybe it's because he had too much of this as a child. Even if his mother was one of the gentle women, he got it from somewhere. The family shrew, whoever she was, sounded like the tap, tap, tap of some female hammer. And you can know this for sure, my lonesome friend—Roger's recall for that sound is not far below the surface.

If a woman persists in her nagging, her man will retreat into his own world. He will barricade himself. At first he'll hear you. But when he gets too much, you've had it. The Lord created men with a trap door in each ear as a defense against brawling women.

So what are the alternatives?

One is to be a good sport about some things. Kristy is a classic example of what I have in mind here. She's a supersentimental somebody. She was raised with affection all over the place. But Bruce is a clod when it comes to the little extras, like remembering anniversaries. When they were first married, Kristy took all this personally. She thought if he loved her enough, Bruce would care enough to remember a few things. You know, cologne, candy, "say it with flowers" now and then. But that's not Bruce. He wasn't raised that way.

So Kristy decided to quit nagging. From now on she would announce, "Tuesday's our anniversary, honey, and you're taking me out for dinner." Then she makes the reservations, buys herself a corsage, dresses up in her best, and off they go for their celebration. It really is *their* celebration, because

Bruce likes it this way. He thinks that's how they do it in any well-run marriage.

I wish I could tell you she's brought him around. It would be nice to report that he remembers now after seventeen years. But he doesn't, he hasn't, he never will. So Kristy does that for him. And he appreciates it. Some women might feel put upon staging it like this. Not Kristy. She appreciates Bruce for all the good things about him. And she accepts the things that will never change.

Theirs is a fine marriage. In fact I'd give it an "A" when it comes to communicating. She talks. He talks. And if you could see them with each other, you'd know there's a lot of togetherness going on here.

—From Charlie W. Shedd, *Talk to Me.* Garden City, N.Y.: Doubleday, 1975.

FOR FURTHER READING:

Wilke, Richard B. *Tell Me Again, I'm Listening.* Nashville: Abingdon, 1973.

Wright, H. Norman. *The Family That Listens.* Wheaton, Ill.: Victor Books, 1978.

NAIL CARE

IT'S AS IMPORTANT for your hands to look beautiful as it is for them to move gracefully. You can have more beautiful hands if you determine to work on them. Wear rubber gloves when you use strong detergents and cleaning agents. Give yourself a daily hand massage, using good hand cream or lotion.

If you have splits, breaks, white spots or

ripples in your fingernails, check your diet. Deficiencies of vitamins, calcium or protein will show up in nails that look unhealthy. So check with your doctor to see if you need vitamin or other dietary supplements.

Some of the good protein boosters which are available nowadays are low in calories and carbohydrates. They will help improve your nails and general health.

Do you constantly break or tear your nails? Using your fingernails as tools can destroy their beauty. Use the end of a pencil to dial the phone. Grasp small objects like hairpins with the cushions of your fingers. Use kitchen gadgets, not your nails, to pry open the tops of containers. Turn light switches off and on and push elevator buttons with your knuckles rather than your fingers. Use a natural nonalkaline soap for dishwashing.

A well-kept manicure requires only thirty minutes once a week, if it is done correctly. To give yourself a professional manicure in the least amount of time, keep all your manicure equipment together in a shoe box, so that you don't have to spend time looking for it. You will need:

1. A nail file with a very fine, "diamond" filing area. Or if that is unavailable, use an emery board
2. A Q-tip or orange stick for cuticles
3. Cuticle conditioner
4. Nail buffer and conditioning cream
5. Fingernail scissors (not nail clippers)
6. Pumice stone (for calluses)
7. Fingernail polish
8. Hand lotion

Before you start filing, look at your hands to see what nail shapes and colors will be best for you. If you have short, wide fingers, almond-shaped nails will be slenderizing. Avoid an intense shade of polish. Leave an uncolored margin along the sides of the nails, to give the optical illusion of narrowness and length.

If you use an emery board for filing, remember that the dark side (which is rougher) should be used on your toenails. The light side is for your fingernails. When you file, try

to achieve a softly ovaled look. A very good length for most nails is one-quarter inch above the back of the finger. Let your nails grow approximately one-eighth inch up on the sides before you begin to file them. Also, file from the side of the nail up to the top of the nail, in one direction only, to avoid tearing.

When coloring your nails, you may want to use a clear base and a top coat, as your polish will then last longer. Brush on polish with three movements to each nail. Start at the center, then do each side. Apply two to three thin coats, letting each dry between coats. Whenever possible, avoid wearing chipped and peeling fingernail polish. Be sure to give your nails plenty of time to dry between coats and after finishing. You may harden the polish by placing your hands under *lightly* flowing cold tap water.

By taking the trouble to keep your hands lovely and feminine and then using them gracefully, you may be able to transmit to others the gentle spirit of God that is within you.

In learning to use the miracle of touch which God has given us, we can pray as did the Psalmist: ". . . the work of our hands, establish thou it" (Psalms 90:17 KJV).

—From Joanne Wallace, *The Image of Loveliness*. Old Tappan, N.J.: Revell, 1978.

FOR FURTHER READING:

Jones, Candy. *Finishing Touches*. New York: Harper & Brothers, 1961.
Pierre, Clara. *Looking Good*. New York: Reader's Digest Press, 1976.
Wallace, Joanne. *Dress With Style*. Old Tappan, N.J.: Revell, 1983.

NUTRITION

IT IS PERFECTLY reasonable to suppose that if one hundred well-adjusted, normal men and women were placed together in a room and told, "ten of you will definitely die within one year," not one person would feel that the statement applied to himself or herself.

Healthy-minded people feel invincible. Given an opportunity to guess at our potential old age, we clearly see past sixty, and most people expect to be active into their mid-eighties. According to the Census-Bureau report on social indicators for 1976, published on December 27, 1977, we find that a woman born in 1974 can be expected to live to be seventy-six years old, and a male born in 1974 might expect to live until sixty-eight years of age.

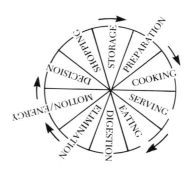

But our life span is affected by the gradually increasing numbers of degenerative diseases—diseases that are not being matched by corresponding scientific skills in finding cures or ways of avoiding these diseases altogether. In other words, the way we are living is beating the medical profession to the finishing post.

Essentially, degeneration comes from what we consume, the amounts we consume, how we consume it, how we void what's left and how we move about in order to use up the energy we have received. Since we humans are vain, or made to be so by social pressures, we tend to look upon nutrition as a means by which we might have:

Slimmer bodies
Whiter teeth
Straighter bones
Better hair
Clearer skin

Item by item, this list can be correlated with certain mineral, vitamin, protein or calorie excess or deficiency, but none of these adjustments can be described as nutrition. Nutrition is the complete cycle. To discuss one without the other is literally to preach malnutrition, because the *whole issue* is not being presented.

Let's begin with the cycle as a whole and take a quick look at the spokes that turn it into an effective wheel.

DECISION

Budget affects most families and often takes first place in *all* decisions related to what's actually eaten. The lower food budgets contain more potential for better food than those calling for more money spent without much control.

Vital good health for every member of the family should be the uppermost decision for the meal planner. Plan for fresh, whole foods with the accent upon vegetables, fruit, nuts, seeds, milk and cheese. Let meat settle into second place.

Plan to phase out all pre-prepared foods and beverages.

Decide to reduce the "dining out" experience, especially at fast-food-service and gourmet-styled establishments. Treat these opportunities as changes in routine rather than as an alternate food source.

Decide to eliminate all foods that cause you concern (subject to the emotional decisions that need family agreement) and don't buy *anything* that's supposed to be good for you until you *know* that it is.

Decide to give what you will save to a reputable world hunger-relief program.

Translate all these decisions into a shopping list and do not buy outside this list.

SHOPPING

Pay a special visit to your local supermarket for research only. Simply go, not to buy, but to read labels and absorb prices. Check *everything* that looks attractive to you. ... The government has insisted that you have the right to know what is in your food.

By law it is now displayed, but if you don't understand what you are being told, it's all pretty useless isn't it?

Shop for the best fresh foods, and if possible, find an organic food source where they *guarantee* the food free of all chemical influence.

Shop within your consumption needs for perishables. It is better to buy perishable green vegetables at least twice a week. You might be able to crisp a wilted green vegetable in cold salty water, but you won't replace its nutrients!

Beware of the word "enriched." This word announces that chemicals have been added to make up for those removed by the manufacturing process. We suggest you buy the food *before* it's altered in the first place.

STORAGE

A rather simplistic message reads,

If mold won't grow on it,
Neither will you!

Hence your whole foods are going to be more easily spoiled than those you have hitherto purchased. Keep a waste list on your refrigerator. Actually admit to all that you have to throw out *before* it is cooked. In a study conducted in Arizona, it was conjectured that if the local figures were a reflection of the national scene, then each year we waste some eight billion dollars on foods that never get to the pan, let alone the plate!

What, we wonder, is this costing you?
Keep a list and you'll know!

PREPARATION

If you *must* peel vegetables, keep the peel and trim in plastic bags for each day and cook them quickly (five minutes at the fast simmer, not boil). Strain and use this vegetable broth for soups and gravies and for cooking other vegetables. After a short while

you'll find you seldom go to the kitchen tap for straight water.

Wash all fruit and vegetables and cut or tear away all faded, wilted or bruised areas *before* you refrigerate. This helps to alert you to the immediate waste from certain vegetables, like leeks. You can also put bruised items into a priority-consumption bowl.

Don't let peeled, cut vegetables sit in cold water ready to be cooked. It is far preferable, if you are forced to prepare them some time ahead, to keep them in a plastic bag under refrigeration until they are ready to be cooked.

Red meats and eggs will cook better if brought to room temperature before cooking. The "younger" the meat, such as suckling pig, chicken, lamb, veal or rabbit, the more likely its spoilage in a warm kitchen.

Aim to have *everything* cut up and weighed or measured before you begin to cook. This simple technique sorts the Chef from the cooks. It's called *mis en place* (or put everything in its right place before you start). Any halfway decent TV cooking show will prove this point more than adequately—these performers don't have time to go looking for something or to peel a clove of garlic while the meat is already cooking!

COOKING

The more we grow to rely upon whole, fresh foods, the more concerned we need to be with retaining their fragile value. We make the decision to eat better in order to have vitality, but if we do all the right things and then dump it all into a pan and destroy all the advantages, we might be better off doing less work and go back to reading cooking directions on labels and popping vitamin pills.

We are trying to get adequate nutrition from the least destructive sources. We know that some forms of protein come complete with fat, which directly or indirectly means cholesterol, which directly or indirectly means some form of heart problem. Thus we reduce the protein from animal sources to a reasonable level: about 3½ to 4 ounces per day, total. We can look to vegetables, seeds, grains and some milk products to produce the major element that our bodies need.

Baking is virtually a thing of the past for our family. We bake bread, but that's just about where it ends. I haven't discovered an "adequate" cookie or cake, and the desserts seem to fade away when fresh fruit and cheese is served.

SERVING

The least time-consuming and least costly element of a good meal is setting the table well. As a capital investment it may look like a problem, but think of the meals and the people you can say "I love you" to!

EATING

Our disposition at the time of eating is vital to both enjoyment and digestion. We simply cannot settle an agitated spirit with antacid tablets!

Eating on the run is an insult to our bodies. We need to settle down for at least ten minutes before eating and to remain seated for at least the same time after the end of the meal.

Chewing is essential, because the larger the piece of food, the more stomach acid will be required to dissolve it. All food should be thoroughly chewed. Compulsive eaters seek only mouth-feel rather than taste satisfaction; they can't gulp the sensations down fast enough, and to chew is frustrating for them. If you had to chew each mouthful twenty times before swallowing, would you find it hard? If you would, then you could be a compulsive eater, but rather than just read about it, why not chew on it and see?

DIGESTION

Digestion and elimination are the only parts of the cycle in which our bodies work

independently of our efforts. Of course, we can make some additions when we have eaten or drunk too much, but the only truly effective *control* is to hunt down the transgressors one by one.

I do not doubt that my digestion is different from yours. I'm sensitive to different foods, and I *feel* my allergies. If I *feel* my new whole-grain cereal in the shape of heartburn, and take an antacid in order to cancel out the signal, then I'm likely to continue with the cereal *and* the antacid.

On the other hand, if I take nothing for my discomfort and suspect the cereal is the culprit, then I'll take action on the cereal. In this case I add milk to the grains a half hour before breakfast to soften the multiple (seven-grain) hard edges—result, no heartburn. I located the source, modified the use and avoided the condition.

We can all take this step, and frankly, we should, no matter how *addicted* we are to indigestion remedies. Indigestion is our body screaming for relief from abuse. We must listen!

ELIMINATION

When the beautifully prepared, balanced and well-chewed food has been swallowed and digested without the need of chemical aids, it still has to be eliminated.

Bowel movements are seldom if ever discussed in cookbooks, but we can't consider nutrition without completing the cycle. A clean, healthy, unaided evacuation of the bowel is essential if you are to experience vitality. Putrefied waste material in stale, toxic layers gets absorbed into the bloodstream and produces a full range of symptoms, all associated with exhaustion and causing us to reach for high-energy foods to keep the blood sugar going. Result: a fat human being with a poor bowel operation who is heading for chronic depression.

Bowels are aided by naturally fiber-filled or "sharped-edged" foods. The much-publicized *miller's bran flakes* and sharp-edged raw *sunflower seeds* are excellent promoters.

They soften the waste matter and stimulate the digestive tract at the same time.

Keep a small bowl of raw, unsalted sunflower seeds mixed with seedless raisins in the kitchen to keep pace with your need to nibble. A few tablespoons of these fellows, well chewed, plus a tablespoon of bran flakes at breakfast mixed with other cereals, and fresh orange juice to drink should certainly get things under way, even in the most obstinate of cases. You'll need to drink more water than usual to get the best value from the change.

Of great importance to the proper cleansing of our system is the fast. This simple means of deprivation has been muddled by many well-meaning folk. Certainly it is good to pray *and* fast, but the fast cannot take the place of a right attitude toward the subject of the prayer. What does happen, I believe, is that one ceases to be self-indulgent for a period. This freedom from self-serving combines with the surplus energy released by arresting the digestive process and produces concentration upon the objective, which is to petition God for a brother or sister in need. When a fast is conducted for cleansing purposes, self-interest is very much uppermost, and the three-to-seven- or even ten-day fasting period can be possible because we are convinced that the benefits to our bodies are real.

I do not believe that you can mix the two fasts. One is spiritual and cuts off our needs because we seek only that Father will help or heal our fellow man. The other is physical and is concerned with cleansing his temple (our body) so that we might be more effective witnesses for our Lord Jesus Christ.

I should make one observation here. The total exclusion of food for the purpose of losing weight is not and cannot be regarded as a fast. Weight loss can be achieved only by turning away from those foods that induced the fat in the first place. This represents a gradual healthy process rather than a swift, cruel pause in a continuing process of bad nutrition that is totally misrepresented as a fast!

MOVEMENT

The reason we need food is to fuel and repair our bodies as we daily move about our lives. The *way* we move determines *how much* we need to eat. Some people move quickly; they dart about. These people are usually thin. Other, taller, broader, heavier people move at a slower pace. Some people walk, others drive everywhere; some take exercise, others watch TV.

The fact is, we were designed to move on our own two feet, and while reclining chairs, TV sets, automobiles and jets are entertaining and convenient, their use has hastened our demise as a health-filled nation.

It is a *fact* that a person who takes exercise craves less sugar. It is a *fact* that exercise, properly conducted, can reduce a diabetic's need for insulin support. It is a *fact* that regular, meaningful exercise will reduce the pulse rate, increase the flexibility of the arteries and reduce hypertension. It's really up to you. Either you move your feet first or they'll move you feet first!

—From Graham Kerr, *The Love Feast.* New York: Simon & Schuster, 1978. Mr. Kerr's most recent book is *The Graham Kerr Step-by-Step Cookbook.*

FOR FURTHER READING:

Lamb, Lawrence E. *Stay Youthful and Fit.* New York: Harper & Row, 1974.

Padus, Emrika. *The Woman's Encyclopedia of Health and Natural Healing.* Emmaus, Pa.: Rodale, 1981.

Tear, Jim, and Jan Houghton Lindsey. *Fed Up With Fat.* Old Tappan, N.J.: Revell, 1978.

OBEDIENCE

Spiritual

Another consideration in the development of our relationship with God is obedience. It is hard to obey someone you do not know, nor even desire to. For this reason, it is important that every Christian understand who God is. As we read the Scriptures, it is good to look for the character, the capability, and the promises of God. As we study, we recognize that God is worthy of the trust we have placed in Him because He is loving, sovereign, omnipotent, holy, merciful, compassionate, faithful, and full of loving-kindness, as well as possessing many other characteristics.

A life of obedience is not a life of following a list of do's and don'ts, but it is allowing God to be original in our lives. As we are sensitive to the leading of the Holy Spirit and follow the direction He gives, God works in and through us. Galatians 3:11 suggests that no one can ever win God's favor by trying to keep the Jewish laws because God has said the only way we can be right in His sight is by faith. The Prophet Habakkuk says that the man who finds life, finds it through trusting God. (*See* Habakkuk 2:4; Hebrews 10:38; Romans 1:17.)

A hymn that is very meaningful to me is "Trust and Obey." The concept of obedience is expressed in a beautiful way:

When we walk with the Lord
In the light of His Word,

What a glory He sheds on our way!
While we do His good will
He abides with us still,
And with all who will trust and obey.

Have you listened to any grandparents recently and seen their excitement as they talk about their grandchildren? Or have you listened to a young man who has just discovered his companion for life? These people can be so full of the joy in their relationships that they couldn't possibly keep still about it.

So our relationship with God can overflow as we share with hearts full of joy, love, and gratitude concerning what God has done for us. Paul says in Colossians 1:28, "So everywhere we go we talk about Christ to all who will listen, warning them and teaching them as well as we know how. We want to be able to present each one to God, perfect because of what Christ has done for each of them" (TLB).

—From Vonette Zachary Bright, *For Such a Time as This.* Old Tappan, N.J.: Revell, 1976.

FOR FURTHER READING:

Elliot, Elisabeth. *Discipline: The Glad Surrender.* Old Tappan: N.J.: Revell, 1982.

Murphey, Cecil B. *Press On: A Disciple's Guide to Spiritual Growth.* Ann Arbor: Servant, 1983.

P

PAIN AND SUFFERING

SUFFERING IS INEVITABLE. None of us can permanently evade it. Yet few, if any, are ever prepared for it when it comes. Our health is one of many things we take for granted. To have a body free of pain, functioning vigorously, enabling us to carry on our pursuits with great ease is an indescribable asset—though only a temporary asset in this world. Illness, accidents, and age can lay waste our bodies and minds ever so quickly.

If health is one of your hallmarks today, do not waste time brooding over the future and torturing yourself over the "what ifs" of life. *Celebrate* its gift and make good use of your energy and vigor. Regard every day of your life as an event to be celebrated, and invest it for the good of others and for the glory of God. Learning how to live life to its fullest will enable a person to suffer without bitterness. After all, if the Lord tarries, none of us will get out of this world alive anyway. Death need not be depressing! It is a statement of fact—a fact that reality verifies daily.

If suffering and pain have overtaken you in your journey then there is good news for you. God has not forsaken you, and your suffering is not pointless. As Samuel declared, "The LORD will not forsake His people."

You may cry out from the depth of your being, "Why? Why me? Why this? Why so soon?" You may feel you have only started to live and now it looks as though everything may be cut short. But the good news of Christ is that you can live meaningfully right up to your death, if death be your present assignment—and, yes, beyond!

Job asked why and rightly so. It hurt to lose everything—his wealth, his family, his friends, and his health. Although he never received an answer for the reason of his suffering, *he discovered that God was in his suffering with him, that it was not senseless, and that he could trust God beyond his limit of understanding.* As great as our pain may be, we can survive as human beings if we know that we are not alone and that from our suffering can come a quality of meaning which will redeem it from pointless agony.

Nothing is wasted in God's economy, and no need goes unnoticed! We can pray for healing and submit to the best medical help available. Yet, for reasons known only to God, some of our cries for physical healing are answered with a *yes* and others with a *no.* Of course, we are aware of the fact that, if He answered every prayer with a yes, we would stay in this world too long. With whole bodies and healthy minds, none would pray, "It is time for me to die."

This world is only a part of the picture. Here we struggle and experience life as a mixture of good and bad, hope and despair, love and selfishness. God's dream for us is to share in His life and His creative resources as His dear children, and this world is too small for the fulfillment of that dream. In this world God confronts us with Himself and His purpose, but gives us the freedom to buy into His dream by faith in His Son, Jesus Christ, or reject His love-offer and pursue our own selfish end. That choice is ours now. To receive Christ as one's Savior and Lord does not bring immediate escape from suffering, but does bring adequate resources for enduring our agony.

Others may suffer more or less than we do. But we do well to remember that suffering is all-encompassing. Suffering is like gas pumped into an empty room, it will fill the room completely whatever its size. Thus suffering fills the human soul, whether the suffering is great or small.

Suffering colors our whole life, but God has given us the power to choose what that color will be—darkness or light, bitterness or hope.

The experience of pain and suffering affords us an unusual opportunity to face ourselves in the core of our being. What are our strengths and weaknesses? What have we lived for and now may die for? What do we consider valuable and truly important? What are we like under great stress?

None of us is so strong that suffering will not threaten to overwhelm us at some point. But we can find, in God's suffering for us and with us, the resources for recovering our dignity and courage.

I do not want to minimize the problem. Suffering is hard—so hard it often seems unbearable and we cry, "I can't go on like this." It is at this point we need to remember that it is not so much the experiences life brings that crush us, as our attitude toward them. We can and do choose our response to life, to its experiences, and to our suffering. To give in to self-pity only destroys our opportunity to make use of the thing that is costing us our lifeblood.

We have no choice over what our suffering does to our body, but we decide what it does to our spirit. If we see ourselves as helpless victims who can do nothing to make our situation better, we may become locked into a self-defeating attitude and paralyze our capabilities of even believing that this attitude can be changed. But if we realize that we have chosen an attitude which hurts instead of helps, and we *want* to, we can change it at any given moment by simply deciding to do so. God has given us that freedom over our destiny and none can take it from us.

—From Creath Davis, *How to Win in a Crisis.* Grand Rapids: Zondervan, 1976.

FOR FURTHER READING:

Narramore, Clyde and Ruth. *How to Handle Pressure.* Wheaton, Ill.: Tyndale, 1975.

Schaeffer, Edith. *Affliction.* Old Tappan, N.J.: Revell, 1978.

PAP TEST

What Happens in a Pap Smear

Actually, what occurs in those few minutes takes longer to explain than it does to experience. First, the physician inserts an instrument called a speculum into the vagina. Once in place, the two shoehornlike prongs are spread apart to permit a clear view of the cervix. Then, with the blunt tip of a depression stick or a cotton swab, the doctor will take two or three sample scrapings: one from the outer cuff of the cervix, one from the area just inside the cervical canal, and possibly one from the vaginal wall.

Aside from some discomfort caused by the pressure of the speculum, you shouldn't feel any pain. For one thing, the cervix has no nerve endings. And second, since the cervix is shedding cells all the time, only this loosened cellular debris is scraped away to be smeared onto slides for microscopic analysis. Indeed, some women remark that the most painful part of the procedure is waiting to hear the results.

And, says Robert Bowser, Ph.D., program director for gynecologic cancer of the National Cancer Institute, even that's uncalled for. The vast majority of Pap smears are normal. Even if a woman is called back for a follow-up test, it doesn't mean she should panic. She could be asked to return for any of a dozen reasons. Maybe the slide wasn't prepared properly. Or she might have a vaginal infection. Or maybe it's some slight abnormality labeled "precancerous" which might disappear on its own.

Unfortunately and understandably, though, there's more than one woman confused by Pap test terminology. After all, what health-minded person can comprehend that a "negative" test result could bring anything but bad news? But it's actually good news. Negative to the physician means negative for disease. It means that the cells of your cervix are normal; there's no sign of cancer.

"Positive," on the other hand, implies the presence of cancer. But again, don't panic. Some physicians use the term "positive" to describe any Class III to Class V abnormality—which . . . covers a lot of ground. Furthermore, any precancerous condition and even early cervical cancer is very treatable and curable. In fact, thinking in terms of cancer or surgery at this point is jumping the gun. No competent doctor would base a diagnosis solely on the findings of a single Pap smear. Besides, physicians tell us, if you've been having Pap tests regularly, chances are *extremely remote that the first hint of trouble is going to signal a serious invasive cancer.*

How Often? Well, It Depends

That brings us back to our original dilemma. How regularly should you have a Pap test to insure early detection?

Well, according to the July/August, 1980, guidelines of the American Cancer Society, all healthy women age 20 and over, and those under 20 who are sexually active, should have a Pap test for two consecutive years. If those tests are both negative—and if the woman is not considered a high risk of cervical cancer because of an early age of sexual intercourse, multiple sexual partners, or a history of genital herpes—then she should continue to have Pap smears taken at least every three years.

Exceptions to the rule, according to the ACS, include women who are at high risk of cervical cancer and therefore should be screened more frequently, and those who are relatively inactive sexually and may consequently prefer longer intervals between the tests.

Your Best Safeguard

Your best safeguard against [cervical cancer] is the Pap smear.

Based on the little we know of cervical cancer, it looks like the Pap smear may be able to detect abnormal cell changes in the cervix at least eight years before a full-fledged cancer develops. With prompt treatment, then, advanced life-threatening cancers can be prevented.

Of course, the Pap smear is only a preliminary test in the screening for cervical cancer. So, if word of suspicious cells calls you back to the examination table and stirrups, here's what to expect from further diagnostic tests:

- *Colposcopy.* That may sound frighteningly invasive, but it's no more hassle than a Pap smear. After a speculum is inserted and the vaginal walls swabbed with a vinegarlike solution to remove mucus, the exposed cervix is viewed through a binocular instrument called a colposcope, which magnifies the surface features. The instrument is held outside the body, so don't freeze up in anticipation of pain. It won't hurt and, in fact, may save you additional and perhaps unnecessary follow-up.

- *Biopsy.* And preferably a colposcope-directed biopsy. Once the problem is located, and evaluated through colposcopy, the physician can take a tissue sample from the suspicious area. That can be done in the office. At most you might feel a little pinch, but it isn't enough to require anesthesia or hospitalization. *No treatment—and least of all, hysterectomy—should be undertaken without a biopsy.*

- *Conization.* If, on colposcopic examination, the physician discovers that the suspicious area reaches into the cervical canal, or if the biopsy results return from the lab labeled moderate to severe dysplasia, it may be necessary to evaluate the extent of disease further by cutting a cone-shaped wedge out of the cervix. Since half of the volume of the cervix is actually removed during this procedure, hospitalization and anesthesia are required. Immediate complication including hemorrhaging and long-term complications such as infertility can result. Obviously, this is not your basic biopsy. Yet, it remains an invaluable diagnostic tool which could save you from a hysterectomy. And, by comparison, the risks are small.

Treatment is then tailored according to the extent of the trouble and the stage of cancer development. As mentioned earlier, it usually takes many years for a full-fledged cervical cancer to take hold. And it isn't even known for fact whether every problem labeled "precancerous" would develop into a cancer. But most are removed as a precautionary measure. Other minuscule lesions diagnosed as "mild dysplasia" may disappear on their own, perhaps a result of some kind of body defense mechanism. But generally speaking, the earlier the diagnosis, the less drastic the treatment and the more effective the cure. It's rare for any diagnosed mild to moderate dysplasia or lesion to require hysterectomy.

—From Emrika Padus, *The Woman's Encyclopedia of Health and Natural Healing.* Emmaus, Pa.: Rodale, 1981.

FOR FURTHER READING:

Fishbein, Anna Mantel, ed. *Modern Woman's Medical Encyclopedia.* Garden City, N.Y.: Doubleday, 1966.

17 Women Doctors, with D. S. Thompson, M.D., as consulting editor. *Everywoman's Health.* Garden City, N.Y.: Doubleday, 1980.

PARENTING

The Declaration of a Real Parent

Being real has not resulted in hair loss or loose joints—a little loose skin maybe—but I'm still altogether. It has, however, worked off a few sharp edges and thinned my skin a bit. As I worked at being real, my facade of perfectionism finally faded. Through the experience of turning from "ideal," I developed guidelines which I named "The Declaration of a Real Parent." Perhaps they can help you stay in tune with reality.

- I am a parent to my children—not a peer.
- I am here to guide and direct my children, not to keep them constantly amused. I am a person, apart from the children, with needs and concerns of my own.
- I understand parenting is not a simple task. There are no magic formulas.
- I will be honest in my discussions with other parents, taking care not to pretend I am the *Mythical, Model Parent.*
- I will be *real*, with my children as well as with other parents in my prayer or support groups.
- I will help other parents in their struggle to be authentic, with a listening ear and with sympathetic understanding.

When we are real, we become transparent. We can care, forgive, love, and be loved in return. If you still have questions about being yourself, ask your family. If there's one thing I've learned through life with my teenagers, it's that no one knows the *real me* like my family!

SIX STEPS TO FINDING THE REAL YOU

1. Be willing to show your warts as well as your beauty marks.
2. Don't be afraid to share true feelings with the people you love and are close to.
3. Allow the free flow of tears and laughter. Don't stifle yourself.
4. Tell your children when you hurt—encourage them to do the same. Show them laughter when you're tickled. Cry in your pain. Shout in your anger. Love in all things.
5. Refuse to isolate yourself as an anomaly or an abnormal parent if your children aren't the people you've reared them to be. There

are many parents, who, like me, need to know they are not alone.

6. If you really want to get radical, share your real self with strangers. You'll find the strangers quickly become friends when you trust them enough to share.

—From Patricia H. Rushford, *Have You Hugged Your Teenager Today?* Old Tappan, N.J.: Revell, 1983.

Disappointed Expectations

Among the many causes of parental explosions are two common and closely related attitudes. Both have to do with unrealistic expectations, first of your children and second of your ability to control your children's behavior.

Disappointed expectations make us all angry. If I expect traffic to move briskly on the way to the airport and it doesn't, I get upset. If in spite of traffic difficulties I get to the airport in time only to find my plane has left, I am angry. In the same way, if I expect my children to behave in certain ways and they don't, then again I am inclined to become inflamed.

Tragically, many parents have unrealistic hopes and expectations of their children, about their careers as well as about everyday things. If you expect Veronica to stop picking her nose the first time you ask, and if Veronica goes on picking her nose, the stage is set for an explosion. Under such circumstances a tense parent faces two possible solutions: (1) to control his or her temper every time Veronica picks her nose; (2) not to expect Veronica to get over her habit right away.

Solution number two is the better one. If you don't have to cope with unrealistic expectations, you have less anger to control. If you can accept the fact that unpleasant as the habit is it will probably take Veronica a little while to get it out of her system and that she may well display her nose picking when you entertain guests, you will not be so tense.

Accepting such a solution may not be easy. It will involve visualizing all the unpleasant situations in which Veronica displays her digital expertise, realizing that the earth will not come to an end whatever lapses she may have. Once you can accept this you will begin to make progress. But it will take practice, practice picturing Veronica picking her nose in front of guests, practice reminding yourself that Veronica is more important to you than they are and that she sometimes forgets. This kind of practice constitutes an exercise in putting yourself in Veronica's shoes. Habits are habits. You may have one or two yourself that you have difficulty controlling—like getting mad.

Please understand that I am not recommending that you ignore Veronica's problem. We are talking now not about how to stop her picking her nose but how not to get mad when she does.

Disappointed expectations, then, may surprise us into explosions. But expectations sit so quietly on our shoulders, so lightly around our belts and seclude themselves so unobtrusively in our pockets that we are unaware of their presence. Unless, check list in hand, we inspect ourselves to bring hidden expectations to light, they will victimize us mercilessly. Let us look at a few of the commoner ones.

Have I been expecting that home will always be a haven of refuge and peace? Many of us do. The expectation is understandable but hardly realistic. In any case it is the parents' responsibility to make the home a haven of peace not for their own benefit but for their family's. It is the parent birds who line the nest with down.

But all question of rights aside, home will not always be a quiet haven. And if fathers and mothers, weary from struggles of the day, expect to have peace at home, they are in for disappointments from time to time.

Have I been expecting more than my child is capable of, accomplishments beyond his or her stage of development? Children mature at different rates. Bowel and bladder control, motor skills, a sense of responsibility and even puberty cannot be predicted with precision. Not all small children walk at twelve months or talk at twenty-four months. Flowers do not open simultaneously in spring. What am I expecting of my child? Is it realistic? If it is not, my child and I may both suffer needless distress because of my anger at not encountering what I thought I had a right to expect.

Am I expecting behavior radically different from that of other children of the same age? Different table manners? A different degree of room tidiness? A different attitude to haircuts and bathing frequency? A different degree of forgetfulness? Or of truthfulness? A lower frequency of sibling hassles and rivalries? A greater immunity to temptations?

We use the word *expect* in different senses of course. When we tell a child, "I expect you to sit up straight at the table!" we are really saying that we want the child to do so and that we don't intend to let him or her get away with anything less. But that is not the kind of expecting we're talking about. We are dealing with unconscious or half-conscious assumptions, with what we thought or imagined should and would happen.

Naturally we want to see certain standards observed by our children. Quite rightly we aim at such standards which may indeed be higher than those we observe in our children's contemporaries (for once again we are not dealing with the question of whether we ought to let standards slide but with how to cope with our feelings when they do). It is a mistake to underestimate an enemy, and if the enemy is contemporary culture, then we are doubly foolish to do so. Our expectations will be dashed and we will be angered because we have been living in a dream world.

Think of it from the child's point of view. He may know what you want. He may even, at times, want it too. But knowing and doing are not the same. Our children are powerfully influenced by culture, are gripped by habits and, like us, have to grapple with fierce temptation. Not all bad behaviors represent deliberate disobedience, rebellion or stubbornness. And even those that do may be the end result of an intense inner struggle. If we are not going to be thrown by their undesirable behavior, we must take hard and frequent looks at them, must try to understand what they are coping with so that we know what to expect.

Some of our expectations may arise from our selfishness. Although we assure ourselves that we want only our children's good, our expectations may in reality have a lot to do with our personal pride and comfort. If this is the case then our anger will be adulterated with bitterness and resentment. It is well to look not only at what we expect of our children but also why we have such expectations.

—From John White, *Parents in Pain.* Downers Grove, Ill.: Inter-Varsity Press, 1979.

Single Parenting

KEEPING YOUR FAMILY INTACT

Is there family life after a marriage breaks up or a spouse dies? Many women are finding that a broken marriage or death of a mate, no matter how devastating, need not result in a broken home. Renewing a sense of family after one parent is gone can be difficult but not impossible. Here are some ways one single parent found to put her family back together again.

1. *Create a Wholesome Atmosphere.* When my marriage ended, I sensed that the quality of our family life was going to be determined in some ways by the attitudes of the people around us. I made it clear from the start that ours was not a broken home, that I was not a swinging single with five short roommates. We were a family, sharing a very difficult experience, but a real family, nonetheless.

Because the year before the separation had been so stressful, I expected the children would be more relaxed once they got used to the situation. I told their teachers to look for

357

some positive changes. Not surprisingly, they found what I told them they were looking for. I discouraged my mother from calling them "those poor little half orphans," introduced the children to other single parent families, and planned a few special events for the first summer to give some substance to my pep talk about a better life.

But I didn't overdo it. Too much pep talk can develop into the divorce-as-a-wonderful-opportunity-for-personal-growth approach and I don't really see divorce that way. I was hurt and angry that my marriage didn't last; my children were hurt and angry, too, and they needed to vent those feelings. In the early months, we cried as much as we laughed; shouted in anger as much as in joy and had three Earnest Discussions for every frivolous one. We continued to be a family, but we had to work out new ways of living together, and that was serious business.

2. *Maintain Order.* In many two-parent homes, each adult takes over areas traditionally labelled as "his" or "hers," and the children are assigned jobs more because it is good for them than because they are needed. But in the single parent family, the children really are needed. This does not mean that the single parent should share the authority in the household with one of her children.

My children, already used to helping around the house, were told just how important they were to the smooth running of our home. They knew it was to their advantage to cooperate (if only to avoid a grouchy mother), but they also knew I could manage alone if I had to and that I stood between them and any real disaster.

3. *Schedule "Unscheduled" Time.* I try to plan for other family needs as well by leaving blocks of time unscheduled for talking, playing a game, reading a story, or other spur-of-the-moment things that make family life a pleasure. Scheduling free time allows me to feel that I am supposed to be relaxing and ensures that I don't cheat my family with obsessive working.

4. *Extend Your Family.* Single parent families do not thrive well in solitude. They need connections with other people to feel part of a larger family and the community.

The ties to extended family are especially important in helping single parents and their children feel they are "normal" and part of a "real" family.

Before they died, my parents lived nearby. My father, crippled by arthritis, was an ideal grandfather, attuned to the pace of small children. My mother happily took the children bargain-hunting at flea markets, passed along to them her librarian's respect for good books, and shared their taste in movies more readily than I can.

We are a little short in the aunt and uncle department, but I have scores of relatives of the second cousin (or first cousin twice removed, depending) variety. Many of them I have come to know only in adulthood, but my children are meeting them early in life, forming strong bonds and learning that the degree of kinship depends more on emotional ties than blood ties.

Close friends are another sort of extended family. We made some very good friends at the single parent camp our church runs each year. If the warmth and caring of Christian friends is important to me, it is probably even more important that my children grow up with the companionship and leadership of other people who are committed to Christ.

5. *Work at Making Memories.* Because single parent families often have some very unhappy experiences in their backgrounds, it is important to create happy times together. I've been fortunate to have work that requires some traveling. When the children were small I took them all with me. As they grew older, I took only a couple at a time (rotating them to be fair) and gave them a chance to concentrate on just one sibling for a few days.

Because my ancestors were not only prolific, but nomads, as well, we have family spread all over the country. Every trip becomes a family reunion, and when we stay home, the family comes to visit. The ties become stronger every year . . . and we are happier for them.

Seventeen years ago, when I first became a parent, I envisioned family life quite differently from the way it turned out. By the time my last child is grown, I will have spend eighty percent of my parenting years as a single parent. It is often difficult, but then it isn't always easy for two parent families, either. It's only as they work around the troubles and take pleasure in the good times that any group of people stays intact and becomes a real family.

—ELIZABETH HORMANN, books editor for *Single Parent*, single parent of five, an adoptive parent, and social worker.

DON'T MAKE YOUR CHILD YOUR CONFIDANT

All of us face decisions which are hard to make. We often feel the need to talk to someone about them. We benefit from talking, and from getting the advice and suggestions of the other person. Nothing wrong with that, unless you turn to your child to be your confidant.

All of us have our moody days and depressed times, and feel the need to talk to someone. Talking makes us feel less lonely, alone, and misunderstood. Talking helps us, but can hurt the child whom you turn to as your confidant.

Some parents find a willing listener in one of their children. The child cares and wants to help and may encourage the parent to talk more. This can be especially true in families of one parent. It's easy for the single parent to confide in a child and for the child to encourage it.

But it is not wise to make your child your confidant. A young child, or even a teenager, is not prepared emotionally or intellectually to handle adult problems.

When a child is used as a confidant, that child tends to grow up too fast. He misses the playful life appropriate to his age. Or, she develops prematurely a serious attitude to life around her and loses some of the relationships with other children her age.

Childhood comes only once and does not benefit from being shortened by a confiding parent. It is better for both child and parent if the parent finds an adult to confide in.

—HUGH BURNS, Th.M., psychotherapist, Clayton Professional Building, Riverdale, GA 30274.

FOR FURTHER READING:

Dobson, James. *Hide or Seek.* Old Tappan, N.J.: Revell, 1979.

Dodson, Fitzhugh. *How to Parent.* New York: New American Library, 1970.

Rushford, Patricia H. *Have You Hugged Your Teenager Today?* Old Tappan, N.J.: Revell, 1983.

PLASTIC SURGERY

PLASTIC SURGERY belongs to everybody . . . who has the money to pay for it. It's stupefyingly expensive. The plastic surgeons, though, know how to play games with insurance companies and can defer your costs by telling Medicaid that the skin hanging down over your eyes is obstructing your vision, the stomach apron is giving you a rash on your thighs, and the clogged sinuses in your big nose interfere with your breathing. It's really nice of them to try to ease the financial burden on you by making a third-party payment possible, but I can't help feeling that if they didn't charge so much and didn't demand the cash up front (like no other branch of medicine), they wouldn't have to manipulate insurance forms so elaborately. One leading plastic surgeon, showing slides of some of his operations to a New York medical class, inserted a shot of his huge estate at the close of his presentation. Very funny—but the message was no joke; this can be a very lucrative profession. But those guys often think of themselves as "artists," not just as surgeons.

The most common question asked about plastic surgery is whether it will hurt. Yes, it will, but the operation itself won't. Plastic surgeons have premedication and local anesthesia down to an art, and even though you have to remain awake during surgery, you barely feel the first Novocain needle, which is the most painful. Noses, eyes, and face lifts are done under local anesthesia. I'm not sure why, except that general anesthesia is a little riskier.

The newest trend is to do whole facial procedures in the office instead of the hospital. This horrifies me for one reason. I once had a patient with a gigantic nose, and I felt compelled to suggest she get it fixed. The plastic surgeon she chose admitted her to the hospital to do, in his words, "the most atrocious nose I've ever seen." He put some local anesthetic into it and a few seconds later noticed she wasn't breathing. She had no pulse or blood pressure. Luckily, they were next to a cardiac surgery room, and part of a team was able to rush over and resuscitate her. She had had a cardiac arrest from an allergic reaction to the anesthesia. This is rare, but a doctor needs only one experience like it in a lifetime to be convinced that when you're doing potentially traumatic surgery—be it abortion, a delivery, or plastic or oral surgery—it's good to have a hospital nearby.

So the pain of surgery, except in cases like that one, is the least of the procedure. The pain afterward is a real shocker, however. "My face didn't feel like me for months," one of my patients said. "When I washed it, I wondered whose face I was washing. It was the weirdest, most uncomfortable sensation I've ever had." But pain never stopped anyone from having babies, and it won't stop anybody determined to change her features from having plastic surgery.

What about disappointment in the outcome? One woman confided to me that her face looked lopsided. It wasn't just the swelling, either. Her eye looked crooked and she couldn't stand what she saw in the mirror. Then one morning about three months after surgery she woke up and fell in love with herself. She said, "My face just suddenly came together. But why didn't the surgeon warn me that I would have the ugly interval?"

Cosmetic surgery for aging—face lifts, chemical peels, and so on—tends to create few psychological problems, but surgery that drastically alters appearance—a nose job or correcting a deformity, for example—might create a few. After all, people's personalities are partially shaped by their appearance, and you can't make a major change in one of your features without a corresponding change in self-image. Psychiatric counseling

is now routinely provided to people who undergo drastic plastic surgery.

—From Barbara Edelstein, M.D., *The Woman Doctor's Medical Guide for Women*. New York: Morrow, 1982.

POSSESSIONS

ROSALIND GOFORTH, in her story of the life she and her husband led as missionaries in China, told of being robbed by bandits of everything they possessed. She wept.

"But my dear," her husband, Jonathan, chided. "They're only *things!*"

"So also none of you can be a disciple of mine without parting with all his possessions," was what Jesus said about things.

It is a stern condition. Few of us fulfill it literally.

I enjoy material things. In the *hytte*, primitive though it would seem to many Americans, we had plenty of comforts. There was a stainless steel sink in the tiny kitchen, which lacked only faucets. It had a drain that ran into plastic containers that Lars emptied every few days. We had a bottled-gas stove on which we cooked and heated water in a big orange teakettle; all our hot water came from this source, to be used for both dishwashing and bathing. Water was collected in a large tank from the roof and carried into the house in a pail. The outhouse was first class—lace curtains at the window, pictures on the wall.

I am back home now, however, and appreciate more than ever a tiled bathroom and a kitchen sink with faucets. Hot water is an extravagant luxury, and I often thank God for it.

It usually takes loss or deprivation in some measure for most of us to count the blessings we so readily take for granted. The loss of material things is not to be compared with the loss of people we love, but most of us have experienced both, and it is things we are considering now.

The first lesson is that things are given by God.

"Make no mistake, my friends. All good giving, every perfect gift, comes from above, from the Father of the lights of heaven."

I often see, shining in the deep blue of the sky just before dawn, the morning star. At twilight the sea sometimes reflects the pale rose and daffodil colors of the sunset. At night I awaken to find the room flooded with moonlight reflected from the sea, from the glass top of my desk by the window, and from the mirror of the dressing table. Flying at thirty thousand feet, I have seen glorious light shining on the towers and castles of thunderheads. What a gift are these lights of heaven! The same Father who gives them also gives us all other good and perfect things.

It is God's nature to give. He can no more "help" giving than He can "help" loving. We can absolutely count on it that He will give us everything in the world that is good for us, that is, everything that can possibly help us to be and do what He wants. How can He not do this?

"He did not spare his own Son, but gave him up for us all; and with this gift how can he fail to lavish upon us all he has to give?"

The second lesson is that things are given us *to be received with thanksgiving.*

God gives. We receive. Animals do this, too, but more directly and simply than we do:

... The earth is full of thy creatures, beasts great and small ...
All of them look expectantly to thee
to give them their food at the proper time;
what thou givest them they gather up;
when thou openest thy hand, they eat their fill.

Because God gives us things indirectly, by enabling us to make them with our own hands (out of things He has made, of course), or to earn the money to buy them, or to receive them through someone else's giving, we are prone to forget that He gave them to us.

"... What do you possess that was not given you? If then you really received it all

as a gift, why take the credit to yourself?"

The taking of credit becomes an absurdity when we remember that not only the brains, abilities, and opportunities for achievement are gifts, but also the very air we breathe and the ability to draw it into our lungs.

We should be thankful. Thanksgiving requires the recognition of the Source. It implies contentment with what is given, not complaint about what is not given. It excludes covetousness. The goodness and love of God choose the gifts, and we say thank you, acknowledging the Thought Behind as well as the thing itself. Covetousness involves suspicion about the goodness and love of God, and even His justice. He has not given me what He gave somebody else. He doesn't notice my need. He doesn't love me as much as He loves him. He isn't fair.

Faith looks up with open hands. "You are giving me this, Lord? Thank You. It is good and acceptable and perfect."

The third lesson is that things can be *material for sacrifice.* This is what is called the eucharistic life. The Father pours out His blessings on us; we, His creatures, receive them with open hands, give thanks, and lift them up as an offering back to Him, thus completing the circle.

When Solomon's temple was about to be built, King David asked who was willing to give with open hands to the Lord. The people responded and gave gold, silver, bronze, iron, and precious stones. David then poured out his praise and thanksgivings:

Thine, O Lord, is the greatness, the power, the glory, the splendour, and the majesty; for everything in heaven and on earth is thine. . . . But what am I, and what is my people, that we should be able to give willingly like this? For everything comes from thee, and it is only of thy gifts that we give to thee.

The people joined in this praise, prostrating themselves before the Lord and the king, and the next day they celebrated with sacrifices of oxen, rams, lambs, and drink offerings, "with great rejoicing."

"... There should be no reluctance, no sense of compulsion; God loves a cheerful giver. And it is in God's power to provide you richly with every good gift; thus you will have ample means in yourselves to meet each and every situation, with enough and to spare for every good cause."

It is said that Hudson Taylor, founder of the China Inland Mission, once a year sorted through everything he owned. Things that he had not used for a year were given away. He believed he would be held accountable for what he retained and there was no reason to retain things someone else could use as long as he himself had not needed them for a year's time.

Some of us are hoarders. Frugality is one thing, hoarding another. Having lived in a country where an ordinary mayonnaise jar was worth fifty cents without the mayonnaise makes me extremely careful about what I throw away. I believe in conserving as many plastic bags and wire twisters for closing them as I can readily use. My stinginess in the use of wax paper and paper towels amounts almost to an obsession. I have been known to dry out the paper towels used for blotting lettuce leaves—but I lived for eleven years in a place where there were no such things, so they are still luxuries to me.

> Instruct those who are rich in this world's goods not to be proud, and not to fix their hopes on so uncertain a thing as money, but upon God. . . . Tell them to do good and to grow rich in noble actions, to be ready to give away and to share, and so acquire a treasure which will form a good foundation for the future. Thus they will grasp the life that is life indeed.

This lesson leads naturally to the fourth, which is that things are given to us *to enjoy for a while.*

Nothing has done more damage to the Christian view of life than the hideous notion that those who are truly spiritual have lost all interest in this world and its beauties. The Bible says, ". . . God . . . endows us richly with all things to enjoy." It also says,

"Do not set your hearts on the godless world or anything in it." It is altogether fitting and proper that we should enjoy things made for us to enjoy. What is not at all fitting or proper is that we should set our hearts on them. Temporal things must be treated as temporal things—received, given thanks for, offered back, but *enjoyed.* They must not be treated like eternal things.

Jesus said, "Beware! Be on your guard against greed of every kind, for even when a man has more than enough, his wealth does not give him life." He went on to tell the story of a man whose crops yielded so much that he had to pull down his barns to build bigger ones. Then he sat back and told himself confidently, ". . . Take life easy, eat, drink, and enjoy yourself.

"But God said to him, 'You fool, this very night you must surrender your life; you have made your money—who will get it now?' That is how it is with the man who amasses wealth for himself and remains a pauper in the sight of God."

"Do not store up for yourselves treasure on earth, where it grows rusty and moth-eaten, and thieves break in to steal it. Store up treasure in heaven, where there is no moth and no rust to spoil it, no thieves to break in and steal. For where your treasure is, there will your heart be also."

I must confess there was a sense of liberation when my silver was gone. I had felt uneasy each time we left the house. There had been a series of burglaries in our neighborhood and we knew we were probably on the list. The police were fairly sure they knew who was doing it, but seemed powerless to do anything about it before or after. When it happened, I was shocked, but very quickly was able to say, "Well, so much for that. Thank You, Lord." My heart was lighter. We spent some of the insurance money on a set of plated silver that I suppose nobody is going to want very badly.

Four lessons, then:

1. Things are given by God.
2. Things are to be received with thanksgiving.

3. Things are material for sacrifice.
4. Things are given us to enjoy for a while.

And there is a fifth: all that belongs to Christ is ours, therefore, as Amy Carmichael wrote, "All that was ever ours is ours forever."

We often say that what is ours belongs to Christ. Do we remember the opposite: that what is His is ours? That seems to me a wonderful truth, almost an incredible truth. If it is so, how can we really "lose" anything? How can we even speak of His having the "right" to *our* possessions?

"Everything belongs to you! Paul, Apollos or Cephas; the world, life, death, the present or the future, everything is yours! For you belong to Christ, and Christ belongs to God!"

"Son, thou art ever with me, and all that I have is thine," the Father says to us. That is riches.

—From Elisabeth Elliot, *Discipline: The Glad Surrender*. Old Tappan, N.J.: Revell, 1982.

POSTPARTUM DEPRESSION

WHEN I was in my early twenties with two babies under four, I needed only one word to describe my life, *fatigue!* I've never been that exhausted before or since those days. As a young mother I remember feeling worn out beyond belief, and I truly believed I would never feel rested again in my life—and that fatigue was *forever.*

The first awful effects of fatigue occurred a few weeks after my first child was born. When I described my symptoms to my friends, they just smiled and said, "Oh, that! It's just 'after-birth blues.' You'll get over it." My feelings of depression were to be treated as if they were a short-term mental problem, which, given time, my mind would outgrow.

I learned much later that "postpartum battle fatigue" has been recognized by doctors since 1875 as a distinct, but generally benign, disorder that affects a large percentage of new mothers. It's also not all "in our heads," but results from a combination of emotional *and* physical factors.

The emotions and the body go through very radical changes during pregnancy. It is no wonder that immediately after giving birth, when we've abruptly lost as much as twenty pounds of baby and fluids, with the hormones at a very low level, and possibly thyroid deficiencies, postpartum blues really hit us. The apprehensions and responsibility of caring for an infant loom before us, and we're at a loss to explain our feelings. We are profoundly overcome. One moment we cry, the next, laugh, and then we find ourselves talking gratefully of how glad we'll be when the baby sleeps through the night.

It's always precisely at this point that some forty-nine-year-old lady like myself comes up to you and feeds you two concepts that utterly gag you.

First: "This is the *best* time of your life!" Then she adds snidely, "You'll just hate it when they get to be teenagers!"

When my daughter-in-love, Teresa, was told this, she said to me, "If *this* is the best time in my life, why am I always crying?"

I had to remind her that women who make these comments are making a statement about *their own lives* and *their own babies*, who are now teenagers. Such an appraisal of life has very little to do with the young mother they are talking to.

Second: "This stage of life will go by very fast. Why, in no time at all the baby will be grown up and married!"

Right. Partially. I say this statement is *partially* correct because *my* babies *are* grown. But when you are living at this stage, with *your* babies, it's extremely difficult for you to see ahead even two years, much less ten or fifteen. Telling you that this time will go quickly is a little like saying, "If you wish hard enough on a star, someone will come in each week and clean and wax your kitchen floor commercially at absolutely no cost."

You are positive this child will never be five years old. Those babies of yours will never toddle off to kindergarten, and you're sure you'll be *forever* knee-deep in diapers, formula, and fatigue!

I've given both Laurie and Teresa this timely Scripture reference. (I'd engrave it on their foreheads if they'd let me.)

And let us not get tired of doing what is right, for after a while we will reap a harvest of blessing if we don't get discouraged and give up.

Galatians 6:9 TLB

—From Joyce Landorf, *Changepoints.* Old Tappan, N.J.: Revell, 1981.

FOR FURTHER READING:

Infant Care. Washington: U.S. Department of Health, Education, and Welfare, 1970.

Todd, Linda. *Labor and Birth.* Minneapolis: International Childbirth Education Association, 1981.

PRAYER

GOD SPEAKS to us through His Word, but to cultivate this relationship we should learn to talk with Him. We communicate with God through prayer; however, the prayers of many people never go much beyond "Now I lay me down to sleep." Many people pray only in emergencies. Others find it boring, so they don't pray at all, while still others neglect prayer because they don't feel worthy. For many, it remains a relatively unknown experience.

Yet Jesus found it necessary to pray; He taught His disciples how to pray. Through history, we find those who have been outstanding in the cause of Christ are those who have prayed. The Scripture admonishes us to pray without ceasing (*see* 1 Thessalonians, 5:17), which means talk to God hundreds of times a day. We are told there is nothing too small for His attention or too great for Him to accomplish.

The importance of prayer is recorded in many verses. In Jeremiah 33:3 God promises us that when we call to Him, He will show us great and mighty things we do not know. James 4:2 tells us that we have not because we ask not. Matthew 7:7 says, "Ask, and it shall be given to you; seek, and you shall find; knock, and it shall be opened to you." In John 16:24, Jesus makes this statement: "Until now you have asked for nothing in My name; ask, and you will receive, that your joy may be made full." The Bible places a very strong emphasis on prayer.

The basic reason people do not pray is that they do not know how to pray. Often when they do pray they don't see answers to prayer. Those who pray must first know that to receive answers they must be rightly related to God. They must belong to Christ (*see* 1 Timothy 2:5).

If I'm walking down the street and a little boy comes to me and says, "Will you please give me a nickel?" even though I've never seen him before, I will probably give him the nickel.

But when my own child says, "Mommy, give me a nickel," I usually know whether he needs it. If he does, I'm obligated as his parent to provide for that need, and even if he doesn't need it, I'll probably give it to him because he asked me, unless he would be harmed by my giving him the nickel.

With the first child, I have the choice; but with my own child, I'm obligated to provide for his needs. Also, because I love him, I will try to please him by giving him what he likes if it is for his best interest.

So it is in our relationship with God. When we receive Christ, we become children of God. Because of our new position, God promises to provide for our needs. But when we have not received Christ as our personal Savior, He is under no obligation to answer our prayers.

Another prerequisite to receiving answers from prayer is to have a clean heart: "If I regard iniquity in my heart, the Lord will not hear me" (Psalms 66:18 KJV). In other words, God will not listen to us if we have not confessed our sin. However, God clearly explains, "If we confess our sins, He is faithful and righteous [just] to forgive us our sins and to cleanse us from all unrighteousness" (1 John 1:9).

The third prerequisite to answered prayer is having a forgiving heart: "And whenever you stand praying, forgive, if you have anything against anyone; so that your Father also who is in heaven may forgive you your transgressions" (Mark 11:25). Many times I have heard someone say, "Oh, you can't expect me to forgive him. I could never forgive what he did to me." Yet God expects us to forgive others so that we can receive His forgiveness and He can answer our prayers.

Those who pray must do so in faith; believing is a prerequisite for answered prayer.

In addition to these basic principles in praying, there are a few key words which will also enable us to pray confidently. First is the word *abide* as found in John 15:7. This verse is important to prayer; I've learned to call it the combination to heaven.

Imagine a bank safe with a gigantic door and a large combination lock on the front. This safe contains the treasures of heaven, God's safe of answers to prayer. But to open the door you have to apply the combination: "If you abide in Me," and turn the big wheel until it clicks, "and My words abide in you," we turn it in the opposite direction until it clicks, "ask whatever you wish," and again turn the combination wheel until it clicks, "and it shall be done for you." Now just take hold of the gigantic handle and open the door. Inside the safe are all of God's good things which are available to us if we simply apply that combination.

By His example and teaching, Jesus encourages us to ask God for specific requests—those which have to do with our needs, our relationships, or anything that concerns us.

God delights in listening to us express our desires to Him. Prayers do not have to be long, nor does a person need to be super-spiritual to talk to God. He simply desires that we come to Him with clean hearts and pure motives.

It is beneficial to keep a prayer list where you record the request, the day requested, and the date answered. This may help to increase your faith as you specifically see the ways in which God is answering your prayers.

It is not necessary to be in any special position to pray. I find some of my greatest times of communication with the Lord are when I'm working with my hands and my mind is free to concentrate on talking to Christ. When I'm washing dishes, preparing meals, driving, or going about other daily tasks, I talk to Him about everything.

I've learned to pray about everything. When unexpected guests come and I don't know what to serve, I'll pray, "Lord, show me what to do." Or when I'm baking and I don't have an ingredient, I'll pray God will show me what I can substitute. This prayer was especially necessary at a dinner party when I ran out of sauce that needed to stand for twenty-four hours. As I prayed, God gave me a creative mind. Instead of the fresh-tomato base, with which I originally started, I duplicated the taste with canned goods and spices I had in my pantry. Just as God gave me the answer in that situation, He gives each of us the ability to think creatively in the times we need it. From my own experience, as well as that of others, I've learned that God becomes a greater reality as we see how He answers prayers.

—From Vonette Zachary Bright, *For Such a Time as This*. Old Tappan, N.J.: Revell, 1976.

FOR FURTHER READING:

Briscoe, Jill. *Hush! Hush!* Grand Rapids: Zondervan, 1978.

Edens, David and Virginia. *Making the Most of Family Worship.* Anderson, Ind.: Warner Press, 1968.

Murphey, Cecil B. *Prayerobics*, Waco, Tex.: Word Books, 1979.

Self, Carolyn Shealy, and William L. Self. *Learning to Pray: A Handbook for Personal and Group Study.* Waco, Tex.: Word Books, 1978.

Shoemaker, Helen Smith. *The Exploding Mystery of Prayer.* New York: Seabury, 1978.

Taylor, Florence M. *As for Me and My Family.* Waco, Tex.: Word Books, 1976.

PREGNANCY

PERHAPS no change in a woman's life is more radical than the experience of being pregnant and giving birth. It is a relatively short experience in terms of time, and though it may be repeated, each pregnancy raises the question of a woman's self-understanding in a new way. Pregnancy and birth involve an identity crisis for a woman. She is challenged to formulate a new self-concept, a new understanding of herself in relation to her physiology, and a new view of the meaning of her fertility. Pregnancy and birth challenge not only the woman's sense of herself as an individual but also her relationship to the father of the child and her anticipated relationship with the baby as its mother. Fundamentally, pregnancy and birth locate a woman in an experience of the body and a perception of the self that is uniquely female. That uniqueness can bring both pride and fear; it links her unalterably with those who have experienced pregnancy and childbirth and separates her from those who will never experience it.

—From Penelope Washbourn, *Becoming Woman.* New York: Harper & Row, 1977.

Complications

The majority of pregnancies are completely normal, but there are some (about 30 percent) in which complications may develop. If left unattended these conditions can become serious, but the main purpose of antenatal care is to detect potential dangers and, where possible, to prevent them from happening.

The chart shows which unusual symptoms should be reported immediately to a doctor and what the possible causes of such symptoms may be.

Danger Signs	Possible Causes
Severe abdominal pain, possibly with slight bleeding, in first few weeks of pregnancy.	Ectopic pregnancy
Vaginal bleeding with or without abdominal pain in the first 28 weeks of pregnancy.	Threatened miscarriage
Vaginal bleeding with or without abdominal pain after the 28th week of pregnancy.	Premature separation of placenta (abruptio placenta, if pain; placenta praevia, if painless)
Severe swelling of fingers and face, with blurred vision and headaches, after the twentieth week of pregnancy.	Toxemia of pregnancy
Gush of water from the vagina at twenty-eighth to thirty-sixth week	Rupture of membranes (bursting of amniotic sac)

DISPLACED PLACENTA

Hemorrhage after the twenty-eighth week may be caused by two fairly rare conditions: (a) *placenta praevia*, in which the placenta lies in the lower part of the uterus; and (b) *abruptio placenta*, in which the placenta separates prematurely from the uterus. A woman with placenta praevia will be hospitalized after the twenty-eighth week. A Cesarian may be necessary, but in 20 percent of cases delivery is normal. Most cases of abruptio placenta continue normally, and in only 25 percent is separation too great for the infant to survive.

Rupture of Amniotic Sac

A sudden gush of water from the vagina after the twenty-eighth week generally means that the amniotic sac in which the baby grows has burst and amniotic fluid is escaping. If this occurs before the twenty-eighth to thirty-sixth week it may often precede premature labor. The woman is hospitalized and drugs or sedatives may be given to discourage labor. After the thirty-sixth week labor will be allowed to continue or will be induced as the baby is sufficiently mature to survive.

Toxemia of Pregnancy

Toxemia of pregnancy is a serious condition that can occur in late pregnancy. It affects 7 to 12 percent of women having their first baby and 3 to 6 percent of those having subsequent children.

Symptoms and Signs. There are three main warnings: (a) edema (swelling due to water retention) of fingers, face, or legs; (b) raised blood pressure; and (c) protein in the urine. Excessive weight gain is also associated with toxemia.

Progress. Toxemia goes through two stages; (a) *Pre-eclampsia.* This rarely occurs before the twentieth week and the conditions are those mentioned above. (Some degree of edema, particularly of the legs, is, however, common in pregnancy. It becomes dangerous when associated with other symptoms.) As pre-eclampsia progresses, vision becomes blurred and the woman will suffer severe headaches; (b) *Eclampsia* is the final and most severe stage and may be fatal. Fits, followed by unconsciousness or coma, are characteristic. It is particularly dangerous for the fetus.

Treatment. Today toxemia rarely develops to a final stage. This is almost entirely due to antenatal care, where the symptoms can be detected early on. For this reason alone regular attendance at the antenatal clinic is vitally important.

Bed rest and a restricted diet is generally sufficient to prevent toxemia from developing. Diuretic tablets may be given to get rid of excess water and salt. For more severe cases hospitalization is necessary so that the condition can be checked.

Ectopic Pregnancy

If the fertilized egg does not reach the uterus within seven days, the tiny armlike protrusions (*chorionic villi*) which will have formed by then will burrow into the wall of the Fallopian tube. The latter will become sorely distended as it can only stretch to a limited extent. The chorionic villi will continue to burrow into the wall in search of nourishment—which is obviously restricted. Eventually they will break through the muscular wall or into an artery causing bleeding, pain, and the loss of the embryo. (Surgery is always necessary.) Occasionally, however, the embryo will escape into the cavity of the abdomen and the chorionic villi will burrow into the wall where eventually a placenta will develop. Healthy babies have occasionally been delivered (by Cesarian section) which have developed within the abdomen.

Ectopic pregnancies are not uncommon and since the same hormones are secreted as in a normal pregnancy causing the naturally anticipated reactions, they are not always detected until discomfort is felt. One in every ten women who has had an ectopic pregnancy is liable to have another. They are often due to prior inflammation of the Fallopian tube.

—From The Diagram Group, *Woman's Body.* New York: Simon & Schuster, 1981.

FOR FURTHER READING:

Padus, Emrika. *The Woman's Encyclopedia of Health and Natural Healing.* Emmaus, Pa.: Rodale, 1981.

PREJUDICE

CLEAR CONFRONTATION of another's prejudices requires that I be aware of, and wary
of, my own.

Before I dare address another on his bias
or her intolerance, I need to recognize my
ever present tendencies to slant the issues,
skew my conclusions, and shape my view-
points in favor of my kind, my kin, etc.

I need to deal with my own prejudging—
whether it be radical, liberal, conservative,
or apathetic. I am all of these on different
issues. I am in process of changing and being
changed. I may be useful in challenging
other's opinions.

Somewhere the ideas began—
that whites think they have divine rights,
that blacks are violent, power-driven,
that Indians are unimportant, dispensable,
that Mexicans are lazy, irresponsible,
that Polacks are stupid, slow-witted,
that Russians are malicious, dishonest,
that Italians are emotional.

Where did the ideas begin? I can't recall
who first implanted the stereotypes in my
mind. Can you identify how these and their
many variants first came to you?

No matter how, where, when I learned
them, if the stereotypes of prejudice are with
me now, I am responsible. If they are still
with you, you are responsible. Such ideas
stay with us because we choose to keep them
with us. We reindoctrinate ourselves with
strange ideas such as, "Black people are biologically different from whites," or, "Minority people are shiftless, lazy, and not to be
trusted."

To keep alive such assumptions as though
they were facts, we simply keep repeating
them, keep telling ourselves that they are
true, keep slipping them into casual conversations:

"Minority children seem to have lower
IQs."

"The Indian has contributed little to our
world."

"The race problem in America is essentially a black problem."

"The race problem in Canada is an Indian
problem."

The words are empty. We know it as we
hear them. Yet the repetition serves to convince ourselves that our prejudices are still
serviceable.

They aren't.

. . . . .

Prejudice is any collection of negative
feelings based on erroneous judgments
which are not readily changed even in the
face of data which disproves them.

Prejudice is any set of negative valuations
based upon a faulty and inflexible general-
ization.

The process of forming these generalizations called prejudices flows as follows:

We categorize to maintain our sanity.
Grouping things, thoughts, and people into
classes is necessary in order to handle the
complexity of our world. The trap lies in our
tendency to exaggerate differences between
groups on a particular characteristic and to
minimize the differences within all groups.

*We stereotype to maintain our equilib-
rium.* It throws us off balance to constantly
be observing differences, so we attribute
certain traits to large human groups. Often
these are images chosen to justify a negative
feeling—fear, threat, inferiority. It is a head
theory to support what the heart wants to
make true.

*We sanitize all incoming data to maintain
purity of opinions.* By being selective on
what we expose ourselves to, we automatically limit our contacts and possibilities. By
being selective with attention, we unconsciously exclude all incompatible data. By
being selective in our recall, we drop out
conflictual facts. So only supportive evidence is admitted and any contradiction is
seen as an exception to the rule which goes
to prove the rule.

*So we discriminate in feeling, then in
thought process, then in action.* And the con-
tradictions go unnoticed.

For example, the traits considered a virtue
in the groups we like (because we are like

them) are seen as a vice when observed in members of unlike groups. If one is a white-Anglo-Saxon protestant, he or she will admire Lincoln for being thrifty, hardworking, eager to learn, ambitious, successful. In a Jew, such traits would be called stingy, miserly, driven, uncharitable, etc.

What beliefs, attitudes, generalizations and stereotypes I carry with me into the next moment are my choice. What prejudices and biases I keep with me are my responsibility. I am free—if I'm willing to accept the freedom inherent in humanness—to leave the past and its self-serving opinions behind me.

I have racist attitudes. I don't like discovering them in myself, so I've become expert at hiding and denying them. Now I know that freedom and healing come as I can own these attitudes, admit my inner confusion, confess my apathy, discard my myths, and make a change.

Life changes from moment to moment. I too can change, unless I choose to be stuck with or to stick by old, narrow, self-defeating ideas and ways of behaving. Healing can come as I become willing to risk the pain of letting go of what I've clung to. Or hung onto. Prejudice is a bulldog grip. It is clenched teeth. It is a spiteful bite that grips the past and its stale ideas as a protection against the present and its realities. It is hanging onto the imaginary security of fantasies that "me and my kind" are superior in some way.

Healing follows a willingness to risk seeing, admitting, smiling at and saying goodbye to old generalizations. Then healing, forgiveness, love, and reconciliation happen.

. . . . .

At the heart of living in unprejudiced patterns, there are central commitments, such as these:

1. Christians—who seriously try to follow Jesus daily in life—will refuse to make distinctions between one race or another,

or to make decisions on the basis of one race being imagined as superior to another.

2. Those who follow Jesus point out dishonesty and discard dishonest beliefs as they discover them. And there is no honest base—biblically, biologically, culturally, or statistically—for fighting or prohibiting interracial marriages.

3. Those who follow Jesus will question and challenge prejudices that separate people, and walls that create distrust between people.

Look at Jesus Christ.

He was born in the most rigidly ethnic culture of all time; born in a fiercely nationalistic nation; born in Galilee, the most bigoted backwoods of that nation; born into a family of snobbish royal lineage; born in a time when revolutionary fanaticism fired every heart with hatred for the Roman oppressors; born in a country practicing the apartheid of rigid segregation between Jews and Samaritans.

Jesus Christ was born in a world peopled with prejudiced, partisan, fanatical, intolerant, obstinate, opinionated, bigoted, dogmatic zealots—Roman, Samaritan, and Jewish. Yet He showed not a trace of it.

Read and reread the documents of His life. There is absolutely nothing to indicate feelings of racial superiority, national prejudice, or personal discrimination.

Those who stand with Jesus Christ stand with all humanity. They discard prejudice whenever, however, and wherever they find it, confronting it in themselves first of all; then, and only then, in the world about them.

—From David Augsburger, *Caring Enough to Confront*. Ventura, Calif.: Regal, 1981.

FOR FURTHER READING:

Jacobs, Joan. *Feelings*. Wheaton, Ill.: Tyndale, 1976.

Wright, H. Norman. *The Christian Use of Emotional Power*. Old Tappan, N.J.: Revell, 1974.

PRESSURE

THE WEIGHT of pressure is not only judged by the size of the load but by the strength of the one who bears it.

A heavy crate can be carried by a large truck with ease, but that same crate when placed upon a child's wagon will crush it. The weaker wagon cannot sustain the heavy weight of pressure that is placed upon it. So it is with your physical well-being. When you suffer from poor health, you are overwhelmed by pressures that are not even considered as such by others who enjoy vibrant health.

Think of it this way. Your health is something like a bridge. If it is sturdy and strong, it can sustain a heavy load; if it is weak, even a lesser load may cause it to collapse.

It's simple logic to recognize that the stronger you are, the more pressure you can bear; and the weaker or more fragile you are, the less you can tolerate. Your physical well-being has a direct bearing upon your reaction to the pressures of life. Poor health places life in a framework of pressure, while good health accepts it as a challenge. How you feel physically affects your sense of pressure more than you probably realize.

Remember times when you felt like a million dollars—wonderful, tremendous! You were convinced you could jump over the moon if you needed to. You felt you could tackle almost anything and it wouldn't throw you.

Then there were those other days: you didn't feel so well, you were tired and your head ached. These were the times, of course, when everything went wrong. At least it seemed that way. Molehills became mountains and any little thing could get you down.

People need stimulation in order to find motivation. Yet, when you're in a fragile physical state, any task demanding initiative becomes a stressful situation. Responsibility takes on the dimension of pressure. It doesn't take much to throw on the panic switch or cause you to crumble.

Your human body, however, is an amazingly flexible organism. It learns to adapt to its shortcomings. Through the years, it may have had its problems, not functioning as efficiently as it should. Perhaps you needed medication or a different diet, or some other corrective measures. Nevertheless, since change is gradual (and therefore subtle), it is easy to accustom yourself to feeling badly. In other words, you develop a tolerance which accepts your physical problems as natural for you. It's entirely possible to feel below par most of the time, and yet not be aware of your low-level physical condition. If you would turn the calendar back to relive a day or a week of your life twenty, ten, or even five years ago, you might be amazed at the difference between how you felt then and the way you drag around now.

So if pressures are getting you down, take a close look at your health. Do you have enough physical stamina to hold up under the stress and strains of life? Do routine responsibilities that others accept without batting an eyelash leave you feeling on the bottom of the pile? If everything you do turns out to be a big energy crisis—*your* energy—chances are that your supply needs medical assistance. You weren't meant to drag around feeling like a flat tire under a two-ton truck. If that's the way you find it, it's time you take some action.

DIVIDING YOUR DUTIES

Delegating sounds like a simple operation, but there's more to it than meets the eye.

In the first place, be sure that the person you choose is capable of handling the job. Incompetency is difficult to tolerate. It can lead to nothing but frustration to all concerned. It could even prove disastrous, causing more work and trouble than you would have had without the "help."

To struggle over something in which one has had no training, or lacks all natural inclination, jeopardizes his emotional security and places him under a great amount of unnecessary stress. To put pressure upon the person who is working to relieve you of pressure, is both ironic and unwise. It's also unethical to reduce your stress at the expense of another. Furthermore, if the person to whom the work has been delegated does not feel confident or comfortable in doing it, he will require on-the-job training and supervision, or run the risk of turning out unsatisfactory work. Either way can be frustrating to you both.

Yet, well trained assistants are not always easy to come by. If the job you wish to delegate is of long duration or will be repeated in the future, it's worth training your own helper, if necessary.

Whether you choose an experienced worker or a novice, one thing is certain: *you* are the one responsible for the finished product. To avoid a bad scene in the end, you'd better paint a clear-cut picture now. You can't be too specific in your instructions.

The fact is, a common complaint among secretaries is that their bosses are too vague about what they want done. "You have to read their minds," one young secretary confided. But "reading" another person's mind is an art that few have mastered. In fact, the only really reliable "mind reader" is the God who created our minds. So, when giving a task to someone, make sure you know what you want done. If it's fuzzy in your mind, it will be fuzzy when you try to explain it to someone else.

So, when you're delegating a job to someone else, don't fail to spell out clearly just what you expect. Explain how you want the job done, and when it must be completed. Write your instructions so there will be no question about what you expect from your assistant. If you will take time to do this, you will eliminate confusion, avoid misunderstandings and the finished product should meet with your approval.

After you've turned the job over to someone who you believe is qualified and competent, leave him alone and let him work.

He's capable, and will do a commendable job without you breathing down his neck, continually checking on him. If you're going to do that, you might as well handle it all yourself, because you're not really delegat-

ing. This doesn't mean that you should be oblivious to his progress or withhold helpful suggestions. It does mean, however, that you must give your helper a vote of confidence and enough freedom to allow him to be his best.

HIRING A HELPER

Sometimes all a person needs is someone or something to get him over the "hump." For example, you find that you are a slave to your house or your garden demands all your spare time. In all probability, it would ease your situation if you hired someone to help you. Perhaps a high school boy would like to earn a little money weeding your flower bed or mowing the lawn. And if you could have a lady do some housework once a week, or even every other week, what a great relief that would be. It might not even be a regular need. Perhaps it's only when you entertain that you feel the necessity for help. If you're having a special dinner party, it might keep your blood pressure from rising, if someone helped in food preparation or in washing the dishes. Your way of life determines your need.

You may feel that you cannot afford to spend money for extra help. Perhaps you consider this a luxury that you can do without. Yet, pressure is hard to endure, and stress makes living a strain. If by hiring a few "helping hands," you can relieve yourself of pressure and reduce the strain, would it not be a wise investment? Your personal well being is worth more than money.

There are times at our office when the staff is deluged with work. Although all of us are busy, the secretaries seem to feel the brunt of it.

"Why don't you bring in some extra help?" I suggest.

I have often explained to our staff that there's no need to struggle under a mountain of work. In our location there are numerous organizations that provide special secretarial help for short periods of employment.

"When you feel under the pressure of

work," I tell them, "phone a secretarial service and employ a typist or two. They can assume a sizable work load and help get you out of a bind. If one or two days will take the pressure off, go ahead and employ them for that length of time. It doesn't cost much to get a little assistance, and it will ease things up for you."

Actually, an organization operates more efficiently and at no greater cost when its employees are not subjected to undue strain or tension. But more important than money is the health and happiness of the people who make up that organization.

"Helping hands" are not always of a human origin. The technology of our modern age offers a staggering number of labor saving devices which are geared to meet almost any imaginable human need. Many busy people find that these mechanical helpers lighten their loads. With less work, there is also less pressure.

. . . . .

THE DO-IT-YOURSELF DILEMMA

To "do it yourself" is a popular concept these days. There are do-it-yourself books and pamphlets on every conceivable subject, and kits of every variety to help you do it. "Foolproof" instructions accompany these kits—and sometimes they prove that you were a fool for ever attempting such a complicated project in the first place!

If you have the time and enjoy a do-it-yourself challenge, go to it and more power to you. But if you are busy and time is of essence, or if projects of manual dexterity cause you frustration, you probably should let someone else "do it." When you "do it," you may save money, but you seldom save time. And if you're pressed for time, doing it yourself will undoubtedly "press" you even harder. If you don't have natural talent or know-how in the area of your project, it could even take a great deal longer—to say nothing of the stress resulting from your frustration.

Although home projects and do it yourself

programs have their merits, one needs to evaluate his time and his ability. It isn't worth doing-it-yourself if it means unwarranted tension and stress.

. . . . .

It's amazing how much a family can get done when the mother and father take the time to teach their children how to work. The next step is to set up job assignments. Of course, parents will need to follow through on these to be sure that each task has been completed and is satisfactory. Children are capable of performing a great variety of duties which come in many sizes and types. Some jobs are appropriate for the very young, others are suitable for pre-teens and still meet the moods and abilities of teenagers. When parents sort out the jobs to be done and assign them according to age and ability, the family workload need not be heavy on anyone.

Not long ago I visited a home where a bulletin board held a prominent spot in the kitchen. On it was posted a list of various work assignments. When I asked about it, the father explained how it functioned.

"We divide up the work around here," he said. "We give the little jobs to the little people and the big jobs to the big people. We list the jobs right here on the board, and any time we find any job not being done (including my own) we require an accounting to the entire family. Most jobs are assigned for two weeks, then we review them. Some jobs continue for several months. It really works out quite well."

The man went on to tell me how before they started this "work distribution" program, his wife was always overworked. He also explained that pressure and tension had often resulted when disgruntled family members were asked to pitch in and work. Now there was never any question about what there was to do or who was responsible to do it.

"The kids really don't mind it, in fact they rather like it," the father told me as he summed up the explanation. "The best thing about it, though, is that work around our home is a family affair and we're all in this thing together."

—From Clyde and Ruth Narramore, *How to Handle Pressure*. Wheaton, Ill.: Tyndale, 1975.

FOR FURTHER READING:

Davis, Creath. *How to Win in a Crisis*. Grand Rapids: Zondervan, 1976.

Hart, Archibald D. *Feeling Free*. Old Tappan, N.J.: Revell, 1979.

LaHaye, Tim. *How to Win Over Depression*. Grand Rapids: Zondervan, 1974.

PRIDE

"GOD OPPOSES the proud" (1 Peter 5:5). This verse shows God's sharp verdict against the proud, for there can scarcely be anything worse than having God not only withdraw His grace from us but even flatly oppose us. Perhaps we complain that we are so spiritually dead, that we have difficulties praying, that God does not answer our prayers. This may be the reason. Because of our pride God opposes us and refuses to answer. Or perhaps we seem to be pursued by misfortune. We cannot succeed in anything we undertake no matter how hard we try. Why? God cannot bless us, because our pride has closed the door to Him.

The enemy tries to make every effort to keep us from recognizing this. For every time we do not bring our sin into the light and repent of it, he gets us in his hands. So in many cases he has covered up our pride. This hidden pride is the most dangerous sin. For instance, we cannot stand it, when people pay little attention to us and do not honour us, but pay honour to someone else. We cannot stand it, when we are not worth anything to others, because we do not have many talents or shining qualities or a charming personality. We cannot stand it, if someone reproaches us and humiliates us in the eyes of others. We cannot stand it, if we do not have a position of leadership and cannot set the

pace. We do not realize that all of this stems from our pride.

On the contrary, we often feel sorry for ourselves, because people do not give us what our talents, education and capabilities deserve, or because we have to do work that is "beneath us." We feel sorry for ourselves, because we have not received the education or training necessary to carry out our job. Or we cannot bear the fact that our parents are uneducated, that we ourselves have not reached a prominent position. All these things oppress us and make us unhappy. We blame the external conditions, and we deceive ourselves about our real motives.

We cannot digest any criticism. We shut ourselves off from other people and may even think it is humility when we persist in this attitude, "I have to deal with this somehow myself." But in our hidden pride we are so mixed up that we cannot find the next step to ask for help and release. Our desire to have others think that we are especially humble and modest can also be hidden pride. We are too concerned about what others think of us. Pride can appear in many different forms. Only the Spirit of God can give us light about them.

Our hidden pride is like hidden poison, which threatens our spiritual life with death and will ruin everything in our lives. We have to make every effort to recognize our pride. By searching our consciences we have to let ourselves be shown the dangerous symptoms. We have to get to the bottom of this and ascertain which situation was difficult for us, because we were humiliated, embarrassed or overlooked.

Some Bible verses can help us get the proper attitude towards our pride:

"Every one who is arrogant is an abomination to the Lord . . ." (Proverbs 16:5).

"Pride goes before destruction, and a haughty spirit before a fall" (Proverbs 16:18).

"The Lord abundantly requites him who acts haughtily" (Psalms 31:23).

"What is exalted among men is an abomination in the sight of God" (Luke 16:15).

It is a dreadful verdict that Jesus pronounces in the last verse over the proud and haughty. They are an abomination to God. That is why there will be dreadful judgment against the proud and lofty in the last days (Isaiah 2:12) and the Lord "Will put an end to the pride of the arrogant, and lay low the haughtiness of the ruthless" (Isaiah 13:11), when He comes again to judge mankind. The proud can await destruction. No matter how high the price, we have to experience redemption from our pride. Otherwise a terrible judgment will await us. We have to be horrified by our sin of pride, which is one of the most satanic sins, because Satan is pride personified. The proud belong to his kingdom. Through their pride they are tilling the ground for many other sins. If we are not determined to make a radical break with our pride and to strive for humility, we will never be free from Satan's nets.

The Word of God gives us clear directives. First, "Humble yourselves therefore under the mighty hand of God" (1 Peter 5:6). In practical life it can look like this: If we are denied an honour, an office, a position of leadership, something that our pride has been striving for, we must humble ourselves beneath the mighty hand of God. We must surrender our will to God; we must yield to everything that humiliates us. We must say, "Yes, Father," to the flaws in our personality, to our insufficient education and talents, to our family situations, to being a sinner again and again, to our own faults reflected in the behaviour of our children, etc. Let us say, "I thank You, Father, for taking pains with me and thinking up this way of humiliation for me so that I can be freed from my pride." If we call to the Lord in this way, we will find that God will answer this prayer.

Then the second thing that Jesus advises us to do: We should humble ourselves as Jesus did, the Son of God, the Lord Most High, at whose feet the angels fall, bringing Him homage. It is written: "Taking the form of a servant . . . he humbled himself" (Philippians 2:7, 8). Now He is calling to us sinful men, who actually deserve nothing more than the place of lowliness, "Whoever humbles himself will be exalted" (Matthew 23:12). Let us respond to Jesus' challenge by

voluntarily humbling ourselves. That will help us to become humble, for when we go Jesus' way of lowliness, some of our pride will crumble. Let us choose freely a lowly position that will humble us. Whenever possible, we should not accept any titles or honours; we should not try to stand out in any group, or strive for positions of honour. On the contrary, let us take advantage of the opportunities to step back and let others receive the honour that we may deserve. Let us be quiet when we have the opportunity to draw attention to ourselves. Above all, let us admit our mistakes and sins to a counsellor, or to others when it is necessary, because that often humiliates us the most. Only true humiliations can really make us humble and free us from pride. Whoever becomes a "friend" of humiliations will find that they have great power. When they are accepted in love for Jesus, they are like a hammer that smashes our pride to pieces.

But it is also necessary to wage an intensive battle of faith against the sinful power of pride, behind which Satan stands, in order to be freed from it. We must act according to the advice of the Holy Scriptures and accept humiliations, but at the same time bring the bondage of pride daily under the blood of the Lamb, who has released us from this spirit of pride. We have to fight a battle of faith against "principalities and powers" without becoming tired and discouraged. We must fight in the knowledge that Jesus will be victorious, for He was victorious on the cross and redeemed us to humility. Then we will experience the fulfillment of God's promise to come and dwell with the humble (Isaiah 57:15).

Jesus could say that He was "lowly in heart" (Matthew 11:29). What radiance there is in the life of a truly humble person: the majesty of Jesus Christ shone forth in Him, the humble and lowly Lord, on His bitter way to Calvary. Could it be that He who was "lowly in heart" would not do everything possible to clothe His disciples with this virtue also? He has the power to make us humble men who bear His radiance and majesty. For this He offered His sacrifice on Calvary. On the cross He trod the head of the serpent under His feet—the serpent who personifies pride. He is Victor over sin and the power of pride. If we call upon the Lamb of God, who overcame our pride, He will make us overcomers too.

—From Basilea Schlink, *You Will Never Be the Same.* Published and copyright 1972, Bethany House Publishers, Minneapolis, Minnesota 55438.

PROCRASTINATION

PROCRASTINATION. It's a big, technical-sounding word that simply means "putting off things until tomorrow." I've wanted to study the subject for a long time, but never got around to it. Nor have I gotten around to a lot of other things. I'm one of the world's worst procrastinators.

My favorite tasks to put off are home repairs and letter writing. You can probably think of your favorites: the laundry, cleaning house, watering the plants, paying the bills.

The worst chore of all, I'm told, is cleaning the oven. Mary, a friend of mine, told me of an experience she had after moving into a new home a few months before. With all the unpacking she had to do, she had put off cleaning her oven. One day Mary's husband turned off the gas to check the water heater. Later, after the gas was turned back on, Mary couldn't get her oven pilot relit. So she called Mrs. Smith, who lived two doors down, to give her a hand. When Mrs. Smith looked into Mary's dirty oven, she gasped and said, "Mary! This oven is so filthy that it's a wonder you haven't started a fire in here! When Mrs. Jones lived here her kitchen must have looked like a pigpen!"

Mary bit her lip and just nodded. She decided not to tell Mrs. Smith that she had brought this stove with her from their previous house!

People procrastinate for lots of reasons. Most of the time we put off things we hate to do. People who have additional responsibilities at church or on the job may have even more opportunities to procrastinate. There's

business correspondence or uninteresting research or papers to correct. Rationalizations are so easy to come up with:

"What I really need right now is a break. I know that means I'll be late with my project, but if I did it now I wouldn't do a good job anyway."

"This TV program only comes on once a year. I can mend clothes any time."

"Ultimately, spending time with my husband is more important than anything else, so it's worth it for me to wait on that job."

"I only have an hour to work, and I know the floors will take several hours, so I'll wait until I have a bigger block of time."

"I want to be available to my kids at all times. They're always my first priority."

"This business letter just arrived, so I don't need to answer it now. I'll wait until several more pile up and answer them all at once."

"Why don't I just admit to myself that I hate doing dishes, instead of acting like I want to get them done?"

"I'm not going to be enslaved by my schedule. Everyone needs some spontaneity in their life. I'm going shopping."

Those who occasionally put off a couple of irritating chores, but basically live an orderly life otherwise, probably don't have too much to worry about. My concern is for people like me with chronic procrastination problems.

Problem procrastinators seem to fall into one of two categories. First are those whose schedules are oppressed by responsibilities they can never find time for. They're not necessarily overworked; they just can't seem to get things done. In the second group are those who have the same problem with one added complication: they can't even find time to do things they *want* to do—such as recreation, hobbies, reading, etc. People in both of these groups, but especially the second, have to work a little harder to overcome their procrastination.

As Christians, procrastination may especially bother us because we sense more keenly the importance of "redeeming the time." Besides the chores of everyday living, we feel the urgency of making an impact on the world for Christ. We often have that extra desire to spend time befriending the neighbors and witnessing to them about our faith in Christ. Jesus himself conveyed that sense of urgency when he said, "The harvest is plentiful but the workers are few" (Matthew 9:37).

While the Bible doesn't say much about the specific issue of procrastination, it does talk about our use of time. In Genesis, God gave Adam and Eve dominion over all creation. Though the created order still belongs to God, he has appointed us to be good stewards, or managers, of it. Time is a part of that created order; therefore we are to be good stewards of God's time.

Procrastination can also result from confused priorities, and the Bible has plenty to say about priorities. "Seek first his kingdom and his righteousness, and all these things will be given to you as well" (Matthew 6:33). God wants us to make him our first priority. "Trust in the Lord with all your heart, and lean not on your own understanding; in all your ways acknowledge him, and he will make your paths straight" (Proverbs 3:5–6). If we yield our time to God's control, he promises to help us use it wisely.

Further scriptural insight on procrastination can be gained by studying how Jesus used his time. Imagine trying to live his hectic schedule for even one day! Religious leaders interrupting him all the time with questions and accusations. People stopping him constantly to be healed or forgiven. With all those demands, was Jesus ever tempted to put off some task? The Bible doesn't say specifically. But we do get the impression that Jesus had no trouble managing his schedule. He never seemed to be in a hurry. He seemed to know exactly what he was to do and that his time on earth to do it was short. He took time out from the crowds to be by himself, to rest, meditate, and talk with his Father. He wasn't able to preach to everyone but never expressed any dismay about it. When Jesus died on the cross, he was able to say, "It is finished." His attitude should be an example to us.

Let's look more closely at some of the un-

derlying causes of procrastination. Many of my reasons for putting things off related to my management of time. I was so disorganized that I practically had no other choice but to procrastinate. My four primary errors:

Overcommitment. I had signed my life away to so many church committees, Bible studies, Sunday school classes, and free-lance projects that I couldn't have gotten everything done even if I did nothing else for eight hours a day. Even though these were worthwhile Christian activities, they left me no time for other priorities. I needed to cut back.

Doing big jobs all at once. I refused to start anything until I thought I had enough time to complete it. Sounds noble, but as a result I wasted each day's spare minutes. On top of it, the job took even longer than the big block of time would allow because I hadn't anticipated things that needed to be done ahead of time. I needed to break up the project into a number of smaller tasks.

Poor concentration. Too many times I tried to read or study with a lot of distractions around. But even when I was alone in a quiet place, my mind wandered easily. I usually thought about other things I had to do. Rather than try to blot them out of my mind, I needed to jot them down somewhere for later reference.

Not setting goals. If I had only made some simple decisions about what I wanted to accomplish that day, I could have tackled the tasks one by one and finished them. But since I hadn't set any goals for myself, I'd watch a little TV, read a magazine, stop at the grocery store, call a friend, and wonder where my day went.

Poor use of time can easily lead to the procrastination habit. Applying some basic time management principles can help you get better organized.

For many procrastinators, these tips and a little time may cure the problem once and for all. Unfortunately, it didn't cure me. The principles worked great—when I chose to follow them. But often I still couldn't make myself get the job done, even something I *wanted* to do. That tipped me off to the possibility that my problem was deeper than one of time management.

After a good deal of searching and talking to other people, I began to identify some of the deeper reasons I procrastinated. Most of them were subconscious feelings that kept me from doing what I wanted to do. Here are a few:

Fear. Whether it's a fear of failure, fear of offending someone, or fear of getting hurt or rejected, fear can be a great immobilizer. My fears usually have to do with making a stupid mistake. I'm afraid to fix the refrigerator myself because I might hook up the wrong wire and burn out the motor. I'm afraid to build shelves or try a new recipe because I might botch it up. I really want to do these things, but my fear prevents me.

Guilt. Sometimes I feel I'm not spending enough time with my family. Often that feeling comes at the same time a project I must complete is due. My "family guilt" takes hold, and I delay the project so I can be with them. But then "late project guilt" sets in and plays against my "family guilt." As a result, I don't plunge wholeheartedly into either activity and still feel guilty about both.

Worry. Though related to fear, worry paralyzes me in a different way. When I worry, I get a vague, nebulous feeling that something bad might happen—sort of a fear of the unknown. And since it's so vague, I have trouble figuring out just what's causing it. Whatever the cause, it keeps me from moving forward.

Obligation. If I agree to do someone a favor—not because I particularly want to but because I feel obligated to—I find it much harder to get around to it. Sometimes I don't realize the extent to which I've obligated myself to some person, group, or organization.

Insecurity. From time to time we all feel that a particular task is too difficult for us. Yet too many people feel that way too often. They complain, "I can't do anything right." These people aren't just admitting their limitations; they're creating them. When they get stuck with a task they feel is impossible to start with, they put it off because they don't have the confidence to surge ahead. As a chronic procrastinator, I've fallen into this trap at times.

Perfectionism. Sometimes I never even start a project because my concern for doing it perfectly makes me spend endless hours researching and worrying over needless details. Only after much agony do I finally get started. In other cases, I'll get two-thirds of the way through a job, then never complete it because I continually want to add some "finishing touch" in order to make it perfect. As a result, I never really finish the project, and I'm never completely satisfied.

Fear, guilt, worry, obligation, insecurity, and perfectionism. These are some of the underlying reasons I procrastinate. What do they all have in common? In every case, I allow something other than myself to control me.

Take perfectionism, for example. When I can never feel reasonably satisfied with a job I've done, no matter how hard I've worked on it, something's wrong. I am being controlled by some impossible external standard, not by my own evaluation of my time and ability. No wonder I put off the job again and again. Why bother finishing it if I'm not going to like it?

A similar dynamic happens with the other reasons, too. When I feel unnecessarily obligated to someone, I'm letting that person control me in some way, even if it's only in my own mind. If I avoid talking to someone because I'm afraid I'll offend her, I'm letting her reaction control me.

How do we get out of this trap of letting others determine our priorities and schedules? The solution obviously requires more than simply rearranging our schedule. A good start might be to ask yourself some of the questions on page 378. Then, if you feel you're procrastinating for deeper reasons, such as the ones mentioned above, try the following steps. They've proved helpful to me, especially when I've felt completely paralyzed by my procrastination.

First, get your feelings out in the open. Are you afraid of something? Worried? Feeling obligated? Simply identifying *why* you're putting off a project will help you understand yourself a lot better.

Second, try to determine the source of that feeling. You may be allowing someone or something other than yourself to control you. Perhaps it's someone you feel obligated to, someone who expects too much of you, or someone you haven't forgiven for hurting you. Or the source may be an experience—a significant mistake or failure that you still haven't forgotten. In a real way, these people or experiences can lead you to procrastinate.

Third, once you've identified and determined the source of your procrastination, ask yourself: do I want that person or experience to control my life, or do I want to decide for myself what my priorities should be? At this point, you need to accept the responsibility for your own actions and take charge of them. Someone else may be the source of your problem, but you're the only one who can, with God's help, do something about it.

It may take awhile for the procrastination habit to change completely. Be happy for the little changes you notice, such as deciding to clean the bathrooms right now. Little changes, over a period of time, add up to big changes. Be patient.

I have another friend, Jean, who hates to clean house. She let her apartment deteriorate until the day some friends were coming to visit. In a whirlwind of activity, she picked up the whole place and threw everything into the bedroom. When her friends arrived, one of them took a quick tour of the apartment, stopped at the bedroom and said, "What does your bedroom look like?"

Before Jean could open her mouth, her friend opened the door. "I was so embarrassed," Jean told me later, "that I almost gave up procrastinating forever. But not quite."

May we all be delivered from horror stories like Jean's. Let's not wait any longer to do something about it.

Tempted to Put Something Off?

Ask yourself these questions . . .

1. *What tasks am I putting off?* Identify not just the task itself (laundry, housecleaning) but the *kind* of task you're avoiding (routine chores, church responsibilities).

2. *Why don't I want to do this task?* Answers here can range from "It makes me feel stupid" to "I'm afraid I'll mess it up" to "It hurts my back."

3. *How does it affect me and others when I put off that task? Is it worth it?* Procrastination affects people in different ways. Some people get antsy and irritable; some get lethargic; others plunge into a pile of "busy work" in order to forget about the job that needs to be done. Are you leaving people hanging who are depending on you? Is the benefit of waiting greater than the benefits of doing it now?

4. *How can I break up this project into several small tasks?* Doing a little cleaning each day is easier than cleaning the whole house in one afternoon. The same principle can apply to business correspondence, laundry, even cooking (when you're preparing a feast). Getting started is often the hardest part of the job.

5. *Can I arrange to work alongside a friend who has similar responsibilities?* The benefit here is obvious: you have companionship and someone to help you pace yourself.

6. *Do I tackle the most unpleasant tasks first each day?* When you get the worst out of the way first, your outlook for the rest of the day will be much brighter.

7. *Have I removed any obstacles that keep me from doing this job?* Examples: TV, radio, telephone, kids, spouse, co-workers, books, magazines.

8. *Have I determined the source of any guilt, worry, or fear that may be at the root of my procrastination?* The source could be a previous experience where you failed miserably. It could be a parent or friend whom you're allowing to impose unnecessary standards or expectations on you. Whatever the

378

source, recognize how consciously or unconsciously it has been controlling you. Then determine not to let it control you any longer. This step does not come easily and may take a long time.

9. *Can I decide for myself to do this job even though I know I won't like it?* This decision helps you to take control of the situation rather than vice-versa.

10. *Do I congratulate myself each time I avoid procrastinating?* An oft-neglected but very important step: each time you have a victory, no matter how small, reward yourself with a short break or a non-fattening snack. The next time an opportunity to procrastinate comes up, remember how good you felt the last time you overcame that urge. Then get to that job right away, and reward yourself again.

—VERNE BECKER, associate editor, *Campus Life* magazine.

R

RAPE

RAPE IS a violent act of hostility and/or sexual gratification in which one person (usually male) coerces another (usually female) into participating in sex acts of various kinds.

MYTHS

Women ask to be raped by the clothing they wear, or by engaging in hitchhiking and going places alone.

Research indicates that dressing a certain way does not invite or protect a person from rape. While some behaviors involve risk, the fact is that about 50 percent of rapes occur in the victim's home.

Anyone can prevent rape if they want to.

Most rapes carry the implicit, if not explicit, threat of death or severe bodily harm. The fear caused by this threat makes many people decide to submit rather than risk mutilation or death. About one-third of the rapes involve a weapon.

Women cry "Rape" to get back at a particular man or men.

The history of rape convictions indicates that a small percentage of those charged are sentenced or imprisoned. In some states a witness is required to get a conviction. In addition, many women reporting rape have been subject to humiliation and abuse both by police and in the courts. Therefore, this form of vengeance is hardly an effective one.

Rape is an impulsive act of sexual gratification.

Many rapists are married or have access to sexual gratification. Some rapes, especially "gang rapes," appear to be premeditated.

While some rapists report a measure of sexual motivation, generally the men rape as a means of exerting power.

Men who rape women are psychotic.

Rapists obviously have behavior problems, but most of them are not "insane" and they can be held accountable for their actions.

Men who rape other men are homosexual.

Men rape men for the same reasons they rape women: to express power and dominance. The victim of a rape, male or female, is just an object: something to be used, humiliated, and dominated. Research indicates that most rapists are heterosexual not homosexual.

Rapists are usually minority men and their victims white women.

The FBI reports that in the United States most rapes occur within racial groups, i.e., white on white, Black on Black, Native American on Native American, etc., rather than between racial groups.

FACTS

- One rape is reported every three minutes in the United States.
- Only 10 to 25 percent of rapes are ever reported.
- 50 percent of rapes occur between people who know each other (friend, neighbor, family member).

—From Council on Women and the Church, United Presbyterian Church, U.S.A. *Myths and Facts About Rape and Battering.*

The Rapist

There is a fairly well-defined picture of the rapist. I am speaking now of the man who goes out with the deliberate intention of finding a victim; the man who snatches an accidental opportunity to rape cannot be so easily categorized. But the intentional rapist falls into a pattern. He is usually young, employed, and apparently normal. He may be married and have children. Somewhere in his life he feels that he has failed to live up to the definition—his own, his parents', society's—of masculinity. Or he feels that he is a failure in his sexual and/or personal relations with his wife or other women. Gang rapists are suspected of having strong—but hidden—homosexual tendencies that are satisfied by watching other men have intercourse, especially anal, with a victim. Massachusetts psychologist Dr. Nicholas Groth says of gang rape, "In part, the rape is motivated by a wish among the men to have sex together and the victim becomes the vehicle for achieving this." Or the rapist may be attempting to assert his machismo, his virility, over a woman who symbolizes the dominance of any woman in his life.

But whatever his problem, he is a weak, sick, unstable character looking for a victim who is weaker than himself whom he can frighten, subdue, hurt and humiliate. In an article he wrote for the January 1975 issue of *Psychology Today*, Dr. Selkin says that, "The ultimate tragedy in rape is the dehumanization of both victim and assailant." He states that the rapist's feelings of omnipotence, guilt, fear of retribution, or anger can be keys to diagnosing and treating his sickness. One rapist interviewed in jail said, "I wish no harm on anyone. If I cannot overcome my sickness, I would not want to live anymore." But as Dr. Selkin observes, "Unfortunately, most rapists can neither admit nor express the fact that they are a menace to society. Even convicted rapists who are serving long prison terms deny their culpability. They tenaciously insist women encourage and enjoy sexual assault. These men will tell you they are the greatest lovers in the world."

—From Martha Yates, *Coping*. Englewood Cliffs, N.J.: Prentice-Hall, 1976.

FOR FURTHER READING:

Ketterman, Grace H., M.D. *How to Teach Your Child About Sex*. Old Tappan, N.J.: Revell, 1981.

17 Women Doctors, with D. S. Thompson, M.D., as consulting editor. *Everywoman's Health*. Garden City, N.Y.: Doubleday, 1980.

Washbourn, Penelope. *Becoming Woman*. New York: Harper & Row, 1977.

READING

HAVE YOU ever sat down and made a list of all the things you read every month, and estimated how much time you spend on each? If you do this, you'll probably find that between newspapers, magazines, and trade publications you spend at least fifty hours a month. Then you have to ask yourself this question, "Considering the some 7,000 books published in America each year, the millions of books in the Library of Congress, and the thousands of periodicals printed each month, am I getting a representative cross-section of the available information in my reading?"

Most men who ask themselves this question end up by rationing themselves to five or ten minutes a day for newspapers, ten or fifteen minutes a day for magazines of all kinds, and at least an hour a day for informative books. If they have been spending a lot of time watching TV they also ration themselves to not more than several hours a week for this medium.

Selecting What to Read

Would you like to be able to read 50,000 words a minute? There are many times when it is easy to do this if you know how. All you have to be able to do is to recognize within one minute that a 50,000 word book does not suit your purposes, and *decide not to read it.* What is important is not to be able to read fast, but to be able to decide what not to read. *Selectivity must be the watchword.*

Here are some of the questions you can ask yourself in order to improve your selectivity:

1. What is this book about? Do I want to explore this subject now?
   —scan the table of contents and the cover flaps.
2. What are the author's qualifications? Is this the sort of person who can help me grow?
   —look at the cover flaps for biography; look at his bibliography to see how up-to-date he is, and what company he keeps.
3. How well does the author organize his material?
   —look at the table of contents, the author's preface, and a few chapter-opening paragraphs: sometimes the author has worked hard in order to make reading easy for you; but if the book has a tortuous style, make sure there is rich pay-dirt before you start mining.

With these three groups of questions you will be able to eliminate almost all the books that would waste your time. Of course, you will miss some gems by using such a coarse screen, but you will be able to handle a big throughput and make perhaps an 80 percent extraction.

These methods of discovering books will prove helpful:

1. Scan book reviews in high calibre periodicals, such as *Scientific American, Harpers, The Atlantic Monthly, Main Currents in Modern Thought, Science,* etc.
2. Scan the bibliographies of the books you read.
3. Browse through book stores and seek the counsel of skilled book dealers.

Abstracting Information

You now have a book in front of you that you want to read. The first thing to remember is that no matter what you do you won't be able to get more than a few of the author's ideas. For that matter, most of the books you will read will have only a few ideas to offer that you can use at the time of reading. The trick is to find these ideas as quickly as possible. "If," as Gertrude Stein said, "a book has been a very true book for you, you will always need it again." When you come back to a book you bring to your second reading more past experience, and are able to abstract a new set of ideas.

This is a useful routine for quickly taking out of a book the information you need.

1. Read the preface and cover flaps for clues about the author's purposes in writing the book, and the ways he uses to get his ideas across.
2. Study the table of contents and make sure you have a rough picture of the book in your mind before you start exploring it. Without this picture you can easily get lost.
3. Scan the book quickly—say in an hour or so—just in order to get to know the author and how he talks. You can't understand what a man means until you've listened to him for a while.
4. Carefully read those parts of the book that look as though they contain the information you are looking for. Often you need only read two or three chapters of a book the first time. Later, if you need more, you can go back for it. Look at a book much as you look at a hardware store; you never expect to buy up the whole store—just a few things you need at the moment.

—From James T. McCay, *The Management of Time.* Englewood Cliffs, N.J.: Prentice-Hall, 1959.

FOR FURTHER READING:

Elliot, Elisabeth. *Discipline: The Glad Surrender.* Old Tappan, N.J.: Revell, 1982.

Murphey, Cecil B. *Press On! A Disciple's Guide to Spiritual Growth.* Ann Arbor: Servant, 1983.

RESENTMENT

IF WE are harboring resentment, grudges, or bitterness against others, the New Testament commands us to put them away. "Let all bitterness and wrath and anger and clamor and slander be put away from you, with all malice, and be kind to one another, tenderhearted, forgiving one another, as God in Christ forgave you" (Ephesians 4:31).

When we hold a grudge against someone, we are holding a claim against them. We write out spiritual IOUs. We keep strict accounts, planning to exact the very last penny. In our ledger, we hold IOUs against our parents (for quarreling between themselves and manipulating us); against brothers and sisters (for belittling us and getting more parental attention, or so it seemed); against spouses (for some petty fault or slip of the tongue); against children (for lack of respect and for turning out different than we planned). We hold IOUs against friends, neighbors, co-workers, acquaintances, and so on. If we are to experience freedom ourselves, we must cancel all these debts. We must deal with our IOUs the way God dealt with his (Colossians 2:14).

GETTING RID OF RESENTMENT

There is a practical way to get rid of resentment. Make a list of all those people toward whom you have resentments. Begin with the people closest to you—parents, spouses, brothers, sisters, and children—and move outwards from there. You might want to list each on a separate slip of paper, and then tear up the IOUs one by one. Forgive each of them, no matter what they have done to offend you.

You may come up against one or two IOUs that you feel you just can't tear up, because the hurt was too big.

.   .   .

Tearing up IOUs is usually a unilateral action. For our part we release people who have offended us. We say by our action that we no longer intend to collect whatever it is we think they owe us. Tearing up IOUs does not mean going to each person toward whom we feel resentful and saying, "I forgive you for the time you did this" or "I don't hold that against you anymore." Usually putting aside resentments and bitterness is something I do privately, between me and the Lord. However, the process can suggest ways of straightening out broken relationships. We should be open to taking further steps if they seem right. Talking over what we think we must do with a person we trust may spare us from making a serious mistake.

The Lord gives us the grace to forgive and forgive generously. We should begin now by tearing up the IOUs we are holding, and we should repeat the process regularly.

We can now add another part to our strategy for getting free from the influence of the flesh:

> We must put aside all resentment, bitterness, and grudges. These are obstacles to our spiritual freedom which prevent us from experiencing the power of the Lord in our lives.

—From Bert Ghezzi, *Getting Free*. Ann Arbor: Servant, 1982.

FOR FURTHER READING:

Wright, H. Norman. *The Christian Use of Emotional Power*. Old Tappan, N.J.: Revell, 1974.

RESPONSIBILITY

Accepting Responsibility

Responsibility is as synonymous with *motherhood* as *love*. Every mother feels overwhelmed by it the moment she brings her tiny infant home from the hospital. That first moment when you are alone in your home, holding your helpless baby—no nurses to summon, no mother to call—can be frightening. Not only do you have the responsibility of changing your baby's diapers, feeding him, of loving him, you stand responsible for his very *life!*

Every day I sat and cradled my boy to my bosom, looking at his gentle, trusting eyes. Wonder filled me when I thought: *I— Sheila—am responsible for Jason's life!* Some days I felt overjoyed, so proud that God entrusted me with such a beautiful little life. But other days I crumbled into tears of dismay; surely I did everything wrong!

Responsibility, will it make me or break me? Will I be challenged, motivated, uplifted? Or will I be buried by its overwhelming weight? Will I be paralyzed by the very natural fears and apprehensions that come with this new role? My own mother has done much to help me balance my sense of responsibility with my fears of "what might happen" to my family.

Until recently I didn't know my mother once lived in fear that something might happen to one of us. She feared we would be hit by a car, fall out of a tree, or become deathly ill. When I first experienced the overwhelming sense of responsibility for Jason, I called mom and said, "I don't know if I can take it! I am so afraid of being a horrible mother. What if I say or do something that emotionally scars Jason for the rest of his life? What if I don't watch him carefully enough, and he has an accident? What if I'm not feeding him the right kinds of foods? And what if . . . ?"

Mom suddenly interrupted me, "Sheila, you can't live in the fear of 'what if . . . ?' It will destroy you. You'll become so paralyzed that neither you nor Jason will find the joy in life God intends you to have. I know how you feel. For years I felt the same way about you and your brother and sisters. Finally I realized that I was doing a disservice to you and to myself, not to mention my faith in God.

"Turn Jason over to God. After all, God loves him even more than you do. God knew that you, with all your strengths and weaknesses, were the ideal mother for Jason. Give Jason to God, and He will fill in all the gaps. Where your love is too protective and too

weak, there God will be, smoothing out your efforts, helping Jason become all He wants him to be."

Through talks like that I've realized the freedom that comes with entrusting your children to God. And in so doing I've discovered that my responsibilities can be enjoyed, not just endured.

The answer lies in the word itself. For if you look at it carefully, responsibility is merely *response-ability,* the ability to respond to my child's needs. If, as a mother, I accept that task, I am being responsible. Beyond that I must turn the outcome of any circumstance or situation over to God.

—From Sheila Schuller Coleman, *Between Mother and Daughter.* Old Tappan, N.J.: Revell, 1982.

RETIREMENT

SINCE ADULTS can now expect to live longer and more vigorous lives than those of previous generations, here are suggestions for making those years of fulfillment.

1. Plan for your retirement by moving gradually into other forms of activity. Determine to keep yourself busy after you leave your lifetime work.
2. Divorce yourself as quickly as possible from your job. You may want to keep alive a few friendships, but don't allow yourself to continue trying to relive your former work. Stop visiting your old place of work.
3. Consider doing part-time or volunteer work. Men, too! Men are now volunteering for work in hospitals and nursing homes that previously was done only by women.
4. Consider moving to a smaller house. Look at the move as a new phase of life and an opportunity to begin an exciting challenge.
5. Have regular physical check-ups. Early discovery and treatment of medical problems can add years to life.

6. Keep physically fit. Especially keep off weight. Older people simply do not need as many calories as they did at age thirty-five. Exercise regularly (ask your doctor how much). Get plenty of fresh air and eat nutritious foods and well-balanced meals. Get enough sleep.

7. Remain socially active. Make new friends. Most churches have golden age groups called anything from Keen-Agers, XYZ clubs, or Golden Agers. Join formal organizations as American Association of Retired Persons (AARP).

8. Remain active at home. Develop new skills or rediscover old hobbies. Travel, if your health and finances permit. Tackle books you've always wanted to read by setting goals for yourself.

9. Stay active in a local congregation. Don't participate only with your own group. Ask your pastor for a job you can do. Mix with younger people. How about assisting in the kindergarten class? Maybe the nursery? Many children today in our mobile society who are isolated from grandparents welcome a grandparent-type contact.

10. Use the phone. My mother, who died in her eighties, remained actively close to a dozen women her age. They belonged to the same church, and because of health, found themselves confined to home, often for days at a time. But they used the telephone. My mother spent at least two hours every morning calling her friends. My mother said, "We cheer each other up."

11. Expand yourself. Try something new. How about a "year of adventure?" One friend determined that once a week she would do something new—something she had never done before. For instance, once she visited a Quaker worship service, another week she went to an amusement center alone. Go back to college. Learn a foreign language.

—From Cecil B. Murphey, *Encyclopedia of Christian Marriage*. Old Tappan, N.J.: Revell, 1983.

FOR FURTHER READING:

Ortlund, Ray and Anne. *The Best Half of Life.* Waco, Tex.: Word Books, 1976.

Pearce, J. Winston. *Ten Good Things I Know About Retirement.* Nashville: Broadman, 1982.

Tournier, Paul. *Learn to Grow Old.* New York: Harper & Row, 1972.

ROLES

Leadership

What is leadership in the home?

There is the "man-is-and-ever-shall-be-the-sole-leader" theory. This view assumes that some superior gift of chromosomes and hormones makes man the natural possessor of unique talents and abilities which fit him to lead out. He is, due to his strength, size, intelligence, and tendency toward dominance, naturally "the boss."

Dominance may effectively give orders and demand control, but it does not lead. Dominant authority serves well as a censor, an enforcer of views, a dispenser of discipline. But that is not leading.

And dominance is not uniquely characteristic of either sex. It is often an evidence of a rigid, authoritative personality. Frequently it is a sign of weakness and insecurity, indicating that the domineering person fears change or challenge so greatly that he/she cannot risk being flexible and is terrified of becoming vulnerable before another personality.

There is the "husband-is-the-head-and-the-head-is-the-leader" theory. The husband may be the "head," but to be head and to be leader are two different things. Headmanship is not synonymous with leadership. The headman may serve as the formal "chief-in-charge," as the recognized "legal name and nominal head" (as does the husband, whose family name becomes the title for social use). But such "headmanship" is much more than a matter of status, rank, or recognition. It accepts the responsibility for failures and successes in the relationship, but does not assume sole authority in decisions and directions.

Nor does the biblical recognition of man as "head" in marriage endow him with authority and right-to-dominate. Some have thought that Paul's patterning of man's role as "head" after Christ's position as "Head-to-the-church" gives great weight to the husband's role.

Does the husband, like Christ, become Lord and Master? The ultimate word? Since the two, man and Christ, are compared, does that give man all the rights and roles of Lord in the home? On the contrary, the purposes of the comparison are specifically stated in both 1 Corinthians 11:1–10, and Ephesians 5:21–33. Headship means responsibility and initiative. Responsibility to act in love. Initiative to act in service. As Christ acted in self-giving love, and self-humbling service

(giving us a whole new meaning to "headship"), so husbands take the initiative in building an atmosphere of loving, self-sacrificing service.

Headmanship is only part of leadership, one facet of one kind of leadership.

Christ cut through our contorted ideas of headship with surgical words:

Among the heathen it is their kings who lord it over them, and their rulers are given the title of 'benefactors.' But it must not be so with you! *Your* greatest man must become like a junior and your leader must be a servant. Who is the greater, the man who sits down to dinner or the man who serves him? Obviously, the man who sits down to dinner—yet *I* am the one who is the servant among you (Luke 22:25–27).

.   .   .

The autocratic personality	The Christ-ocratic personality
gives orders without asking questions, without permitting questions;	asks questions, seeks to truly hear, suggests alternatives;
makes demands, dishes out directives, lays down the law, defensive if challenged.	respects freedom and dignity of others, can affirm the truth clearly and concretely, but nondefensively.
requires compliance regardless of consent or agreement.	values willing cooperation works for open agreement and understanding.
pushes and manipulates one-man rule in over-under position.	leads, attracts, persuades personal relationships in side-by-side identification.
says "you do, you must do, you ought to have done, you'd better do."	says "come, let's do, we might have done, can we try?"

.   .   .

What then is leadership? If it is not something a person is, then it must be something he or she does.

Leadership is accepting responsibilities and performing certain functions in a marriage relationship in a way that advances both persons together toward their goals.

If leadership is "doing certain tasks or functions," then it is obviously not a certain role, a certain sex, or a permanent possession of one of the persons. Leadership alternates; it is a contribution made by either or both together.

If leadership is "helping and serving so that both move forward," then it is an action done by either person in a way that liberates both. It may go unnoticed. It happens best when unrecognized. It is accepted most easily when it is unself-conscious, selfless, self-giving. When it is exercised in the Christ-way of giving help.

Helping another is best defined as giving another the freedom to change, and to change voluntarily. This is a creative exercise in leadership. In contrast, authoritarian dominance prohibits free choice, and inhibits free interchange and the freedom to change.

A "strong" husband may choose a wife whom he can dominate. He resents competition or contradiction. He wants a submissive, compliant mate. As years pass, he may come to resent her submissiveness as a sign of weakness.

Or a dominant wife may choose a man she can "mother." Instead, she smothers. He, tiring of it all, attempts to express his true feelings, only to be beaten down with a word or two. She cannot respect a man who is flattened with one swat. He cannot respond to a woman who clips him when he opens his true feelings. So hostility, morbidity, and often infidelity follow.

.   .   .

Negotiating the responsibilities and the unique ways each person prefers to perform is a marriage-long task. They cannot be negotiated once, then forgotten. People mature, grow, and change. The experiences of life, delightful or difficult, either fit or unfit them to continue interacting in the same ways.

If she married him to fulfill her father's role in her life, her expectations will be a major factor in negotiating their life-style at the time of marriage. Three years of maturing may release her from the father need, to a great extent. Her relationship with her husband can now develop on a totally different base.

If he married her to fulfill the "mother-was-a-good-servant" role of maid, laundress, housewife, and to perform these in silent efficiency, he may later discover that she is a person to be respected as the person she is. Their relationship can begin over again—if new negotiation is possible.

Marriage relationships must each achieve their own balance through honest, fair negotiation. They can maintain that balance only through repeated negotiations. But through it all, certain things do remain constant.

Leadership is a function which should always be shared.

Authority in one area or another is a responsibility which is mutually designated to one or the other through honest negotiation. It can be renegotiated at any time.

Responsibility is delegated by both—to each other. Two people may early work their way through such a division of labor in general terms and may even continue to fulfill the same tasks and roles throughout life. But not necessarily so.

Changes come in work, health, schedule, family, outside responsibilities, and many other areas that call for new negotiations and usually a new division of responsibilities.

If one partner is uncomfortable with the way the relationship is being played out, he/she has a right to blow the whistle and call for a new toss-up. Often this means calling in a referee to clarify the situation.

The referee role cannot be played by any spectator. They quickly take sides, or worse yet, alternate sides as the story unfolds. A counselor is needed who will neither believe nor disbelieve either, but will bring objectivity into the situation and uncover the true feelings of each.

If the relationship is off balance, if one has assumed a primary role at the expense of the other's integrity, then a new set of ground rules will need to be drawn up.

If the isolation of being housebound is driving a wife to distraction, she has every right to express her creativity in work outside the home—provided responsible decisions are made in respect for all the needs of the children.

If a man's work is demanding a lion's share of his time, and the children are growing up with virtually no opportunity to know their father, the wife has a right to call for a reapportionment of his time according to their family's actual values.

If there is conflict of roles, either person who is feeling the pinch has the right to call for open negotiations. If the wife is convinced she must leave the first move to her man, she may wait forever before he recognizes that their life-style is shortchanging her and cutting her off from relationships with others, from meaningful work, and from a sense of fulfillment.

Life together is life shared. Shared love, shared work, shared opportunities, shared leadership, even shared initiative. Man, the nominal head, may function officially for both in public matters of leadership. Woman, recognized as his equal in partnership, leads with, and not against him. Together, they choose to grow.

—From David W. Augsburger, *Cherishable: Love and Marriage.* Scottdale, Pa.: Herald Press, 1971.

Sexual Roles

The problem of confusion of masculine and feminine roles today is often treated as though it were only a problem for women, but it affects both men and women, though obviously in different ways. Many women are trying to escape from stereotypes and to be considered primarily as persons. They certainly do not want to be treated as if they were men or neuters. But since full personhood has for so long been identified with masculine personhood, they often give the impression of trying to be "just like men" or to get beyond being women, and may wonder whether they have been too successful in doing so.

On the other hand, many men feel threatened by women assuming—and sometimes very efficiently—what have been thought of as masculine roles, entering into masculine occupations and expecting to be treated as equals. In addition, they often feel confused as to what sort of attitude to take toward women colleagues, since the familiar patterns of stereotyped behavior to females are clearly inappropriate. A distinguished social psychologist, who is also a nun still clad in a voluminous habit, remarked that the habit seemed to be a distinct asset in making her male colleagues feel at ease with her at meetings, because it removed her, as they felt, from the sphere of man-woman relationships which in their minds had nothing to do with usual academic relations. But, equally, some women, while wishing to be treated as professional equals, are ready at the same time to use the traditional feminine weapons of allurement, tears, and "temperament" in their professional life and still expect the courtesies and privileges traditionally accorded to "the weaker sex."

The difficulties facing both men and women in the present state of confusion about roles are indeed vast and complex, and especially in marriage, as has frequently been pointed out. But perhaps the solution will be found in a new concept of masculine and feminine roles. Hitherto these roles have been chiefly based on what men and women do, or traditionally have done, in our society. Ideas about what they are, or should be, are derived from their occupations. Yet anthropologists tell us both men and women have carried out all the various basic tasks of human life in one or another culture, so that occupation is not a necessary basis for identification.

Perhaps we are in a state of transition toward a concept of masculine and feminine roles based on a better understanding of the masculine and feminine *stances* toward reality. With men and women doing whatever they personally can do best, professions and occupations, arts and sciences would all benefit much more fully than they do now from the contributions of persons with the masculine and persons with the feminine stance. Nobody yet knows what enrichment women might bring, for example, to the whole practice of medicine, or to architecture, or to speculative theology if they felt free and were encouraged to be fully *women* doctors or *women* architects or *women* theologians, rather than feeling more or less forced to assume a masculine stance in their professional work.

It is, therefore, part of our task as Christians to work toward such a goal, to examine our own thinking and existing social patterns, and to do what we can to make personhood primary, with the person's sex seen as a vital element but not its complete determinant. Although in many passages he assumed the stereotype current in his society, St. Paul said that in Christ "there is neither male nor female." This statement should be understood to mean that in the Christian life one's maleness or femaleness is to be subsumed by one's personhood, not eliminated or minimized by it.

—From Mary Perkins Ryan and John Julian Ryan, *Love and Sexuality: A Christian Approach.* New York: Holt, Rinehart & Winston, 1967.

Church Roles

Just as women need to bring their gifts into the professional world as helpers, counselors, comforters, and encouragers, they must also have the freedom to exercise these gifts within the church, where in many instances, women are not being used in the capacities for which they have been uniquely gifted.

I discovered some problems along these lines not too long after I became a Christian. Several months after I began attending church once more, I met Eddie. He called himself a completed Jew and said he knew Jesus as his Messiah. Eddie took me alongside to feed me the spiritual food that enables spiritual babes to grow, teaching me discipline about reading my Bible and teaching me how to pray. Eddie said you could pray anywhere, and I noticed he prayed on the tennis court, if he felt like it, even with his eyes open. He answered hundreds of my questions, never laughing at the most elementary or criticizing the most heretical. He merely pointed me back to God's owners' manual—the Bible—for all my answers. Eddie showed me that God had created me for a purpose and had equipped each of us with special gifts He wanted us to use to accomplish His work in the world. He encouraged me to ask God to reveal my gifts and to trust Him to use me just as He had once used His disciples.

As I began reading my Bible I saw that women were clearly portrayed as spiritual equals with men and that the gifts the Holy Spirit brought at Pentecost were given regardless of sex. The prophet Joel wrote, ". . . I will pour out my spirit on all flesh; your sons and your daughters shall prophesy, your old men shall dream dreams, and your young men shall see visions. Even upon the menservants and maidservants in those days, I will pour out my spirit" (Joel 2:28, 29). I read that Paul said, "For as many of you as were baptized into Christ have put on Christ. There is neither Jew nor Greek, there is neither slave nor free, there is neither male nor female; for you are all one in Christ Jesus" (Galatians 3:27, 28).

As I dug into the Old Testament I found that Hebrew women had enjoyed a substantially elevated position, compared with the women of the nations surrounding Israel. Israelite law protected women, giving them rights and freedom unknown in ancient times. Many women in the Old Testament were greatly admired. Sarah was honored for her faith; Esther and Ruth were revered, with entire books of the Bible recounting their hearts for God; and even Rahab, a harlot, was in the lineage of Jesus because of her courage. Perhaps most striking was the story of Deborah, found in Judges 4 and 5. A remarkably gifted woman, called of God to minister to His people, Deborah not only held authority as a prophetess, but also as the judge of Israel. She led the troops into battle against the Canaanites, interpreted the law, spoke God's word to the people, wrote poetry, and kept house for her husband, Lapidoth, all at the same time. Although the Bible mentions no natural children, it calls her the mother of Israel, and under her rule Israel enjoyed forty years of peace. She was pretty impressive.

Reading in the New Testament, I also saw that Jesus greatly respected women. He had the kind of warm, intimate relationship with them unheard of in that day. Many women were prominent in the activities of the early church, ministering, teaching, and holding positions of spiritual influence. Anna was a prophetess; Mary Magdalene was the first to see the risen Christ, carrying the news to the disciples; Priscilla was an instructor; and Paul entrusted Phoebe, a deaconess and fellow worker with Paul, with his important letter to the church at Rome, where she traveled on a business trip.

At the same time, Paul states in 1 Corinthians 14:34, "The women should keep silence in the churches. For they are not permitted to speak but should be subordinate, as even the law says," and in 1 Timothy 2:11–14: "Let a woman learn in silence with all submissiveness. I permit no woman to teach or to have authority over men; she is to keep silent. For Adam was formed first, then Eve; and Adam was not deceived, but the woman was deceived. . . ." Apparently some women were interrupting the services, speaking in tongues in a disorderly fashion and in general abusing their free position in Christ by exercising their authority over the authority of men, not operating under an order of leadership. But in exhorting these women who were out of order, I wondered if Paul was exhorting every woman for the rest of all time to keep silent in every service of worship. Apparently not, for women who were in order prayed aloud, prophesied,

taught men, and were respected members of the early church, as long as they exhibited that servant attitude Christ exhorted all Christians to have one to another, male and female.

From all I could tell, it seemed there should exist plenty of room within the church for women to function as talented and successful individuals, using their gifts creatively. The church was founded on love. What better place for the feminine need to be warm, nurturing, and to establish strong relationships? The entire structure seemed a wonderful container in which both men and women could develop the masculine and the feminine components in all of us, working side by side as we learned how to love one another. I envisioned women being called upon to exercise their gifts in cooperation with men who had the same gifts, the whole church working together as smoothly as the body of a well-trained athlete. I was very idealistic.

When I discovered I had a teaching gift, administrative gifts, perhaps even a mini gift in evangelism, however, and not the more traditionally feminine gifts of helps and mercy, I discovered that using my gifts put me in the middle of a controversy, in the evangelical church, regarding the role of women. At the heart of the matter seemed to lie a definition of the Greek word *kephale,* or "head," as well as the definition of another controversial word: *submission.* These were difficult concepts to sort out, and I didn't know what to do about using my gifts. I certainly didn't want to put on a Christian mask just as I was becoming convinced for the very first time that God made me the way He did for a reason. It seemed my job to discover what that reason was.

So I began to teach the Bible, and my husband supported me. One thing led to another, and what started as a small lecture series for twenty women tripled in size by the end of the first six weeks. By the end of the year, it had multiplied tenfold. Soon The Storehouse was born, an interdenominational ministry for women. I began speaking at conferences, where at first I was on safe ground. I taught women, and no one objected to that. But then someone pointed out to me that Paul had instructed the older women to teach the younger women, and not the other way around. That brought my first problem. I was a younger woman. A lot of grandmothers came to my class. What did Paul mean by *old?* Was he referring to spiritual or to physical maturity? I received a letter from a very sincere young woman who said, "From my study, I honestly do not see where women are called to be teachers, except in a very narrow sense. I would not go so far as to say that I didn't learn from your teaching, because I did, but I would have been much more comfortable seeing an elderly woman. There are so many areas other than teaching women that we younger ladies can be involved in." I felt frustrated, and I wanted to write her back, "I would love to feel more comfortable, too. It's not easy getting up to speak in front of a group of women. But God has called me to teach, not to feel comfortable."

I noticed that the churches encouraged women to teach children, however, but now I had another problem. I needed to know when a child became a man, because I was beginning to speak on some college campuses, and some churches feel the Bible forbids women to teach men. Was a college-aged man too old for me to teach? Or was it all right as long as he was still in school, but not all right if he had a job? No one seemed to be able to give me a definitive answer.

My problems multiplied. Now the lectures for The Storehouse were on tape, and the women took their tapes home. Soon the first husband appeared at the Bible study. It seemed very rude to ask him to leave because I was not supposed to teach men, so I let him stay. To make matters worse, the tapes were occasionally aired on the conference hour of the local religious radio station, and of course men listened, too. There was no way I could control that, and as many men as women wrote for copies of the tapes they had heard.

The problem of how to use my gifts became intensified when I was next asked to speak at a Sunday-morning worship service. The first time this happened I turned down the pastor's request on the grounds women were to keep silent in the churches. I told him I would gladly speak on a Sunday or Wednesday evening, since those were not official worship services, but his church did not have services on Sunday and Wednesday nights. The second invitation I accepted, however, reasoning that since the spiritual leader—the pastor—had asked me to speak, I would teach under his authority. When I arrived, we discussed where I would stand to speak. If I stood in the pulpit, would it appear I was exercising too much authority? If I stood on the level of the congregation, as a layman, would that be more appropriate? What if they couldn't see me? I'm not very tall. Was it all right for me, as a woman, to stand in a subordinate pulpit instead of the main one? Did it really make any difference at all where I stood? Wasn't what I had to say really more important?

What can a woman of God do when she has a gift God commands her to use and He is changing lives through it, but her gift is controversial? Remembering the story Jesus told about the servant who buried his talent and was judged severely for the mismanagement of all God had given him, I have persevered. If the church does not hesitate to send a woman to evangelize on a foreign field, why is she sometimes not permitted to teach a mixed Sunday-school class? Somewhere in the midst of the controversy, is the church missing the substance of what the Bible teaches about women, and is it losing these women? The United Methodist Church, of which I am a member, recently conducted a survey about women's attitudes toward the church, and they discovered a vast majority of women are not going to their pastors for help in times of crisis. Right now a lot of women face crisis and need the church as never before, to undergird us, to listen to us, and to encourage us to find and to use our gifts, in order that the whole Body of Christ may be strengthened.

I have seen what can happen when a woman takes over a church, exercising the wrong kind of authority, weakening the fellowship, and causing the kind of dissension only a woman can cause. I believe Paul wrote to that type of woman in 1 Corinthians. But scores of other women wish to serve the church in ways other than putting macaroni and cheese on the plastic trays at the church-night supper or embroidering fine linen altar scarves, as important as these tasks are. A woman who is gifted by God and is effective in His service should not be barred from using her gift. Perhaps the time has come for the entire Body of Christ to prayerfully reexamine the role of women from God's perspective, laying aside our divisiveness and our fears, to search out new and creative ways in which women can function in the church.

Women have traditionally been the helpers in the church and over the centuries have served well in this function. We make the casseroles for the covered-dish suppers, work behind the scenes rolling bandages for the sick, sew layettes for the poor, and make hundreds of telephone calls to assure good participation in all the fund-raising projects. We make the draperies for the fellowship hall and polish the candlesticks. We also lead the children's choir, change diapers in the nursery, teach Vacation Bible School, cut up the bread for communion, and arrange the flowers for the sanctuary on Sunday morning. We come to the christenings, weddings, and the funerals that are part of the life of the church and faithfully attend the prayer meetings and choir rehearsals. We have been wonderful nurturers, counselors, and encouragers, especially to the youth of the church.

But in other areas women could function equally well, given the opportunity. I would love to see each church develop a core group of women to visit the sick and the bereaved, on a regular basis, on behalf of the church. They could offer the kind of comfort only a woman can bring, in addition to the often hurried service a busy pastor has to provide because there is no one to help him with his visitation responsibilities. I can see how helpful it would be for him to train and assign a woman to follow up each family who has had a death, coming back to visit in the weeks that follow the funeral, checking on the family, listening to their grief, and staying beside them as they work through that long process. Women have a warmth, concern, and an empathetic understanding that the church could use so much more creatively.

I would also like to see at least one woman on every church committee. If the feminine point of view is essential in arriving at a total picture on any issue and women have been created to complement the masculine side of life, logically, both perspectives should receive a chance to influence decisions that affect the life of the whole Body. Having the counsel of a mature Christian woman can only add to the effectiveness of any committee. Furthermore women discern needs the more rational masculine mind sometimes misses, and we adeptly advocate on behalf of these needs. The church should provide a place where women can exercise these gifts in an appropriate manner.

I can also see the value of a group of specially trained women to assist the pastor with his counseling duties, working beside him in ministry to church members in crisis. The feminine perspective can aid in marriage counseling, in problems with teenagers, and with the depression that often faces women who are single, divorced, or widowed. The majority of parishioners who come to their pastors for counseling are women, and they could be greatly helped by the active listening of another woman, in addition to the spiritual guidance of their pastor.

Women compose half the Body of Christ, and the church must begin using all its parts at full capacity, if it would become the trailblazer, for which it has the potential in the new era dawning between the sexes. After all, God created us male and female in the first place, and to His Body Christ gave the blueprint for how we are to live together in love. Will we miss this opportunity to lead because we are embattled in the intricacies of the meaning of Greek words, instead of searching to expand our vision of God's revelation? God's creation continues, and I believe He means to build it upon the rock of His church, instead of the sands of these shifting times. The church must search for new ways to use God's women, building up a stronger Body of Christ, if it is to be all that it is meant to be in this age.

—From Barbara Rice, *The Power of a Woman's Love.* Old Tappan, N.J.: Revell, 1983.

S

SALVATION

Of Husband

DEVELOP A SPIRITUAL PROGRAM

If you are going to help your husband, you must be strong *yourself*. This means developing your own spiritual life. It is not the weak soldier who wins the battle.

The kind of moral fiber you need is not nourished merely by a little Bible verse and a prayer. It calls for complete surrender to Christ—absolute dedication. You need the very presence and power of God Himself. This begins when you confess your sins and die daily to self. Feelings of arrogance or self-pity have no place. God's best is reserved, not for those whose feelings center around themselves, but rather for those who consider themselves nothing for His sake.

You will gather strength and power as you slip away for a prayer rendezvous with your Lord, enjoy the fellowship of other Christians, attend a Bible-believing church where your soul can be fed, listen to Christian radio programs and read Christ-centered books which bring a rich companionship in Christ.

PUT GOD FIRST

You do have an obligation to your husband, but it does *not* come first. God must occupy first place in your life. This means that there is a line beyond which a Christian wife cannot go in serving her husband and family. *She must not deny her Lord.* If a choice is forced, she must obey God rather than man. Her first loyalty is to Christ, and when her husband's demands are in disharmony with the commandments of God, she is not obligated to obey him.

At this point a sharp question may arise. Your husband may squarely oppose you in your determination to live for Christ. He may leave no loophole that will allow you to acknowledge God or to participate in Christian service.

. . . . .

In many areas of married life, a Christian wife can graciously bend to the will of her husband. But where it touches her Christian stand, there is no room for compromise. A Christian wife can neither maintain a good testimony nor develop spiritually if she bows to the unregenerate desires of her husband. It is fallacious thinking to believe that if she attends a worldly function with him, he will be willing to go to church with her. This is an insidious trick of Satan. If he can persuade the Christian wife to let down the bars in this subtle way, he has won them both. Soon the wife begins to lose out spiritually, while her husband loses respect for her and the Christianity she represents. An ungodly mate may taunt or put on pressure to make his wife relinquish her testimony, but when she stands firm and remains true to the Lord, her husband can see that his wife's profession means something vital to her. He may resent the fact that she will not bend to his unregenerate whims. Yet, he must admire her consistent life. In the long run, it may be his wife's steadfast Christian testimony that will influence him for Christ.

SALVATION

Utilize Each Hour

A wife who really covets her husband for God will trim her life to the goal of utilizing as much time as possible with him. If you are married to an unbeliever, you miss Christian fellowship at home. Although you do need the benefit of Christ-centered activities and congenial Christian friends, there is a danger that your husband will feel left out in the cold. When this happens, he resents Christianity because it has cut him off from his wife. So, if a woman is wise, she will devote a reasonable amount of time to her husband and try to create a pleasant relationship. It may cost you something to tell a friend, "I am going to be home tonight with my husband." But this very loss of your personal freedom may become eternity's great gain.

—From Clyde M. Narramore, *A Woman's World*. Grand Rapids: Zondervan, 1963.

Of Children

Knowing that he is accepted as a son in God's family (John 1:12), the child can enter into the fullest measure of self-acceptance. Knowing that his sins are forgiven (1 John 1:9; Acts 10:43), he becomes able to forgive himself for his own shortcomings. The assurance of eternal life (John 10:27, 28) can banish the haunting fear of death and separation. And, as he is made aware of the power of the indwelling Christ, the child can live in the quiet confidence that, "I can do all things through Christ which strengtheneth me" (Philippians 4:13 KJV).

For his weakness and inabilities, the child can find Christ's strength (2 Corinthians 12:9, 10). For his sin, Christ's sacrifice (1 Peter 1:18, 19). For his fears, Christ's presence—always (Hebrews 13:5, 6; Matthew 28:20). For his feelings of inadequacy and self-rejection, he can find Christ's acceptance and love (Ephesians 1:3–7).

But how do we help preschoolers toward knowing this ultimate confidence? It is obvious that few preschoolers will experience "conversion" in the dramatic "Saul of Tarsus" mode (Acts 9). But they can take a first step on the Christian pilgrimage by personally opening their lives to Jesus Christ. And the Christian parent can help them to develop concepts preparatory to this at a very early age.

Let's clarify something right here: The limits of a child's understanding need not be the limits of his faith. Nobody ever *fully* understands the miracle of God's grace in a person's life. Even the most articulate analyst—a John Calvin or a Jonathan Edwards—cannot state exactly *how* God saves a trusting person. "The wind blows where it likes," Jesus said. "You can hear the sound of it but you have no idea where it comes from and where it goes. Nor can you tell how a man is born by the wind of the Spirit" (John 3:8 J. B. PHILLIPS). I do not know just *how* Christ's death atoned for my sins, but God's Word says that it did—and I exercise saving faith by believing that Word (1 Peter 2:24; Romans 5:6–11).

So the limitations of children's concepts concerning God and sin and salvation need not be a stumbling-block to their receiving Christ into their lives. They can grow into knowledge as they develop and mature in their faith, just as all Christians need to "grow in grace, and in the knowledge of our Lord and Saviour Jesus Christ" (2 Peter 3:18 KJV).

What, then, must a child know in order to make an act of saving faith?

1. *He must have a concept of God.* God as Father, Creator, and Sovereign Lord: these are big concepts. Parents who pray with and for their children; who talk often with them about God, their loving Father; who tell about God's attributes of greatness and goodness in story, conversation, worship, and praise: these parents help children build a framework into which developing concepts can be placed.

The invisibility of God makes teaching about Him different from teaching about the material things in a child's environment. But the parent may have more trouble with this than does the child. To little children, things that are not seen are as real as things that do appear (Hebrews 11:1–6). A little child goes by faith in many areas of life—and as long as his basic trust is not disappointed, he has a resource of faith which is very deep.

"God is everywhere. He is a Spirit—so He does not have to be limited to being in one place at a time. Why, He is here with us right now! Let's talk with Him." The parent who lives in an awareness of the presence of God can introduce that Presence to the child at a very early stage.

For the human need to visualize God, He Himself has supplied the picture. The New International Version puts it: "For God who said, 'Let light shine out of darkness,' made his light shine in our hearts to give us the light of the knowledge of the glory of God in the *face of Christ* (2 Corinthians 4:6, *italics mine; compare* John 1:14–18). And so we tell our children—as God's Word tells us—that while nobody has ever seen God, we can visualize Him and relate to Him in the person of the Lord Jesus Christ.

2. *He must have knowledge of the Lord Jesus Christ.* In a home where Jesus Christ is honored as Lord in the lives of the parents, nothing could be more natural than to teach the little children about the person of Christ. The cycling calendar year, with its high points at Christmas and Easter, makes a natural framework into which to fit the stories of Christ's Incarnation, His life, His death, His Resurrection and Ascension. The stories of Jesus never cease to excite the wonder of little children. Tell them, read them from storybooks, read them from the Gospels, sing them—for if children are to exercise saving faith, they must first know of the Saviour.

Doctrinal elements are easily shared within the framework of the stories—shared in the same way that the writers of the Gospels share them. By pointing to the fulfillment of the Old Testament pictures and prophecies; by drawing conclusions from the "signs and wonders" Jesus performed (John 4:48 KJV); by listening to Jesus' own words—the Gospel writers, and we with them, acknowledge the full deity and the total humanity of Jesus Christ. "Jesus is the Son of God" is the simplest formulation for children. We can share with children that,

though Jesus was once a child and experienced all the frustrations and temptations of childhood, He never sinned. And we can share with them that, as the sinless Son of God, He died in our place, taking the penalty of our sins, and rose again to live forever.

3. *He must be aware of his own sinful self.* The concept of "self" as separate from others is one which develops very early. The idea of "sin" is more easily understood by children than adults realize.

Parents who avoid correcting a child or telling him that he has done wrong for fear of inflicting guilt are, quite simply, missing the point. Children are aware, deeply aware, of the sin nature within them, aware of the conflict between good and evil desires. They live with guilt—without any help from their parents. Forgiveness is as real a need to a child as it is to an adult.

With the concepts of God, self, and sin, and a knowledge of the person of Jesus Christ, a preschool child *may* be ready to receive Christ as Saviour for himself. The opportunity can be afforded at an appropriate time—after a child has shown genuine sorrow for his sin, or has expressed a deep love response to the Lord Jesus. "Would you like to ask Jesus to come into your life?" the parent could ask. If there is no pressure, children respond very honestly. "Not yet," a four-year-old might very well say. Or, "I will when I'm ready."

When a child does answer with a yes, the parent can lead him in a simple prayer, something such as this:

Dear Father,

I know that I am a sinner. I am sorry that I have made You sad so often.

I believe that Jesus, Your Son, died for me and rose again.

Right now, I am asking the Lord Jesus to be my Saviour. Please forgive my sins and give me eternal life.

In Jesus' name I pray.
Thank You.
Amen.

If the child hesitates, pause for further explanation. If his attention shifts, just let the matter drop until another time. When the child does make an act of acceptance and commitment, do not expect a radical transformation. Your parenting is not finished! Discipline, development, and patient teaching will all still have their part in your child's growth.

—From Maxine Hancock, *People in Process*. Old Tappan, N.J.: Revell, 1978.

SAYING NO

IT'S POSSIBLE to say no without being offensive about it. But it takes a little practice. You have to learn to smile while you're doing it. Unfortunately, it's a little like rubbing your head and patting your stomach at the same time.

But you can do it now. You *can* be pleasant, and you *can* be firm. The next time you find yourself in a difficult situation and want out, give a great big smile and shake your head. You'll be surprised how little argument you get in return.

Here's something to think about. Every one of the Ten Commandments except two are negative. They tell us what not to do. Life is made up of dos *and* don'ts. You have to learn to use them both with discretion. Too much salt ruins the meal. Too much pepper makes your tongue burn.

It's not too late to take your life by the reins. Sometimes, in order to stop yourself from going over the cliff, you have to stop and change gears. Think positive! Act positive! Pray positive! Never let the ideal that you're striving for slip out of your mind. But remember that you sometimes have to say no to get those positive results. Here are ten rules to help you.

1. Every morning, before you bring in the paper, or put on the coffee, open the door (or window) and breathe. Really breathe. Throw your arms wide . . . hold your head high . . . and let the fresh strong air of March fill your lungs. Then say to yourself, "Today, I'll be honest with myself."
2. Remember that to deny is not to reject. Know the difference.
3. Give a direct answer to a direct question. Don't be afraid to say no to a child. It can be a healthy reaction to a bad situation. Face it, your offspring aren't always angels. You can love them and still say no.
4. Realize that no is only negative when it's a cop-out. This keeps you from being ashamed to say no to an adult. You're not withdrawing from responsibility. You're re-directing it.
5. Analyze your feelings. Look on the other side of the pancake. If you're feeling negative, look for the positive reaction, then move forward.
6. Never say no, when you mean yes. Never say yes, when you mean no. Make up your mind. You're the only one who can.
7. Don't nag. Say it once and mean it. Nagging is like a drop of acid. Sometimes the damage is not immediately apparent. At first, there's only a slight stain on the cloth. Then one day a hole appears. The result: a complete void in place of something of value.
8. Practice this positive statement: "Yes, I'm saying no!"
9. Learn to smile pleasantly when you shake your head. Scowls only make wrinkles, and there's nothing positive about those.
10. Start reforming today. Start again *every* day for the whole month of March.

Does it sound like a lot to remember? It won't be as hard as you think, because God is right there waiting at every turn of the road. So stop coasting and get yourself in gear. Have the courage of your convictions. You know what kind of person God intended you to be. Don't settle for less.

—From Marilyn Cram Donahue, *A Piece of Me Is Missing*. Wheaton, Ill.: Tyndale, 1978.

FOR FURTHER READING:

Narramore, Clyde and Ruth. *How to Handle Pressure.* Wheaton, Ill.: Tyndale, 1975.

Witmore, Nyla Jane. *I Was An Over Committed Christian.* Wheaton, Ill.: Tyndale, 1979.

SELF

I TOOK MY FIRST algebra course in the ninth grade. I barely passed. I never really understood algebra, even though I learned to do the equations and memorized the formulas. I knew the marvelous formulas for finding the circumference, and I knew all about the hypotenuse of the triangle—at least I knew the facts. But I never quite figured out the reasoning behind it all.

I used to marvel at two of my classmates in particular. Kenneth Snyder had that logical, mathematical mind and hardly used a pencil to arrive at an answer that took me half a page to figure out. Or brainy Janice Hendricksen. The teacher would ask a question—and before I had time to think through which of the formulas to use or why "X" equaled B over C^3, that smart girl popped up with the answer!

How did I feel? Quite inferior and stupid. After class each day I worried about my lack of comprehension. I honestly tried, without success, to figure out *why* and never could. Finally, in order to pass, I settled for *how* to get the right answers.

During ninth grade I took my algebra book home during Christmas vacation. I read the first three chapters at least half a dozen times. I still couldn't understand the abstractions.

I worried about my final grade. I worried about failing for the whole year and being held back. I worried whether I would ever get out of algebra. Most of all, I worried about my own inferiority.

If I had only stopped to put the math course in perspective, I might not have felt so bad. I had always been a good student with excellent grades. Yet because I couldn't do well in algebra, it seemed as though I was

doomed to failure. I saw myself only as one of the dumbest students in the school.

Even at home I felt inferior. I grew up with three brothers and a father. They possessed marvelous innate mechanical abilities. They could tackle anything that required using their hands—and they did it well. I always felt awkward and saw myself as a klutz. After awhile I found ways to ask them to do anything that required mechanical or electrical work. "I'm too dumb to learn," I'd say. In truth, I didn't want to try to learn because I felt I couldn't live up to their standards.

What I didn't realize—and it took years before I did—is that I am a unique person. I am lousy in algebra, and I have to hire someone to do all my mechanical work on the house or car.

Even so, I am not inferior. I'm different, perhaps, but not inferior.

Neither am I superior.

I look at myself and at my unique talents. This self-study tells me that I have gifts Kenneth and Janice never dreamed of. My brothers never measured up to *my* special abilities.

Who am I, then? I am a creation of God. The Bible declares that God made all things. I'm part of "all things" and a special part of his creation.

I have talents that others do not possess. I have a unique combination of abilities, and no other human being in the entire world is quite like me.

A popular saying a decade ago still makes good theological sense: God don't make no junk. That home-spun and grammatically twisted philosophy recognizes that God makes no mistakes. He never created any wasted people. God has a purpose for our lives and offers us the opportunities to fulfill ourselves.

I am me—Cec Murphey. I need only to learn to fulfill the destiny to which God has called me. I begin that fulfillment by accepting myself as unique, as loved, and as special to God.

Here's something I have found helpful in my own prayer time and during other free moments in my day. I say to myself: *I am a unique, unrepeatable, miracle of God!* The more I repeat these words to myself, the more my mind believes them. (I'm convinced we believe what we keep hearing about ourselves.)

The more I repeat these words, the more I recognize that I am special to God. Since I learned that fact, I haven't worried about feeling inferior to anyone else.

Actually, if I feel inferior, it's an indictment against God! It's accusing him of turning out irregular products. And, like that homespun philosopher said, God don't make no junk!

—From Cecil Murphey, "God Don't Make No Junk," *Christian Single*, February 1983.

Self-Love

Knowing the love that God has for us should help us to have a proper and real love for ourselves, a "genuine and joyful" acceptance of ourselves. You should be able to say, "I'm glad to be me." This isn't pride or selfishness, it's just agreeing with God that this part of His creation, too, is very good. "And God saw every thing that He had made, and, behold, it was very good . . ." (Genesis 1:31).

To have a proper love for self is the ability to feel good about yourself. You can recognize and accept your weaknesses and inabilities and deal with your sin. It is to feel comfortable about yourself, to be at peace with yourself, to feel *okay*, acceptable. It is not envying another person's gifts, abilities, temperament. It is to be content to be you, the person you are now for now, but always having the aspiration to become more and more the person God created you to be—more and more like Jesus Christ. It is to have a godly desire to be continually growing as a person, but in the process, knowing that you are now a person of worth, of value, acceptable, lovable.

In addition, we must not only know, understand, and recognize through past experiences, the fact that God loves us; but in the midst of varied and sometimes mysterious events that God allows to touch us, we must

believe God's love now. This is the walk of faith. In the midst of the hard-to-understand circumstances we must continue to believe in the love which has been so faithful in the past. In the midst of distressing situations such as a sudden death of a loved one, a wayward child, broken engagement, an accident, a failure in an assignment, loss of goods, God's love remains ever the same.

—From Verna Birkey, *You Are Very Special.* Old Tappan, N.J.: Revell, 1977.

LEARN TO LOVE YOURSELF

To many people that seems to be a totally wrong concept, and certainly the thought of loving yourself, in the minds of many, is utterly unchristian. Fixed in our minds are the words of Jesus, ". . . If any man will come after me, let him deny himself, and take up his cross, and follow me" (Matthew 16:24). We say with Paul, "I am crucified with Christ . . ." (Galatians 2:20). Also we quote Paul with approval, ". . . I die daily" (1 Corinthians 15:31).

Many people fix in their minds that living the highest life means being dead to themselves—giving themselves—forgetting themselves—losing their lives—suffering for a cause—and on and on. It has been said over and over, "God first, others second, yourself last." Within the right interpretation, all of these expressions are valid and most acceptable.

However, let us remember that Jesus agreed with the lawyer who said, ". . . Thou shalt love the Lord thy God with all thy heart, and with all thy soul, and with all thy strength, and with all thy mind; and thy neighbour as thyself" (Luke 10:27). When we read those words, we are so impressed with the forceful emphasis on our love for God and the fact that next our neighbor is mentioned, that we really miss the key to that entire great statement. Those last two words should be written in bold, capital letters: AS THYSELF! That is where it all begins. Our attitudes and feelings toward God and others begin with our attitudes and feelings toward ourselves. *One:* If you hate yourself, you hate other people, and you hate God. *Two:* If you do not care about yourself, you do not care about other people, and you do not care about God. *Three:* If you love yourself, you love other people, and you love God. The beginning of the whole business of love is *learning to love yourself.*

Never get the idea that loving yourself means excluding others. Genuine self-love is never egocentricity or selfishness. Loving yourself does not mean that you are seeking as much as possible out of life—and willing to give as little as possible. Neither is self-love, pride, arrogance, a sense of superiority, or, an exaggerated feeling of importance. True self-love is mirrored in our attitude toward God and our fellowman. We look at others through the attitudes that we have toward ourselves. "Learn to love yourself" is really the starting place.

OVERCOMING SELF-HATRED

Not only should we be concerned about our attitudes toward God and other people, but in learning to love ourselves, we overcome the damaging emotion of self-hatred. Remembering some bad decision, we say, "I could kick myself for being so stupid." We look back on actions in some yesterday with shame and remorse and deep guilt. We cannot forget—we refuse to forgive. Instead, we relive and rethink, over and over, some wrong we did, until we think ourselves into despair and self-degradation.

There are many other reasons why people hate themselves, such as, discrimination they have received because of their race, or color, or national origin. We depreciate ourselves because we lack the talents someone else possesses. Some people do not have the education that they wanted and they need, and they mourn over opportunities that are now gone.

Learn to love yourself in order to stop hating yourself.

We transfer to others the attitude we have toward ourselves. Loving ourselves, we wish good for other people. Hating ourselves, we want others pulled down to our level. Not being happy with ourselves, we are not happy with anybody else.

It has been well said:

When folks is mean, it ain't that they hate you personal. It's more likely because they are miserable about something in their inside. You got to remember how most of the time when they yell at you or get after you, it ain't you they are yelling at but something inside themselves you never even heard tell of, like some other person has been mean to them, or something they hoped for didn't come true, or they done something they are ashamed even to think of, so they get mad at you just to keep their minds off it.

Boy George in "The Foolkiller"

The truth of the matter is, just for our own self-preservation, we need to learn to love ourselves. Hating ourselves: one, distorts our personalities; two, blocks all happiness out of our lives; three, creates within us negative spirits; four, makes us cynical, complaining, and contentious; and five, ruins all of our relationships with God and our fellowman.

Notice that we are told to "learn to love ourselves." It is not something that comes with just a quick decision. You do not simply say, "I will start loving myself," and find it accomplished. If you wish to play the piano, it takes learning; if you wish to paint beautiful pictures, it takes learning. So it is with loving ourselves.

THREE STEPS TO SELF-LOVE

Being convinced that we need to learn to love ourselves, there are three steps to take, but these steps are neither small, nor are they simple.

First, we must learn to love God. This seems a contradiction of what we have just been saying, but the truth of the matter is, the beginning of self-love is self-forgetting. Our very beginning is in God, and we can love God because the Bible tells us, "We love him, because he first loved us" (1 John 4:19). Love for God does not originate within us; rather it is response to God. He made the world in which we live. He causes the sun to shine and all of creation to keep going. More importantly, God knows each person by name. We make great progress when we realize that God's love does not begin with *mankind*, but with each individual. If God did not love even just one person, then His love for mankind would be incomplete and imperfect.

When one person—any person—every person—realizes that he or she is God's child, does that person dare to hate God's child? In the second place, *we love God because He takes out of our lives the wrong, negative attitudes we have toward ourselves.* Self-hatred, a sense of guilt, a feeling of unworthiness, the realization of past mistakes and sin—all these and more—God forgives and forgets. The Bible says, "... for thou hast cast all my sins behind thy back" (Isaiah 37:17).

When God forgives, sin is gone out of sight and is remembered no more. When God forgives, no person needs to hate self any longer. If God is willing to take us into His loving fellowship, then we can live with ourselves in that same loving fellowship.

The third step is *through fellowship with God.* We realize we are not dependent just on our own selves. We are not alone; we have a fellowship which empowers. We stop saying such things as, "This is beyond me and my abilities." Instead, we begin saying with Paul, "I can do all things through Christ which strengtheneth me" (Philippians 4:13).

When we think of our own littleness, we are constantly defeating ourselves. When we think of the greatness of God, we have confident assurance. We can handle the job that is ours to do. We can make friends; we can face troubles; we can quit hating ourselves. Never forget that God is on the side of success. God is never a party to failure.

So to begin with, in loving God, we come to love ourselves, and through loving ourselves, we can love all mankind.

—From Charles L. Allen, *The Secret of Abundant Living.* Old Tappan, N.J.: Revell, 1980.

FOR FURTHER READING:

Dobson, James. *What Wives Wish Their Husbands Knew About Women.* Wheaton, Ill.: Tyndale, 1975.

Miller, Ella May. *The Peacemakers.* Old Tappan, N.J.: Revell, 1977.

Neff, Mariam. *Discover Your Worth.* Wheaton, Ill.: Victor Books, 1979.

Price, Eugenia. *A Woman's Choice.* Grand Rapids: Zondervan, 1962.

Wallace, Joanne. *The Image of Loveliness.* Old Tappan, N.J.: Revell, 1978.

SEXUAL INTERCOURSE

THE IDEAL situation God intended for us is shown by the blissful words "they were both naked, the man and his wife, and were not ashamed" (Genesis 2:25). Adam and Eve could see each other as they really were, without shame, disappointment, or frustration. The sex relationship God had designed for them brought the blessings of companionship, unity, and delight—and note that this was *before* the command to bear children was given (Genesis 3:16).

God's plan for our pleasure has never changed, and we realize this even more as we consider how we are "fearfully and wonderfully made" (Psalms 139:14). When we discover the many intricate details of our bodies which provide so many intense, wonderful physical sensations for husbands and wives to enjoy together, we can be sure that He intended for us to experience full satisfaction in the marriage relationship.

Some have assumed that the sex act became an unholy practice when sin entered into the world. However, this is ruled out when we see that God's basic counsel on sex in the first chapters of Genesis was repeated by Jesus Christ to the religious leaders of His day: "But from the beginning of the creation God made them male and female. For this cause shall a man leave his father and mother, and cleave to his wife, and they two shall be one flesh. What therefore God hath joined together, let not man put asunder" (Matthew 19:5; Mark 10:6–9). Jesus reemphasized this to His disciples in the next two verses in Mark 10, and again we find these commands reinforced in Ephesians 5:31.

As a matter of fact, the sex relationship in marriage receives such emphasis in the Scriptures that we begin to see it was meant not only to be a wonderful, continuing experience for the husband and wife, but it also was intended to show us something even more wonderful about God and His relationship with us. Ephesians 5:31, 32 spells it out: "For this cause shall a man leave his father and mother, and shall be joined unto his wife, and they two shall be one flesh. This is a great mystery, but I speak concerning Christ and the church." *Thus, the properly and lovingly executed and mutually satisfying sexual union is God's way of demonstrating to us a great spiritual truth.* It speaks to us of the greatest love story ever told—of how Jesus Christ gave Himself for us and is intimately involved with and loves the Church (those who believe in Him). In this framework of understanding between two growing Christians, the sexual relationship can become a time of intimate fellowship as well as delight.

This, of course, explains why the marriage union is the only way man and woman can truly enjoy the riches God has planned for them. Because the relationship is specifically designed to illustrate God's unending love for His people, sexual intercourse must be experienced in the context of a permanent, giving commitment. Anything less shortchanges those involved.

Some people have felt uncomfortable about sex because they somehow equate the sexual desire of men with the sexual drive of animals. They should remember that animals breed according to instinct with biological motivation. But man has intercourse as a whole person. He of all creatures is the only one to use reason in choosing to have sexual relations. Husband and wife are the only creatures capable of gaining spiritual unity and a deeper knowledge of each other through the sexual relationship. Let us realize how the bodies of men and women are designed. Even in the sex act itself we are reminded that this is a relationship of persons, not just bodies, for it is no coincidence that man is the *only* creature of God's creation who relates sexually face-to-face.

Scripture suggests that just as we can know God, so we can know our husband or wife in a deeper, higher, more intimate way through the physical act of marriage. *Know* is the term used in the Bible to define our relationship to God; it also is the term used to designate the intimate union of husband and wife. "Adam *knew* Eve" (Genesis 4:1). Mary, speaking of her virginity, said, "How shall this be, seeing I *know* not a man?" (Luke 1:34). Matthew 1:25 says that Joseph *"knew her not"* until after the birth of Christ. The sex relationship offers no more cherished pleasure than this *knowing* of the one you love. With the understanding that our marriage relationship portrays the truths of our relationship with God, we can become free as never before to express our love for our husband or wife fully through the dynamic opportunity of the sex act.

God's viewpoint comes forth vigorously in 1 Corinthians 7:3–5 where the husband and wife are told they actually *defraud* one another when they refuse to give physical pleasure and satisfaction to their mate. The only activity which is to break regular sexual relations is prayer and fasting for some specific cause, and this is to be only by mutual consent for a very limited time.

Although sin did enter the human race in the Garden and brought with it the possibility of perversion of every good thing (including sex), God's plan for His beloved Creation has continued to operate through the provision of the Redeemer, Jesus Christ. By faith people can choose God's way! It is true that our culture is saturated with sex distorted into lust, and desire has been twisted and deformed, until it appears as a beast running loose in the streets, destroying God-given boundaries. *Nevertheless, our marriage bed is a holy place in the sight of God.* We must be careful to maintain this viewpoint concerning sex in marriage, for it is God's. Hebrews 13:4 says, "Marriage is honorable in all, and the bed undefiled. . . ." We need to treasure and share with our children these positive values God Himself teaches in Scripture concerning the love/sex relationship, always placing sex in marriage in an entirely different light from sex outside of marriage. Sex apart from marriage is spelled out as obviously wrong. Sex in marriage is wonderfully right. Let us never forget it!

I cannot begin to describe the dimensions of the marriage relationship as experienced by the Christian couple who have a total commitment to Jesus Christ, and flowing from that a realization of their own security in spiritual and physical oneness; who have an excitement found only in each other, knowing this is for as long as they live. This genuine, total oneness and completeness somehow cannot be explained to the one who has not yet experienced it. When this kind of relationship exists, many times you will both want to praise our Lord and have communion with Him in prayer, each thanking Him for the other and the complete love you share.

Intended for pleasure—yes, in the fullest meaning of the word. And even then, language does not convey what God has prepared for us!

Positions

Positioning of the couple's bodies should suit their own individuality. There need be no set patterns, although early in marriage, the bride, not having had her tissues stretched from childbearing, may find that some angles of penile insertion will cause discomfort. After several children have been born, the tissues around the vagina will be stretched, and the wife will then be more

comfortable in varied positions. Remember, changing of positions may restore interest and encourage excitement, but these new positions must be comfortable and pleasing for both husband and wife. It is worth noting that the right rhythm of movement is just as important as the right position in attaining a satisfactory response for both partners.

The *male-above position* is by far the most commonly used and gives the husband freedom of movement plus greatest control of strength and rapidity of thrusting. Many couples consider this the most satisfying of all positions. The wife lies on her back with legs extended, comfortably separated. The husband lies on top of her, supporting some of his weight on arms or elbows, his legs inside hers. After insertion of the penis her legs may be moved farther apart, closer together, inside his, or wrapped around his legs or up over his body.

To assume the *female-above position* the husband lies on his back, while the wife straddles his body and leans forward. *She* inserts the penis at about a 45-degree angle and moves back on the shaft, rather than sitting down on it. She then assumes whatever posture is most stimulating and comfortable to her. This position allows the wife by her movements to control the exact timing and degree of thrusting that affords her the most sexual response. The placement of each partner's legs will govern deeper or less deep penetration of the penis, depending on what is preferred. The female-above position gives the husband access to her breasts. He also has free use of his hands to better stimulate the clitoris, if necessary, while they are joined in sexual intercourse. This position is often advantageous for a large husband and a small wife, and is sometimes more comfortable as the abdomen enlarges during pregnancy.

Starting intercourse in the female-above position, the *lateral,* or *side-by-side position* is assumed by the wife leaning forward and shifting her body slightly to the right, placing her right leg between her husband's legs. Her left leg is then flexed over his right leg.

403

Advantages of the lateral position are that each partner has at least one hand free for fondling and caressing. Each is free to thrust or rotate hips. Neither has to support weight with hands and legs, and neither is being "pinned" by the body weight of the other.

The *male-behind position* seldom is used but may be tried on occasion and may also be used during late pregnancy. Both husband and wife lie on their sides facing the same direction with the husband back of the wife. The penis is placed into the vagina from the rear. Disadvantages are that the penis does not contact the clitoris and the couple cannot kiss during intercourse. This position leaves the husband's hands free to caress the body and breasts and stimulate the clitoris.

Frequency

Perhaps there has been a difference of opinion on what frequency of intercourse is desirable. Whatever the two of you together prefer certainly is "normal" for your marriage. If you think your husband seems to require sex a lot more than you do, ponder this illustration: If you were in the desert and you were thirsty, you'd think about a glass of water, wouldn't you? But if you're standing by the refrigerator, and there's a big pitcher of ice-cold water inside the door, and you know you can open the door and get it any time you want to, the need for a drink is not nearly so urgent. Maybe the reason your husband seems never to think of anything besides sex is that he's "in the desert" and "thirsty."

Sometimes you will be very tired and feeling as sexy as an old sock, but your husband will approach you with desire. Secular therapists say a wife should be able to respond, "Sorry, but I'm just not up to it tonight." My own opinion as a Christian wife is that we can depend on the Lord to give us the strength and ability to be as warm and responsive as our husbands desire, no matter how tired we are. As we commit this in prayer, trusting the Lord to give us the

strength to meet our husbands' needs, we often find not only that we can do it, but that we enjoy the experience as well. The heart of the matter is attitude. Please do not be like the lady who told me grimly, "I have never *refused* him." And yet it was obvious that the refusal was there in her heart and even in her voice.

If you find rebellion rising within because of counsel which seems to stress submission to your husband and thus goes against your natural inclination, remember that submission to our God and to our husbands is a supernatural work, the result of our own choice of action *plus* God's power. Psalms 40:8 says, "I delight to do thy will, O my God," and this is the point a wife must reach. Submission is always done *by* you, and not *to* you.

Ritual can become a hindrance to sexual enjoyment. If you and your husband have been having sex always at the same time and exactly the same routine, try a different time and a different approach. As the wife who usually schedules the activities for the family, you can plan times when you and your husband will be rested and ready for each other. Your husband needs energy for a good sexual relationship, and you can sometimes protect him from the exhaustion which comes from adding social activities on top of his daily work load.

—From Ed Wheat, M.D., and Gaye Wheat, *Intended for Pleasure*, Rev. ed. Old Tappan, N.J.: Revell, 1981.

Orgasm

What is an orgasm? An orgasm is not a mystical experience. It is a physical experience, and here is a description of the whole human response cycle:

What happens during the response cycle can be divided into four parts. First, there is the *excitement* phase. It begins as the body reacts to some kind of sexual stimulation. Blood rushes into the clitoris (also the penis) engorging it and causing erection. The rate of breathing increases, nipples become erect, body muscles (some voluntary, some involuntary) tighten, and you may notice a sexual flush or rash. The woman's vagina becomes moist, lubricated by fluid which passes through the vaginal walls from the body cavity in a kind of "sweating" reaction. As it lubricates and becomes more sensitive, the vagina begins a process of lengthening and expansion. The compacted folds and ridges smooth out and the whole cylinder straightens, enlarging and tenting at the upper end to make room for the fully erect penis and the ejaculated semen. This causes the uterus to balloon upward.

Excitement is followed by the *plateau* phase, although it would be hard to say exactly when one phase stops and the next begins. During the plateau phase the changes increase. The rate of breathing increases. Most dramatic is the swelling of the tissues around the outer part of the vagina, which makes the width of the vagina half its normal size, and able to grip the penis. The clitoris elevates like a male erection, and the inner lips change in color from pink to bright red. Both sexes feel increased involuntary muscular tension. The testes in the male move closer to his body. If stimulation continues (about a minute from the time of color changes in the vagina), the changes in your body build up to a climax of heightened feeling and body tension, which suddenly spills over into *orgasm*, a series of genital muscular contractions that release the built-up tension.

Orgasm itself is the third phase. There is a feeling of intense pleasure as the vagina goes into rhythmic muscular contractions which have come down from the top of the uterus; then the intensity tapers off. The number of contractions vary with the intensity of the orgasm. The uterus also contracts rhythmically but the contractions are rarely felt. All the body's muscles respond in some way (even hands and feet, and facial muscles often contract into a grimace).

After the orgasm a kind of final *resolution* (fourth stage) occurs. The swelling of the nipples subsides, the sex flush disappears,

and the clitoris returns to its normal position. It may be as long as a half hour after orgasm before a woman's entire body returns to the state it was in before she was stimulated. If she has reached the plateau stage but has not reached orgasm, it will take much longer. Orgasm can be a very mild experience, almost as mild as a peaceful sigh, or it can be an extreme state of ecstasy with much thrashing about and momentary loss of awareness. It can last a few seconds or half a minute or longer. There is, in brief, no right or wrong way to have one.

—From The Boston Women's Health Collective, *Our Bodies, Ourselves.* New York: Simon & Schuster, 1973.

FOR FURTHER READING:

Burbridge, Branse. *The Sex Thing.* Wheaton, Ill.: Shaw, 1972.

LaHaye, Tim and Beverly. *The Act of Marriage.* Grand Rapids: Zondervan, 1976.

Miles, Herbert J. *Sexual Happiness in Marriage.* Grand Rapids: Zondervan, 1967.

Penner, Clifford and Joyce. *The Gift of Sex.* Waco, Tex.: Word Books, 1981.

Washbourn, Penelope. *Becoming Woman.* New York: Harper & Row, 1977.

Wilke, Richard B. *Tell Me Again, I'm Listening.* Nashville: Abingdon, 1973.

SEXUAL ORGANS

Female

Ovaries (ō′ và rēs). The word *ovary* comes from the Latin word *ova*, which means eggs. The ovaries are the main target organs for the pituitary hormones. At puberty the pituitary secretions carried by the bloodstream signal the ovaries to begin to develop eggs. Soon the ovaries will be in full production to continue for thirty or more years.

There are two ovaries, each suspended near the internal center of the lower body about four to five inches below the waist, halfway between the back of the pelvis and the groin. Each ovary is about the size of a robin's egg. At the time of puberty, the surface of the ovary is smooth. Shimmering through the surface there are many tiny glistening droplets called follicles. Each of these ovarian follicles holds an immature egg, or ovum, that is the female cell of reproduction. The eggs in the droplets are so small they would be only barely visible. They are smaller than the dot on an *i*, and it would take at least two million of them to fill a sewing thimble.

The ovaries have another equally vital function: to produce at least two important hormones of their own. These work together with the pituitary hormones to bring the rest of the reproductive system to maturity and then to keep it in working order.

When a baby girl is born there are about 300,000 to 400,000 follicles in the ovaries, although only about 300 to 400 eggs will ever actually reach maturity and be released from the ovary. If two ova, or eggs, are released at one time and both ova are fertilized, a twin pregnancy may result. These babies would not be identical twins, but would be fraternal twins—merely brothers or sisters born at nearly the same time. Identical twins come from the division of a single fertilized egg, and this always produces identical babies of the same sex.

Oviducts (ō' vĭ dŭkts). The word *oviducts* means "egg ducts." These are also commonly called the fallopian tubes. There are two oviducts, or tubes—one for each ovary. Primarily made of muscle, each of these tubes is about four inches long, and about the same diameter as a small telephone cord.

These muscular oviducts are essential to the transport of the tiny immobile eggs from the ovaries. At the same time, the oviducts provide the meeting ground for the female egg and male sperm which are coming to each other from opposite directions.

An egg coming from the ovary must first of all be caught by the oviduct. Neither oviduct is directly attached to its ovary. Instead, each oviduct has a trumpet-shaped widened opening near the ovary. This opening is rimmed with fingerlike fringes (*fimbria*) that conduct a sweeping motion which carries all before it into the oviduct. After the egg is taken into the opening of the oviduct by the sweeping fringe, waves of muscular contractions continue to aid its transport downstream toward the womb.

The trumpet-shaped opening of the oviduct leads to a passage that is no wider than this hyphen: (-). This internal passage, about the size of the point of a pencil, is lined with minute clumps of brushlike hairs called *cilia*. The size of the cilia, in proportion to the egg, is like that of eyelashes in comparison to an orange. The cilia are the sweepers that help to keep the egg gently flowing toward the womb.

An infection, particularly a venereal infection, may block these fallopian tubes by scarring them on the inside. This may cause a woman to be unable to have children. Sometimes these obstructions can be removed by careful surgery. Tubal obstructions are seen by injecting a liquid which shows clearly on X rays as it flows through the *os*, or mouth, of the cervix, into the uterus and through the tubes. This is called a salpingogram and can be done in a doctor's office or in any hospital X-ray department on an outpatient basis. This procedure may cause some slight pain and discomfort, but nothing that is unbearable. It requires no anesthesia.

In performing sterilization for birth control, the surgeon usually double-ties each tube with silk thread and then removes a section of each of these oviducts or tubes. This requires the opening of the abdomen and is thus a major operation requiring several days' stay in the hospital. However, there is another method which does not require the wife to be hospitalized. Some physicians are able to do laparoscopic surgery in which a Laparoscope, a small lighted tube instrument, is passed through an incision in the area just below the navel. Through another small incision in the lower abdomen, another instrument is inserted with which the surgeon is able to grasp and manipulate each oviduct. While he watches through the

Laparoscope, a loop of the oviduct is grasped and an electrocautery tip is used to burn and do away with about one or two inches of the mid portion of each oviduct. There are some other techniques used to close these oviducts, and one of the simplest ones is to insert through the small lower abdominal incision an instrument with which the oviduct can be manipulated, grasped, and pulled up into a loop, a small circular elastic ring (similar to a small rubber band) then being slipped over this elevated loop, thus very tightly squeezing the oviduct closed in two places. At present the elastic-ring method probably offers the best possibility for success of later surgery to reconstruct the tubes, if the woman decides at a future time that she wants to have another baby. I would not, however, want to convey the idea that any operative sterilization method is reversible. An operation for sterilization should be considered as permanent sterilization. Reconstruction surgery would be a very tedious and delicate major operation and would certainly cause some discomfort.

By describing these methods, I am merely explaining for you how and why certain techniques of birth control work. Whether or not you practice family planning is your decision and yours alone. However, every married couple is entitled to have information about each method of birth control, when making this decision.

Uterus (ū′ tēr ŭs). The Latin word *uterus* means womb or belly. The uterus, usually the size and shape of a small pear, is firm and muscular. It is about four inches long. When the woman is standing, it is suspended in a nearly horizontal position in the body, so that the small end of the pear points toward the tip of the spine, while the bulbous upper end points forward.

During pregnancy, the uterus can expand greatly to accommodate, as we know, up to six babies. This is possible because the uterus has many elastic fibers meshed in with the powerful muscle fibers. These muscles later play an important part in labor by contracting forcefully to deliver the baby.

The outside of the uterus is flesh pink in color. Inside there is a red velvety lining called endometrium, from the Greek "within the womb."

Within the uterus is a narrow triangular cavity surrounded by thick muscular walls. An intrauterine device, commonly called an IUD, can be placed in this cavity as a means of preventing pregnancy.

The two incoming oviduct canals enter at the top of the uterine cavity. The lower part of the uterine cavity that forms the narrowest base is called the cervical canal.

Cervix (sûr′ vĭks). The word *cervix* means neck in Latin, referring to the neck of the uterus. Surrounding the cervical canal, the cervix forms the narrow lower end of the uterus. It can be easily examined by the physician, since about half the cervix projects into the vagina.

Like the rest of the uterus, the cervix is firm and muscular. Medical students are sometimes taught that before the first pregnancy the cervix feels like the tip of the nose, and after childbirth it feels like the point of the chin.

The *cervical os* is the opening of the cervix into the vagina. This passageway is as narrow as the lead in a pencil and is framed by strong muscles. Only under strong pressure, as in childbirth, does the fibroelastic tissue of the cervix dilate to increase the size of the opening. The normally tight passage helps to keep the interior of the uterus virtually germfree, especially since a constant slight current of cleansing moisture flows outward.

This moisture, along with a light scraping of cervical cells, is examined for cancer cells in the Papanicolaou, or Pap, smear. It is recommended that women have a Pap smear about once each year, as the cervix is the site of most of the cancer of the female organs. It takes two to six days to get a final report on the Pap smear. When cervical cancer is found early, more than 90 percent is curable with correct treatment.

Vagina (vȧ jī′ nȧ). The word *vagina* means sheath in Latin. The vagina is a very elastic, sheathlike canal that serves as a passage to and from the sheltered genital organs inside the body. At its upper end, the vagina forms a curving vault that encloses the tip of the cervix. The inner walls of the vagina consist of folds of tissue, which tend to lie in contact. The vagina, normally three to five inches long, can expand easily to receive the penis. Its greatest expansion, of course, occurs during childbirth. The folds contain many tiny glands, which continuously produce a cleansing film of moisture so that the vagina is self-cleansing. For this reason douches are seldom necessary.

Near the external opening of the vagina, there is a concentration of sensory nerves that play a significant role in sexual arousal when stimulated by touch. The opening is encircled by a constrictor muscle that responds to communications from the sensory nerves. This muscle can be tightened and relaxed at will.

The first response to sexual stimulation in a woman is the lubrication of the vagina, which occurs within ten to thirty seconds in the younger woman and within one to three minutes in the older woman. Sexual excitement causes the walls of the upper vagina to be covered with beads of lubricant, like moisture on a cold glass—this in preparation for an easier insertion of the penis.

Knowing the precise location of this natural lubrication can enhance sexual pleasure during the excitement phase, for the knowledgeable husband will gently reach up into the vagina and bring lubricant down to the clitoral area for more enjoyable stimulation. Remember, if the wife is lying on her back, all the lubricant will remain in the upper vagina, unless it is brought down.

Adequate vaginal lubrication is absolutely essential for pleasure during intercourse. If it is not present, the husband will need to apply some form of water-soluble artificial lubricant, such as Johnson & Johnson's K-Y Jelly, obtainable at any drugstore. Be sure to apply the lubricant to the head of the penis and to the outside of the vagina before penetration.

The nursing mother should be aware that her capacity to lubricate may be restricted because of low estrogen levels. This vaginal dryness usually persists as long as she continues to nurse. It may be relieved by her obstetrician's prescription for an estrogen cream to apply up into the vagina. While the capacity for vaginal lubrication does continue throughout the female life cycle, low estrogen levels in the menopausal woman will almost always result in vaginal dryness, requiring the use of K-Y Jelly with every intercourse.

Never think of the vagina as a passive organ, but a very active one. When sexually stimulated, it increases in length and widens to twice its diameter. At the beginning of arousal, the upper vagina expands and the uterus lifts up toward the abdomen. In the second phase, the vagina constricts to conform to the penis. After orgasm the uterus moves downward, so that the cervix rests in the pool of semen deposited in the upper vagina.

Hymen (hī′ mĕn). The *hymen*, which has been given the name of the mythical god of marriage, is a shelflike membrane which surrounds but does not cover the lower opening to the vagina. The hymen has no physiologic function and never grows back after it has been dilated. In some instances, a baby girl is born without a hymen, so that its absence is not necessarily an indication of loss of virginity. But in other cases it is extremely tough and resistant.

The opening in the hymen of a virgin is usually about one inch in diameter (large enough for tampon use). However, for comfortable intercourse, a diameter of about one and one-half inches is needed. Thus, statistically, at the time of their first intercourse, 50 percent of brides experience some pain, but not enough to complain about; 20 percent say they have no pain at all; and 30 percent experience rather severe pain.

About six weeks before marriage, every

woman should have a pelvic examination. A thoughtful, interested physician can give her specific instructions which will help remove much of her fear of physical pain due to intercourse.

If the pelvic examination reveals a thick or tight hymen, the prospective bride may wish to have this tissue stretched, so there will be less difficulty and discomfort during the first intercourse. The physician can do this, or she may use her own fingers to stretch the hymen, according to the physician's instructions; or she may ask for exact instructions and a demonstration of how her husband can carefully stretch the hymen on their wedding night before intercourse.

I believe it is best for the prospective bride to devote a few moments each day for two to four weeks before the wedding in stretching the vaginal opening, so that her initial sexual experience with her husband will be as pleasant and painless as possible.

Here are the directions I give for the vaginal stretching. The woman should slowly insert one finger, well lubricated with K-Y Jelly, all the way to the base of the finger, then gently, very slowly, yet forcibly, press downward and backward against this most resistant part of the hymen. When you finally are able to insert one finger all the way to the base, then try to place two well-lubricated fingers into the vagina, again pressing slowly downward and backward with a quite firm pressure.

If the husband is attempting to stretch the vaginal opening on the wedding night, he should make sure his fingernails are filed very smooth and short, then attempt to insert the tips of three fingers, arranged in a wedge shape and well lubricated with K-Y Jelly. Place the fingertips in the vaginal opening and press down very firmly toward the back, but *very* slowly. This should take from fifteen to thirty minutes to accomplish, moving your fingers only about one-eighth inch at a time, until finally you can insert all three fingers to the base.

This procedure will result in the stretching and possibly even the tearing of small

areas in the vaginal opening. If there happens to be a small area of bleeding, do not be afraid. Simply look for the exact spot that is bleeding, take a piece of tissue, put it on the spot and hold it there with a firm pressure. You will be able to stop whatever bleeding occurs in this manner. If another tear and more bleeding occurs when you have intercourse, you can stop it the same way by holding tissue on the exact spot with a firm pressure. The tissue may be left in place about twelve hours and then soaked loose in warm water to avoid new bleeding. Intercourse can begin again the next day.

After such stretching, the major portion of the remaining hymen lies in a crescent shape across the back of the vaginal opening. Its position is such that it moves farther up over the vaginal opening when the legs are brought upward, and is less in the way when the woman's legs are down flat.

This fact should be kept in mind during your first intercourse. If the husband has difficulty in accomplishing initial entrance, a special position may be helpful. The bride lies on her back with two pillows under the hips, with her legs down as flat as possible to move the hymen more out of the way. The husband faces her and approaches from directly above, so that the penis is in an almost vertical position at first contact. With generous amounts of K-Y Jelly around the vaginal opening and on the head of the penis, he places the tip of the penis near the front of the vaginal opening and slides it almost straight down, attempting to slip past the elastic hymen. If the penis slips into the vagina, then the wife can slowly and intermittently bring her knees up as far as her discomfort will permit. At this point, the husband should no longer force the penis in, but allow her to thrust her pelvis upward and forward against the partially inserted penis, which should still be in an almost vertically straight-down position.

If there is a great deal of pain, as a last resort only, Nupercainal Ointment may be applied around the vaginal opening, especially toward the back, and left for a period of five minutes. This is a local anesthetic ointment available without a prescription, and you may wish to have it on hand, if your physician has warned of a vaginal outlet that seems to be unusually tight.

However, following the procedures I have described should ensure a pleasant first-time experience for the newlyweds in almost every case.

The husband should keep in mind that most pain occurs from entering too quickly, not allowing enough time for the muscles around the vagina to relax. At the time of first intercourse, the husband should not persist in striving to bring his wife to orgasm with his penis in the vagina. If she has some soreness, there is no reason to make this worse. After the penis is inserted, the husband should have his orgasm quickly, withdraw the penis, and stimulate his wife's clitoral area gently with his fingers to bring her to orgasm.

The husband's tender care of his wife at this crucial time will do much to establish an attitude of trust within her, so that in the weeks to come, she will be able to totally relax and let herself go in the enjoyment of his lovemaking.

Urethra (ū rē' thrȧ). The *urethra* is the outlet for the urine from the bladder. The urethral opening is about one-half inch above the vaginal opening and entirely separate from it. It resembles a rounded dimple containing a tiny slit. The urethra is actually a tube that runs beneath the pubic bone and can be easily bruised in the first few days after marriage, unless plenty of lubrication is provided for the penis in the vagina.

This bruising produces what is commonly called "newlywed cystitis" or "honeymoon cystitis" and is characterized by pain in the bladder area, by blood in the urine, and rather severe burning when the urine passes. It is an indication that injury to the urethra has allowed bacteria to grow. This bacteria may ascend to produce a severe bladder infection called cystitis. The infection and resulting pain will clear up much more quickly if the bride increases her intake of

fluids and uses medication as prescribed by her physician. Use of a lubricant such as K-Y Jelly is absolutely essential the first few weeks to help prevent this painful condition caused by bruising.

Some women are especially susceptible to intercourse cystitis, just as others are prone to develop sore throats and colds. A woman's anatomy sets up the conditions under which urinary tract infections easily occur. The urethra can be the recipient of contamination from both the vagina and rectum. The anus provides a hospitable site for bacteria, and from there it is only a short ascent to the bladder and beyond. Women should wash after bowel movements whenever feasible and always wipe from front to back.

Most urinary-tract infections in women occur within forty-eight hours after sexual relations. Thus, voiding within a few minutes after intercourse is important, since this helps rid the urethra of bacteria. Bladder urine is usually sterile and the voiding of urine cleanses the urethral mechanism. When bladder emptying is normal and complete, the ascent of bacteria is avoided. Of course, extra intake of fluid helps this urethral flushing. If frequent episodes of cystitis continue, you will need to see your physician for prescription antibiotics to take just after each intercourse. This allows the elimination of bacteria before they have time to multiply enough to produce infection.

Clitoris (klĭt' ar as). This is the Latin word for "that which is closed in." Closed in by the peak of the labia, the shaft of the clitoris, which is about one inch long, is located about one inch above the entrance to the vagina. At its outer end is a small, rounded body about the size of a pea, which is called the glans, from a Latin word meaning acorn. A fold of skin called the prepuce (prē ' pyōōs) or the clitoral hood partly covers the glans.

The clitoris has been called the trigger of female desire. It is the most keenly sensitive point a woman has for sexual arousal and has, as far as we know, no other function. Sufficient physical stimulation of the clitoris alone will produce orgasm in nearly all women. For this reason, many have thought that contact between the penis and clitoris is the only important factor in achieving orgasm. Operations have been performed to provide greater exposure of the clitoris. Yet such surgery does not help to attain orgasm, and it is apt to cause other problems—for instance, the development of scar tissue, which occurs in any operative procedure. Removal of the clitoral hood exposes the clitoris to trauma, and direct contact with it is likely to bring more discomfort than pleasure.

If sexual stimulation causes pain in the clitoris, there may be some rock-hard particles of dried secretion (smegma) beneath some adhesions of the prepuce. These particles can be easily removed and the adhesions released, using a small metal probe. This is a simple procedure done in the doctor's office, not usually requiring even a local anesthetic. Minor clitoral adhesions can be freed at home using a Q-Tip, preferably following a hot bath.

The clitoris sometimes enlarges when caressed, but there is no need for anxiety if it does not. In a study of hundreds of women able to reach orgasm, more than half showed no visible enlargement of the clitoris. Enlargement was only barely noticeable by either sight or touch in others. Most of the enlargement is in diameter, not in length. The size of the clitoris, or its enlargement, has nothing to do with sexual satisfaction or sexual capacity. During the latter stages of sexual arousal, the clitoris is submerged in the engorged surrounding tissues. Therefore, size is never a significant factor in reaching orgasm.

The important points to remember are:

1. The clitoris must be stimulated either directly or indirectly for the wife to achieve orgasm.
2. The basic physiologic response of orgasm is the same, no matter what the method of stimulation.
3. Women often report a subjective difference in feelings produced by the clitoral

orgasm and feelings produced by the orgasm achieved during vaginal stimulation.

The essential anatomical fact a couple must learn is the exact location of the clitoris. This can be most precisely determined during the time of sexual arousal by sensitively placing well-lubricated fingertips alongside the shaft of the clitoris, as it extends upward onto the pelvic bone. You will be able to feel it as you move your fingers back and forth the length of the shaft. Also move your fingers across the shaft from side to side. It is similar to rolling your fingers across a very small telephone cord. Persistent, loving, gentle, sensitive, well-lubricated stimulation alongside this clitoral shaft will bring almost any wife to orgasm within three to twenty minutes. As orgasm is approached, the tempo of the stimulation needs to increase.

When the clitoris is first stimulated in foreplay, very light, gentle, slow caressing usually gives the most satisfaction. In a few seconds, the glans may become overly sensitive or even irritated, and stroking farther up on the shaft, or at the side of the shaft will give a more pleasurable sensation. While the glans of the clitoris is feeling overly sensitive, the wife may prefer to be stimulated in an entirely different area such as the breasts or the inner thighs before returning to stimulation of the clitoral area.

Labia minora (lā′ bǐ ä mǐ nōr′ ä). *Labia minora* are the Latin words for "small lips." They are two parallel folds of smooth, hairless, soft tissue that connect to the hood over the clitoris and can be most easily identified just above and beside the entrance to the vagina. At times the gentle stroking of these small lips gives a very pleasant sensation. Since these lips are connected directly above the clitoris, when the penis moves in the vagina and against these delicate lips, there is friction, tugging, and pulling which carries sensation to the clitoris. Thus, *direct* stimulation of the clitoris is not always desired or necessary for sexual pleasure. The most con-

411

sistent and easily detected physical sign of the wife's sexual arousal and readiness for intercourse is the expansion of the *labia minora* to two or three times their normal thickness. Expansion is detected by gentle touching with the fingers.

Labia majora (lā' bǐ ä mä jōr' ä). These "major lips" appear as a mound of flesh, lying outside and parallel to the *labia minora*. They are normally over the vaginal opening, providing protection against entrance of the penis or other objects into the unstimulated vagina. With sexual arousal, the major lips lie back and flatten, but you probably will not be able to detect this small change. They are not nearly so sensitive to stimulation as the small lips and the clitoral area.

Mons Veneris (mǒnz věn' ěr ǐs). *Mons Veneris* is Latin for "Mount of Venus." It is a small cushion of fat to serve as a shock absorber over the pubic symphysis (the bony prominence above the peak of the *labia majora*). Caresses in this area are quite pleasing.

—From Ed Wheat, M.D., and Gaye Wheat, *Intended for Pleasure*, Rev. ed. Old Tappan, N.J.: Revell, 1981.

Male

The two *testes* are the male reproductive glands. They hang in an external pouch (the scrotum), which is below and behind the penis. Each testis is a flattened oval in shape, about one and three-quarter inches long and one inch wide.

The scrotum is divided into two separate compartments (scrotal sacs), one for each testis. (Usually the left testis hangs lower than the right, and its scrotal sac is slightly larger.)

The testes make a male sex hormone, testosterone, and sperm cells, which are the male reproduction cells. The sperm cells are needed to fertilize the egg in the female body, if new life is to be produced.

The *epididymides* are found one alongside each testis. A number of small tubes lead to each epididymis from its testis. In the epididymides the young sperm cells (spermatocytes) are stored and develop into mature sperm.

The *vas deferens* are the two tubes—one from each testis—that carry sperm from the testes to the prostate gland. They are about sixteen inches long, and wind upwards from the scrotum into the pelvic cavity. They come together and join with the urethra tube just below the bladder.

The *prostate gland* surrounds the junction of the vas deferens and urethra tubes. Here the sperm cells are mixed with seminal fluid: the liquid in which the sperms are carried out of the body. The resulting mixture is semen: a thick whitish fluid.

The *seminal vesicles* make part of the seminal fluid that the prostate gland mixes with the sperm cells. More seminal fluid is made by the prostate gland itself.

The *urethra* is the tube that carries urine from the bladder to the penis. It is S-shaped and about eight inches long. In the prostate gland it is joined by the vas deferens—so it is also the route by which the semen reaches the penis from the prostate gland.

The *penis* is inserted into the female body during copulation. Most of the penis is made up of spongy tissue, loosely covered with skin.

The urethra tube enters the penis from the body and runs inside it to the tip of the penis.

The external opening in the tip (the meatus) is where semen or urine leaves the body.

In its natural state, the sides of the penis near its tip are covered by a fold of skin, called the foreskin. But this is often removed—usually because of religious or social custom, shortly after birth, but sometimes for medical reasons.

—From The Diagram Group, *Man's Body*. New York: Simon & Schuster, 1981.

FOR FURTHER READING:

Padus, Emrika. *The Woman's Encyclopedia of Health and Natural Healing.* Emmaus, Pa.: Rodale, 1981.

Penner, Clifford and Joyce. *The Gift of Sex.* Waco, Tex.: Word Books, 1981.

Wheat, Ed, M.D. and Gaye Wheat. *Intended for Pleasure*, Rev. ed. Old Tappan, N.J.: Revell, 1981.

SHYNESS

EVEN THOUGH it is common and seen among both rich and poor, shyness is hard to define and not easy to change. By nature, some people tend to be quiet and gentle. They don't feel a need to participate actively in conversations, and they aren't worried about communicating with strangers. These people don't worry about shyness. Others seem to like their shyness. It lets them be "reserved" or "unassuming" and they can enjoy life without the pressures of being noticed.

Very often, however, the shy person is anxious and uncomfortable, at least sometimes. He or she holds back because of insecurity, fear of embarrassment, and a poor self-image. In addition, the Stanford researchers discovered that eighty-five percent of all shy people feel self-conscious— strongly preoccupied with themselves and with the reactions of other people.

All of this would suggest that shyness is a tendency—sometimes mild, often strong—to pull away from others because we feel awkward, fearful, or insecure. According to psychologist Phillip Zimbardo, perhaps the world's greatest expert on this subject, the shy person is really afraid of people, especially people who are threatening for some reason: strangers because of their novelty or uncertainty, authorities because they wield power, or acquaintances who might criticize if we make a social blunder or say something stupid. Perhaps all of us feel at least a little uncomfortable and shy when we meet people who seem to be better dressed, more sophisticated, healthier, or smarter than we are. How common it is to feel uneasy around those who have traveled a lot, are superb hostesses, retain a trim figure, converse without apparent nervousness, or seem to be "on top" of every social situation. Such peo-

ple don't mean to intimidate others, but they often make the rest of us feel very inadequate. When we feel inadequate and threatened, we hold back. That holding back is shyness.

For some people, shyness is so strong and gripping that it can only be dislodged and overcome with the help of a professional counselor. Most of us, however, can rise above shyness on our own or with the help of a friend, especially if we understand and seek to apply some simple principles.

1. *Decide to Change.* Have you ever noticed how much we are influenced by labels? A teacher, parent, or coach may tell us that we are "clumsy," "stupid," or "nervous," and, without giving it much further thought, we believe the labels and act as if they were true.

I wonder how often shyness starts with such a label? A child who is quiet, sensitive, self-conscious, lonely, or—like Carol Burnett—"poor and not very pretty," is often assumed to be shy. Since powerful adults believe this and state it clearly, the child accepts the "shyness" label as well and it sticks for life. Shyness, then, can become an excuse for withdrawing and not reaching out to people. We assume that shyness is inborn, when really it is a pinned-on label that we have meekly accepted without question.

It is probably that our society teaches people to be shy. In countries like China and Israel, shyness is not very common because children are made to feel special, are encouraged to express their ideas freely, and are not in competition with each other. In contrast, Germans, Japanese, Taiwanese, and Americans tend to be more shy, presumably because of an emphasis on competition and the need for approval.

Whatever the reason for our reticence, we're not likely to change until we decide to be different. Those Stanford researchers discovered that shyness, even of the most severe variety, has been and can be changed, but to start we must get rid of the idea that improvement is impossible.

2. *Work at Overcoming Fear.* If shyness

413

is really a fear of people and social situations, it would follow that to reduce shyness we must remove our fears.

Most of us aren't shy when we are at home or when we are doing a job that we know well. Shyness more often comes when we are with people whom we don't know and in situations that are filled with uncertainty.

Think, for example, about how hard it is to apply for a job. The prospective employer is a stranger, and we're in a situation over which we have no control. We fear that we might be embarrassed or rejected by the interviewer, and because of this fear, the little courage which we do take into the personnel office quickly melts like ice on a balmy spring day.

It can be helpful, therefore, to practice the job interview ahead of time. Think about how you will dress and what you will say. You might have to *imagine* yourself going to the office and asking for the interview—before you bring yourself to walk up to the door in person.

Strange as it may seem, it sometimes helps to practice the interview with a friend who tries to act like a personnel manager. You might even pretend to be the interviewer who interviews you. What would you look for in yourself? This is not reality, of course, but there is evidence to suggest that when people *act* with confidence and a calm manner they begin to feel more self-assured—and less shy.

Everybody knows that young children are most often afraid when they are alone. It's the same with adults. We find it easier to attend a party, explore a new shopping center, start college, or visit a different church when someone else goes with us. (Job hunting is often harder because we have to do it by ourselves.) If you can find an understanding friend to help you conquer shyness, the battle will be easier.

As Christians, of course, we already have a friend who is with us at all times. The Bible says nothing about shyness, but it does talk about fear. We read that the perfect love of Christ "casts out" fear, and gives us the confidence to go on. Prayer, therefore, is important if we hope to experience the divine help which enables us to overcome the fear of people and social situations.

3. *Talk to Yourself.* Most of us go through life talking to ourselves. Usually we don't do this out loud, but silently we are constantly making plans, evaluating the world around us, and repeating ideas about what we think we are like.

I wonder how often we create our own problems by telling ourselves things which aren't true. We don't always wait for other people to label us. Over and over again we tell ourselves "I'm no good, I'm a failure, I'm less capable than other people, I'll never succeed." These ideas undercut our own self-esteem, eat away our self-confidence, and increase our shyness.

Several years ago some psychologists proposed a deceptively simple technique called *thought stopping.* As soon as you become aware of a self-defeating thought, say "Stop!"—out loud if nobody else is around. Then try to direct your attention to something else. At first the thoughts will come tumbling into your mind with increasing frequency, but before long they will be less common.

It also helps if you challenge your own thoughts. Who says you are shy? Have you really got good reasons to believe that you are stupid or incompetent? Maybe you've been convincing yourself of some things which aren't true.

Many psychologists believe that we also can counter self-destructive talk by trying to create a "positive mental attitude." For some people, this may work but surely it is better to ponder realistically how we can think. It's realistic to recognize that we have been created by God and are individuals whom he loves with no strings attached. When we confess our sins and failures, he forgives. When we admit that Jesus Christ is God's son, he adopts us as his children and gives us special gifts and abilities which allow us to serve him. We then have every reason to tell ourselves: "I'm not junk. I'm a child of the King. I can do all things through Christ who gives me strength."

That's realistic self-talk. It builds self-confidence and strengthens self-esteem. Research has shown that low self-esteem and shyness go together. When we begin to get a realistic picture of our self-worth as followers of Christ, our self-esteem goes up and shyness begins to fade. That's a message worth telling ourselves and others.

4. *Reach out to Others.* At the end of her interview, Carol Burnett was asked if the experience with shyness had taught her anything which might be passed on to others.

"I tell my three daughters," she replied, "that other people have the same problems you have and not to be so selfish as to think the world revolves around what people think about you. They're not always evaluating and judging you in critical ways. They're thinking about themselves." You have to reach out to people because "when we touch another person ... we are helping ourselves."

Sometimes I think many of us are too introspective and concerned about our own problems. The Bible puts a lot of emphasis on helping others, and it may be that this is the best way for handling shyness.

Do you remember those young people in China and Israel? They tended to be less shy because their parents and teachers gave encouragement and love. There were no "put downs" because somebody's science project wasn't perfect, and there was little concern about who was the best hostess or the most capable student. Mutual caring removed shyness from the kids and probably from the parents as well.

Shyness is more likely to appear when we think we will be evaluated. When we reach out to help and encourage others, their reactions and evaluations hardly concern us, and we feel less shy.

One of my favorite Bible figures is Barnabas. Little is known about him except that he had a reputation for encouraging people. I'd be willing to bet that Barnabas wasn't shy.

—GARY R. COLLINS, chairman of the Division of Pastoral Counseling and Psychology at Trinity Evangelical Divinity School, Deerfield, Ill.

SINGLENESS

THERE ARE various reasons why many girls do not marry. Some prefer to be single. They may have witnessed the unhappiness of their own parents or other married couples, and so do not wish to get "tangled up in that kind of a mess." Some women do not want to sacrifice career ambitions, while others avoid marriage because they cherish their independence. Still others feel that it is not in God's plan for them. But many single girls are not hesitant to express keen disappointment in their fate. In the correspondence that comes to my office each day, it is not uncommon to find a letter from a girl lamenting the fact that she is not married. But for every such letter, we receive several others from women who are married but wish they weren't.

Why does marriage by-pass many fine girls who would like to get married? Some girls are left out because they live in communities or attend churches where there are actually very few men their age. Others miss marriage because they are shy and retiring. More aggressive girls demand the male attention and carry through until they reach the altar.

Still others do not marry because they are expected to care for parents or other family members. They are not free to venture away from the home base, or to make the necessary move to meet eligible men.

The unmarried girl who does assume responsibility for her parents is sometimes forgotten by her brothers and sisters who marry and raise families of their own. They seem to take her for granted and expect her to shoulder parental responsibility by herself.

. . .

Another reason some girls never marry is that they price themselves out of the range of most men. Always looking for a man who measures up to their unrealistic ideal, they let the years slip by without meeting their "Dream Prince." Idealism is fine, but one can go to the extreme. Some girls forget that they themselves are not perfect. This immature point of view has eliminated many who might otherwise have been happily married. Such a visionary ideal may be suitable at sweet sixteen, but it hardly fits into the thinking of one who is an adult. Nevertheless, some women never erase the image of their youth, and all through life they go on searching for an idol of enchantment who does not exist except in the world of their dreams.

.   .   .

Many girls have side-stepped marriage in their choice to follow a career. Business, medicine, law, science, education, Christian service, arts and other fascinating fields present a tempting challenge for many other capable women.

One of the unpleasant ramifications which confronts those who are single is the feeling of being left out. So often there is no place for them. "It is a couple's world," insists Lila. "When you are single, you are a fifth wheel. You don't quite fit."

Another problem faces those who are not married. There is little outlet for love and affection. Although this need may be met to some degree when a woman throws her energies into her interests, hobbies or work, the desire for a family—for a husband and for children—is still unfulfilled. The quest for love and a family often presents serious problems for the woman who is unmarried.

—From Clyde M. Narramore, *A Woman's World.* Grand Rapids: Zondervan, 1963.

Acceptance

I like to wear big, bright hats. I have been known to apply butterfly decals at random over my car. I climbed halfway across the top of Victoria Falls. I've experienced the exhilaration of having my head in the clouds as I flew over the Texas countryside in an old Navy Steerman (an open cockpit biplane). I have a wide circle of friends from newborns to my ninety-seven-year-old grandmother, from a nuclear physicist to a Batonga Chief. I admit it. My life is rich, full, and exciting.

But I also confess that there are times

when I've cried myself to sleep. I've felt utterly alone and desolate. I've had "proof" that nobody really cared, and I've longed with aching intensity for someone with whom to share life. I plead guilty to refraining from doing some things I really want to do because I can't find anyone to do them with me. At such times of loneliness, hurt, and self-pity, I find it easy to believe that these things are due to being single. However, during times of more objective appraisal, I have to conclude that if the "down" things I've just mentioned are due to my singleness, then the "up" things I mentioned first must be also.

In my travels I've visited and talked with people from Tokyo to Cusco and from Katmandu to Capetown. I find hurting, aching loneliness just as prevalent among people who have a spouse, several spouses, or who had a series of spouses, as among those who have or have had no spouse. Thus I am forced to conclude that loneliness is part of being human.

Even though loneliness is part of the human condition, there is still, in many parts of the world, a stigma attached to being single. Several months ago, I had an exhilarating encounter with a woman who'd spent twelve years of her life being considered "unclean" by her people. In addition to her physical hurting, she had suffered social and psychological pain. I met this woman in the Bible, in Matthew 9:20, and saw in her situation an analogy to those persons in our world who do not conform to the "normal pattern" of marriage and, therefore, are misfits. The woman in Matthew 9 had heard about someone who could help her, but because of her affliction she could not publicly approach Christ to openly request healing. Her one hope lay in unobtrusively getting close enough to touch him.

Amazingly, in that great crowd thronging around Jesus, she managed to do just that. Perhaps it was because people who knew her stepped aside when they saw her, for if she touched them, they too would become "unclean." Jesus' back was turned, for he was on his way to restore a dead girl to life. But what about this woman who had suffered for twelve years? Hers was not the kind of ailment that caused death. But it did maim and cripple and keep her from truly living. So she touched the hem of his garment and she straightened up—a whole person at last! But her world came crushing down around her as Jesus demanded to know who had touched him. She didn't know then that Jesus wanted to affirm her action and confirm her wholeness, not condemn her.

It is easy for us singles to feel so maimed by our lives that we do not see the Master, or if we do set out to meet him, to get hung up in the crowd. It's hard work to wiggle through the crowd without others suspecting our hurt or without our facade getting damaged or knocked askew. I am not suggesting that we need to let our hurts hang out all over the place. Rather, I am suggesting that Christ wants to heal the hurt.

From my own experience and from talking to and counseling with many others, I find that coming to accept singleness is a step-by-step journey. As we make that journey, some people turn aside from us because our singleness is something they don't know how to deal with. Others get in the way, trying to get us married off. A pleasant, attractive, thirty-ish man visited a church where I was conducting a singles seminar. He told me that Sunday evening services at his own church had become a problem because various friends frequently brought along two or three "eligible" women for him to meet. Such an "auction block" atmosphere made him feel embarrassed.

First Step: Rebellion

The journey to acceptance of singleness usually begins with rebellion. This is the "mad at the whole world" stage. Refusing to accept the possibility of being single for the rest of one's life, one strikes out at oneself but often hits others in the process.

The stage of rebellion is exemplified by the woman whose attitude says, "I'm going to get married, no matter what."

Also in the rebellion stage would be the man who has been described as a "Welsh rarebit trying to act like a Don Juan, smug in the confidence that he is God's gift to women."

Second Step: Depression

A step beyond rebellion is depression. At this stage, one feels like a reject. It is the "something's wrong with me, I just don't have what it takes" feeling. As one writer put it, "Nobody chose me; I didn't make it. Somebody else was just a little something more. . . ." For some Christians this depression stage may also be connected with a "mad at God" stage. Recently a tearful woman passionately confessed, "I am a committed Christian. I have devotions every day, and I am vitally involved in the church. But right now I'm mad at God. I gave him all I have and he turns around and withholds from me someone to love and care for. He sees that I really need a husband. Why doesn't he let me have one?"

Third Step: Rejection

The step beyond depression, a passive response to not making it, frequently takes one to the more active form of rejection. It says, in effect, that since I didn't make it from "single file to center aisle" I'm going to reject all aisles—left, right, and center. This rejection sometimes takes the form of denial of the desire for marriage. That denial may be expressed in many ways, from an overt, brassy, "Marriage? Who needs it?" to a more subtle bragging, "What could a man add to my life that I don't already have?" I must admit that there are times when, faced with the perpetual question about my lack of a spouse, I am tempted to sarcasm: "Since there obviously aren't enough men to go around, I thought I'd be noble and leave them for those like you who really need them."

FOURTH STEP: REPRESSION

The rejection of marriage is no longer overt and obvious. Now, marriage is something one simply does not think about. The repressed desires, however, come out in many ways. For some it takes the form of sublimation to a job or a career. As I look back now, I have to admit that part of my motivation for getting a doctorate ran something like, "Anyone can get a husband, but not everyone can get a Ph.D." Sometimes repression is expressed through constantly driving to be on top, getting one degree after another, and/or striving for continuous achievement or constant recognition.

For some singles, repression takes the form of playing martyr to parents or other obligations. Someone has well said that the role of martyr might be enjoyable for the person playing it, but it is boring to everyone else. This stage of repression basically involves keeping life so full that feelings do not have time to intrude. Because they are so busy and their life is so full, some singles at this stage may be perceived by others or even perceive themselves as being satisfied with singleness.

FIFTH STEP: ACCEPTANCE

But real satisfaction can only come with the next step: acceptance. I believe that it is impossible to attain this stage without some degree of self-acceptance. In this area the Christian has a tremendous advantage. God created us as we are and he loves us and accepts us as we are. Realizing this frees us from the drive to *make* ourselves acceptable.

There is frequently a crisis time when acceptance comes. It does not come easily and some struggle harder than others. But acceptance comes only at the point where we can honestly say to the Lord: "Okay, I really prefer to be married. That is what society expects, and that's what people who have made it seem to have. I'd like to be in that group, but if it is your will for me to be sin-

gle, I accept that. It's not what I would have chosen, but if you have chosen it for me, then it must be good."

The stage of acceptance seems to be more easily achieved by those who have had the chance to say "no" or have received a negative reply to an invitation to marry. For the woman who feels like she must wait to be chosen, there is an additional sense of helplessness and hopelessness. Still, she should remember that while she may not be able to choose to marry, she does have the freedom to choose not to marry. Each person has likely had some opportunity which could have led to marriage. Nearly anyone can find a spouse if just anyone will do. So whether your choice is due to a clear leading of the Lord, an I-hate-the-opposite-sex syndrome or idealism, you are single by choice.

At the end of a singles retreat, one person put it this way: "I'll take back with me . . . greater satisfaction with being single, seeing that I have chosen singleness as an option." Acceptance comes when you decide as Elva McAllister's delightful book suggests that for whatever reason or duration you are *Free to Be Single.*

To achieve that fifth step is as far as many people ever get. In fact, most people are not aware that there is anything more. I would like to suggest that acceptance gets us within reaching distance, but really touching the hem of Jesus' garment involves another step.

SIXTH STEP: AFFIRMATION

This step says not only that I am single by choice, but that I am comfortable about that choice. It is not just a downhill slide that I cannot prevent. Rather, it is a deliberate walk with the Lord. Indeed, it often becomes an uphill climb but as long as the Lord and I are in it together, that's all that matters. One of my acquaintances, in a note to me put it this way: "I am satisfied with singleness because I look at it as God's *BEST* for me [now]." Her friend wrote, "God has a plan for my life, and now as a single person I am more free to be used of him in areas that I could not be if I were married."

partment of Behavioral Science at Messiah College.

Loneliness

Loneliness can be a severe problem for singles and one that God can help the person to handle. I watched a friend and business colleague wrestle with this. His second marriage had failed. He had been accustomed to coming home to lots of activity. Two preschool boys filled the house with clamor and variety. Now he entered a quiet apartment. Drapes were still closed as he'd left them. There was no clutter to step over, no noisy greeting. Ingenious decorating, carpeted walls and expensive sculptures did not crowd out loneliness. He connected a television to the light switch. Walking in the door would no longer be so overwhelmingly silent.

SEVENTH STEP: CELEBRATION

When the hurting is stopped and we can face life whole, we can take the next step of celebration: not only being comfortable about the choice, but actually thankful for it—able to say, "I am glad the Lord has allowed me to be single these years. In the future many things may change, even my marital status, but for now, I'm glad I'm single. I'm not going to squander that privilege by wasting my time moping around for a spouse to justify my existence, nor will I waste precious moments dreaming about what might have been or may yet be. Rather, I'll celebrate by living each moment to the fullest now."

These are the seven steps to becoming satisfyingly single. Let me hasten to point out that having once been healed and able to face life whole does not mean that there will never be any more problems or hurt or pain. But it does mean that having experienced wholeness we know the steps to retrace when those hurts and problems come. It is probably accurate to say that we go through these steps in cycles. I'm not even sure that they are mutually exclusive. At various times we'll work through our personal acceptance of singleness from "No Way!" (rebellion) through "Yuk!" (depression), past "Count Me Out," (rejection), beyond "Duh!" (repression) to "Okay" (acceptance), and even on to "Right On!" (affirmation), with an occasional "Whoopee!" (celebration).

While not easy, it is possible for singles to be satisfied—even to the point of celebrating their choice of singleness. For Christians, the most important person in their lives was single for all thirty-three years of his earthly life. Whatever one's marital status, life with him can indeed be a celebration.

—DOROTHY GISH, professor of early childhood and family education and chairman of the De-

Many married people also experience loneliness. I asked several women whom they considered their best friend. Not one had a prompt answer. After a long pause, a few named their husbands. A surprising number did not consider their husbands as intimate friends. From the description of their relationships, the husbands sounded more like persons with whom their lives had become entangled, men they would not have married if they had known what they know now. Some would have married the same man, but would have done many things differently. One husband and wife never talk about their feelings. They have not been "one flesh" for over seven years. Each is lonely.

NEEDS

God created each woman. Because He has complete knowledge, He is aware of who will marry and who will remain single. He knows how long a woman will be married and all about the person she will marry. Knowing a woman will remain single does not prevent God from giving her emotional needs that usually are only fulfilled in marriage. God's promises apply to every believer. When He says He will supply all our needs, this applies to the happily married, unhappily married, and the unmarried.

One of the greatest needs of any woman, of any person, is self-worth. In our society, a woman has traditionally been thought to gain worth through marriage. The single woman may feel that she has no significant place in a family-oriented society. However, the needs for self-worth are the same, for marrieds and unmarrieds, as well as the need to be needed and important to another.

—From Mariam Neff, *Discover Your Worth.* Wheaton, Ill.: Victor Books, 1979.

Sexuality

Human sexuality is not something apart from ourselves; it is what we are, our very essence. It is expressed in everything we do. It is the source of most of life's richest joys and fulfillments. God does not deny any of us the enjoyment or development of our sexuality. Christian singles are only denied the genital expression of sexuality; in all other ways we are free to express it to the utmost. And that "utmost" has a very broad scope.

Not that such denial is a small thing. But it is possible, and with God's help, it need not be devastating. It can even be enriching. One thing it is guaranteed to do for us if we are Christians: it will keep us clinging personally and purposefully to God for the rest of our lives. Who are we to dare to refuse a gift like that?

The enjoyment of sexuality, in ourselves and in others, is one of God's loveliest gifts. Those who for Jesus' sake have freely relinquished all right to the pleasures of its physical expression will not find themselves lacking in glad, life-affirming enjoyment of sexuality. In spite of this fact—maybe even because of it—they may develop a depth and richness of personhood, a self-fulfilling experience of life, a quality of self-giving service, a totality of being, as great as or even greater than if they had married.

Such fruition, of course, is not automatic. It springs from our total response to God, which consists of thousands of smaller responses, including our responses to our singleness. We all know Christian singles of whom such fruition is true, and others of whom it is not. Which we are depends on what we do with what we have, and on our personal relationship to God.

—From Margaret Clarkson, *So You're Single.* Wheaton, Ill.: Shaw Pubs., 1978.

FOR FURTHER READING:

Fix, Janet, with Zola Levitt. *For Singles Only.* Old Tappan, N.J.: Revell, 1978.

Hensley, J. Clark. *Coping with Being Single Again.* Nashville: Broadman, 1978.

Smoke, Jim. *Suddenly Single.* Old Tappan, N.J.: Revell, 1982.

Yates, Martha. *Coping.* Englewood Cliffs, N.J.: Prentice-Hall, 1976.

SKIN

Care

When someone looks into our faces, the first thing he sees is our skin. Either it glows healthily and attracts others, or it sags, wrinkles, flakes, breaks out and ruins our whole appearance.

Some of us think we can cure any kind of skin trouble with layers of makeup. But blemishes and dark spots will show through even the thickest foundation creams. Wrinkles, once they have arrived, will not disappear without plastic surgery.

Makeup can help an already-healthy skin look more lovely, but it is no substitute for a good complexion. In order to present a glowing face to the world, you must first concentrate on basic skin care programs that will prevent blemishes and wrinkles. Only then can you make the most of cosmetics.

If we are to reflect the Lord's glory and let Him make us more like Himself, we will want to present to others not just a clean face, but a radiant one, a face that attracts rather than repels.

In today's world, a poor complexion and pale cheeks and lips are ways of causing eyes to turn away from us. An unattractive skin, like a lighthouse with mud-splattered windows, keeps our inner radiance from shining through to those we want to help.

To look our best for God, we may want to shower, dress, comb our hair and apply color to our faces *before* we have our daily quiet time with Him. (But isn't it wonderful to know that He accepts us just the way we are—pin curls, sleepy eyes and all?)

If we know that we look our best, we will be ready to forget ourselves and use our lives in serving the Lord. We are going to look at some ways to improve our complexions in this chapter, so that we can look as lovely as possible.

Skin sins are real, and you may be causing many of them because you don't know what to do to avoid blemishes, dark spots, wrinkles and shiny noses. There is a way for these skin sins to be forgiven. But, just as in our spiritual lives, the first step—a willingness to change—must be taken by us.

Joanne Kanoff, owner of a skin salon, developed the lecture on skin care which I use in my course, and she is also the consultant for this chapter. Skin is the most extensive of your body's organs. It protects the inner organs from foreign elements and helps the body regulate its own temperature.

Your face constantly produces dead cells that must be removed, so you should use either a good scrub or a mask. You must keep your face scrupulously clean. If you apply a used washcloth, a dirty powder puff or even a perspiring hand to your face, you may infect the oil glands that lubricate the skin. Then you will have blemishes.

Your skin also serves to register your emotional state. If you are embarrassed, you blush; if you are angry, you may flush; and if you are frightened, you may turn pale. If you are under stress or excited, you may find your skin telling the world by breaking out in blemishes. Your skin may also register the

fact that your diet is poor, your hormones out of balance, or that you smoke or drink.

One of my students had a perfect complexion as a teenager, but after a few years of marriage, her face erupted with angry red splotches. She and her husband had both used their charge cards so frequently that they were receiving embarrassing phone calls and threats from bill collectors. Stress was causing her blemishes. When she and her husband went to a credit counselor and began finding a way to pay off their debts, her face began to clear up magically, too.

A lot of women buy skin products, use them two to three days, then leave them unopened in their medicine cabinets for two weeks at a time. They wonder why their skin does not improve. You must develop a fixed routine, then follow it every morning and night if you want a lovely skin.

WRINKLES, AGE SPOTS AND YOU

Here is a little bit of wisdom to help you remember the importance of skin care:

At the age of twenty, you have the face God gave you.

At forty, you have the face you are working on.

At sixty, you have the face you deserve.

Our skin is much like a flower. We can either care for the complexion God has given us, we can work on it and make it still more beautiful—or we can neglect it and let it shrivel like a rose hip on a thorny stem.

Most of us live in climates where hot, drying sunshine shrivels our skin and splotches it with chloasmata—those yellowish or yellowish-brown patches sometimes called age or liver spots. Cold winter wind also tends to dry out the moisture in our faces. And the ultraviolet rays of the sun may further age our complexions.

There is a theory that the sun's ultraviolet rays are becoming stronger because we have destroyed the layer of ozone that used to screen them from the earth. While this theory has not been proven, it is a fact that dermatologists are finding more dehydration, skin cancers and chloasmata than ever before, and these skin problems are occurring at earlier ages.

As much as we all love the sun and the great outdoors, we should be aware that they can cause many skin problems. If you don't believe this, notice how the areas of your body that are usually covered by clothing remain soft, unwrinkled and ageless. Then compare them to your hands, which are often exposed to the elements. What a difference! In the middle-Eastern countries where women wear veils on their faces, youthful complexions are retained even into advanced age.

By now you may be wondering if it is possible to sunbathe at all. (Who wants to remain cooped up in the house all summer, looking like some spongy-white toadstool, while others go around gorgeously tanned?) The answer is yes, but tan slowly. However, most of us don't have the patience to do that. We want a glorious brownness all at once.

The best way to sunbathe is to expose yourself to the sun only about ten minutes a day. Sun damage to your skin begins at the point when redness begins to appear. Burned skin is like a rubber band that has been left too long in the sun and becomes discolored. If you try to stretch this faded piece of rubber, it will break in two, simply because the elasticity has been destroyed. The natural elasticity of skin is destroyed when it begins to turn red. The face gets lined and leathery. Eventually it has wrinkles.

Age also causes wrinkles. But you don't have to look older than you are! So do protect yourself from the sun. There are many good sun screens on the market. When you choose one, be sure that it has a sun-screen ingredient called PABA. If you apply a sun block (a product that prevents the sun's rays from coming in contact with your skin), you will never burn or tan, for it offers virtually complete protection against the sun.

Many skin problems come from a combi-nation of taking drugs and exposing oneself to the sun. If you sunbathe while you are taking tranquilizers, you may find chloasma spots appearing on your skin. If you are taking tetracycline to cure your acne, your complexion may burn in patches, giving you a peculiar quilted look. Even aspirin combined with the sun's rays may adversely affect your skin. So stay out of the sun as much as possible while you are taking medications.

Prescriptions for high blood pressure, diabetes and epilepsy may cause skin problems even without exposure to the sun. Always ask your doctor what the side effects of drugs can be.

Nicotine makes the small blood vessels contract, preventing the skin from receiving the blood needed to nourish it. Smoking may increase your tendency to wrinkle. Alcoholic beverages can also affect skin tone and muscles.

Skin care routines must become a daily part of our lives, if we are to look our best. In the next section we'll look at ways of overcoming special problems.

Adequate moisture is essential for a healthy complexion and must be included in any good skin-care program. For instance, when you put a wrinkled, dried-up prune in a glass of oil, it remains as shriveled as ever. If you drop it into water, it plumps up, to become almost as juicy as the original plum. Your skin reacts the same way. Once it becomes dehydrated, only water can restore the moisture. It is true that creams, oils and waxy products will keep the water that is continually being supplied to the outer layers of the skin from evaporating. But they cannot add moisture. Only water can do that.

Air-conditioning and artificial heat continuously dry out our skin. No matter where we go, we can't escape a drying environment. We can restore humidity to a room simply by keeping a bowl of water in it. Better still, simmer a tea kettle on the stove during the winter. You might want to invest in a humidifier. It will make your face more dewy—and your house plants more luxuriant!

THE TROUBLE WITH BLEMISHES

If you are healthy and not under too much stress, if you eat correctly, have your hormones in balance, are not a teenager, and care for your face properly—you probably have no blemishes. But every woman should learn how to care for her skin correctly.

Your complexion has many pores, which are designed to bring oil from the tiny glands at their base to the surface of your skin. Both a whitehead and a blackhead result when a pore becomes plugged. A thin layer of skin covers the top of the whitehead. Whiteheads may be caused by stress or diet.

Blackheads do not have a layer of skin over them. The darkness of the blackhead is caused when the chemicals in the oil of the skin touch the oxygen in the air. This is a chemical reaction. Many people think that a person who has blackheads is dirty. This is not necessarily true. However, the oil in the plugged pore does attract dirt, dust and pollutants from the air. When you press the telephone into your face as you talk, wash with a dirty facecloth or even touch your skin with your hands (even though you just washed them), you are transferring dirt into the open pores.

A blemish (pimple) is a blackhead or a whitehead which has become infected and inflamed, and if you pick or squeeze it, you simply inflame it further. You may spread the infection into your bloodstream, which may then carry the germs elsewhere, causing more blemishes.

If you really can't bear to be seen with a blemish, put warm compresses on it to bring it to a head. *Sterilize* a needle, open the blemish, and allow it to drain by itself. Squeezing can cause scarring.

Another type of blemish, rather uncommon but still possible, is a pocket of oil which collects under the skin. It may result from eating too many dairy or other fatty foods.

Stress-caused blemishes are usually hard, deep, and so painful that they often throb when you bend over. These seldom come to a head. A dermatologist might prescribe tranquilizers for this type of problem. Be sure to ask what the long-range effects will be.

The reason that stress causes blemishes is that your emotions can cause the glands in your skin to secrete oil rapidly and in spurts. The gland becomes plugged with oil below the surface. Many women who never broke out as teenagers start erupting with blemishes at age thirty or so—about the time that they have to care for several small children, a home and a husband.

Good nutrition is a must for a blemish-free skin, just as it is needed for a healthy body. If you have blemishes, you probably should avoid salt, sugar and caffeine. Everyone reacts differently to foods, of course, but many people find that chocolate and cola drinks also cause blemishes.

Be sure to eat plenty of proteins and green, leafy vegetables. Try taking a multiple vitamin. Above all else, avoid greasy foods, such as French fries and hamburgers. Your face could be affected by animal fats even if you don't eat them. If you merely work in a greasy environment, such as a fast-food restaurant, you could develop blemishes.

Skin cells repair themselves while we are asleep, so try to get plenty of rest. If you drink six to eight glasses of water daily and have the proper elimination of food wastes, you should see an improvement in your face within two weeks. To give your skin a clear, healthy look, get plenty of daily exercise so that the blood will flow into your face and cleanse it.

WHICH PRODUCT TO BUY

Beyond following good health rules, the most important thing you can do to stay free of blemishes, wrinkles and other skin problems is to follow a regular program of cleansing your face with cosmetics that are right for you. A good skin-care program always includes daily cleansing, freshening and moisturizing.

It is a good idea to use a scrub or mask at

least once a week. Some women prefer a mask because they feel that the granules in the scrub tend to enlarge the pores and cause dryness. On the other hand, others find that the scrub actually helps cleanse their pores of soil, while removing dead skin. You must find what works best for you. My skin-care teacher prefers a scrub to a mask, because it requires less time.

There are at least two philosophies about which kind of cosmetics to use. For instance, a product that contains waxes and fillers may be up to 80 percent effective as a sun screen and thus may in time prevent many sun-produced wrinkles. However, these waxes and fillers are considered by others to be harmful to the skin. This opposite view maintains that these ingredients clog and enlarge one's pores, and thus recommends a water-based or water-soluble product. The view that water-based cosmetics actually replace the water that evaporates from the skin—and thus help prevent dryness and wrinkles—is supported by most major cosmetic companies.

Eliminate the use of deodorant soaps on your face. Since they kill the natural bacteria that protect your skin, all kinds of foreign bacteria and fungi are free to invade.

Regular household soaps can be harmful, too. They are very alkaline (and hence very drying). Many contain wax fillers or animal fats, which leave a scum on your skin that cannot be removed, even if you rinse thirty times!

If you must wash your face with soap, use a transparent complexion bar that is made especially for the face. However, most complexion bars contain a large amount of glycerine, which is too drying for most skin types.

WHAT KIND OF SKIN DO YOU HAVE?

Choosing a skin-care program depends on what kind of skin that you have.

Normal skin has a balance of oil and moisture on the surface. Oil comes through the pores and moisture through the sweat glands, to mix on the surface and produce a soft, smooth, dewy complexion. Normal skin seldom has blemishes. To keep it looking youthful, simply stay out of the sun, use good cosmetics and include a moisturizer.

Dry skin is very fine grained. It *feels* dry, taut and tight. Broken veins and dry, flaky patches may be seen. While you cannot see any pores, the skin feels coarse and looks thin.

If you are dry-skinned, avoid anything that will further dehydrate your complexion—such as alkaline soaps. Even water is slightly alkaline. Dry skin requires more emollients, because as the water evaporates from the cells, the cells collapse. The result is wrinkles. Try to keep moisture on your face at all times, and add humidity to your home.

Oily skin shines all the time. There are usually large pores around the nose and chin. Frequently there are blackheads, whiteheads and blemishes. Sometimes there is acne, the most severe form of eruptions. Oily skin may appear sallow or yellowish in color and feel thick to the touch. The oily-skinned person may have few wrinkles, but those she does have will be deep. They result from using very strong and dehydrating cleansers, especially in the eye and neck area.

The goal should actually be to remove only the *excess* oil. By removing all the oil from the skin, the oily-skinned person will only cause her glands to start pumping oil at a faster rate. She may find that a lotion cleanser penetrates deeper than a cream cleanser. Oily skins require moisturizers just as much as do dry skins. There are non-oily moisturizers made especially for them.

Most oily-skinned people should use a scrub or a mask more frequently. These two products refine the pores, stimulate the circulation and help bring impurities to the surface.

Combination skin is the most common complexion type. Usually there is oily skin in the "T" area (forehead, nose, and chin). On the cheeks, eyes and neck lies drier skin. A heavy moisturizer would not be needed in the "T" area, but may be required elsewhere.

PRODUCTS AVAILABLE

Once you have chosen good products for your particular skin type, try to get *expert* help on how to use them (not necessarily the saleswoman). Let's look at some of the available products and how they should be used:

Cleanser—removes makeup, dirt and oil and also softens blackheads. Apply this product in an up-and-out movement on the cheeks and chin to avoid pulling your facial skin down and causing wrinkles. When working around the eye, use a circular motion. Start at the tear duct, move over the lid, around the outer corner and in toward the nose. Gentleness is important.

Scrub—designed to stimulate circulation, soften impurities, remove the dead cells.

Mask—designed to stimulate circulation, draw out impurities, tone and firm.

Freshener—removes excess cleanser and oil, may help normalize the pH balance after use of a cleanser. Fresheners help your face accept the moisturizer.

Moisturizer—adds water to skin cells, softens face, plumps cells.

Who should use these products? Virtually every girl from the age of thirteen on up—for it is the years between puberty and the mid-twenties when skin needs the most constant attention to preserve it for the later years.

Always be sure to use puffs made of 100 percent cotton to remove or put on makeup, rather than a dirty powder puff or a paper tissue. The powder puff will carry germs to your pores and create blemishes. The paper tissue contains wood fibers, which scratch the face and break the tiny blood vessels below the surface and may cause permanent damage. Many products which are labeled cotton puffs or cosmetic puffs actually contain part (or even all) synthetic fibers. Be sure that you choose only 100-percent cotton products.

Once you have mastered skin care, you are ready to consider makeup. But always remember, skin care must come before makeup!

—From Joanne Wallace, *The Image of Loveliness.* Old Tappan, N.J.: Revell, 1978.

FOR FURTHER READING:

Jackson, Carole. *Color Me Beautiful.* Washington: Acropolis, 1980.
Pierre, Clara. *Looking Good.* New York: Reader's Digest Press, 1976.
Wallace, Joanne. *Dress With Style.* Old Tappan, N.J.: Revell, 1983.
Wilhelmina. *The New You: How to Maximize Your Total Appearance.* New York: Simon & Schuster, 1978.

SLEEP

WE NEED SLEEP regularly or we become irritable and confused; the nervous system and the whole body are eventually affected. The need for sleep is greatest in infancy; a newborn infant sleeps most of the day. Young children should have eleven to twelve hours of sleep a night; for older children, ten hours is usually sufficient. Adults generally require six to eight hours of sleep. Difficulty in obtaining sufficient sleep is a common problem.

Dreaming: At intervals during sleep, the eyes of the sleeper move under his eyelids as if they were wide open and looking at moving objects. If the person is awakened at this stage, he can usually recall a vivid dream. If he is allowed to continue sleeping, he may later recall nothing. Four other distinct stages occur in normal sleep, marked by changes in electric activity in the brain, in breathing, and other vital signs.

The dreaming stage seems to be very important to our well-being. The subject matter of the few dreams we remember is often so strange and puzzling that we are tempted to try to find a meaning in them. According to PSYCHOANALYSIS, dreaming is a safety valve for repressed fears and desires.

—From *Family Health Guide and Medical Encyclopedia* prepared in association with Benjamin F. Miller, M.D. New York: Reader's Digest Association, 1970.

SOCIAL SECURITY

What the Woman Worker Should Know

A woman who works earns social security protection not only for herself but also for her family.

Even if she is single and has no dependents, the social security credits she earns while she works count toward monthly benefits for the family she may have in the future.

WHILE YOU WORK

You have social security disability and survivors insurance protection while you are working. This means that monthly benefits would be payable if you become disabled or die after having worked long enough under social security.

If you become disabled and can't work for a year or more, you can get disability checks. Your disability payments would start with the 6th full month of your disability—there's a 5-month waiting period for disability benefits—and would continue as long as you are disabled. When you've been eligible for disability payments for 2 consecutive years, you also will have Medicare protection.

(A note about Medicare: While you work, you also earn credits toward Medicare protection for yourself and your family in the event that you or they ever need dialysis treatment or a kidney transplant for permanent kidney failure.)

Your children can get benefits, too, when you're disabled. Under the social security

law, the term "children" includes stepchildren and legally adopted children. Monthly checks are payable to unmarried children who are under 18 (or under 22 if they are full-time students) and to children who became disabled before age 22 and remain disabled.

If he is 62 or older, your husband may qualify for payments when you're disabled.

Both your widower and your children can get monthly survivors checks if you should die. Survivors checks may be payable even if you only have 1½ years of work in the 3 years before you die.

If there are no children, your widower must be either 60 or older *or* between 50 and 60 and disabled to get survivors benefits on your work record.

There's also a lump-sum death payment of $255 that can help pay for funeral expenses.

And, if you have dependent parents 62 or older, they may be eligible for payments if you die.

IF YOU INTERRUPT YOUR CAREER

To get any social security benefits, you need credit for a certain amount of work. The amount of credit you need generally depends on your age when you become disabled, die, or retire. If you stop working before you earn enough social security credits, no benefits will be payable. But credits you have already earned remain on your work record, and you can always go back to work and earn any additional credits you need to get benefits.

This rule applies to both women and men. But it's particularly significant to a woman simply because she may prefer to stay home while she's raising children.

One thing to keep in mind, though, is that the amount of any monthly benefit payable on your record could be affected by years of no earnings. The amount of your benefit—and your family's benefits—is based on your covered earnings over a period of years. If several years of no earnings (or low earnings) have to be counted, then your benefit may be lower than what it would be if you worked throughout your life.

You can retire as early as age 62, if you want to take reduced benefits. Payments to people who retire before age 65 are permanently reduced to take account of the longer period of time they get checks.

If you wait until age 65 to retire, you get full retirement benefits.

If you're married, you can get retirement payments either on your own record or on your husband's. By the same token, your husband can get retirement benefits at 62 or older either on his record or on yours. But, whenever a person is eligible for benefits on more than one work record, the benefit payable is equal to the larger amount. (This same rule applies to children who are eligible for benefits when their parents retire.)

Of course, if you've worked all your adult life and had high earnings, it's likely that your own benefit will be higher than a wife's benefit. At 65, a wife gets 50 percent of what her husband is entitled to at 65. On the other hand, if you stopped working for several years or had low earnings, the wife's payment may be higher. When you apply for retirement benefits, the people in the social security office can tell you whether you will get a higher payment on your own record or on your husband's record.

A wife who has earned her own social security credits also has certain options at retirement. For example, suppose your husband continues to work past 65 and earns too much to get benefits. Or, suppose he's younger than you. You can go ahead and retire on your own record. Then, when he retires, you can take wife's payments if they would be higher.

Or regardless of your husband's age, you can take reduced benefits on your wage record before age 65. But remember, your payment will always be reduced—even if

you take reduced benefits on your own record and then take wife's benefits when your husband retires.

(NOTE: These same benefit rules and options apply to a husband who's eligible for retirement payments on both his own and his wife's work record.)

Finally, there's Medicare. If you are entitled to monthly social security benefits— either on your own record or on your husband's—you will have Medicare hospital insurance protection automatically at age 65. If you're not entitled to benefits, you'll need some credit for work under social security to get hospital insurance without paying a monthly premium.

To get Medicare medical insurance, you enroll for it and pay monthly premiums.

What a Wife Should Know

What about the woman who chooses to make her home and family her career?

She and her family have social security protection through her husband's work, and they can get benefits when he retires, becomes disabled, or dies.

Regardless of your age, you can get payments when your husband becomes disabled or retired if you are caring for a child under 18 or a disabled child who is entitled to benefits.

If you don't have a child in your care, you must be 62 or older to get benefits when your husband becomes disabled or retires.

If you get retirement benefits before 65, the payment amount is reduced. If you wait until age 65 to retire, you get the full wife's benefit, which is 50 percent of the amount your husband is entitled to at 65.

Both you and your husband will have Medicare hospital insurance at 65 if he is entitled to monthly benefits. You can enroll for medical insurance. You will have Medicare at 65 even if your husband is younger than you and still working, provided he is at least 62 and files an application to establish that he will be entitled to benefits when he retires. If your husband is deceased, you'll have Medicare if he would have been entitled to benefits or had worked long enough under social security.

(While your husband is working, he earns credits toward Medicare protection for your family in the event any of you ever need dialysis treatment or a kidney transplant for permanent kidney failure. Also, if he becomes disabled and is entitled to benefits for two years, he would have Medicare protection.)

WIDOW WITH CHILDREN

You can get a widow's benefit at any age if you are caring for a child who is under 18 or disabled and entitled to benefits. Survivors benefits on your husband's record are also payable to unmarried children under 22 who are fulltime students.

Your benefits will stop when you no longer have a child under 18 or disabled in your care. Usually, your benefits also will stop if you remarry before age 60. But, benefits to your children will continue as long as they remain eligible for payments—regardless of whether you remarry.

WIDOW WITHOUT CHILDREN

Even if you do not have dependent children when your husband dies, you can get widows benefits if you are 60 or older.

The amount of your monthly payment will depend on your age when you start getting benefits and the amount your deceased husband would have been entitled to or was receiving when he died.

Widows benefits range from 71½ percent of the deceased husband's benefit amount at age 60 to 100 percent at 65. So, if you start getting benefits at age 65, you'll get 100 percent of the amount your husband would be receiving if he were still alive.

If you're disabled, you can get widows benefits as early as age 50, but your payment will be reduced.

A point to remember: If you are entitled to retirement benefits on your own work record and you receive reduced widows benefits between age 50 and 62, your own retirement benefit at 65 also would be reduced.

REMARRIED WIDOW

Ordinarily, a widow loses her social security rights when she remarries. But, benefits to a widow (or widower) who remarries at 60 or older can continue without any reduction in the amount.

If your new husband gets social security checks, however, you can take a wife's benefit on his record if it would be larger than your widow's payment.

DIVORCEE

You can get benefits when your ex-husband starts collecting retirement or disability payments if you are 62 or older and were married to him at least 10 years.

You may also get payments if your ex-husband dies, provided you are 60 or older (50, if you're disabled) and you were married 10 years or more or you have young children entitled to benefits on his record.

MEDICARE FOR WIDOWS

If you are 50 or older, and you become disabled while getting checks because you have young children in your care, contact social security about eligibility for Medicare. Even though you haven't filed a claim for payments based on the disability (since you are already getting payments as a mother), you could be eligible for Medicare protection if you have been disabled for 2 years or longer.

Social security benefits payable to you when your husband retires or becomes disabled or dies may be reduced by the amount of any pension or annuity you receive based on your work in non-covered public employment.

The offset provision does not apply to wives or widows who would be eligible for public pensions by December 1982 and who qualify for social security dependents' benefits under the law in effect on January 1, 1977.

If You Change Your Name

One important thing to remember about social security is to make sure that your social security record shows your correct name. This is particularly important if you are employed because your employer reports your earnings under the name you give him or her.

Whenever you change the name you use in employment—whether because of marriage, divorce, or other reasons—you should report the change to social security. Otherwise, your earnings won't be properly recorded and you may not receive all the social security credit due you for your work.

Of course, if you choose to continue using your maiden name after marriage, as many women do today, you don't have to report your marriage. Just be sure you use your maiden name consistently throughout your employment.

Even if you don't work, you should report any name change so that your record will show the correct name when you apply for benefits.

To report a name change, all you have to do is fill out a *Request for Change in Social Security Records.* You can get this form at any social security office.

Any time you have questions or need additional information about social security or if you want to apply for benefits, just call one of our offices. The phone number is listed under Social Security Administration in your local telephone directory.

—From U.S. Department of Health, Education, and Welfare, *A Woman's Guide to Social Security.* HEW Publication No. (SSA) 79-10127, January, 1979.

SOUL HEALING

If you ask ten different people what inner healing or soul healing is, you might get ten different answers. They could all be correct, too, as each person would be looking at the subject from his or her own experience.

To me it is God restoring your soul as you learn to practice the presence of Jesus in the past, as well as in the present, and on into the future—helping you to forgive everyone, and setting you free to live at your fullest potential.

"A tall order," you may say. Maybe you won't walk this way constantly, but there are moments when it is possible, and the moments can turn into hours, and hours into days, as you reach for a goal which God has for you. A goal must be something you reach for or you won't stretch and grow.

No, it doesn't happen overnight, but we've been watching people change, sometimes slowly, sometimes with amazing suddenness, as their souls are healed. Jesus is the same in the past, present, and future (*see* Hebrews 13:8). God has been with you always, and He's with you now, but you have to "practice" realizing His presence.

Hope Howard, a daughter in Christ, describes the need for soul healing this way: "It's like having garbage in your kitchen," she says, "and instead of getting rid of it, you throw it into the basement!" As I thought about Hope's description, I realized that most of the garbage we're talking about in soul healing isn't from our own kitchen—it's been contributed by others! So I expanded her illustration a bit.

A person comes to your front door and knocks. You open it, and they hand you a bag of garbage. Not knowing what else to do, you accept it. Someone else knocks at the door, and the scene is repeated. Some of your callers just leave the garbage on the front steps without knocking! Soon your kitchen is overflowing, so you begin to put the bags in the basement. It isn't too long before your house begins to smell horrible!

There are two things you can do. You can grow accustomed to the smell and keep stuffing things into the basement (of your subconscious); or you can call for Jesus, the One who knows how to get rid of it. Just as you can produce rich soil by composting literal garbage, so Jesus, who always knows how to make something good out of something bad, can use the hurts you have suffered to bring you good (see Romans 12:21). The nasty stuff people have been dumping in your life can be used by Jesus to produce good, rich soil in which your life can grow.

What Soul Healing Isn't

I'll be giving further definitions of soul-healing prayer as we go along, but now let's consider a few things it isn't:

1. Soul healing is not reconfessing past sins. Corrie ten Boom teaches that our forgiven sins are cast in the sea of God's forgetfulness, to be remembered against us no more. By the sea, she says, is a little sign: NO FISHING ALLOWED. We're certainly not doing any of that kind of fishing! Those sacks of garbage of our own making—ones we've confessed—have already been handed over to Jesus. It would be silly to try to give something to Jesus that doesn't exist. However, the consequences and results of our wrongdoing, any damage done to others, require correction, and healing, too. And we often need help forgiving ourselves.

2. Soul healing isn't digging around in the basement of your subconscious, but letting God bring things to the main floor of your life as He chooses. Things which have seemingly been forgotten by the conscious mind can be festering in the

unconscious, sending up all kinds of problems. God brings the buried stuff to remembrance so He can heal it; then it loses its power to hurt. He can give us new feelings about the old scenes, so that when they are remembered, the pain is gone. Not only has the wound been cleansed, it's been healed as well.

3. Soul healing isn't giving advice, although as you pray with people, the Holy Spirit may give clearer insight into their problems. If they're looking for advice, they should be directed to qualified professionals: pastors, marriage counselors, doctors, psychologists, or psychiatrists instead of (or in addition to) soul-healing prayer.

4. Soul-healing prayer isn't a psychological gimmick. It doesn't give easy answers which avoid the Cross. It's a supernatural encounter with the crucified and resurrected Lord Jesus. "Certainly He has borne our griefs, and carried our sorrows. . . . He was whipped and bruised for our sins, took our punishment to bring us peace, and through His wounds we are healed" (Isaiah 53:4, 5, paraphrased). Any such healing received is through, in, and because of Jesus.

Faults Need Healing

Are we supposed to pray for others for healing of their souls? The King James Version of the Scripture, James 5:16, reads, "Confess your faults one to another, and pray for one another, that ye may be healed. . . ." [Dennis Bennett] says, "Almost every other translation of the New Testament reads, 'Confess your sins one to another.' The usual Greek word for 'sin' in the New Testament is hamartia. It occurs 172 times. But the word used in James 5:16 is paraptoma, which occurs only 23 times. It is translated 'sin' only four times in the King James Version. Six times it is translated 'offense,' nine 'trespasses,' twice 'fall,' and twice 'fault.' Arndt and Gingrich, in their Greek-English Lexicon of the New Testament, give as the first meaning of parap-

toma, 'a false step.' It can be used to indicate an error, a mistake in judgment, a blunder."

"It seems to me that the translators of the King James Version saw that it couldn't be *sins* we're to confess *to one another.* We confess our sins to *God;* and sins are not *healed,* they are *forgiven.* That's why the word is translated 'fault' rather than 'sin.' We are to admit our *faults* or weaknesses to one another, so we can pray to be *healed.*"

A "fault" is a *defect*—something you cannot help. A hurt in the soul that needs healing would be a "fault," not a sin, although if it is not healed, it can lead to sin.

If you have a faulty tire on your car, and you don't get it fixed, it may cause an accident. *Soul healing is praying for one another's faults to be healed so that there will not later be sins to be forgiven.* It's getting to the problem before the problem gets to you.

A Checklist for Soul Healing

Your soul needs healing if you have been hurt or damaged by another person, experience, or event outside your control. We're not yet living in heaven; we're exposed to the imperfections of ourselves and others, so we can safely say everyone to some degree has needed, presently needs, or will need healing for the soul.

Here is a checklist to help you recognize if you would benefit from healing prayer:

1. Were you greatly embarrassed when a child or young adult?
2. Can you see a pattern of hurtful events beginning early in your life, each building upon the other?
3. Do you have difficulty recalling anything about your childhood? Is it a total blank?
4. Do you wish you were someone else? Do you dislike yourself? Do you wish you had never been born?
5. Do you dislike the opposite sex, or your own sex?
6. Do you have a learning disability such as dyslexia, which was not diagnosed in childhood? Do you, or did you, have another kind of limiting handicap?
7. Are there habits ("besetting sins") that control you?
8. Do you have unreasonable fears?
9. Do you often find your reaction to something said or done is far beyond the stimulus?
10. Do you have a recurring memory of a past hurt? Does it still trouble you to think about it?
11. Are there people you can't forgive? Do you have trouble asking someone else to forgive you?
12. Do you have overwhelming feelings of guilt?
13. Do you find it nearly impossible to admit making a mistake? Do you usually look for someone to blame for what goes wrong in your life?
14. Do you have a nearly continuous feeling of anger inside? Are you usually critical in your remarks or thoughts about others?
15. Do you go on compulsive overeating or drinking binges? compulsive undereating binges?
16. Do you have a fantasy world you escape into?
17. Are you obsessed with sexual thoughts or fantasies?
18. Do you have a physical illness that has no known cause?
19. Do you suffer from depression frequently, or over long periods of time?
20. Do you have frequent nightmares, or troubling recurring dreams?
21. Do you have physical or mental exhaustion from wrestling with inner problems? Do you have difficulty sleeping, or do you want to sleep too much? (Check for physical causes, too.)
22. Are you extremely restless, "on the go" constantly? Unable to sit and relax from time to time? (There's a difference between a healthy "drive" and being driven.)
23. Are you a workaholic? Do you feel guilty if you aren't doing something

"productive"? Are you always striving for the approval of others?

24. Were you an adult before you ever felt loved by another person?

25. Do you often compare yourself with others and end up feeling inadequate and discouraged?

26. Do you have a constant need for physical affection, or do you not like to be touched at all?

27. Do you have a deep sense of inferiority? Do you feel unloved, unapproved of?

28. Do you have a hard time being consistent in your spiritual life?

29. Is it hard to believe God loves you or approves of you?

30. Do you find it difficult to give and receive love?

If a number of items on this list fit you, you will benefit by soul-healing prayer.

—From Rita Bennett, *Emotionally Free.* Old Tappan, N.J.: Revell, 1982.

SPIRITUAL GIFTS

THE SUBJECT of spiritual gifts, important in the life of the Early Church but too often neglected through the centuries, has recently risen into prominence in modern church thinking.

Apostolic believers learned early in their Christian experience the truth about gifts. When the young church at Jerusalem faced the complaint of discrimination in the administration of daily welfare, the apostles urged believers to seek out godly and *gifted* men to handle the problem. So the congregation chose men with the gift of wisdom. The result was an increase in the ministry of the Word and in the number of disciples (Acts 6:1–7).

Paul wrote about gifts in his letters to the Romans, Corinthians, and Ephesians. In fact, these letters give us three major lists of gifts.

Paul taught about gifts from the very beginning of every new church. He wished each assembly to develop spiritually in normal and undelayed fashion. New churches with all new believers had no members adequately mature to qualify as elders or deacons. But thrown on the power of the Holy Spirit to put into practice Paul's teaching on the discernment and discovery of spiritual gifts, some members grew sufficiently to be chosen as elders on Paul's return visit, not long later (Acts 14:21–23). Through the exercise of gifts, saints had been edified.

NO UNGIFTED BELIEVERS

Every child of God has a gift or gifts. Our gifts are assigned us when we are born by the Holy Spirit into the family of God. At the moment of a believer's baptism into the body of Christ at regeneration, he is given a gift which he should exercise for the health of the whole body. Though gifts may lie dormant for months or years, they are given at our spiritual birthday. The word for gift was used by the Greeks to refer to a birthday gift. The presence of gifts from the moment of conversion explains how in the Early Church some could qualify for elder or deacon not long after the founding of a new fellowship.

Paul emphasized the universality of gifts. "Unto *every one of us* is given grace according to the measure of the gift of Christ" (Ephesians 4:7). "The manifestation of the Spirit is *given to every man* to profit withal" (1 Corinthians 12:7).

Without exception, every new believer receives a gift or gifts. Those fresh from heathenism—new believers in Brazil, Zaire, India, and Taiwan—have been given spiritual gifts. Also unschooled converts are the recipients of gifts, for gifts have no relation to education.

Even those with wicked backgrounds are allocated gifts immediately on repentance. Though the Apostle Paul had been a violent persecutor of the church, even to sharing in the death of saints, the Spirit gave him gifts the moment he was saved. The Corinthians possessed gifts in abundance, despite only a few months removal from flagrant sinning (1 Corinthians 6:9–11).

So, you are a gifted child of God. Since you are also given an outlet for your gift, you are a minister too. Three days after confronting Jesus on the Damascus Road, Paul was told by Ananias that his ministry was to bear the name of Jesus before Gentiles and kings (Acts 9:15; 22:15, 21; 26:16–18). For every gift He bestows, the Spirit has planned a sphere of service.

Thus, no child of God should have an inferiority complex. Rather, awareness that he is a gifted child with an area of ministry should meet every child of God's psychological need to feel wanted and to possess a sense of worth. No false humility should make him moan, "I'm a nobody," and lead him to bury his gifts and hear the ultimate verdict: "slothful servant."

To sum up—though not every believer is exercising his gift, nor even knows what it is, nevertheless every child of God has received one or more gifts to be used for the upbuilding of the church, and for which he will one day render account.

Gifts Are Varied

A well-known conductor was holding a rehearsal one night with a vast array of musicians and a hundred-voice choir. The mighty chorus rang out with peal of organ, blare of horns, and clashing of cymbals. Far back in the orchestra the piccolo player thought, "In all this din, it doesn't matter what I do." Suddenly the conductor stopped the music, flinging up his hands. All became quiet. Someone, he knew, had failed to play his instrument. The shrill note of the piccolo had been missed.

Just as many notes are needed to make harmony, and many colors to make a painting, so many gifts are essential for the functioning of the body of Christ. Paul put it, "For the body is not one member, but many" (1 Corinthians 12:14).

We are not born equal. Though we share in the same Holy Spirit, who enables all believers to confess Jesus as Lord (1 Corinthians 12:3), and who has baptized all believers into the body of Christ (v. 13), we are given different spiritual gifts for service. More than once Paul uses the analogy of the human body with its many members—eyes, ears, hands, feet—to illustrate the varied gifts in the church of Christ. "Ye are the body of Christ, and members in particular" (v. 27).

How many different gifts are there? Some list as few as 9; others in the range of 15 to 22; and still others estimate more.

How many gifts are assigned to each believer? At least one, likely more than one, perhaps, several. Could not this be inferred from Christ's parable of the talents in which one man was given one, and another two, and another five? Though one fellow had only one, the other two had a total of seven talents between them.

We can also observe multiple gifts in operation in individuals described in the New Testament. For example, Philip had the gifts of wisdom, showing mercy, evangelism, and perhaps others unrecorded in the sacred record.

Two or more gifts may often operate simultaneously, blending together. Just as a candle on a three-branch candelabra may shine separately and distinctly while the other two remain unlit or two or three may shine jointly, so a person may have just one gift in exercise, or at another time gifts may glow co-mingled.

Not only are we appointed diverse gifts, but we are allocated differing ministries. Since each believer has a different combination of gifts and ministries, it's likely each of us is in some way unlike any other believer in arrangement of spiritual abilities and outlets to serve. We may not be created equal, but we are unique. There will never be another you.

Why do we get differing gifts? And why do we get the particular gifts we do? The sovereign Holy Spirit simply assigns to every man individually as He wills (1 Corinthians 12:11; Ephesians 4:7). "God set the members every one of them in the body, as it hath pleased Him" (1 Corinthians 12:18). Clearly, distribution of gifts is by divine dealing.

Therefore, no one should boast of his gifts. Paul asks, "Who maketh thee to differ from another? and what hast thou that thou didst not receive? now if thou didst receive it, why dost thou glory, as if thou hadst not received it?" (1 Corinthians 4:7). Because our gifts come through the gracious sovereignty of the Spirit, and not through any merit of ours, they should occasion no bragging on our part.

Neither should we follow, nor idolize, nor become the devotees of any human leader out of admiration for his gifts. Paul warns against this error in 1 Corinthians 3, pointing out that those who exercise the gifts must not be allowed to eclipse Him who gave them (see vv. 3–7, 21–23). Leaders are only fellow-servants, gifted by the Spirit for a particular ministry.

This means we should never envy anyone else's gifts—not Billy Graham's evangelism ability nor John Stott's teaching expertise. Rather, we should be content with God's choice of gifts for us. Discontent is really criticism of the way the Spirit runs His church.

Margaret loved to entertain but found teaching impossible. When she accepted God's sovereign wisdom in bestowing on her the gift of hospitality, she entertained frequently, and was a real blessing to her guests. Barbara, on the other hand, enjoyed teaching, but found it hard to entertain. When she accepted her gift of teaching, guilt feelings over failure to entertain as much as Margaret dissolved. Barbara entered zestfully into teaching her Bible classes, also blessing many. Margaret and Barbara thanked God for each other's gifts instead of envying them.

—From Leslie B. Flynn, *19 Gifts of the Spirit.* Wheaton, Ill.: Victor Books, 1974.

Discovering Your Gifts

We shall look at six guidelines that will aid you in discovering the spiritual gifts that God has for you.

1. *Open yourself to God as a channel for his use.* Christians seeking to discover spiritual gifts should begin by affirming that the Holy Spirit dwells within them. Paul wrote to the Christians at Corinth, "Do you not know that your body is a temple of the Holy Spirit within you, which you have from God?" (1 Corinthians 6:19). Spiritual gifts cannot be separated from their source; *all* the spiritual gifts exist in the Holy Spirit. The gifts of the Spirit are not like a cassette which God shoves into you. They result from the operation of the Holy Spirit who dwells within every Christian. Spiritual gifts must always be seen in the light of the inner working of the Holy Spirit.

The Christian's proper attitude to the Spirit's presence is a willing surrender to his gracious working. We begin to discover our spiritual gifts as we consecrate ourselves daily to Christ for his using. The spirit of the following prayer is appropriate: *Jesus, I affirm that you are Lord. I'm your willing instrument to be used as you see fit. Show me what gifts you have for me, and teach me to be responsive.*

Are you unsure of your spiritual gifts? James advised, "If any of you lacks wisdom, let him ask God, who gives to all men generously and without reproaching, and it will be given him" (James 1:5). As you pray about your spiritual gifts, take time to listen to God. Be available. Study the spiritual gifts listed in the New Testament, and then ask God to show you what gifts are yours. You'll be surprised at how readily he responds to your seeking.

2. *Examine your aspirations for Christian service and ministry.* Serving others is, after all, the whole purpose of spiritual gifts. Peter counseled his readers, "As each has received a gift, employ it for one another, as good stewards of God's varied grace" (1 Peter 4:10). Maturing Christians have learned that their greatest satisfaction is not in being served, but in serving. So look at what ministry you are drawn toward . . . which of the spiritual gifts hold a special attraction for you?

Remember that God's normal way of working is to bring excitement into your life, not boredom. An important theme of scripture is that doing God's will satisfies a basic human hunger (John 15:11). Jesus said, for example, "My food is to do the will of him who sent me, and to accomplish his work" (John 4:34). The Holy Spirit generates a desire within us to do God's will. Maturing Christians grow beyond shallow concepts of discipleship that equate unhappiness with serving God.

One important way in which God reveals his will to us is by giving us inner desires. Paul captured this concept in these words: "For God is at work in you, both to will and to work for his good pleasure" (Philippians 2:13). The psalmist expressed this same thought by writing, "Take delight in the LORD, and he will give you the desires of your heart" (Psalms 37:4). God's way is the way of fulfillment—and it is the way of joy! So take seriously your aspirations and spiritual desires. Those inner impulses most likely stem from the promptings of the Holy Spirit.

3. *Identify the needs that you believe to be most crucial in the life of the church.* Another aspect of discovering the spiritual gifts God has for us is the examination of our concerns. God often guides us by creating within us a sense of burden for a task that needs accomplishing or for some need that remains unmet.

The person who is troubled about false doctrines in the church may have the calling to teach. One who is burdened when others are hurting emotionally or physically may have the gift of compassion.

I recently asked a young woman this question: "What do you think is the greatest need in your church?"

She answered, "It concerns me a lot that persons' needs are not met. I think we ought to serve others more than we do."

From observing this young woman and by talking to others about her, it became obvious to me that she had the gift of helps.

A true shepherd becomes concerned when his people are misled, confused, or divided.

Someone with the gift of administration is especially troubled by disorganization and mismanagement. The Christian who has the gift of giving becomes uneasy when resources are unavailable to carry on God's work.

Check out your concerns. God is probably speaking to you and helping you discover your spiritual gifts through the needs you see in the church. As you see opportunities to minister, God will often burden you to get involved personally. If God is leading you to act, he will provide you with the necessary *charismata* for the task.

4. *Evaluate the results of your efforts to serve and to minister.* Gifts, like talents, grow as we use them. A clear indication that God has given you a particular spiritual gift is growth in effectiveness as you exercise that gift.

Questions to ask yourself are:
—Am I developing more competence in this area?
—Do opportunities open up for me to exercise this gift?
—Are my efforts producing good results in the lives of others?

Naturally, not everyone will accept your ministry. (Remember, even Jesus' ministry was rejected by some.) But if you are properly using your spiritual gift, you'll find yourself growing in confidence, in ability, and in effectiveness.

A very good sign that God has given you a spiritual gift is that others within the church are helped by your ministry. False modesty about what God is doing in your life may hinder your spiritual growth. So take an honest look at what God is doing through you. The results of your Christian ministry will serve as a good indication of the gifts God is giving you.

5. *Follow the guidance of the Holy Spirit as he leads you into obedience to Christ.* Jesus said, "He who has my commandments and keeps them, he it is who loves me; and he who loves me will be loved by my Father, and I will love him and manifest myself to him" (John 14:21). Elsewhere, Jesus emphasized the importance of obedience in his par-

able of the talents: "you have been faithful over a little, I will set you over much" (Matthew 25:23).

Obedience to Christ remains crucial to experiencing the fullness of his life. Of course, we should never assume that our obedience will gain us merit; the Christian life rests solidly on grace, not law. Obedience to Christ, however, does open the door for him to lead us into abundant life. Obedience is the root which produces the fruit of a creative life.

God's primary will for each one of us is the sanctification of all aspects of our lives. Paul, inspired by the Holy Spirit, wrote these words: "For this is the will of God, your sanctification ... May the God of peace himself sanctify you wholly; and may your spirit and soul and body be kept sound and blameless at the coming of our Lord Jesus Christ" (1 Thessalonians 4:3; 5:23). Basically, God's will for us relates more to the quality of our *being* than it does with the specifics of our *doing*. Naturally, God does have a personal, customized plan for each one of us; but he also has a general will for all Christians. His will is that the totality of our existence comes under the redeeming lordship of Jesus Christ.

Sometimes we become overly concerned about the spiritual gifts that God wants us to manifest, while overlooking Christ's basic call to obedient discipleship. Obedience to the light we have will lead us into light we do not yet possess. A sure way to know God more clearly is to follow him more nearly. Obedience to present light will lead us into even greater light in the future.

6. *Remain alert to the responses of other Christians.* The New Testament discussions of spiritual gifts always occur within the context of the body of Christ, the church. Christ is the head of the church; and Christians make up the various members of his body, each functioning in a needed way. Working in harmony, the members of the body edify one another and they bring glory to Christ who is the head.

Growing Christians realize that God calls them into fellowship with other members of Christ's church. Since no Christian will

manifest every spiritual gift, we all need one another (1 Corinthians 12:27–31). The individual Christian never exists in isolation; he constitutes but a part of the whole body.

We need constantly to maintain a harmonious relationship with other Christians because others often see our spiritual gifts before we do. The affirmation and support of Christian friends will prove of great help to us in discovering and manifesting our own spiritual gifts. One of the most helpful services we can perform for a fellow Christian is to affirm gifts and graces which we see in him.

If other Christians are not helped by your ministry and if they do not affirm your gift, reevaluate what you are seeking to do. But if the Christian community consistently recognizes and receives your ministry, you may be sure God is working in you through a spiritual gift.

Remember this basic principle: God is more interested in us than we are in him. With this basic principle in mind, be available. If you are open to God, in his own time he will lead you into an understanding of your gifts.

—From Kenneth Kinghorn, *Gifts of the Spirit.* Nashville: Abingdon, 1976.

FOR FURTHER READING:

Wagner, C. Peter. *Your Spiritual Gifts.* Ventura, Calif.: Regal, 1979.

Yohn, Rick. *Beyond Spiritual Gifts.* Wheaton, Ill.: Tyndale, 1976.

SPIRITUAL LIFE

OUR SPIRITUAL lives are not dependent upon our daily devotional times. They are dependent upon Christ Himself. But time spent alone with Him, allowing Him to speak to us through the Bible, is our access to His grace. Grace is always flowing toward us. Always. Our part is to put out our cups to receive it. I like to think of my own devotional hours as receiving hours.

But this receiving must not end when we

close our Bibles. The normal, relaxed Christian life is one that is regulated by a definite rhythm like breathing. Receiving and responding. Receiving and responding.

Perhaps many of you feel that your prayer life is the weakest part of your Christian life. It well may be. I know I considered mine weak for many years. And yet we make a horrible mistake when we think of prayer as separate from our Christian walk. When we walk with a human friend, talking to that friend is an integral part of the walk.

—From Eugenia Price, *Woman to Woman*. Grand Rapids: Zondervan, 1959.

FOR FURTHER READING:

Bright, Vonette Zachary. *For Such a Time as This*. Old Tappan, N.J.: Revell, 1976.

Elliot, Elisabeth. *Discipline: The Glad Surrender*. Old Tappan, N.J.: Revell, 1982.

Murphey, Cecil B. *Press On! A Disciple's Guide to Spiritual Growth*. Ann Arbor: Servant, 1983.

STEPPARENTING

WE ARE ONLY now beginning to see a tremendous increase in remarriage and stepparenting, and it will continue to even greater proportions. Take a look at some interesting facts:

1. One out of every five children in this country is the child of a divorce.
2. Eighty-five percent of divorced persons remarry within five years.
3. In the United States, right now, some 20 million adults are stepparents.

We must be wise enough to understand that given these statistics, there is bound to be an ever-increasing number of adjustments and problems facing stepparents and stepchildren alike.

Add those adjustments and problems to the "wicked-stepmother image" and you've got a pretty depressing starting point. It used to be said that the hardest job in the world

was being a mother. But, after talking to a lot of women, I think I'll change that to say: The hardest job in the world is being a stepmother.

Here are a few suggestions I've gleaned from women who have gone through the stepparenting experience.

1. If it's at all possible, start your new family life in a new or different house. Feelings are closely entwined with a home or apartment, and to start in a new place helps to cut down on old feelings and begins to generate new feelings and emotions.
2. Watch out for the too-high-expectance syndrome. Don't expect instant love, instant involvement, and instant rapport with your stepchildren. A solid relationship takes time. Let love and caring for each other develop slowly. God's timing is rarely ours. Read the Old Testament's greatest piece on waiting, as found in the Book of Habakkuk.
3. Let children participate and share their feelings in deciding what the stepparent will be called. Some children will have no problem with Mom, Mommie, or Mother —others will. First names may be the best route, or invented nicknames; but, whatever—get the child's input. It will speed up the adjustment time.
4. Basic to a good relationship is your ability to call your stepchild "my son" or "my daughter," especially when the child is under ten years of age. This may be difficult at first, but just as you must break away from the image of the "wicked stepmother," referring to your child as yours instead of stepchild, is a pledge of respect, and it helps to lift the child's self-esteem.
5. The tendency to go soft in the area of disciplining your stepchild is normal. However, it can be disastrous. A good way to begin is to let the biological parent do much of the disciplining, and gradually to share the loving responsibility. But, by all means, let all the children know there is

437

only *one set of rules* for all children (mine, his, and ours) and that you and your husband are firmly and unitedly agreed about it!

—From Joyce Landorf, *Changepoints*. Old Tappan, N.J.: Revell, 1981.

STEWARDSHIP

YOU AND I, who are God's people, are to be funnels for God's flow of resources. The Bible says, "Give, and it will be given you ..." (Luke 6:38 RSV). When the spout is blocked at the bottom, because of our stinginess, God can put nothing else in at the top.

Young couples often feel that they just don't have enough to give now. With their incomes low and their desires for furniture and stuff to fill the place where they live, there's just no money to give to the Lord. Such an analysis will prove that there's not enough to give and buy all those other things.

Giving to the Lord is not so much a matter of money as it is trusting God. When we give to the Lord first, we are really telling Him that we have the faith that He will replace it with more than enough to meet our needs. As our needs are met, we'll continue to be His channel for giving resources to others.

Are you trustworthy with what God has given you? Do you acknowledge that everything you have has come because God has made it possible?

A first-off-the-top-of-your-income tithe is the best way I know to prove to yourself and to demonstrate to God that you trust Him. One of my friends says that God is the only business manager in the world who can make 90 percent go farther than 100 percent.

Start your marriage as tithers. Know the joy and blessing of giving to others as you start your life learning to give to each other in marriage. The outflow of money from your new marriage will add to your relation-

ship a certain rare quality that will be meaningful to you and attractive to others.

—From George and Marjean Fooshee, *You Can Beat the Money Squeeze*. Old Tappan, N.J.: Revell, 1980.

FOR FURTHER READING:

Burkett, Larry. *Your Finances in Changing Times*. San Bernardino, Calif.: Campus Crusade for Christ, 1975.

Fooshee, George and Marjean. *You Can Beat the Money Squeeze*. Old Tappan, N.J.: Revell, 1980.

Kilgo, Edith Flowers. *Money Management*. Grand Rapids: Baker Book, 1980.

STRESS

JESUS KNEW what the stress-filled life was all about, even in His relatively slow-moving generation. Excited and sometimes frantic crowds often surrounded Him. On one occasion people had to be lowered through an opening in the roof to see Him (Mark 2:4). Crowds of more than 5,000 gathered to hear Him, to be healed, or to be delivered of demons. Yet the Gospels never paint a picture of a hurried, striving Jesus. Jesus even told His disciples to come apart and rest awhile! He frequently went by Himself to pray. Other times He took His disciples with Him and got away from it all.

If Jesus didn't have to be everything to everybody all the time, why should we? Jesus had His priorities in order. He recognized the Father's will as the most important aspect of His life. He maintained a steady devotional life with the Father. He ministered on a full-time basis, but He kept His life in balance. He took time "to consider the lilies," to smell the flowers, as we say today. The Bible indicates He rested and ate, and He certainly exercised, as walking was the primary way to get around in His day.

Another area of stress unique to Christians occurs when we are concerned whether we're doing the don'ts and not doing the do's.

Guilt may be added to concern if we are participating in practices that are not glorifying to God. Real stress results.

Too often, however, when someone attempts to counsel us on a questionable practice, the counselor's spirit of accusation makes us afraid to discuss our problems or sin. Instead, we keep it to ourselves, and that not only produces stress, but we go on as defeated Christians. Those who counsel must do so lovingly. "Brethren, even if a man is caught in any trespass, you who are spiritual, restore such a one in a spirit of gentleness; each one looking to yourself, lest you too be tempted" (Galatians 6:1).

GETTING RID OF THE SHOULDS

As Christians, we sometimes impose pressures on ourselves that the Lord would not. We get too wrapped up in what we should do to present a good testimony to the unbelieving world.

We think we should work harder and longer at our jobs than anybody else. We should always have a smile on our face so that a downhearted and discouraged world can see that things are going well for us. We must project that we're on top of it all because we have Jesus.

Some say we should never get angry, yet it is true that bottled up anger or frustration contributes to stress. Anger may sometimes be justified, but it must be tempered with self-control (see Galatians 5:23) and carefully expressed (see Ephesians 4:26), or not expressed to other people, but resolved with God alone through prayer. Jesus showed anger and other feelings, including disappointment, discouragement, and loneliness. At other times He entered into joyous celebrations, such as when He contributed to the wedding party by turning water into wine.

Too often Christians try to ignore their feelings, or suppress them—even in their prayers. More than anyone, Jesus could have been caught up in the thinking that He should always be doing His Father's business, but He realized that by living a balanced life He was doing His Father's business. No one knew the depravity of man and his need for a Saviour more than Jesus did, but He was not driven by the lateness of the hour. He knew His own life and ministry would be relatively short. Yet He took time to pray, to fast, to eat, to celebrate, to socialize, to rest, and to meditate. He was faithful to the Father's will.

Too often shoulds are self-imposed—and the reasons for them as well. For example, we should have good marriages, not because we're on center stage and the unbelieving world is watching, but because God ordained the institution and He wants us to enjoy it.

MAKING CHOICES

Theological choices and decisions can create stress. When it comes to matters of eternity, we want to make right decisions. Teachings differ on how we come to God and how we are to worship and live. Some say that a person chooses Christ, others that God chooses us in the sacraments. Still others emphasize good works. Views also vary on spiritual gifts and on modes of worship. Charismatic or noncharismatic? Liturgical or not? What about the end times? Are the doomsday preachers right, and if so, should we stock up on candles and dried foods? Political action groups such as Moral Majority want our support. Is their approach valid? What about Christians participating in civil disobedience? We cannot minimize these questions of faith and practice. They require thought—and even study. Their very urgency can be stressful.

Too often we are caught up with trying to do the "right" thing, and trying to please people instead of the Lord. If we concentrated on living to please Him, we would reduce the stress in our lives immeasurably. Our pressure points may never be altered, but *we* will be. We need to get out of the way and let Jesus respond to the stress in our lives. We forget that the Son has made us free, and part of that contract is freedom from stress.

"It is His character that is taken on, but that does not negate the individual's personality. Both the extrovert and the introvert are to be what they are while becoming more like Christ. This does not mean withdrawal or denial of self as much as it does taking on the positive attributes of His love, compassion, and commitment" (James L. Johnson, *How to Enjoy Life and Not Feel Guilty*, Harvest House, p. 35).

It is to the gentle nudge of the Spirit of God to which we must respond and answer. Each of us hears and responds to Him in a different way, because each of us is unique.

I believe that if we seek to live godly, holy lives, tuned to the Spirit of God, we can receive the mind of Christ regarding every stress-producing situation facing us in the twentieth century. But we must do our part to maintain a balanced lifestyle—one that includes work, ministry, play, and rest in proper proportions.

SATISFACTION OR STRESS?

Work should bring us satisfaction and other good things. "He that tilleth his land shall be satisfied with bread" (Proverbs 12:11). For those of us who aren't farmers, work assures us of having money for buying food. Since work is a gift from God, we must enjoy it and not let it become a vanity (Ecclesiastes 2:11).

Work is clearly one of the chief producers of stress, and much job-related stress is uncontrollable. Work stress has intensified the last 25 years. In the fierce competition of the last two decades, pressure begins at the top of the ladder and works its way down. Quotas are upped, territories expanded, and more is demanded of employees at every level. Expectations constantly increase. There's not much abiding in business.

We hear a lot about job burnout. Prison guards often succumb to stress in less than ten years. The high rate of alcoholism among police officers indicates their job stress is

high. Firemen, waitresses, and secretaries are also singled out. Teachers too are prime candidates for job burnout with 100,000 a year assaulted by students.

A person experiencing job burnout will be more prone to utilize escape tactics such as excessive drinking or eating, or wanting to stay in bed. He will have little enthusiasm for his job, his inefficiency increases, and he will be extremely tired after work. The burnout victim may have various aches and pains, chronic stiff neck or a back problem, insomnia, and even suffer chronic alcoholism, depression, or bleeding ulcers. By that time, the job controls the burnout victim.

This problem is getting so acute that many companies are investing millions of dollars to protect their employees. Some give a 3-month paid leave of absence after ten years of service. Exercise and aerobic dance courses are being made available for employees during the lunch hour. Some companies insist that employees get away from their desk at midday. Others are investing in sports and health equipment or providing jogging trails, tennis courts, softball fields, and swimming pools on the company grounds.

Some companies now realize that our biorhythms are thrown off when we must work varying shifts—that the body doesn't function well when coping with inconsistent routines—and they operate only two workshifts instead of three.

Job burnout knows no economic status. The assembly-line worker must deal with the stress of boredom, the busy executive with the stress of heavy responsibilities, red tape and bureaucracy.

WOMEN HAVE SPECIAL FRUSTRATIONS

Burnout is not limited to men. Skyrocketing inflation and the cost of homes have forced back to work some women who would prefer to be home raising a family. A woman may be assigned a more "lowly" job because she is not "the head of the home." She also can be the brunt of jokes and sexual harassment on the job. Even if she is as qualified as a man, she may never advance very high up the ladder.

The working mother is often concerned that she is unable to spend enough quality time with her children. Unless her job is one she especially wanted, it may not provide the satisfaction she could get in the home, and this can leave her frustrated and angry. Further, unless family members help, her home and job duties make the possibility of a balanced lifestyle remote. Meals may not be as carefully planned and nutritious, family togetherness breaks down, and the only exercise she gets is when she unloads the washing machine.

And yet millions of American women thrive on this type of pace. I have a friend who has won the "Consultant of the Year" award in the employment business four times and each time in a period of a depressed economy when businesses were cutting back on their hiring. When she started in the business in the early 1970s, she was making $575 a month. Now she makes eight times that amount. She admits that she easily gets caught up in the competitive drive to make the most of job placements. Everybody likes to win—even Christians!

She has to work at not letting her job run her life. To get her mind off of herself, her quotas, her placements, and her potential first-place trips to Hawaii, she shows concern for other people. She is an encourager and a good listener. She goes to lunch with friends who are not associated with her job, draws them out, and focuses on them.

Being so other-directed has impressed her work associates, most of whom are not Christians. Following an acceptance speech she gave as "Consultant of the Year," she received a standing ovation. Her life stacked up with the message of her speech.

—From Jan Markell, *Overcoming Stress*. Wheaton, Ill.: Victor Books, 1982.

FOR FURTHER READING:

McCay, James T. *The Management of Time*. Englewood Cliffs, N.J.: Prentice-Hall, 1959.

The Diagram Group. *Man's Body*. New York: Simon & Schuster, 1981.

SUICIDE

What Is Suicide?

The number of suicides is grossly underreported. Families are loath to have the death pronounced a suicide because of the social stigma attached, as well as the loss of life insurance benefits, since policies do not pay face value under these circumstances. Equally important is the fact that authorities do not always agree as to the means of death.

For example, a young man is found dead with a bullet between his eyes. Beside him is a rifle he has had for a year, with equipment for cleaning it. Accident or suicide?

To be classified a suicide, a person must intend to kill himself and he must actually do so. This is easier said than proved. Did the youth in the above incident intend to take his life? What about the celebrated Marilyn Monroe, with her overdose of sleeping pills—was her intention lethal?

The tool to determine intention is a psychological autopsy. Dr. Edwin S. Schneidman, Chief of the Center for Studies of Suicide Prevention in the National Institute of Mental Health, asserts that a team of social scientists must first interview all the people who were close to the victim and record every reaction and recollection while memories are still fresh. "The investigators would know things about the person that many people close to him did not know about him. And they would find out things about him that he did not know about himself!" The interviewers would then write on the certificate the type of death, using N, A, S, H, the abbreviations for *n*atural, *a*ccidental, *s*uicide, *h*omicide.

SLOW SUICIDE

There are those who are suicidal and yet are not recognized as such. These people find life intolerable and unmanageable and participate in death-oriented behavior. The definition of who and what constitutes a suicide should be expanded to make room for

441

that vast and assorted collection of people engaged in "life-shortening activities." They could well be labeled as either a partial, a subintentioned, a submeditated suicide, or a suicide equivalent.

For people commit suicide without being consciously aware they are doing it. Their entire life-style involves a movement toward the brink of self-destruction. The same psychic forces that impel an individual to jump from the roof of a skyscraper may also be responsible for such dangerous habits as overeating, overworking, or heavy smoking. Sooner or later, many of these subintentioned suicides will succeed in killing themselves. Installment-plan suicides may be less obvious, but are just as deadly.

AUTOCIDE

For example, we all know people who constantly drive too fast, cross major arteries against traffic lights, and pass on hills. One place to look out for disguised suicides is on the road. The car serves as an ideal instrument of self-annihilation. The popular wisdom that says, when a car shoots past at ninety, "Man, he's trying to kill himself," may well be correct.

Autocide occurs when a vehicle is used as a method of self-imposed death. Dr. Alfred L. Moseley of the Harvard Medical School concludes that suicides are a "significant though unknown" proportion of the 48,000 annual auto deaths in the United States. And the Federal Center for Studies of Suicide Prevention, Bethesda, Maryland, claims that many drivers play latent, unconscious roles in hastening their own demise. An educated guess is that one quarter of the drivers who die in auto accidents cause them subintentionally by imprudent and excessive risk-taking.

Rescue, Incorporated, has a number of cases in its files of people who attempted to kill themselves by "accidentally" smashing their cars into poles, or trees, or abutments. After studying the personalities and life situations of thirty drivers who died in one-car

crashes, Dr. Robert Litman, of the Los Angeles Suicide Prevention Center, suggests that about five percent of such accidents were deliberate. Thus the family of the deceased escapes the stigma of having a member commit suicide. At the same time, insurance benefits are promptly paid. It is for these reasons that persons who attempt autocide rarely leave suicide notes. The use of the car as a method of self-destruction is peculiarly resistant to later observation, statistics, and analysis.

ALCOHOLISM

Between one-half and two-thirds of the fifty thousand deaths and two million serious injuries on the highways each year are associated with the excessive consumption of alcohol. In a study at the University of Michigan, Dr. Melvin L. Seltzer examined 72 drivers responsible for automobile accidents claiming 82 lives. He discovered not only that a high proportion of the drivers were alcoholics but that there was a significant relation between accidents, alcohol, and suicidal tendencies. In Maryland, during a five-year period, tests were made for alcohol in the blood in 617 of 1455 suicides, and levels of .05 percent or more were found in 35 percent of the victims. Alcohol deepens aggressiveness, which, when turned against one's self, may lead to suicide.

Alcoholism is a form of life-shortening activity in which a physical disease such as cirrhosis is usually listed as the cause of death. Yet, once again, by drinking to excess the alcoholic plays an unconscious and indirect role in his own demise. He lives in a world of desolation, loneliness, fear, and anxiety. Death is the final release from pain.

OTHER FORMS OF SUBINTENTIONED SUICIDE

As usually defined, suicide is the deliberate taking of one's life. It becomes apparent that a larger number of people want to die, but have not reached that state where they will act consciously on a suicidal desire.

Accident-type suicides are not as rare as the casual observer might believe. The accident-prone may believe they are careful, yet they behave in curiously self-destructive ways, such as stabbing themselves with a knife or "accidentally" taking too many sleeping pills.

A person may not be sure that he wants to die. Neither is he convinced that he wishes to live. This ambivalence is demonstrated in a deadly "game" called Russian roulette: By leaving the outcome to external forces (the place of the bullet in the gun), the decision is made for him. The gamble with death is also involved in other daredevil feats, such as auto racing and parachute jumping.

A suicide equivalent may be camouflaged in idealistic and altruistic garb. The martyr may give up his life for the honor of God and country. Unconsciously he may have wished to die. An opportunity presented itself to do so with honor and nobility. He gains our gratitude, not our disdain.

These deaths are not ruled as suicides even though definite unconscious lethal intention is involved. To clarify the situation, the Suicide Prevention Center of Los Angeles has proposed three workable psychological classifications for cause of death. An *unintended* death is one in which an individual plays no active role in his own demise. An *intentioned* death is one in which the victim has an active part in his own death through deliberate or impulsive acts. In the *subintentioned* death the victim plays a partial, unconscious, covert role in his own self-destruction.

There are many ways of committing suicide besides slashing one's wrists, or swallowing poison, or shooting or hanging oneself. Suicide, by any name, is the Number One cause of unnecessary deaths. And in the words of Justice Cardoza: "A cry for help is a summons for rescue."

—From Earl A. Grollman, *Suicide*. Boston: Beacon Press, 1971.

Living As a Suicide Survivor

Few official taboos remain against suicide or against your family. The state doesn't punish you for what your family member has done. Most of the punishment you will receive, if any, will come from your "friends" and your own family.

Suicide survivors consistently report more feelings of stigma and shame than do those experiencing normal grief. However, much of this may be more imagined than real. You will experience some blame, to be sure. Some will be subtle, and some quite blunt, but it will come your way. But don't start seeing an "enemy" behind every rock. Not everyone will feel what you tend to assume they feel. If you start breaking ties with close friends and co-workers over what you think they're thinking, you may well be left on your island of isolation with no one to help you find rescue.

I agree with those who believe in openness and honesty on your part. Most suicide survivors aren't very honest with their close friends about the nature of the death. This only hurts you, because you are always left to wonder if and how much they "know." Such a constant state of not knowing doesn't *help* you work through your grief. It *hinders* you. It leads toward inevitable isolation and loneliness.

.   .   .   .   .

Members of a suicide's family often tend to see the death as a family disgrace, a skeleton to be hidden from view in the closet. They talk of "dishonor," "a blot on our good name," and frequently resort to denial to avoid this perceived shame. The spouse, however, is singled out for the greatest blame. As Phyllis Silverman points out, "The suicide leaves his wife (or her husband) a legacy that keeps her married to him (or him married to her) *because of this guilt by association*" (Phyllis Rolfe Silverman, "Intervention with the Widow of a Suicide," in Cain, ed., *Survivors of Suicide*, p. 210). Women may feel some stigma because they are "without a man" in a male-dominated society. Suicide spouses feel immediately the difference between other widowed spouses and themselves. This often prevents them from getting involved in support groups for widowed spouses. It also poses problems for meeting new friends and for future dating, since "telling" presents some risks to new relationships.

You may be unfortunate enough to live in what Albert Cain and Irene Fast call a "blaming community" (Cain and Fast, "The Legacy of Suicide: Observations on the Pathogenic Impact of Suicide upon Marital Partners," in Cain, ed., *Survivors of Suicide*, p. 148). Schoolmates taunt your children, neighbors heap blame upon you, and your family and in-laws aim their fingers at you. You hear statements like "I'm not surprised it happened" and "She drove him to it." These people dissect your marriage in public. Their goal is to "draw blood" from you

and your children through their malicious gossip. In this extreme kind of situation, which rarely happens, suicide survivors find literally no support for their shattered lives. Their feelings of shame go sky-high. Their grief gets hopelessly stuck because they can't talk about it to anyone. So they retreat into their homes, or change their phone numbers, or eventually move away. If you find yourself in this kind of situation, I see no point in continuing to be the bull's-eye for their target practice. Moving away is no disgrace when you do it for the right reasons. In this case, your move isn't made out of denial, but rather as protection for you and your family. Remember, you and your children are your first priority.

—From John H. Hewett, *After Suicide*. Philadelphia: Westminster, 1980.

FOR FURTHER READING:

Deffner, Donald L. *The Possible Years*. St. Louis: Concordia, 1973.

T

TELEVISION

USUALLY IT'S THE specifics of television that bother us. We are disturbed by the off-color jokes in the comedy or the crescendo of pre-Christmas toy commercials.

But some researchers who have no particular religious orientation to their thinking, would point us in a different direction. George Gerbner and his associates at the University of Pennsylvania contend that the effects of any particular aspect of television ought not to be our greatest concern. Rather, Gerbner suggests, we should notice how television shapes our way of looking at the world. Television, he argues, is like Christianity: it fashions our whole way of thinking.

That is thought provoking. It makes us ask which is shaping our thinking more—Christianity or secular television? Has television become an obstacle to our forming a Christian mind?

Research evidence compiled by professional observers such as Gerbner over the last 30 years confirms that television indeed has an impact on our view of the world. It shapes people's thinking about what sex is like, how affluent the people around them are, how dangerous the world is, what political questions are important, and so on. It is only reasonable to conclude that our huge investment in the medium—50,000 to 75,-000 hours or more in an average American's lifetime—is also having an impact on our thinking about more fundamental aspects of reality.

Television's power to cultivate an entire view of reality is a challenge that most Christians have not reckoned with. The danger is that while holding the correct set of beliefs about God and his Word we may be allowing something quite different to shape our minds.

When we spend time with television, we are casually and rather passively exposing our minds to a world that, simply, ignores God. The realities of the Christian revelations, which in the scriptural view tower over the landscape like gigantic monuments, are all but invisible to television's near-sighted eye.

In the television world, for instance, it is of no importance whether God made all things or not. Documentaries probe political and economic issues without posing such questions as, What are God's purposes in this area of life, and, How can men and women best serve them? In television entertainment's world of police stations and fancy apartments, no one speaks of creation or, apparently, thinks of it. Just as the television world is peopled by higher proportions of law enforcement workers, professionals, and affluent folks than the real world, it is also inhabited by a race of people who for the most part do not care whether they are living in a purposive creation or a cosmic accident.

Creative man, not creator God, fills the screen. When was the last time a late-night talk show featured a guest whose prominence lay in his uncompromising obedience to God? Guests are not chosen for their exemplary submission to God's will or their keen understanding of his intentions for some department of life. They are chosen for *their* creativity, their own original achievements, their striking expressions of individuality.

Daily Christian life flows from an awareness of being a creature, made with a purpose, cared for by God. This consciousness ought to suffuse the Christian's outlook as blood courses through his veins. But for many of us, this awareness is submerged in the stream of images from television, which, while rising occasionally to heights of technical artistry in showing this beautiful world of movement and color, nowhere relates its fragmented images to the Artist who lies behind them.

In contrast to the men and women of the Scriptures, many Christians today sense only weakly the way God intervenes in the world and in each individual life. Most Christians find it difficult to develop a daily awareness of God as sovereign Lord who holds the initiative in his dealings with us. This difficulty is worsened as we immerse ourselves in the television view of the world, where there is absent an awareness of God's ability to work his will in every circumstance of life. On television, God never does anything.

Not only God, but evil also recedes from view in the television world. In a story, a boy feigns blindness to escape a brutal father and win adoption in a better home—a powerful case for lying, made at an emotional level that resists rational refutation. In another story, a married soldier far from home enters an adulterous liaison with a woman of great sensitivity—again, a powerful emotional case for wrongdoing. Such programming makes it harder rather than easier to see what is right about righteousness and wrong about wrongdoing.

This moral confusion weakens the conviction that *any* behavior can be seriously and profoundly wrong. The Christian has more than a moral code. He or she recognizes the gravity of wrongdoing—its ungratefulness, its wickedness, its eternal folly. The Christian ought to be angered at serious sin. But as one writer, Stephen Clark, has noted, Christians are too often angry about that which offends *them* and complacent about that which offends *God*. We get angrier at being cut off on the expressway than by abuse directed at God's law. This shows a failure to develop a mature Christian mentality that sees serious wrongdoing as the personal affront to God which, in fact, it is.

No doubt our minds have been affected by spending so many hours on the moral tableland of the television world, where sin is flattened into insignificance, rather than in the scriptural world, where the collision of righteousness and evil has carved a landscape of soaring peaks and dizzying chasms.

In many cases, our thinking also lacks a grasp of the dynamics of good and evil. We know that sin is the world's root problem, that human society apart from God is locked in a system of evil that Scripture calls "the world," and that society has fallen under the power of "the prince of this world." But to a large extent we have not integrated this knowledge in our minds. Our thinking has not been refashioned so that we are able to see our families, careers, and workplaces in those terms.

While television is not the only cause of our difficulty, it is certainly a factor, and a greater one the more time we spend with it. As television sees it, the world has its problems, but they are not beyond the ability of well-intentioned, highly trained individuals to deal with.

If television cannot cope with sin, neither can it face up to redemption. It tells us that life can be improved but not transformed. One of television's underlying messages is "the world is the world is the world." This is all there is, and this is all there is going to be. On the one hand, it's not so bad, television says: situation comedies show us that deep down, everyone is just folks; documentaries show us good, competent people hard at work to bring progress. But don't hope for anything radically better: the soaps display people's endless, tedious unfaithfulnesses; the news reveals society's central institutions, especially the government, as incapable of controlling the course of events.

The television view of the world is similar to some schools of psychology. These theories view man without taking into account either original sin or re-creation in Christ. They examine what can go wrong in the psyche of fallen man; and they propose what can be done short of starting all over. Similarly, television presents human society without illuminating either its bondage to evil or redemption in Christ. Psychological journals do not offer case studies of how men and women have died in Christ and been raised to new life with God. Television does not dramatize their stories.

The television world's view of reality is at odds with Christianity in many ways. But to say that television world is "secular" is to touch at once on all the ways that the medium implicitly repudiates the realities of revelation—God as purposeful creator and intervener, the nature of mankind's predicament, and re-creation in Christ. All these realities presuppose an order of existence above the natural world, an age beyond this "saeculum."

A secular current flows powerfully through all the major institutions of our society—government, school, business, the mass media. Against this current, Christians do not easily maintain a biblical world view. In American society today it is not easy to speak publicly, or even think, about events in light of eternity.

Once again, the problem for many of us is that our beliefs have not changed our thinking. We believe in eternity, but we tend not to see our lives and society from an eternal perspective. "How will this matter look in the very long run, at the judgment?" "How then will I wish I had acted now?" "How does Christian hope change the way I must view this suffering?" Our minds too rarely run down such channels.

By its nature, secular television blocks the development of this mentality. Television presents images of this world in a way that says, This is all there is. The mind remains trapped in the ideals, desires, and anxieties of this life.

These are what Malcolm Muggeridge calls "diversions" from the path of faith in God. Muggeridge puts it forcefully:

"I think that diversions are more difficult to deal with than ever before because the fantasies of life have been given such extraordinary outward and visible shape, even to the point where you can see them on the TV screen for three or four hours a day, these fantasies of power, of leisure, of carnality. Western men and women live in that world of images almost as long as any other, and it is a fearful thing. That is why you find among the young this extraordinary despair, because they feel there is no escape for them—no escape into reality."

The Great Commandment is that we should love God with all our mind and heart and strength. To love God with our minds means to have our minds formed by his Word, to have our thinking conformed to his way of seeing things. It is precisely with this that television interferes. To spend many hours with television is to fail to love God. At some point between our turning on the television for a little entertainment after dinner and our turning it off at the end of the evening, we enter a receptive communion with the images and messages of a secular culture. We begin with relaxing, and end with loving the world.

The early Christians were sensitive to the imaginative power of pagan poetry, drama, and popular entertainments, and they dealt with them cautiously if at all. Augustine described his interior life as "a limitless forest, full of unexpected dangers"; he was conscious of the complexities of the mind and the unpredictable ways that images and memories can tempt us and lead us astray. Unfortunately, many of us today have lost this sense of how vulnerable our minds can be to the influences of the world.

Basically we are not on the defensive against the world—although defense is necessary—because we have been caught up in God's transforming work. He is making our minds and hearts new.

What he requires is our cooperation. We are to seek the things that are above, where Christ is. This involves allowing God to make his truth present to our minds in many practical ways through what we read, what we watch, what we listen to. Then he transforms our minds, and we come to view life from the perspective of being in Christ. We come to know God's will. We come to know the height and breadth of his love.

We jeopardize this process of transformation by heavy involvement with television. Let us instead take control of this interference and cooperate with God giving us a new mind and heart.

—From Kevin Perrotta, *Taming the TV Habit.* Ann Arbor: Servant, 1982.

Soap Operas

"A soap opera is a kind of a sandwich whose recipe is simple enough," wrote James Thurber. "Between thick slices of advertising, spread twelve minutes of dialogue, add predicament, villainy, and female suffering in equal measure, throw in a dash of nobility, sprinkle with tears, season with organ music, cover with a rich announcer sauce, and serve five times a week."

Except for the organ—and possibly the announcer—today's television soap operas remain fundamentally unchanged. For just about fifty years, these serialized dramas have entertained, educated, and involved Americans from every walk of life with their stories. People laugh with them; they cry with them; they get things out of their systems with soap operas. The soaps are a purely American art form and a kind of emotional catharsis; phenomena that touch the lives of an estimated 35 million people each day.

"More hours are spent watching the soaps," according to one reporter, "than are spent working by all the farmers in the United States each day. More time is spent watching these daytime serials than is spent working by all federal, state, and local government officials put together. More time is spent watching soaps than is spent working by all the automobile and steel workers in America."

There is really no typical soap opera viewer, at least not anymore. A great diversity in age group, education, and economic standing is represented in the audience, where thirty percent of today's viewers are men.

The soap opera got its name, of course, because its earliest sponsors were manufacturers of different brands of soap. Today, commercials still spill over into the storylines, with flushable diapers quickly followed by throwaway spouses and disposable marriages.

Soap opera life is lived at the level of the most universally felt fears, frustrations, and desires. No one's life is dedicated to a cause, to political passion, intellectual curiosity, status, or success-seeking. People care little about satisfying hobbies, sports, or popular diversions. Life's boring details are omitted, for soap opera life is a life in outline . . . a life devoid of real life's ruts and routines.

Telephones never ring unless a lover or confidant is calling; milkmen, laundrymen, and exterminators never intrude in their immaculate homes. There are never any bills to pay or groceries to be bought. No one ever has to go to the cleaners, or have his or her car inspected, or take out the trash.

Work hardly affects the development of soap opera storylines, where the economic value system is a distorted picture of the American world of work. Soaps can be accused of discrimination against the man—or woman—who works with his or her hands, and the fact of employment is but another device to establish soap characters as real people.

Traditional values of American democracy are usually upheld on the "stories." There is a reliance on the judicial system, stress on law and order, and a belief in free enterprise. Any character who breaks the law is eventually punished. Sin is to be avoided; virtue is rewarded in the long run, and for every crime of commission there is a punishment. Although infidelity and divorce do occur frequently on soap operas, they are not condoned, but rather are sources of great anxiety and soul searching. Strict standards of decency in language, dress, and human sexuality are more often than not maintained.

The religion of Soapland is a domestic religion, one that asks no more than simple goodness and kindness to one's fellow man. And, while religion, per se, is respectfully mentioned from time to time on today's dramatized serials, the church is not portrayed as a driving force in most people's lives. But in times of trouble, perplexity, or serious illness, God is thought of more frequently.

By and large, Soapland is a good place to live. Generally speaking, if something is wrong, it is not beyond resolve or redemption. Although the presence of so many evil people certainly provides an opportunity for adventure, evil, itself, is always defeated. Good people who continue to strive against all adversity emerge victorious.

Dan Wakefield, popular storyteller and author of the book *All Her Children*, goes as far as to claim that Old Testament scriptures are the stern father to all soap operas. Indeed, it would seem that with all of the plagues, incest, miracles, fears, and retributions, the essential New Testament message—forgiveness—is lost on daytime television.

The unhappiness that many people see as central to the soap opera is, perhaps, the key to its basic appeal. Although sustained misery is not really a soap opera characteristic, prolonged anxiety is. Unlike other television programs, soap opera people agonize over their decisions and worry about what the results of their actions will be.

The central idea behind all of the daytime dramas is that personal happiness is possible today for the person who continues to strive for it. The soaps preach that the only way of life that can bring happiness in this world is a life of the heart, a life of emotional commitment to other people. This leads one Christian critic to observe that the subject matter of soaps is not so much the concern, as is the underlying point of view. "Soaps reinforce the twentieth century point of view that morals are relative," she suggests.

Critics usually assign two basic reasons to why people watch soap operas: One reason, they say, is to escape from life and its dreary realities; the other is to learn how to cope with one's own life more effectively.

Viewers look to the soaps for models—who to be, how to think, and how to solve their problems. They identify with the characters. Sometimes they feel that they or someone they know looks like a character in the story; other times, something in their own lives somehow resembles what they see on TV.

There is a great deal to be learned from the soaps about how to handle one's life and affairs. Individually we are limited in our knowledge about how other people live. Yet, only soap operas attempt to offer a detailed, day-by-day dramatization of the way other people behave in personal and intimate situations.

No other type of television programming shows its audience how other parents advise their children about marriage, how deeply one friend should question another about a drinking problem, or how much a father need tell his children about his marital difficulties.

The daytime serials attempt to define standards of acceptable social etiquette. They demonstrate how to arrange parties, make and break dates, honor the holidays and memories of loved ones, and cope with children leaving home. Ruth Warrick, who plays Phoebe Tyler on "All My Children," gets to the heart of the matter when she says that, ". . . basically we're animated Dear Abby's, always giving advice."

One critic was moved to conclude that, ". . . the soaps are the only place on television where you may see adult topics explored in a dramatic context, as if they were problems that involved real people." When one prominent soap couple decided to adopt a baby, an Ohio woman wrote in to offer them her own six-month-old; she was sure her child would be getting a good home. Another woman sent a letter to Eileen Fulton, the actress who plays Lisa Coleman on "As the World Turns." "Please tell me where you buy your clothes, how you do your hair, what perfume you use," she begged, "I want to model my life after yours."

A major criticism leveled at the soaps is that they create problems where none in fact exist. Some viewers—basically happy and healthy in their own lives—internalize the problems they see on the tube and make them their own. One housewife stopped watching soap operas after her family questioned her changing moods. "I came to realize that I was actually feeling anxiety over characters in my favorite story," she explained. "I knew it was a serious problem when I became very depressed over the illness of a character. It had just become too real."

Addictive fantasy has its own brand of realism, according to Dr. John Lion, a psychiatrist at the University of Maryland. Lion believes that soaps enable viewers to see human beings in "a very emotional way, the way we really are," and he recommends the soap operas to patients with "an overglamorized view of the world."

In a society torn between a need to keep up with changing realities and a desire to stick to the tried and the true, soap operas present a view of life which viewers can share.

In their book, *The Soaps*, Madeleine Edmondson and David Rounds conclude, "Most forms of entertainment are morally neutral. They make no attempt to raise questions of meaning and value. Soaps, on the other hand, have always addressed themselves primarily to exactly these questions. The situations and events dealt with by the soaps force the viewer to consider and answer some of the time honored philosophical questions: What is happiness? What is love? How can we reconcile ourselves to misfortune, accept death, justify what seems like a crushing and incomprehensible fate? What do we live for anyway? And, is it all worthwhile?"

Raising these questions is often helpful, yet viewers may be hurt by accepting the answers of the soaps instead of the scriptures. Joan Huyser, a Christian soap opera critic believes that, "Because of their point of view, soaps raise false expectations. They lead one to believe that comfort and happi-

ness come from self, from a certain view of blissful love, from an ever present friend and from social status."

"We attempt to find ultimate meaning for our existence in television, but such meaning is not there to be found," conclude George C. Conklin and Linda W. McFadden of Pacific School of Religion, Berkeley, California, in an article on television and theology.

"Placing television and its uses in a Christian theological perspective," they write, "helps us to see that our stewardship of television is an issue of human community. All of us—sponsors, producers, and viewers—share responsibility for what television is and how it is used."

Ultimately, each of us must look at our needs, commitments, and priorities as we consider the place of soap operas in our daily lives. Do soaps represent entertainment, education, companionship, or habit? The answers to these questions will help you decide if soap operas are worth your while.

Do you experience an increased pulse rate during the opening music of your favorite soap opera? Do you break out in hives at the thought of missing an episode? Then beware, you may be suffering from soap opera addiction.

Soap operas themselves may be entertaining, informative, and horizon-expanding. But they can also be addictive. How can you tell if your afternoon pastime has become a habit? Consider these questions:

1. Do you regularly plan your daily activities so that you are within range of a television set during soap opera time?
2. Do you become irritated when the phone rings or someone comes to the door while you are watching your favorite soap?
3. Have you ever turned down an invitation because you would have to miss a soap opera?
4. Do you feel anxious on Friday afternoons, knowing that you will have to wait two days for another episode?
5. Do you become worried or concerned about soap opera characters and their problems?

If you answered yes to these questions, you could be hooked. Take a minute to consider your priorities. If soap operas are nudging out the things in your life that are really important, you may need to re-establish your commitments.

—BRUCE H. JOFFE

FOR FURTHER READING:

Hancock, Maxine. *People in Process.* Old Tappan, N.J.: Revell, 1978.

THOUGHTS

Control of Thoughts

Romans tells us *Do not be conformed to this world, but be transformed by the renewal of your mind . . .* (*see* verse 12:2). This passage is talking about a renovation, a complete change for the better. The word *renewal* here means *to make new from above.* Man's thoughts, imaginations, and reasonings are changed through the working of the Holy Spirit. As Dr. Bernard Ramm puts it, "The Spirit establishes the direct connection from the mind of God to the mind of the Christian."

The *first step* in controlling your thoughts comes from the ministry of the Holy Spirit in your life. This reflects, however, upon *your own willingness* to let the Holy Spirit work in your life and to stop trying to run your life by yourself. Renewal of the mind brings about a spiritual transformation in the life of the Christian.

The *second step* in the process is to consider the direction of your thought-life itself. What do you think about? As suggested by Proverbs 23:7, *What a man thinks in his heart, so is he.* As we build up storehouses of memories, knowledge, and experience we seem to retain and remember those things which we concentrated upon the most. We are largely responsible for the things we let our minds dwell upon.

The *third step* is to realize that the Christian *does not* have to be dominated by the thinking of the old mind, the old pattern. He has been set free. *God has not given us the spirit of fear, but of power, and of love, and of a sound mind* (*see* 2 Timothy 1:7). Soundness means that the new mind can do what it is supposed to do. It can fulfill its function.

The *fourth step* is to let your mind be filled with the mind of Christ. There are three Scripture passages which place definite responsibility upon the Christian in this regard. In Philippians 2:5 KJV, Paul commands, *Let this mind be in you, which was also in Christ Jesus.* This could be translated: *Be constantly thinking this in yourselves* or *Reflect in your own minds, the mind of Christ Jesus.* The meaning here for the words *this mind be* is "to have understanding, to be wise, to direct one's mind to a thing, to seek or strive for."

The *fifth step* is this: In order to sustain the new thinking pattern it is important for the Christian to fill his mind with those thoughts and resources which will help him. Scripture itself fills this need.

> How can a young man keep his way pure? By guarding it according to thy word. With my whole heart I seek thee; let me not wander from thy commandments! I have laid up thy word in my heart, that I might not sin against thee.
> Psalms 119:9–11 RSV

We are also told to *desire the sincere milk of the word, that you may grow* (*see* 1 Peter 2:2). The Word of God is the safeguard against sins of the mind. Solomon said to commit your works upon the Lord. (*He will cause your thoughts to become agreeable to His will*) *so shall your plans be established and succeed* (*see* Proverbs 16:3 AMPLIFIED). An attitude of yielding and dependence upon God is a first step.

In addition to studying the Word of God, the *sixth step* is to strengthen our minds through prayer.

> Have no anxiety about anything, but in everything by prayer and supplication

451

with thanksgiving let your requests be made known to God. And the peace of God, which passes all understanding, will keep your hearts and minds in Christ Jesus.

                        Philippians 4:6, 7 RSV

Hitherto you have asked nothing in my name; ask, and you will receive, that your joy may be full.

                        John 16:24 RSV

Ask, and it will be given you, seek and you will find, knock, and it will be opened to you. For every one who asks receives, and he who seeks finds, and to him who knocks it will be opened.

                        Matthew 7:7, 8 RSV

God will keep our minds and He will answer us. But it is up to us to ask.

The new birth is the starting point for our emotional control. Bringing our thoughts under the control of the Holy Spirit is the final step.

—From H. Norman Wright, *The Christian Use of Emotional Power*. Old Tappan, N.J.: Revell, 1974.

TIME MANAGEMENT

To GET downright philosophical about time you'll realize that without it, you cease to be. In addition to eternal life, time is one of the most precious gifts God has given us. Yet, we tend to waste much of it.

A very wise man, Alexander Woollcott, once said, "Many of us spend half our time wishing for things we could have if we didn't spend half our time wishing."

Unfortunately, many people don't even spend their time wishing—they simply spend it in front of the TV set watching soaps and other nondetergents.

In a recent study it was found that the average homemaker watches daytime television an average of three hours daily. That becomes fifteen hours a week, based on a five-day week, or sixty-seven hours a month. On a yearly basis, those figures calculate to about 800 hours—or roughly one whole month, day and night, of solid TV watching.

If that astounds you, you'll be even more astounded to learn that the average family watches television not three hours a day, but six! That makes two solid months out of every year dedicated to watching the tube.

With that enormous chunk of time gone, it's no wonder we hear so many people saying, "I don't have time to . . ."

In order to combat that problem, I'd like you to keep track of how you spend every minute of your time for the next seven days. The object of this exercise is to see where you are wasting valuable time and how you can better use that time to set daily goals, and improve productivity and the quality of your life. On the next page is the chart you will use. Begin filling in the chart now and continue for the rest of the day. Then copy this chart on six pieces of paper and fill in one each day. After seven days, you will see a pattern that will reveal whether or not you are wasting time. If you are, you will want to reschedule your time in a way that allows you to be more productive and also promotes your goal of developing an ageless attitude.

Time	Detailed account of how time is spent
6:00	
6:30	
7:00	
7:30	
8:00	
8:30	
9:00	
9:30	
10:00	
10:30	
11:00	
11:30	
12:00	
12:30	
1:00	
1:30	
2:00	
2:30	
3:00	
3:30	
4:00	
4:30	
5:00	
5:30	
6:00	

6:30

7:00

7:30

8:00

8:30

9:00

9:30

10:00

10:30

11:00

11:30

12:00

Here is a sample of how to fill in your time chart:

7:30   up, shower, exercise, makeup, dress
8:00   coffee, read Bible
8:30   breakfast, TV talk show
9:00   TV, phone Leone, coffee & newspaper
9:30   TV, iron, phone Lotti, and so forth

After seven days, make some new charts and record your time schedule as it changes. It will undoubtedly take you a few weeks to develop a more productive schedule, so don't be discouraged. If the new one doesn't work, change it again. Be open to change. *Having an ageless attitude means being flexible.*

GOAL SETTING

Finding more time is worthless, however, unless you use it productively. And to do that, you will want to make a practice of setting goals. But first, let's define *goals*—

they should not be confused with activities. Busywork is not goal setting. You cannot "do" a goal. Most of our busywork can be classified as *activities*—things we do.

Activities are those things which we do daily. They comprise necessities such as washing the dishes, cooking, running to the market, and so on. We do them easily and regularly.

The difference between activities and daily goals is that the latter achieves something we are not accustomed to doing.

In addition, it is possible to have *daily goals*. For instance, if you have been used to thinking negatively about yourself and your goal is to become aware of and change those attitudes daily, that is a daily goal.

You may also have *short-term goals*. These take longer than a day to accomplish; they may take as long as six months. The daily goals may be the steps by which you accomplish your short-term goals.

For instance, if you decide to change your self-image from that of an impatient, cross woman to that of a gentle, loving spirit who can accept herself, a six-month goal would be appropriate. However, you can clearly see that daily goals are needed to accomplish your short-term goal. You cannot accomplish a goal of any magnitude without working on it daily. For example, to become gentle and loving, your daily goal would include awareness of your negative responses. The second daily goal is to memorize and repeat a Bible verse that emphasizes patience and kindness. Then pray that God will help you be that kind of person.

Short-term goals are a necessary part of a vital life, but you must also have *long-term goals* if you are to feel a sense of accomplishment and satisfaction about your life. Too many people look back with regret and begin numerous sentences with, "If only I'd ..." or "I wish I had ..." because they drifted through life without a plan, rather than directing their own life through the setting and attaining of lifetime goals.

Long-term goals are the things you'll look back upon with a sense of accomplishment. These, too, will be specific goals, as are the short-term and daily goals, but obviously will take much longer to accomplish.

As an example, a long-term goal that might be five years away could be a trip to Europe to see where your ancestors were born. Or, you might want a career goal, such as progressing from waitress to restaurant manager or going to college and graduating. Perhaps you didn't graduate from high school and have always wanted your diploma.

While all of these are long-term goals, they are accomplished by setting short-term goals that will facilitate your plan to accomplish the long-range one.

Once you learn to set realistic, attainable goals, your possibilities are limitless. Only your lack of imagination and initiative will hold you back.

Once you learn to understand and set goals, your life will take on the kind of meaning that may have been missing all these years. I recommend that you read Alan Lakein's book *How to Get Control of Your Time and Your Life* for a most thorough understanding of goal setting. This is a vital subject that is well worth the time it will take you to research it.

Right now, take a minute to jot down some tentative goals—ones that are attainable. Remember, goals can always be changed; you aren't tied into them forever. Having a goal is the important part.

Daily goals:

Short-term goals:

Long-term goals:

—From *Ruby MacDonald's Forty Plus and Feeling Fabulous Book.* Old Tappan, N.J.: Revell, 1982.

Scheduling

Some of us are more organized than others. Some of us like to work in a more structured framework than others. Adapt this to whatever your personal needs may be. You have to allow yourself lots of free time, especially when your children are small. If you are a person who receives many telephone calls, you must allow time to talk on the telephone. If there are people or situations that are constantly interrupting you, you have to schedule time for interruptions. If you are a highly regimented person and find your schedule is very organized, then your activities will be easier to schedule.

There are certain cautions to be aware of in scheduling. Don't try to emulate other people, but do what God wants you to do. When you are accomplishing what He has asked of you, you are highly motivated and you find that you have time for what He wants you to accomplish, not necessarily what everybody else wants you to. Recognize that God has made you a very unique individual. He has given you certain talents and capabilities.

Perhaps another pitfall could be best described as "Everybody get out of my way, here I come with my schedule." Being available to your family is part of time management, yet it is sometimes impossible to plan. So I caution you not to overplan; allow yourself time for the unexpected so that your schedule doesn't "run you" but you "run it."

A planned, Spirit-controlled life results in having the satisfaction of knowing that you're doing what you want to do and are living a fulfilled, meaningful life. It means choosing several things that you really enjoy doing and accounting for them in your schedule. It includes doing the humdrum variety of things which have to be done—and all of us have those projects—with more enthusiasm. You will find that those projects go much faster, are much easier, and in the end are more productive because you know that God wants you to do them. That helps you to desire to complete these goals. It is through the planned life that we find ourselves developing into the persons whom we want to be and whom God wants us to be.

—From Vonette Zachary Bright, *For Such a Time as This*. Old Tappan, N.J.: Revell, 1976.

FOR FURTHER READING:

Bowman, George M. *Clock Wise*. Old Tappan, N.J.: Revell, 1979.

Donahue, Marilyn Cram. *A Piece of Me Is Missing*. Wheaton, Ill.: Tyndale, 1978.

Kilgo, Edith Flowers. *Handbook for Christian Homemakers*. Grand Rapids: Baker Book, 1982.

Tchividjian, Gigi. *A Woman's Quest for Serenity*. Old Tappan, N.J.: Revell, 1981.

TOBACCO

CONSIDER the medical effects of tobacco upon yourselves.

1. The carbon monoxide in inhaled smoke significantly reduces the ability of hemoglobin in the blood cells to take up oxygen from the lungs and deliver it to the body's tissues.
2. Tests have shown that as few as ten inhalations of smoke increases resistance in the air passages of the lungs, and this choked-up condition persists for an hour after each cigarette.
3. Tiny hairlike cilia, which act as brooms to sweep out the windpipe and bronchial tubes, become paralyzed by smoke, and without this natural defense the lungs become vulnerable to airborne bacteria, viruses, dust particles and chemical pollutants.
4. The lung capacity of habitual smokers gradually shrinks because thickened air sacs throughout the lungs become less efficient in oxygen and carbon-dioxide exchange.
5. Because of tobacco tar in cigarettes, smokers become five times more vulnerable to, and much more affected by, such conditions as chronic bronchitis, emphysema, asthma, and respiratory allergies than do nonsmokers.
6. Nicotine in tobacco is a supertoxic, very lethal poison. As little as five drops can kill an adult. It acts as rapidly as cyanide. Fortunately, most of it is burned in smoking, but what remains stimulates the sympathetic nervous system, causing it to send more adrenal and other hormones to the heart than it needs. This eventually causes irritation and scarring in the heart muscle, narrowing of the coronary arteries, and a greatly increased chance of bloodclot formation. These conditions eventually end up in a heart attack, and the average age for such victims is getting younger every year.
7. Recent research shows evidence that the combination of smoking and taking birth-control pills reduces the natural resistance of premenopausal women to heart attacks, thereby making them almost as vulnerable as men.

   There are potentially dangerous risks for pregnant women who smoke, too. They are more liable to have intrauterine bleeding with fetal death or premature delivery of an underweight baby with an increased chance of its death in the first few months of life.
8. The statistical connection between tobacco tar and lung cancer is so well es-

tablished now that no other comment is needed. Remember, though, that with its pain, nausea, coughing up blood, weight loss, and partial asphyxiation, having terminal lung cancer is not a very comfortable way to die. The price of a lifetime of smoking is a deathtime of agony.

A word of encouragement: If you give up smoking, almost all toxic effects will disappear within a few weeks, but, of course, destroyed lung tissue can never be regenerated. Some smokers have tried switching to cigars or a pipe, but these are still quite harmful to the lungs, especially if you continue to inhale, though less so than cigarettes. However, they are more likely than cigarettes to cause cancers of the mouth and tongue, because smoke from them is hotter and the concentration of tar is greater. If you can't quit, try to get started on a vigorous physical-conditioning program which will at least help to reduce some of the potential and actual harmful effects of tobacco by increasing lung efficiency and by strengthening the heart.

Let me briefly give you a few scary statistics. If you smoke one twenty-cigarette pack daily, you are eight times more likely to get lung cancer; twenty times more likely with two packs daily than a nonsmoker. Upon discovery of this cancer, only 20 percent are considered operable, and of these only 30 percent or seven people out of a hundred, survive five years.

Smoking's most dangerous effect, statistically, however, is not its effect on the lungs, but on the heart and blood vessels. Sudden death from heart attack has in some instances been found to be as much as sixteen times greater in heavy smokers than nonsmokers. Another study found that the overall death rate from all causes was six times greater in smokers. Life insurance actuarial statistics show that the average fifty-year-old who has smoked one pack daily since age twenty-one has a life expectancy eight and a half years shorter than the nonsmoker. That works out to twenty and one half minutes of life lost for every cigarette!

That's not all. Smokers also incur three times the risk of suffering from a stroke and are twenty times more likely to have disabling constrictions in the arteries of the legs. Blood pressure rises ten to fifteen mm. Hg. in smokers, and they have more peptic ulcers, which heal more slowly. In addition to lung cancer, smokers develop more cancers in the mouth, tongue, lips, esophagus, larynx, pharynx, kidneys, and bladder. Tobacco also has an inhibiting effect on sexual libido. This is often unrecognized by the smoker, who tends to ascribe his lost potency to age or other problems. When he quits smoking, unexpected improvement in this area is a pleasant surprise.

How to quit? It takes motivation and courage. Here are some hopefully helpful suggestions.

There are several systems that use conditioning therapy, with self-imposed rewards for success and penalties for failure. These take several weeks, but work well if you stick with it. The Schick Stop-Smoking Clinics use aversion therapy in which taking certain controlled substances so alters the taste of cigarettes that one quickly loses all desire to smoke again. That is thoroughly unpleasant, but quick and effective.

Hypnosis can sometimes be effective, though I have some reservations. Occasionally, after treatment, an alternative habit may develop, such as nail biting, gum chewing, excessive coffee drinking, or taking tranquilizers, if any underlying problems are not dealt with. Also Christians generally are resistant to the prospect of submitting control of their minds to another person. For these reasons, although I don't recommend a trial of hypnotherapy, I strongly urge anyone intent on giving it a try to go to a well-qualified person, preferably a psychiatrist or other medical doctor.

The department of psychiatry of your local county or city hospital should be able to advise you what number to call to obtain one of these therapies.

"Cold turkey," or ending smoking abruptly by yourself, is the quickest, but the most painful. If you choose this method, pick a definite date: the first of next month, a birthday, an anniversary. It helps the significance of the commitment. Withdrawal symptoms, such as craving, last from two to three weeks, and you may experience temporary nervousness, sleep disturbance, fatigue, slight weight gain, and inability to concentrate. But stick with it. The long-term benefits of quitting far outweigh the brief discomfort period.

Cutting down gradually is less painful, but may take several weeks. In my view this is the best method, if you can be both patient and determined. Use of the four-stage filter system which progressively reduces the tar and nicotine inhaled has helped some to quit over a period of a few weeks. Try also these tested and effective methods which have worked for many who have attended Smoke Enders classes.

1. Realize that smoking is a learned habit and, therefore, through the behavior modification of constant practice, you can relearn the habit of nonsmoking.
2. Motivation is essential. Establish your incentive to quit. Write down a list of reasons: health needs, economics, self-concept, aesthetics, effect on others, example to your children, self-mastery, and so-forth. Be positive. Have the attitude that you are achieving something, not that you are denying yourself something.
3. Keep a cigarette count sheet and carefully record every one you use, at what time, under what circumstances, and how you are feeling. Keep the sheet wrapped round your pack and don't light up until you've noted it down.
4. Start breaking the habit by carrying your pack in a different place. At home or in the office store them out of easy reach. Start smoking without inhaling. Hold the cigarette in the hand you don't usually use. Do not carry matches or lighters. Take fewer puffs and use only half the cigarette, or even less. Mix a variety of different brands of cigarettes in your pack. This will begin to make smoking unpleasant.
5. Pick substitute habits to meet needs formerly met by smoking. (This does not include pot, alcohol, or eating!) When you desire a smoke, wait at least five minutes before giving in. Try these distractions first; the desire might go away: Find something small you can play with with your fingers. Take a short but brisk walk, if you can get out. In the office do some isometrics or knee bends. Half a dozen slow, very deep breaths held for a few seconds both at the full and empty points are very therapeutic.
6. Agree with yourself that you will smoke at least one less cigarette tomorrow than today. Again, don't regard this as a sacrifice or feel sorry for yourself. Be glad you're actually succeeding in quitting. The end is in sight. Drink plenty of water to wash the nicotine out of your body.
7. Set a definite date in the near future for your absolute last cigarette. Tell many close friends of your resolve. Such public commitment will bolster your determination. Find a friend who has also successfully quit smoking and encourage each other to stick with it.
8. Committed Christian believers have one additional resource: the power of the indwelling Holy Spirit. "Praise the Lord and Pass the Ammunition" we used to sing in World War II. Any battle in this life needs a combination of personal courage, effort, and determination, with God's invoked strength and help. "God helps those who help themselves" is a well-known, though nonbiblical truism commonly used in our culture. "Fortune favors the brave," is a similar secular motto of a prep school I attended in England.

As Christians, we don't believe in luck, but God so often does seem to bless those who strive to serve Him.

—From O. Quentin Hyder, M.D., *Shape Up.* Old Tappan, N.J.: Revell, 1979.

TOUCHING

TOD ANDREWS died early one April morning. Immediately after receiving the news I rushed to see his widow. Mable tried to talk, but her voice faltered and cracked. Gray eyes filled with tears.

Then Mable hugged me. I encircled her with my arms. For several minutes, no words passed between us. Finally she straightened up. With a handkerchief she dabbed her eyes. She said huskily, "Thank you . . . for being here."

As I relive that experience, I recall other scenes, times when words couldn't quite convey the depth of feeling.

Our home church held a farewell service for us when we left for Africa. One by one members came by and shook our hands. Suddenly Bernice hugged me tightly. "I want to tell you how much I love you and Shirley, but I can't find the words," she half-whispered and squeezed me again.

Last summer we concluded a church leaders' retreat. At our closing exercise, each one held a chunk of French bread, then went to every other person, individually, and took a piece from each other's bread. Then each pronounced a benediction upon the other: "The Lord bless you and keep you" or "May his Spirit always lead you."

During the two-day retreat I had felt especially close to Lamar. He and I had been in a prayer group for the two days and prayed together several times. As he started to speak to me, he stammered slightly and then impulsively hugged me. I thought to myself, "You've given me a beautiful benediction."

Incidents like this have made me realize the importance of human touch. In fact, I have a kind of motto. When I'm with people and words don't seem to convey all that needs to be said, then I try this approach: *When in doubt, hug 'em!*

It works. Not because it's premeditated. Not because it's a gimmick. It works because it's an expression of caring.

Physical touch conveys so much. By the mere touch of a hand we express love, happiness, anger, agitation. Ever have someone grab you by the arm in a menacing way? Or poke a forefinger against your chest?

The Bible presents an amazing amount of information about the touch of the human hand. In the Old Testament offerings, the high priest laid his hands on the sacrificial animal, then confessed the sins of the people. By that action he symbolically transferred the guilt of the nation onto the lamb.

Elisha was called to the home of a young boy who had died. The prophet stretched himself out on top of the child, breathed into his mouth, and life returned.

The New Testament abounds with the stories of Jesus touching people. Can you imagine the furor when Jesus laid his hand on a leper? Leprosy was an incurable disease feared by the people. No normal person came close to a leper. In fact, when a leper approached other people, he or she had to cry out, "Unclean!" then quickly passed on as far away as possible.

But Jesus defied all customs. He reached out and physically touched a diseased man (Matthew 8:1–3). The gospel accounts are filled with Jesus making physical contact with people, from healings to blessing little children.

In most churches, the ordination to the office of minister has always been effected by the laying on of human hands. Church officers usually go through a similar experience. New church members customarily receive "the right hand of fellowship."

Mere physical touch says, "You are one with us. We identify with you." Then we look at our sophisticated world and we're afraid to get too close to people. Afraid to touch. Afraid to open ourselves. We keep our distance and retreat inside. I'm not suggesting meaningless backslapping or senseless hugging or excuses for sexual seductions. But I advocate freedom—freedom to express care.

In my first pastorate a number of children in the neighborhood got to know me. Some of them attended our Sunday school. Meeting them on the street, it was not unusual for Dawn to hug me or Tom to grab me. One little pre-schooler jumped at me, encircled me with her arms, pulled me down to her level and said, "Give me some sugar!" and then waited for a kiss.

For me, touch symbolizes our attitudes. The more uptight a man is, the more his physical body shows it through limited gestures, lips that scarcely move and hands that never reach out. A woman sits stiffly or moves backward as you come closer to her. They're both afraid of physical contact.

Then I think of Jesus. Children sat on his lap. He laid his hands on them. He touched lepers, the blind, the lame—all kinds of people. His touch brought physical healing, but liberated the soul as well.

People need our touch. They need our liberating and caring expressions.

Remember the story of the Good Samaritan? A dying man lay by the roadside, but the religious Jews passed by, unwilling to touch him, unwilling to defile themselves. Then an alien, a Samaritan, appeared. He picked up the man, cleansed his wounds, and showed mercy. That's the ministry God calls us to—the ministry of touch. We do it symbolically when we talk about touching lives. But we also need to give others our physical touch.

I encounter people all the time. Sometimes we want to offer comfort but words seem inadequate. *But I can sometimes say it with a hug!*

—From Cecil B. Murphey, *When in Doubt, Hug 'Em!* Atlanta: John Knox, 1978.

Hands

It is indeed sad that many Americans have not learned to use their sense of touch to express love. We know that a loving hand on a sick person's forehead or a grieving person's shoulder often works wonders. Jesus used his hand to heal the ear of the high priest's servant in the Garden of Gethsemane (Luke 22:51). And the woman who had internal bleeding for twelve years instinctively knew that she would be healed if she could just touch Jesus' robe (Matthew 9:20, 21).

Scientific studies prove that babies who are not touched, caressed, hugged and cuddled often die. Love, expressed through touching, is therefore a basic human need.

But why are we so afraid to show our love to others in this way?

Perhaps you don't use your hands to express love because you are afraid of seeming like a clinging vine. However, you will be interested to hear that a study of eighty male and female college students showed that the higher the subject's self-esteem, the more intimate he or she was in communicating through touch, especially when relating to a female. If you pat others on the shoulder or the back, you are proving yourself more relaxed and confident than if you hold back.

A lot of people make fun of those who talk with their hands, saying that they lack word power, but scientists have found that those who have a high rate of hand movements or gestures are actually more fluent than others.

Don't be afraid to use your hands as God intended them to be used! Let them express the love in your heart, the gentleness and gracefulness that reaches out to other people. You will become more beautiful if you do!

If you want more touch in your family, then *you* be the one to instigate it. When sitting beside your husband on the sofa, take his hand. When a child sits beside you, pick him up and place him on your lap, or put your arms around him. Others learn from our loving example. The movements of your hands can attract or repel others. Here are some important do's and don'ts:

1. The proper position of the hand when it is relaxed and at your side is to let the profile show. Your thumb should be relaxed and pointed straight down. The four fingers should be slightly curved toward the body.
2. Never use your fingers to point. If you want to indicate something with your hands, move the whole hand in the desired direction with the palm open and up.
3. Try for more graceful hand movements. When you reach to pick up something, move your wrist first and let the fingers follow. The arm should move in an arch, and the fingers should be relaxed. A bit of

practice will make this movement seem more *natural*. Think how ballet dancers move their arms up and down slowly and gracefully, like the wings of a bird. Practice until it does not seem affected.

—From Joanne Wallace, *The Image of Loveliness*. Old Tappan, N.J.: Revell, 1978.

TRAVEL

Sources of Information

National tourist organizations are official arms of foreign governments and usually headquartered in New York, with branch offices in such major cities across the country as Los Angeles, Chicago, Boston, Atlanta, San Francisco, or Houston. These bureaus are rich sources of free information, but their function should not be confused with travel agencies, whose agents can do everything from planning your itinerary to notifying the hotel you'd like a board under your bed. Some tourist offices provide more helpful literature than others. I have seen everything from seductive color brochures that give no specifics, to plain xeroxed sheets with detailed walking tours. Some countries just know how to sell what they've got. The French recognize that we go to France to eat, so they have myriad restaurant guides for all price ranges. Although the word "bargain" should be excised from almost every country's vocabulary, Hong Kong still offers good buys. Logically, Hong Kong's tourist bureau offers a comprehensive shopping guide. The Italians push their history and, among other items, have a first-rate map to Rome's historical monuments, museums, and catacombs, with extensive historical notes.

The material you receive will vary according to what is available and, equally important, *how you ask for it*. The ideal method is to talk with a representative in person. If you are researching via the mail, write early and give a deadline by which you need the information. Most of the travel literature you will receive is sent third class, so you want your request in the "action pile," not the "futures" department.

Because there is nothing quite so confusing as getting an avalanche of generalizations, make your questions as specific as possible when you write, call, or go in to seek information. Instead of asking for hotels in Paris, for instance, indicate how much you want to spend, if you want a breakfast-included arrangement, if you prefer small, family-run establishments or large modern quarters. Ask for information about special events. Many countries have year-long celebrations for the birth—or death—of musicians, saints, philosophers, war heroes, etc., and if the trend to turn chefs into national heroes continues, we may see national holidays for Escoffier or Paul Bocuse. Fetes mark the anniversary of the founding, liberating, or destruction of a city, the building of a famous church. If you are traveling with children, request information on activities or places of special interest. Some countries—Denmark and Ireland, for example—have farm vacations which are particularly suited to kids, and others have guides specializing in sight-seeing for kids so you can have a two-hour meal without a hamburger in sight.

The airlines also have a windfall of free or low-cost information. Call your local reservations office and ask what is available. They might suggest that you contact their tour department, write to the main office, or they may take your name and address and send booklets to your directly. Some airlines, like Pan American, have small guidebooks to capital cities and the environs. Japan Airlines, for instance, puts out "Business in Japan" and "The Woman's Guide to the Orient." Air India will even tell you how to wrap a sari.

. . . While plowing through this "helpful propaganda" remember that ad agencies and public relations companies have spent billions to seduce you with words and pictures. Rarely will you find any critical evaluations. Have you ever seen a picture of a tourist with third-degree burns from lying in the sun? You must read the fine print, note the asterisks, and ask as many questions as you think necessary. Be wary of the possible hidden meaning of these adjectives: pleasant (without character); comfortable (worn); colorful (teeming); peaceful (boring). Is the work *completed* on the newly remodeled wing, or will you be lodged in the old, crumbling section? Is the balcony more than a window ledge? Do you have to contort your body to see the water in an ocean- or lakeview room? Does "extensive convention facilities" mean you will be sandwiched between the five hundred cash-register salesmen wearing badges? Is the special children's program more than just hamburgers on the menu? What does "year-round sunshine" or "occasional showers" mean?

The Travel Agent

Even if you were the world's most assiduous researcher, it's unlikely that you could ever amass and *evaluate* all the information about your trip as well as the skilled travel agent with his constant access to travel industry literature and "fam trips"—familiarization trips—that provide firsthand experience. The operative word here, however, is *skilled.* The field of travel agents attracts as many hucksters and opportunists as the health food business. Some of the most common "nonprofessionals" are businessmen using the agency for tax benefits and free trips; people selling paradise cheap, with only a box office number for identification; or "outside travel agency salesmen" who trade in stolen tickets. Those types are a minority, but awareness that they do exist is part of your self-protection.

The bona fide professional belongs to the American Society of Travel Agents. The elite travel agent will also have CTC, or "Certified Travel Counselor," after his name, which means he has completed the two-year course of the Institute of Certified Travel Agents. If you have any suspicions about the agency you are considering, ask if the local Better Business Bureau has any complaints on file, or write to the American

Society of Travel Agents, Consumer Affairs Department, 711 Fifth Avenue, New York, N.Y. 10022. You're being intelligent, not snoopy.

Don't be embarrassed to "interview" the prospective agent. However, you can't expect a mind reader. What you want is someone who can translate your ideas—as vague as they may be—into concrete plans. Does he/she seem willing to take enough time to ask you the important questions: your interests, your budget, your anxieties, if any, about food, types of accommodations, customs relating to women, or political situations in certain parts of the world? Anyone who minimizes the differences between travel agents on the grounds that they all get the same kind of information is taking the easy way out. But even the best agents aren't miracle workers. Each piece of information you provide will help them come up with the right trip for you. A travel agent, like an interior designer, works best when he has all the pertinent information. In order to make a bedroom function most effectively, for instance, your designer would have to know if you read in bed in order to have a good reading light, or if you pile magazines, books, a radio, phone, flowers, by your bed in order to give you a large-enough table. I would recommend you divulge the following to your travel agent:

1. Tell him/her the purpose of your trip. Try to list *all* the elements you'd like to have. You may be doing yourself a disservice by stressing the importance of a secluded beach and neglecting to say you're passionate about gambling, that you care about good food, or that you feel uncomfortable unless you speak the language and you're only fluent in English.
2. Outline your budget, and how you want to apportion the funds.
3. Explain what *you* mean by a "one-star" hotel. Hotel classifications are so diverse that first class in one country might be the equivalent of third class in another. The agent also has *his* own interpretation of

such terms as luxury, standard, budget, old, charming, etc.

4. Several destinations may suit your needs. Listen to all the possibilities, and be flexible enough to consider a new idea. No one would go so far afield as to suggest ice fishing in Newfoundland when you've asked for ancient temples.

5. What does the price of the tour or package arrangements include: tips, taxes, admission fees to museums, transfers from airports to hotels, sightseeing, meals? You don't want to find out after you get there that dinner is "an extra."

6. Go over any cancellation clauses in package plans and ask your agent to translate from "legalese."

Inexpensive air fares often require advance booking so talk to an agent early enough to take advantage of them.

It won't cost you anything to use a travel agent—with a few stipulations. A travel agent is paid on a commission basis from airlines, hotels, and large tour operators. There is a set commission fee, for example, on domestic and international flights, so you needn't worry that he'll book you on an airline managed by his cousin Morris who gives him a higher fee. You can even have a travel agent book you a flight from New York to California and nothing more—at no cost—although some agents prefer not to do it because of the small commission rate. On any kind of booking, you may be charged for long-distance telephone calls or cables.

An agent usually has one self-protection rule. If you ask the agent to plot an individualized itinerary for you, he may ask for a nonrefundable deposit, perhaps 10–15 percent of the estimated cost, to be applied to the cost of the tour. He's protecting himself against the client who takes the professionally planned itinerary and books the trip himself, meaning the agent will not receive any commissions, and in essence has planned the trip for free. The deposit also helps separate the people who realize they are paying for an agent's expertise from those just looking for general information or an "armchair" trip.

HOW A TRAVEL AGENT USUALLY WORKS

1. You talk, sketch out and decide on an individual itinerary or a package tour.

2. When you pay the agent a deposit on the total amount, you are given a receipt and an invoice telling you when the remaining balance is due.

3. A few days later the agent will show you a completed itinerary, and if it suits you, he will then check the availability of hotels and transportation and make the bookings. In the event of space problems he will consult you and suggest alternatives.

4. The arrangements are made through a tour operator, companies that specialize in putting together transportation and land arrangements, a corresponding travel agent at the destination, or with personal contacts at hotels.

5. He will inform you if visas are necessary and process the forms for you through a visa service.

6. He will tell you what shots are required, if any; have passport forms on hand to show you how to fill them out, and usually will collect information about your destination from the tourist offices.

When you leave the office for your trip, your travel folder should include:

1. A detailed itinerary.

2. Airline, rail, cruise tickets.

3. Original vouchers for you, copies to the corresponding agent (you will have the phone number and an agency contact), and copies to the reservations manager at the hotel. The voucher, in fact, is a replacement for the money you have paid to the travel agent at home, and it will be marked "prepaid" with the exact amount in dollars. It will specify what you are entitled to; if you will be met at the airport in a motor coach or limousine; the kind of room accommodations you will have; if

breakfast is included; sightseeing tours and any special requests, whether it's a particular interest like jewelry auctions or having kosher or vegetarian meals. If you don't know how long you want to stay in a hotel, the agent will usually give you a voucher for one night, and notify the hotel that if you decide to stay on you will pay the additional cost on departure.

4. Travel and baggage insurance forms to fill out and mail back to the agent. Baggage insurance covers lost luggage. But let's say you have an airline ticket with specific departure and return dates. If for some "good" reason you have to return early, or postpone the trip, you forfeit the cheaper fare. Your travel agent can sell you a policy that will cover the additional cost of the ticket. Ask the agent what the insurance company considers a "good" reason—illness, a death in the family, etc.

—From Dena Kaye, *The Traveling Woman*. Garden City, N.Y.: Doubleday, 1980.

Tips for Travelers

IN PREPARING TO TRAVEL

1. Make a checklist weeks before you plan to travel. It could look something like this:

   Hotel/Motel Reservations (Date) _____
   _____
   _____
   Tickets _____
   Currency _____
   Traveler's Checks _____
   Credit Cards _____
   _____

2. Make a personal list of items to pack in each suitcase. Paste/tape the list on the inside top. Check each item as it is packed.

3. Take only what you need. You or someone else will have to lug, carry, or push your luggage. The lighter the load, the easier for everyone.

4. Confirm all reservations.

5. Make arrangements for mail and any other deliveries. (In many cities the post office will hold mail if you request it.) Have a friend or relative check your home/apartment daily.

6. Leave your itinerary with someone, so you can be contacted in case of emergency.

7. Research the place/places you plan to visit. Know in advance the things you want to see.

8. Let the children help plan the trip. Show them on a map where they live now, where they're going, the total miles, the miles each day, etc. It's a good opportunity not only for family togetherness, but for an informal learning experience for them.

WHILE TRAVELING

1. Appoint one family member to make a final check of the room where you stay. After all luggage is cleared out and everyone gone, one person needs to check bathrooms, closets, and under the beds for any mistakenly left items.

2. Give yourself plenty of time. Allow time for unseen delays. If traveling by car, don't set your next stopping place so far away that you will have to exceed the speed limit in order to reach your destination by a specified time.

3. Remind yourself to be courteous to and tolerant of people who are different. It's not a matter of right or wrong, only a difference in culture or custom.

4. Include quiet games or reading material for children. They easily become bored on long trips.

5. Plan for a few minutes of worship together as a family unit.

AFTER RETURNING

1. Don't impose on friends to hear all the details of your trip. If they're interested, they'll let you know.

2. If you show slides of your travel, keep the presentation brief. Not many people are interested in "the tiny rock in the bottom left hand corner reminds me that . . ." or "the thin fellow standing in the back row is named. . . ."

3. You are not an expert on another section of the United States or of the world. Naturally you have opinions and personal observations. Share them as such.

—From Cecil B. Murphey, *Devotions for Travelers*. Old Tappan, N.J.: Revell, 1982.

U

UTERUS

THE UTERUS is the baby carriage of the pelvis. It has a specific, generally short-term use and comes in handy only during a relatively small segment of a woman's life. Yet it is the organ that gives the most trouble to the post-reproductive female. It is a small, muscular, pear-shaped structure that in its good days had the miraculous ability to stretch to many times its normal size and encompass a fetus, and the unique ability to shed its lining (called the endometrium) at monthly intervals. It doesn't seem to manufacture any hormones itself except perhaps the prostoglandins, but it's the target organ for the ovarian hormones and the gonadotrophins. It would be nice if it would just quietly shrivel up and die when it is no longer needed, but female organs are rarely very accommodating, and some of the most annoying and costly female illnesses arise during the uterus's slow demise.

Uterine disease is usually manifested in two ways: by tumor formation or by bleeding.

THE BUMPY, LUMPY UTERUS

Most tumors of the uterus are benign. These are called fibroid tumors and are quite common in women over forty. They form in the muscle wall of the uterus, sometimes jutting into the uterine cavity (the lumen), where they can disrupt the lining and cause bleeding. A majority of fibroid tumors, however, simply grow outward and cause no symptoms. Your gynecologist can feel them at your yearly pelvic exam. Removing them

or not is your choice. You can have either a hysterectomy (removal of the uterus with or without the ovaries) or a hysterotomy (scooping out only the tumor, the technique to use if you still want children). Or you can just sit on them.

I am presently sitting on a fibroid tumor the size of a grapefruit, and my gynecologist is eyeing me expectantly. It doesn't hurt or bleed or block any vital organ, though it does make my bladder a little more irritable. The risk I am taking is that the tumor will block my kidneys, or will grow more rapidly or become malignant—which is about as likely as gallstones leading to gallbladder cancer (not too likely). Why am I so stubborn? Well, fibroid tumors are common in women and usually get smaller after age fifty, when the amount of estrogen in the body diminishes. It's not that I'm afraid of surgery. Hysterectomy is the most common major operation in women, and today's gynecological surgeons are decent technicians. But I hate general anesthesia and the six-week post-op convalescence when you can't exercise or drive and *can* eat. If they could get me back to work in two weeks, I'd be strongly tempted to undergo the knife.

THE BLEEDING UTERUS

The most common cause of uterine bleeding is the monthly menstrual cycle. This occurs at regular intervals when the uterus sheds its lining, the endometrium. The quantity of blood lost varies from individual to individual. Some women are known as heavy

466

bleeders; others have only a scanty flow. However, excess bleeding at any time, bleeding or spotting between periods for more than one cycle, or any bleeding after menopause can be a sign of disease.

The most common source of excessive bleeding in the over-forty female is a benign condition called DUB (dysfunctional uterine bleeding), caused by a hormonal imbalance. There is an excessive buildup of the endometrial lining, which alters the regularity and amount of blood flow. Usually it's a good idea to have a D and C (dilation and curettage or more informally, dusting and cleaning), a minor surgical procedure in which the cervix is dilated and the wall of the uterus is scraped. This procedure is useful in making a diagnosis—the removed tissue can be examined under a microscope to determine if it is malignant—and as therapy, because it removes the excess tissue from the wall of the uterus, leaving a normal base.

Incidentally, a D and C can be done in a doctor's office, but don't believe that "it won't hurt a bit." Even with the best local anesthesia, you'll have cramps afterward.

Occasionally, a "chemical" D and C is done instead of a surgical one; high doses of progesterone are injected or administered by pill for seven to ten days and then abruptly stopped. This induces the uterus to slough off its lining. But progesterone in large doses is a hateful drug. It causes bloating, depression, headaches, nausea, and weight gain.

Excessive bleeding from DUB lasts from ten to twenty-one days and can cause spotting, oozing, clotting, and hemorrhaging. You get sick of stained underwear and relentless changing of tampons. If you've had several trials of hormonal therapy and several D and C's and still the problem persists, you might get fed up with the whole messy business and opt for hysterectomy. The problem would pass eventually, but who knows how long that would take? If it's making you tired, cranky, and chapped, there's nothing wrong with having the . . . thing removed.

—From Barbara Edelstein, M.D., *The Woman Doctor's Medical Guide for Women*. New York: Morrow, 1982.

V

VACATIONS

THE WORD *vacation* means a time of rest, but for most of us it is anything but restful. Clothing must be purchased and packed, car repairs made, traveler's checks bought, and afterwards, charge account bills paid.

Yet vacation is one of the best ideas ever to come to the working world. People need time off from their regular activities to recharge themselves.

Jesus recognized the need for a period of time away from the routine of daily work. While His work was of immense importance, He knew that the physical bodies of He and His disciples could not take the pace of constant work and no relaxation. After a particularly difficult time for the apostles Jesus "said unto them, Come ye yourselves apart into a desert place, and rest a while: for there were many coming and going, and they had no leisure so much as to eat" (Mark 6:31).

A vacation, in the truest sense of the word, is not a period of hustle and bustle, but rather a time of physical rest and mental reflection. While traveling and engaging in recreational activities may be a means of attaining some of the mental and physical rest needed, a real vacation is one which leaves the family relaxed and with a good attitude.

But marriage counselors point out that the two-week vacation period is one of the most dangerous times of the year as far as marital harmony is concerned. For some reason, most marriages cannot bear the strain of two solid weeks of unrelieved togetherness. Vacation time frequently turns into a time of battle with parents squabbling and children sulking.

Financial counselors suspect that financial strain is another reason for vacation upsets. Incredible as it may seem, those families who are the most deeply in debt are the ones who may be vacationing the most often and in the most expensive manner. The vacation is rationalized on the basis of "Let's get away for a while and forget our money worries."

If you are trying to run from money worries, the hundreds of dollars you may spend will not bring happiness. The best way to get the most value for your vacation dollar is to plan your vacation with worthwhile motives in mind.

WHAT SHALL WE DO ON VACATION?

The kinds of vacations available to you are as varied as the seashells you collected on the beach last summer. You can take a sports oriented vacation with a concentration of golf or tennis, a back-to-nature vacation with the emphasis on hiking, horseback riding, and camping, or a rest-and-recharge vacation with beautiful scenery and little to do, or even a remodeling vacation during which you paint your house. The choice is yours, but the presence or absence of money should not be the determining factor, because with careful planning you will be able to achieve the results you want, even on a limited budget.

With ample funds you can go to an exotic island and golf on a secluded course, however, if your funds aren't so ample you can still accomplish your goal. The difference is you will be staying at home and playing golf on the public course. Whatever the current shape of your budget, the kind of vacation you want to enjoy is possible, provided you are able to be flexible in your choice of location.

The best way to get the most vacation value for your dollar is to select the kind of vacation that pleases you and to scale it up or down to fit your budget.

If fishing is what you want to do, then by all means do it, but you don't have to do it in South America. With the exception of oceanside or skiing vacations, any activity you might choose is probably available to you on either a local level or only a day's drive away.

What Shall We Wear?

Second in importance only to "Where shall we go?" is "What shall we wear?" Other than Christmas and back-to-school time, the period of time preceding a vacation probably accounts for more clothing purchases than any other time of the year.

In order to economize it is necessary to pinpoint both your destination and your lifestyle. If you decide to undertake something new, such as skiing, you may find yourself investing more in clothing and equipment than in the actual vacation. Therefore, when planning a vacation which involves some activity you have not participated in previously, take into consideration the cost of the clothing and equipment involved as well as the expenses of the vacation itself.

Most shoppers who buy new clothing for vacation make two major mistakes: they buy too much or they buy the wrong items. The first place you will need to go shopping when you are planning your vacation, is in your own closet. Look to see what useable outfits you already own, and plan your purchases around them. Everybody likes new things to wear on vacation, but cutting down on vacation clothing is one of the most effective means of holding down the cost of a vacation.

What Kind of Transportation?

One of the major expenses involved with a vacation is the matter of getting there. Let's look at some of the options available to you in the transportation department.

1. *By Car.* For most of us the favored method of vacation travel is by family car. Even with the cost of gasoline rising almost daily, it is still cheaper to go by car if you have to transport a group to your destination.

How then can we get the most economy for the family vehicle? First, before ever pulling out of the driveway, make certain the car is in tiptop running shape. Are the brakes sound and the battery reliable? Do such things as windshield wipers, headlights, taillights, and turn signals work effectively? Do you have a jack and a useable spare tire? Is the car free of mechanical defects? Are the tires free of signs of excessive wear?

The best way to avoid financial disaster on a trip is to take care of all known automotive problems before you go. Should you have to spend one day of your vacation standing around a greasy garage, you will know how important preventive maintenance really is. Not only will you likely pay an exorbitant price for the repairs you will need, you will also pay the price of having missed a day's entertainment or relaxation.

On some interstate highways there has been a great deal of fraud perpetrated on vacationers by unscrupulous service station operators. While most states are cracking down on these notorious operations, some still exist. Don't leave your car unattended at a service station. Doing so means that you may get charged for more gasoline or oil than you actually bought. It also gives these con artists a chance to puncture your radiator hose or slit your fan belt so they can sell you a new one.

Increasing gasoline mileage is an important means of cutting vacation costs and three ways of boosting gasoline mileage can be done by any traveler: (1) Before you go on vacation have your car tuned up and have new spark plugs and a new air filter installed. These measures can increase gasoline mileage significantly. Also, have the oil changed. This doesn't affect the gasoline mileage, but it does prevent some other costly problems. (2) Don't overload your car. Not only does too much weight cost you in terms of tires and shock absorbers, but it also decreases your gasoline efficiency. (3) Drive the speed limit and maintain a smooth, even pace. Starting and stopping quickly burns up extra gasoline, and driving too fast not only leaves you open for a speeding ticket but increases your car's consumption of fuel.

Good tires are vital to your family's safety. Therefore the purchase of new tires may be an integral part of your vacation expense. Since you know in advance that vacation season is coming, make it a point to purchase the best tires you can afford during the months they are on sale. Plan ahead in order to get the best prices. You won't find the same bargains in June, July, and August as you will in March and April.

—From Edith Flowers Kilgo, *Money Management*. Grand Rapids: Baker Book, 1980.

FOR FURTHER READING:

Collins, Gary R. (editor). *Living and Growing Together*. Waco, Tex.: Word Books, 1976.

VALUES

Christian Values

"Do not neglect to do good and to share what you have . . ."—Hebrews 13:16

What are your values? What is important in your life? Doing good? Sharing? Being honest? Loving justice? Peace? Mercy? Faith?

Now consider the ways in which you came to prize those values. Were your parents a major example for you? Friends? Teachers? The probability is great that many of your cherished values have been transmitted (that means "handed-over") to you in part by members of your extended family. On the other hand you have been, and continue to be, exercising some choice in the formation of your value structure. Among conflicting values you are constantly choosing, and hopefully you are growing in the process.

Can values be learned? A debate among social scientists now centers on this topic, as on the attendant one: "If values are learned, how does this process take place?" Some argue that values are really determined by heredity, or by circumstances over which one has no control. Others consider change and growth not only possible, but even begin to offer ways of getting at that re-orientation of people in living situations.

Perhaps we cannot resolve once for all that conflict, but we can focus on clear, accepted Christian values among ourselves. We can encourage each other, as well as the children in our "family," to increase in sensitivity and grow morally. Take this clear word from the writer of Hebrews, for example: "Do not neglect to do good and to share what you have." Or consider the classic statement of the chief virtues by Paul in 1 Corinthians 13:13: "So faith, hope, love abide, these three; but the greatest of these is love." In these instances and many others, we have clear statements of Christian values. How do we incorporate these values, and others we can name easily, in our living? What about the inconsistencies and the need for growth?

To supply just one illustration, at a recent session with adults in a church school one man spoke of his situation with some dismay: "Something's wrong! When people ask me about it, I tell them how much I love my family and how important they are in my life. But when I figure how I spend my time, I find I don't act as though they were so important at all. My energies go elsewhere." His group of church school colleagues had been discussing the case of a family breaking up. Members of the group could have greeted this man's self-revelation in a variety of ways. They could have ignored him, scoffed at him, or scolded him. Instead they listened, and one person signaled hearing him: "The priorities seem mixed up. . . ." Conversation moved along with the man still included in it. And subsequently, he began to act more the caring parent and spouse.

The church group, in this situation, seems both to have helped the man clarify his present enacted values and move toward the formation of values he would move to act upon. What is true for a Christian person is also true for a Christian community. Its values often need to be clarified, but they are also formed within the church. There are numerous guides on "value clarification" available for use in schools and churches. Through growing in the faith, Christian families at the nuclear and congregational levels can come to develop and act on Christian values as well as clarifying present commitments.

All too often, however, the families in which we participate are abdicating responsibility for the valuing process. At the same time social forces—mobility and haste in American life, dehumanizing movie and television programming, role confusions, racial tension on a world wide basis, and family separations on a large scale—are occupying a center stage today unparalleled in human history.

The church is not now aiding in value formation as it used to.

. . . . .

It is unrealistic to expect immediate change in the cultural situation of all persons. But we can center consciously on supporting and encouraging Christian patterns of living that prize and seek to embody central values in our tradition—love for others, for instance. We must discover methods to understand better what the Christian idea of love requires of us in situations of conflict and decision.

We can likewise seek to live in a consciously Christian manner ourselves, learn-ing from other believers and from people we trust the ways in which to cope and creatively deal with our daily commitments and possibilities. Discussions of values in Bible study, in peer groups, with families and friends, can help clarify and even form (sometimes "re-form") the values on which we seek to depend.

—From Louis and Carolyn Weeks and Robert A. and Alice F. Evans, *Casebook for Christian Living.* Atlanta: John Knox, 1977.

FOR FURTHER READING:

Hancock, Maxine. *People in Process.* Old Tappan, N.J.: Revell, 1978.

VENEREAL DISEASE
(Sexually Transmitted Disease)

Gonorrhea

The most common form of VD is gonorrhea. It is caused by a germ that can be easily identified under an ordinary microscope. In the female cervix and vagina, this germ may live without causing much discomfort, though it often causes severe infection and great pain. During sexual intercourse with a woman who is infected with this germ, it is almost certain to infect the man's urethra and penis. This infection causes severe pain upon urination and a thick, yellowish discharge. The condition will, in time, tend to improve, but meanwhile he will infect anyone with whom he has sexual contact. Each, in turn, will infect other sexual contacts, and an epidemic is underway.

Though this germ is developing a resistance to the antibiotics that can kill it, gonorrhea is still quite easily cured by proper medical care. When untreated, however, it may cause such inflammation and scarring of the sensitive tissues in the reproductive tract, that sterility may result. A person so damaged may never be able to have children. A baby born to a mother who carries

471

this germ in her vagina during its delivery is very likely to develop a serious eye infection. It is obvious that, when untreated, this disease has extremely serious complications that can be completely avoided by good medical care.

Venereal Warts

Another common form of VD is known as venereal warts. This disease causes the growth of wartlike tissue that is ugly and annoying, though not painful. The warts grow in a coarse, grayish brown cluster about the penis or on the labia. They are caused by a virus and must be treated by a physician, but they are entirely curable.

Syphilis

The most serious type of VD, because of its long-range complications, is syphilis. It is caused by a corkscrew shaped microscopic germ called a "spirochete." When this germ enters a human body through a scratch or even an irritated area of mucous membrane in the reproductive tract or elsewhere, it will cause a sore. This sore is only slightly painful, and for this reason, it may be dismissed as not being serious enough to require medical care. It heals very slowly, and is round with a raised border that causes it to look a bit like a paper punch has been used to make it. The sore may be on the skin in the genital area where it can be easily seen, or it can develop internally, where it may go unnoticed.

Because this lesion is not too bothersome, and if it happens to be inside a woman's vagina, she will probably not even know it is there. Syphilis, therefore, is often neglected and left untreated. When untreated, the germ will slowly migrate through the bloodstream or body tissues to any part of the body where it lies dormant. Years later, a crippling form of arthritis may develop, a serious brain infection causing permanent loss of normal mental functioning can occur, or a baby born to an untreated syphilitic mother is almost certain to have serious birth de-

fects. The other results are too many to list. The important fact is that syphilis can be cured. It needs careful, long-term follow-up, but it is completely curable.

Vaginal Infections

There are two common vaginal infections that are not usually spread through sexual intercourse, though they may be. They are caused by microorganisms called yeast and Trichomonas. Both of these infections can be easily picked up in a bathtub or from swimming. They commonly occur after long or intensive treatment with antibiotics. They produce a vaginal discharge that causes severe itching and burning. Since the urethra and urinary bladder are very close to the vagina, there may be a bladder infection as well.

Treatment of these diseases is best recommended by your physician. He can prescribe medication to be inserted in the vagina and may order oral medication to completely cure them. Though men rarely have any symptoms of these infections, they may carry the organisms. A husband and wife can bounce this sort of infection back and forth between them without any other sexual exposure. In such cases, oral treatment is necessary for both spouses.

—From Grace H. Ketterman, M.D., *How to Teach Your Child About Sex.* Old Tappan, N.J.: Revell, 1981.

Herpes Simplex II

Herpes simplex II or herpes progenitalis, is caused by a virus that is related to the one responsible for cold sores. Genital herpes has become a major problem in recent years, in large part because there is no effective treatment for the disease. Many individuals who contract genital herpes have outbreaks of fluid-filled blisters on the genitals periodically for many years. The disease is transmitted by sexual contact during such an outbreak. If a pregnant woman delivers during an outbreak of herpes progenitalis, the newborn infant may contract the disease. In newborns, genital herpes can cause severe problems and can be fatal. Caesarian delivery is recommended for any woman with active lesions. In addition, women with genital herpes should have a Pap smear every six months, since the Herpes simplex II virus is associated with an increased incidence of cervical cancer.

Prevention: The best way to prevent spread of the disease is to abstain from sexual activity during an outbreak. The use of condoms also helps prevent spread of genital herpes.

—From Ernest L. Wynder, M.D., ed., *The Book of Health.* New York: Watts, 1981.

FOR FURTHER READING:

Bianzaco, Andre, M.D., *VD: Facts You Should Know.* New York: Lothrop, Lee & Shepard, 1970.
Ketterman, Grace H., M.D., *How to Teach Your Child About Sex.* Old Tappan, N.J.: Revell, 1981.
17 Women Doctors, with D. S. Thompson, M.D., as consulting editor. *Everywoman's Health.* Garden City, N.Y.: Doubleday, 1980.

W

WEDDINGS

Christian

What is the difference between a marriage ceremony performed by a minister of the gospel and one performed by a justice of the peace? What makes a *Christian* wedding different?

When a couple has a sincere appreciation of marriage as the fulfillment of God's plan for their lives, their marriage is a religious ceremony. Most Christian/religious ceremonies say something such as "Marriage was instituted by God" and it is the oldest institution in the world because God said that it was not good for the man to live by himself (*see* Genesis 2:23, 24).

God planned for marriage to make people happy and fulfilled. Marriage is honorable (Hebrews 13:4). It is a picture or type of the relationship between Jesus Christ and the church (*see* Ephesians 5:23–27).

A ceremony performed by a Christian minister acknowledges God as the creator of life and the planner of perfect relationships. A justice of the peace fulfills legal requirements; a Christian minister fulfills God's purpose in the act of joining one man and one woman in the state of matrimony.

When two Christians marry, the original commitment each made to Christ takes on a deeper significance as it is expanded to include a commitment to each other. A miracle happens as each is transformed into a part of the other. Biblically, this is called "becoming one flesh" (Genesis 2:24).

—Shirley Murphey

WEIGHT CONTROL

Reasons to Lose

Like smoking and drinking, eating to excess is learned behavior, and can, therefore, be unlearned. Motivation or incentive is an absolute prerequisite. You've got to *want* to eat less. Determination to persist is another essential ingredient for success. Making a list of good reasons to lose weight helps you to maintain progress. Make your own list. It might include some of these:

1. *Aesthetics*—you look better and appear more attractive if you're not fat.
2. *Economics*—junk foods are costly in comparison with their nutritional value.
3. *Example to your children*—whose attitudes and beliefs about food are learned from their parents.
4. *Self-mastery*—are you controlling or being controlled?
5. *Health*—your knowledge of the medical dangers of obesity.
6. *Well-being*—you feel physically so much better when you're not overweight.
7. *God's will for your life*—do you want to live for Him? If so, fat or fit? Remember, your body is His temple.

Let your attitude be positive and self-reinforcing. Don't think of dieting as a deprivation of pleasure, but rather the positive achievement of a better self-image, a personality capable of discipline and mastery, and a Christian living victoriously for God.

What learned behavior stimulates you to eat? Is it your cultural habits inherited or absorbed from your parents or from peers or from advertising? Or is it the sight or smell of food, a vending machine, the time of day, or some emotional upset? Try to distinguish in yourself between stimulation of the appetite and actual hunger. We all so often eat when we are not really hungry. We often just crave something in the mouth—food, drink, chewing gum, or a cigarette. Freud called it oral regression. That's just about it, so often, just infantile thumbsucking—regressing back to the comfort, the satisfaction, and the sense of security of something, anything, in the mouth!

—From O. Quentin Hyder, M.D., *Shape Up.* Old Tappan, N.J.: Revell, 1979.

Special Problems of Women

As a woman doctor treating dieters, I have discovered that there are three categories of people: overweight women, thin women, and men.

An overweight woman is one who is more than 15 percent heavier than her ideal weight, an excess which usually represents an increase in fat, not muscle. The problem can range from a slight tendency to put on a few extra pounds to a gross obesity that has gone out of control; but once a woman manifests the trait to any extent, she must henceforth always consider herself as having at least the potential to be severely overweight.

Thin women, on the other hand, have been endowed by nature with bodies which burn fat rapidly and efficiently; if they happen to acquire a few extra pounds, they tend to return to normal again very quickly. These women gain weight very seldom, and lose it effortlessly. Listening to them, however, one would think they were constantly wrestling with the specter of obesity. They complain endlessly about the agonies of losing five pounds, while boasting of their expertise as dieters. They can always tell you which are the best, the quickest, the healthiest, the most strenuous diets. Their smug authority would be comical if it weren't for its devastating effect on the fat women who lis-

ten to them and feel frustrated and guilty because they can't go home and duplicate their success.

Nothing is more annoying for a woman with a weight problem than listening to a fashionably skinny friend "ex-pound" her favorite diet as she picks up a piece of chocolate cake; it's simultaneously infuriating and depressing. What we need constantly to keep in mind is that it is not superior willpower or self-discipline that keeps such a person thin, but simply the luck of the draw when metabolisms were being passed out.

.   .   .   .   .

Comparing male and female weight loss is like comparing apples and oranges; they are both fruit, but there the similarity ends. If you're an overweight woman who has struggled unsuccessfully with diet books and diet plans devised by male diet doctors, I'm willing to bet that a big part of the reason you're still fat is that you've never been told this simple fact: men lose weight almost twice as fast as women do. They burn calories twice as fast for the same amount of exertion. The reason is that a woman's body is naturally composed of a higher proportion of fat to muscle tissue than a man's, and muscle mass burns five more calories per pound to maintain itself than fat or connective tissue.

This means that while a woman's appetite is the same as a man's, she needs only half the amount of food to maintain her weight. How can an overweight woman fail to get discouraged when doctors ignore such a fundamental truth of biology and instead place the blame for her inability to lose weight as fast and consistently as her husband can on her self-indulgence and lack of willpower?

.   .   .   .   .

It is *much, much harder for an overweight woman to lose weight than it is for a naturally thin woman, or for any man.* I used to ask women to bring their husbands with them to my office so that I could enlist their aid and support. I would spend hours talking to them about their wives' physiology and problems with fat storage, only to have them nod in a bored way as they waited for an opening to tell me how *they* lost weight by simply switching from beer to Bourbon or from steak to fish, or when they had to work overtime for a month. It soon became apparent to me that even though these men lived with and loved these women, they could not comprehend what was going on in their wives' bodies. Whether the husbands were of normal weight or overweight, they understood fat only in terms of their own metabolic systems.

We burn 10 to 15 calories per pound of body weight where men burn from 17 to 20 doing the same thing, yet our appetites are identical. We are classified as overweight if we are between 10 and 15 percent above ideal weight; but ideal weights are usually calculated from life insurance charts, which up to this decade have been overwhelmingly male and oriented toward the upper middle class.

I compute female ideal weight differently. I use 5 feet as a baseline of 100 pounds; for every inch of height over 5 feet, a female adds five pounds. A woman 5'3" tall, for example, should weigh 115 pounds. I also take body build into consideration. There should be a difference of about 10 pounds between women with small and medium frames. (Since I see very few Amazons around, I rarely classify females as large.) I also add a pound for every five years past 25 years old. If you are a female 5'5" tall with a small frame, 35 years old, you should weigh between 127 and 132 pounds. You will then be *cosmetically thin.* If you are 15 percent above this weight, you are overweight, *cosmetically overweight.*

The point at which the problem ceases to be one of cosmetic overweight and becomes a matter of health has yet to be determined; that is why I don't impose my own standards of weight on anyone else. Some women want to be superthin, others want only to go down a few dress sizes, still others simply want to feel better. I let my patients decide for themselves what kind of bodies they want;

all I am is the tool to help them achieve their aim.

Overweight ought to be a disease of prevention. But if it can't be prevented, it should be put under control as early as possible.

Let's look at some of the reasons why women are the fatter sex:

1. *Biological*—There is no escaping the fact that we were designed as baby receptacles, so nature has seen to it that we will never be without fat. She has decreed that we will always be padded with a soft cushion of subcutaneous (under the skin) fat, in case the fetus needs extra food, protection, and heat. It doesn't matter if you never exercise your biological function and go through life without bearing a child; nature will pad you anyway, just in case. That is why it's so difficult to lose those last few pounds remaining between you and your lean body mass.

2. *Hormonal*—The female hormones that give you your beautiful skin and good bones and protect you against heart attacks are the same ones that make it easier for you than it is for a man to convert food into fat. Estrogens and progesterones are naturally fat-producing and fat-hoarding hormones. Even if you have your ovaries (which produce the hormones) removed, the adrenal glands will take over and secrete estrogen-like hormones for the maintenance of body fat.

If you're taking birth-control pills (whose operative ingredient is estrogen), you will be 10 percent more likely to convert food into fat if your weight is normal, and close to 20 percent more likely if you tend toward overweight—and this is not even taking into account the fluid-retaining properties of both estrogen and progesterone. These propensities for making you fatter are present in all female hormones, both natural and synthetic.

3. *Social—The "Home-Baby-Eat Syndrome"*—The responsibility of feeding a family three meals a day means having to think about food morning, noon, and night—buying it, preparing it, seeing that it gets eaten, cleaning up afterwards. Every

housewife spends a lot of time in the kitchen, where she is constantly exposed to temptation, especially if she prides herself on her cooking. It's easy to deceive oneself into thinking that it's all for the sake of one's husband and kids, but how many good cooks don't also love to eat? Still, you can't put all the blame on proximity. A chronic overeater will manage to get her excess calories somehow, even if she works outside her home during the day; she'll overeat when she gets home at night, or she may spend the weekend baking bread and cookies to make up for lost time. Maybe her husband enjoys cooking as a hobby; then of course she has to eat everything he makes so as not to hurt his feelings. It will be interesting to see what happens now that sex roles are being reversed in so many areas. If men move into the kitchen, will we have thinner females and fatter males? And what will happen when the formerly thin grandmother is cast in the role of baby-sitter for her working daughter? Will she also become overweight?

I feel, though, that the social role of wife and homemaker is not as important a factor in obesity as women would have us believe. Inappropriate responses to food cues plague the would-be dieter, whether she is in her own home, or another's or at a job. Since food is always available—if only from the candy machine at the office—the overweight woman will always find a reason why she should eat it!

4. *Body makeup*—As if all the above didn't give men a sufficiently unfair advantage, women also require fewer calories. Some authorities claim that women require two calories less per pound of body weight than men, but I think it is actually closer to five calories. The reason is that more calories are needed to sustain large muscle mass in a male than to sustain fat in a female. Men are usually heavier and taller than women, but even the smallest man has more muscle per unit of weight than the largest woman.

5. *Appetite*—Nor has nature even bothered to equalize the difference in the way men and women burn calories by giving the woman a smaller appetite. Appetite, unfor-tunately, depends entirely on the individual; so many psychological variables influence hunger that it is almost impossible to measure appetite objectively. All we can be sure of is that a woman can, and will, often eat as much or more than a man, even though she requires fewer calories.

Everything I have been saying here applies to all women. Multiply it by two, add a triggering mechanism for overeating sugars and starches, stir in a dash of carbohydrate intolerance, and you have the stew in which the overweight woman finds herself.

—From Barbara Edelstein, M.D., *The Woman Doctor's Diet for Women.* Englewood Cliffs, N.J.: Prentice-Hall, 1977.

Overeating

Why do *you* overeat?

Have you ever thought your problem was unique and separate from the rest of the world? If your thin friends had the life of troubles that you had, they'd gain weight, too, you think.

Have you ever thought nobody suffers like you do? This way of thinking says everybody has a happier and better life than you and eating is all you've got. The notion that others are happier, better off and leading lives of comparative ease is not true at all. There is also a mistaken belief that it's not as hard for others to lose weight as it is for you. Everyone who has ever gone on a weight-loss program has had to struggle with temptation, deny themselves and go without.

That's what it says in the Word anyhow. In 1 Corinthians 10:13 it says:

No temptation has overtaken you but such as is common to man.

This verse is telling us that we are in a human realm of existence and the problems that beset us are all within this human realm. There's no superhuman task for us to undertake when we are within the confines of this realm. That's why the Lord tells us in Matthew 17:20 that if we have the faith as a grain of a mustard seed, nothing is impossible to us.

There is not a single temptation that is beyond human resistance.

. . and God is faithful, who will not allow you to be tempted beyond what you are able, but with the temptation will provide the way of escape also, that you may be able to endure it.—1 Corinthians 10:13

With the temptation God always provides a way of escaping its power over you so that you may endure and not fall.

The reason many of us don't grab hold of this promise is because we want to be excused from our Christian responsibility to think and act like Christians.

What Makes Us Do It?

Has anyone or anything made you angry lately? Anyone or anything made you upset, worried, furious, miserable, frustrated, depressed or anxious?

Have you ever noticed the way children behave when they've been caught doing something they shouldn't be doing? One of the first things they might say is, "Oh, he/she made me do it!" Two small boys invade the cookie jar and when Mother happens on the scene, they both point at the other and say in harmony, "*He* made me do it!"

It's the mature person who can stop blaming people and situations for his/her own sins. The responsibility for our happiness is on our own shoulders. Nobody else holds it for us. We do.

People don't actually *make* you angry. You make yourself angry. Imagine driving in your car with a friend. This friend is telling you every turn and stop to make, as if you had never been behind a wheel before. He is being a backseat driver *par excellence*.

You think to yourself, "This guy is really making me angry. In a minute I'll explode."

Explode you may, but not because he makes you angry. You may want to throw your Indy 500 trophy at him, as well as your international chauffeur's license, but please, as you do, say the truth and tell him, "I *make*

myself angry when you tell me how to drive."

Nobody else *makes* you anything. You make *yourself* feel, think, say, act and do what you do. Nobody else actually makes you overeat. You overeat because of you.

You *condition* yourself to eat what you eat, where you eat, how much you eat and when you eat.

What It Means to Be Conditioned

If you have had several happy experiences eating and watching TV, there is an automatic trigger inside your brain that will tell you *eat* when you get in front of the TV. You only need to see a TV set turned on and you'll feel like eating something. If you have paperwork to do and you've conditioned yourself to eat while working, you'll find yourself thinking of food as you work. If you have made a habit of eating when you're depressed, upset, lonely or worried, your brain will tell you *eat* when you are in these states of mind. You've conditioned yourself to eat when you encounter these stressful circumstances.

Now, here's the good news. You can decondition yourself. You can develop new habits so that your brain does not think *food* when you are in certain situations or places or engaging in certain activities. One woman says that she doesn't overeat at all during the day when she is on the job, but the minute she walks into her apartment, she starts to eat, and doesn't stop until she goes to bed.

Somewhere along the line she conditioned herself to think food and home are inseparable. On the job she didn't think about eating, but once home, her "eat" trigger was pushed and off she went, eating everything in sight.

Home should not mean food to us. Home is a million things, and eating is only one of the things we do there. Those experiences as a child when Mother cooked up those feasts in her kitchen and all the family rallied around the table for family time, with food as the main attraction, may still remain in your memory. So you spend your years trying to relive these childhood experiences. Or maybe relaxation means food to you. When you arrive home after a day of pressure and hard work, you want to relax. Relaxation means food, so you not only eat, but you overeat.

You can end these lifetime patterns and develop new ones. You re-condition yourself.

Check if you do any of the following:

—— Eat while watching TV.

—— Eat while driving the car.

—— Eat while studying or doing paper-work.

—— Eat while reading.

—— Eat while on the job.

—— Eat while shopping.

—— Eat while preparing a meal.

—— Eat when cleaning up after a meal.

—— Eat more alone than with others.

—— Eat before going to bed.

—— Get out of bed in the middle of the night to eat.

—— Eat more on weekends than during the week.

—— Eat more at night than during the day.

—— Skip breakfast but gorge later on in the day.

Many books on dieting will tell you to substitute those fattening snacks you've been eating during these times for low-cal snacks. This is acceptable, but it is not breaking the patterns that have been set up in your response system. If you really want mastery over these habits in your life, end them.

Don't eat while watching TV. (Do your nails, sew, whittle, carve or paint something instead.)

Don't eat while driving the car. (Wait until you get to a restaurant, home, or wait until a certain time.)

Don't eat while studying or doing paper-work. (A glass of water will be terrific.)

Don't eat while reading. (Be good to yourself. Enjoy your book without getting fat.)

Don't eat while on the job. (Wait until lunch or dinner and reward yourself with thinness.)

Don't eat while shopping. (Your body will love you for it.)

Don't eat while preparing a meal. (Your body doesn't want you to put more into it than it needs.)

Don't eat while cleaning up after a meal. (You are not a garbage disposal; you are a beautiful human being.)

Don't eat more alone than when you're with others. (Be good to yourself at all times, not just in front of others.)

Don't get out of bed in the middle of the night to eat. (Your stomach deserves a rest.)

Don't eat before going to bed. (Think beautiful thoughts instead and have a Jesus snack in the Word.)

Don't eat more on weekends than during the week. (Discover your "triggers" and put an end to them.)

Don't eat more at night than during the day. (Do something fun instead of eating.)

Don't skip breakfast and gorge at other times. (Breakfast is energy time. You are too special to go without your a.m. energy.)

The only danger in substituting carrots for potato chips as a snack is that you may eat carrots for a while, but then go back to potato chips again. The habit hasn't been dealt with. If you end the habit, you've gotten to the source of things.

You may have a string of Freudian excuses for overeating and being fat, but these don't have to keep you fat. You can change your behavior if you really want to. It doesn't matter what your mother fed you when you were just a tot, or what you went without as an adolescent, or what your family eating patterns were. You can say NO to those old habits and stop analyzing and making excuses for them.

God says He will *provide a way of escape* for you. If you are a compulsive eater, God will *provide a way of escape.* If you are an impulsive eater, God will *provide a way of escape.* That's what it says in 1 Corinthians 10:13. He is right now providing a way of escape for you if you will take it.

PRACTICAL HELPS FOR THOSE TOUGH TIMES OF TEMPTATION

1. Tell your friends you're on a special eating program when they invite you for

dinner. Tell them exactly what you *may* eat and what you may not. Don't use this opportunity to binge. Your friends will be happy to cooperate when they see it is important to you.

2. When you eat in a restaurant, do not examine the menu. Plan what you'll order before you get there. Think of the many lovely foods you can plan your meal from. A large salad with strips of turkey and cheese; cottage cheese; lean meat; chicken without the skin; broiled fish with no butter; a baked potato with no butter; fresh fruit. Don't use eating out as an excuse to binge. Remember, you are a very special person. You deserve to be good to yourself.

3. Other people may not have yielded their eating habits to the Lord yet. Don't worry yourself about them. You be the obedient one and praise the Lord you are. If others want to eat fattening and unhealthy foods, you don't have to join them. You eat your salad and broiled fish and thank Jesus you've taken the escape He has provided for you!

4. Count your calories. Count them *before* you eat them. Be in control of things.

5. Don't buy fattening junk foods. If your family insists on these foods, let them buy them. One woman told her husband, "Those snacks and junk foods will have to come out of the entertainment money because my grocery money must go for *food.*"

6. Cut up carrots, celery and cauliflower immediately and keep in a plastic container in the refrigerator to have some ready healthy "fast food" on hand.

7. At church dinners, potlucks, showers, weddings and other food-oriented activities, pack your own nutritious and scrumptious eats in plastic containers and bags. Slip into the kitchen and put your food on a plate like the others have—things like fresh fruit with lemon dressing, cold sliced turkey, shredded cheese, crisp vegetable salad. Carry a thermos of mint tea or another herb tea so you don't

have to put Kool-Aid or some sugary punch into your body.

8. You don't have to substitute chemical sweeteners for sugar. You don't have to put the artificial sweeteners in your precious body. You don't have to drink artificially sweetened sodas or drinks. You can use honey and maple syrup as sweeteners and for your cooking and baking needs, and eat plenty of fresh fruit. Drink fresh fruit juices without sugar. Praise the Lord for your health and beauty.

You are a unique and special person—a very important person. You deserve to have good things. Those good things do *not* include fattening and harmful foods.

You are His workmanship, created in Christ Jesus for good works (Ephesians 2:10). You are unique as a person created with His very own hands. He loves your soul, your spirit *and your body.* He knows your body. He formed you. It's important to Him that it operate and function well.

For thou didst form my inward parts;
Thou didst weave me in my mother's womb.
I will give thanks to Thee, for I am fearfully and wonderfully made;
Wonderful are Thy works,
And my soul knows it very well.
My frame was not hidden from Thee,
When I was made in secret,
And skillfully wrought in the depths of the earth.—Psalm 139:13–15.

You have begun your weight loss program and you're going to lose every ounce you intend to lose. Remember that. You're going to stick with it no matter how long it takes. There may be a million temptations, but He is continually providing a way of escape for you. The Word of God will take first place over the thing you're tempted to eat. You'll speak the Word to yourself and love it far more than that thing you almost ate.

The Lord will accomplish that which concerns me (Psalm 138:8) is your promise and your strength.

You are unique and special, and your problems are human. They are the same problems and struggles we all face. You are *never* alone when you are losing weight.

You are never alone when you are exercising self-control. Somebody else right now is saying no to dessert, too. Someone else right now has found that way the Lord provides the overeater for escape—as you are discovering.

—From Marie Chapian, *Free to Be Thin*. Published and copyright 1979, Bethany House Publishers, Minneapolis, Minnesota 55438.

Appetite vs. Hunger

One of the things that overweight persons have never gotten clear in their minds is that there is a vast difference between *hunger* and *appetite* (the desire for certain foods).

Very few normal American families know what real hunger is. They may not eat "high on the hog" all the time, but they usually find enough food available to them to keep from really being hungry.

Each body has a weight-regulating system that controls the body's need for food. Medical science has identified its specific area in the brain. It's known as the hypothalamus. The term *appestat* has been coined to refer to it. It's an automatic regulator in the same sense that a thermostat regulates temperature.

When the appestat is functioning properly, the desire to eat has a direct relationship to the amount of energy used. If you do more, it directs you to eat more. Do less and it will tell you to eat less.

It is an ideal mechanism, except that it can be tilted out of balance after extended periods of improper dietary habits. To bring it back into functioning order, where it will reliably tell you how much food you need, it must be given a period of time during which the obese person eats less food than previously and eats more nutritiously.

After a bout with illness where smaller amounts of food have been eaten, many people find that their appetites have temporarily diminished. They feel as if their stomachs have shrunken. What has really happened is that the appestat control has been given a short opportunity to begin to regulate the person's need for food.

But because habits usually dictate how we behave, the habit of eating more than we need (our *appetites*, in other words) soon takes us back into the same pattern of eating more than our bodies need, and the appestat is again short-circuited.

—From Jim Tear and Jan Houghton Lindsey, *Fed Up With Fat*. Old Tappan, N.J.: Revell, 1978.

Behavior Modification

What we're really talking about when we talk about changing habits is *behavior modification*. When we use that term it immediately conjures up in many people's minds B. F. Skinner and his behavioral experiments and the Russian scientist Dr. Ivan Pavlov and his dogs.

While we may not agree with all of the conclusions these behavioral scientists have come up with, their theories have shown how we humans can be conditioned to change our responses to *learned* habits.

In Pavlov's experiments with behavioral modification he demonstrated how dogs could be made to salivate when a bell was rung even though no food was present. He did this by first ringing a bell each time he fed the dogs. This imprinted on the dogs' memories the association between the bell ringing and food being given. After a period of time, he began to ring the bell but not give any food. The dogs' saliva, necessary for digestion but impossible to produce at will, began flowing at the sound of the bell alone.

The dogs had acquired a new habit. They had learned a response over which they had no control. It was now programmed into their subconscious memories and had become what is known as a *conditioned reflex*.

It may be hard to see the comparison between dogs and their reactions and human beings, but the principle of acquiring new habits works in much the same way in the human brain.

481

The human mind is divided into two parts: the *instinctive mind* and the *reasoning mind.* The instinctive mind is mostly subconscious and is what we refer to as *memory.* Its function is largely the storing up of sense experiences as they occur. Using information received from the five senses, it records experiences and stores them in the subconscious mind, where they become memory.

The instinctive mind is much like a tape recorder. It observes, listens, and records, but makes no conscious analysis about the information fed into it. But as the information it receives piles up certain habits, responses, and attitudes develop.

The reasoning mind is the part of us that analyzes causes and effects, even when they are not clearly related, and out of it comes our creative thinking. It is more like a computer which is able to reason, analyze, create, draw rational conclusions, and make moral judgments.

The prevalent philosophy of society today is that whatever feels good, tastes good, doesn't hurt anybody else, and works is okay to do. This is what is known as a *pragmatic* view of life.

The dictionary defines pragmatism as "a philosophy that makes practical consequences the test of truth."

With that rationale, behavioral scientists could use behavior modification to manipulate a whole society into believing and behaving in "truth," as defined by them.

We can already see results of this by the way children are convinced, through constant repetition on television, that only one cereal is fit for them to eat. Just let mom try to buy something else if she's got her child along with her, and she will see how his behavior has been conditioned by what he's been bombarded with on TV.

Behavior modification assumes that experiences are determinative of who we are and how we must act. Experience is a powerful teacher, as can be seen by Pavlov's behavioral experiments with dogs. But when it comes to man, there is another key element that must be taken into consideration in changing our behavior.

A human being is not an animal. One of the main distinguishing factors of man is that he has been given moral reasoning ability by his Creator. This means that he has the ability to gather data, analyze it, and make a rational moral judgment about whether it is right or wrong.

Man can fail to exercise this function of his mind or so distort its use that black becomes white or everything fades into gray, but nevertheless, if he is thinking correctly, his moral judgment should have a predominant place in determining his behavior.

We live in an age of no absolutes. Man has lost sight of the fact that his life is meant to be lived by principles, values, and correct moral decisions.

The decline in the role of moral reason can be traced almost proportionately to the decline of the teaching of biblical principles. The Ten Commandments and the Golden Rule, "Do unto others as you would have them do unto you," are "old hat" and outdated today. The kids don't hear these truths at home, in school, or even in many churches, so they have discarded their validity in their lives. Those kids grow into adults with the same views.

Perhaps you're wondering what all this information has to do with losing weight.

Let me tell you, it has *everything* to do with how successful and permanent your weight loss will be. Unless your decision to get your life together and lose weight is predicated on the fact that it's the best thing to do and the right thing for you, no one can permanently change your habits or behavior. With the moral reasoning ability given to you by God, you must analyze the problems you are presently coping with (overweight or whatever), determine what is the *right* thing to do about it and then, with that moral reinforcement, set about relearning the new habits.

New habits can only be learned if the learner is willing to stick with the program long enough to give it time to work. No one is going to be around to stand over you and make you do things the right way. That's where your having learned to live by principles and truth will cause you to triumph over old habits.

—From Jim Tear and Jan Houghton Lindsey, *Fed Up With Fat.* Old Tappan, N.J.: Revell, 1978.

Importance of Exercise

How does one get rid of fat? Easy, you say. Just follow Dr. XYZ's super don't-eat-ever diet, and it will come off rapidly and easily. Success is guaranteed within sixty days or sooner, right?

Wrong! True, you can lose weight on a crash diet. But losing *weight* is not what you who are overfat need to do. You need to get rid of *fat*, not *weight*.

With a crash diet you lose muscle and water and some fat, but confirmed studies show that 99-plus percent of those who lose weight by diet alone will regain it. Not only that, you regain the weight as 100 percent fat! *Crash dieting is one of the surest ways to gain fat, not lose it.* Weight loss solely by dieting means you will lose muscle and fat but regain only the fat. Sooner or later you will have a net gain in fat!

It is important to realize that we are all bombarded daily by powerful advertising "hype" about diets and dieting. We have a rash of new miracle diets each year that draw millions of gullible takers. Where I come from we believe in miracles, but the miracle of losing fat comes slowly and steadily in every instance I have ever seen. Sudden hurry-up diets are almost always flagrant examples of bad diet advice.

In "miracle" diets that have been popularized in recent months and years, the dieter's calorie-and-protein intake is cut to starvation levels. True, you can shed pounds quickly with these diets, but while you are battling the bulges of flab, you are running the risk of losing valuable muscle mass that is so important to the entire body, especially the heart. At least one study has shown that such diets have been associated with heart irregularities that resulted in the deaths of fifty-eight women. One popular diet drink provides a daily supply of under 400 calories

(starvation level) and less than forty grams of protein (well below the recommended minimum of sixty grams). Persons on this kind of weight-loss plan may experience irregular heart rhythms within a week of starting the diet.

Such miracle diets claim to include vitamin-and-mineral supplements, but they do not alter the bad effects of inadequate dietary protein. Such diets also claim there will be no sufficient muscle loss, but as a medical doctor who has spent many years in nutritional and weight-control work, I say categorically this is pure hogwash.

The miracle-diet substances or plans preach nutritional nonsense and propagate inaccuracies that can result in life-threatening side effects. For example, one untruth is that undigested food accumulates and becomes fat, while digested food cannot cause weight gain. Precisely the opposite is true. Another myth states that enzymes cannot work together and often cancel each other out in the digestive tract. Again, the facts are exactly the opposite.

In short, *don't use miracle diets!* In the long run they do not work, and they can cause serious harm.

I know what your next question is going to be, and it's a very logical one: "If I can't count on dieting only and miracle diets are downright dangerous, what *can* I do?"

The answer is simple, but it may not thrill you. You don't get rid of fat by diet only. Dieting is important but it is secondary. When trying to lose fat, your primary weapon is aerobic exercise. Aerobic exercise is the kind anyone can do. Aerobic exercises are long, slow, easy, endurance-type activities. I repeat, you do not have to be an Olympic champion to engage in aerobic exercise that fits your abilities and life-style.

Please note that when I talk about aerobic exercise, I am not including calisthenics or stretching activities. The exercises you see on TV shows are usually calisthenics or stretching of some kind. These are excellent, but do almost nothing to help you lose fat. Also, spot-reducing aids such as hip-shaker belts at your local health spa do nothing whatsoever to burn fat either, not even in

Desirable Weights

Weight in Pounds According to Frame (In Indoor Clothing)

	HEIGHT (with shoes on) 1-inch heels		SMALL FRAME	MEDIUM FRAME	LARGE FRAME
	Feet	Inches			
Men	5	2	112–120	118–129	126–141
of Ages 25	5	3	115–123	121–133	129–144
and Over	5	4	118–126	124–136	132–148
	5	5	121–129	127–139	135–152
	5	6	124–133	130–143	138–156
	5	7	128–137	134–147	142–161
	5	8	132–141	138–152	147–166
	5	9	136–145	142–156	151–170
	5	10	140–150	146–160	155–174
	5	11	144–154	150–165	159–179
	6	0	148–158	154–170	164–184
	6	1	152–162	158–175	168–189
	6	2	156–167	162–180	173–194
	6	3	160–171	167–185	178–199
	6	4	164–175	172–190	182–204

	HEIGHT (with shoes on) 2-inch heels		SMALL FRAME	MEDIUM FRAME	LARGE FRAME
	Feet	Inches			
Women	4	10	92–98	96–107	104–119
of Ages 25	4	11	94–101	98–110	106–122
and Over	5	0	96–104	101–113	109–125
	5	1	99–107	104–116	112–128
	5	2	102–110	107–119	115–131
	5	3	105–113	110–122	118–134
	5	4	108–116	113–126	121–138
	5	5	111–119	116–130	125–142
	5	6	114–123	120–135	129–146
	5	7	118–127	124–139	133–150
	5	8	122–131	128–143	137–154
	5	9	126–135	132–147	141–158
	5	10	130–140	136–151	145–163
	5	11	134–144	140–155	149–168
	6	0	138–148	144–159	153–173

For girls between 18 and 25, subtract 1 pound for each year under 25.

Metropolitan Life Insurance Co., *Four Steps to Weight Control*, 1969.

the spot where you are being jostled. When you want to lose fat, engage in aerobic exercise. These are the long, slow, endurance exercises such as walking, jogging, bicycling, and swimming.

As director of Student Health Services at Oral Roberts University for the last ten years, I have seen mild and easy aerobic exercise (note the *mild* and the *easy*) work with hundreds of men and women. Daily, my staff and I guide overfat people in losing weight *and fat*, while toning and building muscles through good nutrition, proper diet, sports activities, and aerobic exercises that are right for the individual. Yes, it's slower than the miracle crash diets, but it's safer and more effective over the long haul. The weight stays off. There is no regaining of pounds that are composed of more fat than previously.

As for aerobics being "only for kids," nothing is further from the truth. People of any age can participate in the long, slow, endurance type of aerobic exercise at their own speed and in their own way.

I will say it one more time. *Dieting is helpful, but the way to lose weight, the way to lose fat and keep it off, is through exercise.* And by exercise I mean aerobic activity, carried out regularly for the rest of your life.

—From Jim Krafft, M.D., *Flab: The Answer Book.* Old Tappan, N.J.: Revell, 1983.

FOR FURTHER READING:

Gundry, Patricia. *The Complete Woman.* Garden City, N.Y.: Doubleday, 1981.

Krafft, Jim, M.D. *Flab: The Answer Book.* Old Tappan, N.J.: Revell, 1983.

Murphey, Cecil B. *Fitness: The Answer Book.* Old Tappan, N.J.: Revell, 1983.

Wise, Karen. *God Knows I Won't Be Fat Again.* Nashville: Nelson, 1978.

WIDOWHOOD

IN THE OLD romantic novels, a bereft lover frequently died of a broken heart.

Don't count on it. It doesn't happen that way, and those of us who are widows have been left to cope with a life unlike anything we could ever have imagined.

All of us, at one time or another during our married lives, have tried to picture what it would be like if our husbands died. Believe me, the reality is something for which the most vivid imagination cannot prepare you.

You can—and I hope, will—make practical preparations for the state of widowhood, but there is little you can do in advance that will brace you for the wrenching emotions of grief and sorrow you will suffer.

It's a pity there cannot be some wise, all-knowing personage to induct us into widowhood; someone who can warn us of the strange, lost feelings we will endure; who can map the pitfalls ahead of us; and who can caution us to beware of the searing agonies ahead.

But there is no such person or ceremony. We are thrust into limbo by the death of our mates, and become overnight, different women. Lonely, frightened, alone—women apart.

A widow is a mutant, grafted onto the species: a source of anxiety and discomfort to a society that favors pairs and couples. We are neither maid nor married, yet we carry about with us all of the appurtenances of marriage—the name, the ring, the possessions, the children. Each one of us feels alone and helpless, and we wonder, "Am I the only woman who feels this way? Am I the only one tortured by these fears and doubts about my life alone?" The answer, of course, is "No." You are *not* unique. Other women have suffered as you are suffering, and they have become normally functioning human beings once more; so will you.

It isn't easy. You will not arrive at that state soon, or without additional scars. You will suffer intense grief, sorrow, rebellion, and anger. But you will live through it. You will survive, and you will, incredibly, adapt to your new life alone. Gradually you will begin to see ahead a glimmer of your ultimate goal—acceptance.

I hope your marriage was happy, I hope

that you had many years together; however many they were, they were too short. But you will have to face the fact that from now on you will be living with memories. Treasure them, but don't burden yourself with them. We all wish that we had been a little sweeter or more patient or more loving. But we are only human. Don't torture yourself with regrets and remorse. If you had a good marriage, he understood and forgave, and the way you might have responded on a given occasion days or months or years ago did not subtract one minute from his life. He loved you—remember that.

The hardest thing for you now is to face the trite fact that, although he is dead, life does go on; you are alive and must make a life for yourself, alone.

Consider yourself blessed indeed if you have children still living at home. They will give you a reason for living when it seems that there can no longer be one. The simple mechanics involved in managing a family household will *make* you get up each day and accomplish something, no matter how little.

And that is no minor feat, because you will find yourself beset by a plague of mental paralysis.

After that week of near-hypnosis following your husband's death and burial, you suddenly find yourself gripped by the most exhausting let-down. You have held yourself together while you planned the funeral. You greeted and talked with all the callers; you maintained a facade of calm acceptance and stability. Now the funeral is over. The flowers have withered and the callers have gone, and the doubts and fears descend upon you like dark birds of prey.

For a while you—and society—have held them at bay. There had been, hanging protectively between you, the tapestry of death, woven of the small, everyday things society has devised to ease those who are grief-stricken back into the routine of daily life. There have been the decisions to be made about the casket, the funeral, the songs and verses, the flowers, the pallbearers. These details following a death keep the

mind and hands busy, and that is their purpose.

—From Martha Yates, *Coping.* Englewood Cliffs, N.J.: Prentice-Hall, 1976.

FOR FURTHER READING:

Hardisty, George and Margaret. *How to Plan Your Estate.* Lafayette, Calif.: Carodyn, 1983.

Padus, Emrika. *The Woman's Encyclopedia of Health and Natural Healing.* Emmaus, Pa.: Rodale, 1981.

WILLS

EVERY DAY people die without a will, trust, or any provision for what is to be done with their property or their minor children, so the law must step in to meet the emergency.

Our laws, for the most part, are written by legislators and interpreted by judges. Most of these people are attorneys. When these attorneys leave their places in government, or in the court system, they may retire or return to the practice of law, using the very laws they wrote and interpreted, to deal with your affairs.

Are laymen, then, simply pawns in a system, for the most part set up by, run for, and administered by attorneys?

Laws are just rules for people to live by. They apply to all—attorneys and laymen alike—and are most often written to try to remedy a need. When people don't obey the rules, both the rule breaker and the innocent suffer.

WHY NOT JUST LET IT HAPPEN?

All right. Let it happen as it will if you prefer, but be aware of this: The State has a plan all ready to go that will take care of the transfer of your things if you become incapacitated or die before you've made your own plan as with a living trust or a will.

If the deceased (the one who dies) leaves

no instructions, the State *gives* the instructions, based on laws decided upon by lawmakers. These instructions from the State Legislature are known as *laws of intestacy, laws of intestate succession,* or *laws of descent and distribution.*

Sometimes these legislative directions will give a result you *would* have wanted anyway, but often that is not the case. It is not unusual for very unexpected and unfair results to occur:

Andy died without a will, leaving a mother and sister surviving him. His wife, Bonnie, had passed away the year before. Bonnie had left five children by a former spouse. Andy's five stepchildren were all adult, had never lived with Andy and were relatively well-to-do. They were strangers to Andy, actually. The property Andy left had been acquired during his marriage to Bonnie and by their joint efforts in a community property state. The law of intestate succession specified that all of Andy's property belonged to his stepchildren and none of it to Andy's needy mother and devoted sister.

You may agree or disagree with the result, but that is really not the point. The point is, do you want to be the one to decide where your property is to go at your death, or in the case of small children without parents, who will rear them? Or do you want that decision to be made by someone for you?

But That Isn't the Worst of It

When both parents die, and they fail to give instructions or indicate their preference, the Court must find a guardian to take the children. The Court, in the absence of parents, looks to relatives. If any are available and willing, the one they choose may have been just the choice the parents would *not* have wanted. That's too bad. They can't be consulted now. At least it probably is better than the complete stranger the Court appoints in the absence of a relative after the

child has been a ward of the Juvenile Court. Or is it? Sometimes relatives tend to fight over children, appearing to want them, but once they have them, the resentments toward having to care for them begin to mount.

Besides not having the say as to where your children are to go, both the one appointed by the Court to wind up the affairs of your estate and the guardian must be bonded. This is an added expense your estate must bear and one you should have avoided.

In addition, the guardian and your child or children will have many problems to face when you are gone—problems you probably wouldn't wish on an enemy, let alone on your loved ones.

To Sum It Up

Some undesirable results of intestate succession laws are as follows:

1. Your surviving spouse and children may have to share ownership of your estate;
2. You lose the opportunity of specifying who or what will receive any of your property or specific items of your property;
3. You lose the opportunity of waiving bond for both guardian and executor;
4. You lose the opportunity of setting up a trust for care of your children;
5. You lose the opportunity of choosing a trustee and guardian who will be sympathetic to the spiritual as well as the physical needs of your children;
6. You lose the opportunity of planning your estate so as to minimize tax and administration expense;
7. These laws make no allowance for you to fulfill your obligations of charitable stewardship (giving to charities);
8. They include no allowance for friends.

There are many other negatives and very few positives to a course of no planning.

Normally anyone who can understand what he or she is doing, and who is not a minor, *can* make a will. Some states have special provisions regarding age, marriage status, and other exceptions, so you should check your own state law in this regard.

Anyone who now owns or expects someday, prior to death, to own property or be responsible for minor children or other dependents *should* make a will.

Whether you are *single* or *married*, the need to make out a will is definite, and it should be done as soon as possible.

Once you have decided to go ahead with a will, you should find a lawyer.

If you have someone prepare your will for you, that is, practice law on your behalf, that person must be a licensed attorney and in compliance with the laws of your state regulating persons who practice law.

Remarriage

Whether remarriage follows death or divorce, both parties should consider estate planning to take care of their new circumstances and responsibilities, as a Number One priority. One fellow stated:

> My wife and I have our own separate property from prior marriages. We desire that the property go to our respective children by these former marriages. We both have wills to this effect, executed before our present marriage. Should the wills be updated?

Yes. Both of you should make new wills or amend the old ones by codicil just as soon as possible. The laws of the various states differ as to the rights you have to each other's property.

But you should not leave this for the law to resolve, perhaps after expensive court litigation. This should be the subject of a new estate plan. You and your wife should provide for what is to be done with all your properties, separate or otherwise, so that both of you and your children will be served properly. Your attorney can show you what you can and must do in this regard.

—From George and Margaret Hardisty, *How to Plan Your Estate*. Lafayette, Calif.: Carodyn, 1983.

FOR FURTHER READING:

Fooshee, George Jr. *You Can Be Financially Free*, Old Tappan, N.J.: Revell, 1976.

Hardisty, George and Margaret. *How to Plan Your Estate*. Lafayette, Calif.: Carodyn, 1983.

Yates, Martha. *Coping*. Englewood Cliffs, N.J.: Prentice-Hall, 1976.

WITNESSING

WITNESSING for Christ offers a crowning experience in your Christian growth. The definition of a witness is quite simple: a person who knows something from personal observation or experience and who merely states the truth and circumstances of this fact. Similarly, a Christian witness speaks of a personal salvation experience, based upon the person and atoning work of Jesus Christ. This does not mean arguing or instructing. It merely involves your telling what has happened to you. This cannot be debated. The religious leaders of Israel, for example, could not dislodge the simple man whose back-to-the-wall statement rang out deathless across the whole church age: "Whereas once I was blind, now I see."

Actually, your influence as a Christian woman is very important. As you witness for the Lord you are doing these things: You are helping others to learn about the only One who can save them from their sins, and you are being obedient to God. A mandate for all witnessing is found in Romans 1:16: "For I am not ashamed of the gospel of Christ; for it is the power of God unto salvation to everyone that believeth; to the Jew first, and also to the Greek."

How can you be a witness in your own home or office? This is not the problem it first seems to be, when you think of the lives you touch each day.

Perhaps you would like to give an attractive tract to a fellow-worker or to those who call at your door. Some Christians have found that Christian books and magazines are among the best ways to influence others for Christ. But regardless of your methods, witnessing is not something to be labored. It is the natural overflowing of love for Christ.

—From Clyde M. Narramore, *A Woman's World*. Grand Rapids: Zondervan, 1963.

WORK

LET ME SUGGEST five questions each of us should periodically ask ourselves about our job.

1. *Why am I here in this job?* Do you feel you are in your present job because of an accident? Because you happened to answer an ad, or your brother-in-law got tired of having you sit around and found you a job? Because of ambition? These attitudes certainly undercut any sense of Christian vocation. We should feel we are in our work because God has called us to it, in just as real a way as He has called any bishop, clergyman, or priest.

Several months ago a man asked me to call on him in his large office in New York City. He said, "A year ago I turned my life over to Jesus Christ. It happened in my church." He then described the change that had begun to happen in his home—new communication between him and his wife; deeper understanding of his teen-age daughter. There were many other evidences of his new commitment.

Then he said, "I find now, a year later, that I am still behind the same desk doing the same job in the same way, and I suspect something is wrong. If Christ has come in as Lord of my life, things ought to be very different in what I do eight or ten hours a day." He was right, of course. Now he is exploring, along with some other men, the opportunities and strategy for Christian ministry in daily work.

We must dispense with the myth that commitment to Christ means becoming a clergyman or that work done inside a church building or in a church organization is more holy, somehow, then work done in the market place. Christ came to give us a sense of calling in everyday work. This is where the world is changed, and where the Kingdom is built.

Jesus Himself was a working man, and He called twelve working men to be His initial disciples. He could have been born into a priestly family, but He was not. We must understand the really radical thing God has done in Jesus Christ, in wanting to build a new world and a new Kingdom primarily through committed working men.

2. *For whom am I working?* Are you working for God, or for men? You cannot really serve both. When we are addicted to people's praise and thanks and rewards, we are in a real way under the tyranny of men and are working for them.

Often I feel terribly sorry for the wives and mothers in the world who work such long hours and never seem to be finished with their chores. If they are working for the appreciation and thanks of their families, they seldom or never get it. But when we work for God, we are free to serve others no matter how unreasonable or thankless they may be. Our reward is God Himself saying to us, "Well done, good and faithful servant."

Daily chores take on new meaning when we work for God rather than men. One woman has this inscription over her kitchen sink: "Divine services held here three times daily." What a marvelous freedom in washing greasy pots and pans, not for those who eat from them, but for a Lord who puts a woman into a home to serve a family for Him!

We need continually to ask ourselves whether we are willing to risk our jobs and our financial security in obedience to Jesus Christ. When we really work for God, and know that it is He to whom we are responsible, and from whom we get our reward, we are then free to be His people in any given situation.

3. *What am I working for?* Wages? Prestige? Or am I working to do the will of God? This has much to say about our motives.

Christ's own life gives us a key. When He found people abusing others in the temple, He came in and violently upset the status quo. But when people wished to destroy *Him*, He let them drive nails into His hands. Perhaps this is the kind of freedom Christian men and women need in their jobs; not to protect their own interests, but to look to the interests of others; to protest when innocent people are being hurt, but not to protest for self-preservation. This freedom comes only when we can answer the question, "What am I working for?" with "To do the will of God."

Where is your security? Is it in the person who pays your salary or do you see him only as an agent whom God at this time has chosen to supply your needs? You cannot really love your boss or paymaster until you see him as God's agent. If you see him as your provider, then you cannot be honest with him, and fear and resentment are bound to color your relationship.

I have a wonderful Chinese friend, Moses Chow. His father was one of two sons in a family in pre-communist China. He had become a Christian and was told by his father that if he persisted in following this "new god," he would be disinherited.

There was wealth in the family, but Moses' father could choose only where he had found life, and life abundant. So, in his determination to follow Jesus Christ, he was disinherited and left China.

Moses Chow told us that his father went on to make a new home in a new country in the Far East, and has been quite successful as a Christian businessman. He left the security of the world and trusted God, who was able to provide. Meanwhile, Moses' grandfather and others fell victim to communism and lost everything. We don't follow God *because* He makes us secure, but our security is in God—even in economic matters.

4. *With whom am I working?* God wants us always to be aware of the people next to us. It's not enough just to work honestly and industriously, for Christ calls us to be a priesthood of believers who willingly take responsibility for those who are our neighbors.

A railroad engineer came to his minister and asked to be put to work as a new Christian. The minister told the engineer that there was no position in the church open at the present time, but that there was a job, and it involved the question, "Is your fireman a Christian?"

This is the concept of the priesthood of believers, when we see that our primary job is not to be an elder, deacon, or vestryman in the church, but to be a priest to the man next to us in our daily work. This is where we need to recapture the marvelous vision God has for the priesthood of the laity.

God calls the laity to do a job the clergy cannot do in many instances. In a parish I once served, a close friend who was a doctor became quite ill. Though I visited him almost daily, I saw no improvement and no benefit from my visits. One day I went to see this Christian doctor and found him greatly improved and free from fear.

I asked him what had happened, and he told me of a visit he had had a few hours before from one of the senior surgeons in the area who had prayed with him and given him a prescription. The prescription was to read Joshua 1:9. My friend had been visibly touched by God, and not through a clergyman but through a brother physician.

5. *What kind of place am I in?* Jesus Christ, by His very call to accept Him as Lord and Saviour, has brought us inside a revolutionary movement, so that the place we are in assumes tremendous importance.

No job is too menial to be of importance to a communist! Shouldn't this same thing be true for any Christian trying to build a worldwide Kingdom? Even a chambermaid making beds in a hotel can influence guests who go out and make decisions of worldwide importance. Christians should ask God to show them the nature of the place they are in. How important is the particular store, shop, industry, or service which is theirs? What could God do through that particular organization to change His world?

490

Recently I was speaking with a Congregational minister in New England. He told me of meeting with a group of high school students who wanted to know how to live their faith more effectively. He asked them to think hypothetically what they would do in their school if they were communists.

They brainstormed for a time and came up with a number of things they could do to sabotage the school: cut classes, sow discord, obstruct education in all kinds of ways, from telling lies to smoking in the basement.

Suddenly, one of the boys said, "Wait a minute, isn't this just what we are doing now!" It was a wonderful eye-opener for these young people to begin to see their high school as a place where Christ could begin to change the world through them. Later on they began to discuss just what it meant to be Christ's people, building a Kingdom in their own school.

There is a revolution going on in the world. Jesus Christ Himself is the leader, and when we accept Him as our Lord, He calls us into it with Him. He needs us. He wants us to see our jobs with the eyes of faith and understanding as something far more than a means of earning a livelihood. Our jobs are places where, as revolutionaries, we help to accomplish His revolution in the hearts and lives of men everywhere.

—From Bruce Larson, *Dare to Live Now.* Grand Rapids: Zondervan, 1965.

WORKING WOMAN

Back to Work

After years of volunteer work for her church and community, Marian Burden took a paying job—and now she does professionally what she did philanthropically for more than 20 years.

Her work is interesting because as director of public relations for Bloomingdale's in Hackensack, New Jersey, Marian works closely with people. Her position, which came as a direct result of her volunteer efforts, puts her in touch with all types of people as she plans store promotions, tours, seminars and art exhibits.

"When I was first married, my husband was in public relations," Marian explains, "and because I wanted to understand his work, I began taking courses and applying what I learned to the programming and publicity area of church and community work."

Much of Marian's volunteer work centered around the First Presbyterian Church of Ridgewood, New Jersey, where she, her husband and their four sons attend services.

"While I worked for the church and other civic groups, I always directed my efforts to promoting, publicizing, administering and raising funds," she says. "For instance, for some time I was involved in public relations for the Synod of New Jersey and, all the while I was raising my sons, I devoted a good many hours to the Woman's Guild. While teaching in Sunday School, I set up a formal morning worship for children so they could learn about adult services."

Later, Marian coordinated an innovative fair for the church that drew wide publicity. Afterwards, a friend who knew that Bloomingdale's was looking for a creative administrator to direct publicity suggested that Marian apply.

Marian had never thought about a full-time job before, but when she added up the cost of educating her four sons, it sounded like a practical—and rewarding—idea.

More women like Marian are taking jobs each year as Christian women follow a nationwide trend. But in spite of this changing role, many of them still ask themselves, "Should I or shouldn't I work?" and, "If I take a job, can I still be the kind of woman I have always been?"

While struggling for the answers, they get the job jitters and inevitably ask, "Who would hire me?"

Naturally, not every woman who wants to work can move into an executive position such as Marian Burden's. But if you decide to look for work, here are 10 steps to ease those job jitters.

1. *Evaluate Yourself.* An honest appraisal in which you evaluate your needs, desires and background is vitally important. Ask yourself questions such as: What personal assets do I have? At what do I excel? What are my primary interests and hobbies? What kind of training and experience do I have? What are my reasons for wanting to work? What will working cost me in clothing, transportation, extra household expenses and taxes? The answers to these questions will help you decide just which jobs are right for you.

2. *Research the Market.* Research jobs that are available for women with your background by studying the Help Wanted ads in a number of newspapers. These ads will show you just what is available and what salary range you can expect. Borrow books about jobs from your public library and concentrate your reading on those that interest you. Write down the requirements of each position you might consider. This kind of research will help you pinpoint areas to further investigate.

Depending on your talents, skills and education, spot check jobs for which you may already be qualified. Some to keep in mind are: bank teller, credit investigator, typist, stenographer, secretary or bookkeeper. In addition, there are selling jobs in insurance, real estate and travel. Food services also offer employment for caterers, clerks and cashiers in hotels and restaurants, company and school cafeterias. Finally, if you do have the training, work is readily available for medical technicians, dental assistants, programmers, proofreaders and keypunch operators, to name a few.

3. *Ask for Support.* Talk to people working in jobs that interest you to learn how they got started. Attend job seminars or enroll in counseling or exploring workshops sponsored by your community college. Fees are usually nominal, and some job counseling may be free.

One woman who had worked for years as a volunteer church secretary enrolled in an exploring course and discovered that her real interest was in the medical field, not in office work. As a result, she found someone to replace her in the church office and took courses to become an x-ray technician.

4. *Get the Training.* You may have to spend some time and money brushing up on skills you already have or learning new ones to prepare you for today's job market. Fortunately, many colleges offer continuing education courses in degree or non-degree programs. The class schedules are flexible, and educational counseling is often available. In addition, some financial aid is available for part-time students.

Another woman who worked for her church and community while her four children were small enrolled in college for the first time when her youngest started school. She majored in recreation and hoped to work with nursing home residents. Today she is a physical therapist at a geriatrics center.

If the job you would like does not require a four-year degree, look into two-year colleges, vocational or adult schools. Training is also available at business, trade and technical schools, which are listed in the Yellow Pages. If you can't get training before taking a job, try to find employment in a company that offers on-the-job training. Then, you can pick up skills while you work and take courses at night or on the weekends if you have the time and inclination.

5. *Review Your Experience.* You may not think you have any skills, but running a household, paying bills, dealing with doctors and dentists, and serving on a church committee have probably given you potential business skills that can be further cultivated in a job.

6. *Try Part-Time First.* One of the benefits of part-time or temporary work is that you can use either of these options to explore a variety of fields. In many part-time jobs, and in all temporary ones, you are paid by the hour. An exception to this are some professionals who do receive a salary for part-time work.

Part-time employment can also help you and your family adjust to the idea of you working. It offers outside stimulation and can provide you with valuable training.

7. *Prepare a Resume.* Many times, a potential employer will see your resume before meeting you. Therefore, it should be clear, concise and interesting. There are a number of publications available from your library or bookstore that can guide you in writing a job-winning resume.

8. *Practice for the Interview.* You are "on stage" during a job interview, so practice at home first. Think about the questions you may be asked and prepare your answers. If you know someone who works in a personnel office, ask for a list of topics that may be covered. To help you get started on your practice interview, here are some typical questions: What would you like to be doing professionally in five years? Are you willing to take courses or go through training? Can you work under pressure? Will you be able to work overtime?

Answer all questions in a positive, personable way and make it clear to the interviewer that you are serious about a job. Be enthusiastic and leave your personal problems at home.

9. *Follow All Leads.* Compile a list of firms and nonprofit agencies where you might find work. To make this list, consult the Yellow Pages and your local chamber of commerce. Contact by letter or in person the head of the department that interests you, instead of going through the personnel office. Eventually you'll be sent there, but having other contacts first can sometimes make your route smoother. Read the want ads regularly and reply promptly. Register at private and state employment agencies. Look for news items about businesses that plan to move to your area and establish a network of people who can help you by telling everyone you know that you're looking for a job.

10. *Change Your Attitude.* Instead of succumbing to the job jitters, lift yourself psychologically and spiritually by telling yourself that you can do it. Too many women fear that they won't measure up in a job. Most of these fears are unfounded. Remember that years of coping with a home, children, church and community work help prepare a woman to handle many challenges she may face on her job.

Marian Burden is a good example.

"In my case, I think being involved in church work helped me develop more tolerance and compassion for the people I meet in my job. Through church work I learned to cope with various situations.

"If you decide to work," she advises, "be prepared to start as an apprentice. It takes a while to get your feet wet, so be willing to pay your dues. Once that first step is taken, the rest falls into place."

—ROBERTA ROESCH, award-winning author of several books and hundreds of magazine and newspaper articles and features.

Resume

A quick glance through the Employment Want Ads will indicate that the more interesting, challenging, and better paying jobs require resumes. What is a resume? Simply a summary of skills—an easy way for a prospective employer to assess an applicant's qualifications. Thus you'll want to do everything that you can to make your resume a neat, attractive package that represents you as a valuable employee.

Before you begin to write your resume, decide on your objective, or the kind of job you want to apply for, and write it out at the top of the paper just under your name, address, and phone number.

Then summarize the skills that you have which will qualify you for that particular job. For instance, if you're applying for a job as a receptionist, write under your summary, *skilled at appointment making, scheduling, handling phones and people.* If secretarial skills are required, be sure to put down your typing and shorthand speeds.

If you're applying for a job as a recreational therapist in a nursing home, highlight any involvement you have had with the elderly, as well as all experience you have in planning recreation programs for any age. Mention your personal strengths, such as imagination, enthusiasm, and special ability to relate to older people.

A resume is no place for modesty. Rather it is an opportunity for you to promote yourself to a prospective employer before having to face her or him. (That will come later if she likes your resume—because a good resume will get you a foot in the door of a personnel office.)

Homemakers, you'll be amazed at the skills you've developed over ten to twenty years of running households, scheduling activities, and keeping accounts. So summarize everything you're good at that would relate to the job you're applying for, whether you ever got paid for it or not.

After your summary, you must itemize any specific work experience that you have had. If you've never had a paying job, mention your volunteer activities such as organizing the PTA carnival, serving as a volunteer receptionist in your local hospital, or running a Vacation Bible School. Be very specific in your job descriptions, mentioning, for example, that you had to recruit, train, order materials, and prepare the facilities for 200 children for the VBS. That should qualify you for a number of responsibilities.

Obviously, if you have a strong employment history you should list your jobs in chronological order. But don't include dates of employment if the dates might be a negative factor, such as indicating very short employment periods or long gaps between jobs. Put the name and location of the firm you worked for and specify your particular responsibilities in that job.

After your experience, employers are usually interested in your education. If you have any degrees, mention them in your summary, then under a separate heading for education include your high school and college (if you attended one) with the years you graduated and the location of each school. Do not mention your high school activities unless you did something outstanding like win a national speech contest.

Scholastic achievements are worth mentioning as is your grade point average if it was over 3.0, but resist the impulse to note that you were a varsity cheerleader or on the drill team. Don't forget to include any seminars or adult education courses which would make you a more valuable employee.

Personal data is the last thing you itemize on your resume, and it is important to accentuate the positive and eliminate the negative. For instance, if you are under forty-five include your age, otherwise forget it. If you're married, say so; divorced, no need to mention it. Be sure to include any hobbies, sports, and talents which might make you sound more interesting, such as orchid culture, racquetball, or oil painting. And if you're a marathon runner or a former beauty queen, say so. Mention your club affiliations if you have room, since they will help in your all-round character picture.

Too many women feel they are only capable of low-paying sales jobs when the employment field is wide open to them if they would take some time to study the Want Ads and put together an attractive resume (no more than two pages unless you're applying for a corporate position). Carefully check for spelling and punctuation errors, and type it or have it typed neatly on good quality bond paper (no onion skin or erasable bond). Photostat several copies, mail them out with a cover letter, and start preparing for your interviews.

A cover letter should accompany every resume you send. It should explain why you are writing and what are your qualifications. Use your personalized cover letter to spark an employer's interest in you as a valuable asset.

Address your cover letter to the employer, not the personnel manager. Ask for an interview and refer to your resume without duplicating the information in it.

Good luck! Your professional-looking resume is the first step toward that exciting new job.

—LINDA SCHIWITZ, a free-lance writer living in El Cajon, California.

Two-Career Family

Despite agreement between spouses that a wife should work or follow a career, it takes a man of unusual ego to accept the fact that his wife has outstanding career potential. In most cases, the career of the wife is secondary to that of the husband. Frequently, wives with professional training follow the moves demanded by their husband's career and pick up whatever job they can find when the family moves to a new location. An executive who is also an engineer and a scientist told us that her husband was one of only two or three men she had met during her life who accepted her interests in traditionally male disciplines and adjusted his career to her own strong career drive. She called him "a rare beast indeed!" Another woman who began her career in her forties in a field related to her husband's work and then began to outstrip him in some ways confessed that professional jealousy had been a problem between them. "I think the problem has resolved itself. He had to be assured that his role was not diminished because mine was increased."

Recent secular literature on working couples indicates that conflicts about family and career will be severest at mid-career and that couples are likely to sacrifice their families for their work when they first start out and are trying to get established. In fact, such couples are better off professionally if they have no children. If both partners rank their career first, conflict will be inevitable, whereas if one gives more attention to the family (usually the wife), potential conflict is reduced. Working in related or similar fields can make communication easier, but there can be rivalry, and in some cases, the home becomes an extension of the office. Rivalry and conflict can be particularly intense if the woman earns more than the man. Generally if partners are at different stages of their careers, they tend to be more supportive and less competitive. Finally, job-flexibility, mutual support, and good communication between spouses increase the chances that a two-career couple can succeed at work and at home.

Very few of the Christian women we interviewed showed this kind of thorough-going commitment to a two-career marriage where work was an all-consuming activity. Most couples maintained a commitment to a number of people, activities, and service involvements. We were told that family came first and that couples worked hard at giving good care to their children. They admitted that spending time together could be a problem when work loads were heavy or family commitments were great. "Providing quality time for each other is always the thing that goes on the back burner. That's something we have to work on." A marriage counselor told us, "You have to take time to communicate, and that seems to be the big problem. You make time for the things you want to do, so something's got to give if you want time for something else. What I've heard a lot of people saying is that they're aware they haven't made time for each other because they're so busy running here and there and doing things with the children or doing housework or whatever."

GUILT

Working women frequently experience gnawing guilt, especially if they work because they want to, not because they have to. Guilt is intensified if a person has not really thought through why she is working or if there is a conflict with her spouse or family about her job. Guilt is frequently the result of a set of "shoulds" which we internalize as we grow up; "shoulds" which come to us from our upbringing, from societal pressure, from our belief-system. If we carry around the "baggage" of too many shoulds, we waste a lot of psychic and emotional energy trying to live up to unrealistic ideals which have little to do with God's expectations. Some psychologists maintain that a system of shoulds can tyrannize the individual, locking her into a rigid life system which makes adaptation to the changing circumstances of life almost impossible. Sometimes compulsive shoulds are a sign that we don't really accept ourselves and that we subconsciously think neither God nor our family accepts us, either.

Molly, a homemaker in Maryland, told us, "Society says you've got to be the perfect mother, the perfect housekeeper, the perfect lover, the perfect career woman. Whether you're a homemaker or a career woman, if you try to raise a family, you can't do everything. You've got to decide what is important to you." When we think about our feelings, we often discover that we are experiencing false guilt which is based on a set of priorities made up of inherited "shoulds."

Working mothers seem to feel guiltiest about themselves and their children. One woman blurted out to us, "I tend to feel guilty when I'm doing something I enjoy. Isn't that awful?" Another admitted, "It's been very difficult for me to learn that rest and relaxation are part of life." Although Scripture sets forth the principle that rest from work is good and necessary, many women feel that mothers should never relax or have time to themselves. There is a subtle form of "workaholism" related to the "super-mom" mentality in middle-class American society. In this ideal of motherhood, the super-mom is at the beck and call of the entire family and always puts others first, even if she also works outside the home.

—From Patricia Ward and Martha Stout, *Christian Women at Work*. Grand Rapids: Zondervan, 1981.

Historical Background

WOMEN ENTER THE PROFESSIONS

Medicine was the exclusive prerogative of men up to the middle of the nineteenth century with two exceptions—large numbers of midwives who assisted in bringing into the world the large numbers of babies being born, and the dispensers of home remedies and poultices on a neighborly basis who were both cheaper and more accessible than

doctors. The latter group could hardly be termed professionals. As the supply of trained male physicians increased, the midwives lost prestige and their numbers diminished. At the same time there was a "felt need" for women physicians. Why? Because in a day more modest than ours, many women so disliked to consult a man on their intimate ailments or expose their bodies to the male gaze that they would go without a doctor if they could defer this necessity.

Who did it first? Dr. Elizabeth Blackwell (1821–1910) has long had this reputation, with her sister Emily a close second. What a remarkable family the Blackwells must have been! They were the sisters of Henry and Sam Blackwell, and thus the sisters-in-law of Lucy Stone and Antoinette Brown. But were they really the first woman doctors? It depends on how we reckon it.

Long before Elizabeth Blackwell, apparently from about 1835, Harriot Hunt (1805–1875) had been practicing medicine illegally because she could not induce a medical school to accept her on account of her sex. She was no novice. She had acquired a medical education by private instruction and was so successful that she built up a very lucrative practice. As a result, she had property to be taxed. Feeling keenly the injustice of "taxation without representation" because women were denied the vote, she sent in her taxes every year with a written protest to this effect, and kept it up for more than twenty-five years.

Harriot Hunt did eventually receive an M.D. degree though later than Elizabeth Blackwell. Denied admission at Harvard in 1847, she tried again in 1850 and almost succeeded. She was about to be admitted when it was discovered that a Negro man had also applied. To take such a risk on two such "never befores" was too much! Miss Hunt was asked to withdraw her application and complied. However, a Female Medical College had been started in Boston in 1848, mainly to give scientific training to midwives, and two years later one with the same name but a higher academic level was opened in Philadelphia. In 1835 the Philadelphia school conferred on her an M.D. degree.

. . . . .

Once the barriers were down, more women became physicians. In law the movement was slower and followed a somewhat different course. Apparently not many women felt attracted to this profession, whether from sensing that they would be at a disadvantage in legal battles with men or from lack of feeling a primary need in this field. By the 1870s, when women began in any numbers to take up this profession, it was relatively easy to be admitted to law school but very difficult to be admitted to the bar.

Apparently the first woman to be graduated from a law school was Ada Kepley, from Union College in Chicago, in 1870, but I know nothing more of her. However, the year before that, Mrs. Arabella Mansfield had been admitted to the bar in Iowa, having acquired the requisite qualifications in a private office. The terms under which she was admitted should have become normative for her sex, though they did not. The Court held that the statute providing for the licensing of "any white male person" of proper qualifications could be extended to her because of another statute specifying that "words importing the masculine gender only may be extended to females." Had this statute and this interpretation become universal, the woman suffrage battle could have ended then and there, and the Equal Rights Amendment for which women have contended since 1923 would not be necessary!

By the 1870 decade the public had become fairly well accustomed to women doctors, but aspiring women lawyers still had to struggle to acquire an opportunity to employ their skills beyond clerical work in law offices. The best known of those who won the battle to secure recognition and something like equality was Belva Lockwood.

Mrs. Lockwood (1830–1917), married at eighteen to U. H. McNall and widowed at twenty-two, was a teacher and school administrator for sixteen years. During this period she did much teaching and other work in her local church along with her school duties, and during the Civil War was very active in organizing the relief activities of women. In 1868 she was married again to Dr. Ezekiel Lockwood and moved to Washington, D.C. After birth and death of a child, finding no consolation in this bereavement except in mental exertion, she decided to study law. She applied for admission to Columbia College but was refused on the ground that "her presence would distract the attention of the students." The next year the National University Law School was opened with provision made for admitting a few women students. There she received her law degree.

Getting admitted to the bar was another matter, but after some wangling the Supreme Court of the District of Columbia licensed her to practice. The Court of Claims in 1875 refused her application on the ground, first, that she was a woman and second, that she was a married woman with legal rights vested solely in her husband. She then began working to get a bill passed by Congress that would admit women to the bar of the United States Supreme Court. It took three years, but she succeeded and was the first recipient of this honor. Well known by this time as a lawyer, she did much to promote temperance, peace, and woman suffrage.

A considerable amount can be said of the preaching and ordination of women.

. . . . .

We have had occasion to speak of the preaching of Lucretia Mott, Quaker, and Mary Livermore, Universalist. These two groups, because of their greater freedom from ecclesiastical dogma and control, seem to have produced more women preachers in the nineteenth century than any of the more conventional denominations. The Congregational Church with its emphasis on local self-government was also open to this possibility, and this church ordained the first woman on September 15, 1853.

. . . . .

Another pioneer woman preacher was Olympia Brown (1835–1926), a younger contemporary of Antoinette and a Universalist. Educated at Mount Holyoke Seminary and Antioch College, she was admitted with some reluctance to the theological school of St. Lawrence University at Canton, N.Y., and was ordained there upon her graduation in 1863. She is credited with unusual intellectual acumen. She held several pastorates, married John H. Willis though she kept her maiden name, and demonstrated that it was quite possible to combine a successful pastorate with marriage and motherhood. Her Alma Mater did her belated honor by celebrating the centennial of her ordination with considerable publicity, a bronze plaque, and a scholarship established in her name.

—From Georgia Elma Harkness, *Women in Church and Society.* Nashville: Abingdon, 1972.

Equal Opportunity

Since the 1960s the United States Government has made it increasingly clear—through legislation, Executive orders, and judicial decisions—that equal opportunity for women in employment and education is a Federal goal. Congress first expressed the goal in 1963 with passage of the Equal Pay Act, which amended the Fair Labor Standards Act. With this and other amendments, the Fair Labor Standards Act broadly prohibits wage discrimination based on sex in public and private employment.

. . . . .

Women still earn considerably less than men. Despite their increasing presence in the work force and in educational programs and despite Federal protection, data from 1975 indicate that even when they both work full time, year round, the average woman worker earns only about three-fifths

of what a man earns. On the average, black and Hispanic women earn even less than white women. In fact, the male-female average wage gap is greater than it was in 1960, before the passage of the Equal Pay Act. In 1977 female college graduates, including those with advanced degrees, who worked full time year round had a median income below that of male high school dropouts.

Women are segregated in low-paying dead-end jobs. Despite the heterogeneity of the female work force, 1976 statistics indicate that 78.5 percent of all women are concentrated in clerical, sales, service, and blue-collar jobs, with 55.9 percent of women concentrated in just two occupational categories—clerical and service. In 1978 "Women were 80 percent of all clerical workers ... but only 6 percent of all craft workers; 63 percent of service workers but only 43 percent of professional and technical workers; and 64 percent of retail sales workers but only 23 percent of nonfarm managers and administrators." To achieve an occupational distribution identical to that of white men, it has been estimated that 66 percent of white women, 69 percent of black women, and 80 percent of Puerto Rican women would have to change occupations. According to Ralph Smith, acting Director of the National Commission for Employment Policy, "The extreme form of occupational segregation in which women remained at home may have ended years ago, but the majority are still doing 'women's work.'"

Women are much less likely than men to hold full-time jobs. Only 41.4 percent of the women in the labor force in 1975 held full-time, year-round jobs, compared with 63.9 percent of the men in the labor force. Women were 70 percent of all part-time workers (persons who work less than 35 hours per week) in 1977. Voluntary part-time work increased approximately three times faster than full-time work from 1965 to 1977, and most of those taking part-time jobs were women.

Women's access to job opportunities is restricted. Despite their increasing presence in the work force, women still have considerably more difficulty than men in finding jobs.

In 1977, for example, men's rate of participation in the labor force was 30 percent higher than women's, and the average unemployment rate for white men was 5.5 percent. In the same year, the unemployment rate for white women was 7.3 percent; for black women it was 14 percent, reflecting the effects of both sex and race. The largest difference in unemployment between men and women was among prime-age workers, those ranging in age from 25 to 44.

Women are much less likely to complete college than men. Even among the relatively young population, significant differences in college completion rates persist. In 1976, for example, 34 percent of white men between the ages of 24 and 29 had completed at least 4 years of college; in the same year, the completion rate for white women of comparable age was two-thirds the rate of white men; for black women it was one-third.

Women still do not receive education or training that is as advanced as men's. In 1978 a higher proportion of female than male undergraduates were enrolled in public 2-year colleges. According to sociologists Barbara Heyns and Joyce Adair Bird, the most prestigious universities "remain the preserve of the most traditional students, in terms of sex, race, and age," i.e., young white men. Moreover, although nearly half of all undergraduate degrees were awarded to women in 1976–77, they received only 24 percent of the doctorates and 19 percent of first professional degrees during that year.

Women are underrepresented in Federal employment and training programs. Although they were 56 percent of the population eligible to participate in federally supported programs under Titles I, II, and VI of CETA in 1977, women were only 44 percent of the participants. Moreover, they were least represented in the programs that provide participants with jobs, which are also the most expensive programs to operate.

—From United States Commission on Civil Rights, *Child Care and Equal Opportunity for Women.* Clearinghouse Publication No. 67, June 1981.

FOR FURTHER READING:

Elliot, Elisabeth. *Discipline: The Glad Surrender.* Old Tappan, N.J.: Revell, 1982.

Getz, Gene A. *The Measure of a Woman.* Ventura, Calif.: Regal, 1977.

Miller, Ella May. *The Peacemakers.* Old Tappan, N.J.: Revell, 1977.

Neff, Mariam. *Discover Your Worth.* Wheaton, Ill.: Victor Books, 1979.

WORRY

Practical Tips for Worriers

1. At least three times each day I will remind myself, "God loves *me.*" These words remind me that because he loves me, he also helps me with my problems.
2. I can tell Jesus Christ every worry. If it's big enough to trouble me, it's big enough to tell the Lord.
3. I need not worry about mistakes and sins of the past. When I start to worry, I will remind myself, "I am free from my past. God has forgiven me."
4. I will learn not to worry about my health by remembering that God created my body and God gave me life. I am his.
5. Because new relationships and new experiences start me worrying, when I go into any new area of life I will tell myself, "Jesus is with me. I need not worry."
6. Worries give me the grasshopper complex—the worries seem like giants and I am like an insect. But with God on my side, I am the giant; my worries are the insects.
7. I will search out people who will listen and ask them not only to hear my worries, but to help me bear them through their loving counsel and physical presence.
8. I will get involved in a physical exercise program. I will not spend my time sitting and thinking about my problems.

Physical exercise is one of the best medicines I can take.

9. When I worry constantly, I will ask myself, "Is this the *real* worry?" Often small anxieties mask deeper problems. Through my own inner probings and with the help of the Holy Spirit, I will discover my real causes for worry.

10. When I can't sleep because of worry, I will learn relaxation techniques. As my body relaxes, my mind will also relax.

11. I worry about people not liking me and rejecting me. Instead of worrying about the people who don't respond to me, I will give thanks to God for the close friends who do care about me.

12. I worry because I think about my problems. I will memorize at least four Bible verses to repeat when I am tempted to worry. (Examples: Philippians 4:13; 4:8, 9; John 14:27; James 1:5; Hebrews 2:18; 13:6.)

13. When I worry and doubt God's reality or his concern for me, I will tell God about my doubts and ask his help to conquer them.

14. I will not allow Murphy's Law to control my life ("If anything can go wrong, it will"), but I will live by Murph*ey*'s New Law: "If anything can go right, it probably will."

15. I will erase three words from my vocabulary: *should, must, ought.* Only God has the right to lay those demands upon me.

16. I win over worry by taking little steps. Each time I can conquer the tendency to worry over anything, it makes me stronger so I can win over the next worry that comes along.

17. "Put on a happy face," went the words of a popular song. I will practice smiling. Whenever I look in the mirror, I will smile. The smile on my face will strengthen me against the worries in my mind.

18. It is not merely immediate worries that trouble me. It's a habit of worry. I will work toward breaking that negative cycle.

19. No matter how difficult my problems, I

can repeat the two special words: *But God.* They will give me help and assurance.

—From Cecil B. Murphey, *Devotions for Worriers.* Old Tappan, N.J.: Revell, 1982.

FOR FURTHER READING:

Carlson, Dwight L., M.D. *How to Win Over Fatigue.* Old Tappan, N.J.: Revell, 1974.

Davis, Creath. *How to Win in a Crisis.* Grand Rapids: Zondervan, 1976.

Hart, Archibald D. *Feeling Free.* Old Tappan, N.J.: Revell, 1979.

Stoop, David. *Self-Talk.* Old Tappan, N.J.: Revell, 1982.

WORSHIP

CHRISTIANS NEED to understand the spiritual enrichment that worship brings into the life of the believer. William Temple says, "To worship is to quicken the conscience by the holiness of God, to feed the mind with the truth of God, to purge the imagination by the beauty of God, to open the heart to the love of God, to devote the will to the purpose of God."

Worship involves relationship with God, and it is experienced as a person acknowledges the presence of God at any time, in any place.

Albert Orsborn beautifully expresses the desire of one who has worshiped:

Let the beauty of Jesus be seen in me,
All His wonderful passion and purity;
O Thou Spirit divine,
All my nature refine,
Till the beauty of Jesus be seen in me.

Personal worship is implemented by eliminating from our minds all worldly preoccupations and quietly entering God's presence. There our fears, prejudices, tangents, and rebellions will be corrected and balanced by the Holy Spirit.

Worship becomes more meaningful when

a special place is made a sanctuary. God said to Moses: "Put off thy shoes from off thy feet, for the place whereon thou standest is holy ground" (Exodus 3:5 KJV). One obvious sanctuary in nature is, perhaps, one of the most overlooked places—your backyard, your own patch of holy ground! In the midst of a busy working day, sanctuary may be in the quietness of a lunch hour listening to music. Housewives and mothers have found spir-

itual sanctuary even while hands are washing dishes. Relaxation and quietness provide tranquility for thought. On mountains, near the sea, in church, or in a rocking chair, one can be still and know.

—From David and Virginia Edens, *Making the Most of Family Worship*. Nashville: Broadman Press, 1968, pp. 12–13.

Index